African Americans in the U.S. Economy

African Americans in the U.S. Economy

EDITED BY
CECILIA A. CONRAD, JOHN WHITEHEAD,
PATRICK MASON, AND JAMES STEWART

ROWMAN & LITTLEFIELD PUBLISHERS, INC.
Lanham • Boulder • New York • Toronto • Oxford

ROWMAN & LITTLEFIELD PUBLISHERS, INC.

Published in the United States of America
by Rowman & Littlefield Publishers, Inc.
A wholly owned subsidiary of The Rowman & Littlefield Publishing Group, Inc.
4501 Forbes Boulevard, Suite 200, Lanham, MD 20706
www.rowmanlittlefield.com

P.O. Box 317, Oxford OX2 9RU, UK

British Library Cataloguing in Publication Information Available

Library of Congress Cataloging-in-Publication Data

African Americans in the U.S. economy / edited by Cecilia Conrad . . . [et al].
   p. cm.
  Includes references and index.
  ISBN 0-7425-4377-3 (cloth : alk. paper)—ISBN 0-7425-4378-1 (pbk. : alk. paper)
   1. African Americans—Economic conditions.   I. Title: African Americans in the
US economy. II. Conrad, Cecilia, 1955–
E185.8.A34 2005
330.9'0089'96073—dc22

                                       2004018357

Printed in the United States of America

♾™ The paper used in this publication meets the minimum requirements of American
National Standard for Information Sciences—Permanence of Paper for Printed Library
Materials, ANSI/NISO Z39.48-1992.

Dedication

This volume is dedicated to Robert Span Browne (1925–2004). Bob established the gold benchmarking standard for scholars aspiring to undertake serious study of the economic circumstances of black Americans. Moreover, Bob demonstrated that understanding social dynamics was necessary, but not sufficient, to achieve social change. He dedicated his entire professional life to the development and operation of institutions designed to enhance economic outcomes for marginalized groups.

Bob founded the Black Economic Research Center (BERC) in 1969 as a type of "economic laboratory" where young black economists conducted a variety of research projects and, concurrently, produced the *Review of Black Political Economy*. His successes at institution building are further documented by continuing efforts toward addressing the inequities experienced by black farmers, which were spearheaded by the Federation of Southern Cooperatives/Land Assistance Fund. Bob Browne laid the groundwork for this initiative in 1971 through the creation of the Emergency Land Fund (ELF). He expanded the focus on self-help and preserving and enhancing community economic resources by creating the Twenty-First Century Foundation, which has provided approximately $2 million in funding for projects and organizations.

Bob Browne was also one of the foremost experts on African economic integration. From 1980 to 1982, he served as the first U.S. executive director of the African Development Bank in Abidjan. He also served as a senior research fellow in the African Studies and Research Center at Howard University, and later as a Ford Foundation research fellow at Howard. He and Robert Cummings from Howard University published a seminal work in 1984, *Lagos Plan of Action vs. the Berg Report*, which compared the plan for a continent-wide economic community drawn up by African leaders with an alternative scenario produced by the World Bank. Bob worked as staff director for a House Banking subcommittee on international development from 1986 to 1991, and during the past decade, he served as consultant and advisor for numerous organizations. In 2004 he co-chaired the G8-Africa project for the Council on Foreign Relations.

Bob Browne's writings in the *Review* explored a wide range of topics including barriers to black participation in the U.S. economy, cash flows in the ghetto community, the political economic challenges and prospects for black economic development, economics education, and community development corporations. This volume is a testimonial to Bob's seminal role in establishing a solid tradition of engaged and focused scholarship examining economic dimensions of the black experience. Many of the chapters in this volume offer updates to several issues that Bob flagged for systematic inquiry some thirty-five years ago. It is our hope that this collection further contributes to the institutionalization of the intellectual and activist legacies of Bob Browne and, in addition, serves as a catalyst for motivating additional analysis of the topics that he identified as critical for enhancing the economic well-being of African Americans.

Contents

PART III

Theories of Racial Discrimination, Inequality, and Economic Progress

PART IV

Current Economic Status of African Americans: Hard Evidence of Economic Discrimination and Inequality

PART V

Globalization and Its Impact on the Economic Well-Being of African Americans and Latinos

PART VI

Black Capitalism: Entrepreneurs and Consumers

PART VII

Education, Employment, Training, and Social Welfare: Alternative Public Policy Approaches in the Struggle to Achieve Racial Equality

PART VIII

Understanding Black Reparations

PART IX

African American Economic Development and Urban Revitalization Strategies

Preface

Over the past several decades, academic discourse on racial inequality has focused primarily on political and social issues with significantly less attention to the complex interplay between race and economics. *African Americans in the U.S. Economy* represents a contribution to recent scholarship that seeks to lessen this imbalance.

This project builds on important thematic precedents established by the *Review of Black Political Economy*. From 1970 to the present, the *Review* has been the only professional organ wholly committed to the publication of research examining the intricate role of race in economic life. Influenced by the pathbreaking studies conducted by the many scholars responsible for the *Review*'s success, this volume is designed primarily to provide a political-economic analysis of the past and present economic status of African Americans.

The broad range of topics explored in this volume reflects the multifaceted approach to issues of race, racial inequality, and the operation of the U.S. capitalist economy that has characterized most issues of the *Review*. A multidisciplinary design and theoretical orientation are employed that apply principles and methods adapted from political economy investigations. The book's multidisciplinary framework blends knowledge from history, economics, political science, sociology, and other disciplines to generate new insights about the persistence of racial economic inequality and discrimination. We present a distinct black political economic model of the relationship between race and economic outcomes that draws on and further extends several decades of scholarship by our colleagues in the National Economics Association.

The forty-three chapters in this volume represent the work of some of the nation's most distinguished scholars on the topics presented, covering a range of contemporary economic issues. The individual chapters cover several well-defined areas, including black employment and unemployment, labor market discrimination, black capitalism and entrepreneurship, public policy and racial economic inequality, urban revitalization, and black economic development. While the chapter authors present the topics from a variety of public policy and theoretical perspectives, their work shares a common premise—race matters. Indeed, many of the chapters show that racial discrimination persists despite the optimistic expectations generated by standard economic analysis and despite the widespread publicity to the contrary.

In editing this volume, we have tried to make each chapter as reader-friendly as possible. We have worked closely with each contributor to ensure that individual chapters are written in a style free of the complex and technical jargon that characterizes scholarly economics journals and most economics textbooks. We have done so, however, without sacrificing our commitment to the scholarly integrity, theoretical coherence, and empirical rigor that the data and topics presented require. Although the book is accessible and relevant to a range of students and to the general public, its methodological sophistication and its practical and theoretical knowledge should be appealing to academicians and practitioners alike. It can be used as either a primary or a supplementary text for university and community college courses in economics, ethnic studies, political science, sociology, and urban studies.

The development of this book has stretched over a two-year period, during which we have communicated regularly to complete the final manuscript. Thus, this project truly represents a collaborative effort—from the selection and arrangement of the chapters, to the writing of the introduction, to the final editing phase.

Throughout the development of the book, we received valuable assistance from the contributors, including their reviews of companion chapters. We thank them for their support.

ACKNOWLEDGMENTS

Our deepest thanks go to Gary Dymski of the University of California–Riverside, Mary King of Portand State University, and Marc Kitchel of City College of San Francisco. Each provided invaluably helpful comments on most of the chapters, as well as important support and encouragement during all stages of our project.

Other colleagues and friends provided us with valuable information and materials, read and commented on various sections of the book, and gave us special assistance that only the most talented teachers can offer. Monica Bosson, Deborah Goldsmith, George Moss, and Laura Walsh of City College of San Francisco gave us detailed comments and editorial assistance on many sections of the book, resulting in many improvements. Manuel Pastor, of the University of California–Santa Cruz, provided important economic research on the Latino population of the United States and assisted with the integration of this ethnic group into key sections of the book. Aguibou Yansane, of San Francisco State University, read the final three sections of the book and commented extensively.

Many others read and offered suggestions on particular chapters: Randy Albelda, Darlene Alioto, Robert Allen, Andrew Barlow, Timothy Bates, Michael Best, Peter Bohmer, Thomas Boston, Robert Browne, William A. Darity, Richard Edwards, Paula England, Curtis Haynes, Jane Humphries, Dennis Johnson, Preston Justice, Tim Killikilley, Heng Kuang, David Landes, Dave Littleton, Manning Marable, Susan McElroy, Tami Ohler, Debra Porter, Jim Robinson, Bruce Smith, Robert Weems Jr., and Jessica Williams.

At the early and later stages of this project, we drew on the talents and perseverance of research assistants. David Burns, Helen Beckon, Danielle Herring, Tony Tiu, and Janelle Wright provided clerical support, library and Internet research assistance, and other technical help critical to the completion of the final manuscript. These individuals with Claudia Sitgraves and Michael Enriquez, doctoral candidates at the University of California–Berkeley, also contributed to the development of the study guide that accompanies our book.

We further wish to acknowledge the substantive assistance of the Social Sciences Department and the School of Behavioral and Social Sciences at City College of San Francisco, the African American Studies Program at Florida State University, and the Department of Economics at Pomona College. Sandra Handler, former dean of the School of Behavioral and Social Sciences; Debra Porter, assistant to dean of liberal arts at City College of San Francisco; and Ule Jackson and Shamuna Malik, staff members of the African American Studies Program at Florida State University were especially helpful.

Cecilia A. Conrad
John Whitehead
Patrick Mason
James Stewart

Black Political Economy: An Introduction

Despite over three hundred years of participation in the U.S. economy, African Americans continue to be excluded from the full realization of the American dream. African Americans represented 12.3 percent of the U.S. population in 2000 but received only 9 percent of the income and owned only 3 percent of the assets. With the exception of the American Indians, African Americans have the highest poverty rates of any racial and ethnic group.[1] Racial inequality persists despite the passage of civil rights and equal employment opportunity legislation, the convergence of black–white school completion rates, and the predictions of economists that racial discrimination cannot thrive in a free market economy. Yet, economics textbooks, particularly those for introductory students, are either silent about the economic influence of race or provide only a cursory overview of Gary Becker's theory of discrimination.[2] Becker, a Nobel Prize–winning economist, conducted a thought experiment in the 1950s: what would happen if employers, workers, or consumers were willing to forfeit profits, wages, or utility to avoid an economic exchange with someone of a different race? Becker argued that in the highly stylized world of orthodox economic theory, the racial animus of white employers, employees, and consumers would not lead to persistent racial discrimination. Instead, Becker believed that when employers, employees, and consumers did not possess market power, discrimination would disappear rather swiftly from the market.

Moreover, economic historians—or the so-called New Institutionalists—who wish to explain the economic success of North America and Western Europe on the one hand and the poverty of Africa on the other hand steadfastly ignore the role of the slave trade and the long-term practice of chattel slavery in the Americas.[3]

The standard argument is that rich countries are rich because of private ownership of capital, competitive markets, and civic institutions that are able to enforce contracts. African countries are poor because they lack sufficient private ownership of capital; they do not have competitive markets; and their civic institutions are not sufficient to enforce private contracts.

Becker's theory and the work of the New Institutionalists has had a powerful impact on how economists and other social scientists think about the relationship between race and economic status. Because Becker's theory predicts that race does not matter, scholars of racial inequality have focused on developing explanations other than race for persistent racial differences in economic status.

This book takes a different approach. The chapters in this book begin with the premise that race matters—and then proceed with an analysis of the implications of race and racism for the economic status of African Americans and for the operation of the American economy. This approach challenges the adequacy of neoclassical, mainstream economic analysis as a useful paradigm in explaining the persistence of racial inequality; hence, it also challenges the validity of the neoclassical paradigm for explaining the general distribution of income and wealth, the operation of labor and capital markets, and the competitive process. The intellectual origins of this approach lie in the last three decades of scholarship generated by black political economists in the African diaspora. James Stewart and Major Coleman, drawing on these three decades of scholarship, identify two major foci of the black political economy paradigm, "(1) the role of economic forces in intensifying or mitigating conflicts between 'racial' groups, and (2) the extent to which economic institutions can be viably organized and operated while simultaneously accommodating sustained patterns of racial stratification." The chapters in our book build on and significantly extend the principles, terminology, and methods derived from Stewart and Coleman's work and other variants of the black political economy paradigm.

The chapters in this book span the ideological spectrum of economics, from neoclassical theory to Marxian analysis of class. While most of the chapters focus on the economic impact of racism on African Americans, not all of the authors are economists, nor are they exclusively African American. Although the authors begin with the shared premise that race matters, they do not always agree about its implications for the economic status of African Americans, nor do they agree about the appropriate public policies to ameliorate its effects. For example, one author advocates school vouchers to improve black educational attainment; another opposes it. Some authors promote black capitalism as a strategy for black economic advancement, whereas others not only question the ability of black-owned firms to create employment but also worry that black capitalism worsens class divisions within the black community.

UNDERSTANDING RACIAL INEQUALITY

Despite the diversity of perspectives represented in this volume, several broad themes do emerge. The first is that neoclassical economic theory cannot adequately explain racial differences in economic status. Neoclassical economic theory argues that, first, competitive markets will eliminate discrimination; and, second, that black–white income disparities are caused by racial differences in culture, tastes, and innate abilities; or by racial differences in investments in education, training, and other activities that increase productive capacity. Although the authors represented in this volume generally concede that differences in education and training contribute to black–white economic inequality, they challenge the conclusion that competitive markets will eliminate discrimination or create a level playing field. They point to the persistence of gaps in earnings and employment status among blacks and whites with the same education and training as evidence that racial bias continues to constrain the choices and opportunities of African Americans. For example, in chapter 14, Susan Williams McElroy reports that the median earnings of black male high school graduates in 2001 were nearly $7,500 less than the median earnings of white male high school graduates.

Competitive markets not only fail to erase the effects of racial discrimination, but they tend to reproduce the inequality that racial bias creates. For example, the lower earnings of African Americans combine with racial bias in credit markets to create racial differences in wealth. Even if racial bias were eliminated in both the labor and the credit market, the difference in wealth of black and white households would persist. As Gary Dymski and Patrick Mason conclude, "If all personal bias against black applicants for capital and credit were to disappear tomorrow, the huge racial wealth gap would remain; and this alone would insure that credit and capital flows are lower in the black community; and this leads to fewer opportunities for capital accumulation and wealth-building."

A second broad theme in this book is that history matters. Because competitive markets tend to reproduce inequality, restrictions on economic opportunities in the past affect the present. Profits from the Atlantic slave trade and from plantation slavery not only fueled U.S. economic growth in the 1800s but also contributed to the contemporary prosperity of the United States and Europe and to the economic stagnation in many African countries. Slavery has long-term consequences for the descendants of slaves, for slave owners, and for those who were neither slaves nor slave owners but who enjoyed privileges associated with white skin. Long after emancipation, African Americans continued to be denied full social citizenship in the United States. In the South, improvements in the education of white school children were financed by paying black teachers low salaries and by spending little on textbooks and other supplies for black children. Even as blacks escaped the political and economic repression of the South to enter the industrial workforce of the North, they were met with racial hostility. White workers acted to exclude black workers from union membership and from industrial workplaces. Eligibility rules for New Deal social insurance programs such as Social Security and unemployment insurance excluded the occupations in which most African Americans worked.

This history of racial oppression and exclusion created the conditions under which African Americans participate in the contemporary U.S. economy. The emasculating effects of slavery, Jim Crow, and continuing racial discrimination in labor markets contribute to the high proportion of black families headed by women. The denial of full social citizenship to persons of African descent for nearly two centuries created the racial differences in wealth observed today. As Thomas M. Shapiro and Jessica L. Kenty-Drane conclude, "African-Americans cannot earn themselves out of the racial wealth gap. The huge racial wealth gap is a historical legacy that the past continually visits upon current generations."

This history has also left African Americans especially vulnerable to structural changes in the U.S. and the global economy, the third broad theme in this book. Globalization in particular poses new challenges to the economic prospects of people of African descent. Globalization has been a powerful force in creating a new global village, characterized by increasing cooperation, cultural exchanges, and democratic practices among inhabitants. This and other features of globalization have created new possibilities for the struggle against fear, ignorance, and white privilege. However, globalization has also led to a move away from the welfare state, to the disappearance of key industries and high-wage jobs from minority communities, and to increased competition for low skill jobs. These features of globalization have contributed to the widening social inequality within the African American community and between blacks and whites.

As described, most conservative economists believe that competitive markets are self-correcting and that the effects of racial discrimination will disappear over time and without government action. Once again, this book offers a different perspective, of which the fourth theme is that a laissez-faire approach will not reduce racial inequality.[4] The authors in this book advocate traditional forms of intervention, such as enforcing antidiscrimination laws and endorsing new strategies.

Much of the improvement in black economic status since the 1960s has required government intervention through equal employment opportunity legislation, minority contracting programs, equal credit laws, and so forth. However, while some African Americans achieved middle-income status, the economic status of others has deteriorated. High unemployment, low wages, inferior schooling, and the related problems of poverty and welfare dependency plague many African Americans. To reverse the tendency toward growing inequality, unconventional and unpopular policies (such as reparations) may be required.

A final broad theme that emerges from the chapters of this book is that social capital matters. Paraphrasing Shondra Nash and Cedric Herring in this volume, social capital "consists of cohesive community networks that indicate trust and cooperation based on a common culture and goals, group loyalty, a sense of identity and belonging, and coordinated actions." Social capital is a critical ingredient to community economic development strategies, and institutions such as churches, community-based businesses, and cooperative organizations help to build and sustain social capital. Black-owned businesses, regardless of location or industry, are more likely to hire African Americans as employees than are businesses not owned by blacks. The black church has given birth to colleges and universities as well as to mutual aid societies that have developed into black-owned insurance companies that exist today. In a 1990 survey, 71 percent of black clergy reported that their churches were engaged in community-outreach programs, including day care, job search, substance abuse prevention, food and clothing distribution, and so forth. Many churches have spun off community development corporations to develop housing and entrepreneurial ventures. Other community-based organizations have played similar roles. In a critique of a conservative free market proposals for inner-city revitalization, John Whitehead and David Landes write, "Inner-city economic revitalization requires considerably more than the provision of a favorable environment for attracting private profit-seeking mainstream firms. In fact, the over thirty years of research on inner-city revitalization suggests that revitalization initiatives must be comprehensive and holistic, extending beyond economic issues. The motor of a local revitalization initiative may be economic development, but crucial to its success may be programs in such areas as family support, improved public education, drug rehabilitation, mental health, environmental clean-up, and community policing."

ABOUT THIS BOOK

The forty-three chapters in this book are organized into nine subsections: part I, Slavery and the Early Formation of Black Labor; part II, Organized Labor and African Americans; part III, Theories of Racial Discrimination, Inequality, and Economic Progress; part IV, Current Economic Status of African Americans; part V, Globalization and Its Impact on the Economic Well-Being of Americans and Latinos; part VI, Black Capitalism; part VII, Education, Employment, Training, and Social Welfare; part VIII, Understanding Black Reparations; and part IX, African American Economic Development and Urban Revitalization Strategies. Even though the text focuses on the African American population, we have included important research on other major racial–ethnic groups; but, owing to data limitations, the text gives little attention to the smaller racial–ethnic groups, such as Arab Americans, Korean Americans, Filipino Americans, and indigenous Hawaiians. Much more research is needed to develop a truly comprehensive multicultural economics text, and we hope this volume will contribute to this new social research.

Part I examines the historical role played by blacks in the building of the U.S. economy and in the emergence of the black working class. It documents the development of a capitalist world system dependent on slavery and the importance of black slaves to American economic development. Philip Foner describes the origins of the international slave trade and its role in financing the British industrial revolution. William Darity Jr. links the wealth created by the slave trade to the contemporary prosperity of the United States and Europe and to the economic stagnation of many African countries.

James Stewart focuses specific attention on how black labor was mobilized on plantations to generate profits that fueled economic growth in the Southern and the Northern states.

The last two chapters in part I provide accounts of the economic circumstances of African Americans following the Civil War. Daniel Fusfeld and Timothy Bates describe the operation of the Southern sharecropping system, which led to the superexploitation of black sharecroppers and their condition of chronic debt. Philip Foner examines how World War I created new employment opportunities for blacks in the urban North, spurring the large-scale emigration of blacks from the South.

Part II continues the examination of black labor in the post–Civil War period. It chronicles the early attempts to recruit black workers into organized labor and the racist union practices that excluded blacks from most trade unions in the period immediately following the Civil War. William Harris describes the history of blacks and trade unions. Philip Foner recounts how the exclusion of blacks from white unions led to the formation of the Brotherhood of Sleeping Car Porters. In the final chapter of part II, James Stewart provides a detailed case study of attempts to overcome racism within the United Steel Workers of America during the pivotal years 1948–1970.

Part III builds on this historical foundation to analyze the economic status of African Americans. Part III presents and critiques the major theories of discrimination and racial economic inequality. John Whitehead's chapter compares conservative and liberal theories of discrimination, highlighting the strengths and weaknesses of each theory. Whitehead concludes that neither conservatives nor liberals have developed an adequate theoretical model of how capitalism can exploit a racial distribution of resources. Peter Bohmer's chapter continues Whitehead's discussion of the capitalism–racism nexus by looking at its treatment within the Marxist theory of racism and racial inequality. Timothy Bates and Daniel Fusfeld present a radical version of the crowding model. They argue that the crowding of black workers into the secondary, low-wage job sector worsens black–white income differentials and contributes to other racial differences in economic outcomes. Mary King's chapter presents a unique twist to the analysis of racial economic disparities by looking at racial violence as a tool for economic repression and for the enforcement of unequal property rights in "whiteness." James Stewart and Major Coleman conclude this section with a chapter that introduces the black political economy model that highlights the economic value of racial identity and examines the linkages between racial identity production and economic disparities. The model's interpretation of persistent racial inequality differs significantly from the explanations emerging from the other models discussed.

Parts IV, V, and VI examine economic outcomes for African Americans today. In the first chapter of part IV, Susan Williams McElroy discusses the relationship between education and labor market outcomes. Her research demonstrates that, while educational attainment plays a crucial role in labor market outcomes, it does not fully account for disparities in earnings for race–gender groups. In the chapter "Persistent Racial Discrimination in the Labor Market," Patrick Mason challenges Becker's prediction that competitive markets will destroy racial discrimination within the labor market, through an examination of the relationship between the racial wage gap and changes in the quality and the quantity of schooling. In a second paper, coauthored with Gary Dymski, Mason shifts attention from labor markets to financial markets, examining racial differences in access to credit. The next two chapters focus on the economic status of African American women: Cecilia Conrad describes the movement of black women into clerical and sales jobs after 1960, a change she attributes to the enforcement of equal employment laws and the narrowing wage gap between black and white women, which she attributes to legislation and to improvements in educational attainment. Cecilia Conrad and Mary King then focus on the status of one group of African American women—single mothers who maintain families—and they examine the economic and social factors contributing to the high proportion of black families headed by single women. The differences in income, access to credit, and family structure described in these five chapters have long-term consequences for the accumulation of wealth. Hence, it is appropriate

that part IV concludes with Thomas Shapiro and Jessica Kenty-Drane's chapter on racial differences in the accumulation of wealth.

The chapters in part V examine the impact of globalization on the socioeconomic well-being of people of color in the United States with particular attention to African Americans. Peter Dorman gives an in-depth analysis of the impact of increased capital mobility on employment in black and Latino communities. Jessica Gordon Nembhard, Steven Pitts, and Patrick Mason describe the consequences of corporate-driven globalization for economic inequality within the black community. The remaining three chapters focus on specific aspects of globalization: the shrinkage of the public sector (Mary King), immigration (Steven Shulman and Robert Smith), and the expansion of the penal system (Andrew Barlow).

Part VI examines the characteristics of black-owned businesses, from barbershops to hip-hop entrepreneurs, and debates the merits of black capitalism as a strategy for black economic advancement. Manning Marable describes the early history of black-owned businesses. The next two chapters examine the current status of black-owned businesses (Cecilia Conrad) and banks (Gary Dymski and Robert Weems Jr.). Part VI continues with two provocative chapters, written by Robert Weems Jr. and by Dipannita Basu, on hip-hop culture and its implications for black business development. In the final chapter of part VI, Earl Ofari Hutchinson worries that black capitalism will exacerbate class divisions among African Americans. He cautions that black capitalism by itself will not have a major impact on black economic well-being because of the small size of the black-owned business sector.

The remaining sections of the book suggest alternative strategies for improving the economic position of African Americans. Part VII examines public policies to improve the educational attainment and incomes of individual blacks. Howard Fuller and Louis Schubert each debate the merits of school voucher programs, and Michael Stoll and Bernard Anderson each identify effective policies to increase black youth employment prospects. Linda Burnham discusses the consequences of welfare reform for black families.

Part VIII explores critical aspects of the

growing and controversial reparations movement. Robert Allen presents an overview of past and present black efforts to obtain reparations. Richard America uses a general theory of restitution to make the case that reparations are due to African Americans, and he discusses policy options for payment. William Darity Jr. and Dania Frank discuss precedents for reparations payments to blacks emerging from the experiences of Americans Indians, Japanese Americans, and Jews.

Part IX presents various economic development and revitalization strategies to address some of the challenges that face African Americans in the dawn of the new millennium. John Whitehead and David Landes emphasize the importance of attracting debt and equity capital to support the development of minority businesses that are linked to high-growth sectors of the economy. The Whitehead and Landes chapter and the chapter by Kalima Rose advocate equitable development strategies. Rose shows how equitable development strategies can be used to lessen the adverse effects of gentrification that often accompanies community revitalization efforts. The next chapters discuss the job and wealth creation potential of the black church (Shondrah Nash and Cedric Herring) and of black-owned businesses (Thomas Boston). In the final chapter of this section, John Whitehead and James Stewart examine the potential role of black athletes as a funding source for broad-based inner-city investment initiatives.

Taken as a whole, the volume provides a comprehensive overview of the historical, contemporary, and prospective economic challenges that have confronted and currently confront African Americans in an ever-evolving global capitalist regime. The range and detail of the information presented in the various chapters provide a solid foundation for developing new approaches that can move our society toward providing true equal economic opportunity for all.

NOTES

1. Using data from the 2000 census of the population, poverty rates were 8.1 percent for non-Hispanic whites, 12.6 percent for Asians, 17.7 percent for native Hawaiians and Pacific Islanders, 24.9 percent of blacks or African Americans, 25.7 percent for American Indians and Alaskan Natives, and 22.6 percent for Hispanic or Latinos (who may be of any race). Information available at www.census.gov/prod/2003pubs/c2kbr-19.pdf.

2. The quantitative coverage of race and gender may have increased, but a survey of textbooks and economics journals from 1972 to 1987 finds a decline in the serious treatment of discrimination.

3. An illustration of the New Institutionalist perspective on African economic development is an article by Stephen Haber, Douglass C. North, and Barry Weingast, "If Economists Are So Smart, Why Is Africa So Poor?" (*Wall Street Journal,* July 30, 2003). They argue that the problem is not financial or resource constraints but the need to craft political institutions that limit the discretion of government. No reference is made regarding the role of the slave trade or colonialism on the development of those institutions.

4. A laissez-faire policy is one where the government does not actively intervene in the workings of the competitive market.

PART I

Slavery and the Early Formation
of Black Labor

1

The International Slave Trade

PHILIP S. FONER

This chapter examines the origins and the expansion of the international slave trade and its role in financing the Industrial Revolution in England. The instability of other sources of labor in the New World colonies is described along with the processes by which trade in enslaved Africans came to dominate other trade relationships with Africa. The international slave trade is shown to have transformed the institution of slavery into a purely economic enterprise that fueled intense competition among European nations for dominance. This chapter argues that the British victory in this competition facilitated the amassing of enormous profits that underwrote the rapid development of industrial enterprises.

The discovery of America added an entirely new dimension to the demand for slaves. By the sixteenth century, the demand for cheap labor to exploit the new continent's resources had created an enormous market for slaves, and the slave traffic in Africa changed from an accessory to the older trades to a major economic enterprise, providing enormous profits for the rising European capitalist class. Africa would continue to supply gold dust, ivory, dye, woods, animal skins, tortoise shells, beeswax, and bamboo canes; but so lucrative was the slave trade that no other form of commerce could compete with it. Henceforth what money-hungry European merchants demanded from Africa was human beings for slaves, and the demand did not slacken for two hundred years.

In a number of European possessions in the New World, especially in the English West Indian and North American colonies, the immediate successor of the Indian slave was not the Negro but the landless poor white of Europe. Promoters of colonization appealed to hard-pressed tenants, craftsmen, farm hands, unemployed artisans, and agricultural laborers to start

a new life in the New World. Many responded eagerly and came over under the terms of a labor contract or indenture that bound them to service for a specified term, usually from five to seven years, in return for their passage. But there were others who came, not of their own volition, but as victims of a highly organized, thriving kidnapping business, which dragged them off the streets of large cities—grown men and women and young boys and girls—and brought them in chains aboard a ship. Many more, such as the victims of the then-heavy sentences for petty misdemeanors or destitution, were sold from the crowded prisons by a government eager to rid itself of costly public charges. Still others received court sentences for deportation or, given their choice, accepted indenture rather than long prison terms or the gallows.

A constant stream of poor whites from Spain, Portugal, France, and especially England moved to the colonies of the New World, but they failed to satisfy the tobacco and sugar plantations' voracious appetite for labor. Many ran away into the wilderness or countryside and were thus lost to their masters. Most had come over hoping to become landowners. At the end of seven years, when they became free, many did acquire land; others, leaving before their contracts expired, had little difficulty disappearing into the mass of free citizens.

What the plantations needed was a cheap and stable labor supply, and slavery met this need. Slavery was a lifetime status; moreover, it was passed on to the slaves' children. The owner was not limited by the expiration of the indenture or by the inconvenience of hiring a new worker. Men and women with black skins could be held for a lifetime of service. An indentured white worker, after eluding his master, might be assimilated in the mass of free workers. Because of their color, runaway Negro slaves could be more easily recognized and captured. Even when they had attained freedom, they were viewed with suspicion when seeking work and were sometimes thrown back into slavery. As blacks, they were held to be descended from Ham, the accursed son of Noah; as pagans, their "savagery" and "barbarism" placed them beyond the pale of civilization, and the usual rites of Christian conduct did not apply to them. As Eric Williams points out, the owners of plantations "would have gone to the moon, if necessary, for labor." But they had Africa, with its seemingly unlimited cheap labor supply. In a 1764 essay entitled "On the Populousness of Africa," a British official on the Gold Coast wrote, "Africa not only can continue supplying the West Indies in the quantities she has hitherto, but, if necessity required it, could spare thousands, nay, millions more, and go on doing the same to the end of time." It was to Africa that the European colonists turned.

THE ATLANTIC SLAVE TRADE

For a short time the Portuguese were preeminent in deriving profits from the transportation of slaves to the New World. In 1493 the pope had issued a series of papal bulls that established a line of demarcation between the colonial possessions of Spain and Portugal. The West, including the New World, went to Spain; and the East, including Africa and most of the lands in Asia, to Portugal. (A year later, in the Treaty of Tordesillas, Portugal was permitted ownership of Brazil, its sole possession in the New World.) Since the papal judgment excluded Spain from Africa, Spain was never able to supply its own colonies with slaves. Even if Spain had been inclined to ignore the papal division, the country would have found it difficult to engage in the slave trade. Although Spain's gold and silver helped to finance the European economic revolution then in progress, its own social system remained basically feudal, and the country lacked the capital and industry to make itself independent. Spain had to rely on foreigners to populate its colonies with slaves.

After 1640 the official Spanish contract to supply slaves to its colonies, the *Asiento do Negros,* was awarded to various contractors in turn; and although Portuguese merchants were often able to purchase the exclusive privilege, their monopoly over the trade with the Spanish possessions was broken. While an illegal trade in slaves flourished and the official policy of exclusiveness was difficult to enforce, the *Asiento* became a highly coveted and bitterly contested prize among nearly all the European powers. There is some question about whether the *Asiento* was prized for the profits to be made on the slave trade or for the opportunity it provided for illicit sale of other goods in Spanish America in return for silver. Probably both were factors.

England and Holland emerged earliest as capitalist countries: during the sixteenth century the merchant capitalists in both countries achieved preeminence over the landed aristocracy; and during the revolutions of the seventeenth century, they became the dominant force in the state and assumed direction of its policies. For this rising class, the slave trade and the slave plantations in the New World provided an important source of wealth in the crucial period of primitive, or original, accumulation of capital. Nevertheless, in the early years of the slave trade, none of the maritime countries of northern Europe showed much interest in becoming directly involved. Not that they had any scruples, but the high cost of the African slave trade made it unattractive until the end of the sixteenth century. Between 1620 and 1650 the English, Dutch, and French all established colonies in the Caribbean. Sugar cultivation was introduced into these colonies during the 1640s, and the Caribbean Islands rapidly developed into large-scale sugar producers. As sugar consumption soared, the vast profits from sugar production quickly justified the high cost of slave importation from Africa. The demand for slaves increased at a phenomenal rate. Having now become a highly profitable business, the slave trade inevitably attracted all maritime Europe. "Strange," writes Eric Williams, "that an article like sugar, so sweet and necessary to human existence, should have occasioned such crimes and bloodshed!"

As early as the sixteenth century, the British and French were staging occasional raids on Portuguese slavers, but they posed no real threat to Portuguese dominance of the slave coast. The arrival of the Dutch in the seventeenth century, with a formidable navy and the capital and shipping resources of the Dutch West Indian Company, was another matter. The Dutch seized Portuguese vessels on the high seas, established contacts with Africans who opposed the Portuguese, and set up permanent settlements of their own on the Guinea Coast. By the middle of the seventeenth century, the Dutch navy had seized all of the Portuguese forts on the Gold Coast and had even added Luanda and northeastern Brazil to their overseas dominions. Although Portugal lost its preeminent commercial position in West Africa, it soon regained control of Angola and Brazil. The Congo and Angola remained in the hands of the Portuguese and continued to supply Brazil until the end of the slave trade.

In the course of the seventeenth century, other European nations competed for African slaves and built posts along the West African coast: Sweden, Denmark, France, England, even Brandenburg (a province of present-day Germany). Jean Baptiste Colbert's West Indian Company, representing the France of Louis XIV, occupied the mouth of the Senegal River, where it established an important center. Although the company failed, a successor was formed that in 1677 captured from the Dutch the important island base of Gorée, near Cape Verde. By the last quarter of the seventeenth century, the Dutch position on the slave coasts, so strong in midcentury, was being challenged by England and France.

The English were the chief competitors of the Dutch, and they soon replaced them as the dominant power in the slave trade. English merchants were slow to enter the traffic, for they enjoyed a lucrative trade in gold and ivory with the African tribes and feared that the slave trade might cause a disruption in this commerce. When in the mid-sixteenth century an Englishman, John Lok, carried off five Negroes from the Guinea Coast under the justification that they "were a people of beastly living, without God, law, religion or commonwealth," the trade in gold and ivory was halted, and the London merchants forced Lok to return his booty to help them reestablish their trade. No such difficulty, however, confronted Sir John Hawkins in 1562, when he encroached on the Portuguese monopoly of Africa, acquired three hundred Negroes on the Guinea Coast, and carried his "good merchandise" across the Atlantic on a ship called the *Jesus*. Aboard this vessel, the psalms of David, the Lord's Prayer, and the Creed were recited every evening in the English tongue. Amid these religious surroundings, the Negroes were herded together in pest-ridden holes. Those who survived were sold to the Spaniards in Hispaniola.

Queen Elizabeth, when she first heard of Hawkins's venture, commented that it "was detestable and would call down vengeance from the heavens upon the undertakers." But when Hawkins came to see her and informed her of his "prosperous success . . . and much gaine to him-selfe," she not only forgave him but became a shareholder in his second slaving voyage. After his first venture, Hawkins formed an African company with the leading citizens of London. According to Philip II's Spanish envoy to London, Hawkins's second voyage "brought him 60 per cent profit." As a result, his chronicler happily wrote, "His name therefore be praised, for evermore! Amen."

On three occasions Hawkins sailed with his human cargo to the New World—in 1562, 1564, and 1568; and although he attracted increasingly wealthy and powerful backers, he did not inspire many Englishmen to emulate him. As yet, England had no colonies. In the early seventeenth century, when it did acquire such colonies (in the West Indies and in North America), the colonists obtained their small numbers of Africans from the slave traders of other European nations. But with the introduction of sugarcane in Barbados in 1641 and the occupation of Jamaica by the

British in 1655, the demand for Negroes grew to the point where the English themselves began to transport large numbers of slaves from Africa. The lucrative business was handled by chartered companies. The Royal African Company, chartered in 1672 with the backing of the Duke of York (later King James II), was given a monopoly of the English trade between Cape Blanco on the north and the Cape of Good Hope on the south for one thousand years. No subject of the Crown other than the company was to visit West Africa except with the company's permission, and the company was authorized to seize ships and cargo infringing on its monopoly. In return, the company promised to supply England's American colonial possessions with three thousand slaves each year.

The Royal African Company established forts along the African coast; but the Dutch opposed the English intrusion, and the two European nations fought an undeclared war over the African trade, with the British emerging victorious. Between 1673 and 1711 the Royal African Company delivered about ninety thousand slaves to England's West Indian and North American colonies, but the company was powerless against the competition of freebooters. The coast was too long and the number of forts too few to prevent interlopers from operating. Some traders bought licenses from the company, but many successfully evaded the attempts to enforce the monopoly privilege and thus profitably carried slaves to the West Indies. In 1712, after a long and bitter controversy waged between the Royal African Company and the separate traders, Parliament refused to confirm the company's monopoly. In 1731 the Royal African Company abandoned the slave trade and specialized only in the ivory and gold dust trade. After 1712 any Englishman, including any in the colonies, was free to engage in the African trade.

In the first edition of the *Encyclopaedia Britannica,* published in London in 1771, there is the following entry under *African company:* "A society of merchants, established by King Charles II for trading to Africa; which trade is now laid open to all his majesty's subjects, paying 10 *per cent,* for maintaining the forts." The fact that this trade was in human merchandise was thus concealed.

With the ever-increasing demands of the sugar plantations, the volume of the British slave trade skyrocketed. The British colonies imported 2,130,000 Africans from 1680 to 1786, and the island of Jamaica absorbed as many as 610,000 slaves from 1700 to 1786. Between 1712 and 1721, Bristol ships alone carried 160,950 slaves to the sugar plantations.

But British slave traders did not stop at providing laborers for England's colonial possessions. In 1713, as a result of her victory in the War of Spanish Succession, England was conceded the *Asiento,* the exclusive right to carry slaves to the Spanish colonies, for thirty years. British traders were quick to take advantage of the privilege. At the same time, they were furnishing slaves to the French West Indian colonies. It was estimated in 1788 that of the annual British export of slaves from Africa, two-thirds were sold to foreigners; and according to one authority, during the whole of the eighteenth century, British slave traders furnished the sugar planters of France and Spain with a half-million Africans.

With its powerful navy, industries capable of supplying the necessary goods, and unlimited resources in capital for investments, England emerged as the most powerful nation in the slave trade. For most of three centuries—from the last quarter of the seventeenth century until the middle of the nineteenth—the English dominated the trade, although at various times the French, Dutch, Portuguese, and Americans were active competitors.

If Liverpool was practically built on traffic in slavery, so too was the African trade a key factor in the rise of British industry. The triangular trade, of which the slave trade was the cornerstone, involved the barter of manufactured goods for African slaves; these were in turn sold in the West Indies in exchange for either sugar or bills of exchange payable in England. The New England slave trade in the mid-eighteenth century was three-cornered, as the British trade was. But only three commodities were usually involved: rum, slaves, and molasses. Rum was shipped from Newport, Salem, Boston, and New York to the west coast of Africa. Here it was exchanged for Negroes, who were shipped across the Atlantic to the West Indies and sold mainly for molasses, which would be carried back to New England to be distilled into more rum, to buy more slaves, and so on and on.

The triangular trade stimulated the growth of industries such as shipping, iron, woolen, linen, and cotton goods; and the manufacture of cotton goods for the purchase of slaves provided the initial stimulus for the emergence of Manchester as the great cotton-manufacturing center of the world. The trade in slaves provided employment for thousands of British seamen, ship carpenters, riggers, sail makers, ironmongers, rope makers; and makers of cotton, linen, and woolen goods, silk handkerchiefs, guns and ammunition, hardware, and household utensils of all kinds. Even though there were some Europeans who saw that the huge sale of firearms to Africans in exchange for slaves might boomerang by enabling Africans to resist, the inexorable requirements of the slave trade overcame such concerns. As Basil Davidson notes, "Huge quantities of firearms were poured into West Africa during the major period of the slave trade. . . . At the height of the eighteenth century commerce, gunsmiths in Birmingham [England] alone were exporting muskets to Africa at the rate of between 100,000 and 150,000 a year."

The profits from the triangular trade provided one of the major sources for the accumulation of capital that financed the Industrial Revolution in England. Merchants who made money in the African trade invested their profits in banking and in a variety of other industries, thereby providing the capital necessary for the "takeoff" of England's great industrial development. In the first volume of his classic work *Capital,* Karl Marx points out that—with the discovery of gold and silver in America, the enslavement of the Indian population, and the beginning of "the conquest and lotting" of the East Indies—"the turning of Africa into a warren for the commercial hunting of black skins signalized the rosy dawn of the era of capitalistic production. These idyllic proceedings are the chief moments of primitive accumulation." As Marx points out, all capitalist societies have needed as a condition for their early development, what he called "the primitive accumulation of capital." This was a relatively swift, open plundering of wealth to prime the pump, to launch the building of the factory system. In the European countries the slave trade was a primary source of the primitive accumulation of capital, and on this—to no small extent—the British, French, and Dutch capitalist systems were built. Thus, Marx speaks in *Capital* of European capitalism emerging out of the "bloody womb" of African slavery.

2

Africa, Europe, and the Origins of Uneven Development: The Role of Slavery

WILLIAM A. DARITY JR.

This chapter describes the economic foundations of the Atlantic slave trade and the role of trade and slavery in generating European and American economic growth and their contemporary prosperity. Conversely, the devastating effects of the slave trade on Africa, and its continuing effects, are also discussed. It is suggested that the linkage between historical and contemporary patterns of inequality provides support for the reparations movement.

The world is sharply divided between rich and poor nations. Among the richest are the nations of Europe and the nations formed by European occupation, settlement, and subsequent political domination. The latter group includes the United States, Canada, Australia, and New Zealand. Among the poorest are many of the nations of the African continent.

The gap is staggering. For example, Britain's per-capita income in 1999 exceeded $20,000 while Ghana, a former British colony, had a per-capita income of less than $2,000. Belgium's per-capita income exceeded $25,000 while the Congo, a former Belgian colony, had a per-capita income less than $1,000. Another former European colony, Sierra Leone, had a per-capita income of a mere $448 (United Nations Development Program 2001, 141–144).

How did these vast differences in standards of living come about? Are they the result of historical accident? Are they the result of European cultural and intellectual superiority? Can they be explained by differences in geography and natural resources?

The answer is, none of the above. The gap is due primarily to the long-term effects of the Atlantic slave trade that transported enslaved Africans to the New World between the sixteenth and nineteenth centuries. Enslaved Africans' labor on plantations in the New World fueled the rise of European industry. Specifically, the first industrial power, Britain, can trace much of its early manufacturing strength to the slave trade and to the slave plantation system. Colonial North America's economy was anchored on slave-grown sugar as the critical input to the production of molasses and rum for domestic sale and especially for export. The beginnings of French industrialization can also be found in the slavery trade. It is clear that African economic backwardness finds its beginnings there as well.

This perspective is far from uniquely my own. The fullest presentation of this vision of how the world's wealth got to be so unequally divided is in the work of three intellectuals from the West Indies whom I refer to as the Caribbean school of scholarship: Eric Williams, C. L. R. James, and Walter Rodney. Williams, the first postindependence prime minister of Trinidad and Tobago, wrote a classic study, *Capitalism and Slavery*, which detailed the specific ways in which British economic development was spurred by the slavery trade, culminating in the consolidation of the British industrial revolution by the end of the eighteenth century. C. L. R. James's *Black Jacobins*, still the definitive study of the Haitian slave revolution, demonstrates specifically how French industry grew from its strong linkages to the slavery trade. And Rodney's book *How Europe Underdeveloped Africa* (1972), demonstrates how African economic development was stunted by the impact of the slave trade on the continent.

This essay summarizes and extends several of the arguments advanced in those classic works. It describes the economic motives that precipitated the initial establishment, consolidation, and expansion of the Atlantic slave trade. The stimulus to European manufacturing industries resulting from the slave trade and from the expansion of plantation slavery is also explored. The devastating effects of the slave trade on stability and economic development in Africa are also discussed, providing a basis for understanding the current disparities in income levels between African countries and their aforementioned Western counterparts.

THE MERCANTILIST FOUNDATIONS OF THE ATLANTIC SLAVE TRADE

To understand the motives behind the Europeans' participation in the enslavement of Africans and their use of enslaved Africans as plantation laborers in the Americas, one must understand the ideology of mercantilism, which informed the thinking of the European elites who designed national policies for their respective countries throughout most of the years of the Atlantic slave trade.

Merchantilist intellectuals identified two goals for national policy: military power and economic wealth. Economic wealth was associated with the expansion of manufacturing activities and the growth of exports of manufactured goods. Mercantilist thinkers generally embraced the idea that if their nation was to improve its position in either of these two areas—that is, be-

come stronger militarily or accumulate greater national wealth—other countries would have to become weaker or poorer. In short, mercantilists saw the international arena as one that operated under the principle of what political scientists call a *zero-sum game*, a scenario where the value of any gains to the winner are offset exactly by a loss of equal value to the loser.

Thus, mercantilism saw all nations as fundamentally in conflict with one another. Not only was military power linked to the goal of dominance on the high seas via naval warfare, but economic strength was linked to the goal of dominating international trade via commercial warfare. Britain was the first nation to achieve sustained industrialization precisely because it was the most effective at waging both types of mercantilist wars. Economic historian Joseph Inikori put it precisely:

> In the end Britain won [the cut-throat military struggle among Western European nations], cornered the lion's share of the opportunities, and developed the industries and financial institutions to launch the first capitalist economy in the world, thanks to African slaves whose forced specialisation in the production of commodities for Atlantic commerce was the foundation of the Atlantic system. (28)

Slavery played a central role in a strategy based on mercantilist goals because of the importance attributed to the development of colonial possessions. Colonies were valued because they were a potential source of mineral wealth and raw materials that could not be grown at home, which could be transformed into final, manufactured goods for export. Thus, over the course of the slave trade, the Americas became a major source of gold and silver as well as raw sugar, tobacco, and cotton. Colonies could also function as guaranteed markets for the export products of the home country. Furthermore, imperial rule could control the pace of industrialization in the colonies to ensure that they themselves did not become competitors in producing manufactured goods.

For colonies to perform these vital functions, they required a labor force. The indigenous populations were inadequate in numbers and kind. The European invasion of the Americas had decimated the Native Americans; particularly devastating were the actions of the Spanish "conquistadors," who wrought destruction by war and disease. The natives also knew the terrain and could often escape forced labor by fleeing further inland from the plantation and mining sites.

The European sources of labor were inadequate in numbers for two reasons. First, the price of voluntary migrants was too high to be cost-effective in producing the labor force "needed" to develop the Americas as a colonial breadbasket. Second, although some Europeans were kidnapped and put into the equivalent status of slave laborers in the Americas, to do this on an extensive basis would have depleted the home labor force in European countries. That in turn would have meant a rising price of labor in the home countries, making the cost of domestically produced goods more expensive and less competitive on the international market. Certainly mass emigration, forced or otherwise, was inconsistent with the populationist instincts widely shared by mercantilist thinkers.

Forced labor of Africa's peoples afforded the solution for the mercantilists. The reason was not that Africans were better suited to be slave laborers or were better adapted to the climate of the Caribbean plantations; the reason was that the process of slavery made Africans available in large numbers at prices that made plantation agriculture in the Americas profitable. Oliver Cox (1970, 332) observed, "Sometimes, probably because of its very obviousness, it is not realized that the slave trade was simply a way of recruiting labour for the purpose of exploiting the great natural resource of America." It was brutal recruitment and forced recruitment, but recruitment nonetheless. Williams (1994, 9), his words dripping with irony, noted that "the [native] reservoir was limited, the African inexhaustible. Negroes therefore were stolen in Africa to work the lands stolen from the Indians in America."

Some Africans were clearly implicated in the trade in slaves, serving as merchants of the trade on the African coast or as raiders who procured slaves by capturing others in the interior of the continent. But the demand that prompted the emergence of a complex supply network came from the mercantilist-inspired vision of the needs of colonial development in the Americas. Moreover, all Africans were confronted with a prisoner's dilemma after the trade got underway: either play a role in the network of slavers or be confronted with the much-greater risk of being enslaved oneself.

According to Eric Williams, the enslavement of black people was primarily motivated by economic factors—most notably, the practical requirements dictated by European greed for profits from the colonial system. Eric Williams was also correct in his contention that the enslavement of Africans produced antiblack racism. The enslavement of Africans in the interval from the sixteenth through the nineteenth centuries was the incubator for the emergence of antiblack racism in the New World. The central attributes of this type of racism were the beliefs in the intellectual, moral, and cultural inferiority of black people. Those beliefs have obviously outlived slavery.

Britain's success in playing the mercantilist game was phenomenal. For instance, Britain managed to run sustained trade surpluses with Portugal and Spain that had to be financed by bullion obtained by mineral wealth that was procured by slave labor in the mines of colonial America. A. W. Birnie (1935, 175, 180) estimates that in the early eighteenth century the Portuguese trade alone brought into London fifty thousand pounds worth of bullion from the mines of Brazil each week. Thus, the mineral wealth of Brazil was transferred to Britain, although Brazil was not a British colony. The influx of bullion helped keep interest rates low in Britain, thus preserving cheap credit conditions for manufacturers.

The triangular trade and the slave plantation system were critical for the buildup of British manufactures and the British acquisition of raw materials. Britain's major industrial cities—Liverpool, Manchester, Birmingham, and Bristol—all experienced rapid growth due to the direct or indirect stimulus of the slave trade. Liverpool was the home of the most extensive range of firms engaged in the slave trade. They obtained firearms from Birmingham and cotton textiles from Manchester so that they could be exchanged for slaves on the west African coast.

Of course, Manchester also imported slave-grown raw cotton to produce the textile output, thus receiving what Eric Williams called a "double stimulus." Bristol was a major naval and industrial shipyard, with vessels used in the slave trade made locally. The West Indian markets were an important outlet for English ironmongers. They produced the tools utilized in plantation agriculture. Moreover, they produced the chains used to imprison enslaved Africans at the transport sites on the African coast and during the middle passage. Furniture and pottery makers also benefited.

The growth in the importance of Africa and the Americas as receiving sites for British-manufactured exports, particularly manufactured goods other than textiles, is revealed clearly in the table reproduced from a paper by Joseph Inikori (1987) based on Ralph Davis's research (1969). By the 1770s the major export recipients for English manufactures, apart from woolen goods or textiles, were Africa and the Americas. By then Africa and the Americas ranked second to southern Europe as purchasing sites for English textiles. Table 2.1 clearly demonstrates the dramatic growth in the relative importance of Africa and the Americas as importers of English goods.

The economic gains resulting from this slavery-based economic expansion were massive. Even a conservative estimate of British profits from the slave trade in the interval 1784–1786 (£318,000) as a share of gross investment expenditures was three times as great as the share of profits from the auto industry in gross invest-ment expenditures in the United States in the 1980s. The ratio of profits from commodities made for export to the Americas and Africa to gross investment expenditures in Britain, again in 1784–1786, was 0.12, whereas the ratio of *all* manufacturing profits to gross investment in the United States two hundred years later was 0.10 (Darity 1990).

The financial sector also received a major boost from the slave trade. In particular, the British insurance industry developed rapidly by providing protection against losses for owners of slave-trading vessels. Williams (1994, 98–105) identifies the insurer Lloyds of London and the Barclays Bank as major British financial institutions that grew from the springboard of their direct connections to the slave trade. The same was true of banking firms based in Glasgow, Scotland.

C. L. R. James's work suggests that the positive impact of the slavery trade on France's economic development should not be underestimated. He identifies the growth of the cities of Nantes and Bordeaux as specifically tied to the stimulus they received from their merchants' involvement in the slave trade. Wine and brandy in Bordeaux utilized slave-grown sugars. James (1963, 48) reports that by the mid-eighteenth century there were "16 factories [refining] 10,000 tons of raw sugar from San Domingo [modern-day Haiti] every year, using nearly 4,000 tons of charcoal." Hence, there was a backward linkage and stimulus for the coal-mining industry as well. Similar effects can be identified for Holland and even Germany, although for the latter indirectly via trade linkages.

Table 2.1   Regional Distribution of English-Manufactured Exports, 1699–1774: Three-Year Averages (in thousands £)

	Rest of Europe		Southern Europe		Americas and Africa	
	WG	OG	WG	OG	WG	OG
1699–1701	1,544	383	1,201	73	185	290
1722–1724	986	141	1,606	226	30	337
1752–1754	1,326	257	1,954	390	374	1,197
1772–1774	963	650	1,667	337	1,148	2,533

Source: Inikori (1987).
Note: WG = woolen goods; OG = other goods.

THE ATLANTIC SLAVE TRADE: THE FOUNDATIONS OF ARRESTED DEVELOPMENT IN AFRICA

While the slave trade clearly enriched European countries—whether those actively involved in or those indirectly linked to this trade—the question still remains: What were the consequences of the Atlantic slave trade for Africa? Africa experienced an inversion of the economic benefits experienced by Europe from the slave trade. The vast, forced out-migration led to a comparative depopulation of the continent. The labor force for the development of a manufacturing sector was not present, had there even been the financial capacity to build such a sector. Furthermore, depopulation undermined the presence of sufficient density of population to produce the market demand that would have provided the necessary stimulus for the growth of industry.

Capture of slaves by raids and by warfare on communities led to the destruction of communities and to the disruption and destabilization of African civilization. To conduct the captures, the slave raiders would obtain firearms, trading slaves to get guns. Hence, what Inikori calls a slave–gun cycle got underway: slaves were exchanged to get firearms that were used to procure more slaves who were then traded for more firearms and so on. Imports of firearms, however, were certainly not productive inputs in other types of commercial activities.

The major commercial activity on the continent in the eighteenth century, apart from agricultural production, was the export of Africans into slavery. This activity did not have the rich web of backward and forward linkages that promoted the development of a wide array of industrial activities in Europe. While some individual traders grew quite wealthy, for the continent as a whole the slave trade was an economic disaster. Indeed, the slave export industry functioned as an enclave sector largely disconnected from other economic activities, apart from draining human resources from them.

CONCLUSION

As suggested in the introduction, the vast economic disparities we observe to this day between the European and the African orbit of nations is not accidental, nor is it attributable to European cognitive superiority. These disparities are also not the result of differences in climate or in the endowments of natural resources. Pure and simple, current inequalities were forged in the crucible of the slave trade, a key instrument of mercantilist policy in the period of the rise and the operation of the Atlantic economy. Profits generated by the slave trade and by plantation slavery provided the fuel for a continuing and self-perpetuating pattern of uneven development that will, in the absence of radical interventions, victimize people of African descent throughout the twenty-first century. It is this understanding that provides momentum for the reparations movement discussed in other chapters.

NOTE

William A. Darity Jr. is a Boshamer Professor of Economics at the University of North Carolina–Chapel Hill, as well as a research professor of public policy studies at Duke University.

REFERENCES

Birnie, A. W. 1935. *An Economic History of the British Isles.* London: Methuen.

Cox, Oliver. 1970. *Caste, Class, and Race.* London: Modern Reader.

Darity, William A., Jr. 1990. "British Industry and the West Indies Plantations." *Social Science History* 14, no. 1 (Spring): 117–149.

———. 2000. "Mercantilism, Slavery and the Industrial Revolution." In *Caribbean Slavery in the Atlantic World: A Student Reader,* ed. Verene Shepherd and Hilary Beckles, 480–492. Kingston, West Indies: Ian Randle (originally published in 1982).

Davis, Ralph. 1969. "English Foreign Trade, 1660–1700." In *The Growth of English Overseas Trade in the Seventeenth and Eighteenth Cen-*

turies, ed. Walter Minchenton. London: Croom Helm.

Inikori, Joseph. 1987. "Slavery and the Development of Industrial Capitalism in England." In *British Capitalism and Caribbean Slavery: The Legacy of Eric Williams,* ed. Barbara Solow and Stanley Engerman. Cambridge: Cambridge University Press.

———. 1993. *Slavery and the Rise of Capitalism: The 1993 Elsa Goveia Memorial Lecture.* Mona: Department of History, University of the West Indies.

James, C. L. R. 1963. *The Black Jacobins: Toussaint L'Ouverture and the San Domingo Revolution.* 2nd rev. ed. New York: Random House (originally published in 1936).

Rodney, Walter. 1972. *How Europe Underdeveloped Africa.* London: Bogle L'Ouverture.

United Nations Development Program. 2001. *Human Development Report 2001.* New York: Oxford University Press.

Williams, Eric. 1994. *Capitalism and Slavery.* Chapel Hill: University of North Carolina Press (originally published 1944).

3

The Critical Role of African Americans in the Development of the Pre–Civil War U.S. Economy

JAMES B. STEWART

This chapter examines how the institution of slavery was used to coerce blacks to play a major role in generating pre–Civil War regional and national economic growth. The important role of the Atlantic slave trade in establishing the conditions for the expansion of plantation slavery is first described. The discussion then focuses on the processes associated with plantation agriculture that facilitated exploitation of black labor and ingenuity. As explained, the outcome of these processes was the significant profits that fueled Southern and national economic growth. Also investigated are the conditions imposed on enslaved blacks, which limited their later ability to benefit substantially from emancipation. Three factors have combined to institutionalize the continually expanding black–white wealth disparities: slavery-induced impairments; public policies providing no land, compensation, or other assets to emancipated blacks; and a regime characterized by racial hostility in which economic, political, and social gains by blacks were under constant attack. This linkage between historical exploitation under slavery and current wealth disparities provides an important justification for reparations payments to compensate African Americans for losses suffered during and after slavery.

This chapter examines the critical role played by enslaved blacks in generating pre–Civil War regional and national economic growth. The starting point is the exploration of the impact of the Atlantic slave trade and the expansion of plantation slavery on the economic development and performance of colonies in what is now the United States. Traditional and contemporary historical studies of slavery—particularly the new body of knowledge generated through statistical, or cliometric, methods—help us to understand how the system of slave-based plantation agricul-

ture evolved, as well as its linkage to the U.S. national and other Western economies. This system generated substantial profits through the exploitation of black labor that fueled Southern and national economic growth. It is this pattern of exploitation that is the principal focus of this chapter.

Also reviewed are the efforts to quantify the losses experienced by blacks and the gains experienced by whites. Such estimates can be thought of as providing upper limits for contemporary reparations claims. Selected pre– and post–Civil War economic outcomes are compared to provide another perspective on the contributions of blacks to pre–Civil War economic growth. In addition, various post–Civil War economic initiatives undertaken by blacks are discussed to show how slavery limited opportunities for broad contributions to America's economic life and growth. Highlighted are implications from the study of contemporary debates about reparations.

CONTRIBUTIONS OF THE ATLANTIC SLAVE TRADE TO COLONIAL ECONOMIC DEVELOPMENT

W. E. B. DuBois, arguably the preeminent figure among African American scholars, asserts that the slave trade provided the foundations of European development for over four hundred years. "From 1442 to 1860, nearly half a millennium," DuBois insists, "the Christian world fattened on the stealing of human souls" (1904, 303). There is no doubt that the exploitation of enslaved Africans was especially vital to the development and performance of the U.S. economy in the latter decades of the eighteenth century and the first decade of the nineteenth century. Lorenzo Greene (1942, 68) declares that on the eve of the American Revolution the slave trade formed the very basis of the economic life of New England. According to Greene, "The vast sugar, molasses and rum trade, shipbuilding, the distilleries, a great many of the fisheries, the employment of artisans and seamen, even agriculture—all were dependent on the slave traffic" (69). DuBois (1896, 28–29) describes the trade in enslaved Africans as "a perfect circle":

> Owners of slavers carried slaves to South Carolina, and brought home naval stores for their shipbuilding; or to the West Indies, and brought home molasses; or to other colonies, and brought home hogs heads. The molasses were made into the highly prized New England rum, and shipped in those hogsheads to Africa for more slaves. Thus, the rum-distilling industry indicates to some extent the activity of new England in the slave-trade.

Ronald Bailey (1992, 209) observes, "Although relatively small in numbers, African slaves were connected to almost every aspect of the New England economy, working as house servants, in agricultural production, and in industry."

Robert Fogel (1989, 18) indicates that between 1502 and the 1860s "about 9,900,000 Africans were forcefully transported across the Atlantic." There are, of course, heated disagreements about the actual number of Africans who were seized from Africa and enslaved in the West, with some writers asserting that the number was much larger than that claimed by Fogel. The number of enslaved Africans entering what is now the United States was a small fraction of the total number of Africans who were captured and transported to the Western hemisphere. Over 75 percent of all enslaved Africans were imported into the Western hemisphere between 1451 and 1810, and the colonies that eventually became the United States accounted for only about 7 percent of that total (Fogel 1989, 18). Brazil was the final destination for the largest proportion of Africans transported across the Atlantic, accounting for about 41 percent of the total. According to Fogel, the "great majority of the slaves brought into the British, French, and Dutch Caribbean colonies were engaged in sugar production and its ancillary industries" (1989, 21).

In contrast, sugar cultivation played a relatively minor role in the development of slavery in the U.S. colonies. In 1760 about two-thirds of the enslaved Africans in the North American colonies were used in the cultivation of tobacco, rice, and indigo (Fogel 1989, 29). Africans imported into the Chesapeake region—namely, Virginia and Maryland—were central to tobacco production. The efficiency of tobacco production was enhanced through the use of the gang labor system, which involved strict supervision by overseers. South Carolina, however, became a major base of rice production (Trotter 2001, 65). Because many of the Africans who were imported into the low country of colonial South Carolina had knowledge of rice-growing techniques, rice cultivation exploited the human skills and knowledge—that is, the human capital—of enslaved Africans, in addition to their labor. The technology of rice production, with the skills and knowledge possessed by newly arrived Africans, enabled the use of the task system to organize work, rather than the gang system employed in tobacco production (Trotter 2001, 67). The task system provided enslaved Africans with greater latitude than the gang system did, permitting them "to set their own pace as long as they performed a set number of specified tasks" (69). Completing tasks early allowed enslaved Africans to "carve out time for themselves for cultivating their own crops, participating in the market economy, and increasing their level of autonomy" (69). Although more latitude may have existed under the task system than under the gang system, this did not mean that overall conditions faced by enslaved Africans were less severe in the lower South: "Tobacco cultivation was a difficult and arduous process that frequently strained 'every nerve' of the bondsmen and -women, but life and labor were even more difficult in the Lower South, where rice production dominated during the colonial era" (67).

Although the Atlantic slave trade was outlawed after 1807, it had already played a major role in establishing the foundations for expansion of a U.S. economy dependent on slave labor that would prosper until the onset of the Civil War. Bailey (1992, 207, 221) asserts that "the growth of the textile industry in New England between 1790 and 1860 . . . was strongly connected, through various routes, to the slave trade and the slave-based Atlantic economic system" and that this industry "was central to the industrial revolution in the U.S." In 1816, large-scale manufacturing in New England employed approximately five thousand workers, about 1 percent of the total U.S. workforce; by 1840, these figures had grown to one hundred thousand, about 14 percent of the workforce. Zevin (1971, 123) notes that "this remarkable explosion of industrial activity was dominated in every sense by the expansion of the cotton textile component of manufacturing." Although cotton textile production in New England was not directly dependent on maritime activities as such, there is no question that the capital undergirding the industry was generated through profits connected to the Atlantic slave trade Bailey (1992, 234). Joseph Inkori (1992) suggests that domestic textile production in New England increasingly displaced textile imports from England as the rapid settlement of areas west of the original colonies proceeded.

COTTON IS KING! BLACKS AND THE GROWTH OF THE SOUTHERN ECONOMY, 1820–1860

Studies examining the political economy of slavery between 1820 and 1860 have been marked by controversies that cloud recognition of the important contributions by blacks to the Southern and the national economic development. Researchers debate whether plantation owners were precapitalist landed gentry or shrewd capitalists; what the relative productivity was of enslaved blacks compared to free workers; and whether resistance by blacks had any measurable effect on plantation output. On one point, however, there is little dispute—the invention of the cotton gin precipitated a dramatic increase in the demand for enslaved labor that transformed the Southern economy.

The invention of the cotton gin in 1793 led to a wholesale restructuring of the Southern economy. Joe Trotter (2001, 151) explains that the cotton gin lowered the cost of cotton production, inducing landowners to shift production away from rice, indigo, and tobacco. Trotter declares, "The cotton gin enabled planters to expand the production of cotton beyond the coastal areas of Georgia and the Carolinas, into the interior where short-staple cotton dominated" (151). The demand for enslaved blacks to produce cotton increased dramatically, but the abolition of the Atlantic slave trade drastically limited the importation of enslaved Africans. (The trade was not totally eliminated, however—slightly more than fifty thousand Africans were illegally transported into the United States between 1808 and the beginning of the Civil War.)

The problem of ensuring an adequate labor supply was solved in part by the large-scale relocation of blacks—"as the demand for slave labor escalated, nearly 1 million Blacks migrated under the lash from the Upper to the Lower South" (Trotter 2001, 152). This massive redeployment of labor resources was facilitated by a well-organized internal slave trade that involved small and large urban-based operations. The population of enslaved blacks involved in cotton cultivation also grew through "natural" reproduction. Disagreements continue about the extent to which breeding efforts by planters contributed to population growth. Trotter insists, "Under the impact of growing demands for slave labor, many planters adopted a 'breeding mentality'" (2001, 152). However, Fogel counters, "Abolitionist claims that the high U.S. fertility rate was the consequence of the efforts of planters to manipulate the breeding of slaves as they did their cattle and to take advantage of changing market conditions, including the closing of the slave trade, cannot account . . . for trends in fertility within the United States" (1989, 151). Irrespective of the prevalence of breeding, "over the half century from 1810 to 1860 the [South's] demand for slaves increased twentyfold" (Fogel 1989, 64). By 1860 there were approximately four million enslaved blacks in the South, owned by almost four hundred thousand white families, representing possibly two million individuals, out of a population of eight million whites. The distribution of slave ownership was highly uneven, with 12 percent of slave-owning families owning slightly over 50 percent of the slaves.

The economic impact of the massive exploitation of black labor on output was remarkable. Cotton production increased dramatically: 300,000 bales in 1820; 700,000 in 1830; 2.0 million in 1850; 4.5 million in 1860 (Trotter 2001, 151). Douglass North (1961) suggests that the South's cotton economy was a leading sector of the nation's antebellum economy in part because cotton growers relied on outside interests to market crops, which provided employment for Northern commercial interests and stimulated food production in the Ohio valley.

Although disagreements persist about the level of profits generated by the slave-based economy, there is a general consensus that the system was profitable and that most plantations earned at least average profits when compared to other enterprises. Robert Fogel and Stanley Engerman (1971) argue that most large-scale slave owners earned a 10 percent return on their investments, a figure comparable to normal profit levels of Northern industrial enterprises. Management of large plantations took on some of the characteristics of managing industrial enterprises and involved similar problems. Smith insists,

The plantation owner aimed to maximize his profits by employing an overseer or manager of labor and by attempting to persuade him to look to the long-term maximization of plantation output. Overseers, however, tended to undermine planters efforts at profit maximization because they were paid fixed wages and received bonuses for short-term increases in cash crops. As a result, many planters assumed the dual role of planter-overseer in the Old South. (1998, 65)

Economic growth continued in the South even during the latter stages of the slavery regime. Per-capita income of the South grew at an annual rate of 1.7 percent between 1840 and 1860—a third faster than in the North (Fogel 1989, 87–88). The extent to which profitability and growth resulted from the efficiency of plantation agriculture is disputed. For example, Gavin Wright insists that the high regional growth rate experienced by the antebellum South did not result from the efficiency of labor extracted from enslaved Blacks but instead from "the extraordinary growth of the world demand for cotton between 1820 and 1860" (1976, 303).

Agricultural profits were generated disproportionately by intermediate and large plantations (respectively employing sixteen to twenty slaves and more than twenty slaves), where the gang labor system was used (Fogel 1989, 74–75). The highest levels of efficiency—that is, the maximum output per unit of labor—"were generally in those states that attracted the bulk of the interstate slave traffic" (75). Fogel insists that "the intermediate and large slave plantations of the cotton belt were nearly twice as efficient as the free farms . . . in 1860" (75). Slave owners used a combination of methods to extract desired levels of output from enslaved laborers. One technique involved altering the capital:labor ratio to increase labor productivity. Mark Smith notes that beginning in the 1830s planters attempted to "modernize slavery through the introduction of labor-saving equipment and modern management techniques" (1998, 10). Robert Fogel and Stanley Engerman maintain "expenditures on farming implements and machinery per improved acre were 25% higher in the seven leading cotton states than they were for the nation as a whole" (1974, 255).

In general, exploitation of black labor involved coercing artificially high levels of productivity per hour compared to free workers rather than requiring more hours of work per year. Fogel estimates that the productivity of enslaved blacks was "a third higher than that of free laborers" (1989, 187). John Olson (1992, 234–235) finds that although enslaved blacks worked fewer hours per year than free workers did in either the North or the South, they worked 94 percent harder each hour. It is important to recognize that conditions differed by region and by size of plantation, with the worst conditions generally associated with cotton production under conditions of gang labor.

Planters used a combination of violence and positive incentives to extract high levels of work effort. Trotter argues that "under the lash of the whip, 'gang' laborers had few incentives to work harder or faster" (2001, 165). Stephen Crawford (1992, 536) maintains that somewhere between 36 and 45 percent of enslaved blacks were on plantations where frequent physical punishment was employed. Various researchers, including Kenneth Stampp (1956), have described various modes of resistance by enslaved blacks to the inhumane work regime imposed on them, including revolts, sabotage, and work slowdowns. Eugene Genovese (1974) suggests that day-to-day struggle for improvement of conditions, rather than revolutionary assaults, was the chief form of resistance. Fogel is skeptical of claims of effective resistance, arguing that "even if day-to-day resistance was rife . . . [it] could reduce but not cancel out the greater intensity of gang labor" (1989, 159).

Plantation owners regularly used incentives to complement physical punishment. Fogel asserts, "The variety of positive incentives that masters developed to elicit the cooperation of slaves in their productive enterprises are evidence that naked force, indispensable as it was for the effective functioning of gang-system slavery, was not enough" (1989, 189). These incentives included prizes for the most cotton picked in a day, year-end bonuses, occupations involving greater prestige and responsibility, time off, and plots of land.

One of the most controversial issues in the slavery literature is the extent to which the family life of enslaved blacks was manipulated to serve planters' interests. Early scholars insisted that the institution of slavery precluded efforts by enslaved blacks to establish stable family relationships. As an example, E. Franklin Frazier (1966, 88) could see only "loose ties that had held men and women together in a nominal marriage relation during slavery" among enslaved blacks involved in agricultural labor. Contemporary scholars—such as John Blassingame, Eugene Genovese, and Herbert Gutman—have painted quite a different picture, one of remarkable family resilience in the face of continuing assaults and creativity in establishing other institutions (see Blassingame 1972; Genovese 1974; Gutman 1976). According to Trotter (2001, 186), "Enslaved families enabled black men and women to demonstrate their love for each other, offer each other and their children a modicum of protection, and initiate the young into the intricacies of human bondage and resistance."

More recent research has provided new evidence that partially reconciles the competing viewpoints. Stephen Crawford (1980) finds that a surprisingly high proportion (two-thirds) of enslaved adolescent blacks lived in two-parent families. At the same time, the other third lived in households where one or both parents were absent, typically as a result of one or both parents having been sold and relocated via the internal slave trade. Family life appears to have been more stable on larger plantations. Crawford reports that families headed by mothers only were 50 percent more frequent on plantations with fifteen or fewer slaves than they were on larger ones. Smaller plantations also had a disproportionately larger share of households where the father and mother lived on different plantations. Smith provides a useful summary statement: "The larger the number of slaves, the greater their opportunity for resisting slavery, for establishing bonds of community, and for cultivating their own culture" (1998, 43). To put this general observation into perspective, Fogel (1989, 185) reminds us that in 1850 there were only 125 plantations with 250 or more enslaved blacks, and only 20 percent of enslaved blacks were located on plantations with fifty or more of their compatriots.

In assessing the contributions of blacks to pre–Civil War economic growth, it is important to recognize that black labor was exploited outside of plantation agriculture as well. A useful context for discussing this issue is provided by Fogel's claim (1989, 101) that although the nonagricultural sector accounted for less than a quarter of Southern output in 1840, it was the source of about 40 percent of all the increase in the region's per-capita income during the last two decades of the antebellum era. We know also, as Mark Smith (1998, 74) observes, that "the South had about one-third of the nation's railroad mileage in 1860 and the network was financed primarily from southern and not northern investment capital." Not only was this rail network self-financed, enslaved blacks supplied the labor used in its construction. As noted by Starobin (1970), the South accounted for approximately 20 percent of invested industrial capital in the 1850s. Southern industry, such as textile manufacturing, made extensive use of slave labor and was intricately tied to slave labor. In the 1850s, between 160,000 and 260,000 slaves worked in industry, with four-fifths owned directly by industrial entrepreneurs. Starobin reports that industries employing slave labor were more profitable than were similar industries employing either integrated slave–free workforces or free workforces.

Slavery was a normal feature of Southern cities. In 1860 there were approximately seventy thousand urban slaves. The population of free and enslaved blacks in Southern cities was declining between 1850 and 1860, as the demand for agricultural labor increased. Put succinctly, enslaved blacks were relocated from the cities to plantations because redeployment into cotton production yielded greater returns to owners. In discussing slavery in urban areas, Wade (1964) has noted that public control replaced private supervision by owners because many enslaved blacks were allowed to "hire their own time" and to "live out" (find their own residence). These arrangements reduced the costs to owners of maintaining involvement in negotiating contractual arrangements for the employment of enslaved blacks and for providing for their subsistence. It also allowed enslaved blacks with such arrangements to capture some of the returns from their human capital. Owners were often paid fixed amounts that were less than the amounts earned, even after accounting for maintenance expenses. Trotter observes, "Artisans were the most numerous of the self-hirees," including "carpenters, tailors, seamstresses, and mechanics" (2001, 167). Roger Ransom and Richard Sutch provide a useful reminder that "only about 6 percent of adult male slaves held occupations above those of agricultural worker, unskilled laborer, or house servant" (1977, 15).

The sizable number of enslaved blacks with technical skills is a reminder that exploitation of enslaved blacks was not restricted to physical labor. As an example, many enslaved blacks working in metal, wood, or machinery developed new or improved technologies but were unable to obtain a patent because they were not U.S. citizens. Intellectual property rights of black inventors were typically appropriated by owners, although in some cases owners were unable to obtain patents for devices designed by enslaved blacks because they were not the actual innovators. Studies by Louis Haber and Vivian Sammons document the range of inventions by blacks during the slavery regime—including patents requested by Henry Blair (a free black) for a corn planter (1834) and a cotton planter (1836)—and provide evidence of black involvement in developing technologies contributing to economic growth and development (Haber 1970; Sammons 1990).

Another particularly pernicious form of forced appropriation involved the required transfers of wealth accumulated by blacks to purchase property rights in themselves and their kin in search of freedom and family cohesiveness. Robert Fogel observes, "Available evidence indicates that most manumissions during the late antebellum era were due to free Blacks who first purchased their relatives and then freed them" (1989, 194).

MEASURING GAINS TO WHITES AND LOSSES TO BLACKS

Despite the mountain of evidence chronicling exploitation of enslaved blacks under the U.S.

slavery regime, developing reliable estimates of the income and wealth generated directly and indirectly by this baneful system is difficult. Some of the produced income financed conspicuous consumption by planters, who would spend excessively on luxury items. Other income was converted into personal wealth holdings—namely, financial assets and real estate. Some income provided capital that financed large-scale industrial ventures, often in partnership with Northern interests. Accounting for the outcomes of these flows and transactions is problematic because much of the accumulated wealth of the slave regime was destroyed by the Civil War.

Ransom and Sutch (1990) estimate that enslaved blacks accounted for about 15 percent of the total private assets in the U.S. economy in the two decades preceding the Civil War. Robert Fogel (1989) reports that the top 1 percent of wealth holders in the South were generally rural planters operating businesses based on slave labor. These economic elites were richer, on average, than their Northern counterparts by a factor of about two to one. Moreover, the big planters of the cotton belt were generally consolidating their economic positions during the late antebellum era. The percentage of Southern households owning slaves declined from 36 percent in 1830 to 25 percent in 1860. Between 1850 and 1870 the real wealth of the typical gang system planter increased by 70 percent (Fogel 1989, 84). Toward the lower segments of the wealth distribution, the typical cotton belt farmer owned eight slaves, but enslaved blacks represented only about 50 percent of total wealth of these farmers (82). At the bottom of the wealth distribution, "The ordinary laborer . . . was too poor to purchase a single adult slave, let alone the land and other capital employed on the average farm in the cotton belt" (82).

While whites at the bottom of the wealth distribution may not have benefited materially from slavery as much as elites did, they were nevertheless beneficiaries of overall growth. Average wealth of nonslaveholding farmers in the South was several times greater than that of Northern laborers (Fogel 1989, 82). It can be argued that white Northern laborers were exploited by the emergent pattern of industrialization. As William Darity observes, "Karl Marx would have argued that the freedom of the wage laborers is also illusory. For Marx, wage labor was no more than wage slavery" (1990, 7). This was certainly true in the first half of the nineteenth century. At the same time there was a fundamental asymmetry between the situation of enslaved blacks and that of white Northern wage laborers. Each white ethnic group was eventually initiated into the fraternity of whiteness, which conferred access to enlarged income and wealth-generating opportunities, or what legal scholars such as Cheryl Harris (1993) define as property rights in whiteness that were, and continue to be, inaccessible to blacks.

Several efforts have been made to measure the gains accrued to whites and the losses experienced by blacks that are attributable to the slavery regime. Richard Vedder, Lowell Gallaway, and David Klingman (1990) estimate that approximately 25 percent of the total income in the Southern states was attributable to slave exploitation. According to their calculations, which assume a constant 7.51 percent return to slaveowners, enslaved blacks received about 50 percent of their marginal product in 1820; but this figure had declined to 32 percent by 1860. The authors calculate that the total wealth accumulated from slavery by the onset of the Civil War was about $3.2 million in 1859 dollars, which is the same figure calculated by Ransom and Sutch (1990). James Marketti (1990) has also estimated the losses incurred by Africans, resulting from enslavement during the 1790–1860 period. He finds that the value ranges from $2.1 billion to $4.7 billion (in 1983 dollars). Using similar techniques, Larry Neal (1990) calculates a figure of $1.4 trillion.

One factor that these various calculations overlook is the potential incremental income that could have been generated if systematic restrictions on human capital accumulation had not been in place. Laws restricting the education of enslaved blacks were first passed in the 1820s. Ransom and Sutch estimate that "probably no more than 2 to 5 percent of adolescent and adult slaves could read and write on the eve of the Civil War, and those were largely self-educated" (1977, 15).

The dietary practices employed by owners had perhaps even more detrimental effects on human capital accumulation, in addition to basic mortality patterns. Robert Fogel insists "excess death rates of children under 5 . . . accounted for nearly all the difference between the overall death rates of U.S. slaves and U.S. whites during the late antebellum era" (1989, 144). Fogel also contends that the available evidence indicates that surviving infants were disproportionately undersized and that small babies failed "to exhibit much catch up growth between birth and age 3 [suggesting] chronic undernourishment during these ages" (143). Infants' postnatal problems originated with the malnourishment of pregnant women who were subjected to "the intense routine of the gang system down to the eve of childbirth" (145). Pregnant women were not provided with nutritional supplementation that might have compensated for such high levels of physical activity. As a consequence, they generally failed to achieve sufficient weight gains "that would yield average birth weights and forestall infant death rates" (145).

Although Fogel does not make the logical connection, surviving black infants suffered short- and long-term complications as a result of prenatal and postnatal nutritional deficiencies. These conditions included impaired learning skills and chronic health problems that hampered efforts to accumulate human capital and compete in post–Civil War labor markets. We now know, as documented in the Center on Hunger and Poverty's *Statement on the Link between Nutrition and Cognitive Development in Children* (1998, 5), that "undernutrition—even in its 'milder' forms—during any period of childhood can have detrimental effects on the cognitive development of children and their later productivity as adults" (see also Brown and Pollitt, 1996). When undernutrition is coupled with the oppressive conditions associated with slavery, the results are even more disastrous. The center's report notes that "undernutrition along with environmental factors associated with poverty can permanently retard physical growth, brain development, and cognitive functioning [and] the longer a child's nutritional, emotional and educational needs go unmet, the greater the overall cognitive deficits" (8–9). In the case of very low birthweight infants, "permanent cognitive deficiencies associated with smaller head circumference may reflect diminished brain growth" (7). The center's report maintains that

"the greatest costs associated with undernutrition among children are the more intangible . . . opportunity costs—the costs of lost opportunity in which productivity with financial benefits would otherwise occur" (7). These opportunity costs are quite large because, as described by Robert Waterland and Cutberto Garza (1999), childhood malnutrition has lifelong consequences through its effects on the body's metabolism. These effects create increased morbidity and mortality risk associated with obesity, cardiovascular disease, high blood pressure, and diabetes. There is no question that these adverse health conditions resulted in significant losses for blacks in the post–Civil War economy.

THE LEGACY OF SLAVERY AND THE LATE-NINETEENTH-CENTURY ECONOMIC STATUS OF BLACK AMERICANS

The economic performance of the South deteriorated drastically during the 1860s and 1870s. Despite the exploitative dimensions of sharecropping and tenant farming, emancipation reduced the capacity of Southern interests to exploit black labor. Emancipation enabled blacks to significantly increase the portion of income actually received from agricultural pursuits. Ransom and Sutch suggest that Blacks' share of agricultural output "rose from 22 percent provided slaves on large plantations for their subsistence to . . . approximately 56 percent . . . received by black sharecroppers and tenant farmers in 1879" (1977, 4).

At the same time, blacks reduced their labor force participation and their hours of work—they "duplicated (perhaps emulated) the work–leisure patterns of other free Americans" (Ransom and Sutch 1977, 6). Hours worked declined for all age–gender cohorts, and "the cumulative effect was quite spectacular," with the decline in hours ranging "between 28 and 37 percent per capita" (6). However, Fogel notes that "by 1880 the labor force participation rate of blacks was probably quite close to prewar levels" (1989, 100). Moreover, "black and white farmers, equally endowed with capital and land, were equally productive in the 1880s and 1890s," and "whether black or white, farmers who toiled on small farms after the war were considerably less productive than the gang-system laborers of prewar times" (100).

Blacks were, however, unable to participate in postwar economic development solely on their own terms. As noted by Ranson and Sutch, "The economic institutions established in the post-emancipation era effectively operated to keep the black population a landless agricultural labor force operating tenant farms with a backward and unprogressive technology" (1977, 198). Furthermore, opportunities to acquire human capital and pursue economic ventures outside agriculture remained restricted.

Opportunities to acquire human capital and pursue economic ventures outside agriculture remained restricted. Despite efforts by the Freedmen's Bureau and other organizations, "in 1870 nearly 80 percent of black children aged ten to fourteen could neither read nor write [and] in 1880 over three-quarters of the black children in rural districts were not learning to write" (27–28). The absence of significant investment in the education of black children perpetuated high illiteracy rates among adults, which "remained over 80 percent . . . in 1880, and over 75 percent as late as 1890" (28). Moreover, not much progress was made in reducing the nutritional deficits that characterized the slavery experience. "Though the diet was probably a bit more varied than the rations of slaves forty years earlier, it still consisted primarily of corn and pork . . . that contained too little protein and too much fuel value," and working members of tenant farm families fared even less well than did hired field laborers (11).

Illiteracy was also a barrier to black artisans who attempted to take advantage of the skills acquired during slavery. Ransom and Sutch argue that "it is likely . . . many slave 'artisans' were illiterate [and]. . . . Probably found illiteracy a major obstacle to pursuing artisan trades independently" (1977, 35). Despite the barriers, black artisans fought to attain literacy, as documented by the fact that the literacy rate among artisans was four times higher than that among farm laborers (35).

Despite legal and other institutional restrictions, several examples illustrate how formerly enslaved blacks demonstrated entrepreneurship and innovativeness in carving out a space for themselves and in contributing to economic growth in the post–Civil War period. Janet Hermann (1981) and Joe Trotter (2001) describe how formerly enslaved blacks Benjamin and Isaiah Montgomery used their experience in operating six plantations in Davis Bend, Mississippi, during the Civil War years (two belonged to Confederate president Jefferson Davis and a relative) as a foundation for the establishment of the all-black town Mound Bayou, Mississippi. A similar development, researched by Elizabeth Bethel (1981), occurred in Promiseland, South Carolina. Post–Civil War black migration helped to provide markets that spurred transcontinental trade. Nell Painter (1977) has described the so-called exoduster movement during the late 1870s, which prompted two hundred thousand blacks to migrate from the South to the Midwest. Kenneth Hamilton (1991) has shown how this movement led to the establishment of several all-black towns, including Boley, Oklahoma.

Having gained citizenship, black inventors were finally able to assert intellectual property rights and obtain patents for inventions that improved, for example, the efficiency of railroads, manufacturing processes, and agriculture (see Haber 1970; Sammons 1990). Unfortunately, most black inventors had difficulty in capitalizing on their ingenuity due to limited access to investment capital. This phenomenon reflects, in part, institutional barriers to black wealth accumulation.

Comparisons of pre– and post–Civil War wealth distributions illustrate the nature of such barriers. The average personal estate in the South for whites fell dramatically from 1860 to 1870, primarily as a result of black emancipation (Soltow 1975, 140). However, maldistribution of landownership was only minimally affected by the war. The top 1 percent of wealthholders owned 29 percent of the real estate in 1860 and 27 percent in 1870 (140). Ransom and Sutch contend that "ownership of land was not fragmented in the process of subdividing the holdings into tenant farms" (1977, 78). Data from the 1900 census indicate further that landholding remained concentrated at the end of the century (80). Property assessment data for Southern states confirm large racial differences in property ownership. Average per-capita property assessments for blacks were $9.73 in 1880, compared to $269.18 for whites. Comparable figures in 1890, 1900, and 1910 were, respectively, $13.16, $19.75, and $23.88 for blacks; and $312.37, $296.25, and $321.22 for whites (Ng 2001). The dramatic disparity in wealth holdings between blacks and whites constitutes one of the most enduring legacies of the exploitation experienced by blacks during slavery.

CONCLUSION

The evidence presented in this chapter documents how the institution of slavery was used to coerce blacks to play a major role in generating pre–Civil War economic growth in the United States. Slavery enabled much of the product of black labor to be appropriated by various nonblack interests. Not only were the products of black labor and ingenuity appropriated by Whites, but conditions were imposed on blacks that left a continuing legacy of racial inequality in economic and noneconomic outcomes. Faced with a variety of structural barriers and individual impediments at the end of the Civil War, blacks have struggled to increase incomes and improve economic welfare. The difficulty of this struggle cannot be overstated, for, as emphasized by Roger Ransom and Richard Sutch, "unlike the indentured servants of Colonial America, blacks received no freedom dues; land redistribution was aborted and blacks were forced to begin their lives as free men and women without money, without tools, without work animals, without assets of any kind [and] their economic, political, and social freedom was under constant attack by the dominant white society, determined to preserve racial inequalities" (1977, 198). And, as shown in this chapter, newly emancipated blacks were forced to face the postwar world with physical and mental impairments deriving from the abuses associated with slavery.

Public discussion of reparations proposals to compensate African Americans for these experiences has intensified in recent years. In this chapter, the efforts to quantify losses experienced by blacks and the gains experienced by whites discussed can be thought of as providing upper limits for contemporary reparations claims. Research

by William Darity, Patrick Mason, and James Stewart (2001) indicates that a significant reduction in wealth inequality between blacks and whites requires a large-scale reparations-type wealth redistribution. Only such a redistribution is likely to generate the magnitude of funds necessary to overcome the long-term adverse health consequences among blacks that have their origins in the system of chattel slavery.

REFERENCES

Bailey, R. 1992. "The Slave(ry) Trade and the Development of Capitalism in the United States: The Textile Industry in New England." In *The Atlantic Slave Trade, Effects on Economies, Societies, and Peoples in Africa, the Americas, and Europe*, ed. J. Inkori and S. Engerman, 205–246. Durham, N.C.: Duke University Press.

Bethel, E. 1981. *Promiseland: A Century of Life in a Negro Community*. Philadelphia: Temple University Press.

Blassingame, J. 1972. *The Slave Community: Plantation Life in the Antebellum South*. New York: Oxford University Press.

Brown, J., and D. Pollitt. 1996. "Malnutrition, Poverty, and Intellectual Development." *Scientific American* 274:38–43.

Center on Hunger and Poverty. 1998. "Statement on the Link between Nutrition and Cognitive Development in Children." Waltham, Mass.: Center on Hunger and Poverty. Available at www.centeronhunger.org/pubs/cognitive.html.

Crawford, S. 1980. "Quantified Memory: A Study of the WPA and Fisk University Slave Narrative Collections." Ph.D. diss., University of Chicago.

———. 1992. "Punishments and Rewards." In *Without Consent or Contract: The Rise and Fall of American Slavery*. Vol. 2: *Conditions of Slave Life and the Transition to Freedom Technical Papers*, ed. R. Fogel and S. Engerman, 536–550. New York: W. W. Norton.

Darity, W. 1990. "Forty Acres and a Mule: Placing a Price Tag on Oppression." In *The Wealth of Races, The Present Value of Benefits from Past Injustices*, ed. R. America, 4–13. Westport, Conn.: Greenwood Press.

Darity, W., P. Mason, and J. Stewart. 2001. "The Economics of Identity: The Origin and Persistence of Racial Norm." Unpublished manuscript.

DuBois, W. E. B. 1896. *The Suppression of the African Slave Trade to the United States, 1638–1870.* London: Longmans, Green.

———. 1904. "The Development of a People." *International Journal of Ethics* 14:292–311.

Fogel, R. 1989. *Without Consent or Contract: The Rise and Fall of American Slavery.* New York: W. W. Norton.

Fogel, R. and S. Engerman, eds. 1971. *The Reinterpretation of American Economic History.* New York: Harper and Row.

———. 1974. *Time on the Cross: The Economics of American Negro Slavery.* 2 vols. Boston: Little, Brown.

Frazier, E. F. 1966. *The Negro Family in the United States.* Revised and abridged ed. Chicago: University of Chicago Press (originally published in 1939).

Genovese, E. 1974. *Roll, Jordan, Roll: The World the Slaves Made.* New York: Pantheon Books.

Greene, L. 1942. *The Negro in Colonial New England, 1620–1776.* New York: Columbia University Press.

Gutman, H. 1976. *The Black Family in Slavery and Freedom, 1750–1925.* New York: Pantheon Books.

Haber, L. 1970. *Black Pioneers of Science and Invention.* New York: Harcourt, Brace and World.

Hamilton, K. 1991. *Black Towns and Profit: Promotion and Development in the Trans-Appalachian West, 1877–1915.* Urbana: University of Illinois Press.

Harris, C. 1993. "Whiteness as Property." *Harvard Law Review* 106, no. 8 (June): 1709–1791.

Hermann, J. 1981. *The Pursuit of a Dream.* New York: Oxford University Press.

Inkori, J. 1992. "Slavery and the Revolution in Cotton Textile Production in England." In *The Atlantic Slave Trade, Effects on Economies, Societies, and Peoples in Africa, the Americas, and Europe,* ed. J. Inkori and S. Engerman, 145–181. Durham, N.C.: Duke University Press.

Marketti, J. 1990. "Estimated Present Value of Income Diverted during Slavery." In *The Wealth of Races, The Present Value of Benefits from Past Injustices,* ed. R. America, 107–123. Westport, Conn.: Greenwood Press.

Neal, L. 1990. "A Calculation and Comparison of the Current Benefits of Slavery and an Analysis of Who Benefits." In *The Wealth of Races: The Present Value of Benefits from Past Injustices,* ed. R. America, 91–105. Westport, Conn.: Greenwood Press.

Ng, K. 2001. "Wealth Redistribution, Race, and Southern Public Schools, 1880–1910." *Education Policy Analysis Archives* 9, no. 16 (May 13).

North, D. 1961. *The Economic Growth of the United States, 1790–1860.* Englewood Cliffs, N.J.: Prentice-Hall.

Olson, J. 1992. "Clock Time versus Real Time: A Comparison of the Lengths of the Northern and Southern Agricultural Work Years." In *Without Consent or Contract: The Rise and Fall of American Slavery.* Vol. 1: *Conditions of Slave Life and the Transition to Freedom Technical Papers,* ed. R. Fogel and S. Engerman, 216–240. New York: W. W. Norton.

Painter, N. 1977. *Exodusters: Black Migration to Kansas after Reconstruction.* New York: Knopf.

Ransom, R., and R. Sutch. 1977. *One Kind of Freedom: The Economic Consequences of Emancipation.* New York: Cambridge University Press.

———. 1990. "Who Pays for Slavery." In *The Wealth of Races: The Present Value of Benefits from Past Injustices,* ed. R. America, 31–54. Westport, Conn.: Greenwood Press.

Sammons, V. 1990. *Blacks in Science and Medicine.* New York: Hemisphere Publishing.

Smith, M. 1998. *Debating Slavery, Economy, and Society in the Antebellum American South.* Cambridge: Cambridge University Press.

Soltow, L. 1975. *Men and Wealth in the United States, 1850–1870.* New Haven, Conn.: Yale University Press.

Stampp, K. 1956. *The Peculiar Institution: Slavery in the Antebellum South.* New York: Vintage Books.

Starobin, R. 1970. *Industrial Slavery in the Old South.* New York: Oxford University Press.

Trotter, J. 2001. *The African American Experience.* Boston: Houghton Mifflin.

Vedder, R., L. Galloway, and D. Klingman. "Black Exploitation and White Benefits: The Civil War Income Revolution." In *The Wealth of Races: The Present Value of Benefits from Past Injustices,* ed. R. America, 125–137. Westport, Conn.: Greenwood Press.

Wade, R. 1964. *Slavery in the Cities: The South, 1820–1860.* New York: Oxford University Press.

Waterland, R., and C. Garza. 1999. "Potential Mechanisms of Metabolic Imprinting That Lead to Chronic Disease." *American Journal of Clinical Nutrition* 69:179–197.

Wright, G. 1976. "Prosperity, Progress, and American Slavery." In *Reckoning with Slavery: A Critical Study in the Quantitative History of American Negro Slavery,* ed. P. David et al., 302–336. New York: Oxford University Press.

Zevin, R. 1971. "The Growth of Cotton Textile Production after 1815." In *The Reinterpretation of American Economic History,* ed. R. Fogel and S. Engerman, 122–147. New York: Harper and Row.

4

The Black Sharecropping System and Its Decline

DANIEL FUSFELD and TIMOTHY BATES

This chapter traces changes in the organization of Southern agricultural labor from Reconstruction until the 1950s. Landowners, enabled by state laws, manipulated tenancy arrangements to keep the livelihood of poor blacks and whites linked directly to cotton cultivation. Blacks were disproportionately found in sharecropping, the most oppressive condition, in which the farmer paid for the use of the land by "sharing" crops with the landlord (typically 50 percent). Federal agricultural policies led to the displacement of many tenants during the 1930s, whereas others had their benefits reduced or expropriated by unscrupulous landowners. As agriculture became increasingly mechanized and cotton declined in importance, tenancy arrangements were eliminated, and millions of uprooted blacks migrated to Northern urban areas.

After the Civil War, cotton was raised increasingly by a system of sharecropping, whereby tenants worked the land "on halves." In 1880, 64 percent of all Southern farms were owner operated, but this figure was lower in the Cotton Belt. The percentage of farms operated by owners fell steadily, reaching 53 percent in 1900 and 44 percent in 1930.[1] The majority of tenants worked on small holdings rather than large plantations, and white tenants were more numerous than blacks were. Whites, however, were most commonly working on the small holdings in hilly regions and in areas with less-fertile soil. The plantations, which relied more heavily on cotton than did the small farms dominated the rich bottomlands, where soil fertility was greatest. Unlike the majority population on small farms, the majority of plantation tenants were black.

Southern agricultural workers who did not own land were of four types: cash tenants, share tenants, share croppers, and wage laborers. The most affluent agricultural workers were tenants who paid a cash rental for the use of the land. These tenants owned their own equipment and made their own decisions about growing and marketing crops. Cash tenants were the least common type of black agricultural workers. Share tenants, because they owned some of their own equipment, were able to rent land on the basis of paying the owner between one-fourth and one-third of the crop raised. Sharecroppers, in contrast, had nothing to offer but their own labor. The landowner provided the sharecropper with the mules and equipment necessary to raise a cotton crop, and in return the sharecropper paid, as rent, about one-half of the cotton crop. In addition, share tenants and croppers had to pay (out of their personal share of the crop) for seed, fertilizer, and food supplies that were provided to them by the landowner. Share tenants and croppers were provided with a two- or three-room wooden shack, and they were often allowed to raise vegetable gardens for personal use. The poorest agricultural workers were wage laborers. They were not guaranteed any fixed amount of work; they were employed by the day when they were needed; and they may or may not have been provided with a shack to live in. As the traditional cotton economy deteriorated in the 1920s and 1930s, blacks were increasingly downgraded from share tenant and cropper status to the wage labor status. Early agricultural mechanization also encouraged downgrading to wage labor status.

Share tenants and croppers were designated as farmers in the census, but they closely resembled ordinary laborers in many ways. They were told what crops to plant, when to plant them, and the number of acres to be planted. Especially on the large plantations, their work would be regularly supervised by the landlord or his agents. Share tenants and croppers were entrepreneurs, however, in one important sense: they carried a considerable share of the risk involved in raising and marketing the crop. When the crop was bad or when prices for cotton were particularly low, the cropper might find himself at harvest time with no remaining cash after the landlord had charged him for food, seed, and fertilizer. The tenant would then be entirely dependent on home-raised produce plus cash advances or credit arranged by the landlord. Living in a perpetual state of indebtedness to the landowner was not uncommon. When the cotton crop was sold, the tenant had to take the landlord's word for the price that was obtained. Furthermore, the landlord not only kept all accounts on credit and all supplies advanced to the tenant, but he also determined the rate of interest charged on all advances. Tenants were not allowed to question or even to check the accuracy of the landlord's accounting for crop proceeds, advances, and interest charges. When the landlords themselves were close to bankruptcy, the temptation to cheat the tenants at settlement time must have been particularly strong. Blatant cheating of tenants, though, would have made it difficult for the landowner to attract and hold good workers.

The advancing of food, clothing, and supplies to sharecroppers was quite normal because these workers typically had no resources of their own—otherwise they would not have been sharecroppers. The cropper would most commonly receive credit from the landlord, usually at a particular store or commissary, to purchase food and other necessities up to a certain amount each month. Since this restricted the cropper to purchase only

at the store where credit was available, it was an easy matter to considerably mark up prices on tenant purchases. A study of the Mississippi Delta area in 1936 showed that the average subsistence advance per year was roughly $94 for sharecroppers and $138 for share tenants. An additional $68 and $145, respectively, were advanced to sharecroppers and share tenants for seed and fertilizer.[2] A flat 10 percent interest rate was normally charged on these advances at settlement time, after the crop was sold in the fall. Since the duration of the advance was much less than one year, the effective annual rate of interest paid by share tenants and croppers was several times the 10 percent rate. The burden of paying 20 to 30 percent interest for goods purchased on credit at high prices kept many of the tenants in a perpetual state of indebtedness. Under these circumstances, it was difficult to accumulate the wealth that would allow for upward mobility to share tenant or cash tenant status, much less actual landownership.

Some incentive was necessary to keep up the laboring efforts of the share tenants and croppers. Since the share tenants owned their own mules and equipment, they faced the threat of losing these to the landlord if their cotton crop was not sufficient to pay off debts at harvest time. For the cropper, there was the threat of being thrown out by the landlord if one did not appear to be working diligently on the cotton crop. Finally, there was always the possibility of producing a big crop when cotton prices were high, enabling the tenant to pay off the landlord's advances and to have enough cash to live on without further credit. Once clear of debt at usurious interest rates and high commissary prices, the tenant could then perhaps accumulate enough money to become a cash tenant, to buy an automobile, or even to purchase land. Enough black share tenants and croppers achieved such improved economic status, especially if they worked for honest landlords, to serve as examples for the payoffs of hard work. At the other extreme, the perpetual failure to escape indebtedness and to get ahead created many disillusioned tenants whose chief concern was merely to get by. It was difficult for the sharecroppers to escape from their status. State legislation made it virtually impossible for share tenant and cropper families to leave the land except in the fall after harvest time. Although debt peonage had been declared illegal by the Supreme Court in 1911, similar types of bondage were common. Tenants who were in debt to their landlords could be prevented from moving away until they paid off the indebtedness. This practice was made effective by gentlemen's agreements among landlords in that they would accept tenants from other planters only if the move was approved by the present landlord. Since dishonest landowners could readily keep their tenants in debt, the only possible escape was often to flee the community entirely. Tenants' dissatisfaction with landlords did in fact generate their frequent moving from place to place, with whites being generally more mobile than blacks and with the lowest class of tenants being more mobile than cash and share tenants. Indeed, in 1934 black sharecroppers in the Cotton Belt counties of Georgia were estimated to have a median residence length of less than three years.[3] Frequent moving from place to place made it difficult to develop a good vegetable garden; it certainly did not encourage sound soil conservation practices.

Overall, the share tenants and croppers in the Cotton Belt lived poor lives, and their chances for upward mobility were slim. With the landowner having the power to determine crops, planting and harvesting times, cultivation techniques, and final crop marketing, independent decision making by tenants was certainly not encouraged. Many planters discouraged tenants from developing good gardens, fearing that vegetable gardening would interfere with cotton cultivation; some landlords would not even permit tenant gardens. The tenant had no incentive to improve his living quarters because all improvements were the landlord's property. Many landlords looked down on efforts by black families to educate their children, preferring that the youngsters work in the cotton fields. Tenant families resided in wooden shacks that had glassless and screenless windows as well as leaky roofs. Black tenant families were often provided with open privies, but about one-third of them had no privies at all. Diet was dominated by the three *M*s—meat, meal, and molasses—foods rich in fats and low in vitamin content. Fat salt pork followed by cornmeal typically accounted for over 60 percent (and up to 70 percent) of the caloric intake of black tenant families.[4] Particularly among families that did not raise gardens for personal use, this diet frequently caused such vitamin deficiency diseases as pellagra. Poor diet also produced high susceptibility to contagious diseases, low vitality, and a high death rate. Black tenant families suffered from an extremely high incidence of tuberculosis when they moved to congested urban ghettos.

Incentives that did exist under this system were often perverse: it was to the tenant's advantage to rob the soil of its fertility. The tenant's incentive was to make no repairs or investments that were likely to outlive his tenure at his present residence. Once he had decided to move, the tenant found it to his advantage to burn planks from the porch floor as firewood and to take along any moveable materials that had not succumbed to the ravages of earlier tenants. The result was exhausted soil and buildings unfit for human habitation, but the soil often continued to be used for cotton cultivation and the buildings housed more groups of tenant families. The result was a growing group of tenants with the attitude of "What's the use of trying?"

The white landowner, of course, rationalized his privileged position by claiming that the tenants were childlike and improvident, willing to work only when in need of food. He had to tell his tenants what to plant, how to plant it, and when to harvest it. Why, if he did not keep an eye on them, they might starve to death. The typical tenants, according to the typical landlord, would not even bother to grow a garden unless they were told to do so. Tenants were seen as naturally lazy and shiftless, incapable of making a living without supervision; tenants would not even fix their own leaky roofs. In financial matters, the landlord must maintain a watchful eye on tenant money; otherwise, the tenant would throw it away on foolish expenditures. Sweet benevolence—at 30 percent interest rates. The Southern planters' rationale for sharecropping closely resembled their rationale for slavery.

BAD TIMES

Periodic bad times were a normal part of life in the Cotton Belt. The early 1890s, for example, produced several years of particularly poor weather, whereas the early twentieth century brought severe boll weevil invasions that devastated the crop in parts of the western Cotton Belt.

During these bad times, the tenants fell deeper in debt to the landlords, and the landlords assumed an increased indebtedness with such creditors as banks and insurance companies. Some of the weaker planters failed during these periods, but the system in general continued, waiting for high prices and large cotton crops to restore profitability and reduce the debt burden. World War I produced high cotton prices, generating prosperity even in regions where crops had been reduced by boll weevil infestation. Many tenants actually shared in this wartime prosperity.

During the 1920s and early 1930s, however, the Cotton Belt was devastated by disasters of nature and the marketplace. Year after year of poor crops combined with low cotton prices drove planters and tenants deeper into debt. Prices of cotton lands plummeted in value, and hundreds of banks that had financed landowners were themselves driven into bankruptcy by the prolonged Cotton Belt depression. As credit dried up and as millions of acres of land fell into the hands of creditors, the landlord's traditional willingness to provide for his tenants through advances of food and supplies became less and less common. Creditors such as life insurance companies acquired land when plantation owners defaulted on their loans, and these new owners had no interest in supplying food, seed, and fertilizer to sharecropper families. They wanted to rent the land to cash tenants, but the sharecroppers could not afford to feed themselves, much less pay cash rents. When landowner advances were not forthcoming, many tenants had no way to plant a crop, or even to survive, so

they left for villages and urban areas. Fortunate tenants with relatives in the cities were frequently provided with sufficient transportation money to leave the Cotton Belt, often moving to Northern cities where their relatives were enjoying the benefits of a strong job market during the 1920s.

Greene County, Georgia, provides an extreme example of the combined impacts of boll weevil infestation and low cotton prices (see Table 4.1).[5]

During the ten years following 1924, the annual cotton crop fluctuated between forty-four hundred and eighty-seven hundred bales. Greene County was quite prosperous at the end of World War I. The boll weevil invasion of the early 1920s, however, devastated cotton yields, and consistently low prices for the meager crop drove most of the large planters into bankruptcy. Thousands of tenant families left the county entirely, and large tracts of cotton land reverted to brush and pines by the late 1920s. By 1925, land prices had dropped to one-fifth of their 1919 level, and pine sawlogs had displaced cotton as the leading agricultural cash crop in the county. Traditional Cotton Belt agriculture never again reached more than a fraction of its former self in Greene County; most of the old plantation owners were gone for good, and the tenant families had scattered. By 1927, nearly sixteen thousand acres had been sold by the sheriff for back taxes; the unpaid taxes amounted to $5,870, less than thirty-seven cents per acre on average. Throughout Georgia and South Carolina, many cotton farms and plantations were permanently abandoned during the 1920s.

The reduced output of cotton would have produced, via supply-and-demand forces in the marketplace, sharply higher prices in earlier times. In the 1920s, however, the United States

Table 4.1   Number of Cotton Bales Ginned per Year in Greene County, Georgia

Year	Bales
1918	18,773
1919	20,030
1920	13,414
1921	1,487
1922	333
1923	1,490
1924	4,279

was losing its share of the world cotton market to aggressively expanding cotton producers in Egypt, India, Brazil, and a host of other countries (over 50 percent of U.S. crop was sold abroad). Nations such as Russia and China were expanding cotton production rapidly to meet their domestic needs, while cotton cultivation was springing up in new producing areas such as Nigeria and Uganda. Domestically, a new kind of cotton cultivation was spreading in Texas and Oklahoma that was more mechanized and less dependent on tenant labor than cotton production in the deep South.

Depression in the early 1930s produced even lower demand for cotton and hence even lower prices. A study of two thousand cotton-production tenant families in Mississippi, Alabama, Texas, and South Carolina found that average cash income in 1933 was $105.43.[6] In that year the federal government instituted a series of agricultural programs, particularly the Agricultural Adjustment Program (AAA), that were destined to push tens of thousands of black families out of tenancy. With its overall objective to raise and stabilize farm income, the AAA paid direct subsidies to farmers who agreed to reduce their cotton crop acreages. Landlords, of course, divided the reduced cotton acreage among fewer tenants and expelled thousands of now-superfluous tenants from their lands. Government payments to compensate farmers for their acreage reductions were supposed to be shared between the tenant and the landowner, according to the usual share of the crop that each received. The landlord was given the responsibility for paying the tenant his portion of the government money. Since tenants were often deeply in debt to their landlords, their share of the funds was not given to them—it was merely applied to their outstanding debt. Other landlords simply cheated the tenants out of their rightful portion. One major problem regarding administration of the AAA program, which was administered at the county level, was that blacks were politically powerless throughout the Cotton Belt. A 1937 study by the Brookings Institution concluded that the AAA had "found no way of writing a contract that would guarantee the cropper his share in the benefit payments."[7] Overall, the landlord had been given a strong economic incentive to reduce their tenant labor force when they drastically reduced their cotton acreage, and they had been given much of the responsibility for administering the AAA programs. The results were predictable.

Two additional strategies for taking the tenants' share of AAA benefit payments were mechanization and reduction of tenants to wage labor status; the two were closely interrelated. Tenants who were reduced to wage laborers were not entitled to a portion of the government subsidies. Increased mechanization was aided directly by the AAA's success in raising cotton prices and by the income supplement that benefit payments provided to landowners. In the mid- to late 1930s, sales of farm equipment increased dramatically in all parts of the United States. Over one-third of all the tractors in use in U.S. agriculture during early 1938 had been produced between 1935 and 1937. Farm equipment sales jumped from $90 million in 1932 to over $507 million in 1937.[8] During the 1930s, the number of tractors on southern farms increased by 86 percent, while the number of tractors in non-Southern states increased by 67 percent.[9] Mechanization was particularly rapid in Oklahoma and Texas. As mechanization increased in the Cotton Belt, the demand for tenants fell and the numbers of employed wage laborers rose.

The mechanization of cotton farming was actually a three-stage process that started in the 1930s and reached completion in the mid-1950s. The older method of cotton production utilized mule power for soil preparation at planting time and hand power for weeding and picking the crop. This labor-intensive technology dominated until the early 1940s but declined rapidly during the late 1930s. The first stage of mechanization entailed using tractors to prepare the soil for planting; weeding and picking were still done by hand, increasingly by wage laborers. Texas in the 1930s began to rely on Mexican migrant labor for cotton picking. This first stage of mechanization was dominant throughout the 1940s, although it began to lose ground to the second stage later in the decade. The second stage of mechanization utilized tractor power for soil preparation and crop cultivation; herbicides largely replaced hand weeding, but picking was still done by hand. The second stage was dominant in the early 1950s only; perfection of mechanized cotton-picking equipment caused elimination in the 1950s of the only remaining labor-intensive step—handpicking the cotton. The need for vast numbers of workers in the Cotton Belt was thus eliminated by the mid-1950s. From 1940 to 1960, output per man hour in cotton production increased more than threefold.[10] In Mississippi alone, nearly one million people left agriculture, a decline of 62 percent in two decades.

Mechanization was aided in the 1930s by government-sponsored agencies that increased the availability and reduced the cost of credit to farmers. Overall, acreage-reduction programs increased crop prices; government payments compensated landowners for acres not planted in cash crops; and farm incomes were increased. The combination of higher farm incomes and easier access to credit made it possible for many landowners to finance mechanization of their operations. Mechanization reduced the need for agricultural workers, and those who were employed in the remaining labor-intensive phases of crop production were able to find work fewer days each year relative to the premechanization phase of farming. The 1940 census revealed that the number of Southern tenants declined by 342,000 during the 1930s decade, and 192,000 of these displaced tenants (including croppers) were black.

As blacks were increasingly pushed out of tenant status, some remained in their plantation shacks and worked as wage laborers part of the year. Others moved to local villages and tried to make a living from a combination of part-time agricultural work, nonfarm employment, and relief. Some displaced tenants left the Cotton Belt entirely, moving to Southern and Northern cities where employment was sparse but where government relief was more available than it had been in the rural South. Those who tried to survive as agricultural workers found that the landowners were largely unconcerned about any lack of life's necessities that they might experience in the farming slack seasons. The wage laborer was on his own; his ability to survive in the South was no longer of much concern to the planters. Cheap labor could be hired in abundance by Southern planters throughout the depression decade. The later 1930s, however, were relatively good times for one group of black agricultural workers. Those remaining share tenants and croppers benefited directly from the higher cotton prices resulting from the AAA's acreage-reduction programs. These tenants also shared in the prosperity of high World War II cotton prices, but they were displaced en masse in the years following the war.

NOTES

1. Gurmar Myrdal, *An American Dilemma* (New York: Harper, 1962), 242.

2. Myrdal, *An American Dilemma*, 247.

3. Arthur Raper, *Preface to Peasantry* (Chapel Hill: University of North Carolina Press, 1936), 161.

4. Charles Johnson, Edwin Embree, and W. W. Alexander, *The Collapse of Cotton Tenancy* (Chapel Hill: University of North Carolina Press, 1935), 17.

5. Raper, *Preface to Peasantry*, 202.

6. Johnson, Embree, and Alexander, *The Collapse of Cotton Tenancy*, 12.

7. Edwin Nourse, Joseph Davis, and John Black, *Three Years of the Agricultural Adjustment Administration* (Washington, D.C.: Brookings Institution, 1937), 342.

8. C. Horace Hamilton, "The Social Effects of Recent Trends in the Mechanization of Agriculture," *Rural Sociology* 4, no. 1 (1939): 3.

9. Myrdal, *An American Dilemma*, 1248.

10. Richard Day, "The Economics of Technological Change and the Demise of the Sharecropper," *American Economic Review* 57, no. 3 (1967): 427–428.

5

The Rise of the Black Industrial
Working Class, 1915–1918

PHILIP S. FONER

This chapter describes and analyzes the periods of African American migration to the urbanized North. Before the turn of the century, the African American community lay overwhelmingly in the South and was overwhelmingly engaged in agriculture. Most of those engaged in agriculture in the South were propertyless and mobile. The immense wartime demand for labor drew black workers north to the cities, where they encountered resistance from trade unions and various European ethnic groups. The postwar recession fell hardest on black workers, exposing the vulnerability of their gains. Nevertheless, the migration to the cities was a major step forward for African American labor.

Before 1915 the treatment of the Southern Negro caused a steady trickle northward. From 1916 to 1918 the trickle became a flood that brought hundreds of thousands of blacks to the North. Earlier migrations to Northern cities had come from the upper South. Now blacks came in from all over Dixie, with the Deep South having the heaviest representation.

Many explanations have been advanced to account for the great migration of Negroes during World War I. Surely the general status of the Negro in the South—the lack of political rights, the social subordination, the economic peonage, the poor educational facilities, the intimidation, and segregation—contributed prominently. But the fundamental motivating force, as in the migration of any people, was economic—the great magnet of employment opportunities. In 1913–1914 the country had been in a minor depression, but beginning in 1915 American industry—largely concentrated in the North—entered a period of great prosperity, stimulated by the demands of the war in Europe and by the later war needs of the United States itself. A great demand for labor arose in such industries as steel, meatpacking, automobile manufacture, munitions, shipyards, mines, transportation enterprises, and many others that directly or indirectly played a role in war production.

In the past the immigrant masses had provided the industrial North with a cheap, readily available labor supply. But the war drastically curtailed the flow of immigrants: the volume declined from 1,218,480 in 1914 to 326,700 in 1915; 298,826 in 1916; 295,403 in 1917; and 110,618 in 1918. Moreover, a half-million immigrants already in the United States left for Europe between 1915 and 1918 to serve in the armed forces of their native lands. With more than four million men drafted into the armed services of the United States when war was declared on Germany in April 1917, the need became acute for workers to take the more skilled jobs of the draftees and to fill unskilled jobs as well.

In the half-century between emancipation and the outbreak of World War I, blacks, with few exceptions, had been unable to get work in the North except in domestic and personal occupations. But now, with the nation's usual labor force enormously depleted, Northern industrialists eagerly turned to the Southern Negroes, women as well as men, the only untapped source of common labor remaining in the country.

An intensive campaign was launched to recruit Southern blacks. American firms had employed labor recruiters for work among European peasants for decades, but this was the first time agents went South to bring black peasants to the North. The agents, sent by railroad and steel companies, initiated the migration by promising high wages, offering transportation subsidies, and distributing leaflets such as the following, scattered throughout Alabama:

Are you happy with your pay envelope? Would you like to go North where the laboring man shares the profits with the Boss? Are you satisfied with your condition here? Has your family all the comforts they should have during these prosperous times or are you just making "Both Ends Meet" while the other fellow is growing rich on your labor? ... Let's Go Back North. Where no trouble or labor exists, no strikes, no lock outs, large coal, good wages, fair treatment, two weeks pay, good houses. If you haven't got all these things you had better see us. Will send you where you can have all these things. All colored ministers can go free. Will advance you money if necessary. Go now. While you have the chance.[1]

This particular agent offered to pay not only the cost of transporting the worker but also the fare for his family, the freight charges on his household goods, and a "reasonable amount" of what he owed in his present town.

Northern industries had also asked the National Urban League's assistance in enlisting black labor as a replacement for the dwindling number of immigrant workers. The league helped to recruit blacks for Northern industry and aided them in their adjustment to life in the North.

The black press (more than four hundred periodicals) stimulated the trek of blacks northward. The *Chicago Defender* was the most influential voice, reaching thousands of Southern Negroes with blistering attacks on life in the South and with glowing reports of the high wages and better social conditions in the "Negro Heaven," north of the Mason-Dixon line. Letters from blacks who had already moved North were especially influential. In some states the demand for labor had sent wages for the unskilled as high as thirty-six cents an hour, and even the eighteen-to-twenty-cents hourly wage for unskilled workers on the railroads was considerably above what blacks commanded in the South. In Chicago, Saint Louis, East Saint Louis, Detroit, and Milwaukee, a black worker could make more money in a week than he could for a month's hard toil in the South, where farm laborers averaged fifty to eighty cents a day and where those who worked on cottonseed-oil mills, sawmills, and turpentine refineries received only slightly more. Further, the ravages of the boll weevil and the disastrous crop failure of 1916 had left thousands of agricultural laborers and sharecroppers without the means of subsistence. As landlords by the hundreds dismissed their tenants and laborers, the lure of a living wage in the North became irresistible.

With the improving economic situation after 1916, Southern landowners began to fear that the mass departure of Southern blacks would deplete their usual labor supply. "If the Negroes go," asked the *Montgomery Advertiser* in September 1916, "where shall we get labor to take their places?"[2] Legislation was enacted on local and state levels to protect the cheap labor supply. Recruiters were charged prohibitive license fees and subjected to strict regulations, with heavy fines and imprisonment imposed for violators. To stop the migration, DuBois notes, the South "mobilized all the machinery of modern oppression: taxes, city ordinances, licenses, state laws, municipal regulations, wholesale arrests, and, of course, the peculiar Southern method of the mob and lyncher."[3]

But such efforts came too late and were too easily circumvented to stem the northward tide of blacks. Ray Stannard Baker wrote, "Trains were backed into Southern cities and hundreds of Negroes were gathered up in a day, loaded into cars and whirled away to the North. Instances are given showing that Negro teamsters left their horses standing in the streets or deserted their jobs and went to the trains without notifying their employers or even going home."[4]

Black workers rushed to the mines of West Virginia and to the industries of New Jersey, Pennsylvania, New York, Ohio, and Illinois. Between 1910 and 1920 the black population in Chicago increased from 44,000 to 109,000; in New York, from 92,000 to 152,000; in Detroit, from 6,000 to 41,000; and in Philadelphia, from 84,000 to 134,000. The labor-recruiting efforts of Chicago's packing houses and the Illinois Central Railroad, with the appeals of the *Chicago Defender,* made Chicago a magnet for penniless sharecroppers of the South. Some moved along to Detroit, where the pressure of wartime needs forced open the automobile plants to Negroes. In April 1917, a survey of twenty of the largest firms of Detroit, mostly manufacturers of automobiles and automobile accessories, showed a total of 2,874 black workers employed. Only two years before, black employment in industrial Detroit had been practically nonexistent.

The decade 1910 to 1920 saw a net increase of 322,000 Southern-born blacks living in the North, exceeding the aggregate increase of the preceding forty years. Although the increase is less than the general estimates made at the height of the migration, it is still an impressive figure. Even more impressive is the fact that the booming wartime labor demands of rail lines, factories, foundries, mines, and packing houses—at a time when the normal supply of cheap labor was shut off—opened these industries for the first time to the black worker. Thus, with the outbreak of World War I and the great migration of 1915–1918, the first black industrial working class in the United States came into existence.

In 1920, manufacturing industries in Chicago had a workforce in which 16 percent of the workers were black, with black representation rising to 23 percent in nonmanufacturing industries. The number of black workers in American industry nearly doubled from 1910 to 1920, from 551,825 to 901,181. The largest gain occurred in iron and steel, automotive, mining, shipbuilding, and meatpacking occupations. A smaller increase occurred in trade and transportation activities,

mainly among railroad workers engaged in road repair and maintenance of way work. Negro longshoremen increased from 16,405 in 1910 to 27,400 in 1920, and there was also a rise in the number of black chauffeurs, hack drivers, and garage workers.

Between 1890 and 1920 the number of black workers in agriculture and in domestic and personal service increased by 552,634, or 20.5 percent. During the same three decades, the number of Negroes engaged in manufacturing and in mechanical work, trade, and transportation grew from 354,091 to 1,354,838, an increase of 282.5 percent. In 1920, one-third of all gainfully employed Negroes were working in American industry.

The employment of blacks in occupations opened by the wartime demand helped, as Herbert J. Seligman put it, to "dispel the myth that the American Negro was at best an agricultural laborer and that complicated industrial processes overtaxed his abilities."[5] A contemporary government study of the migration, based on interviews with employment managers and executives in Northern industry, found them so worried by the acute labor shortage that they were in no mood for mythology. "The majority of executives interviewed were favorable to the experiment with Negro employment in the North, and were sympathetic to suggestions concerning selection, training, housing and recreation for the newcomers."[6]

The demand for black labor slackened when the war came to an end. The nation's war industries, which had depended heavily on cheap, unskilled Negro labor, were dismantled and reconverted to peacetime production, resulting in a mass discharge of black workers. In one week the American Steel Company in East St. Louis, Illinois, reduced its workforce from 1,282 to 25. Almost seven hundred of the discharged men were Negroes. As millions of whites returned to the ranks of industrial labor from the armed forces, employers did not hesitate to replace their black workers. Former Negro servicemen were not so lucky: in April 1919, the Division of Negro Economics announced that 99 percent of Chicago's black veterans were still unemployed, with little prospect of work in the immediate future. The same situation faced black ex-servicemen in other large industrial cities.

In Chicago, where as many as ten thousand black laborers were out of work, the local Association of Commerce wired to the Southern Chambers of Commerce: "Are you in need of Negro labor? Large surplus here, both returned soldiers and civilian Negroes ready to work."[7] Actually, despite the demand for black labor in the South during the postwar months, very few blacks left the industrial centers of the Midwest and Northeast to take jobs offered by Southern employers.

The 1921 economic depression made the situation even more acute for black workers. In Detroit, black unemployment rates were five times as high as those of native white workers and twice as high as those of foreign-born whites. "Colored workers are the last to be hired, and first to be fired," the superintendent of the Colored Branch of the New York State Employment Bureau declared in February 1921. "Always discriminated against by some employers, the present condition of unemployment is causing great suffering among the colored people."[8]

But the influx of Negro workers from the South did not cease. Economic recovery and the gradual elimination of foreign immigrant competition due to the passage of restrictive immigration laws in 1921 and 1924 brought a second migration out of the South in the years 1922 to 1924. More than a half-million Negroes took their scanty belongings and left for the North, most of them to stay. As William Graves told the Chicago Union League Club, "The Negro permanency in industry is no longer debatable."[9]

Yet the status of this workforce was that of unskilled labor. "Everywhere," wrote Roger Baldwin in 1919, "the Negroes had the hardest and most disagreeable jobs."[10] Employers in the South and the North agreed that the work whites usually shunned was reserved for blacks. The superintendent of a Kentucky plow factory expressed the Southern view: "Negroes do work white men won't do, such as common labor; heavy, hot, and dirty work; pouring crucibles; work in the grinding room; and so on. Negroes are employed because they are cheaper. . . . The negro does a different grade of work and makes about 10 cents an hour less."[11] A coke-works

foreman in a Pennsylvania steel mill used almost the same language: "They are well fitted for this hot work, and we keep them because we appreciate this ability in them. . . . The door machines and the jam cutting are the most undesirable; it is hard to get white men to do this kind of work."[12] It was rare to find an industrialist like Henry Ford, who, in an effort to maintain influence with the black community, allowed a few blacks in his plants to be upgraded to skilled positions. The majority of black workers in the automobile industry, as in all industry, were confined to unskilled jobs.

This state of affairs was established during the war by employers and unions, often with government approval. The railroad lines and the railroad brotherhoods had worked out unwritten agreements confining blacks to low-level and menial occupations in railway work. When the federal government assumed control of the nation's rail network late in December 1917, it simply sanctioned the informal agreements between railroad management and the unions by prohibiting the hiring or advancing of Negroes to positions they had not occupied in the past. Under the so-called Atlanta agreement, the Brotherhood of Railway Trainmen and the U.S. Railroad Administration—under the threat by the trainmen to tie up the Southern railroad network—agreed on rules relating to seniority, job classification, and the composition of train crews that resulted in driving many blacks from positions they had long held on the railroads and relegating them to menial jobs.

In various shipyards around the country, employers and unions, again with government sanction, agreed not to give blacks positions above that of common laborer. Black carpenters, reamers, riveters, pipefitters, and drillers found it almost impossible to get work in the shipyards, even though men were badly needed in these occupations. Skilled blacks were forced to accept jobs as helpers to white craftsmen or as "fillers" in tasks demanding few or no skills. A skilled black shipyard worker complained to the federal government: "If . . . we are not fit to have a position as mechanics and officials then I contend we are not good enough to fight for the country."[13] A black riveter, unable to find employment at his trade in a California shipyard, wrote,

We don't ask Social Equality, we only ask an Equal chance to take our part in the Industrial world, to be given the right and opportunity to perform the work, which Almighty God saw fit to give us the brains and strength to do and for which hundreds of years in the most cruel school of slavery qualified and made us to do. . . .

I beg of you to take up this matter at once, don't let the word be taken from the shipyards of America that . . . discrimination is being made in the matter of even Negro labor. What will our boys feel that they have to fight for, what hopes have they to look forward to when after the war they return and the work is done.[14]

Nothing was done during the war by employers, unions, or the federal government to eliminate the racial prejudice that prevented blacks from being hired as skilled workers. A survey published in August 1917, found "Negro graduate engineers and electricians and experienced carpenters, painters and shipbuilders doing the work of porters, elevator men and janitors."[15] A year later, the situation was reported unchanged, and it continued after the war. A study published in 1921 by the Department of Labor, covering twenty-three establishments in five basic industries—foundries; coke ovens; glass manufacturing; iron and steel and their products; and slaughtering and meatpacking—disclosed that of eighty-five occupations in which five or more Negroes and five or more whites were employed, only eight of the occupations open to blacks were in skilled categories. Another observer of the Negro labor scene estimated in the mid-1920s that only 5 percent of black industrial workers were in skilled jobs and 10 percent in semiskilled positions.

While almost all black workers in industry were being kept at the level of unskilled occupations, the number of Negro artisans was declining. Between 1910 and 1920 the number of skilled blacks in the building trades increased by less than four thousand. Black plumbers, gasfitters, and steamfitters increased by only one thousand. During the same period, the number of black blacksmiths, forgemen and pressmen, builders and building contractors, millers, pressmen and plate printers, roofers and slaters, sawyers, stonemasons, and bricklayers decreased.

The decline of the Negro artisans was largely the result of factors that had been operating since the turn of the century. Most important was the hostile attitude of trade unions, which encouraged white workingmen to push the blacks out of skilled occupations and to discourage black apprenticeships. In 1920 the total of white apprentices in all skilled trades was put at 144,177. The total of black apprentices was 2,067.

There is no doubt that the black worker had achieved a great industrial advance between World War I and the mid-1920s. Certainly, too, even work in the lowest industrial occupations was for many blacks an improvement over peonage in agriculture or domestic service. Even though an increased cost of living often wiped out a good part of the gains in wages, it was generally agreed that the black worker substantially improved his economic conditions by moving into Northern industry. But the door to semiskilled and skilled occupations remained shut for the black worker. One reason for this was the racism of white employers.[16] Another important reason, as we shall see in the following chapter, was the economic and racial prejudice of the white trade unions that dominated most of the occupations in question.

NOTES

1. Handbills of Jones-Maddox Labor Agency, Bessemer, Alabama, Record Group 174, Files of the Secretary of Labor, National Archives; also quoted in John D. Finney Jr., "A Study of Negro Labor during and after World War 1" (unpublished Ph.D. dissertation, Georgetown University, 1957), 81.

2. *Montgomery Advertiser,* reprinted in *Literary Digest,* October 7, 1916.

3. W. E. B. DuBois, *Darkwater* (New York: 1919), 43.

4. Ray Stannard Baker, "The Negro Goes North," *World's Work* 34 (July 1917): 315.

5. Herbert J. Seligman, "The Negro in Industry," *Socialist Review* 8 (February 1920): 169.

6. U.S. Department of Labor, *Negro Migration in 1916–1917* (Washington, D.C.: 1919), 124.

7. William M. Tuttle Jr., *Race Riot: Chicago in the Red Summer of 1919* (New York: Atheneum, 1970), 130–132.

8. *New York Call,* February 14, 1921.

9. Quoted in Harold M. Baron, "The Demand for Negro Labor: Historical Notes on the Political Economy of Racism," *Radical America* 5 (March–April 1971): 21–22.

10. Roger Baldwin, quoted in Seligman, "Negro in Industry," 170.

11. Sterling D. Spero and Abram L. Harris, *The Black Worker: A Study of the Negro and the Labor Movement* (New York: Columbia University Press, 1931), 169.

12. Horace R. Cayton and George S. Mitchell, *Black Workers and the New Unions* (Chapel Hill: University of North Carolina Press, 1939), 31.

13. George Carmody to Charles Schwab, September 18, 1918, Records of U.S. Shipping Board, Record Group 32, National Archives.

14. S. L. Mash to L. C. Marshall, August 30, 1918, Records of U.S. Shipping Board, Record Group 32, National Archives.

15. *New York Call,* August 9, 1917.

16. On March 19, 1920, the *New York Call* carried an item on the New York Telephone Company's refusal to hire Negroes to meet a labor shortage. When a field secretary for the League for Democracy asked the assistant to the company's vice president why he did not fill the one thousand openings it claimed it had with black women, he replied that while he "personally had no objection to colored employees, the white operators would leave en masse if they had to work side by side with colored girls." Informed that white girls were working with colored girls throughout the city, the executive stuck to his guns. "The sense of the interview with Mr. Schultz," the field secretary reported, "was that the telephone company would rather suffer complete demoralization than employ Negro girls as operators. In fact he stated as much."

PART II

Organized Labor and
African Americans

6

An Uncertain Tradition: Blacks and Unions, 1865–1925

WILLIAM HARRIS

George Pullman founded the Pullman Palace Car Company in 1867 with the idea that railroad travelers should ride in comfort. In the early years of the company, Pullman hired only black men, many recently freed from slavery, as porters to provide service to the white passengers. While Pullman counted on blacks as a cheap and docile labor force, he could not have foreseen that by the mid-1920s these same porters would form an independent union. This chapter traces the labor history that led to the formation of the Brotherhood of Sleeping Car Porters. It chronicles the early efforts to organize black and white workers together as well as the racist union practices that excluded blacks from most trade unions. The author also discusses conflicts within the black community between those who urged black workers to cooperate with white management for the sake of jobs and those who believed that white and black workers shared a common cause.

In the years immediately following the Civil War, as some men moved to complete the transcontinental railway and speed the transfer of commodities from one place to another, others emphasized the movement of people. They envisioned great rewards in catering to the comforts of railroad travelers. One such individual was George M. Pullman, who visualized a railway system that would move passengers across the country in optimum comfort. Pullman had experimented unsuccessfully with sleeping cars before the Civil War and was now determined to make good on his conviction that long-distance rail travel did not have to be miserable.[1] Pullman's service would provide the finest equipment and personal servants, a luxury many passengers did not have at home. In 1867 he founded the Pullman Palace Car Company and his dream became reality.[2]

The service that Pullman initiated made it possible for passengers to board one of his cars and forget the small worries that often trouble people traveling great distances. Company employees, whom Pullman chose to call *porters*, stowed the passengers' baggage and thereafter ministered to all of their needs and wants, including even the shining of their shoes. Pullman's combination of attentive servants and the utmost in modern machinery captured the fancy of the American traveling public. Through the years, the Pullman Company became a giant among the nation's corporations.

The porters whom Pullman hired during the first years of his company were all black men, many of them recently freed from slavery. The practice of hiring blacks continued until the turn of the century; by that time, the word *porter* became synonymous with blacks.[3] Among the reasons Pullman decided to hire only black men as porters, three stand out: the feeling of "elegance" whites were said to experience in having black servants; the fact that blacks were cheap labor; and the accepted social distance between the races.[4] Pullman officials were aware that blacks had been traditionally assigned service roles and that it was a mark of status among whites to be served by them.

By the beginning of World War I, the Pullman Company employed approximately twelve thousand porters, most of whom lived in Northern urban areas. Thinking that Southern blacks would make better servants, Pullman recruited its porters in the South and transferred them to areas where they were needed. Most porters went North alone and eventually sent for their families, often including relatives other than wives and children.

Though Pullman became the largest single employer of blacks in the United States and held numerous outstanding credits among African Americans, at least a few blacks resented company practices. They believed, for example, that the company hired blacks as porters to continue the servant–master relationship that had existed during slavery. A. Philip Randolph, who later led in organizing the Brotherhood of Sleeping Car Porters, often expressed this view during the 1920s when he spoke of early Pullman service. Writing in 1928, he accused the Pullman Company of having conspired to keep porters shrouded in slavery-imposed ignorance of their rights as workers. He saw little difference between the company's attitude and that of Southern landowners who took advantage of the freedmen through tenancy and enforcement of vagrancy laws:

> Burdened with the heritage of slave psychology, fearing lest they be plunged back into the sinister system of chattel slavery, they were easily induced to accept any wage system, however small and miserable, expecting to solicit gratitude from a sympathetic traveling public. In the year of the beginning of Pullman, 1867, Negroes were not only incapable of thinking in terms of collective bargaining . . . but they were uncertain of their freedom. In such a state of civil, political, and economic uncertainty, why wouldn't Pullman seek to get them to work on a semi-feudalistic basis?[5]

Since blacks formed an easily identifiable group, it is likely that Pullman managers consciously considered their ex-slave status when deciding to use only black men to provide personal services on sleeping cars. Though the company's position was that it hired blacks out of concern for their welfare, the fact is that Pullman hired very few of them in its repair and erection shops; in addition, management explicitly excluded blacks from service as conductors.

George Pullman's success enabled him to underline his strong commitment to precision and orderly society, a commitment that extended to include some of his employees. To provide what he considered to be the environment in which people should live and work, he built the community of Pullman, Illinois, for his shop employees. The company included in its town everything the founder thought working-class people needed, even libraries and museums to enhance their cultural development.

Pullman expected the same orderliness that existed in his town to prevail on the job and in relations between company and employees. Personal audiences of employees before the boss should settle all disputes, and labor organizations had no place in company affairs. This attitude was typical in American industrial relations at the time, but few companies had a policy as intransigent as Pullman's. The company's reaction to employees' activities during the great railroad strike of 1894 established the point.[6] The major importance of the strike to Pullman was that it disrupted the order that existed in the Pullman Company and marked the beginning of a new era in its labor–management relations. No longer could the company claim that harmony and goodwill prevailed.

The Pullman strike had far greater impact than just the changes it fostered in the Pullman Company. After Eugene V. Debs and his followers entered the strife, it came to embrace the major railways with termini in Chicago and stands as a major juncture in the development of labor–management relations in the railroad industry. Moreover, the strike marked a defeat for efforts to improve relations between black and white workers and dashed the hopes of those who longed for a breakup of the craft organizations in favor of more broadly based unions. Debs, who had resigned his post as secretary of the Brotherhood of Locomotive Firemen the preceding year so that he could organize the American Railway Union (an industrial union that sought to obliterate craft lines), failed in his effort to convince union members to include black railroaders in the movement. Thus, few if any blacks participated in the strike of 1894.

Debs's inability to convince his associates in the union to make common cause with black railroaders by organizing them into the union was not unusual. Indeed, the major unions of operating railroad employees—the Brotherhood of Locomotive Engineers, the Order of Railway Conductors, the Brotherhood of Locomotive Firemen, and the Brotherhood of Railway Trainmen—prohibited black membership by their constitutions.[7] Considering themselves the aristocracy of American workers and employed in the nation's major industry of the time, operating employees on the railroads remained aloof even during the general labor movement, refusing formal association with either the Knights of Labor or the more recently organized American Federation of Labor. Largely because of the skills required for their jobs, the railroad unions were able to restrict entrance to their ranks through strict apprenticeship, and they generally eschewed strikes and militant unionism, preferring to improve wages and working conditions of members through quiet negotiations with management.

Beginning in 1869 a new federation of unions, the Knights of Labor, actively recruited black workers. These activities represented a ray of hope and encouraged some national black leaders, such as Frederick Douglass and T. Thomas Fortune, to endorse their efforts.[8] Many original Knights were disgruntled trade unionists who had tired of the narrow craft orientation of their former organizations. Operating in secret local assemblies and employing as their motto "An injury to one is the concern of all," the Knights of Labor sought to create solidarity among all classes of workers, regardless of race and, eventually, sex. Thus the Knights made particularly strong efforts to organize African American workers, notably in occupations that employed large numbers of blacks. It sent organizers, black and white, into the South to recruit members, and it insisted that the rank and file extend brotherhood across racial lines. By its peak year, 1886, between sixty thousand and ninety thousand African Americans belonged to the Knights of Labor out of a total membership estimated at seven hundred thousand.[9]

The craft unions of skilled workers never accepted the principles or the leadership of the Knights of Labor, and in 1881 they came together at Pittsburgh to form their own union movement. This group, the American Federation of Labor (AFL), soon became the dominant force in organized labor. Although organized along craft lines, thus placing a premium on skilled labor that marked the federation as exclusive and discriminatory, the AFL did not clearly define its attitude toward black workers during its first years.

Most studies of trade union policies toward admission of African American workers point out the difficulty that these conflicting elements caused for leaders of organized labor—namely, racial hostility on the one hand and the desirability of workers' unity on the other. Member unions of the AFL controlled their own membership, and even then final decisions on whether to admit an applicant rested with the local to which he applied. Under such conditions, personal bias could play a much larger part in determining a union's makeup than if members were recruited at the national level. National leaders could continue to emphasize the need for labor solidarity and write constitutions that extended membership privileges to black and white workers, whereas locals continued to exclude African Americans.[10]

Though leaders of the AFL could act only as a moral force on the question of admission of blacks into unions, their views did create the general atmosphere in which the trade union movement developed. The dominant figure in the AFL was Samuel Gompers, president of the Cigar Makers' Union when he took part in founding the federation in 1881. Chosen president of the new organization, Gompers was to serve in that capacity every year, except one, until his death in 1924. Though initially encouraging racial cooperation, the AFL by 1900 had become a bastion in the development and maintenance of racism in the United States.

One of Gompers's biographers, Bernard Mandel, maintains that during the 1890s Gompers underwent an evolution in his attitude toward blacks and their participation in the labor movement. Mandel writes that, during the federation's early years, the AFL leader actually insisted on organizing blacks and argued with Southern unionists that the organization of African American workers was not a matter of "recognizing social equality, but a question of absolute necessity."[11] Through the 1880s and into the 1890s, Gompers maintained that blacks served as strikebreakers and shunned organized labor mainly because white unionists refused to join in common cause with them. After 1896 the leader changed his view on this issue and assigned responsibility directly to blacks themselves for their failure to hold union membership. Gompers's interest in retaining his position in the AFL and in upholding the craft nature of the federation was partly responsible for his shift.

Gompers explained that he could not accept black workers into the AFL and could not insist that affiliated unions grant them equal rights, because Southern whites would not tolerate blacks as equal. Still, it was Gompers who proposed at the convention of 1900 that the AFL support segregation and create "federal" unions for black workers, a proposal the delegates passed.[12] Gompers claimed that he recommended this new procedure to organize blacks who could not join regular unions, but this was only a subterfuge. Implementation of this policy would lead only to results unfavorable to African Americans. Segregation into impotent unions, under the direct supervision of the nearest white local of a particular craft, denied blacks job protection. They had no representation at international meetings, nor did they have direct input in decisions on wages and working conditions. Furthermore, white locals controlled admission to apprenticeship in trades, a lever they used eventually to eliminate blacks from certain crafts.

The problems of labor organizations and black workers had long perplexed black spokesmen. If some recognized the necessity that blacks gain employment under any circumstances, many others had come to believe that organized labor should be respected. Even after the AFL convention of 1900 gave official sanction to segregated locals for blacks, some black leaders had continued to push for membership of African Americans in craft unions, while oth-

ers urged cooperation between black workers and white capitalists. The Niagara movement, a loose organization of black radicals under the leadership of W. E. B. DuBois, discussed economic conditions of blacks at its meeting in Boston in 1907 and resolved that the interests of black and white workers were identical. The movement reportedly assured African Americans that "the cause of labor is the cause of black men, and the black man's cause is labor's own."[13] At the same time, others took an opposite view. The Tuskegee movement and the views of its leader, Booker T. Washington, weighed heavily on black thought. Washington had convinced a whole generation of blacks that their best interest and hope for advancement lay in the Tuskegee philosophy—that is, working hard and amassing capital. The Tuskegee philosophy had no place in its teachings for organized labor, and Washington and his followers advised blacks to line up with the great captains of industry.[14]

Though Northern whites had long been hostile toward black workers, the relatively few blacks in the region during the nineteenth and early twentieth centuries had not made the organization of African Americans a major issue there. But around 1910 blacks began to trickle North in ever-increasing numbers, to escape hardships in the South and to gain employment in the allegedly plentiful jobs available in the North. By the time of American entry in World War I, the trickle had become a flood, and Northern white unionists became alarmed over increasing competition from blacks. Delegates to the AFL conventions of 1916 and 1917 alerted the leadership to the increasing number of blacks in jobs previously held only by whites, suggesting that the federation take steps to organize the newly arrived blacks and thwart what the unionists saw as efforts on the part of management to import African Americans to obstruct the work of organized labor. The delegates passed such resolutions in both years, though Gompers and the AFL's executive council refused to implement them.[15] Delegates at AFL conventions might pass such resolutions, but for blacks, the East St. Louis race riot of July 1917 brought realities sharply into focus. This riot, in which organized workers were conspicuous, ended in death for numerous blacks, whereas many more were injured. It served to widen the gap between organized whites and unorganized African American workers.[16]

If arrival of blacks into Northern urban regions raised a new sense of urgency among white labor leaders, black leaders showed a heightened interest in economic matters and the relationship between African Americans and organized labor. The ambivalence and uncertainty of previous decades remained, and different groups continued to offer various and sometimes contradictory remedies to the plight of urban blacks. Some, like the National Urban League (NUL), which had been founded in 1911 specifically to ease the transition of blacks from rural to urban life, at first counseled a close relationship between blacks and employers. The league view was that the immediate economic need of newly urbanized African Americans was to find jobs. The National Association for the Advancement of Colored People (NAACP) shared the view that blacks needed work to survive, but some leaders of the association also recognized the right of workers to organize and bargain collectively.[17] There was still another view of how best to improve conditions for blacks. Some spokesmen called on blacks to oppose the AFL, form labor unions of their own, and affiliate with Industrial Workers of the World. Thus the World War I period saw influential blacks either calling for membership in the AFL or emphasizing independent black unions, all the while others were advocating for a radical change in the American economic and social order.

The NUL–NAACP group endeavored during World War I to improve relations between black workers and organized labor and to enhance the position of African Americans with the federal government. Their most successful effort came in 1918 when the two organizations, with assistance from other representative black leaders, secured from the U.S. Department of Labor a specially created department: the Division of Negro Economics. Under the directorship of Dr. George Edmund Haynes, the first executive director of the NUL and a professor of sociology at Fisk University, the Division of Negro Economics was intended to keep the Secretary of Labor informed on conditions among African American workers, to devise methods to end difficulties caused by racial discrimination, and to strengthen the participation of blacks in war industries.

After securing minor concessions from the Department of Labor, black leaders met twice with representatives of the AFL. The most important meeting came in the April 1918. At the conference, Gompers reaffirmed the federation's published wish to have all workers organized within the AFL. He promised to use his prestige to help break down racial prejudice among whites, and he called on black spokesmen to use their "influence to show Negro workingmen advantages of collective bargaining and the value of affiliation with the AFL."[18] Unwilling to settle for high-sounding rhetoric, NAACP and NUL leaders offered specific proposals that would improve the position of black workers within the AFL. They encouraged Gompers to publish his views on bringing blacks into the organized labor movement; they called on federal leaders to hold periodic meetings with representative African Americans; they suggested that Gompers push a resolution through the next AFL convention confirming his wish that blacks be organized; and they recommended that the federation hire black organizers.[19] The AFL convention endorsed the principle of these proposals in 1918 but made clear that in so doing "no fault is or can be found with work done in the past" with regard to blacks.[20]

Black leaders did not give up on the organized labor movement after passage of the meaningless resolution at the convention of 1918. Both the NAACP and the NUL devoted much time to economic problems at their 1919 conventions. This marked the first time the NAACP discussed labor problems in the convention.[21] The NUL did more than simply discuss working conditions among blacks and problems they faced with organized labor. It advised blacks that they should seek membership in unions, but when that was "not possible they should band together to bargain with employers and organized labor alike."[22] In 1924 the NAACP called on "white unions to stop bluffing [on admitting blacks] and for black laborers to stop cutting off their noses to spite their faces" by joining with management in labor disputes. The association solemnly warned white labor leaders that unless steps were soon taken to ease discrimination, "the position gained by organized labor in this country is threatened with irreparable loss."[23]

While leaders of the NAACP and the NUL argued for cooperation between blacks and organized labor, other African Americans, particularly during the late years of World War I, began experimenting with independent all-black unions. In his study of trade unionism, Ira Reid found that at least nineteen independent black unions with a minimum membership of 12,585 had developed during the war period. The most successful such activity among blacks came in the railroad industry, which operated under federal direction during the war. The government's positive endorsement of railroad union activity encouraged this development. Two unions—the Brotherhood of Dining Car Employees, under the leadership of Reinzi B. Lemus; and the Railway Men's International Benevolent Industrial Association, under Robert L. Mays—achieved meaningful benefits for their members and helped increase trade union awareness among black employees. The Railway Men's Association intended to serve as a conglomerate organization for all classes of black railroaders who were denied membership in the unions of their craft. Lemus's dining car employees' union restricted coverage to that particular class.[24]

Among black employees who benefited from the interest in independent unionism were the Pullman porters. Intelligent men, the porters did not remain untouched by the debate that raged about them. Conflicting pressures tossed them about as they assessed their own confused situation. Some porters believed that workers had the right to organize to protect their interests; others thought jobs belonged to the employers and that employees worked at the owners' sufferance. Only in later years would the depth of the schism between the two groups become apparent. To the general public, the porters appeared a united and harmonious group. Most people assumed that the Pullman Company paid them well and that they enjoyed favorable working conditions.[25] Many active porters, as well as former ones, encouraged the belief that they were happy with their situation. Indeed, as Perry Howard put it, they considered Pullman service a "badge of honor among the Race and the Pullman porter coming into contact with 35,000,000 passengers

[was] a missionary for his people."[26] Both the company and the numerous black spokesmen put pressure on porters to conduct themselves in a manner that would reflect favorably on Pullman and black people in general. Some porters were unduly impressed with the dubious prestige that came from serving important whites, often bragging to other porters and friends that one noted person or another had been in their cars.

Although a number of porters expressed satisfaction with their jobs and although the white press and portions of the black press promoted the idea of contentment, some porters were unhappy with conditions at Pullman. They had sporadically expressed their grievances to the company during the early years of the twentieth century and had even given some thought to forming a union.[27] Lack of leadership, however, as well as the company's adamant opposition to unionism, made any such attempt dangerous as well as futile.

As in most labor–management disputes in the 1920s, wages formed the porters' major grievance.[28] In 1926, for example, at a time when the government estimated that to maintain an adequate standard of living the average family residing in urban America needed an annual income of $2,088, a porter's base pay totaled $810 per year.[29] In addition, porters received tips, which, according to a survey conducted by the Labor Bureau of New York for the Brotherhood of Sleeping Car Porters, amounted to an average of about $600 annually. From this income the company required porters to buy their own uniforms during the first ten years of service. Uniforms and other job-related expenses—such as the cost of shoe polish for their clients—amounted to approximately $33 per month. For their $67.50 monthly wage, Pullman expected porters to provide about four hundred hours of service, not including time spent preparing cars for passengers or readying them for storage after runs.[30]

Shortly after the war, the porters attempted to improve their position through collective bargaining. The most serious attempt came in 1920, when several porters formed the Pullman Porters and Maids Protective Association (PPMPA). The company responded by seizing the initiative. Giving the appearance of not opposing unions, it presented the porters with an employee representation plan (ERP), an impressive title for what was in fact a company union. In addition, Pullman allowed the PPMPA to remain intact, though the benevolent association functioned as a powerless fraternal organization with secret passwords and a modest scheme for sickness and death benefits.[31] The ERP was typical of the company unions that sprang up around the country to challenge orthodox trade unions for influence among workers.

Establishment of the ERP and the simultaneous defusing of the PPMPA in 1920 silenced some of the dissident voices; but by 1924 the talk had resumed. Several porters presented the company with a petition requesting that porters' monthly wages be raised to $100. Concurrently, Robert Mays's Railway Men's Association made energetic efforts to recruit porters.

Pullman's director of employee relations, F. L. Simmons, believed the porters' petition meant that Mays had met with some success among the service employees. As a countermeasure, he suggested that the president of the company allow the porters to present their petition through the ERP, thus giving the company time to decide on a plan of action.[32] President Edward F. Carry accepted Simmons's recommendation and offered to negotiate with representatives of porters and maids at a meeting scheduled for March 1924. For the company, the conference would serve the dual purpose of responding to the porters' petition while staving off Mays's movement by proving to the employees that machinery already existed for handling their grievances.

Pullman wished to bind porters and maids to an agreement in 1924, before Mays and his group could become strong enough to cause trouble for the company. Consequently, it raised the porters' pay by five dollars per month, about an 8 percent increase.[33] Carry believed the company had done its service employees a favor by negotiating with them through the ERP. He wrote Simmons about the benevolence of company unions that protected porters and other black workers from the cruelty and avarice of white unionists.[34]

By 1924, then, porters, like most blacks, remained ambivalent about trade unionism and lacked the essential element of leadership needed to change their conditions. The porters obviously recognized that they needed an organization if they were to improve their situation. Still, they were willing to place their hopes in the goodwill of their employer. Pullman officials had good reason to believe that they had succeeded in quieting most of the porters' concern while staving off the intrusion of orthodox unionism.

Like the situation at Pullman, the general picture of the relationship between blacks and organized labor remained confused by the mid-1920s. Of course, a majority of the rank-and-file white unionists still deeply resented blacks and widely held the view that blacks were poor risks in time of industrial strife. They used black strikebreaking as evidence to justify this point of view. Some black spokesmen, particularly those from the professional classes, agreed that black strikebreakers had been responsible in the past for defeating strikes, but they were by no means apologetic about that fact. Strikebreaking, they argued, had been the only course available when whites had denied blacks access to jobs by excluding them from membership in unions and by closing apprenticeship to young blacks. Abram L. Harris, for example, believed that blacks became strikebreakers in an attempt to find "relief from economic slavery."[35] Whatever the merits of the arguments, it was clear that such deep racial animosity could be overcome only by strong leadership from both sides. The challenge was all the greater because influential voices—black and white—continued to advise blacks to maintain their alliance with white capitalists.[36]

The most prolific and perhaps most influential exponent of this view was Kelly Miller, dean of the College of Arts and Sciences at Howard University, a spokesman for the old school, which Randolph and others argued had outlived its usefulness and should step aside for the "New Negro." Randolph recognized that Miller had been a "constant fighter in the interest of civil rights" but pointed out that he "fawn[ed] before the altar of big business and glorified the so-called capitalists' benefactions to the race, apparently unmindful of the service black labor is to white capitalists."[37]

In a major statement on blacks and trade unionism in 1925, Miller argued that African Americans would find their most faithful friends among the great employers. He maintained that though a superficial logic aligned black and white workers, existing racial animosities would make such liaisons impossible. Thus blacks should follow the "good sense that array[ed] them on the side of capital."

T. Arnold Hill, who became the first director of the NUL's Department of Industrial Relations in 1925, formulated far different views on blacks and labor. Hill had joined the NUL in 1914 as assistant to the executive director, Eugene K. Jones, and went to Chicago in 1916 to help establish the league's branch. He became executive secretary of the Chicago Urban League, where he remained until he returned to New York City in 1925.[38] From his new position Hill chided AFL officials to make good on their pronouncements of nondiscrimination, and he joined efforts of other blacks to break down antiunion views among African Americans.[39]

Like Miller, Hill saw the personal hostilities that job competition engendered between black and white workers; in contrast to Miller, Hill recognized that this individual competition among blacks and whites was not the essence of racism in American society. Far more important than racial animosity on the personal level was the institutionalization of the hatred. Workers had little power to control or influence major institutions. That power lay in the hands of Miller's "great employers of labor." When Miller called on blacks to seek the capitalists' "protection," he was appealing to the very group that maintained his people in the lowliest of positions by excluding them from schools, jobs, and participation in government.

Even as Hill was formulating a prolabor stance for the NUL, several other developments were occurring that indicated the strong desire of some African Americans to improve their economic conditions through unionism. Not only did the NUL create its Department of Industrial Relations, but black communists established the American Negro Labor Congress; Frank R. Crosswaith founded the Trade Union Committee for Organizing Negro Workers (TUC); and in August, porters organized the Brotherhood of Sleeping Car Porters.

Frank Crosswaith, a black New York socialist, put the finishing touches on the TUC, a broad-based organization that included such diverse elements as the NAACP and the socialist unions, early in 1925.[40] The Garland Fund and the AFL provided financial support to Crosswaith's group, which was intended to serve as a liaison between blacks and organized labor and to provide requisite leadership to smooth differences between the two groups.[41] The TUC called again for the AFL to hire black organizers to recruit black workers. Hill, author of the proposal, expected such appointments to "remove a large portion of the opposition raised by Negro workers to the AFL," an opposition rooted in the AFL's refusal (despite the rhetoric of its national leaders) to admit blacks to equal membership.[42] The committee expended much effort in trying to improve the image of organized labor for blacks. One way to do this was to encourage the NAACP and the NUL, the two most visible black organizations in New York, to organize their office staffs. When put on the spot in this way, the two organizations responded differently: the NUL acquiesced and allowed the committee's organizers to talk with its employees, whereas the NAACP refused to permit a similar session with its workers.[43]

Impetus for encouraging union organization among black workers came from still another direction when the American Communist Party convened the American Negro Labor Congress (ANLC) in Chicago. The congress vowed to create independent all-black unions so powerful that the AFL could no longer afford to keep them out.[44] But in reaching this position, the Communist Party faced a dilemma. It believed in the solidarity of all workers, and on the surface it could not support the idea of all-black unions; yet, the party recognized that prevailing hostilities between blacks and whites made integrated unions impractical. Expediency dictated that the communists go on with the organization of blacks in whatever manner possible, worrying about solidarity later. In any event, the congress never reached a substantial portion of the black population.

Most black and white labor leaders rushed to condemn the ANLC. Green considered the congress detrimental to the interests of organized labor as well as black workers, warning both groups to stay away from it. Leaders of the NUL chided Green for having given the ANLC more attention than it deserved, suggesting in *Opportunity* that the congress had introduced no new grievances and pointing out that blacks "never paid attention to communist arguments."[45] Randolph and his colleagues at the *Messenger* shared the league's distrust of communism. The magazine editorialized against the congress, warning blacks against being "lured up blind alleys by irresponsible labor talkers." In direct reference to the communists and ANLC, the *Messenger* argued that no "labor movement in America among white or black workers can solve the problems of American workers, white or black, whose seal of control is outside the country."[46] On this issue, as on others, DuBois stood almost alone. He saw the Chicago meeting as one of the most significant gatherings in recent black history. As far as he was concerned, progress of black people was more important than the vehicle through which progress was achieved.[47]

If these new organizations of 1925 served only to stimulate debate on the question of blacks and trade unions and were of only ephemeral duration, they clearly announced that the struggle had begun in earnest. No longer could leaders of the AFL and local unions deny blacks membership without being called on to explain their stance, nor would black workers in the future hear only advice that they should maintain personal loyalty to their employers. It would be left to the Brotherhood of Sleeping Car Porters to lead efforts in breaking down barriers of animosity between black and white workers and in bringing African Americans into the mainstream of trade unionism.

NOTES

1. Almont Lindsey, *The Pullman Strike: The Story of a Unique Experiment and of a Great Labor Upheaval* (Chicago: University of Chicago Press, 1942), 21–22.

2. Joseph Husband, *The Story of the Pullman Car* (Chicago: A. C. McClure, 1917), 47.

3. Sterling D. Spero and Abram L. Harris, *The Black Worker: The Negro and the Labor Movement* (New York: Columbia University Press, 1931), 430.

4. Brailsford R. Brazeal, *The Brotherhood of Sleeping Car Porters* (New York: Harper and Brothers, 1946).

5. *Chicago Defender*, December 29, 1928.

6. Lindsey, *Pullman Strike*, 94–96.

7. F. E. Wolfe, *Admission to American Trade Unions* (Baltimore: Johns Hopkins University Press, 1912), 119–120; W. E. B. DuBois, ed., *The Negro Artisan* (Atlanta, Ga.: Atlanta University Publications, 1920), 167–168.

8. Emma Lou Thronbrough, *T. Thomas Fortune: Militant Journalist* (Chicago: University of Chicago Press, 1972), 81–82, writes of Fortune's flirtation with the Knights of Labor but emphasizes that economics remained for him a secondary question of racial justice. August Meier, *Negro Thought in America, 1880–1915* (Ann Arbor: University of Michigan Press, 1963), 46–48, has a good discussion of Fortune's economic philosophy. See also T. Thomas Fortune, *Black and White* (1884), for Fortune's own statement of his views. For Douglass's views on the Knights, see Philip S. Foner, *The Life and Writings of Frederick Douglass* (New York: International, 1943), 4:342.

9. Sidney H. Kessler, "The Organization of Negroes in the Knights of Labor," *Journal of Negro History* 37 (July 1952): 248–276.

10. Wolfe, *Admission to American Trade Unions*, chapter 6, discusses procedures used by the unions to discriminate against black workers. See chapter 1 for his discussion of general requirements for admission of workers into national unions. See also DuBois, *The Negro Artisan*, 171, for discussion of the importance of local unions in determining union membership.

11. Bernard Mandel, "Samuel Gompers and the Negro Workers, 1886–1914," *Journal of Negro History* 40 (January 1955): 34–60 (quote from 40).

12. AFL Convention, *Report of the Proceedings* (October 1900), 12–13.

13. Quoted in Abram L. Harris, "Should the BSCP [Brotherhood of Sleeping Car Porters] Join the AFL" (unpublished manuscript in National Association for the Advancement of Colored People Papers, Library of Congress), 14. It should be pointed out that trade unionism was not a major concern of the Niagaraites. Some of their statements fail to mention black workers at all, emphasizing instead improvements in education and civil rights.

14. Spero and Harris, *Black Worker*, 50. On occasion Washington went beyond merely cautioning blacks against labor unions and warning them of the necessity of remaining loyal to their employers. He advised blacks to become strikebreakers if doing so would enable them to gain employment. But, as

on so many other issues in his career, Washington was inconsistent. In an article in *Atlantic Monthly* 111 (June 1913): 656–667, he allowed the possibility that white labor unionists were changing attitudes toward blacks and proposed a qualified support of trade union efforts.

15. AFL Convention, *Report of the Proceedings* (November 1916): 148.

16. Elliott Rudwick, *Race Riot at East St. Louis, Illinois, July 2, 1917* (Carbondale: Southern Illinois University Press, 1964), especially chapters 3–5.

17. Nancy J. Weiss, *The National Urban League, 1910–1940* (New York: Oxford University Press, 1974), 89–91, 100–101, 123–128; Charles Hint Kellogg, *The NAACP: A History of the National Association for the Advancement of Colored People, 1909–1920* (Baltimore: Johns Hopkins University Press, 1967), 1:34–35, 266–271.

18. Quoted in Reid, *Negro Membership*, 27. See also Kellogg, *The NAACP*, 1:68; Weiss, *National Urban League*, 208–209; Finney, "Negro Labor during and after World War I," 283–293; and NAACP, *Annual Report* (1917–1918): 69–70.

19. Reid, *Negro Membership*, 27–29.

20. Reid, *Negro Membership*, 29. Though the NAACP took part in the negotiations that led to dubious concession, it is still questionable how concerned the association was for organized labor and the economic conditions of blacks. In its *Annual Report* (1919), the NAACP listed its "Program for 1919." The right of blacks to earn a living is eighth on a list of nine items, after "equal rights to parks, libraries, etc." and just "an end to color hyphenation."

21. *Crisis* 18 (June 1919): 89. NAACP founders considered making unionism the topic of their first meeting in 1910 but decided against it on the advice of William English Walling and DuBois, both of whom thought political and social issues more important. See Kellogg, *The NAACP*, 1:34–36.

22. Quoted in C. H. Wesley, *Negro Labor in the United States, 1850–1925: A Study in American Economic History* (New York: Vanguard Press, 1927), 278.

23. NAACP, *Annual Report* (1924): 48–49.

24. Reid, *Negro Membership*, 118–127, discusses independent black union activities during the war period (see 123 for membership figures). See also Spero and Harris, *Black Worker*, 116–127; and Finney, "Negro Labor during and after World War I," 341–351.

25. Spero and Harris, *Black Worker*, 431; Murray Kempton, *Part of Our Time: Some Ruins and Monuments of the Thirties* (New York: Simon and Schuster, 1955).

26. Ibid., October 31, 1925.

27. An article in *Messenger* 8 (September 1926): 284–285, discusses early attempts to organize porters into unions. Frank Boyd, author of the piece, was a representative of the Brotherhood of Sleeping Car Porters, and so one might question the seriousness of some of the grievances he listed and the impact of these organizational efforts on porters. Brazeal, *The Brotherhood*, 6–14, also discusses the porters' grievances and their early attempts to solve them through organization.

28. A. Philip Randolph, "The Case of the Pullman Porters," *Messenger* 7 (1925): 254.

29. *Messenger* 8 (January 1926): 10.

30. Labor Bureau, "Survey of Wages, Tips and Working Conditions of Pullman Porters" (New York: Labor Bureau, 1926). Copy in Negro Labor Committee Record Group, Pap Schomburg Branch, New York Public Library (hereafter cited NLCRG).

31. Untilled and undated statement [1921], Pullman Company Papers, Chicago (hereafter cited PC). The PPMPA became the Pullman Porters Benefit Association.

32. F. L. Simmons to E. F. Carry, January 15, 1924, PC.

33. F. L. Simmons to E. F. Carry, January 15, 1924, PC.

34. Carry to Simmons, April 2, 1924, PC.

35. Abram L. Harris, "The Negro Worker," *Labor Age* 19 (February 1930): 5; George A. Price, "The New Leadership," *Messenger* 8 (June 1926): 169.

36. Kelly Miller, "The Negro as a Working Man," *American Mercury* 6 (November 1925): 310–313. Horace R. Cayton and George S. Mitchell, *Black Workers and the New Unions* (Chapel Hill: University of North Carolina Press, 1939), 378, wrote that this was a widely held view among upper-class blacks. They shared Miller's view that white employers cared more for black workers than did white trade unionists.

37. A. Philip Randolph, "Economic Radicalism," *Opportunity* 4 (February 1926): 63.

38. *Who's Who in Colored America*, 5th ed., 255. Arvarh F. Strickland, *History of the Chicago Urban League* (Urbana: University of Illinois Press, 1966), has the best discussion of Hill's activities in Chicago.

39. Weiss, *National Urban League*, chapter 12, discusses league efforts to find jobs for blacks in the white industrial sector. See especially, 181–191, for

comments on the employment efforts of the Department of Industrial Relations.

40. Frank R. Crosswaith, "The Trade Union Committee for Organizing Negro Workers," *Messenger* 7 (August 1925): 296. Weiss, *National Urban League,* 211, argues that Hill's activities did not necessarily represent a prolabor attitude on the part of the league; rather, the league supported efforts to improve relations between blacks and organized labor out of a feeling of necessity.

41. The TUC report to the Garland Fund, January 1, 1926, NLCRG. The Garland fund donated a total of $2,435 to TUC during 1925. See Elizabeth G. Flynn to Thomas J. Curtis, May 7, and Flynn to Crosswaith, June 29, 1925, NLCRG.

42. The TUC report to the Garland Fund, January 1, 1926, NLCRG. This proposal is spelled out in greater detail in a letter to Hugh Frayne, AFL general organizer for New York, from several black trade unionists (including Randolph and Crosswaith), as well as James Weldon Johnson of the NAACP and Hill of the Urban League. National Urban League Papers, Manuscripts Division, Library of Congress.

43. The TUC executive secretary's report to the executive committee, September 22, 1925, 4, NLCRG. The activities of the TUC continued until early 1926; then Crosswaith began to spend most of his time working with the porters. In the original draft of the report, Crosswaith wrote that he "was sure" that continued conversations with Johnson would make possible organizational meetings with NAACP office personnel. The final version read "I hope." As it turned out, he was overly optimistic even to hope.

44. Theodore Draper, *American Communism and Soviet Russia* (New York: Viking, 1960), 331–332, 346; *Time* 6 (November 9, 1925): 8. The magazine quotes Lovett Fort-Whiteman, national organizer of ANLC, as having declared, "The Negro people as a race are of no importance, but as an industrial class they are one of the most important races in the world. The fundamental aim of the American Negro Labor Congress is to mobilize—to organize the industrial strength of the Negro into a fighting weapon."

45. *Opportunity* 3 (December 1925): 354.

46. *Messenger* 7 (July 1925): 261, 275.

47. *Crisis* 31 (December 1925): 60.

7

The Brotherhood of Sleeping Car Porters
PHILIP S. FONER

In 1929, the Brotherhood of Sleeping Car Porters held its first national convention and elected A. Philip Randolph as its first president. In 1925, Randolph, with several Pullman porters, launched the independent black union to deal with the low wages and substandard working conditions of the members. This chapter discusses the brotherhood's early history, from its organizational drives to its affiliation in 1928 with the American Federation of Labor (AFL).

At the 1928 AFL convention, the white delegates were startled and somewhat shocked when a black union applied for an international charter. The application was presented by A. Philip Randolph, the dynamic socialist who had left journalism to organize the Brotherhood of Sleeping Car Porters. At the time of the application, the Pullman porters had undergone three difficult years as an independent union.

Randolph and a few score of Pullman porters launched the brotherhood on August 25, 1925, in New York's Harlem. Its intention was to deal with the low wages, long hours, lack of adequate rest on trips, lack of bargaining power, and job insecurity in the porters' work. The porters had specific grievances as well: they were required to remain on call at sign-out offices for several hours per day without pay; porters in charge often had to perform conductors' work without adequate compensation for extra services; and the Pullman employee representation plan did nothing to correct injustices.

When federal control of the railroads ended in 1920, the Pullman Company, eager to stifle the porters' efforts to organize, introduced the employee representation plan, which in the words of company president E. F. Carey was "offered to our employees for the purpose of handling expedi-

tiously and settling promptly and fairly all questions which arise as to wages, working conditions, and such matters as may be important to the welfare of the employees."[1] Basically, the plan was a company union. Like the antiunion schemes adopted by many other American companies during the postwar years, it included a promise not to discriminate against workers for membership in any union or fraternal order but insisted that "the right to hire and discharge shall be invested exclusively in the company." The workers' representatives could appeal a discharge as a grievance to the Bureau of Industrial Relations, whose decision was to be "final"—though the bureau was simply the company's personnel department. Its chairman, who supervised the entire employee representation plan, was appointed by the company; and the company controlled the operation of the plan by financing it and by supervising the election of representatives.

It was not long before some of the porters' representatives saw the plan for what it truly was: a device to put a benevolent face on the Pullman Company and to discourage union consciousness. Some of the porters were ready to organize a real union but were deterred by a fear of losing their jobs. In 1925, Ashley L. Totten, one of the militant employee representatives under the plan, heard A. Philip Randolph speak and was impressed by the socialist editor. He initiated a one-man campaign to sell the porters to Randolph, and Randolph to the porters. At the first meeting to launch the union movement, held privately in New York, Randolph presided, read the motions he had drawn up in advance, and then voted for approval himself so that those present could not be accused later by a company spy, certain to be there, of supporting a union. A series of similar meetings followed, culminating in the establishment of a "National Committee to Organize Pullman Porters into the Brotherhood of Sleeping Car Porters." Randolph was invited to become general organizer; W. H. Des Verney, who for thirty years had been an operating porter, was chosen to assist Randolph; and Roy Lancaster, a former official of the employee representation plan, became secretary-treasurer.

From the beginning, the *Messenger* served as the spark for the brotherhood's organizational drive and the voice through which porters could anonymously express their grievances and desires. Porters operating between New York and Chicago risked discharge by serving as underground couriers, delivering bundles of the *Messenger* with its descriptions of the porters' grievances and its presentation of the brotherhood's program. They carried leaflets and confidential communiques to the brotherhood nucleus already operating in Chicago.

It was not easy to win recruits for the brotherhood. Although unemployment had decreased by the mid-twenties, blacks were still feeling its effects. A large number of out-of-work blacks were eager to become Pullman porters; indeed, it was often the only job a black college graduate could land. Those who were already porters were reluctant to risk their jobs, and the company's welfare workers—ex-porters who paid visits to porters and their families and usually received twice the salary of the average porter—were quick to point out that Randolph, not being a Pullman porter and hence immune against the company's bitter hostility to unions, had nothing to lose. Welfare workers, antiunion porters, and company inspectors rode the trains on which union men worked and invented charges of rule violations against them, which often led to their discharge. To overcome the fear this practice created, the brotherhood had to assure the porters that the membership list was carefully guarded.

Despite the stiff opposition of the Pullman Company, many porters were convinced that they needed a real union to end the outrageous conditions under which they labored. There were fifteen thousand Pullman porters traveling all over the country. Those assigned to regular runs began work at $67.00 a month; if they remained in the service for fifteen years, they would thereafter receive $94.50. Tips increased the actual earnings, but the cost of uniform, shoe polish, meals, and so forth was deducted from their wages. Their eleven thousand miles of travel per month usually meant four hundred hours, excluding preparatory time and time spent at the terminals. To aggravate the situation, porters often "doubled out" or ran "in charge" of a car, taking increased responsibility under unfavorable physical conditions for added pay at a diminishing rate. Many of the Pullman porters realized that only through collective bargaining could they hope for redress.

The rally publicly launching the brotherhood on August 25, 1925, in Harlem's Elk Hall, was hailed by the *Amsterdam News* as "the greatest labor mass meeting ever held of, for and by Negro working men." It drafted a set of demands and announced that the porters would settle for nothing less than the following:

1. recognition of the brotherhood (which, of course, meant abolition of the employee representation plan);
2. an increase in wages to $150 a month, with the abolition of tipping;
3. a 240-hour month and relief from unreasonable doubling out; and
4. pay for preparation time.

In August 1936, Frank Crosswaith, a veteran black socialist labor organizer who had been present at the meeting, eloquently declared:

> The soldiers of labor's cause must never be permitted to forget that fateful August night eleven years ago, when enveloped by the suffocating heat of a summer's night and the stifling smoke from a hundred cigars, cigarettes and a few pipes, several hundred Pullman Porters defiantly threw down the gauntlet of

battle to the nation's mightiest industrial monarch.

He went on to praise the porters for demonstrating "a courage hitherto unsuspected among Negroes in industrial warfare" and for awakening "the labor movement to the serious menace of the company union."[2] Though there were more than a few porters who did not dare to fight the company and face discharge, and though some were even spies for the powerful corporation, these black workers in the main merited Crosswaith's words of praise.

The brotherhood's first organizing drive in Chicago—headed by Milton P. Webster, a Republican leader in the city and a former Pullman porter himself—met with a magnificent response. But the majority of local black leaders were unenthusiastic. They argued that the porters could never successfully challenge the Pullman Company; that the company, because of its long record of hiring black workers, was a benefactor to the race and should be supported and not attacked; and that blacks should not, in so many words, bite the hand that fed them. The company made sure to distribute such statements by influential Negroes to rank-and-file porters, adding in its own releases that the brotherhood porter "nucleus" was made up of "derelicts who have been dismissed for incompetency," "traditional gripers," and "morons"; and that Randolph was an "outsider," a "Communist agitator," and a "threat to our American way of life." Lancaster and Totten were fired, and Des Verney resigned before he could be dismissed.

Spearheading the attack for the Pullman Company was Perry Howard—a black Chicago attorney, Republican National Committee man, and agent for the Department of Justice. Howard, an orator in the style of Booker T. Washington and an advocate of the expansion of segregation in government employment, challenged Randolph to a public debate in Chicago with the avowed purpose of "blasting and demolishing the Brotherhood and its leadership once and for all." The hall was packed with Negro workers, and Howard was lustily booed while Randolph received an ovation.

The debate occasioned not a single line in the Chicago papers, but word-of-mouth accounts among the porters gave the infant brotherhood much-needed publicity. This marked the beginning of a nationwide offensive against the employee representation plan. Ashley Totten drew on his wide experience and firsthand knowledge as a former official of the plan to blast its iniquities via the *Messenger,* leaflets, and speeches during an organizing tour across the country. Randolph and Totten swept victoriously through St. Paul and Minneapolis, Seattle and Spokane, Portland (Oregon), Oakland, San Francisco, Los Angeles, Salt Lake City, Denver, St. Louis, and Kansas City, leaving in their wake an ever-increasing army of converts to the brotherhood. At the risk of their jobs, porters began assuming active roles in the union.

At first the Pullman Company did not take the brotherhood seriously, viewing it as just another of the many fly-by-night efforts of the porters to unionize. But as the brotherhood gained recruits, the company struck back viciously. Brotherhood stalwarts, several with decades of service as porters, were "dishonorably" discharged; thugs hired by the company struck down brotherhood organizers in broad daylight; and the black press was subsidized to launch an all-out offensive against the union. The *Chicago Whip* (which Randolph termed derisively the "Flip") and the *Chicago Defender* (which he called the "Surrender") not only advised porters to support the company union but urged members of the black community at large to "align themselves with the wealthier classes in America" as their only hope of salvation.[3] The *Argus of Saint Louis,* to that time a poorly financed publication, blossomed out in an increased size; its editorials flayed the brotherhood "reds"; and it ran front-page stories presenting Pullman as the "benefactor of the Negro race." The Pullman Company placed half-page advertisements in the *Argus* and distributed copies free to porters. Following an investigation for *Labor Age,* Robert W. Dunn wrote that "praise of the company has come from negro papers all over the country in which advertising has been carefully purchased in return for a 'correct' editorial policy."[4]

In the face of opposition from "respectable" black circles, of the prompt firing of all who aided the organizing drive, and of the physical attacks on organizers, nuclei were established in several cities. Boston, Randolph acknowledged, was a "hard nut to crack" because porters there, like other New England workers, were steeped in conservatism and had feared dire consequences for themselves from unionization, especially if it failed. But a nucleus appeared nonetheless.

With the Ku Klux Klan operating in high gear in the South, the brotherhood restricted its organizational drives below the Mason-Dixon line to a porter "underground," which made contact with the personnel of southbound trains and distributed literature explaining the union's program. When an organizer was finally dispatched to Jacksonville, the Pullman Company used its influence to hale him into court on a charge of preaching racial equality by distributing the *Messenger*. Given the choice of leaving Jacksonville within twenty-four hours or serving a term at a convict camp, he left at the advice of the brotherhood. Organization of the South would have to wait for some break in the hostile climate.

To counter the antiunionism of the black papers, ministers, and political leaders, the brotherhood sponsored labor institutes and Negro labor conferences in the larger cities throughout the country. The discussions centered on the grievances of the porters and the need for black workers in general to unionize. By the end of 1926, more than half the porters had pledged allegiance to the brotherhood. Pullman chose to ignore the fact and continued to deal with employees through its company union. However, it did step up its social welfare program of summer picnics, parades, and Christmas parties. To deprive the brotherhood of one of its most effective organizing weapons—the porters' starvation wages—Pullman called a wage conference in 1926 and permitted the porters to elect delegates. At the conference, porters were granted an 8 percent wage raise. Company officials were quick to point out that the employee representation plan was responsible for the porters' pay rise. They neglected to mention that, in the election of delegates to the wage conference, the company had noted the name of every porter who failed to vote and that these porters, assumed to be brotherhood members, were then threatened, suspended, or dismissed.

The company's concessions did not deter the brotherhood. In 1927 it pressed for the demands it had formulated two years before, but it was easier to formulate a series of demands than to actually win the porters' support for an all-out drive to realize them. Beset by company spies and detectives, and subject to procompany propaganda in much of the black press and in most of their churches, many porters and their families dropped away. Only underground cells of solid, tried members continued to function; but their number was diminished whenever a cell was penetrated by a company spy and when the identified cell members were dismissed. To let the black porters know that they were not indispensable, the Pullman Company began hiring a few Chinese, Mexican, and Filipino porters. The brotherhood tried to reassure the black porters that U.S. immigration laws made this company threat meaningless, but the threat did have an effect.

With shrinking membership and a corresponding decline in dues, the brotherhood was forced to close many of its branch offices. It appeared that the efforts to unionize the black porters would have the same fate as Randolph's previous attempts to organize blacks into unions. But the brotherhood's long months of work and its courageous battles in the face of Pullman's vicious counteroffensive had won the admiration of many labor and liberal publications, which recalled Pullman's infamous record in the great strike of 1894 and urged support of the effort to curb the power of that longtime foe of unionism. Financial support came from a number of needle trades (the garment industry businesses where needles are the tools of the workers), unions, and from the Chicago Federation of Labor, whose president, John Fitzpatrick, spoke at public meetings and over the radio on behalf of the brotherhood. Soon other officials of the AFL, including William Green, joined the supporting chorus. Worried about the influence of communists in the Negro working class, they saw the brotherhood, whose leadership was bitterly anticommunist, as a bastion against the American Negro Labor Congress.

Although most of the black papers continued to be hostile, the *Crisis*, the *New York Age*, the *Amsterdam News*, and other black journals rallied to the brotherhood's defense and sponsored benefits that netted the organization its much-needed funds (the *Pittsburgh Courier*, formerly a champion of the brotherhood, did an about-face however and declared that the company had properly refused to recognize the union because Randolph was a socialist). The National Association for the Advancement of Colored People and locals of the National Urban League endorsed the brotherhood, and some black churches even permitted it to use their buildings for meetings. Most important of all, many black workers came to see the brotherhood as a symbol of the Negro's claim to dignity, respect, and a decent livelihood and as a test of the ability of black workers to build and maintain an effective union. "The Fight of the Pullman porters is the all absorbing topic wherever two or more Negroes gather in Harlem," one report said.[5] Many blacks knew the words of "The Marching Song of the Fighting Brotherhood," set to the tune of "My Old Kentucky Home":

We will sing one song of the meek and
    humble slave
The horn-handed son of toil
He's lolling hard from the cradle to the grave
But his masters reap the profit of his toil.
Then we'll sing one song of our one Big
    Brotherhood
The hope of the Porter, and Maids
It's coming fast
It is sweeping sea and wood
To the terror of the grafters and the slaves.
(Chorus)
Organize! Oh Porters come organize your
    might,
Then we'll sing one song of our one Big
    Brotherhood,
Full of beauty, full of love and light.[6]

In its hour of stress, the brotherhood had the support of the porters' wives and female relatives organized in the Colored Women's Economic Council. The council formed women's auxiliaries in various cities, staging rallies, bazaars, picnics, boat rides, theater benefits, and other types of fund-raising socials. Of particular importance was the help the auxiliaries gave to porters' families who had suffered because of Pullman dismissals.

Encouraged by this support, the brotherhood moved against the Pullman Company on a government level. On May 20, 1926, the Railway Labor Act became law. It provided for "the prompt disposition" of all disputes between railroad carriers and their employees. In case of a dispute, the act called on the two sides to meet in joint conference to "make and maintain agreements" on rates of pay, rules, and working conditions. Employee and employer representatives were to be designated without "interference, influence, or coercion," and any dispute that could not be resolved in conference was to be submitted to a federal board of mediation.

After trying vainly to get E. F. Carey, the president of the Pullman Company, to meet with the brotherhood as the "designated and authorized" bargaining agent of the porters, Randolph appealed on October 15, 1927, to the Railroad Mediation Board to settle the dispute between the company and the brotherhood. At the same time, the brotherhood invoked the quasi-judicial powers of the Interstate Commerce Commission against the system of tipping as a substitute for adequate wages, urging the commission to compel the Pullman Company "to cease and desist from directly or indirectly informing or instructing applicants for positions as porters that they may expect increment to their wages from passengers" on the ground that this was a violation of the Interstate Commerce Act.[7]

The brotherhood met with failure in both appeals. In August 1927, the Railroad Mediation Board announced that the parties had failed to reach agreement through mediation and thus recommended arbitration. But arbitration was voluntary, and the Pullman Company rejected the board's recommendation, which closed the first appeal.[8] Then, in March 1928, the commission ruled by a vote of four to three that it did not have jurisdiction in the dispute between the Pullman Company and the brotherhood. All Randolph accomplished by the toadying tone of his letter was to convince the company that the brotherhood was weak and that its demand for recognition could be ignored.

Faced with dwindling membership, depleted funds, and a government clearly unwilling to stand up for the black workers, the brotherhood announced that it would strike the Pullman Company as the only remaining way to compel recognition of the workers' right to collective bargaining. The strategy was to force president Calvin Coolidge to set up an emergency board under section 10 of the Railroad Labor Act to investigate the dispute and report its findings to him; then, confident that the findings would support the brotherhood, Randolph and the members could rally public opinion to induce the president to put them into effect.

The threatened strike made news in every paper the country over, and denunciations of Pullman's system of tipping as a substitute for proper wages filled many columns. Heywood Broun, in the *New York Herald Tribune,* called the Pullman Company "a panhandler" and said that "some federal police officers should take away the tin can from the corporation and confiscate its pencils. . . . I'm tired of tipping the Pullman Company."[9]

But the brotherhood strategy came to naught. The Railroad Mediation Board ruled that section 10 of the Railway Labor Act did not apply in the dispute between the union and the Pullman Company and that "in the Board's judgment, an emergency as provided for in the said section does not exist in this case."[10] Many porters, fed up with the company's stalling and the government's do-nothing policy, urged the brotherhood to go ahead with the strike, indicating their willingness to risk the consequences. Randolph, in a newspaper interview, announced that "this is the first time we have threatened a strike and we intend to go through with it if our men favor doing so."[11] The brotherhood then took a strike vote, and the results were astounding, indicating how many porters were ready to prove that they were not so-called Uncle Toms. By a vote of 6,053 to 17, the strike was approved.

But Randolph began to have second thoughts. The strike vote had indicated that the porters were willing to walk out if need be to secure their rights and win their demands, but "a strike vote doesn't mean that the porters will necessarily strike," he declared.[12] Randolph was aware that the company was building a huge mechanism to cope with a strike, should one be called; but most influential in his decision to disregard the vote of the porters was the advice he received from William Green, who said that "a strike at this time would play into the hands of the Pullman Company" and counseled instead "a campaign of education and public enlightenment regarding the justice of your cause and the seriousness of your grievances."[13] On June 8, 1928, the brotherhood's leadership called off the strike.

Randolph's decision not to go forward after being empowered to do so by the membership was a serious blow to the morale of the porters. But the brotherhood's leader argued that the mere threat of a strike had brought the union a great gain, since it had "reversed the concept of the American public stereotype of a shuffling, tip-taking porter to an upstanding American worker, demanding his right to organize a union of his own, as well as a living wage." The communists, who had long been critical of the "craft isolation" of the "present leadership of the Brotherhood of Sleeping Car Porters," claimed a sellout and charged that it smacked of "typical AFL and Railroad Brotherhood type of leadership." They called on the porters to replace the leaders with "a militant, class conscious leadership."[14] For years to come, black communists pointed to the calling off of the strike as a blow to the entire black working class. "The chances of success were very bright," the *Liberator,* a black communist weekly, declared on July 20, 1931. "The rank and file of the porters were very militant. The Randolph leadership and the AFL called the strike off, betraying Negro workers in the interest of the labor fakers."

Brailsford R. Brazeal, in his history of the union, agrees with the interpretation of the brotherhood leadership that the mere threat of a strike had produced gains for the union and adds that "this was the first time in the history of the United States that a large mass of Negroes, submarginal workers, conditioned as inferiors, threatened to project a strike on a national scale under Negro leadership."[15]

The sagging morale of the porters received a lift as a result of a court decree compelling the Texas and New Orleans Railroad to disband its company union. This ruling was the result of a petition by the Brotherhood of Railway Clerks charging that the Texas and New Orleans Railroad financed and otherwise controlled its employees' representation in violation of the Railway Labor Act of 1926. The Texas decision, which was eventually upheld by the U.S. Supreme Court, encouraged the brotherhood leadership in the conviction that, despite losses in membership and funds and the many long and bitter struggles and disappointments that lay ahead, the battle against Pullman's company unionism would succeed. With this conviction, the brotherhood applied to the AFL's executive council for an international charter.

By 1925 Randolph had become as conciliatory toward the AFL as he had once been critical. Already in 1923, he had attempted to mend his bridges with Samuel Gompers (a founding member and then president of the AFL), whom he had condemned as the symbol of all that was evil in the federation, by inviting him to contribute articles to the *Messenger*. From the beginning of William Green's presidency in 1924, Randolph sought his advice, support, and practical know-how in building the brotherhood. As mentioned, Green, who was especially disturbed by communist efforts to influence the black workers, regarded the success of the fledgling brotherhood and its affiliation with the AFL as a way of ensuring that, if blacks were to be organized, it would be under "wise leadership." The brotherhood's leadership, sorely in need of Green's financial assistance and moral support and sharing much of his aversion toward the communists, found it beneficial to cultivate harmonious relations. Most of the AFL internationals did not share Green's enthusiasm for the brotherhood, recalling Randolph's earlier attacks on their unions and not forgetting that, while anticommunist, he was still a socialist. But since the porters' union did not threaten the segregated job structure or their monopoly, they were prepared to support the entry of the brotherhood within the "House of Labor."[16]

But the idea of admitting the Negro union as an equal was too much for the internationals to swallow. Consequently, when the Hotel and Restaurant Employees' International claimed jurisdiction over the brotherhood on the ground that the Pullman porters were hotel workers on wheels, the white internationals backed its claim. Randolph was already subject to sharp criticism for calling off the strike. He knew that if he consented to tie the brotherhood to an organization such as the Hotel and Restaurant Employees' International, which had a constitutional provision establishing the inferior status of black workers, his leadership would be jeopardized. He rejected the "feasible solution" offered by the AFL, and the porters gave him a resounding vote of confidence. At conferences before the AFL's executive council, Randolph made it clear that the brotherhood would never consent to be just another dues-paying "Jim Crow auxiliary."[17] The AFL international was equally firm in refusing to relinquish its jurisdictional claim. A compromise was finally reached in which Randolph, "to establish a beachhead," affiliated thirteen of the brotherhood's largest divisions as "federal unions" of the federation.[18]

Sections of the Negro press, with various black politicians and clergymen, denounced Randolph for having anything at all to do with the AFL, citing its general exclusion for most black workers and for its Jim Crow status for the rest. But Randolph was criticized most of all for accepting federal union status when experience had proved it to be a type of unionism that completely hamstrung the efforts of black workers to improve their standards. The communists termed Randolph's acquiescence another indication of the bankruptcy of the brotherhood leadership.

Randolph defended his decision as fundamentally sound. As the delegate of the New York division, he would gain entrance to AFL conventions. Once there, he could study at close hand this "American version of the labor movement" and wage a battle to remove the stumbling blocks it placed in the way of unionizing black workers. Randolph saw the sleeping car porters as "the spearhead which will make possible organization of Negro workers."[19] He was convinced that the brotherhood could best do so within the federation.

In 1929 the brotherhood called its first national convention in Chicago, at which it adopted a constitution and held its first election of officers. Randolph was elected president, Milton P. Webster first vice-president, and Roy Lancaster secretary-treasurer. The union was all but defunct at the time: the membership had declined to the vanishing point after the Pullman Company fired or suspended every porter found to have voted in favor of the strike. But Randolph was determined that the union of black workers must not fail. "We are making history for our race," he emphasized in a letter to Webster. "We are sounding the tocsin for a new race freedom." In another letter to Webster, dated August 27, 1928, he gave this advice on how to recount the formation and early history of the brotherhood:

> One thing I would stress very fundamentally though, and that is that never again will Negroes permit white people to select their leaders for them. I would make it very emphatic that upon that principle we shall not compromise, not only with respect to the Pullman porters but with any Negro movement. Negroes will no more permit white people to select their leaders than will white people permit Negroes to select theirs. I would emphasize the fact, too, that the Pullman porters organization is a Negro movement, and that it stands for the self-expression and interest of Negroes by Negroes for Negroes. I would also indicate . . . that it would not matter what the opposition would be, that the question of rights of Negroes to choose their own leaders is as fundamental as the right of life itself.[20]

NOTES

This chapter is reprinted from Philip S. Foner's *Organized Labor and the Black Worker,* 1619–1973, pages 129–135, 177–186. Copyright © 1974 by International Publishers. Reproduced with permission of Greenwood Publishing Group, Inc., Westport, Conn.

1. *Labor Age* 15 (March 1926): 2.
2. *Black Worker,* August 1936.
3. *Chicago Whip,* May 15, 1926.
4. There were a few exceptions, most notably, the *New York Amsterdam News,* the *Chicago Bee,* the *Kansas City Call,* and for a time the *Pittsburgh Courier.* Robert Dunn, "Pullman 'Company Union' Slavery," *Labor Age* 15 (March 1926): 3.
5. *New Leader,* January 16, 1926.
6. *Messenger,* August 1926, 223.
7. *Railway Age,* March 17, 1928, 28.
8. In reaching this decision, the Pullman Company seized on Randolph's tactical blunder in his sending it a fifteen-page letter in which he assured the company that it stood to benefit immensely from recognizing the brotherhood. "Under the influence of the Brotherhood," he emphasized, "discipline would flow from the principle of attraction, instead of coercion." Randolph conceded that the company had the right to require discipline from the porters and pledged that, if recognized, the brotherhood would do more for the company to maintain discipline than would any company union. In all, the brotherhood would cooperate to the full "to build a bigger and better Pullman industry to serve the nation." A. Philip Randolph to John R. Morron, June 4, 1927, Lowell M. Greenlaw Papers, Chicago Historical Society.
9. Quoted in A. Philip Randolph, "Story of the Porter," *Silver Jubilee Anniversary Folder* (Chicago: 1950), 9.
10. Randolph, "Story of the Porter," 9–10.
11. *New York Evening Journal,* March 15, 1928.
12. *Messenger,* April 1928, 90.
13. *Chicago Defender,* June 16, 1928.
14. Communist leaflet quoted in *New Leader,* June 16, 1928.
15. Brailsford R. Brazeal, *The Brotherhood of Sleeping Car Porters* (New York: Harper and Brothers, 1946), 87.
16. Even the railroad brotherhoods favored affiliation of the brotherhood with the AFL, where it would be kept by jurisdiction rules from encroaching on railroad jobs set aside for whites only. To a number of black papers and politicians, news of the prospective affiliation with the AFL was enough to kick up another storm of criticism of the brotherhood. The *Chicago Defender* denounced the brotherhood for wanting to join the federation, which it called "paradoxically plutocratic and communistic." Through the *Louisville News,* a black politician urged the brotherhood to have nothing to do with the AFL and, instead, "to seek to win the Pullman Company officials." *Chicago Defender,* August 20, 1927; *Louisville News,* December 26, 1925.
17. Brotherhood of Sleeping Car Porters, executive council minutes, New York headquarters, 1929.
18. *Proceedings of the AFL Convention, 1928,* 137–139.
19. *Proceedings of the AFL Convention, 1928,* 384–385.
20. A. Philip Randolph to M. P. Webster, August 3, 1926, and August 27, 1928, Brotherhood of Sleeping Car Porters Papers, Chicago Historical Society.

8

Civil Rights and Organized Labor: The Case of the United Steelworkers of America, 1948–1970

JAMES B. STEWART

This study examines the activities of the Civil Rights Committee of the United Steel Workers of America (USWA) from its inception in 1948 through 1970. The inquiry is designed to shed insights into factors contributing to surprisingly limited cooperation between the labor movement and civil rights organizations. The analysis reveals that although the USWA established bureaucratic mechanisms to address civil rights issues, its effectiveness was stymied by bureaucratic inertia and the inability to adapt to new mandates associated with the enforcement of civil rights legislation. In addition, dissatisfied black workers aggressively challenged the union to make good on its stated commitments to racial equality. This chapter suggests that renewed cooperation may now be possible as civil rights organizations and labor unions face increasing pressures induced by the continuing expansion of global economic networks.

Organized labor has had a longstanding interest and active involvement in efforts to promote the civil rights of groups facing discrimination. Despite this fact, the degree of cooperation between organized labor and civil rights advocacy groups has been largely episodic. Over time, the two constituencies have developed different approaches to addressing civil rights issues, demonstrating how it is often difficult to resolve seemingly competing foci, despite what would appear to be clearly overlapping interests. There was, of course, extensive collaboration between organized labor and civil rights advocacy organizations during the civil rights movement; however, before and after that time, less cooperation has been the norm.

The increasing economic vulnerability experienced by racial and ethnic minorities and workers has forced organizations representing both groups to expand their traditional agendas. As an example, civil rights organizations are increasingly focusing on issues of economic empowerment, with concerns about the deteriorating employment prospects of blacks at the top of the new agenda and with large numbers of unorganized black workers in the South constituting a potential vital constituency for organized labor. If organized labor and traditional civil rights groups are to be in the vanguard of forces generating a new movement for economic justice, then it is important to examine the historical and contemporary sources of friction on employment-related issues. Doing so will serve as a necessary precursor to their forging an effective coalition to confront current political and economic challenges associated with globalization.

This study explores some of the bases for limited labor–civil rights cooperation by examining the activities of the Civil Rights Committee of the United Steel Workers of America (USWA). The USWA's executive board created the committee in June 1948 to promote the union's civil rights policies and objectives. It is important to scrutinize the Civil Rights Committee for several reasons. First are the opposing interpretations of the union's degree of commitment to racial equality. Second is the opportunity to examine the degree of correlation between the USWA's active involvement in supporting the civil rights movement on many fronts—including at the national, district, and local level—and the status of its own black workers. Third, and particularly important to the concerns of this investigation, is that despite all of these visible efforts, USWA's national leadership faced significant internal challenges from organized groups of black workers who remained critical of the union's efforts. Understanding the reasons for these challenges can provide important hints with respect to the development of strategies to strengthen the contemporary ties among black workers, black communities, and organized labor.

In the first section of this chapter, I discuss elements of the Wagner Act that create potential difficulties in addressing civil rights issues. Then I explore the record regarding organized labor's early commitment to equality. The detailed examination of the activities of the Civil Rights Committee is thus subdivided into two periods: 1948–1964 and 1964–1970. In the final section, I consider implications of contemporary efforts to address the concerns of workers and marginalized racial/ethnic minorities.

THE WAGNER ACT AND CIVIL RIGHTS

Melvyn Dubofsky (1996, 14) has examined the various criticisms of the Wagner Act in the context of what he describes as "the tension between the rights of workers (citizens) as individuals and as members of a collective (unions), between liberty as a product of narrowing public power and the consequence of positive state action, between the elected public government and private voluntary governance." Dubofsky argues that "just at the moment that the American state chose through the Wagner Act to legitimate the collective power of workers, employers and their political advocates reinvigorated the concept of constitutionally protected individual rights as a restraint on the collective power of working people" (13).

Linking this assessment to the legislative and judicial products emanating from the civil rights movement, Dubofsky observes,

> For almost thirty years, however, the federal courts usually interpreted labor law and industrial relations policy to buttress the power and influence of trade unions—and sometimes employers—against the will and desire of individual workers. In the aftermath of the civil rights movement and congressional civil rights legislation of the mid-1960s, federal jurists began to rule in favor of individual African-American workers and women workers who had been victimized both by unions and employers (in some decisions, judges awarded new rights to such workers on a class rather than individual basis). (13)

A second type of explanation for the tension between civil rights and organized labor extends the focus on the Wagner Act and asserts that labor unions' potential to address racial grievances was stifled by the creation of alternative vehicles outside the collective-bargaining framework. As a case in point, Nelson Lichtenstein (1995) has argued that the creation of structures that provided avenues for individual workers to seek redress outside the collective-bargaining framework is a major culprit that has contributed to weakening the labor movement and to the dilution of synergies between the civil rights movement and organized labor. Specifically, he suggests,

> The 1963 March on Washington signals the moment when workrights underwent a fundamental shift in their meaning and method. Indeed, the summer of 1963 may well be taken as the moment when the discourse of American liberalism shifted decisively out of the New Deal/laborite orbit and into a world in which the racial divide colored all politics. From the early 1960s

onward the most efficacious and legitimate defense of American job rights would be found not as a collective initiative, as codified in the Wagner Act and advanced by the trade unions, but as an individual claim to a worker's civil rights based on one's distinctive race, gender or other attribute. From a legislative point of view the decisive moment in this transformation came when, during the great political opening that followed the Birmingham demonstrations of May 1963, legislation governing fair employment practices was rolled into the 1964 civil rights laws as Title VII. (1995, 5)

Lichtenstein insists that these events unleashed a broad-based emphasis on "rights consciousness" that gradually encompassed a variety of groups other than blacks, and he complains that "at the very moment in which this great right consciousness was being carried forward, the model of collective action embodied in the Wagner Act was reaching a virtual dead end, in the legislature, in the courts and as opinion polls have repeatedly demonstrated, among the general population as well" (1995, 7). He asserts further that "during the 1960s and 1970s—the very years in which civil rights law was being codified—Congress did nothing to liberalize labor relations law" and that "the courts turned the very idea of the industrial democracy which had once occupied the very heart of the collective-bargaining process into an exclusionary principle which exempted unionized workers from many of the statuary rights which those same courts and legislatures had begun to create or enforce" (7–8).

ORGANIZED LABOR AND RACIAL EQUALITY

Although problems with the Wagner Act and the emergence of alternative venues seeking relief from discrimination have hampered organized labor's efforts in the civil rights arena, it is important that one examine the degree of labor's commitment to racial equality. As noted by Michael Goldfield (1993), there is ongoing disagreement regarding the extent to which the racial practices of the Congress of Industrial Organizations (CIO) unions were significantly more egalitarian than those of the American Federation of Labor (AFL), which was notorious for its racism. At the extreme, as summarized by Goldfield,

CIO unions, even during their prime, were merely another vehicle for maintaining white employment, white possession of more desirable jobs, and other white privileges, their differences from AFL unions largely due to the industrial milieu in which the CIO operated. Thus, the CIO unions were themselves a major obstacle to African-American advancement— part of the problem, not part of the solution. (1993, 1)

Goldfield, via an analysis focusing exclusively on the activity of CIO unions in the South, advances the general thesis that CIO unions were in fact originally more egalitarian than AFL unions were, primarily because of the influence of the communists and other leftists. Black workers were generally more active in leadership and in organizing efforts when they were members of unions influenced by left-wing ideologies. As the influence of the Left eroded, so did mainstream CIO unions' commitment to authentic racial egalitarianism. Goldfield is particularly critical of the treatment of the Mine, Mill, and Smelter Workers by the Steelworkers. He cautions, however, against making blanket assessments, arguing that "any attempt to evaluate the racial practices of the CIO as a whole, its component unions, and various fractions [sic] within it must be multidimensional and systematic, not merely anecdotal" (1993, 6). There are, of course, competing interpretations of the extent to which the CIO was committed to racial equality. Stein (1991), in particular, offers a much more generous assessment.

The upshot of Goldfield's analysis for present purposes is that the uneven record of organized labor in combating discrimination within its own ranks as well as its often willing acceptance of explicitly discriminatory practices in the workplace constitute an important source of the tension between traditional civil rights advocates and organized labor, independent of the issues of the disjunction between the remedies available to aggrieved workers under the Wagner Act and civil rights legislation. Discriminatory practices sanctioned and accepted by the union, both in the workplace and within the union organization itself, often coexisted among formal structures charged with fighting discrimination as well as within the active and visible support by top union leaders for civil rights initiatives outside the employment arena. The various federal, state, and local legislative and administrative interventions designed to promote racial equality had profound influences not only on how individual workers sought relief from discrimination but also on how unions sought to align their rhetoric and internal practices.

Internal challenges to the USWA's initiatives emerged partially as a result of the workers' heightened expectations, conditioned in part by the USWA's establishment of mechanisms touted as vehicles to promote racial equality. Once these mechanisms were established, however, there was substantial ambiguity regarding the appropriate role for local and district union officials, whose actions were often perceived by rank-and-file members as reflecting a wavering of commitment. The challenges also reflected the failure of the USWA to achieve any meaningful diversity in its leadership structure. Moreover, external legal and administrative challenges forced the USWA to assume the posture of a subject of inquiry, rather than a partner in enforcing antidiscrimination statutes, when several USWA locals were named as codefendants in high-profile discrimination cases filed by individual workers with the Equal Employment Opportunity Commission.

CIVIL RIGHTS IN THE USWA, 1948–1964

The establishment of the USWA Civil Rights Committee was mandated by resolution at the USWA's Fourth Annual Constitutional Convention in 1948.[1] Designated as chairman was Thomas Shane (director of USWA District 29, Detroit area) and, as secretary, his brother Francis, who had been appointed as the USWA's first civil rights secretary in 1947 by president Philip Murray. One of the committee's first initiatives

was the convening of a series of one-day conferences held on successive Sundays between January 29 and February 26, 1950, in Pittsburgh, Chicago, Los Angeles, Philadelphia, and Birmingham (Alabama) to examine "fair employment practices in American industry."[2] The typical agenda for these conferences, which were cosponsored with the CIO Committee to Abolish Discrimination, involved presentations by Thomas Shane and representatives of the National Association for the Advancement of Colored People, the local Fair Employment Practices Commission, top leaders of the USWA, and other important community leaders.[3]

This particular approach to the establishment of an internal mechanism to promote racial equality has its roots in the Committee to Abolish Racial Discrimination (CARD), established by the CIO in 1942. Marshall Stevenson (1993) has provided important perspectives on CARD, which are quite useful for the present investigation. He characterizes CARD, in part, as "a response by the national leadership to pressure from black unionists in the CIO to do more to promote its professed policy of nondiscrimination and racial egalitarianism" (47). More significant, Stevenson observes,

> Backed by the CIO executive board's mandate, CARD sought to implement a systematic educational program in each CIO affiliate designed to show the ill effects of race prejudice among the rank and file and union leadership. CARD attempted to promote greater access to jobs for African Americans by constantly stressing that affiliates should negotiate racially nondiscriminatory contracts. It continued to support the major civil rights legislation of the day—antilynching, antipolltax, and the creation of a permanent [Fair Employment Practices Commission]. (48)

Many of the elements of CARD's program were replicated in the work of the USWA Civil Rights Committee. The USWA's commitment to this basic direction was reaffirmed at the Fifth Constitutional Convention of USWA, which pledged to continue the struggle to achieve the full, equal enforcement of all the rights guaranteed in the U.S. Constitution, regardless of race, color, creed, or national origin. More specifically, the resolution adopted at this convention stated, "We promise full support to the Civil Rights Committee of the USWA, created by our Union to implement the activities of our organization in this field." For present purposes, it is significant to note that the resolution demanded, in part, "the passage of federal and state fair employment practices acts."[4]

One dimension of the committee's efforts involved an examination of racial employment practices within the steel industry. A mail survey was conducted in 1950.[5] The responses to this survey are revealing and warrant a much more detailed scrutiny than is possible here. It is useful, however, to highlight a few representative responses. Several unions reported that the organization of workers had led to the reduction or elimination of past patterns of discrimination in hiring and job placement. A significant number of locals reported that formal grievance procedures constituted the primary mechanisms through which nondiscriminatory hiring patterns had been instituted. Despite perceptions of efficacy of the grievance procedures, some locals reported opposition on the part of white workers to efforts to promote equality (*USWA Archive*, box 3, file 21).

The results of this survey generally suggest that the USWA's organizing campaigns and its policy of negotiating nondiscrimination clauses in all contracts had borne fruit in terms of reducing racial discrimination experienced by black workers. However, several cautions are in order. First, many of the responses asserted that there had been no discrimination before or following USWA affiliation, suggesting a certain lack of credibility. Second, many of the responses indicated that there were minute populations of minority workers, a fact that several respondents themselves correlated with the absence of discrimination. Third, the majority of the responses were from locals located in the North; given the earlier discussion of the status of blacks in Southern unions, it is important to give this matter special attention.

The survey was one of several impetuses for a nationwide series of clinical conferences on human relations sponsored in 1951 and 1952 by the USA-CIO Civil Rights Committees. The locales for these conferences were Detroit, Beaver (Pennsylvania), Chicago, Gary, Columbus, Cleveland, and Cincinnati. The conference held in Gary on May 12, 1951, explored the general topic of civil rights in the unions.[6] One component of the program required participants to engage in small-group discussions organized around three themes: a specific personal problem encountered on the job, the reasons why the union is concerned with issues of discrimination, and the sources of prejudices.

Such internal education efforts were pursued with aggressive efforts to create federal, state, and local bodies to monitor fair employment practices. As an illustration, an August 1953 memorandum from Francis Shane to David MacDonald describes the USWA's involvement in the fair employment practices campaigns from January 1953 through July 1953. Legislation was introduced in eleven states, and "the United Steelworkers of America worked in cooperation with state and local committees for fair employment, where such committees existed, to secure the introduction and enactment of fair employment practices legislation which contained enforcement provisions, and in areas where joint committees were not organized the Union initiated independent action."[7] In addition to these state and local efforts, Shane also reported that "the Union continued to work with the Leadership Conference on Civil Rights in an effort to secure a Federal law for enforcing fair employment practices."[8]

Despite particularly intensive involvement in the campaigns in California, Illinois, Michigan, Ohio, and Pennsylvania, Shane reported that all of the campaigns had been unsuccessful. In addition, legislation failed to pass in five of the six other states. Shane provided an extensive and sophisticated analysis of the reasons for these outcomes, identifying poor organization and limited finances as the major culprits, with "extreme difficulty . . . in getting top flight people to assume positions of leadership in the various campaigns."[9]

Shane proposed the convening of a one-day conference of USWA staff representatives "to more effectively organize our resources for future municipal, state and federal [fair employment practices] campaigns." The proposed conference was convened on September 29, 1953, in Pittsburgh. Gradually the fair employment practices campaign began to bear fruit, as exemplified by the creation of the Pennsylvania Fair Employment Practice Commission. A policy committee met on October 11, 1955, to develop recommendations for commission membership. The struggle for institutionalization of fair employment practices was not the only battle that the USWA Civil Rights Committee waged during 1955. On August 31, 1955, Rayfield Mooty, president of Local 3911, wrote Francis Shane requesting assistance in seeking justice in the lynching murder of Emmett Till, who was "the grandson of Henry Spearman, a steel worker and member of Local No. 3314."[10] Mooty would later play an instrumental role in the ad hoc committee of steelworkers, which would question the depth of the USWA's commitment to eradicating discrimination within the union's ranks. In his capacity as chairman of the Allegheny County Council on Civil Rights, Shane wrote to United States attorney general Herbert Brownell on September 26, 1955, requesting that Brownell "immediately use the power of your office to help bring an end to the series of violent incidents in which the civil rights of many citizens have been violated and, which if allowed to continue, will encourage an even more flagrant disregard for the rights of the individual."[11] Shane went on to assert that "the brutal lynch murder of Emmett Louis Till in Tallahatchie County, Mississippi and the subsequent trial and acquittal of those who were charged with implication in the crime have brought into focus for the entire world to see the vicious and premeditated steps that bigoted and prejudiced people in the United States are taking to deny their fellow men equal justice both under and before the law."[12]

The Civil Rights Committee was not the only component of the USWA organization that intervened in the Emmett Till lynching case. As an example, Local 1011 adopted a resolution calling for "the bringing to justice the kidnapping murderers of young Emmett Till in Sumner, Mississippi." Copies of the resolution were to be sent to the U.S. attorney general, the attorney general of Mississippi, the National Association for the Advancement of Colored People, and Francis Shane.[13]

The Civil Rights Committee also explored some creative, externally oriented educational strategies to promote racial equality. The minutes of the April 9, 1957, quarterly meeting include a summary of plans for a film "based on a civil rights speech made by President MacDonald at the Eighth Constitutional Convention of the United Steelworkers of America on September 19, 1956 in Los Angeles."[14] The minutes also provide an update on the "We Humans" educational project, an exhibit that was successfully presented in the Pittsburgh public and parochial schools and was being considered for possible adoption in Los Angeles and Chicago.

The range of activities described to this point is exemplary of the approach to the promotion of racial equality undertaken by the USWA Civil Rights Committee throughout the pre-1964 period. As indicated, these activities included internal assessments of the effects of union organization on hiring and promotion practices; internal education campaigns targeted primarily at middle-level leadership (district officials and local presidents); externally focused advocacy for federal, state, and local fair employment legislation; lobbying for nondiscrimination statutes in nonemployment arenas (e.g., housing) and for protection against random racial violence (i.e., antilynching legislation); and externally focused human relations educational projects.

The preceding discussion provides information useful for clarifying several issues raised by the debates and competing interpretations of the USWA civil rights activities. Consistent with the perspective advanced by Lichtenstein, there is clear evidence that the provisions of the Wagner Act, coupled with USWA's general policy of bargaining for nondiscrimination clauses in contracts, did improve the circumstances of many black workers. It is clear, however, that these incremental improvements were layered on top of a preexisting pattern of pervasive racial discrimination. The limited commitment of the USWA to plantwide seniority arrangements would allow only slow changes in occupational distributions, leading inevitably to unrealized expectations for many black workers.

The USWA central office empowered local organizing and bargaining efforts, and there is some evidence of creative and forceful civil rights initiatives originating at the local level, catalyzed by the Civil Rights Committee. At the same time, however, there was clearly perceptual dissonance between black workers and local white union officials with respect to the extent of change and to the efficacy of the available grievance procedures. The USWA Civil Rights Committee had neither the sophistication nor the mechanisms to assess the credibility of the reports it received regarding racial equality because it had no direct links with rank-and-file black workers. The committee was unable to operate outside the existing chain of command, which included few individuals with the sensitivities necessary to articulate the broad concerns of black workers in the spirit of Dubofsky's discussion about the tensions between rights of workers as workers and workers as citizens. This problem would come back to haunt the USWA in the post-1964 period.

THE CIVIL RIGHTS ACT OF 1964: MEETING NEW CHALLENGES

The passage of the Civil Rights Act on July 2, 1964, had a profound effect on the approach taken by the USWA in promoting fair employment practices and other civil rights initiatives. It precipitated an expansion of the Civil Rights Committee's efforts, including initiation of a massive educational campaign designed to prepare the USWA for aggressive implementation of Title VII provisions. On August 7, 1964, the committee sent a letter to all directors, staff representatives, local presidents, recording secretaries, and chairmen of local civil rights committees "outlining . . . responsibilities for implementing the law and listing the first of a series of projects the Committee was planning to develop comprehensive support for Title VII implementation."[15] A December 27, 1965, memorandum sent to all district and local officials called on each local to "comply with its constitutional obligation to establish a Local Union Civil Rights Committee" and to "expand our areas of concern to include . . . causes and effects of racial discrimination—such as poverty, slum housing and inadequate educational opportunities."[16] As of the end of 1965,

about 2,150 of the 2,800 locals had not yet established such a committee.[17] Each district director had been requested to appoint a district civil rights coordinator, whose role was in part to oversee the activities of the local committees.[18] The first meeting of the district civil rights coordinators was held on March 11, 1966, in Pittsburgh.[19]

The Civil Rights Committee itself was reorganized, ending Francis Shane's role as the USWA's point person on fair employment issues. Under the new structure, there were fourteen members, all men; the committee membership would remain all male until Helen Mraz, who had served as president of Local 3745 at the National Can Corporation plant in Chicago for fifteen years, was appointed in 1967.[20] Curtis Strong, vice president and grievance committeeman of Local 1014, was appointed to the International Committee on Civil Rights on January 16, 1966.[21]

Under the revised organizational structure, the chairman of the Civil Rights Committee was designated to be filled by an international officer rather than a district director. Vice president Joseph Molony was named chairman, and international secretary-treasurer Thomas Murray continued as secretary. A new position was created—director of the Civil Rights Committee, which was filled by Alex Fuller (District 29), who had helped found the ad hoc committee of black steelworkers, a dissident organization mentioned previously. Fuller had been chairman of the Michigan Fair Employment Practices Commission and vice president of the Wayne County Industry Union Council. He had also served as chairman of I. W. Abel's successful campaign to oust David MacDonald as USWA international president.[22]

As noted, the USWA's civil rights efforts had always centered on the negotiation of broad nondiscrimination clauses in all contracts. A civil rights complaint form was developed with a set of procedures for handling complaints, including determining if a complaint was grievable under enforceable contract provisions and informing complainants of possible internal and external filing to ensure that the statute of limitations did not expire. The functions of the local committees and the procedures for handling complaints were codified in a pamphlet entitled *Civil Rights Guide-*

lines. The foreword of this pamphlet indicated that it was "designed as a guide to Civil Rights Committees, local union officers and members . . . [to answer] the most frequently asked questions about the organization and function of a Civil Rights Committee in a local union and the procedures to be followed in civil rights matters on the job, in the union, and in the community."[23]

A major controversy erupted surrounding the proposed distribution of these pamphlets at a District 31 civil rights conference. District 31 was the home base for the ad hoc movement. In a letter dated May 4, 1967, the leaders of the ad hoc group demanded a meeting with Alex Fuller to resolve the controversy. It is not clear whether the meeting was held, but the ad hoc committee followed up with an August letter to USWA president I. W. Abel, seeking implementation of a "three-point program." The three points of contention were, first, the absence of black representation on the executive board; second, the limited employment of blacks within the district and national offices; and, third, the need for reorganization of the Civil Rights Committee. The letter went on to declare that "the undersigned having been duly authorized by the Delegates represented by Ad Hoc Committee conference held July 29th–30th, 1967 in Birmingham, Ala., again petition you for a conference to review the progress made in the overall area of our (3) three point program and to make recommendations to further implement it."[24]

Communications earlier in the year from ad hoc representatives to USWA officials had complained about barriers to promotion that black workers faced and the fact that black professional employees were absent within USWA itself. The concerns raised clearly had merit. At this time there were no black members of the USWA executive board. The equal employment opportunity report (EEO-1 report) filed by the USWA indicated that none of the district directors were black and that only 50 of the 765 employees in the district directors offices were black. In the international headquarters, only 22 of the 336 employees were black, and only two of the black employees were classified as professionals.[25]

Molony's noncommittal response, dated January 27, may well have been a principal catalyst spurring organization of the Ad Hoc Committee

Conference held in Birmingham, July 29–30, 1967.[26] An official call was mailed to approximately 150 black steelworkers on July 11, 1967, and about 70 persons attended the conference, most from the Birmingham area. The resolution adopted at the conference is notable for its challenge to the manner in which the USWA had approached the issue of promoting fair employment practices through existing mechanisms. It therefore proposed an alternative approach:

THEREFORE BE IT RESOLVED THAT the Local Civil Rights Committee, the District Civil Rights Coordinator and the International Civil Rights Committee be given recognition in the Basic Labor agreement existing between all companies and the USWA.

BE IT FURTHER RESOLVED to the extent that said Union Representative shall have authority to discuss and Resolve such Civil Rights matters with the appropriate representative of management, that may arise from time to time.

BE IT FINALLY RESOLVED that provision be made in the Labor Agreement and or the International Constitution that the complainant's case shall be processed through successive steps, even to arbitration or the International Convention floor for adjudication.[27]

The ad hoc committee's proposed approach to the internal management of fair employment issues was clearly at odds with the existing approach of the USWA. The continuing call for such a radical change in policy and practices signaled the existence of significant discontent within the ranks. This internal controversy was occurring at the same time the USWA had to negotiate the role of existing mechanisms vis-à-vis the new regulatory bodies established under Title VII and related state and local legislation. Thus, a "Consultative Conference on Implementation of Title VII of the Civil Rights Act of 1964 with State Fair Employment and Civil Rights Agencies" was held in Chicago, April 20–21, 1966. The conference was cosponsored by the United Auto Workers; the United Packinghouse Workers; the United Rubber Workers; the United Steel Workers; and the Oil, Chemical, and

Atomic Workers. The ostensible goal of the conference was to develop "meaningful understandings between the five Unions and the State Agencies, that will serve to further our mutual interest in the cause of fair employment practices across the country."[28] A second objective was "to perfect our contract language, education and other machinery at the plant level, so that the day may arrive when this alignment of State, Government Agencies and Labor, can achieve a brotherhood of full equality and full rights for all citizens."[29] In discussing the outcomes of this conference, Alex Fuller was quoted in a newspaper article to have said that the USWA would work with federal officials on preventive and corrective programs.[30] Fuller went on to observe that the majority of discrimination claims arise in the area of seniority. The USWA focused considerable attention on these matters, developing internal position papers regarding merging seniority lines and transfers to support negotiations with the Equal Employment Opportunity Commission at a meeting held on February 17, 1967.[31]

For present purposes it is useful to quote at length some critical language from the policy statement that emerged from the consultative conference:

> As we view the whole concept of "Equality of Opportunity," creating dialogue and working together on complaints is but one aspect of the broader area which must be explored on the path to creating and implementing affirmative action at the State and local levels. Indisputably, surging beyond this horizon means the interpreting to State Agencies the Unions' concepts, as well as their struggle pursuant to our *philosophy of seniority, grievance machinery, and contractual policies.* Here lies a great area and a significant challenge in which we can explore together as we pursue definitive affirmative action.[32]

The statement clearly signaled future problem areas—that is, conflicts over segregated seniority lines, the use of grievance procedures to address racial discrimination charges, and the extent to which contractual agreements could shield discriminatory behavior. The unions did agree not to oppose workers' efforts to seek relief from discrimination through legal challenges, as long as the union's rights were not infringed:

> While the Unions have traditionally supported Civil Rights Legislation and Fair Employment Practices Legislation at the Federal and State levels. . . . It should be clearly understood that the Unions, in their administration and implementation of their constitutional guarantees and contractual responsibilities, will encourage and urge its members to utilize such constitutional guarantees and contractual remedies in the resolvement of problems alleging practices of discrimination at the local union and plant level. The Unions, while urging their members to take full advantage of the Unions' constitutional guarantees and contractual provisions, will work with State Agencies in preserving the public right of its local union members-employees to take advantage of State Laws as well as Title VII of the Civil Rights Act of 1964. Notwithstanding these constitutional guarantees and contractual responsibilities, the Unions will cooperate with their members who find it necessary to seek relief under both State and Federal Fair Employment practices Legislation.[33]

In return, the unions sought early access to information about charges of discrimination filed with the agencies by union members against employers and the unions themselves:

> We believe that this commitment on behalf of the Unions to State Agencies deserves a response in relationship to certain interpretations of *"confidentiality"* by the State Agencies. The Unions believe that because of union-management contract relationships, Unions are inescapably interested and indeed are an integral part of the *investigatory mechanism* as State Agencies pursue their responsibilities. Therefore, if we are to really achieve meaningful dialogue and affirmative action between the Agencies and the Unions, it is imperative that the Agencies at the inception of their *investigatory procedures* forthwith notify the Unions involved of a pending complaint, as well as other parties at interest which, of course, is not within the public domain.[34]

The USWA had continuing problems obtaining information from the Equal Employment Opportunity Commission about charges filed, as well as coordinating its internal investigative processes. Serious problems arose in connection with two cases in 1967. The commission informed the USWA that complaints of unlawful employment practices had been lodged against the U.S. Steel plant in Fairfield, Alabama, and against the local union. The charges claimed that labor pools denied black employees "the full benefits of their seniority and opportunities for promotion equal with those enjoyed by white employees," that the company regularly rejected bids of senior black employees in favor of less-senior white bidders, and that the union had failed to seek redress for these practices.[35] This case had been discussed extensively at the May 15, 1967, meeting of the Civil Rights Committee. The minutes note that efforts to resolve this case had been unsuccessful.

The minutes also referenced another case originating at the Bethlehem Steel plant in Sparrows Point, Md., involving allegations of discrimination in hiring, promotion, transfers, and segregated facilities in the locker rooms and toilets. USWA Civil Rights Committee officials had met with company representatives and were optimistic about prospects for resolution.[36]

The local community and the rank and file exhibited much less patience with the company. The Congress on Racial Equality took a leading role in organizing the Steel and Shipyard Workers Committee to confront the company head on. The strategy included the "'Demand Your Job Rights' Freedom March and Ride" from Baltimore to Washington, D.C., on May 25 and 26.[37] A newspaper article in the *Worker* dated June 18, 1967, stated that "over 200 angry Negro steel and shipyard workers converged on the Department of Labor last week and walked away with an agreement one of the negotiators described as 'the beginning of a new day for black steelworkers and black workers generally.'"[38] The settlement resulted from negotiations between secretary of labor Willard Wirtz; representatives of the workers' committee; Lincoln Lynch, national congress director; and James Farmer, former congress director. As part of the settlement, Wirtz "agreed to withhold certification and seek cancellation of a Defense Department contract . . . unless an agreement is reached covering the Negro workers grievances."[39] According to the newspaper article, "A number of steel union officials walked in the picket line. But part of the workers' complaints were directed at the union, which they said that had failed to wage an effective fight for them."[40] Lynch is reported to have said that the workers "would have to seek redress both inside and outside the union" and that "the object must be to force the company along the lines of the Newport News agreement."[41] The Newport News agreement was the result of a suit filed by the National Association for the Advancement of Colored People Legal Defense Fund charging the company with failure to comply with the executive order outlawing discrimination among recipients of federal contracts. Although the case was still in litigation, an interim agreement had been reached "whereby Negro workers would be upgraded into craft and supervisory positions."[42]

Both the Fairfield and Sparrows Point cases highlighted weaknesses in the overall approach of the USWA to pursuing fair employment practices. In the wake of this development the Civil Rights Committee began to take a harder line with Bethlehem Steel. As an illustration, Bethlehem Steel's offer to hire one hundred youth for summer jobs was characterized as "a grandstand play of the worst kind," in a draft statement dated July 14, 1967. The statement asserted, "The company knew its 'offer' would be impossible for either it or the union to honor because it would violate the contract provisions covering wage rates and job standards which both sides are legally bound to respect."[43] The statement concluded, "We of the United Steelworkers of America have a long and proud record in the two areas of community service and human relations. We resent any attempt to besmirch that record by asking us, under the guise of civic duty, to join in exploiting labor for the clear benefit of private management. We stand ready to assist and cooperate in any worthwhile community endeavor but we will not be a party to any brazen effort to bamboozle the public in a manner that is self-defeating."[44]

The Civil Rights Committee attempted to improve the coordination of the national efforts with the local civil rights committees at the Sparrows Point plants. This resulted in a less-positive assessment of company actions. Strong's assessment differed markedly from that conveyed in the earlier reports, noting "I believe the company is consciously evading the proposition of hiring and promoting Negroes [*sic*] to jobs heretofore denied them."[45] Interestingly, Strong also observed that "the Local Union Committees, on the whole, are not versed enough in the contract to be able to differentiate between a grievance and a civil rights violation, and I believe there is a need for instruction in this area by the staff or other informed personnel."[46]

Strong's observation provides a useful segue to the implications of the preceding discussion for the issues raised in the introduction. There was no inherent reason why the establishment of external mechanisms to enforce nondiscrimination in employment would be correlated with the declining efficacy of the internal mechanisms associated with the Wagner Act. As revealed, the USWA never truly understood the concerns of its rank-and-file black workers that were linked to the broader forces swirling around them outside the workplace, including the civil rights movement and the black power movement. In the minds of many black workers, subtle distinctions between grievances and civil rights violations were irrelevant—the key objective was reducing oppression quickly and effectively. Rational individuals would be expected to gravitate toward mechanisms for redress of complaints that offered the least bureaucratic resistance, exhibited the greatest potential for generating relief, and exhibited the greatest respect for the culture of the victimized. The internal procedures of the USWA and its approach to ensuring racial equality in the workplace came up short on all three measures when compared to the available external mechanisms.

Unfortunately, the USWA still failed to grasp these complexities throughout the rest of the decade, with predictable results. It maintained a commitment to its existing approaches, focusing on incremental refinements as suggested in the civil rights resolution adopted at the Fifteenth Constitutional Convention in 1970. This resolution stated in part,

We have made important steps toward broadening seniority systems and making other adjustments regarding such matters as training, apprenticeship and testing. These steps are essential to the achievement of equal opportunity. We are mindful that not every plant and not every contract has been brought in line with equal opportunity needs regarding these matters, and we call upon all levels of our membership to obtain compliance with such standards. . . . Some traditional systems of seniority or apprenticeship do not lend themselves to equal opportunity. Where this is the case, it is the duty of our Union to make such revisions or overhaul seniority rules as will be consistent with the law, with our own policies and with the rights of all our members. Liberal provisions for transfer, for manning new departments, for entrance into training programs are but a few of the things needed in our plants.[47]

At the same time, however, the resolution went on to assert that

some government agencies and private groups are contending that certain seniority practices are discriminatory and unlawful. Most of these challenges are without merit. Some have disclosed real problems. In such instances our Union has sought to obtain agreements consistent with our equal opportunity policies. Despite these efforts, we have been rebuffed by some government agencies and lengthy lawsuits or administrative proceedings have resulted. It is our hope and expectation that these conflicts will soon be resolved on the basis of remedial measures which enable all of our members to feel that they are receiving non-discriminatory and constructive treatment at the work place.[48]

As of April 1971, there were 1,843 local union civil rights committees, compared to 650 in 1965.[49] However, as of April 1970, there were only 89 black employees out of 1,124 employees on the central USWA staff.[50] The disjunction between institutionalization of civil rights activities at the local level and limited diversity in the USWA leadership structure was a recipe for increasing internal tensions.

The ad hoc committee, now chaired by Ray-field Mooty, held a two-day conference on July 12 and 13, 1969, to "discuss the problems of getting Black representatives in top offices in the nation-wide union."[51] A newspaper article noted that "at the USW's 14th annual convention, held in Chicago's Amphitheatre just two weeks before the traumatic Democratic National Convention, dissatisfied Black workers staged a protest demonstration outside the convention headquarters to attract public attention to their cause."[52] A June 2, 1971, memorandum from Curtis Strong to Alex Fuller described a demonstration on June 1 in Gary, Indiana, by a group of approximately 150 predominately black and Latino steelworkers from Locals 1010, 1011, 1014, and 1016. The protest was conducted under the rubric of the "black caucus" and involved picketing the USWA subdistrict headquarters in Gary for nine hours. According to Strong, "The purpose of the demonstration was to focus attention on the lack of blacks in positions of influence in the USWA, as well as the appointment of a non-black to the sub-district Director's position in District 31."[53] This matter had been brewing for at least a year and involved issues regarding the appropriate handling of civil rights complaints. According to a June 11, 1970, letter from Curtis Strong to Alex Fuller, "The local union charged the company with failure to exchange minutes of meetings, failure to answer Civil Rights complaints, and failure to allow the Union to make in-depth investigations of alleged discriminatory practices. The Union also charged the company with being unwilling to agree to any type of procedure for the joint Civil Rights Committee." The local civil rights committee had in fact been bypassed in discussions between the district union leadership and company officials.[54] The offices of District 30 were picketed by a local black protest organization named the Movement for Opportunity, several of whose leaders were members of Local 4315. Strong indicated, "The present main project is Bryant Air Conditioning and the USW. . . . The stated goals of the Bryant–USW project is to eliminate discriminatory hiring and employment practices by the Company and to eliminate the Anti-Black policies of the Union."[55]

The inability of the USWA to deal effectively with these types of internal conflicts exacerbated its inability to respond effectively to the massive political and economic transformation of the U.S. economy in the 1970s and the intensification of efforts by various groups to assert rightful claims for social justice. Of course, the USWA was not alone in its inability to deal with these issues. The basic posture taken by the USWA toward intermixing traditional collective-bargaining mechanisms with civil rights enforcement vehicles was shared with other major unions, as documented by the fact that the United Auto Workers; the United Packinghouse Workers; the United Rubber Workers; and the Oil, Chemical, and Atomic Workers were cosigners of the policy statement that emerged from the 1966 Consultative Conference on Implementation of Title VII of the Civil Rights Act of 1964.[56] Furthermore, the revolutionary union movement among black autoworkers clearly demonstrates that internal tensions surrounding race were not restricted to the USWA (see Georgakas and Surkin 1975).

CONCLUSION

The most critical question that remains is not what the USWA and other unions could have done differently to avoid the types of problems that have been described. The real question is whether organized labor has gained sufficient insights from the experiences of the 1960s and 1970s to build a rejuvenated labor movement, one that effectively integrates traditional concerns with the sociocultural interests of workers and one that will be shaped by the dramatic demographic changes that are underway.

Consistent with the perspectives advanced by Nelson Lichtenstein in the post-1964 period, the provisions of the Wagner Act and their application by the USWA became less important in addressing the concerns of black workers than had been the case before the passage of the Civil Rights Act. However, as the previous discussion reveals, this phenomenon was as much the result of the union's unwillingness to adapt its approach to collective bargaining and workplace rights as the imposition of an external mechanism for seeking relief that usurped the power of internal mechanisms. In addition, and consistent with

Michael Goldfield's critique, the USWA was too willing to accept existing patterns of inequity in job assignments and promotions that resulted from its collective-bargaining posture regarding seniority rights. Moreover, even when internal bureaucratic structures were designed and introduced to address civil rights issues directly, the effectiveness of these vehicles was stymied by bureaucratic inertia and the lack of a solid commitment from a leadership that manifested much less diversity than did its constituency. There were many individuals who fought hard to promote equality, but their efforts could not have been effective without a mandate from the highest levels of the USWA leadership to go beyond superficial educational and data-collection activities.

Alvin and Heidi Toffler (1995, 53) have provided useful food for thought in exploring how unions must change to meet the challenges of the twenty-first century:

> Unions, primarily designed for the crafts or for mass manufacturing, need to be totally transformed or else replaced by new-style organizations more appropriate to the super-symbolic economy. To survive they will have to support rather than resist such things as work-at-home programs, flextime and job sharing.

There are certainly signs that some important changes are occurring within organized labor. For present purposes, two of the most significant initiatives are efforts by the AFL-CIO to establish alliances with black ministers and the new economic education project being developed by the AFL-CIO. Developing alliances between organized labor and black church leaders reflects the type of holistic approach to the pursuit of racial equity that black workers were seeking during the 1960s. The economic education project is designed to inform union members more effectively about the forces responsible for their worsening economic plight. If successful, it may reverse the political fragmentation within the rank and file that has weakened organized labor's power in the political arena. In discussing race and gender, the outline of the new program acknowledges the changing demographics and asserts that "the labor movement must stand for inclusion and social justice. . . . Workers must have access to jobs and training, and must receive equitable pay, regardless of their race, gender or sexual orientation. The results of past and current discrimination must be remedied by methods which include affirmative action" (AFL-CIO n.d.). The outline also declares, "Unions play a crucial role in uniting workers of all races and both genders around their common interests as workers. When unions have been at their best, reducing wage and job quality differences between workers of different races and genders has been an important goal of our policies, and we must redouble our efforts in these areas" (AFL-CIO n.d.).

Further development of such educational approaches and coalition-building initiatives are likely to serve the interests of workers more effectively in the next century than decrying the erosion of the efficacy of the Wagner Act. In essence, organized labor has two choices in confronting the realities of the twenty-first century: walking backward into the future with eyes fixated on the past; or facing the future head-on by developing new, proactive strategies to address the increasing complexities of the workplace and the nature of work itself that integrate issues of race, ethnic, and gender equity in culturally authentic and systematic ways.

NOTES

The present study makes extensive use of material contained in the *United Steelworkers of America Archive*, Historical Collections and Labor Archives, Penn State University, University Park, Pennsylvania, hereinafter cited as *USWA Archive*. In addition, the Civil Rights Committee eventually changed its name to the Civil Rights Department, but for the sake of simplicity, the original name is used throughout.

1. Denise Conklin, "United Steelworkers of America Civil Rights Department 1945–1971," *USWA Archive* (1988): 3.

2. Letter from Francis Shane, December 19, 1949, *USWA Archive*, box 3, file 26.

3. "Suggested Program Form, Conference on Fair Employment Practices Sponsored by United Steelworkers of America and Its Committee on Civil Rights," Broadwood Hotel, Philadephia, February 19, 1950, *USWA Archive*, box 3, file 24.

4. "Civil Rights," U.S. Convention Civil Rights Resolution, 1950, *USWA Archive*, box 3, file 24.

5. Thomas Shane to all union presidents, directors, and staff representatives, February 17, 1950, *USWA Archive*, box 3, file 21.

6. "Fourth Clinical Conference on Human Relations, United Steelworkers of America, District No. 31, Gary, Indiana, May 12, 1951," *USWA Archive*, box 2, file 20. Information about the other clinical conferences can be found in box 2, files 17, 18, 19, 21, and 22.

7. Memorandum from Francis Shane to David McDonald regarding fair employment practices campaigns, January 1, 1953, through August 1, 1953, *USWA Archive*, box 5, file 8.

8. Memorandum from Francis Shane to David McDonald, *USWA Archive*, box 5, file 8. At this time, the conference comprised fifty-two national organizations representing labor, religion, and education groups, as well as veteran, fraternal, civic, and community groups.

9. Memorandum from Francis Shane to David McDonald, *USWA Archive*, box 5, file 8.

10. Rayfield Mooty to Frank Shane, August 31, 1955, *USWA Archive*, box 7, file 53.

11. Francis Shane to Herbert Brownell, September 26, 1955, *USWA Archive*, box 7, file 53.

12. Francis Shane to Herbert Brownell, *USWA Archive*, box 7, file 53.

13. "Resolution on Justice in Mississippi," n.d., *USWA Archive*, box 7, file 53.

14. Minutes of regular quarterly meeting, United Steelworkers of America, Committee on Civil Rights, April 9, 1957, Pittsburgh, Pennsylvania, *USWA Archive*, box 9, file 5.

15. Memorandum from J. Edward White to Alex Fuller, January 7, 1966, *USWA Archive*, box 11, file 32.

16. Letter to all U.S. district directors, staff representatives, local union presidents, recording secretaries and chairmen and members of civil rights committees in the United States, December 27, 1965, *USWA Archive*, box 9, file 35.

17. Memorandum from J. Edward White to Alex Fuller, January 7, 1966, *USWA Archive*, box 11, file 32.

18. Memorandum from J. Edward White to Alex Fuller, *USWA Archive*, box 11, file 32.

19. To district civil rights coordinators from Joseph Molony, February 10, 1966, *USWA Archive*, box 12, file 3.

20. "Woman USWA Leader Named to Committee on Civil Rights," *Steel Labor*, February 1967, *USWA Archive*, box 13, file 8.

21. From Alex Fuller to Rayfield Mooty, February 8, 1966, *USWA Archive*, box 11, file 32.

22. Program of testimonial banquet honoring Rep. K. Leroy Irvis and welcoming Alexander Fuller, Pittsburgh, Pennsylvania, February 12, 1966, *USWA Archive*, box 19, file 31.

23. Civil rights guidelines, United Steelworkers of America, n.d., *USWA Archive*, box 27, file 1.

24. From Hugh Henderson and Rayfield Mooty to I. W. Abel, n.d., *USWA Archive*, box 12, file 54.

25. Employer information report EEO-1, United Steelworkers of America, n.d., *USWA Archive*, box 13, file 14.

26. From Joseph Molony to Thomas Johnson, January 27, 1967, *USWA Archive*, box 12, file 54.

27. Resolution on civil rights, n.d., *USWA Archive*, box 12, file 54.

28. "Program, Consultative Conference on Implementation of Title VII of the Civil Rights Act of 19.64 with State Fair Employment and Civil Rights Agencies, April 20–21, 1966," *USWA Archive*, box 12, file 1.

29. "Program, Consultative Conference," *USWA Archive*, box 12, file 1.

30. "USW Puts Rights Drive in High Gear," *Pittsburgh Press*, April 27, 1967, *USWA Archive*, box 13, file 8.

31. "Preparation for Shulman Meeting Feb. 17," n.d., *USWA Archive*, box 13, file 11.

32. Draft of policy statement of consultative conference, Wednesday and Thursday, April 20–21, 1966, Chicago Sheraton Hotel, Chicago, Illinois, by five international unions, n.d., *USWA Archive*, box 12, file 2.

33. Draft of policy statement of consultative conference, *USWA Archive*, box 12, file 2.

34. Draft of policy statement of consultative conference, *USWA Archive*, box 12, file 2.

35. Decision in the matter of United States Steel Corportion, Fairfield, Alabama, and United Steelworkers of America and its affiliated local unions representing employees of the United States Steel Corporation, Fairfield, Alabama, n.d., *USWA Archive*, box 13, file 11.

36. Decision in the matter of United States Steel Corportion, box 13, file 11.

37. Flier with heading "Better Jobs Now, Thousands of Black Workers Qualify for Better Jobs at Sparrows Point," n.d., *USWA Archive*, box 12, file 64.

38. "Bethlehem Steel's Negro Workers Win

Govt. Pledge Against Bias," *Worker*, June 18, 1967, *USWA Archive*, box 12, file 64.

39. "Bethlehem Steel's Negro Workers," *USWA Archive*, box 12, file 64.

40. "Bethlehem Steel's Negro Workers," *USWA Archive*, box 12, file 64.

41. "Bethlehem Steel's Negro Workers," *USWA Archive*, box 12, file 64.

42. "Bethlehem Steel's Negro Workers," *USWA Archive*, box 12, file 64.

43. Draft statement, July 14, 1967, *USWA Archive*, box 12, file 64.

44. Draft statement, July 14, 1967, *USWA Archive*, box 12, file 64.

45. Draft statement, July 14, 1967, *USWA Archive*, box 12, file 64.

46. Draft statement, July 14, 1967, *USWA Archive*, box 12, file 64.

47. Civil rights policy resolution, Fifteenth Constitutional Convention of the United Steelworkers of America, September, 1970, *USWA Archive*, box 24, file 11.

48. Civil rights policy resolution, *USWA Archive*, box 24, file 11.

49. Memorandum from Harold C. Sanderson to Alex Fuller, April 2, 1971, *USWA Archive*, box 26, file 32.

50. Equal Employment Opportunity Commission, employer information report EEO-1, United Steelworkers of America, n.d., *USWA Archive*, box 24, file 2.

51. "Black Steelworkers Unite against White Supremacy in Steel Unions," *Muhammad Speaks*, June 27, 1969, *USWA Archive*, box 24, file 11.

52. "Black Steelworkers Unite," *USWA Archive*, box 24, file 11.

53. Memorandum from Curtis Strong to Alex Fuller, June 2, 1971, *USWA Archive*, box 26, file 24.

54. From Curtis Strong to Alex Fuller, June 11, 1970, *USWA Archive*, box 23, file 32.

55. From Curtis Strong to Alex Fuller, June 11, 1970, *USWA Archive*, box 23, file 32.

56. Draft of policy statement of consultative conference, *USWA Archive*, box 12, file 2.

REFERENCES

AFL-CIO. n.d. "Economics Education: What Is Our Message, What Are Our Goals." Mimeo.

Dubosfsky, M. 1996. "A Fatal Flaw: Individual Rights and the Wagner Act." Paper presented at the Labor History Workshop, April 17, Penn State University, University Park, Pennsylvania.

Georgakas, D., and M. Surkin. 1975. *Detroit, I Do Mind Dying: A Study in Urban Revolution*. New York: St. Martin's Press.

Goldfield, M. 1993. "Race and the CIO: The Possibilities for Racial Egalitarianism during the 1930s and 1940s." *International Labor and Working-Class History* 44 (Fall): 1–32.

Lichtenstein, N. 1995. "Civil Rights Culture and the Eclipse of Job Rights in the American Workplace." Paper presented at the Labor History Workshop, November 5, Penn State University, University Park, Pennsylvania.

Stein, J. 1991. "Southern Workers in National Unions: Birmingham Steelworkers, 1936–1951." In *Organized Labor in the Twentieth Century South*, ed. Robert Zieger, 183–222. Knoxville: University of Tennessee Press.

Stevenson, M. 1993. "Beyond Theoretical Models: The Limited Possibilities of Racial Egalitarianism." *International Labor and Working-Class History* 44 (Fall): 45–52.

Toffler, A., and H. Toffler. 1995. *Creating a New Civilization: The Politics of the Third Wave*. Atlanta: Turner Publishing.

United Steel Workers of America (USWA) Archive. Historical Collections and Labor Archives, Penn State University, University Park, Pennsylvania.

PART III

Theories of Racial Discrimination, Inequality, and Economic Progress

9

Racial Economic Inequality and Discrimination: Conservative and Liberal Paradigms Revisited
JOHN WHITEHEAD

This chapter focuses on the economic organization of "race"—how and why racial economic outcomes have persisted in the U.S. capitalist economy. The author presents two theoretical models: the conservative discrimination model and the liberal model. Conservatives link black–white income differentials to African Americans' making poor individual choices, particularly in areas that affect their level of "human capital" endowments. Liberals also use the theory of human capital but tend to focus on social causes in explaining racial economic outcomes. The author concludes that the conservative and the liberal model lacks a thorough analysis of how capitalism can exploit a race-based distribution of resources.

The persistence of racial discrimination and inequality has economic, cultural, political, and psychological dimensions. This chapter focuses chiefly on the economic aspect. I first examine the general characteristics of the conservative theory of discrimination and its view that capitalist competition will lead to the elimination of discrimination. I then review Thomas Sowell's conservative political economic analysis of racial inequality. Finally, I look at the liberal treatment of racial economic outcomes as developed through the writings of several prominent Keynesian economists. Although most conservative and liberal models reveal considerable technical competence, they all lack a comprehensive treatment of the relationship between capitalism and racism.

THE CONSERVATIVE/FREE-MARKET PARADIGM

A conservative/free-market analysis of racial discrimination was put forth by Milton Friedman in his *Capitalism and Freedom* (1962).[1] In Friedman's view, the forces of competition in a capitalist economy will eliminate discrimination within the competitive firm. He states that a firm's use of noneconomic information such as "race" is costly. According to Friedman,

> There is an economic incentive in a free market to separate economic efficiency from other characteristics of the individual. A businessman or an entrepreneur who expresses preference in his [*sic*] business activities that are not related to productive efficiency is at a disadvantage compared to other individuals who do not have such preferences.
>
> Hence, in a free market they will tend to drive him out. . . . The man who objects to buying from or working alongside a Negro, for example, thereby limits his range of choice. He will generally have to pay a higher price for what he buys or receive a lower return for his work.[2]

Friedman's reasoning proceeds as follows. Suppose a firm prefers white workers to equally qualified black workers. If this firm decides to hire only white workers, it will decrease its labor supply and, as a result, increase its recruitment and wage costs. This firm will also face a higher per-unit labor cost since, to some extent, it will be relying on less-efficient white workers. At the same time, a nondiscriminating firm will have an incentive to hire equally or more productive black workers at a lower wage rate. With a lower wage cost, the nondiscriminating firm could sell its product at a lower cost and eventually drive the discriminating firm out of business. In theory, then, there are strong incentives for firms to not discriminate.[3]

An extension of the conservative model can be found in the concept of human capital. Human capital is defined as investments in education, training, and other activities that raise the productive capacity of people.[4] Conservatives argue that black–white income disparities are caused by racial differences in human capital, not by racial discrimination within the labor market. Specifically, the conservative theory of human capital attributes the lower income of blacks to their supposed below-average productivity. Moreover, the assumed lower black productivity is caused by blacks' having smaller or qualitatively inferior investments in human capital than whites do.[5] Ultimately, black–white income differentials are seen as the result of blacks' making bad individual and group choices, particularly in areas that affect their attainment of human capital.[6] Conservatives therefore argue that black–white income differences can be narrowed by individual blacks' making greater investments in human capital.[7]

Many conservatives argue that cultural choices account for much of the black–white human capital gap. The so-called black underclass culture is said to reproduce dysfunctional behaviors, such as living for immediate gratification rather than planning for the future, surviving on welfare rather than accepting a regular job, and (for unmarried women) bearing and raising children without the help of a husband. This so-called culture of poverty is seen as a major obstacle to black economic progress because, among other things, it discourages African Americans from investing the time and money required to increase their human capital. For example, the children of black female-headed families drop out of school earlier than do other children. In general, conservatives argue that black cultural, family, and community values not only discourage education and other human capital attainment before entering the labor market but also encourage bad work habits after becoming employed. Conservatives differ to the primary source of black underclass culture but agree that it is a major reason for the persistence of black–white income differentials.

Conservatives are quite critical of government programs designed to aid blacks and other minorities. Since conservatives believe that competitive market forces are sufficient to discourage discriminatory hiring practices, they see no need for government intervention to improve the status of racial minorities.[8] Conservatives argue that government intervention limits individual freedom and disrupts the efficient allocation of scarce resources.[9]

Black conservative economist Thomas Sowell contends that government programs perceived as beneficial to blacks actually hurt them. Minimum wage, rent controls, and publicly financed schooling are seen as interfering with the free market system and as leading to high unemployment rates, housing shortages, inferior schooling, and other negative outcomes that disproportionately affect low-income blacks.[10] Sowell's harshest criticism, however, is directed against affirmative action. Sowell sees affirmative action as causing white resentment toward blacks and as hurting highly qualified blacks by making it appear as if their success did not come through their own talents. He takes a similar approach to busing: attempting to achieve integration through busing is a disaster since it leads to a white backlash and the conclusion that all black schools are inferior.[11]

Sowell maintains that ethnic groups with the greatest economic success have had the least participation in U.S. politics. The ethnic group cited frequently in this regard is the Asian minority population in the United States, who allegedly "make it" through hard work and little political involvement. Sowell also believes that black emphasis on politics and civil rights has brought blacks short-term gains at the cost of economic deterioration. At the same time, self-sufficiency and the acquisition of education and marketable skills are the true paths to economic prosperity.[12]

Sowell offers "historical evidence" to support his claim regarding the impact of the civil rights struggle. First, he claims that black economic retrogression caused by civil rights legislation is apparent by the fact that in 1969, before the start of numerical quotas, the black–white family income ratio was 62 percent. It declined to 60 percent by 1977. Secondly, his data suggest that black occupational gains were greater in the 1940s and the 1950s, when there was very little civil rights legislation, than during the years following the Civil Rights Act of 1964.[13] The facts, he concludes, show that civil rights legislation has resulted in very few economic benefits and indeed has not been a factor in the reduction of racial economic inequality.

Weaknesses of Conservative Racial Analysis

Competition eliminates racial discrimination within the firm. The view that competition eliminates racial discrimination fails to consider various reasons why a firm might discriminate despite competitive market forces.[14] In the first place, hiring black workers may affront white workers and cause them to produce less or to take other actions that disrupt efficient operations of the firm. Second, employment dealing with the public may be unavailable to blacks because of the realization that their employment may result in the loss of white customers. For example, a white investor may refuse to use a black stockbroker. Third, training costs can multiply when blacks are quitting due to racial harassment by white coworkers. Fourth, the highly sensitive and confidential nature of managerial decision making requires a great deal of trust and cooperation among managers. Hence, managers tend to hire individuals with backgrounds similar to their own—for example, upper class, white, and male.[15] Fifth, discriminatory behavior by a firm's management team can create disunity among workers and as a result weaken their bargaining power. That is, discriminatory practices that generate differences in employment conditions, occupations, and wages between black and white workers discourage collective action to raise the wages of all workers.

Furthermore, firms recognize that some groups of workers are more desperate for employment than others and will accept relatively low wages. In this situation, firms will have a strong incentive to engage in wage discrimination if they have clear information about racial differentials in employment opportunities. If sufficiently large numbers of firms limit employment opportunities for black workers, other firms can then pay blacks lower wages because each firm will know that black workers have fewer employment opportunities than white workers do.[16]

Black human capital deficiencies and cultural choices explain most of the racial income gap. The conservative human capital argument is not supported by statistical evidence. Human capital differences, as measured by years of education, cannot explain black–white income differentials. Blacks have lower income than whites do even when both groups have the same level of education. Consider, for example, the median annual income in 1999 for year-round, full-time workers between twenty-five and sixty-four years old. Black males with a bachelor's degree earned only 78 percent of what white males with the same level of education earned.[17] The race–gender gap for college-educated females was smaller: black females earned 94 percent of the income of similarly educated white females.[18] The race–gender gap for high school graduates showed a similar statistical disparity: black males with high school diplomas earned only 79 percent of what similar white males earned, and black female graduates earned 91 percent of what similar white females earned.[19] These and other statistical disparities suggest that the human capital argument can at best explain only part of the black–white income gap.

Conservative human capital and cultural arguments pose several conceptual problems. First, they assume that it is possible to separate cultural patterns, family structure, and education from racial discrimination. Second, they assume that black educational deficiencies and single female-headed households are cultural choices and not the result of racial discrimination. Third, they in-

fer a causal relationship from the apparent correlation between low income on the one hand and
black educational deficiencies and single-parent
households on the other—that is, black culture
causes low education and female-headed households, which in turn results in low income.

These assumptions on which human capital
and cultural arguments rest are contradicted by
strong evidence that black culture is in part
shaped by socioeconomic conditions, including
racial discrimination and isolation. African
American scholars have shown in this volume and
elsewhere that the growth of black single-parent
households is largely the result of labor market
discrimination facing the black population, especially black males. Past and present discrimination has clearly crowded many black males into
low-paying jobs that do not provide sufficient
money to maintain a family and, hence, to meet
one of the primary obligations associated with
"masculinity" in the United States.

Black low-educational attainment is also
largely caused by discrimination. Many schools in
black inner-city neighborhoods have contributed
little to black human capital attainment because
of their low per-pupil funding, high allocation of
marginal teachers, and soft curriculum that does
not prepare high-potential black students for college. Black students who attend nominally integrated schools are often inappropriately tracked
into non-college-preparatory classes or special
education. A strong case can be made that it is not
black cultural patterns but, rather, the reproduction of premarket discrimination in the U.S.
school system that is the primary cause of the low
level of educational attainment among blacks.

*The civil rights movement resulted in few eco-
nomic benefits for blacks.* Conservative racial
analysis, as informed by the work of Thomas
Sowell, lacks an understanding of the evolution
of the civil rights movement and its impact on
black economic progress. It is clear that the civil
rights struggles of the 1950s and the 1960s as
well as the black power movement of the late
1960s resulted in significant black economic
gains.[20] On the supply side of the economy, civil
rights victories resulted in an unparalleled rise in
education and job-training opportunities for
blacks, which in turn improved the quality of

black labor. On the demand side, employment
discrimination, though it still exists, has lessened
considerably because of civil rights legislation.

Moreover, Sowell's claim that black progress
was greater in the 1940s and 1950s than during
the civil rights era ignores historical reality—
namely, that civil rights activities were present
during this period as well. The civil rights movement rose to a new height with a threatened
march on Washington, D.C., by A. Phillip Randolph and the Brotherhood of Sleeping Car
Porters in 1941 to protest employment discrimination. This threatened march, involving as many
as one hundred thousand blacks, forced President
Roosevelt to issue executive order 8802 calling for
all defense contracts to include clauses requiring
nondiscriminatory practices.[21] The brotherhood
also played a key role in organizing the 1955
Montgomery bus boycott, which sparked the formation of the modern civil rights movement.
Therefore, the civil rights movement did not start
with the passage of the Civil Rights Act in 1964, as
Sowell's analysis suggests.

THE LIBERAL PARADIGM

The liberal paradigm offers a different explanation of racial economic outcomes. Liberal analysis—as seen through the writings of Gunnar
Myrdal, John Kenneth Galbraith, Lester Thurow,
William J. Wilson, and others—suggests that
racial economic inequality results from forces
beyond the control of the individual. Conservative analysis, as we have seen, looks at individuals
and their human capital choices in explaining
black–white disparities in income, wealth, and
educational attainment.[22] Liberals argue from an
entirely different perspective by suggesting that
past virulent forms of discrimination, deep-
rooted changes in the economy, and broad social
forces play a critical role in the reproduction of
black poverty and racial economic inequality.[23]

Liberal racial analysis is strongly influenced by
Gunnar Myrdal's now-classic study, *An American
Dilemma* (1944).[24] In it, Myrdal emphasizes the
self-reinforcing conditions that keep blacks at the
bottom rung of the economic ladder. He states
that if whites believe blacks are inferior, they will
then limit black access to education and employ-

ment. With limited education, blacks will have low levels of productivity, which will in turn justify and reinforce the process of their exclusion from decent jobs and other opportunities. Faced with several disadvantages, the story goes, blacks will not be motivated as a group and will develop many dysfunctional behaviors. Myrdal reasons that all of these outcomes reinforce one another and lead to a vicious cycle of poverty that he calls the "cumulative process."[25] He also recognizes that this cycle will have negative effects on several generations and that it is much stronger than the countervailing market forces that act to reduce discriminatory outcomes.[26]

Myrdal's analysis and recent liberal treatments of racism suggest that government intervention is needed to break the persistence of negative racial economic outcomes. Liberals believe that although capitalist competition promotes efficiency, it tends to reinforce income inequality along class and racial lines. They also believe that competitive market forces, though often helpful, are not strong enough to eradicate black poverty and labor market discrimination. Consequently, liberals hope to counteract these negative economic outcomes through government intervention—transfer payments, progressive taxes, direct subsidies, and so forth—and through specific education and employment-training initiatives. Liberals agree, in general, that education and training for blacks would improve their labor market skills as well as their chances of receiving decent jobs that pay a "living wage."

Lester Thurow and other Keynesian liberals emphasize that education by itself will not guarantee improved employment prospects for blacks and other minorities. Indeed, in Thurow's view, highly trained and educated blacks may be excluded from high-paying primary sector jobs on the basis of statistical discrimination.[27] Suppose, for example, employers believe that, on average, white workers are more productive than black workers are. Then it is "statistically safer" to hire all whites, even though a significant number of blacks can outperform a significant number of whites.[28] In practice, this type of discrimination occurs when an employer judges an applicant's qualifications in terms of the average characteristics of the racial group to which that individual belongs rather than on the applicant's individual qualifications. Moreover, an employer is especially likely to practice statistical discrimination when the cost of obtaining individualized productivity information is high.[29] In this situation, firms tend to rationalize that although there are a significant number of qualified blacks, it is not worth the added cost to identify them.[30]

Affirmative action legislation is the major public policy effort to address current discrimination, the intergenerational effects of past discrimination, and many other racial economic outcomes.[31] Even though there is broad disagreement in liberal circles regarding the use of de facto quotas, most liberals believe that affirmative action guidelines are still needed to force firms to develop information-gathering strategies that identify qualified minority applicants. Liberals also support affirmative action guidelines that require private firms doing business with government to publicize job openings to qualified minority applicants and to those minorities who are underemployed because of labor market discrimination. The effort to bring job information to disadvantaged groups tends to improve the allocation of black labor among industries and occupations.

Government intervention is also needed to cope with the effects of structural changes in the U.S. economy. These changes include a continuing shift from manufacturing to service-industry and high-technology employment, as well as a movement of population and industry out of central-city areas toward suburban areas. Liberals are in agreement that poor blacks in particular have been negatively affected by these changes.[32] The reason is that employment in the advanced-services and high-technology sectors requires high levels of education and training, which most inner-city blacks do not have. In addition, the movement of jobs to the suburbs has meant that a growing number of inner-city blacks are not in the right location to acquire jobs. These changes, *ceteris paribus,* reinforce the growth and the marginalization of the black "urban poor."

Most important, there is growing research that shows a causal link between recent structural changes and a growing economic-class schism within the African American population. Furthermore, many scholars who accept this research

contend that race-specific policies such as affirmative action fail to address black economic impoverishment in the new American economy.
These scholars believe that race-specific policies,
while beneficial to many high-income and educated blacks before the late 1970s, have done little
to reverse the negative impact of economic restructuring on less-educated, low-income blacks.

In response to the growth in inequality among
African Americans, many liberal scholars advocate class-specific, rather than race-specific, government policies.[33] Such policies are aimed at
reducing class income inequality caused by structural changes in the economy. A prominent pro-
ponent of class-specific policies is sociologist
William Julius Wilson. In Wilson's view, class has
become more important than race in determining black socioeconomic well-being and advancement. Specifically, Wilson's thesis is this:

> Although racial oppression . . . was a salient
> and important feature during the pre-
> industrial and industrial period of race re-
> lations in the Unites States, the problems of
> the subordination for certain segments of
> the black population and the experience of
> social advancement for others are directly
> linked with economic classes in the modern
> industrial period.[34]

Wilson also observes that the African American class structure closely resembles that of
whites and that the economic status and mobility
of the poor in both groups are largely determined
by the dynamics of economic restructuring. Most
poor blacks are now faced with employment
problems similar to less-educated poor whites
that are in the same declining job market. Thus,
according to Wilson and his followers, government policymakers must "move beyond race-
specific policies to address the problems of the
truly disadvantaged."[35]

Politicians and public policy advocates who
are in agreement with Wilson's policy agenda support pro-growth initiatives, which aid the economically disadvantaged regardless of their race.
For example, such advocates support expanding
government funding for educational services that
involve training and retraining the "urban poor"
for entry-level jobs in the high-growth sectors of

the economy. They also support funding transportation services that would bring inner-city residents to suburban job sites at a low cost, and they
support as well the increased production of low-
cost housing units in suburban areas.[36] At the
same time, Wilson and other liberals call for additional funding of family support programs and
child care services patterned on European models, which are not solely focused on aiding the
poor and "to which the more advantaged groups
of all races can positively relate."[37]

A central focus of the liberal pro-growth
agenda is the implementation of government
economic policies aimed at moving the economy to a full employment level. As the economy
approaches full employment, the resultant tight
labor market will open job opportunities for
blacks and other minorities.[38] Likewise, tight labor markets—in which the number of job vacancies exceeds the number of workers seeking
employment—will lessen the competitive struggle for jobs between various ethnic groups. In
general, a modern, Keynesian-based liberal
analysis assumes that the maintenance of full
employment and a tight labor market is possible
without any fundamental change in the capitalist economy.

Most present-day liberals reject the classical
Marxist view that racism can be largely explained
in terms of the class–profit dynamics of a capitalist economy. They also dismiss the view that the
end of poverty and racial discrimination can only
come about through a fundamental transformation of the capitalist economic system. For instance, modern liberal racial analysis has not
moved beyond Robert Heilbroner's early formulation that it is

> possible to envisage the substantial allevia-
> tion—perhaps even the virtual elimination
> of poverty, partly through income transfer-
> ence and partly through the creation of a
> more benign environment within the limits
> of capitalism.[39]

Modern liberal racial analysis is also informed by Galbraith's position that "the low
level of educational qualifications among Negroes . . . [reflects] not discrimination *per se* by
the industrial (capitalist) system but prior disad-

vantages in schools and environment."[40] However much liberals differ among themselves regarding the causes of racial discrimination, they agree that it is not capitalism per se that creates and reinforces it.

Galbraith's comments reveal a significant weakness in liberal analysis by treating the U.S. educational system in isolation from its socioeconomic environment. Liberals refuse to acknowledge that schools have evolved in the United States to support the desires of capitalist employers for a disciplined and docile labor force. They also refuse to acknowledge that the U.S. education system is designed to facilitate the reproduction of white privilege and the related concentration of minorities into secondary labor markets with the least desirable and lowest-paying jobs.

Major Weaknesses of Liberal Racial Analysis

Capitalist development is only marginally responsible for racism. Liberal racial analysis suffers from overwhelming weaknesses in its treatment of racism within a capitalist economy. First of all, liberals claim that capitalism has not benefited much from racism and, indeed, is only marginally responsible for its development. Second, and closely related, they claim it is possible to virtually eliminate racial outcomes within a capitalist market economy.

Despite what liberals claim, the development of racism can be largely traced to various stages of capitalist development. The reproduction of racism developed with the rise of capitalism during its stage of primitive accumulation. Institutional arrangements central to the development of this stage of capitalism included the wealth derived from the trade of kidnapped Africans and the subsequent slave production of exchange commodities. Hence, racism that evolved with the enslavement of black people is as old as capitalism and is inextricably linked with its history.

Liberal claims are weakened by the capitalism–racism nexus in the postslavery period as well. It is clear, as several scholars in this volume have shown, that postslavery capitalism reaped considerable economic and political benefits from racism. It is also clear that modern capitalism

may reduce racial discrimination but cannot eliminate it as long as some segments of the U.S. capitalist class have a vested interest in its reproduction. Liberals do not understand this significant fact, nor do they understand that capitalist development molds, controls, and reinforces various socioeconomic outcomes to the persistent detriment of blacks and other people of color. Racism is deeply embedded in capitalist development, and its destruction will require considerably more than modest interventionist efforts, as many liberals claim.

Government-managed redistribution and tight labor markets are the cure for ending black poverty and racial economic inequality. Most liberals, perhaps due to their commitment to reformist politics, overlook evidence that there are significant institutional barriers to achieving an equitable, nonracial distribution of income through government transfer payments and tax policies. One major barrier to government-induced redistribution is the regressive nature of the U.S. tax system. Currently, most U.S. taxes are moderately progressive in theory yet highly regressive in practice. A second barrier is the large number of tax loopholes—including the relatively low tax on capital gains—that are available to high-income groups but not generally available to the typical worker whose income derives from wages. Unfortunately, these and other barriers are deeply rooted in the U.S. capitalist system and explain why the liberal agenda of government-induced redistribution has not borne fruit.

Furthermore, many researchers question the ability of government pro-growth policies and tight labor markets to improve the economic well-being of blacks at the end of the employment queue. Robert Cherry's research, for example, suggests that the strong economic growth during the Clinton–Gore years, which led to relatively tight labor markets and low unemployment, "did not substantially improve the employment situation of black men."[41] His research also suggests that black employment increases will be "robust" only when labor markets have tightened to the point that nonblack labor resources are being fully employed, leaving capitalist firms with no other option but to hire from the pool of unemployed black workers.[42]

Race is no longer a major factor in determining black life chances; therefore, race-specific policies should cease to exist. Wilson's description of a growing income inequality in the African American community is on target, but his views on race and race-specific policies need reworking. There is no doubt that economic racial oppression has lessened considerably since the 1960s, yet it is a serious mistake to believe that racism has declined to such an extent that race-specific policies are no longer needed. To put forth such a view requires that one ignore clear and convincing evidence that racism still operates, that it has taken on a life of its own, and that it still needs to be challenged.[43]

First, there is ample evidence of vast racial discrimination in the rental and sale of housing units throughout the United States. There is also related evidence of widespread mortgage-lending discrimination against poor and middle-class blacks.[44] Second, the weight of discrimination-specific labor market research supports the existence of current and widespread employment and occupational discrimination against the black population as a whole.[45] Michael Fix and Raymond Sturk show in their book *Clear and Convincing Evidence: Measurement of Discrimination in America* that whites receive job interviews at a rate 22 percent higher than equally qualified blacks and job offers at a rate 415 percent higher.[46] Other studies have shown similar evidence of labor market discrimination against middle-class[47] and poor blacks.[48]

CONCLUSION

The conservative and liberal models of discrimination contain a combination of similar and dissimilar elements. In the conservative model, the main body of ideas includes the following:

1. competition between capitalists will lead to the elimination of discrimination;
2. differences in human capital (and cultural patterns) have a far more important effect on black–white income differentials than racism; and
3. antiracist government programs disrupt the efficient allocation of scarce resources

and actually hurt blacks and other minorities.

In contrast, the main corpus of liberal tenets include these:

1. statistical discrimination can occur if an employer believes that average black productivity is lower than average white productivity;
2. past virulent forms of discrimination have had deleterious effects on successive generations of blacks;
3. government programs are needed to address the effects of economic restructuring and the accumulated disadvantages facing people of color; and
4. government intervention can help bring the economy to a full employment level and thereby reduce the competition for jobs between various ethnic groups.

This chapter suggests that neither conservatives nor liberals have developed a comprehensive treatment of how capitalism is an exploitative system that reaps political and economic benefits from a racial distribution of resources. Moreover, since conservatives and liberals accept capitalist social relations and class-structured institutions, their models ignore how the end of racism is incompatible with the maintenance of the capitalist system. Thus, from a black political economy perspective, these models share a weakness in not being relevant to black economic progress. At the dawn of the global capitalist state, conservatives and liberals alike address the persistence of racial economic inequality within models capable of, at best, piecemeal solutions. Far from being paradigms of social justice, conservatism and liberalism have become dinosaurs in the current global struggle to end racial discrimination and exploitation. Racism is woven deeply into the fabric of American society and will not be cured in the foreseeable future without major changes in the U.S. political economy.

NOTES

I wish to thank Cecilia Conrad, Deborah Goldsmith, Mary King, Marc Kitchel, James Stewart, and

Laura Walsh for reading several drafts of this chapter, and providing important feedback. I am especially indebted to Patrick Mason whose very detailed and insightful comments and suggestions led to a complete reworking of this chapter.

1. Friedman, "Capitalism and Discrimination," 108–118.

2. Friedman, "Capitalism and Discrimination," 126.

3. See Feiner, *Race and Gender*, 23.

4. The theory of human capital was systemized by Becker, *Human Capital.*

5. Fusfeld and Bates, *The Political Economy of the Urban Ghetto*, 177–178.

6. Some conservatives even go so far as to argue that blacks' lower human capital and incomes are the result of blacks having a lower level of innate ability.

7. Some conservatives also posit that the racial income gap would be smaller if blacks improved on "basic traits" that are valued in the labor market—for example, punctuality, low absenteeism, and self-initiative.

8. Feiner, *Race and Gender*, 23.

9. It has been argued, for example, that using tax dollars to finance public education promotes inefficiency in educational markets and narrows the choices available to parents. Conservatives point out that parents who send their children to private school pay twice for education—tuition to the private school and taxes to support the public school system. This extra payment narrows the range of choices available to low- and middle-income parents in particular and places very little competitive pressure on public schools to improve the quality of their instruction.

10. See Leiman, *The Political Economy of Racism*, 209.

11. Sowell, *Civil Rights*, 61–72.

12. Sowell's views recall those of Booker T. Washington, in which economics comes first, then political rights and social legislation. One crucial difference, however, is that Booker T. Washington had a strong base in the black community because of his relentless struggle in building black institutions.

13. Sowell, *Civil Rights*, 8.

14. A firm's manpower decisions must take into account the reactions, including prejudices, of its workers, managers, and market of buyers. This is put nicely by Herbert Blumer as follows: "Openings in managerial positions may be barred to qualified members of a subordinate race not because of prejudice but because of a rational realization that their employment would affront others and disrupt efficient operation. Credit may be refused to entrepreneurs emerging out of the subordinate racial group solely because their racial makeup implies possible credit risks. . . . Employment may be refused to subordinate racial members as salesmen, professionals, receptionists, and similar types of employment dealing with the public solely because of the resentment which it is believed their presence might awaken. These are typical kinds of rational decisions—decisions which are guided just as much by the aim of efficient operation and economic return as if they took into account only the productive capacity of the individual racial member. They show clearly that the rational operation of industrial enterprises which are introduced into a racially ordered society may call for deferential respect for the canons and sensibilities of that racial order." Blumer, "Industrialization and Race Relations," 232–233.

15. See Schiller, *The Economics of Poverty and Discrimination*, 203.

16. In addition, if blacks as a group are perceived as having below-average productivity, it may be cheaper for an employer to hire all whites. The reason is that an employer might be able to reduce cost by assuming individual blacks have these below-average group characteristics, especially if the cost of obtaining accurate productivity information on prospective employees is high. In other words, a nondiscriminating firm that goes through the trouble of acquiring information on individual blacks will incur costs that a discriminating firm avoids. Thus, precisely the same grounds on which conservatives predict the elimination of discrimination—namely, competition between capitalists—may in fact promote discrimination.

17. U.S. census data referenced in McElroy, "Race and Gender Differences."

18. McElroy, "Race and Gender Differences."

19. McElroy, "Race and Gender Differences."

20. See Boston, *Race, Class, and Conservatism*, 155.

21. Foner, *Organized Labor and the Black Worker*, 238–244.

22. Conservatives focus on linking black–white human capital differentials to blacks' making bad individual choices. Liberals focus on human capital but tend to look at social causes of the unequal distribution of human capital—for example, unequal access to good schools, lack of college scholarships, and differences in family incomes.

23. Feiner, *Race and Gender*, 24.

24. Myrdal, *An American Dilemma*.

25. Lester Thurow took Myrdal's cumulative causation idea even further, with his description of a white monopoly on education, hiring, training, promotion, and credit decisions. Discrimination in each of these areas reinforces discrimination in all of the others—that is, someone who attends poorly attended schools has a harder time than others in getting the education needed for promotion at work, therefore has a lower income and will have a harder time getting credit for buying a house or starting a business.

26. Cherry, *Discrimination*, 29.

27. Thurow, *Generating Inequality*, 88.

28. Cherry, *Discrimination*, 37; and Thurow, *Generating Inequality*, 174–175.

29. Albelda, Drago, and Shulman, *Unlevel Playing Fields*, 94.

30. Weakness of statistical discrimination argument?

31. Cherry, *Discrimination*, 39.

32. Kasarda, "Entry-Level Jobs," 21–40.

33. Wilson, *The Declining Significance of Race*. Wilson's work has elicited considerable reaction from scholars across the intellectual spectrum. His work is essentially in the liberal tradition and examines the relationship between capitalism and racism in terms of historical stages.

34. Wilson, *The Declining Significance of Race*, 144.

35. Wilson, *The Truly Disadvantaged*, 138.

36. Feiner, *Race and Gender*, 25.

37. Wilson, *The Truly Disadvantaged*, 155.

38. The steady flow of job opportunities in a tight labor market is associated with the maintenance of a high level of aggregate demand.

39. Heilbroner, *The Limits of American Capitalism*, 79.

40. Galbraith, *The New Industrial State*, 254–255.

41. Cherry, "Black Male Employment," 7.

42. Cherry, "Black Male Employment," 10.

43. Such a position rearticulates the racial politics of the Reagan–Bush years in a centrist, Clinton–Gore framework, which emphasizes moderate redistribution and cultural universalism and which seeks to downplay underlying racial conflict.

44. The release of a definitive study by the Federal Reserve Bank of Boston in 1992 established beyond a reasonable doubt that banks discriminate along racial lines when making mortgage loans.

45. Mason, "Male Interracial Wage Differentials"; Darity and Mason, "Evidence on Discrimination."

46. Fix and Sturk, *Clear and Convincing Evidence*, 73.

47. Bendix, Jackson, and Renosa, "Measuring Employment Discrimination," 86–87.

48. Kirschenman and Nickerman, "We'd Love to Hire Them, But. . . ."

BIBLIOGRAPHY

Albelda, Randy, Robert Drago, and Steven Shulman. *Unlevel Playing Fields: Understanding Wage Inequality and Discriminating*. New York: McGraw-Hill, 1997.

Becker, Gary S. *Human Capital: A Theoretical and Empirical Analysis with Special Reference to Education*. New York: National Bureau of Economic Research, 1964.

Bendix, Marc, Charles Jackson, and Victor Renosa. "Measuring Employment Discrimination through Controlled Experiments." In *African Americans in Postindustrial Labor Markets*, ed. James Stewart. New Brunswick, N.J.: Transaction Publishers, 1997.

Blumer, Herbert. "Industrialization and Race Relations." In *Industrialization and Race Relations*, ed. Guy Hunter. 2nd ed. Oxford: Oxford University Press, 1970.

Boston, Thomas. *Race, Class, and Conservatism*. Boston: Unwin-Hyman, 1980.

Cherry, Robert. "Black Male Employment and the Tightening of Labor Markets." Unpublished paper.

———. *Discrimination: Its Economic Impact on Blacks, Women, and Jews*. Lexington, Mass.: Lexington Books, 1989.

Darity, William, Jr., and Patrick Mason. "Evidence on Discrimination in Employment: Codes of Color, Codes of Gender." *Journal of Economic Perspectives* 12, no. 2 (Spring 1998): 63–90.

Feiner, Susan F. *Race and Gender in the American Economy*. Englewood Cliffs, N.J.: Prentice-Hall, 1994.

Fix, Michael, and Raymond Sturk, eds. *Clear and Convincing Evidence: Measurement of Discrimination in America*. Washington, D.C.: Urban Institute Press, 1993.

Foner, Philip S. *Organized Labor and the Black Worker, 1619–1981*. New York: International Publications, 1981.

Friedman, Milton. "Capitalism and Discrimination." In *Capitalism and Freedom*. Chicago: University of Chicago Press, 1962.

Fusfeld, Daniel R., and Timothy Bates. *The Political Economy of the Urban Ghetto*. Carbondale, Ill.: Southern Illinois University Press, 1984.

Galbraith, John Kenneth. *The New Industrial State*. Boston: Houghton Mifflin, 1967.

Heilbroner, Robert. *The Limits of American Capitalism*. New York: Harper and Row, 1966.

Kasarda, John D. "Entry-Level Jobs, Mobility, and Urban Minority Unemployment." *Urban Affairs Quarterly* (September 1983): 21–40.

Kirschenman, Joleen, and Kathryn Nickerman. "We'd Love to Hire Them, But. . . . The Meaning of Race for Employers." In *The Urban Underclass*, ed. C. Jencks and P. Peterson. Washington, D.C.: Brookings Institution, 1992.

Leiman, Melvin. *The Political Economy of Racism*. Boulder, Colo.: Pluto Press, 1993.

Mason, Patrick. "Male Interracial Wage Differentials: Competing Explanations." *Cambridge Journal of Economics* 23 (May 1999): 1–39.

McElroy, Susan Williams. "Race and Gender Differences in the U.S. Labor Market: The Impact of Educational Attainment" (chapter 14 of this volume).

Myrdal, Gunner. *An American Dilemma: The Negro Problem and Modern Democracy*. New York: Harper and Row, 1944.

Schiller, Bradley R. *The Economics of Poverty and Discrimination*. Englewood Cliffs, N.J.: Prentice-Hall, 1995.

Sowell, Thomas. *Civil Rights: Rhetoric or Reality?* New York: William Morrow, 1984.

Thurow, Lester. *Generating Inequality: Mechanisms of Distribution in the American Economy*. New York: Basic Books, 1975.

Wilson, William J. *The Declining Significance of Race: Blacks and Changing Institutions*. 2nd ed. Chicago: University of Chicago Press, 1980.

———. *The Truly Disadvantaged: The Inner City, the Underclass, and Public Policy*. Chicago: University of Chicago Press, 1987.

10

Marxist Theory of Racism and Racial Inequality

PETER BOHMER

This chapter examines the Marxist theory that racism serves the interests of the capitalist or employer class by dividing black and white workers and by reducing their potential unity and bargaining power. The author concludes that the strength of the Marxist theory of racism is its focus on the historical and close relation between capitalism and racism. Its weakness is the underestimation of the importance of racial and other nonclass groupings in the perpetuation and possible elimination of racism.

Racism directed against African Americans and other people of color has been a central and continuing feature of U.S. society.[1] Its forms have changed, but we need to look no further than infant mortality rates and life expectancies; unemployment, poverty rates, and incomes; and stereotypes in the mass media to understand that racism and racial inequality remain. In the framework presented here, racism is analyzed historically as a central aspect of the economic system. In this chapter, I examine the Marxist theory that racism serves the interests of the capitalist or employer class by dividing black and white workers and by reducing their potential unity and thus their bargaining power. I also examine a closely related theory, that of segmented labor markets. Although these theories need to be modified, they have continued relevance today for examining racism and U.S. society.

ORTHODOX MARXIST: RACISM DIVIDES THE WORKING CLASS

Much of the social analysis that focuses on the injustices and inequalities in U.S. society has been influenced by the ideas of Karl Marx and the Marxist tradition.[2] Central to Marxism is the understanding that capitalism is an economic system with two major classes: the capitalist class and the working class. The capitalist class owns and controls the means of production and capital and continually tries to increase its profits. The working class, which is the majority of the population, sells its labor power, its capacity to work, in return for a wage. Profits come largely from paying employees less than the value they add to production, a scenario Marx called exploitation.

Class conflict between capitalists and workers

is inherent in a capitalist system. Workers try to raise their wages and improve their working conditions. Employers try to limit wages and increase the amount of work done per hour. The employer has the upper hand because workers fear losing their jobs and the unemployment that awaits them.

Exploitation in the Marxist sense can only be ended by the working class overthrowing capitalism. Workers can, however, improve their economic situation by forming unions and other organizations. The more disunity among workers, the weaker their ability to effectively challenge the employer. This insight is central to the Marxist analysis of racism, which focuses on attempts by capitalists to divide the black and the white workers. If white workers identify primarily as whites, rather than as workers, they will not act in their common class interests with black workers. The way to end racial oppression and class exploitation is by forming an interracial and united working class.

Racism in the United States is defined as the systematic oppression of African Americans and other people of color and the related ideology of white supremacy and black inferiority.[3] These two aspects of racism have shaped U.S. society from the early 1600s until the present.

The origins of racism in the United States are directly traced to the European conquest of the Americas, to a rapidly expanding capitalism in Western Europe and the British colonies (which were to become the United States), seeking cheap and growing supplies of food, beverages, tobacco, and especially cotton. These needs were met by a system of production in the Americas based on land seized from its inhabitants, American Indians; and the kidnapping, transporting, and selling into slavery of millions of Africans. The slave trade created much of the wealth subsequently invested in textile, shipbuilding, and other emerging capitalist enterprises in the northeastern United States and in Europe. Marxists called this the "primitive accumulation of capital."[4]

By the late seventeenth century, slavery became the established labor system for the production of these agricultural commodities. African people became enslaved not because of European aversion to blackness but because more labor could be coerced from Africans than from either American Indian or European indentured servants. African societies did not have the political and military strength to resist the seizure of its people. The ideology of black inferiority developed as a rationalization or justification for slavery; it was not the cause of slavery.[5] This racist ideology spread throughout the United States.

The following periods are pivotal for the changes in, and the reproduction of, postslavery racism.

1. The defeat of Reconstruction in 1876 by the Southern planter class and its ability to regain control of the labor of blacks led to a new system of racial oppression. Southern planters defeated the alliance of blacks and poor whites as the North withdrew their support for Reconstruction.[6] Jim Crow was the social and political system established by the 1890s that consolidated white planter hegemony in all spheres. It was the segregationist system that dominated the South and influenced most of the country until the 1960s. The 1896 Supreme Court decision *Plessy v. Ferguson,* which ruled that segregation was constitutional, was its legal foundation. The purpose of Jim Crow was the domination and coercive control over black agricultural labor. Sharecropping and tenant farming were the most common forms for the organization and exploitation of black labor. They produced much of the profits and wealth of the Southern upper class.

2. The growing concentration of capital (corporate or monopoly capitalism) led to increased competition among the European powers for new sources of profits. They colonized most of Africa and increased the colonization of Asia in the late nineteenth and early twentieth century. This led to an elaborate ideology of Western cultural, if not biological superiority, over nonwhite people—the white man's burden.[7]

Racist ideology, U.S. imperialist expansion and ambitions, and efforts by an increasingly powerful monopoly capitalist class to divide workers by race and ethnicity led to a great oppression of black people and a virulent racist ideology. Segregation and lynching increased in the early 1900s. Most unions excluded blacks. Black employment grew in industries such as steel and meatpacking but declined in the skilled trades.[8]

3. After World War II, and as a result of the vast reduction in labor required by a far more mecha-

nized Southern agriculture, the economic necessity of Jim Crow to the Southern elite declined. By the mid-1960s, this made it easier for the interracial civil rights movement to force an openly segregationist system out of existence. However, the racial divisions between blacks and whites and the increased exploitation of blacks served capitalist interests and continue to be reproduced.[9]

The direction of causality from profit seeking and the accumulation of capital; the oppression of black people; the racist ideology that justifies racial oppression—all have continued up to and including the present period. Within this framework, racism supports capitalism in several ways:

1. It permits employers to pay lower wages to black employees than to white. The difference between the wages of blacks and whites measures the superexploitation of black workers and the superprofits of capital.[10] For example, if the average wage of white workers is $13 per hour and black workers $9 per hour, then $4 per hour measures the superexploitation of black workers and the superprofits of the employer. Different pay for similar work within a firm is often disguised by slightly different job titles and by making some departments primarily white and others primarily black.

2. Racist ideology, promoted by the elites, is accepted in varying degrees by most white workers. This so-called false consciousness of white workers decreases the ability of workers to unite across racial lines and struggle as a unified group for better wages, benefits, and conditions. Racism makes it easier for employers to play one group against the other, to reduce the average wage, and to maximize employer control and profits.[11] Paying lower wages to black workers exacerbates racial divisions.

3. Blacks are disproportionately unemployed.[12] Racist ideology makes black unemployment more acceptable than white unemployment to white society. It is therefore easier to maintain higher unemployment—in Marxist terms, a larger reserve army of labor—than if whites and blacks shared unemployment equally. By reducing workers' bargaining power, higher unemployment lowers the average wage and thus increases the profit rate. In recessions, employers can provide a cushion to white employees by disproportionately laying off blacks.

In a boom, unemployed blacks are available to meet the expanded demand for labor.

In the Marxist or class-based analysis of racism in the United States, the dominant tendency is for the working class to be fragmented and divided racially, both in material conditions and in ideology. An opposite effect of capitalist accumulation—the erosion of racial, ethnic, gender, and other differences—also exists but is much weaker.

A weakness of this perspective is its focus on the class interests of employers as a whole in perpetuating racism. It does not demonstrate, first, that it is in the best interests of individual employers to discriminate; or, second, that employers as a whole use plausible mechanisms to ensure that the behavior of individual employers coincides with the interests of the group. The analysis often moves from a demonstration that racism is in the interests of employers as a class to a conclusion that the necessary outcome must be racist yet void of evidence regarding the steps by which employer interests are realized. Several models have been developed to address this particular weakness.

MARXIST MODELS OF RACIAL INEQUALITY IN EARNINGS

Marxist models of racial discrimination have been developed to rectify this shortcoming and to critique the implications derived from Gary Becker and Milton Friedman's conclusion that capitalism and racism are incompatible. These class-based models show the interests of employers as a class coincide with the interests of the individual employer to pay lower wages to blacks than to whites. The models focus on one central aspect of racism, that capitalism uses racism to divide workers.

Based on Marx's analysis that production is a social as well as a technical process, these models show that an individual employer can make more profit from a racially divided working class than from one that is united. In these models, the level of wages and the average production per worker depend on workers' bargaining power as well as on the technology. More worker bargaining power means higher wages and lower profits, and less bargaining power means lower wages and higher profits. This provides a microeconomic foundation, consistent with profit-maximizing behavior, of disparate on-the-job treatment of equally skilled black and white workers. It also explains why black workers will not replace white workers, even if the latter can be paid lower wages. These ideas are developed most thoroughly in Michael Reich's *Racial Inequality.*[13]

By hiring white workers and black workers but by paying a lower wage to the black workers, employers as a class gain via racism and racial inequality, and each individual employer maximizes profits. Paying unequal wages in a firm based on race divides workers and makes unity weaker than it would be if all workers received the same wage or if the workforce was racially homogeneous. The resulting disunity from racial division lowers average wages and increases profits. At a certain point, however, firms do not hire more lower-paid black workers to replace white workers because doing so would lead to more black worker militancy, possibly raising the overall level of wages. Alternatively, though with similar results, the disunity of workers caused by different wages paid to blacks and whites leads to increased profits. The reason in the latter case is that the employers are able to get workers to work harder and faster and produce more than they would have otherwise.

Doing careful econometric analysis, Michael Reich shows that the data on racial inequality is consistent with and provides support for this theory.[14] Using data primarily from the 1970 census, he compares urban areas. He demonstrates that greater racial inequality causes lower average earnings of white workers and higher profit rates. He uses the ratio of black-to-white earnings as a measure of racial inequality and racism. In cities in the U.S. South, where the gaps between the wages of blacks and whites are greatest, wages of whites are lowest and profits highest. Reich empirically demonstrates that not only do black workers lose from racism but so do all workers, as their incomes are reduced.[15] If the wages of blacks equaled that of whites, not only would the wages of blacks be higher but so would the wages of whites.

When synthesized with the historical analysis of racism, these models provide insight into the reasons for the reproduction of black–white earnings inequality.[16] They demonstrate that cap-italists divide the working class and that the correct strategy for the increase of racial and overall equality (between employees and employers) is an alliance of black and other workers of color with white workers against their common exploiter: capital.

There are a number of problems, however. This model downplays the role and importance of black people and black organizations in challenging racial inequality and exploitation. Also missing is a convincing explanation of why white workers often accept or support racial inequality and a racist ideology. Since, in this framework, the incomes of white as well as black workers are lowered, claiming white workers have false consciousness is not a sufficient explanation of their racism.

Although this class-based approach to racism provides insight into the reproduction of racial and overall inequality, it leads to class reductionism and excessive economic determinism. Class reductionism considers central only movements and issues directly related to class struggle between the working and capitalist class. Economic determinism means that the economy determines the politics, culture, consciousness, and struggles of a society; it minimizes the autonomous role of culture and race.

In the class-based approaches to racism, there is little analysis of the role and situation of black and white women and how it has differed from that of black and white men. Gender is almost completely disregarded, and there is little investigation of the relation between gender, race, and class oppression.

Recent developments in Marxist theory have led to a fuller analysis of racism.[17] These include theorizing the importance of non-class-based groupings, such as by gender and ethnicity. Culture, ideology, consciousness, and the state are examined as more than reflections of the economic base. They are important aspects of society that influence, and are influenced by, the entire social formation.

SEGMENTED LABOR MARKETS

A second class-based framework for analyzing racial inequality, whose origins are Marxist and institutionalist, is the theory of segmented, or dual, labor markets.[18]

In segmentation theory, there are three distinct labor markets. First, in the secondary labor market, wages and benefits are low and job tenure is short with high turnover. There are few job ladders, and labor control is simple and direct. Examples include most work in fast-food restaurants and in garment factories. In the primary subordinate labor market, most employees are members of unions; pay is significantly above the minimum wage and rises with tenure; and benefits include health, pension, and paid vacation time. Promotion within clearly defined job ladders usually occurs from within the firm and follows bureaucratically established norms, as do layoffs and promotions. Seniority plays an important role. Turnover is low, although unemployment for the goods-producing members of this segment is quite sensitive to the business cycle. Examples of jobs in the primary subordinate segment include blue-collar work in heavy industry and the majority of government employment. In the primary independent segment, the employee internalizes work norms and experiences more autonomy and less direct supervision than that found in other labor segments. Credentials are often needed for entry into this segment. Evaluation, control, and promotion follow bureaucratic norms. Unemployment is low, although there may be considerable movement between employers. Most professional and managerial work is part of the primary independent segment.

Central to labor market segmentation theory is not just the clustering of jobs into three categories but also the employees' lack of mobility between segments. Race plays a role only in determining one's placement into a respective labor market segment. The higher rate of black unemployment and the lower earnings than that of whites are primarily the result of blacks' underrepresentation in the primary labor market and the high concentration of black women and men in the secondary labor market. Except for this racially biased placement, labor market segmentation, not race, determine employment, earnings, promotion, occupational mobility, and job tenure.

The power of labor market segmentation theory lies in its ability to explain the lower earnings and higher unemployment rates of blacks compared to whites.[19] It also explains blacks' more rapid earnings growth during the 1960s and early 1970s via the increased demand for labor in the primary labor market, which led to upward mobility for some blacks from the secondary labor market. It aids in understanding the stagnation in black-to-white earnings since the early 1970s and the more rapid growth of unemployment for blacks than for whites. Reasons include the reduced entry into the primary labor market from the secondary labor market and the overall decline of jobs in the primary subordinate labor market, an important site of employment for black men.

Another plus is that this theory is not dependent on assuming, as the neoclassical theory does, that employers have an unexplained "taste for discrimination"; or, as in the class-based models, that the bargaining power of employees with their employers is decreased when black and white workers receive different wages.

The principal weakness of labor market segmentation theory—one admitted by its adherents—is the absence of an explicit theory of racism. Such a theory is necessary to explain how and why blacks are concentrated in lower segments, why mobility between labor segments differs unfavorably toward blacks, and what accounts for the relative distribution of blacks and whites within each segment. If black-to-white inequality were primarily the result of placement in different labor markets, one would expect small differences in earnings and unemployment rates by race within each segment. This is not the case. As Rumberger and Carnoy conclude, "Black workers even in primary sector jobs face labor market conditions characteristic of the secondary labor market."[20]

A theory of segmented, or dual, labor markets can complement but not supplement a theory of racism. The latter is necessary to explain the different treatment of blacks and whites within each labor market segment and the causes of the concentration of blacks in the secondary labor market. Synthesizing labor market segmentation theory with the particular racial dynamics of past and present U.S.

society would be quite insightful in explaining racial inequality in income and employment.

The power of the class-based theories of racism reviewed here is their ability to demonstrate that racial discrimination follows from the logic and history of U.S. capitalism and that its continuation is consistent with the likely behavior of employers. The main weakness of the theory, that racism divides the working class, is its underestimation of the importance of racial and other nonclass groupings in the perpetuation and the possible elimination of racism. Multiracial working-class organizations are emphasized as the primary vehicle for ending oppression. Organizations of black people as vehicles to end racism are downplayed, as is the role of white people in perpetuating racism.

NOTES

Many of the ideas presented in this chapter are developed in my doctoral dissertation "The Impact of Public Sector Employment on Racial Inequality: 1950 to 1984" (University of Massachusetts, 1985), primarily chapter 3.

1. In this chapter, I focus mainly on racism toward African Americans. I use the terms *black* and *African American* interchangeably. With *people of color,* sometimes referred to as *minorities,* I am referring to people whose origins are non-European, including American Indians, Asian Americans, African Americans, and Latinos. These various "racial" groups—white, Latino, black—are socially constructed categories that shape one's life and interactions with others but are biologically meaningless. There is only the human race, not a white race, a black race, and so forth. See Robert Miles, *Racism* (London: Routledge, 1989); for a history of people of color in the United States, see Ronald Takaki, *A Different Mirror: A History of Multicultural America* (Boston: Little, Brown and Company, 1993).

2. There is a huge Marxist literature. I suggest, as a start, Robert Tucker, ed., *The Marx-Engels Reader,* 2nd ed. (New York: W. W. Norton, 1978); Robert Heilbroner, *Marxism For and Against* (New York: W. W. Norton, 1980); and Paul Sweezy, *Four Lectures on Marxism* (New York: Monthly Review, 1981).

3. The definition of racism does not only refer to racism against African Americans. The distinct as-

pects of racial oppression and the ideology of racism need to be analyzed with regard to each racial group: Latino, Indian, and so forth.

4. See Lloyd Hogan, *Principles of Black Political Economy* (Boston: Routledge and Kegan Paul, 1984), chapter 5 for the centrality of the slave trade and of slave labor in the development of U.S. and European capitalism. See C. L. R. James, *The Black Jacobins* (New York: Vintage, 1963) for an outstanding Marxist study of the importance of slavery in the development of capitalism in France in the eighteenth century.

5. James Geschwender, *Racial Stratification in America* (Dubuque, Iowa: Wm. C. Brown, 1978), chapter 6.

6. For excellent analyses of reconstruction see Harold Baron, "Demand for Black Labor," *Radical America* (March–April 1971): 12–16; Eric Foner, *Reconstruction, 1863–1877* (New York: Harper and Row, 1988); and particularly, W. E. B. DuBois, *Black Reconstruction in America 1860–1880* (New York: Atheneum, 1975).

7. Robert Allen, *Reluctant Reformers* (Garden City, N.Y.: Anchor/Doubleday, 1975), 278–296.

8. For a critique of most unions in the late nineteenth and the early twentieth century, see Philip Foner, *Organized Labor and the Black Worker* (New York: International Publishers, 1976), 64–128; and Michael Goldfield, *The Color of Politics* (New York: New Press, 1997), chapter 5.

9. The Marxist term is *superexploitation.* It means that superexploited workers receive less than the going wage rate even though their productivity is similar to that of other workers. This discrepancy generates excess profits for employers.

10. William Foster, *The Negro People in American History* (New York: International Publishers, 1954), chapter 48; Victor Perlo, *Economics of Racism, USA* (New York: International Publishers, 1976), chapters 5, 9. For the definition of *superexploitation,* see endnote 9.

11. Perlo, *Economics of Racism,* chapter 10; Michael Reich, *Racial Inequality* (Princeton, N.J.: Princeton University Press, 1981).

12. Paul Baran and Paul Sweezy, *Monopoly Capital* (New York: Monthly Review, 1966), chapter 9; Donald Harris, "The Black Ghetto as Colony," *Review of Black Political Economy* (1972).

13. Reich, *Racial Inequality.* See also, similar models by Samuel Bowles, "The Production Process in a Competitive Economy," *American Economic Review* (March 1985); and John Roemer,

"Divide-and-Conquer: Microfoundations of a Marxist Theory of Wage Discrimination," *Bell Journal of Economics* (Autumn 1979).

14. Reich, *Racial Inequality,* chapter 7.

15. One of Reich's explanations is that high-wage racial inequality reduces and weakens unionization, which lowers the average wage. He concludes that the causality between unions and racial equality goes in both directions. Racial equality furthers unionization, and higher unionization increases racial equality in earnings. Reich finds the relation that greater racial equality in earnings causes higher overall wages holds between urban areas for 1960 and 1970. He has not updated this study.

16. I believe these models of racial discrimination have some explanatory power in explaining the low-income and high-poverty rates of Latinos and Latinas.

17. See Cedric Robinson, *Black Marxism* (London: Zed Press, 1983); A. Sivandan, *Communities of Resistance: Writings on Black Struggles for Socialism* (London: Verso, 1990); Robert Miles *Racism after "Race Relations"* (New York: Routledge, 1993).

18. See David Gordon, *Theories of Poverty and Unemployment* (Lexington, Mass.: D. C. Heath, 1972), chapter 4, for the diverse origins and early development of this theory. The early writings usually considered two labor markets: the secondary and the primary. This framework was called the theory of dual-labor markets. Later writings, particularly those whose foundation is Marxist, consider three markets, by dividing the primary labor market into a primary independent and primary subordinate labor market. This is the practice that I follow.

19. David Gordon cited in D. Gordon, R. Edwards, and M. Reich, *Segmented Work, Divided Workers* (Cambridge: Cambridge University Press, 1982), 210–212, estimates the size and racial composition of each labor market segment from the 1970 census. Gordon estimates that 60 percent of the employed black population work in the secondary labor market, almost twice the 32 percent of all employed, non-Latino whites who work in this segment.

20. Russell Rumberger and Martin Carnoy, "Segmentation in the U.S. Labor Market: Its Effect on the Mobility and Earnings of Blacks and Whites," *Cambridge Journal of Economics* (June 1980): 129.

11

The Crowding Hypothesis

TIMOTHY BATES and DANIEL FUSFELD

This chapter discusses the crowding of black workers into the secondary, low-wage labor market. Using supply and demand theory in labor markets, the authors illustrate the effects of crowding, including the following: lower wages in the secondary market relative to higher wages in the primary market; reduced work incentives and therefore lower labor force participation rates for minority workers than for white workers; the movement of minority groups into criminal occupations; and lower wages for minority workers in the primary, high-wage sector when compared to that of white workers. The authors then discuss barriers to workers who move from the secondary to the primary labor market. Crowding is then compared to other forms of coerced labor where the white majority benefits.

Black workers have traditionally been restricted to low-wage occupations requiring relatively little skill. This pattern was changed in part by the entry of a limited number of blacks into industrial employment, particularly during the two world wars, and by the increased black employment in white-collar jobs during the 1950s and 1960s. But these breakthroughs into new sectors of the labor market were relatively limited. For the most part, blacks and other minority groups are found heavily in the secondary sector of the labor market, rather than the primary.

The secondary sector of the labor market comprises service and industrial occupations. The jobs are low paid, relatively unskilled, and often unstable: employment is affected by seasonal and cyclical instability. Jobs are relatively labor intensive, which means that worker productivity is low. Firms are often small and markets are competitive. These businesses tend to compete by "squeezing" labor. Most of the secondary labor market is not unionized.

When any minority group is crowded into a relatively small number of occupations, wage rates are depressed in those occupations because of the artificially increased supply of labor. Meanwhile, the supply of labor in other occupations is decreased, leading to higher wage rates somewhat higher than they would otherwise be in those occupations. Thus, workers in the white majority can benefit from the crowding of black workers into menial occupations. Analysis of this phenomenon was first developed in modern economics during the drive for women's rights in the period from 1890 to 1925 and culminated in Francis Y. Edgeworth's classic 1922 article on equal pay for men and women.[1]

To illustrate the hypothesis, we start with two occupations that require the same level of skills, and we examine the results in a color-blind economy and those in an economy with racial discrimination. In the color-blind economy (assuming equal competition in the labor market), the forces of supply and demand result in the same wage rate in the two occupations. Any wage differential will cause labor to shift from one to the other, since skill levels are the same until wages are equalized. Furthermore, employers will hire workers in each occupation to the point at which the amount added to total revenue by the additional worker is equal to the wage paid; the theory of marginal productivity applies here. The results are shown in Figure 11.1.

Now we close one occupation to blacks and force them into jobs in the other occupation, reserving the closed occupation for whites. Wage rates in the two occupations will differ, and the numbers employed will also shift. Wages fall in the occupation into which the minority group is crowded, as shown in Figure 11.2. Meanwhile, wages rise in the occupation from which minorities are excluded, as shown in Figure 11.3.

A number of corollary propositions follow from this analysis of crowding. First, total employment need not be reduced. Wages will fall in the crowded occupation until all those who are willing to work at those wages are employed. Similarly, the higher wage in the other occupa-

tion will clear the market and ensure employment of all willing workers. These conclusions assume, however, that the level of aggregate demand is sustained at full-employment levels to ensure jobs for the entire workforce. The white workers who earn higher wages need not fear unemployment as long as the national economy is healthy.

A more important corollary is the effect on work incentives among the minority group. Since wages in the crowded occupation will be abnormally low, the incentive to work will be reduced, as against leisure time or irregular occupations. As a result, labor force participation rates among the minority wages encourage a greater amount of work as compared to leisure. This expected result is consistent with the empirical finding that labor force participation rates are higher among whites than among blacks.

Related to this phenomenon is the movement of minority groups into criminal occupa-

Figure 11.1   Color-blind economy: Two occupations with similar skill levels.

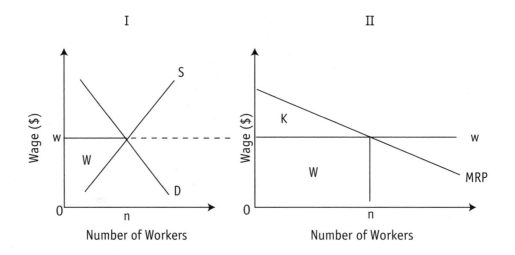

Wages in both occupations are the same, since skills are interchangeable. In diagram I the wage in both occupations is determined by the interaction of demand and supply at level *w*, while *n* workers are employed. *W* is the total wage bill. Diagram II shows the individual employer hiring *n* workers at wage *w*, given the marginal revenue product (MRP; the marginal revenue product is the name given to the additional revenues obtained by adding one unit of a factor of production to a fixed amount of other factors, for example, adding an additional worker to the existing work force in a manufacturing plant). *W* is the total wage bill of the individual employer, and *K* is the amount retained for payments to other factors of production, such as capital.

Figure 11.2   "Crowding" reduces wage rates in occupation A.

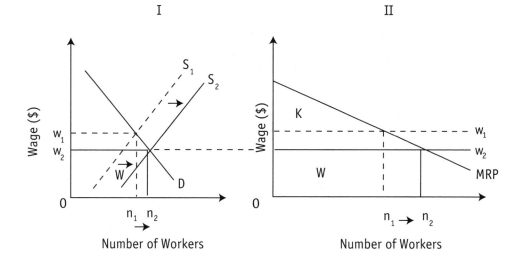

In diagram I the increase in supply of labor in occupation A due to "crowding" shifts the supply curve from S_1 to S_2, with demand conditions remaining unchanged. The wage falls from w_1 to w_2, and the number employed increases from n_1 to n_2. The total amount of wage paid, W, may or may not increase. In diagram II the individual employer increases the number of workers he hires from n_1 to n_2. The wage bill, W, may or may not increase. However, the value of the marginal product has fallen, since w_2 is less than w_1. As we shall see, this indicates a misallocation of resources from society's point of view. In addition, the amount paid to other factors (K) rises.

tions. Low wages and exclusion from high-wage occupations provide incentives to try for the rewards available from crime. This channeling of minorities into crime by economic forces has been characteristic of our history, attracting immigrant minorities from the Irish to the Jews to the Italians and now to the blacks and the Hispanics. The majority of any minority group have always been honest and law-abiding citizens, but there are strong economic incentives that draw a large proportion of minority groups into criminal activities.

Another result of crowding is payment of substandard wages to minority employees when they are able to get jobs in the high-wage occupations. The alternative employment for a black engineer is a low-wage, menial occupation. He is therefore willing to accept less than the standard wage for engineers. Employers are aware of this situation, and enough of them take advantage of it to create the pattern of unequal wage rates for the same job between whites and blacks, men and women,

and other groups subjected to crowding. In recent years there has been some modification of this unequal pay syndrome because of federal government pressure on firms producing under government contract, but differential pay is still prevalent.

Crowding of minority groups into menial occupations brings about a noticeable misallocation of resources. Employment in the low-wage occupations is greater than it would be without crowding, although there is less employment in other occupations. This can be seen by referring back to Figures 11.2 and 11.3. Low wages in the crowded occupations result in more employment there; high wages in other occupations are accompanied by reduced employment in those jobs. At the same time, a larger total return to other factors of production (K in Figure 11.2) encourages expanded employment in the crowded occupations, while a smaller total return to the other factors in the noncrowded occupations (K in Figure 11.3) reduces employment there. The result is

Figure 11.3   "Crowding" of the minority in occupation A causes wages to rise in occupation B.

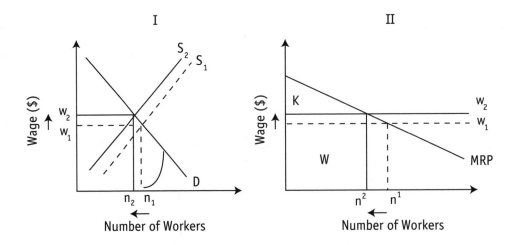

In diagram I the decreased supply of workers in occupation B due to exclusion of blacks shifts the supply curve to the left of S_1 to S_2. With no change in demand the wage rate increases from w_1 to w_2, and employment falls from n_1 to n_2. These changes are reflected in diagram II in individual employers' reordering of their activities. They hire fewer workers because of the higher wage rate (n_1 falls to n_2). Labor productivity at the margin is higher than it was before (w_2 is greater than w_1). While the total wage bill ($W1$) may or may not change, the amount paid to other factors of production ($K1$) is reduced.

misallocation of all kinds of resources into the low-wage occupations and industries. Both labor and capital could be shifted to uses in which returns are higher. This is a loss that must be borne by everyone. Although it is not obvious at first glance that overexpansion of low-wage industries and overemployment in low-wage occupations are harmful to the economy as a whole, that is in fact the case. Shifting a worker from an occupation in which he or she produces goods worth $3.50 per hour to one in which he or she produces $5.50 per hour brings a net benefit of $2.00 per hour to the economy as a whole.

Crowding should not bring the employer any special benefits or losses if competition prevails. Even though the firm pays low wages to some workers, competition will push profits down to the normal level. Only if the employer is in a monopolistic position can it gain from crowding and then only if it hires enough low-wage workers to more than offset the higher amounts it pays in other occupations.

The chief gainers from crowding are workers from the majority population. They earn more than they would if greater competition for jobs from minority groups were present. This has always been true and helps to explain why workers seek to maintain segregated occupational patterns.

The crowding hypothesis has been criticized on the same grounds as Becker's theory of discrimination: profit-seeking employers will hire low-wage workers from the secondary labor market to replace higher-paid workers. This reduces and ultimately eliminates the wage differential between the two. Empirical evidence, however, does not support this criticism. The difference between wage ranges in the primary and secondary sectors of the labor market widened during the 1970s. It tended to narrow in the 1950s and 1960s, when labor markets were relatively tight, but it widened when unemployment rates rose during the 1970s. There does not seem to be a consistent tendency for employers to substitute workers from the low-wage secondary sector of the labor market for higher-paid primary workers.

There are good reasons why workers do not move readily from the secondary to the primary sector of the labor market. Workers in the primary sector learn to work regular hours, report to work on time, take regular and specified work breaks, and respect the authority and discipline of the supervisor or the assembly line. By contrast, work in the secondary sector is often irregular; supervision is less rigorous; hours are less regular; and time requirements are less strict. Workers who learn the more-flexible routines of the secondary labor market need to learn new work habits and patterns of discipline when moving into the primary sector. During the transition period, their productivity is reduced, and the employer's costs of training and supervision are increased. After the transition period, their productivity may be just as great as that of other workers, but we would expect more to drop out during the period of transition (which adds to hiring costs) and that employers would have little incentive to hire them in the first place. These considerations help to explain why tight labor markets are a key condition for the movement of workers from the secondary to the primary sector of the labor market.

A second factor is the relatively high degree of unionization in the primary labor market. The natural desire of labor unions to protect the jobs and wage rates of their members leads them to oppose the hiring of "substandard" workers— those willing to work for lower wages. An employer who insisted on doing so would arouse antagonism on the part of the existing workforce and the union leadership. Each would be more difficult to deal with in collective bargaining. Employers, then, feel pressures from the existing workforce and its union representatives to hire new workers at wage rates equal to those paid to the existing workforce. An employer who did otherwise would face the prospect of heightened worker unrest and perhaps a costly strike. Even if a union were not present, such hiring policies could readily lead to unionization of employees. It is easier to continue hiring workers who are already in the primary workforce.

The hiring process itself adds to the barriers between the secondary and primary sectors of the labor market. The employer usually knows little about a prospective employee beyond age, sex, race, education, and what the employee or references can tell about experience in other jobs. These characteristics must be matched against the requirements of the job and the work habits required. If regular on-time attendance is mandatory and the employer's experience indicates that workers from the secondary sector of the labor market are a poor risk in that respect, those workers will be put near the bottom of the list of potential employees. Workers who have had jobs in which they learned the proper work habits will be placed near the top of the list. Thus, workers already in the primary sector of the labor market will tend to stay there, and workers in the secondary sector will have difficulty in getting out. This "statistical discrimination," to use Thurow's phrase, causes the characteristics of a worker's peer group to determine the worker's employment prospects, rather than his or her individual characteristics.[2]

The process of being relegated to inferior, secondary-sector employment creates a self-fulfilling prophecy: rejection from better jobs leads to employment in the secondary labor market. Low-paying work that is unskilled and often unstable teaches employees bad work habits and negative attitudes toward employers; these traits in turn lead primary-sector employers to view blacks as less-reliable workers. Blacks treated as such are often less-stable workers, and their discriminatory treatment in the high-wage sectors may persist because actual labor market performance appears to confirm employer stereotypes.

CROWDING AND ECONOMIC OPPORTUNITY

Opening opportunities for blacks in high-level occupations may appear to be the policy that would diminish and ultimately eliminate crowding, but that is not necessarily the case. In the 1960s, for example, under the impact of sustained economic growth, the civil rights movement, and government-sponsored affirmative action hiring programs, there was a significant increase in the number of blacks in high-level occupations. Between 1960 and 1969, the number of black men over twenty-five years old in professional and technical occupations increased by 1.07 percent. In managerial occupations, the number increased by 117 percent. Other large increases occurred in employment as trade workers (52 percent) and sales personnel (42 percent). All of these percentage increases were greater than the percentage increase in black men over twenty-five years of age in the labor force as a whole. During the 1970s, in a stagnant economy and a changed political environment, these gains largely ceased. Blacks continued to move into high-level occupations but at a rate about the same as the increase in the black population of working age; that is, the proportion of blacks in the primary sector of the labor force did not increase significantly. The bulk of the black population remained in the secondary labor market, crowded in the low-wage occupations.

It is quite possible for new opportunities to open for minority groups, whereas the bulk of the minority remains crowded in menial occupations. Imagine a hypothetical urban metropolitan area in which 10 percent of the jobs are in low-wage occupations; 10 percent of the labor force is black; and all of the blacks are employed in the low-wage sector. It is a hypothetical situation of "perfect" crowding. Now let the local demand for labor expand at a given rate, say 5 percent annually, but let the black population and workforce expand at a 10 percent annual rate while the white population grows by only 5 percent each year. Assuming no change in output per worker, we would expect several changes in the city's economy:

1. The overall unemployment rate will rise because overall population growth is more rapid than the rate of growth in the demand for labor. But the increase in unemployment will be concentrated quite heavily among blacks. The black low-wage sector of the economy grows at a 5 percent rate while the labor force crowded into that sector grows twice as rapidly. The white labor force, however, grows no more rapidly than the number of jobs in its sector of the workforce.

2. Simultaneously, employment in the low-wage sector will increase relative to employment in the high-wage sector. The high unemployment rate among blacks will push wages down in the low-wage sector, enabling employers to employ more workers there. This effect will mitigate the increase in black unemployment.

3. Some blacks may find employment in the white sector of the economy, even though the low-wage sector remains black. It is quite possible for blacks to move into such occupational categories as managerial, professional, technical, crafts, and sales without significantly modifying the process by which the bulk of the black labor force is crowded into menial occupations.

4. This movement of blacks into the high-wage sector will displace whites. While unemployment will rise, some whites will "skid" into low-wage jobs from which blacks will be "bumped" into unemployment or out of the labor force entirely. This process will increase the black–white antagonisms that are one of the underlying causes of crowding.

These expected effects of crowding are in general agreement with the historical record. As blacks moved North into urban areas from 1910 to the present, the proportion of blacks in the workforce increased. This population movement, with the process of crowding, led to an initially black-predominated labor force in the low-wage sector. This was followed by an upward shift in the unemployment rate for blacks, as compared with whites; by expansion of the low-wage sector itself; and by a movement of some blacks into the high-wage sector, particularly during periods of tightness in the labor market. But this upward movement of some blacks was accompanied by the ghettoization of most blacks and by an intensification of the economic conditions that sustain the urban ghetto and the process of crowding.

Lack of alternative opportunities is the chief economic factor that preserves the process of crowding. But simply opening opportunities for a portion of the crowded minority does not necessarily stop the process. Reality is far more complex. As we indicated in point 4, opportunities in the high-wage sector may even worsen the crowding process for others. Thus, hiring black college professors, for example, does not significantly modify the crowding of the bulk of the black labor force in low-wage occupations. Nor does the hiring of a female corporate executive modify the process by which the secretarial and clerk jobs are reserved largely for women. More than affirmative action hiring procedures are needed.

CROWDING AND COERCED LABOR

The crowding of blacks and other minority groups in low-wage occupations is a modern and sophisticated version of coerced labor. It is a phenomenon found throughout history, with slavery being its most obvious form. Labor is coerced by the law that declares slaves to be property, enabling owners to exploit them much as horses and cows are used to produce for humans. Serfdom, in its many forms of dependent peasantry, is another ancient form of coerced labor. The military draft is a contemporary form. The essential element in all types of coerced labor is exploitation of the worker who receives less than he or she otherwise would if free to do something else.

For coerced labor to exist, alternative opportunities for the worker must be absent or substantially reduced. If the slave, serf, or draftee can evade the system, he or she cannot be coerced into accepting substandard pay. Thus, most systems of coerced labor use the power of the state—through its armies, police, and penal system—to limit the opportunities available to those subject to coerced labor and to force them to remain in their exploited condition.

But not always. Consider the sharecropping and debt tenure system in the South, which was implemented after the Civil War and which remained strong through the 1940s—some remnants still survive today. This system was enforced by economic forces, legal constraints, and community pressures that were often more informal than formal. This chapter is not the place for a history and an analysis of the sharecropping and debt tenure system in the South, but the chief elements are important because many blacks in this country came from that background. A sharecropper used the land owned by someone else, with the landlord often supplying seed and tools and sometimes living expenses. In return, the landlord received a share of the receipts after being reimbursed for the cost of seed and sustenance. This system emerged after the Civil War, when former slaveowners had land

but no labor and when the former slaves had labor but no land. The system was open to much abuse. The black farmer had little education, and the white landowner usually sold the crop and kept the books.

Simple sharecropping grew into a system of debt tenure. After a bad crop year the tenant might not have earned enough to carry him to the next harvest and to provide seed for the next crop. Money for those purposes would have to be borrowed, either from the landlord or a storekeeper in town. Debt could then become a way of tying the tenant to the land. Debts had to be settled before a family was allowed to leave the land, and the debts had a habit of persisting from year to year. This cycle happened throughout the rural South, with poor whites as well as poor blacks—in much the same way as the biblical Joseph was able to enslave the Egyptian peasantry for the pharaohs by using the stored surplus of seven fat years to make loans during the ensuing seven lean years.

Although sharecropping and debt tenure were used to tie labor to the land, lack of opportunity elsewhere was one of the chief reasons for the long retention of coerced labor in the South. Industry was slow in developing; poverty prevented acquisition of Western land; and Northern industry was surfeited with unskilled laborers from Europe. Only with the cessation of immigration and the start of World War I did economic opportunity open the way to ending the coerced labor of the rural South. The black population of the South was able to migrate North to opportunity—and to the urban ghetto.

There, a different form of coerced labor appeared. By excluding blacks from high-paying occupations and crowding them into menial jobs, the pattern of exploitation continued but in a different form. The pattern can be found in Southern cities as early as the 1890s, when the great depression of the decade, particularly strong in agriculture, forced significant numbers of blacks off Southern farms in spite of sharecropping and debt tenure. Moving into Southern cities, they were met with an upsurge of Jim Crow legislation that imposed rigid segregation and largely eliminated their right to vote.[3] Concurrently, blacks were driven out of a number of urban occupations they had hitherto filled—such as the construction trades, long-shoring, and barbering—and were crowded into the menial and low-wage occupations in which they are now found. When industry developed, blacks were largely excluded from the factory jobs, except at the lowest custodial level. This happened, for example, in the steel industry in Birmingham and in textiles and furniture manufacturing in the Carolinas. Opportunities that might have broken the grip of sharecropping in the rural South were more rapidly closed off in the cities by restricting high-paying jobs to whites and by crowding blacks into relatively few low-wage occupations.

Similar developments occurred in the North during and after the First World War. The black migration to Northern cities led to the closing of some occupations to blacks in which they had already found a foothold and to their restriction to low-wage occupations. This form of economic exploitation was accompanied by residential segregation. Restrictive covenants in real estate deeds and residential zoning as means of excluding blacks from specific neighborhoods were first used on a large scale in the 1920s. Loss of the franchise and pervasive Jim Crow legislation were never a major feature of the Northern reaction, but the results were similar. A pattern of coerced labor based on tradition, custom, and the attitudes of white workers and employers emerged, enforced in part by labor unions but more rigidly by customary practices in the labor market and the educational system.

White racism in unions, however, has also undermined the economic status of white workers. Utilizing blacks as strikebreakers helped companies to break strikes and weaken unions in the late nineteenth and early twentieth centuries. Since World War II, black–white worker antagonisms have severely weakened union-organizing efforts in the southeastern United States. Failure to organize widely in the South meant that large union wage gains in the late 1940s and 1950s widened North–South wage differentials. This in turn encouraged some unionized industries to expand their Southern manufacturing operations.[4] The resultant regional shift in manufacturing activity weakened the overall union movement and exacerbated unemployment among workers, white and black, in heavily unionized regions.

At the root of the problem are the forces that create and sustain the ghetto economy and its force of low-wage labor. Coercion of that portion of the labor force does not depend on law but is built into the structure and functioning of the economy as a whole. The form of coerced labor has changed, but coercion has persisted. The intensity of exploitation has diminished, but the fact remains that blacks have been kept in a disadvantaged position. They are no longer property. They are no longer held in thrall by a combination of economic circumstance and legal constraint, but they are oppressed by an economic system that relegates them largely to crowded occupations and low-wage jobs.

A variety of interconnected social and economic processes support the modern practice of coerced labor. One factor is the historical legacy of much of the black population, which was denied the investment in education and work skills available to most whites. The human capital disadvantages of blacks are in part the result of generations of substandard education and lack of access to high-skilled jobs. This process is still at work in the poverty areas of America's cities.

A second factor is racial prejudice and antagonism, which has historically deprived blacks of equal opportunities. These white attitudes toward blacks are noticeably strong among low- and middle-income whites, whose economic status is threatened as blacks seek to rise in the economic and social order. The most obvious manifestation of these white attitudes is the so-called white flight from central-city areas as blacks move in.

A third factor is stressed in these chapters. The ghetto economy itself preserves and strengthens the existing economic status of the entire black community. The white community benefits from the low-wage labor that is the ghetto's chief export, and white workers benefit from the crowding of black workers in low-wage occupations. A self-sustaining economic process that benefits the white community, supported by the heritage of history and white attitudes, is the modern source of coerced black labor.

CONCLUSION

It is easy and comforting to attribute economic discrimination to faults in the people who discriminate and to those who are discriminated against. Remove prejudices (the taste for discrimination) by education, and counter its effects by legally mandated hiring policies. Promote the accumulation of human capital on the part of minority groups so that they can qualify for high-level jobs. Change people to solve the problem. The implication is that there is nothing particularly wrong with the way the institutional structure of the economy functions.

Those approaches to the problem are clearly inadequate. The theory of the taste for discrimination does not adequately account for the continuing economic disparities between blacks and whites. The theory of human capital can explain only a relatively small portion of those disparities. We must turn instead to an examination of the institutional structure of the economy, where we find two processes at work that enable us to understand the complex nature of the problem.

One is the ghetto itself. It is an integral part of the broad economy, providing a low-wage labor force that benefits the economy outside the ghetto. At the same time, social processes at work in the ghetto provide for its perpetuation, depriving the bulk of the low-wage labor force of the human capital and work habits necessary for success outside the ghetto in the more affluent sector of the economy.

The crowding of blacks and other minority groups in low-wage occupations is the second process at work. It has its roots in the same economic force that created the ghetto: the benefit of whites. Self-perpetuating forces are also at work in the crowding process. Workers are crowded into occupations requiring little skill, and unemployment rates are high. Trapped in the secondary labor market, there is little incentive to acquire skills for which there is little use.

These institutional structures and the economic processes they embody interact with racial hostility and a lack of human capital in a process of mutual causation. Ghettoization and labor market crowding are causes *and* effects of racial antagonisms and lack of human capital on the part of blacks and other minority groups. Likewise, racial antagonisms and lack of human capital are at once causes and effects of ghettoization and labor market crowding. Yet the fundamental cause is economic: the white majority benefits.

NOTES

1. Francis Y. Edgeworth, "Equal Pay to Men and Women for Equal Work," *Economic Journal* 31 (December 1922): 431–457. Edgeworth's analysis builds on the work of Millicent Fawcett, including "The Position of Women in Economic Life," in *After-War Problems,* ed. W. H. Dawson (London: Allen and Unwin, 1917), 191–215; and "Equal Pay for Equal Work," *Economic Journal* 28 (March 1918): 1–6. Frank W. Taussig's concept of noncompeting groups is somewhat similar. See Taussig, *Principles of Economics,* vol. 2 (New York: Macmillan, 1946), 234–235; and Norval D. Glenn, "Occupational Benefits to Whites from the Subordination of Negroes," *American Sociological Review* 28, no. 3 (1963): 443–448. Barbara Bergmann develops the crowding hypotheses in "Effect on White Incomes of Discrimination in Employment," *Journal of Political Economy* 29, no. 2 (1971): 294–313.

2. Lester C. Thurow, *Generating Inequality: Mechanisms of Distribution in the U.S. Economy* (New York: Basic Books), 170–177.

3. C. Vann Woodward, *The Strange Career of Jim Crow* (New York: Oxford University Press, 1955), is the standard treatment of the rapid spread of Jim Crow laws and the disfranchisement of blacks during the 1890s in the South. Woodward, however, fails to note the importance of the black migration to cities and gives inadequate attention to the changes in occupations and economic opportunity that occurred.

4. Michael Reich, *Racial Inequality: A Political-Economic Analysis* (Princeton, N.J.: Princeton University Press, 1981), 268–304.

12

"Keeping People in Their Place": The Economics of Racial Violence

MARY C. KING

Economists have ignored violence in their analyses of racial economic disparities, but it is obvious that a great deal of interracial violence has been economically motivated and has had economic consequences. One way to understand racial violence economically is to see it as enforcing unwritten property rights in "whiteness" that include ownership of jobs, occupations, business and educational opportunities, real estate, and white women. U.S. history is replete with examples of violence by whites against people of color to maintain these property rights. It is also possible to see racial violence by people of color against whites, such as the "race riots" of the late 1960s, as a challenge to these property rights in whiteness. Indeed, African American men have made most economic progress vis-à-vis white men during the riot years of the late 1960s and immediately in the aftermath of the Los Angeles riots following the acquittal of the police officers who beat Rodney King.

U.S. history is bloody, and many of its most horrifying chapters deal with race. Yet economists generally do not think about violence when studying the sources of racial economic inequalities in this country. It seems obvious though that racial violence, historically and currently, is often economically motivated, with clear economic consequences.

One way to think about violence in an economic context is to see it as action taken to maintain unwritten "property rights" in race, gender, and class privileges. Legal scholars Derrick Bell and Cheryl Harris, working in a tradition called *critical race theory*, have developed the idea of property in "whiteness," the concept that being white has been a form of property. Whites have had ownership of the best jobs, occupations, land, and education by virtue of being white. Racial violence by whites against people of color has enforced property rights in whiteness.

It is also possible to see racial violence instigated by people of color against whites as a challenge to unwritten property rights in whiteness. For example, the race riots of the late 1960s may have served as a way for African Americans to dispute racial boundaries politically and economically.

THE IDEA OF PROPERTY RIGHTS IN WHITENESS

Cheryl Harris traces the historical evolution of property in whiteness, starting with the claim that "the origins of property rights in the United States are rooted in racial domination"; that is, blacks were enslaved, but whites had self-ownership (1993, 1716). Native American land was taken by force and considered legal by Europeans who did not recognize Native American property rights. Until the civil rights era, "whiteness determined whether one could vote, travel freely, attend schools, obtain work, and indeed, defined the structure of social relations along the entire spectrum of interactions between the individual and society" (Harris 1993, 1745). Harris thinks that present-day opposition to affirmative action is a continued assertion of a property right in whiteness, of expectations of economic positioning that cannot be taken away.

The concept of property rights in whiteness is easily extended to property rights in masculinity—"It's a man's world"—as well as in class and sexual orientation. Color, sex, class, and sexual orientation all have much to do with where a person can feel safe and who will be violently confronted if they try to share a job, space, or other perk of property rights in whiteness, masculinity, straightness, or class.

The idea of property rights in whiteness is easily contained in economists' and lawyers' common understanding of property rights (see Darity, Mason, and Stewart 2000). An economic understanding of property rights goes beyond those written into the law to include anything a person has the "ability to enjoy" (Barzel 1997, 3). Traditional legal understandings of property allow property to be metaphysical as well as physical—for example, rights as well as tangible objects—and modern legal theories include property in the form of "jobs, entitlements, occupational licenses, contracts, subsidies . . . intellectual property, business goodwill, and advanced earnings potential from graduate degrees" (Harris 1993, 1728).

Some property rights in whiteness have been written into the law, starting with slavery. Segregation in housing, education, accommodation, and employment were all legally based. Antimiscegenation laws that prohibited marriage between whites and people of color kept property in the "white family," privileging claims by a white man's brother over his nonwhite widow, even when she was publicly acknowledged to be the primary person responsible for creating the wealth (Pascoe 1999).

Racial violence has been employed to defend white men's property rights in white women. The preponderance of lynchings of African Americans have been overtly motivated by suspicion of a black man's sexual interest in a white woman. Other issues, such as desegregation of education and housing, are frequently articulated in terms of sexuality with a presumption of white male sexual ownership of white women.

When we think about the economics of racial violence in the United States, we have to include the full spectrum of violence, whether state sponsored, state tolerated, or illegal. The U.S. government made use of violence to enforce the legal apparatus of slavery. Police brutality is illegal but has been widely tolerated, serving to "keep people in their place." Vigilante violence has played a large role in our history as well. While these actions are illegal, the perpetrators often operated with near impunity, even with the covert sanction or unofficial participation of the authorities.

So far, I have been discussing only physical violence. However, institutions that maintain high poverty rates, poor housing, inadequate medical care, and inferior education can also be regarded as violence to people and their opportunity to fully develop their human capacities. A much longer chapter would be needed to explore a more comprehensive understanding of violence that included these institutions.

A BRIEF HISTORY OF RACIAL VIOLENCE AGAINST PEOPLE OF COLOR IN THE UNITED STATES

A common experience of people of color in the United States has been a lack of legal standing in the court system. Many states have had laws that disqualified Indians, Asians, blacks, and mulattos as witnesses (see Chan 1991). The result was widespread indifference to crimes against people of color. In 1854 the California Supreme Court went so far as to strike down the conviction of a white man for the murder of a Chinese because the evidence had come from Chinese witnesses (Chan 1991).

Native Americans

Historian Howard Zinn (1995) describes the actions of "Columbus and his successors" as genocide, the literal decimation of the Indian population of the United States and Canada from ten million to less than one million. Policies of war and massacre were followed by forced schooling in government-run boarding schools and a legal system in which the testimony of Indians and other people of color carried no weight so that Indians were murdered or cheated with relative impunity (Amott and Matthaei 1996; Hogan 1990; Wilson 1994). More recently Native American communities have challenged the placement of Indian children with white families; sterilization abuse; the violent repression of the American Indian Movement; and a law enforcement atmosphere many regard as extremely hostile to Indians, particularly in the northern Plains states (see Amott and Matthaei 1996; Churchill and Vander Wall 1990; Crow Dog and Erdoes 1990; Matthiessen 1983, 1984).

African Americans

The history of violence against African Americans in the United States has to start with 246 years of slavery, from 1619 to 1865. That pregnant women were overworked, that their breast-feeding was forcefully shortened, and that children received purposefully poor nutrition generated significantly high mortality rates among infants and children: "children from the slums of Lagos . . . and Bangladesh had an environment for growth superior to that of American slave children" (Steckel 1986a, 430; see also Steckel 1986b). Whippings, rape, and murder figured in short life expectancies (Jones 1985). Jones asserts that "cruelty derived . . . from a basic premise of the slave system itself: the use of violence to achieve a productive labor force" (20).

Vigilante and mob violence, rapes, lynchings, race riots, and attacks on successful businesses and farms marked the decades following emancipation. In 1892 journalist and activist Ida B. Wells stated, "Lynching was merely an excuse to get rid of Negroes who were acquiring wealth and property and thus keep the race terrorized and 'keep the nigger down'" (Jones 1998, 333). Political organizing was consistently met with violence, often by legal authorities (see Carson 1981). Allston and Ferrie (1993) point out that Southern landowners benefited from maintaining an environment of racial violence, since black sharecroppers would be more dependent on landowners who could provide some protection from mob violence or speak with local police on behalf of "their" tenants.

Currently, police brutality, hate crimes, and harassment of African Americans in occupations such as firefighting continue to be routinely reported in the news. The apparently racially based discrepancies in policing and sentencing related to America's so-called war on drugs implicate the government in the violent control of black communities and the destruction of the economic potential of thousands of young people.

Chicanos

The first and largest group of Latinos to reside in the United States became American citizens by virtue of the 1848 Treaty of Guadalupe Hidalgo, which marked the end of the Mexican–American War and brought the northern half of the territory of Mexico into the United States. Mexicans who stayed were to become U.S. citizens, with guarantees that they would retain their property rights, language, religion, and culture (Defreitas 1991; McWilliams 1968; Zinn 1995). But most of what the Mexicans owned was soon lost, through a combination of economic pressure, legal manipulation, and violence. Acuna (1981) relentlessly documents episode after episode of lynching. Especially notorious were the Texas Rangers, who operated as paid thugs for Anglo landowners (Samora, Bernal, and Pena 1979).

Official and semiofficial violence against the Mexican American community, similar to that periodically directed against the African American community but less well known, recurred regularly throughout our history. Particularly infamous are the 1943 "zoot-suit race riots" of Los Angeles, during which hundreds of American sailors descended on the Chicano community for five nights in a row, savagely beating and stripping young Chicanos wearing zoot suits. Zoot-suit disturbances were touched off in San Diego, Philadelphia, Chicago, and Evansville (Indiana) later in the month; and major race riots in Harlem, Detroit, and Beaumont (Texas) later that summer (McWilliams 1968, 256).

Police brutality, excessive force on the part of immigration officials, and vigilante beatings of immigrant workers continue today, as do the high incarceration rates of Latinos.

Asian Americans

The second half of the nineteenth century was characterized by recurrent violence against Asians in the Western states, where most Asians lived at the time. The first targets were Chinese miners in California during the 1850s (Chan 1991). Chinese were murdered throughout the West for their gold; others were targets because they were perceived as an illegitimate source of competition for jobs or businesses, as were Japanese, Koreans, and Filipinos.

Several factors help to account for the violence that Asian immigrants experienced. Quite apart from the racism and nativism that fueled such attacks, the outbreaks were efforts by Euro-American workers to find scapegoats for their problems. It is no coincidence that the incidents tended to occur during years of economic crisis (Chan 1991, 53).

Asians are still vulnerable to violent attack based on the perception of economic competition—domestically, as has been the case for Vietnamese fishers in California and Texas; and internationally, as in the case of Vincent Chin, whose murder was apparently motivated by animosity at the success of the Japanese automakers in the United States (Chan 1991). The idea that Asians illegitimately take work or wealth from more-deserving members of the community is part of what underlay the targeting of Korean grocers during the rioting in Los Angeles in 1992 following the acquittal of the police officers who beat Rodney King.

CHALLENGING PROPERTY RIGHTS IN WHITENESS WITH VIOLENCE

So, the historical record provides substantial evidence of racial violence used to protect property rights in whiteness. It is also possible that violence has been a tool to challenge these property rights—for example, during the race riots of the late 1960s.

The late 1960s were a period of significant racial unrest in this country. One measure of this is the number of race riots that occurred. Two sociologists, Susan Olzak and Elizabeth West, directed a research team to comb the *New York Times* daily newspapers for the years between 1954 and 1992, noting all reports of racial conflict, including race riots.[1] They defined *race riots* as "large-scale and hostile crowd actions that are distinguished by (a) involvement of large numbers of persons (50–100); (b) the presence of weapons, such as firebombs, guns, or other lethal weapons (carried by rioters); and (c) long durations, lasting from two hours to several days, in most cases" (1995, 13). Nearly two-thirds of the race riots they found, as reported in the *New York Times* during this nearly forty-year period, happened in three consecutive years: 1966, 1967, and 1968.

These three years are the very years during which black men's median incomes jumped from a plateau at just over half those of white men to a plateau of about 60 percent, as illustrated in figure 12.1. Black men's incomes from all sources—earnings, savings, property, stocks, government benefits—had bounced between 47 and 55 percent of white men's incomes for years, from 1948 through 1966 (U.S. Bureau of the Census n.d.). Then, in the late 1960s, black men's incomes rose against white men's to between 58 and 60 percent and stayed at that level through 1992, after which they rose to about 66 percent for several years.

Black women had been making significant gains on white women through the 1950s and early 1960s, but their incomes relative to white women's grew fastest during the late 1960s, and they experienced no net progress—even reversals—after the late 1960s. (Black women's progress vis-à-vis white

Figure 12.1   Median incomes of black women and men as a proportion of same-sex whites, 1948–1997.

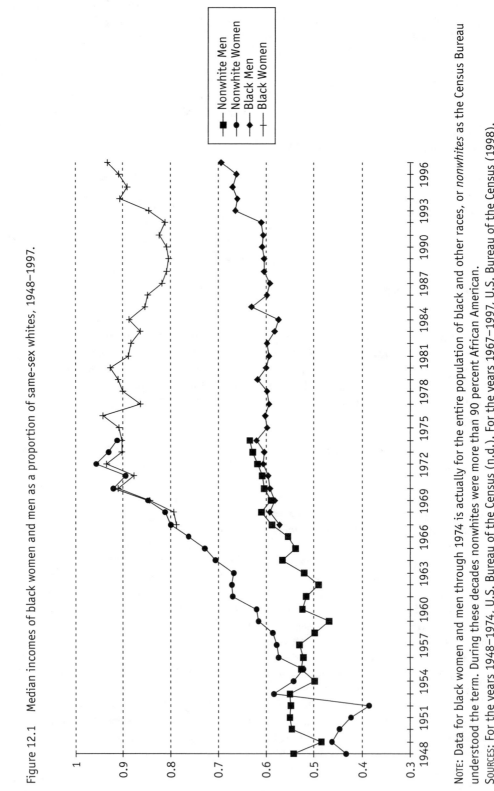

NOTE: Data for black women and men through 1974 is actually for the entire population of black and other races, or *nonwhites* as the Census Bureau understood the term. During these decades nonwhites were more than 90 percent African American.

SOURCES: For the years 1948–1974, U.S. Bureau of the Census (n.d.). For the years 1967–1997, U.S. Bureau of the Census (1998).

Table 12.1   Changes in the Racial Annual Income Ratio and Incidence of Race Riots in the Region, by Sex: 1965–1988

	Men	*Women*
Riot this year	0.012	0.011
Riot last year	0.008	0.011
Riot two years ago	0.006	0.018
Riot three years ago	0.006	0.012
No incident	−0.003	−0.003

Source: Author's calculations from the data derived by Mare and Winship (1990).
Note: The figures represent the average difference in the ratio of black men's to white men's annual incomes in the twenty-two state groups identified in the Mare–Winship (1990) sample of the Current Populations Surveys, 1964–1988.

men has been more even and gradual, as their incomes have risen from 20 percent of white men's in 1940 to 50 percent in 1997.)

Another way to get a sense of the correlation between race riots and income gains for African Americans is to look at gains in particular places. A summary of a state-focused analysis for the years 1965 to 1988 appears in Table 12.1 (see King 2003 for more details). What the figures show is that black women and black men seem to have increased their incomes relative to whites of the same sex in states where there were race riots in any of the four prior years, but they experienced a relative decline in states and years without riots.

Also interesting is the jump in black men's and women's relative earnings immediately after the 1992 riots in Los Angeles. The years of the 1990s were years of expansion and falling unemployment, which often result in higher earnings across the board and in better black earnings relative to whites. However, earnings did not rise in general until later in the expansion (Mishel, Bernstein, and Schmitt 2001) Certainly the Los Angeles riots had some parallels with the riots of the late 1960s, as each involved widely televised coverage of official violence against African Americans.

While nothing is proved by the coincidence of the riot years and the rapid black economic progress, it may well be that the riots have been important in motivating changes by white employers. However, many economists credit low unemployment rates with black economic progress during late 1960s and the late 1990s—

but low unemployment rates are not like the weather, unaffected by economic policy. Michael Reich (1988) thinks that the demands of people active in the civil rights era pushed policymakers to make decisions that created low unemployment. This view is quite compatible with the idea that black violence challenged white property rights in jobs, occupations, and education, thereby resulting in increased incomes for African Americans.

And while economists have not focused on violence as a means of enforcing or challenging racial economic disparities, other people have, as is clear in this passage from Grace Edwards-Yearwood's novel *In the Shadow of the Peacock*:

> It was the cry of alarm being heard in the streets, and on television at dinnertime, that had got Celia hired. It was the clenched fist raised high that no one wanted to see. It was the threat of violence, real and imagined, that propelled company recruiters to black campuses with orders to bring back ten tokens, dead or alive, one for every other department. No one wanted to step off the 8:20 from Larchmont to find Grand Central in flames. (1988, 182)

NOTE

1. Data collection was supported by two National Science Foundation grants: SES-9196229 Sociology Program, National Science Foundation, "Racial Conflict in South Africa and the United

States," Susan Olzak, principal investigator; and SES-8420173, Sociology Program, National Science Foundation, "Dynamics of Ethnic Mobilization," Susan Olzak, principal investigator.

REFERENCES

Acuna, Rodolfo. 1981. *Occupied America: A History of Chicanos.* New York: Harper and Row.

Allston, Lee J., and Joseph P. Ferrie. 1993. "Paternalism in Agricultural Labor Contracts in the U.S. South: Implications for the Growth of the Welfare State." *American Economic Review* 83, no. 4: 852–876.

Amott, Teresa, and Julie Matthaei. 1996. *Race, Gender, and Work: A Multicultural Economic History of Women in the United States.* 2nd ed. Boston: South End Press.

Barzel, Yoram. 1997. *Economic Analysis of Property Rights.* 2nd ed. Cambridge: Cambridge University Press.

Carson, Clayborne. 1981. *In Struggle: SNCC and the Black Awakening of the 1960s.* Cambridge, Mass.: Harvard University Press.

Chan, Sucheng. 1991. *Asian Americans: An Interpretive History.* Boston: Twayne Publishers.

Churchill, Ward, and Jim Vander Wall. 1990. *The Cointelpro Papers: Documents from the FBI's Secret Wars against Domestic Dissent.* Boston: South End Press.

Crow Dog, Mary, and Richard Erdoes. 1990. *Lakota Woman.* New York: Grove Weidenfeld.

Darity, William A., Jr., Patrick L. Mason, and James B. Stewart. 2000. "The Economics of Identity: The Origin and Persistence of Racial Norms." Unpublished paper.

DeFreitas, Gregory. 1991. *Inequality at Work: Hispanics in the U.S. Labor Force.* New York: Oxford University Press.

Edwards-Yearwood, Grace. 1988. *In the Shadow of the Peacock.* New York: McGraw-Hill.

Harris, Cheryl I. 1993. "Whiteness as Property." *Harvard Law Review* 106, no. 8: 1707–1791.

Hogan, Linda. 1990. *Mean Spirit: A Novel.* New York: Atheneum.

Jones, Jacqueline. 1985. *Labor of Love, Labor of Sorrow: Black Women, Work, and the Family, from Slavery to the Present.* New York: Vintage Books.

———. 1998. *American Work: Four Centuries of Black and White Labor.* New York: W. W. Norton.

King, Mary C. 1999. "Keeping People in Their Place: An Exploratory Analysis of the Role of Violence in the Maintenance of 'Property Rights' in Race and Gender Privileges in the U.S." *Review of Radical Political Economics* 31, no. 3: 1–11.

———. 2003. "Race Riots and Black Economic Progress." *Review of Black Political Economy* 30, no. 4: 51–86.

Mare, Robert D., and Christopher Winship. 1990. *Current Population Surveys: Uniform March Files, 1964–1988.* Computer file. Madison: University of Wisconsin, Center for Demography and Ecology (producer), 1989; Ann Arbor , Mich.: Interuniversity Consortium for Political and Social Research (distributor).

Matthiessen, Peter. 1983. *In the Spirit of Crazy Horse.* New York: Viking Press.

———. 1984. *Indian Country.* New York: Viking Press.

McWilliams, Carey. 1968. *North from Mexico: The Spanish-Speaking People of the United States.* New York: Greenwood Press.

Mishel, Lawrence, Jared Bernstein, and John Schmitt. 2001. *The State of Working America, 2000/2001.* Ithaca, N.Y.: Industry Labor Relations Press.

Olzak, Susan, and Elizabeth West. 1995. "Ethnic Collective Action in Contemporary Urban U.S.: Project Description and Coding Manual." Unpublished manuscript, Stanford University.

Pascoe, Peggy. 1999. "Race, Gender, and the Privileges of Property: On the Significance of Miscegenation Law in the U.S. West." In *Over the Edge: Remapping the American West,* ed. Valerie J. Matsumoto and Blake Allmendinger, 215–230. Berkeley: University of California Press.

Reich, Michael. 1988. "Postwar Racial Income Differences: Trends and Theories." In *Three Worlds of Labor Economics,* ed. Garth Mangum and Peter Philips, 144–167. Armonk, N.Y.: M. E. Sharpe.

Samora, Julian, Joe Bernal, and Albert Pena. 1979. *Gunpowder Justice: A Reassessment of the Texas Rangers.* Notre Dame, Ind.: University of Notre Dame Press.

Steckel, Richard H. 1986a. "A Dreadful Childhood: The Excess Mortality of American Slaves." *Social Science History* 10, no. 4: 427–465.

———. 1986b. "A Peculiar Population: The Nutrition, Health, and Mortality of American Slaves from Childhood to Maturity." *Journal of Economic History* 46, no 3: 721–742.

U.S. Bureau of the Census. 1960. *Historical Statistics of the United States: Colonial Times to 1957.*

Washington, D.C.: U.S. Government Printing Office.

———. 1998. *Measuring 50 Years of Economic Change Using the March Current Population Survey.* Current Population Reports P60-203. Washington, D.C.: U.S. Government Printing Office.

———. n.d. *The Social and Economic Status of the Black Population in the United States: An Historical View, 1790–1978.* Current Population Reports P23-80. Washington, D.C.: U.S. Government Printing Office.

Williams, Juan. 1987. *Eyes on the Prize: America's Civil Rights Years, 1954–1965.* New York: Penguin Books.

Wilson, Terry P. 1994. "Osage Women, 1870–1980." In *Peoples of Color in the American West,* ed. Sucheng Chen, Douglas Henry Daniels, Mario T. Garcia, and Terry P. Wilson, 182–198. Lexington, Mass.: D. C. Heath and Company.

Zinn, Howard. 1995. *A People's History of the United States, 1492–Present.* 2nd ed. New York: HarperPerennial.

13

The Black Political Economy Paradigm and the Dynamics of Racial Economic Inequality

JAMES B. STEWART and MAJOR COLEMAN

This chapter uses a black political economy (BPE) paradigm to examine the economic implications of racial stratification and the forces that perpetuate racial disparities. In the BPE paradigm, racial identity is treated as a produced form of individual and group property that has income and wealth-generating characteristics. Collective identity is shown to have economic value, and as a consequence, groups forego income and wealth to protect identity production. As a consequence, reductions in intergroup income and wealth differentials will not automatically lead to the erosion of traditional patterns of collective identification. The BPE paradigm is used to interpret contemporary trends in employment, residential segregation, and incarceration rates. Fundamental issues likely to affect the success of long-term efforts to combat racial stratification and intergroup conflict are discussed.

This chapter presents the core elements of a distinctive black political economy (BPE) paradigm that illuminates key aspects of the contemporary and prospective economic status of African Americans. The two major foci of the BPE paradigm are, first, the role of economic forces in intensifying or mitigating conflicts between "racial" groups; and, second, the extent to which economic institutions can be viably organized and operated while accommodating sustained patterns of racial stratification. While other theoretical frameworks explore one or both of these issues, the BPE paradigm not only addresses both simultaneously in a logically consistent manner, but it also offers credible interpretations of contemporary stylized facts about racial economic inequality.

As traditional racial classifications as well as their role in public policy come under increasing attack, it is important that economic studies

of racial disparities reflect emerging conceptions of racial identity. The growing number of persons of mixed "racial" ancestry has prompted a significant expansion in the number of racial–ethnic designations included in the 2000 population census. Some who have championed this official reworking of previously used racial categories have seen it as signaling the beginning of the end for governmental use of traditional racial categorizations in developing and assessing public policies. However, analysis of the 2000 census data seems to suggest that DuBois's "color line" (1903) remains almost as indelible at the dawn of the twenty-first century as it was a century ago. In the 2000 census, 216,537,642 persons chose *white* as one of their racial classifications, whereas only 2.3 percent of this group chose any other racial classification. Similarly, 34,557,034 chose *black* or *African American* as one of their racial classifications, whereas only 5.4 percent of this group chose any other racial classification.

The continuing attachment of many individuals' to traditional racial classifications suggests that collective identity is a potentially important dimension of economic behavior. The importance of collective economic interests among African Americans originates in the communal traditions of traditional African societies. The pursuit of potential gains from collective action has been reinforced by the common patterns of oppression experienced by individuals during historical periods from the era of slavery until the present. Conversely, the collective economic interests of whites derive from the ideology of white racial superiority and wide access to economic rents generated at the expense of African Americans and other nonwhite groups. The BPE paradigm presented in this chapter facilitates the examination of the conflicts surrounding racial identity and how they contribute to interracial disparities in economic outcomes.

The next section outlines the treatment of racial identity in the BPE paradigm, using comparisons to other approaches to clarify critical distinctions. The third section presents theoretical perspectives on the dynamics of identity-influenced economic conflicts, followed by case study interpretations of selected current patterns of racial economic inequality. The concluding section suggests directions for further inquiry.

KEY DISTINGUISHING FEATURES OF THE BPE PARADIGM

The BPE paradigm treats racial identity as a form of individual and group property having income and wealth-generating characteristics. Race is conceptualized as a produced form of personal identity whose supply and demand are responsive to changes in production costs and budget constraints. However, individual choice does not guarantee social recognition or acceptance. Others' ascriptions of racial identity may differ from that desired by an individual, and those ascriptions can influence economic opportunities and outcomes.

The treatment of race and racial identity in the BPE paradigm differs markedly from what is found in other economic approaches. Neoclassical economists typically think of social identities as characteristics of an individual that are not economically productive but that may have economic consequences. As a result, the scrutiny of race is relegated to a secondary status relative to other forces deemed to be more important for economic decision making. As an illustration, economist Kenneth Arrow, a Nobel laureate, captures the essence of the standard neoclassical approach to examining race as follows:

> The black steel worker may be thought of as producing blackness as well as steel, both evaluated in the market. We are singling out the former as a special subject for analysis because somehow we think it is appropriate for the steel industry to produce steel and not for it to produce a black or white work force. (Arrow 1974, 4)

The decentering of race in traditional economic analysis has shaped how neoclassical economists approach the study of racial inequality. The neoclassical approach is encapsulated into what can be characterized as the subfield of the "economics of discrimination." This subfield has its origins in the notion of a "taste for discrimination," introduced by another Nobel economic laureate, Gary Becker (1957).

Becker's well-known "taste," or preference, theory of discrimination asks a rather simple question: if there is a subset of individuals within society who regard economic association with other racially distinct individuals as an economic bad, will these tastes for discrimination have a sustained impact on economic outcomes? The individuals with a preference for discrimination may be consumers, employers, or employees. Becker argues that, although this form of bigotry may produce a certain degree of segregation, such preferences do not produce sustained interracial differences in wages, employment, or occupational attainment when the general conditions for a competitive economy are met. The key conclusion flowing from Becker's model is that the competitive forces of the market undermine the economic impact of irrational preferences. For Becker, bigotry is an irrational preference: it is exogenously given and can only be maintained at a prohibitive cost to the employer, employee, or consumer because nondiscriminating owners of capital will choose profits over racism in making resource-allocation decisions. Presumably, discriminating owners either will be forced out of business or will modify their behavior to be competitive, although the period over which such market adjustments could be expected to occur is never formally specified.

At least two major issues raise serious questions about the operational usefulness of the neoclassical approach for interpreting the forces that produce racial economic inequality in the real world and for offering viable recommendations for reducing such inequality. The first issue is the extent to which market imperfections limit the type of antidiscriminatory responses predicted by the competitive model. Many studies continue to find evidence of labor market discrimination as well as discrimination in other economic activities, including human capital investment options and choice of residence. In response, proponents of the BPE paradigm ask the following questions:

1. Does the persistence of discrimination simply imply that markets are not sufficiently competitive to achieve the predicted outcome?
2. If noncompetitive markets are the norm in the United States, have discriminating agents developed ways to adapt institutions to accommodate discriminatory preferences such that losses in efficiency are minimized?
3. Have discriminating agents found strategies to shift the burden of economic losses resulting from discriminatory practices onto the victims?
4. If structural adaptations are possible that allow relatively costless discrimination to operate (from the vantage point of discriminators), do members of a dominant group have any incentive either to seek information about the social costs of discrimination and racial stratification or to undertake actions to mitigate them?

Mason (1995, 1999), Williams (1991), and Darity and Williams (1985) have demonstrated convincingly that competition is not only consistent with discrimination but that competition creates material incentives to persistently reproduce discriminatory behavior. The BPE paradigm builds on these important findings.

A second issue treated inadequately in the neoclassical paradigm is the presumed irrationality of so-called tastes for discrimination. Becker does not treat the origin of a taste for discrimination, or bigotry, as an economic question. However, as will be demonstrated, when racial identity is conceptualized in economic terms, the presumed power of competitive markets to punish decisions based solely on racial preferences is diminished considerably. Whites who benefit directly or indirectly from discrimination that victimizes other groups have few incentives to oppose systems of racial domination and in fact can easily become avid supporters. Darity and Williams argue, for example, that "workers can . . . concentrate and consolidate, particularly by ethnicity or race . . . via control of training, evaluation, information, and the definition of jobs," which allows "winners in early rounds of labor market competition . . . [to] insulate themselves from the most recent recruits to the wage labor force" (1985, 259–260).

In the BPE paradigm the norms of collective racial identity emerge as a critical mass of persons engaged in own-group altruism and other-group antagonism. Once a sufficiently large number of persons begins to engage in racialized behavior, there are increasing economic incentives for all persons to engage in racialized behavior. Racialized behavior spreads throughout society because individuals observe that own-group altruism and other-group antagonism is an income-increasing strategy relative to individualist behavior, where neither altruism nor antagonism is involved in exchange with other persons. Moreover, each agent's payoff to racialized behavior increases with the mean wealth of the agent's group. Income and wealth inequality increase the incentives for racialized behavior.

The aggregate constellation of behaviors and values of individuals who actively identify with a particular racial classification constitutes what can be described as *collective racial identity*. The existence of this type of quasi-kinship-based affiliation emerges from innate human instincts. However, it is social institutions that codify definitions of, and the boundaries between, racial groups. In the United States, the record of governmental specification of rules of racial classification associated with peoples of African descent is well known. Such classifications were established through legislation and through court decisions. The categories *mulatto, quadroon,* and *octoroon* were purported to designate an individual's degree of African ancestry. These were given official status not only to distinguish patterns of descent but also to assign differential opportunities.

Collective racial identity, as conceptualized in the BPE paradigm, is not easily categorized using traditional economic terminology. Collective racial identity has some characteristics similar to what economists term *externalities*—that is, output created by other productive activities. This collective identity has a positive value for those who identify with it or benefit unconsciously from its existence, but it can have negative effects on those who identify with a different racial–cultural identity. However, collective racial identity also has dimensions that are like "public goods," which are nonexcludable and nonrival in consumption. Once public goods exist, they are there for all to enjoy. So it is often the most rational strategy for private actors to let others go first and seek to enjoy the good without contributing to its production. This is the dilemma of public goods. Without some sort of collective-action mechanism, such goods risk being underproduced. Conversely, without collective action, public bads—pollution, noise, street crime, risky bank lending, and so on—risk being overproduced. In the BPE paradigm, efforts to neutralize the negative effects of externalities associated with the reproduction of racial identities constitute a major source of interracial conflicts in the United States. Economic discrimination and other forms of disparate treatment serve as means to reduce negative externalities perceived by the more-powerful groups as emanating from the cultural identity reproduction of less-powerful groups (Stewart 1995).

INDIVIDUAL RACIAL IDENTITY, COLLECTIVE IDENTITY, AND INDIVIDUAL DECISION MAKING

One of the critical issues addressed by the BPE paradigm is how economic competition among racial groups affects the distribution of goods and opportunities among people. When traditional economists think about how members characterized as belonging to the same racial group behave, they often have in mind a form of affiliation similar to voluntary membership in an organization. This perspective has led some commentators to suggest that the historical exploitation of blacks has produced short-term collective efforts to overcome oppression but no persisting solidarity capable of influencing economic activity. In this view, collective efforts erode once barriers facing individuals are removed.

Stewart (1976, 1995) and Darity, Mason, and Stewart (2003) have developed models that demonstrate how individual decisions regarding economic well-being are influenced by considerations related to racial identity. In these models the economic opportunities available to an individual agent vary depending on the extent to which active group identification influences that agent's economic decisions. Such choices are, of course, constrained by social custom, history, and other factors. Notions of "white privilege" and "property rights in whiteness" convey the reality that persons socially identified as white have an economic safety net or a group insurance unavailable to nonwhites even if they choose to identify with nonwhites as their primary reference group. Conversely, institutional phenotypic discrimination potentially imposes a type of "tax" on the economic opportunities and outcomes of nonwhites even if their economic behavior and other characteristics mirror those of similarly situated whites. Governmental action establishes the upper and lower bounds of such taxes. Governmental action can, for example, protect the interests of whites by creating quasi-separate jurisdictions that allow the availability of high-value public goods to be restricted. To illustrate, within some large urban school districts, it is not unusual to find well-endowed public schools populated principally by white students while the majority of schools are resource poor.

As noted, collective racial identity is partly an "externality" that has a positive value for those who identify with it or derive its benefits unconsciously; but such an identity is assessed negatively by those who identify with a different racial–cultural identity or find the cultural production process distasteful. The magnitude of the negative effects generally increases with the frequency and duration of contacts with members of other racial–cultural groups and the degree of overlap in identity characteristics between groups. Some elements of another culture's racial–cultural group identity can be experienced through commodities as opposed to direct contact. Thus, well-designed consumption technologies allow the positive characteristics of other groups' cultural products to be consumed or experienced without experiencing the negative external effects associated with direct interaction with the products' originators. The clearest example of this phenomenon is the attraction of hip hop music to suburban white youth who reside in largely segregated enclaves.

Another way of describing these dynamics has been suggested by Okonkwo (1973), who argues that the presence of whites in a particular area who discriminate against blacks inflicts an external diseconomy on a community of "aware" blacks. The term *aware* can be interpreted to mean those for whom the production of cultural identity has explicit value. From this vantage point, discriminatory behavior by groups in conflict becomes one manifestation of efforts to adjust the social environment to reduce the impact of perceived externalities associated with cultural production by other groups. In fact, Okonkwo suggests such an interpretation: "The assumption that discrimination is an externality will in general cut both ways, so that Blacks will appear as a public bad."

Individuals with similar cultural production functions have an incentive to engage in collective behavior to reduce the negative externalities associated with other groups' cultural production. Such intergroup competition can lead to tensions even in the absence of competition for, or maldistribution of, economic resources. It is important to recognize, however, that persisting resource maldistributions will inevitably exacerbate intergroup tensions.

Albert Breton (1974) has shown how people will commit resources to political efforts to reduce what he describes as "economic coercion." Such coercion involves the discomfort or reduced sense of economic well-being experienced by a person when one's expectations of gains resulting from economic policies deviate from the actual flow of goods and services received. Breton argues that when people experience a sufficiently high level of discomfort, they will commit time and resources to political activities in an effort to alter the policy that is perceived to be the source of their discomfort. In a similar vein, the BPE paradigm suggests that individuals and groups will commit economic and noneconomic resources to political activities of various sorts to configure their environments so that cultural identity production can occur without undesired external influences.[1]

The effect of another group's cultural production activities on a person's own-group cultural production thus constitutes a type of quasi-economic coercion that engenders responses similar to those described by Breton. Differences in wealth, or more broadly resource endowments, as well as different traditions of political behavior lead to differences in the types of political activities undertaken by different groups. African Americans often exhibit a preference for political activities such as demonstrations because these are relatively lower-cost options than paying political lobbyists and because they allow the intensity of concern to be expressed. In addition, numerical minority status reduces the effectiveness of bloc voting. In contrast, voting is an effective political instrument for whites because of their numerical majority status (until the mid-twenty-first century) and because the objectives of racial domination and subordination guarantee alignment between actions of elected officials and their individual and collective well-being.

Competition for economic resources is typically layered on top of competition for social space. Thus, when so-called middle-class blacks seek to escape the cultural production environment in central cities, they often wind up residing in racially segregated suburban enclaves. In the initial stages of suburban residential demographic transformation, the cultural production of the first black residents is likely to have little effect on white residents. The income levels and socialization of the initial cohort of black residents is often more like that of their white counterparts than those blacks who subsequently relocate to the neighborhood. As cultural production competition intensifies, some whites will choose to relocate and more will exercise this option as the demographic transition proceeds.

The BPE paradigm also suggests why school desegregation efforts typically entailed relocation of black students in relatively small numbers to predominantly white districts. This pattern minimized the negative externalities associated with the activities of the relocated students on white students, while allowing the existing cultural production process to proceed with minimal disruptions. Of course, this policy disrupted the cultural production processes of the relocated black students.

In general, concentrations of people with similar cultural production functions create opportunities to take advantage of economies of scale. As an example, if there are enough residents in a given area, a black church can be established or an independent black school. Thus the size of the local black population and its characteristics become important parameters in the location decisions of highly mobile black professionals. This phenomenon helps explain the high level of black return migration to the South and the especially magnetic attraction of the Atlanta metropolitan area. In addition, black middle-class parents are increasingly selecting historically black institutions of higher education for their offspring, although their class status would presumably allow so-called integrated options. The goal seems to be to ensure that some minimal level of group identity is produced with the acquisition of general human

capital. Further, parents seek to avoid their children's exposure to the negative externalities and derivative intergroup conflicts associated with cultural production processes operative in many traditionally white institutions.

Cultural production externalities are obviously more important in some activities than they are in others. These externalities are particularly important in the marriage market, although interracial relationships and marriages are increasing. They are also important in competition for positions with high levels of prestige and power and in the case of religious observances. There is an old adage that the most segregated hour in the week is eleven o'clock on Sunday morning. Cultural production externalities appear to be least problematic in professional athletics, although racial stratification appears to be present in playing positions in some sports and even more so in the ownership, management, and coaching ranks.

The importance of cultural production externalities in the workplace depends on the degree of workers' identification with the profession, organization, and occupation relative to the intensity of their racial group identification. As in athletics, high potential returns from cooperative behavior may overwhelm the effects of negative cultural production externalities. In general, employers attempt to create a quasi-artificial enterprise identity that serves as an alternative or complement to the principal reference groups with which workers identify, such as race or religious affiliation. Similar to the process described earlier, this identity is a joint product—that is, an externality generated with the firm's income-generating activities. Within a bureaucratic organization, individuals are expected to monitor their cultural production to minimize the generation of negative externalities that adversely affect productivity and worker solidarity. These expectations create a disproportionate hardship on those whose cultural production functions are more dissimilar from the cultural norms. This problem can cut both ways; as an example, a white employee in a black-owned firm with a majority black workforce may have to adapt his or her typical cultural production in uncomfortable ways. However, the converse is more typical—that is, black employees feel pressure to modify cultural identity production to reduce variation from white norms.

The work environment can be structured to minimize the effects of cultural production conflicts on income-generating activities. Various techniques are used to accomplish this end. As noted, racial segregation and occupational crowding were popular strategies during the pre–civil rights movement era. More recently, diversity training has become the principal technique for avoiding intergroup conflicts. Those who are unable to modify cultural production functions run the risk of termination, and blacks may well face the most difficult problems in making acceptable adaptations.

Outside the world of work, friendship across racial–cultural groups is feasible to the extent that overt differences in racial identity production are small compared to the collective positive externalities resulting from other sources of affinity. At the same time, it is possible that racial–cultural identity production strategies may be bifurcated. Individuals may employ one strategy when dealing face-to-face with members of another group, while making investments in their identity of origin when interacting with family members and other friends. One method to avoid cognitive dissonance when employing a bifurcated production strategy is to discount cultural production by someone with a different racial background. One example is the "you are not like the others" syndrome. To some extent, interracial marriages constitute an extreme case of this adaptation strategy. It is important to recognize, however, that distinctive phenotypic characteristics and unique cultural attributes are likely to be always with us. However, the transformation of these attributes into economic property and competing racial identities is not a law of nature; but a close examination of some contemporary patterns of racial inequality suggests that the underlying processes will be difficult to transform.

THE BPE PARADIGM AND THE DYNAMICS OF CONTEMPORARY RACIAL ECONOMIC INEQUALITY

As noted, the second major area of concern for the BPE paradigm is how institutions are organized and operated to achieve acceptable levels of efficiency while accommodating patterns of racial domination that are critical to the normal functioning of the U.S. political economy. In the United States, this accommodation involves, among other adaptations, minimizing the degree to which whites are exposed to undesirable identity production externalities produced by other groups, especially those by blacks. Racial disparities and racial discrimination are endemic features of the U.S. economy and social systems. Discrimination based on race, per se, is infused into a myriad of institutional practices in ways that are virtually impossible to totally neutralize or eradicate.

The term *racial stratification* is used in the BPE paradigm to describe the general process by which race is used as a criterion to assign roles and positions in organizations and institutions. Racial stratification in economic institutions leads to the disproportionate assignment of high-status positions—those associated with control over allocation of resources, distribution of economic benefits, and high incomes—to members of the dominant group. The collective outcome of the operation of stratification processes across organizations is the institutionalization of a hierarchy of dominant and subordinate statuses among racial groups.

The extent of racial stratification that exists within a given organization or in the society more generally depends on the balance of political power between dominant and subordinate groups, which may differ across organizations at a given point in time. Structural changes in the economic system, political upheavals, and other major transformative events and processes can disrupt racial stratification processes and alter the short-term balance of political power—that is, create a social disequilibrium. Recognition of the dynamic character of racial stratification processes differentiates the BPE paradigm from most other analytical approaches that explore the role of structural forces in perpetuating racial economic inequality. For example, some analysts, including many economists, point to the civil rights movement, subsequent black electoral gains, and new residential and occupational mobility to declare the formal end of the legacy of historical forms of racial domination/subordination. They claim that discrimination, as typically conceived, is no longer a major factor contributing to the observed racial disparities. Instead, they place the blame for the persistence of these disparities on the victims themselves; that is, individuals are failing to respond appropriately to market opportunities. The institutions that socialize individuals—such as family and friendship networks—are also criticized for encouraging and reinforcing behavior that is unresponsive to market signals and incentives.

The BPE paradigm provides a different explanation for the persistence of racial and economic disparities. The simple BPE paradigm answer is that the interventions forced by the civil rights movement were never intended to eliminate previous disparities. Rather, new formal and informal rules, policies, and procedures were instituted in response to changes in the balance of power precipitated by the civil rights movement. While opportunities were created during the early years that did indeed produce some measurable gains, the subsequent reconsolidation of the preexisting racial order reinvigorated racial stratification processes.

The efforts since the mid-1960s to reestablish the previous racial order have involved an intense and ongoing political and legal battle between proponents of equalizing opportunities and those adherents to the old racial order. Opponents of equity efforts have masked their objectives in language touting so-called color-blind policies. Relentless attacks on so-called affirmative action educational and employment policies have mobilized employee resistance to efforts to reduce stratification within organizations and a weakened commitment on the part of managers to reducing stratification.

The willingness of white workers to buy into the antistratification reduction rhetoric is driven to a large extent by the need to find a scapegoat for the declining quality of life engendered by globalization pressures. As an example, employers have responded to global competition by reducing benefits for low-income workers. Less than one-fifth of low-income workers have access to employer-sponsored pension plans.

Legal sanctions against job and occupational discrimination have enabled many blacks to move into supervisory roles. A large number of

white males resent the growing presence of Blacks as authority figures and view them as interlopers illegitimately occupying these high-status positions. The term "angry white male syndrome" has been coined to describe this phenomenon. From the vantage point of the BPE paradigm, the most intriguing charge is the claim that many blacks who now occupy high-status positions are unqualified or underqualified.[2] This rhetorical tactic clearly signals that one of the major underlying tensions in the workplace is the disruption of the traditional status hierarchy of positions with whites in high-status occupations and blacks in low-level jobs. The disruption of the traditional status hierarchy of positions and the angry-white-male syndrome are particularly prominent since the collapse of Jim Crow in the South and the relatively successful interventions to reduce job and occupational discrimination in the North.

Another illustration of how formal and informal rules, policies, and procedures have contributed to the persistence of racial disparities after the civil rights movement is the case of residential segregation. In contrast to the limited capacity to avoid racial interaction in the workplace, whites are much more able to avoid interaction with blacks in residential settings. The efforts of individual whites to avoid the negative externalities perceived to be associated with black cultural production are manifested in persistent high levels of racial residential segregation. Hypersegregation persists despite equal housing legislation and public programs designed to reduce residential segregation. Blacks living in metropolitan areas with black populations of one million people or greater are especially likely to live in segregated neighborhoods. Detroit, New York, Chicago, and Philadelphia rank, respectively, second, fourth, fifth, and eighteenth in degree of black–white segregation out of 310 metropolitan areas (Census Scope n.d.). This pattern simply suggests that high levels of black identity production increase incentives for whites to relocate to avoid negative effects on their own identity production.

Residential segregation contributes to the problem of *spatial mismatch*, a term first introduced by economist John Kain in 1968. Spatial mismatch describes the phenomenon where the suburbanization of jobs coupled with restrictions on the residential options open to blacks creates a surplus of workers relative to the available jobs in inner-city neighborhoods, resulting in joblessness, low wages, and long commutes for black workers. Raphael and Stoll (2002) observe that metropolitan areas with high levels of black–white residential segregation exhibit a high degree of spatial mismatch between blacks and jobs. Krovi and Barnes (2000) find that African Americans generally have the longest travel times to work in all regions of the country where public transit is available and that low-income minorities have longer travel times than low-income whites do.

It is important to recognize that spatial mismatch patterns are more complex than the historical pattern of inner-city residents' having difficulty traveling to suburban job sites. Downward pressure on incomes and on the status of all workers induced by global competition has trickled down in ways that are intensifying conflicts over valuable commercial and residential space in urban areas. Intense political battles have been, and are being, waged for control of city government by globalization-friendly constituents who want to make cities more attractive to global corporations.

Compounding the problem of spatial mismatch is the growing presence of new sources of easily controllable sources of labor to fill low-paying, low-status jobs, especially those in the services sector. The representation of foreign-born workers in the labor force has been growing faster than their population representation has, and immigrants are disproportionately employed in business services, construction, nondurable and durable manufacturing, health care, and personal services. The proportion of foreign-born workers is higher than that of native-born workers in service occupations (19.2 percent versus 13.2 percent); in operating, fabricating, and laboring occupations (18.7 percent versus 12.7 percent); precision production, craft, and repair occupations (12.1 percent versus 10.5 percent); and farming, forestry, and fishing occupations (4.5 percent versus 2.1 percent; U.S. Census Bureau, 2001). From the vantage point of the BPE paradigm, there are several reasons why immigrants are preferred over domestic black workers. Immigrants present much less potential status competition than blacks do. The cultural identity production of immigrants is perceived to generate fewer negative externalities for whites than that of blacks. Finally it is easier to maintain social control (racial stratification) through immigration laws and manipulation of residency status.

Black males are drastically overrepresented in all state prison populations compared to whites and Hispanics. Many traditional analysts attribute this pattern to disproportionate criminal tendencies among blacks deriving from the failure of the socializing institutions to cultivate a respect for law and order. However, the BPE paradigm raises the issue of whether this pattern is itself part and parcel of the system of social control. Cohen and Canelo-Cacho (1994) estimate that the reduction in violent crime due to increases in imprisonment of violent offenders since 1975 has been no more than 10 percent. Spelman (1994) finds that current incarceration rates avert perhaps no more than 8 percent of crimes. One alternative explanation for high incarceration rates among black males is the transformation of this population into economic commodities that are fueling the growth of the prison–industrial complex. Many of the new prisons warehousing blacks are located in rural, predominantly white areas that have lost much of their mining and manufacturing employment bases to industrial shifts. Prisons provide new sources of revenue, and the presence of large numbers of black inmates is acceptable to local white residents because black cultural production is stringently controlled and status differences between inmates and the local population are sharply defined. In fact, the presence of large populations of black inmates constitutes a positive input into white cultural identity production as other sources of status have been diminished. More generally, the images of black criminality in the media, including the infamous "Willie Horton" presidential campaign ad, fuel white perceptions about the extent of negative externalities associated with black cultural identity production and reinforce segregation and stratification processes.

Some of the more-revealing data suggesting the underlying racial stratification motives associated with incarceration policies are embedded in comparisons of prison operating expenditures per inmate with the costs of educating disadvantaged students. Prison operating costs in 1996 ranged from $13,977 in Georgia to $37,825 in Minnesota (Stephan 1999). Now compare those numbers to $10,000, which is one estimate of the maximum cost associated with ensuring that a student residing in an environment characterized by concentrated poverty can meet the new "No Child Left Behind" standards ("Inadequate Funding Makes NCLB Worse" 2003). Between 1985 and 1996 state educational expenditure increased by 3.6 percent per year, compared to 7.3 percent for prisons, excluding costs of prison construction (U.S. Bureau of the Census n.d.). The apparent choice of incarceration over education, even given unfavorable cost–benefit ratios, suggests that separating black males from the population at large serves an important social control function.

Most traditional analysts focus on the analysis of criminal behavior and crime reduction strategies. In contrast, the BPE paradigm emphasizes how these patterns interact with various public policies in ways that disrupt black cultural identity production. Shihadeh and Ousey (1996, 649) maintain that inner-city crime is linked directly to the process of suburbanization, which "contributes to the disinvestments and decline of black communities in the city," increases social isolation, and "thereby engender[s] high crime rates." Clear (1996) argues that incarceration involves the entry and exit of adults from families, leading to a change in economic circumstances of those families—a change that may force relocation. Clear insists further, "each prisoner represents an economic asset that has been removed from that community and placed elsewhere" who is no longer spending money in the community (9). Moreover, most ex-offenders are likely to return to their neighborhoods on release, and "these ex-offenders are more likely to be unemployed or underemployed, adding to the local unemployment rate and the chronic difficulties ex-convicts face in finding and retaining work" (9).

The preceding discussion provides only a partial overview of the range of stratification processes with which the BPE paradigm is concerned. Nevertheless, it demonstrates that the BPE provides a more comprehensive analysis of the dynamics of racial stratification than its competitors and can thus facilitate the development of more functional strategies to change the status quo.

CONCLUSION

The BPE paradigm suggests several fundamental issues that must be addressed in efforts to develop strategies to combat racial stratification and intergroup conflict. First, in a world characterized by cultural differences and inequitable distribution of economic resources, intergroup conflict in economic as well as noneconomic settings is an endogenous characteristic of the social space rather than an exogenous contaminant of market allocation processes and individual decision making. Second, collective identity has economic value, and groups will forego income and wealth to protect identity production. Third, reductions in intergroup income and wealth differentials will not automatically lead to the erosion of traditional patterns of collective identification. Fourth, as long as investments in racial identity generate differential returns for different identities, significant racial stratification will persist. Fifth, incentives for engaging in cooperative intergroup behavior can reduce the potentially negative dimensions of interracial contact and create alternatives to traditional racial identification. And sixth, movement toward more egalitarian inter- and intraracial distributions of wealth must be a major element in any earnest attempt to reduce racial conflict.

By specifying the mechanisms through which racial inequalities are perpetuated, the BPE paradigm lays the foundation for additional research in the subfield of stratification economics. Further analyses employing stratification paradigms have the potential to produce new insights regarding strategies to achieve significant reductions in interracial economic inequality.

NOTES

The authors are deeply indebted to Cecelia Conrad, Patrick Mason, and John Whitehead for their extensive and incisive comments on earlier drafts. The final version incorporates key refinements that would not have been possible without a major cooperative effort.

1. Cultural production is the process by which cultural identity is created. The cultural production function might include inputs such as modes of speech or dress, choices of entertainment and food, and neighborhood location.

2. The idea of unqualified or underqualified black workers or students seems to be very real in the minds of whites. Research reported by Coleman (2003) indicates that 75 percent of whites believe that it is very likely or somewhat likely that less-qualified blacks get jobs or promotions before more qualified whites do. In addition, 78 percent of whites believe it is very likely or somewhat likely that less-qualified blacks get admitted to colleges or universities ahead of more-qualified whites. Regardless of what many whites may think, nearly all of the available evidence indicates that black employees are as qualified as whites and in some cases more qualified. Coleman (2003) recognizes that if black workers are underqualified or unqualified, there should be some measurable costs at the market level as a result of deficiency in skills, qualifications, performance, or productivity.

REFERENCES

Arrow, Kenneth. 1974. "The Theory of Discrimination." In *Discrimination in Labor Markets*, ed. Orley Ashenfelter and Albert Rees. Princeton, N.J.: Princeton University Press.

Becker, Gary. 1957. *The Economics of Discrimination*. Chicago: University of Chicago Press.

Breton, Albert. 1974. *The Economic Theory of Representative Government*. Chicago: Aldine Publishing.

Census Scope. n.d. "Segregation Dissimilarity Indices, U.S. Metro Areas Ranked by White/Black Dissimilarity Index." Available at www.censusscope.org/us/rank_dissimilarity_white_black.html.

Clear, Todd. 1996. "Backfire: When Incarceration Increases Crime." Available at www.doc.state.ok.us/DOCS/OCJRC/Ocjrc96/Ocjrc7.htm.

Cohen, Jacqueline, and Jose Canela-Cacho. 1994. "Incapacitation and Violent Crime." In *Understanding and Preventing Violence*, ed. Albert Reiss

and Jeffrey Roth, 4:296–338. Washington, D.C.: National Academy of Sciences.

Coleman, Major G. 2003. "African American Popular Wisdom versus the Qualification Question: Is Affirmative Action Merit-Based?" *Western Journal of Black Studies* 27 (Spring): 35–44.

Darity, William, Patrick Mason, and James Stewart. 2003. "The Economics of Identity: The Origin and Persistence of Racial Norms." Unpublished manuscript.

Darity, William, and Rhonda Williams. (1985). "Peddlers Forever? Culture, Competition, and Discrimination." *Papers and Proceedings of the American Economic Review* 75, no. 2 (May): 256–261.

DuBois, William E. B. 1903. *The Souls of Black Folk: Essays and Sketches*. Chicago: A. C. McClurg.

"Inadequate Funding Makes NCLB Worse." 2003. *FairTest Examiner* (Winter/Spring), available at http://fairtest.org/examarts/Wint-Spring%2003%20double/Funding.html.

Kain, John. 1968. "Housing Segregation, Negro Employment, and Metropolitan Decentralization." *Quarterly Journal of Economics* 82:175–197.

Krovi, Ravindra, and Claude Barnes. 2000. "Work-Related Travel Patterns of People of Color." In *Travel Patterns of People of Color*. Columbus, Ohio: Battelle.

Mason, Patrick L. 1995. "Race, Competition, and Differential Wages." *Cambridge Journal of Economics* 19, no. 4 (August): 545–568.

———. 1997. "Race, Culture, and Skill: Interracial Wage Differences among African Americans, Latinos, and Whites." *Review of Black Political Economy* 25 (Winter): 5–39.

———. 1999. "Competing Explanations of Male Interracial Wage Differentials: Missing Variables Models versus Job Competition." *Cambridge Journal of Economics* (May).

———. 2004. "Persistent Racial Discrimination in the Labor Market," chapter 15 of this volume.

Okonkwo, Ubadigbo. 1973. "The Economics of Ethnic Discrimination." *Review of Black Political Economy* 3, no. 2: 1–18.

Raphael, Steven, and Michael Stoll. 2002. *Modest Progress: The Narrowing Spatial Mismatch between Blacks and Jobs in the 1990s*. Living Census Series. Washington, D.C.: Brookings Institution.

Shihadeh, Edward, and Graham Ousey. 1996.

"Metropolitan Expansion and Black Social Dislocation: The Link between Suburbanization and Center-City Crime." *Social Forces* 75, no 2: 649–666.

Spelman, William. 1994. *Criminal Incapacitation.* New York: Plenum.

Stephan, James. 1999. *State Prison Expenditures, 1996.* NCJ 172211 (August). Washington, D.C.: U.S. Department of Justice.

Stewart, James. 1976. "An Analysis of the Impacts of Structural Variables on the Relative Levels of Economic Welfare of the Black Populations of the United States and the Republic of South Africa." Ph.D. diss., Department of Economics, University of Notre Dame.

———. 1995. "Toward Broader Involvement of Black Economists in Discussions of Race and Public Policy: A Plea for a Reconceptualization of Race and Power in Economic Theory, NEA Presidential Address, 1994." *Review of Black Political Economy* 23, no. 3: 13–36.

U.S. Bureau of the Census. 2001. *Profile of the Foreign-Born Population in the United States: 2000.* Current Population Reports P23-206. Washington, D.C.: U.S. Government Printing Office.

———. n.d. "State Government Finances, 1985–1996." Available at www.ojp.usdoj.gov/bjs/pub/pdf/spe96.pdf.

Williams, R. 1991. "Competition, Discrimination and Differential Wage Rates: On the Continued Relevance of Marxian Theory to the Analysis of Earnings and Employment Inequality." In *New Approaches to the Economic and Social Analysis of Discrimination,* ed. R. Cornwall and P. Wunnava, 65–92. New York: Praeger.

PART IV

Current Economic Status of African Americans: Hard Evidence of Economic Discrimination and Inequality

14

Race and Gender Differences in the U.S. Labor Market: The Impact of Educational Attainment

SUSAN WILLIAMS McELROY

This chapter analyzes differences in labor force participation, unemployment, and earnings by race, gender, and race–gender groups in the United States. In particular, it addresses how differences in labor market outcomes vary by educational attainment level. This research demonstrates that educational attainment plays a crucial role in labor market outcomes. Further and more important, differences in labor market outcomes among race–gender groups also vary according to education level.

This chapter analyzes differences in labor market outcomes by race, gender, and race–gender groups in the United States. In particular, it examines how differences in labor force participation, unemployment, and earnings vary by educational attainment level.

Labor market outcomes differ noticeably along these dimensions. For example, men have higher labor force participation rates than women do, and blacks have higher unemployment rates than do whites.[1] Furthermore, groups of persons who are of the same racial or ethnic group but of different genders have noticeable differences in labor participation and unemployment. For example, one observes differences between African American males and African American females. At the same time, groups of persons who are of the same gender (females, for example) but of different racial and ethnic groups also have different labor market statuses and experiences. For example, black women have higher rates of labor force participation than white women do, but black men have lower rates of labor force participation than white men have.

The question this chapter asks is how educa-tional attainment affects these differences in outcomes. It first compares labor force participation rates and unemployment rates for race–gender groups with the same educational attainment. Next, it reviews how earnings differ by race and gender within educational categories. Finally, it considers how occupation varies by race–gender groups in the U.S. labor market and how the occupational distribution of race–gender groups differs by educational attainment. It concludes that educational attainment plays a crucial role in labor market outcomes.

DIFFERENCES IN LABOR FORCE PARTICIPATION AND UNEMPLOYMENT BY RACE–GENDER GROUPS

Everyone in the population falls into one of three mutually exclusive groups based on employment status: employed, unemployed, or not in the paid labor force. An individual who is employed has a job and is working for pay. To be counted among the unemployed, an individual must be without work and must be actively looking for work. Finally, some persons, such as full-time students or homemakers, are not in the paid labor force at all.

From individual-level data, one can derive indicators of how well various demographic groups are faring in the labor market. Labor force participation and unemployment rates are examples of such labor market indicators. The labor force participation rate is a ratio—the labor force divided by the number of persons in the population expressed as a percentage. The labor force consists of persons sixteen years of age or older who are not in institutions and who are either employed or unemployed and actively seeking work. The unemployment rate is also a ratio—the number of unemployed persons divided by the number of persons in the labor force, expressed as a percentage.

Labor force participation rates and unemployment rates vary by race, gender, and race–gender as documented in Table 14.1. We first discuss labor force participation rates and then consider unemployment rates. In 2001, the labor force participation rate of the population age twenty-five and over was 67.4 percent. Males (all races combined) had a higher labor force participation rate than women had (all races combined). Thus, on aver-age, men were more likely than women to be in the paid labor force. However, comparing men to women in terms of labor force participation obscures important differences across race and race–gender.

Within race, gender matters; and within gender, race matters. For example, the labor force participation rate of whites (males and females together) was 67.1 percent in 2001, but white males had a higher labor force participation rate (76.1 percent) than white women had (58.8 percent). Among blacks, the gender difference in labor force participation is noticeably smaller, with 72.5 percent of black males in the paid labor force as compared with 64.8 percent of black females. Thus, for blacks and whites alike, females had lower rates of labor force participation than men did; but among blacks, the gender gap in labor force participation is smaller than it is among whites. Hispanics (males and females) have a labor force participation rate of 69.7 percent, but Hispanic women are considerably less likely to be in the paid labor force (57.6 percent) than are Hispanic men (82.5 percent).

What difference does education make to labor force participation rates? Economic theory predicts that persons with more education will have higher rates of labor force participation be-

Table 14.1   Labor Force Participation and Unemployment Rates by Race–Gender Groups: 2001 Annual Averages

	Labor force participation rate (%)	Unemployment rate (%)
Total (all races, male and female)	67.4	3.7
Male, all races	75.9	3.6
Females, all races	59.7	3.7
Whites, males and females	67.1	3.3
White males	76.1	3.2
White females	58.8	3.3
Blacks, males and females	68.2	6.3
Black males	72.5	6.7
Black females	64.8	5.9
Hispanics, males and females[a]	69.7	5.3
Hispanic males[a]	82.5	4.6
Hispanic females[a]	57.6	6.3

Source: U.S. Bureau of Labor Statistics (2001).

Note: Data are for persons aged sixteen years and over.

[a]*Hispanic* here refers to an ethnic category; as such, Hispanics may be of any race.

cause for them the opportunity cost of *not* being in the paid labor force is higher than for persons with less education. In other words, because more highly educated persons have higher average earnings, a person with a college degree, for example, foregoes higher earnings than does a high school graduate when he or she does not participate in the paid labor market.[2] In fact, the data confirm that across race–gender groups, persons with more education have higher labor force participation rates.

As Figure 14.1 reveals for black, white, and Hispanic males and females, the higher the level of education, the higher the labor force participation rate of the race–gender education group.[3] In 2001, for example, 74.3 percent of white male high school graduates aged twenty-five years and over were in the paid labor force, while 84.1 percent of white male college graduates of this age were. Both of these race–gender education groups (white male high school graduates and white male college graduates) had higher rates of labor force participation than did white males in the same age group who had not completed a high school (57.0 percent labor force participation rate). The same pattern applies to the other race–gender groups represented in Figure 14.1; that is, college graduates have higher labor force participation rates than do high school graduates. Similarly, high school graduates have higher labor force participation rates than do persons who have not completed high school.

Does education matter for differences in labor force participation across race–gender groups, and if so, how much? The data again reveal the central role of educational attainment. Comparing the labor force participation rates of white males to those of persons of other race–gender groups within education levels makes this point clear. For instance, compare black males to white males. Among high school graduates, the labor force participation rates of black and white males are essentially equal (74.3 percent for white males and 74.4 percent for black males). The same is

Figure 14.1   Labor force participation rates by educational level for race–gender groups, 2001.

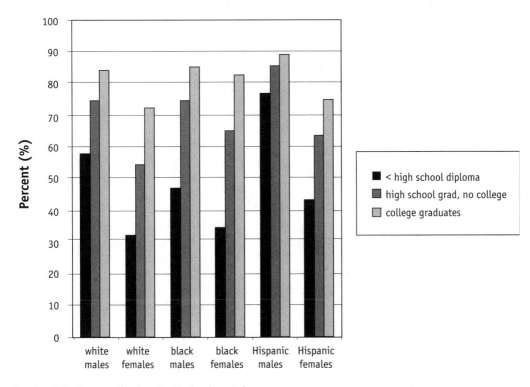

SOURCE: U.S. Bureau of Labor Statistics (2002a).

true for college graduates. White male college graduates have a labor force participation rate of 84.1 percent, and black male college graduates have a labor force participation rate of 85.6 percent. Thus, at the college graduate level, the labor force participation rates of black and white males barely differ at all. Yet, marked differences in labor force participation rates of black and white males do exist at the lower education level—namely, at the level of less than a high school diploma. White males who have not completed high school have a labor force participation rate that is 1.22 times higher than the corresponding rate for black males in this education category. The labor force participation rates of white males and black males who have less than a high school diploma are 57.0 percent and 46.6 percent, respectively.

Education is not as useful in explaining gender differences in labor force participation rates. Women have lower labor force participation rates than men do at every level of educational attainment. However, education is related to size of the gender gap. Gender differences in labor force participation appear to be greatest for persons with less than a high school diploma.

We consider now the following questions. First, how do unemployment rates differ according to race, gender, and race–gender groups? Second, does education matter for race–gender group differences in unemployment, and if so, how much? In 2001, 3.7 percent of workers in the U.S. labor force were unemployed.[4] As Table 14.1 indicates, unemployment rates are quite different across race, with blacks having an unemployment rate that is about twice as high (6.3 percent) as the white unemployment rate (3.3 percent). Hispanics had an unemployment rate lower than the black unemployment rate and higher than the white unemployment rate. White men and women have equal unemployment rates, but there are gender differences among blacks and Hispanics. Among blacks, males have a higher unemployment rate (6.7 percent) than black females do (5.9 percent). Among Hispanics, females are more likely to be unemployed (unemployment rate of 6.3 percent) than men are (unemployment rate of 4.6 percent). Unemployment rates by race–gender groups, while certainly informative, hide the differences in unemployment rates by education

level within race–gender groups. As shown in Figure 14.2, across race–gender groups, persons in the lower education groups have appreciably higher unemployment rates than persons who have completed more schooling. Specifically, persons with less than a high school diploma have the highest unemployment rates; college graduates have the lowest unemployment rates; and high school graduates fall in between.

In relative terms, black–white differences in unemployment rates are greater for the lower education groups, and this fact applies to males as well as females. For example, black female college graduates experienced a 3.0 percent unemployment rate in 2001, markedly lower than the unemployment rate of either black female high school graduates (9.2 percent) or black females who had not completed high school (18.2 percent). Another example is white females, for whom the unemployment rate of those with less education than a high school diploma (10.0 percent) was higher than the unemployment rate of high school graduates (4.2 percent) and college graduates (2.3 percent).

Black–white differences in unemployment within gender show again the important role of educational attainment in labor market outcomes and that racial differences in labor market outcomes are determined in part by education. As an example, when we compare black female unemployment to white female unemployment in relative terms, we find that the racial gap in unemployment rates is larger at the lower education levels—that is, less than high school diploma and high school graduate—than at the higher education level of college graduates. In 2001, the unemployment rate of black women with less than a high school diploma was 1.8 times higher than the unemployment rate of white women in the same education group; the unemployment rate of black female high school graduates was 2.2 times higher than the unemployment rate of white female high school graduates; and the unemployment rate for black female college graduates was 1.3 times higher than the unemployment rate for white female college graduates. Comparing black male unemployment rates to white male unemployment rates and black female unemployment rates to white male unemployment rates reveals a similar pattern.

Figure 14.2   Unemployment rates by educational level for selected race–gender groups, 2001.

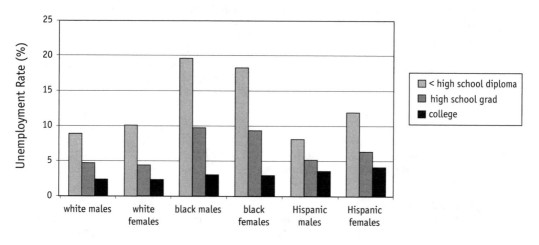

Source: U.S. Bureau of Labor Statistics (2002a).

In general, persons with less than a high school diploma have weaker attachments to the labor force, as measured by labor force participation and unemployment, than do those with higher levels of educational attainment. Differences in educational attainment help to explain racial differences in labor force participation rates and unemployment rates for racial groups but provide little insight into gender differences.

DIFFERENCES IN EARNINGS BY RACE–GENDER GROUPS

Educational attainment is strongly linked to earnings, and this is true across race–gender groups in the U.S. labor market. Table 14.2 presents median annual earnings in 1999 by educational attainment for persons aged twenty-five to sixty-four by race–gender groups for year-round, full-time workers for the following race–gender groups: non-Hispanic white males, non-Hispanic white females, non-Hispanic black males, non-Hispanic black females, Hispanic males, Hispanic females, and Asian/Pacific Islander males, and Asian/Pacific Islander females.[5] *Year-round* is defined as working fifty or more weeks per year, and *full-time* is defined as working thirty-five or more hours per week.[6] Earnings estimates for year-round, full-time

workers are used because, in this way, one avoids mixing part-time and full-time workers and mixing seasonal workers and full-year workers.[7] Table 14.2 shows that across race–gender groups, higher education levels are associated with higher earnings. High school graduates earn more on average than persons who have not completed high school.[8] College graduates earn more on average than high school graduates do.[9]

The earnings differentials by race–gender groups are sizable. If all educational attainment categories are taken together, non-Hispanic white males had the highest median annual earnings of the eight race–gender groups represented in the table. Asian/Pacific Islander males were the race–gender group with the next-highest average earnings and earned ninety-two cents for every dollar that non-Hispanic white males earned.[10] Non-Hispanic black males earned 75 percent of what non-Hispanic white males earn, or seventy-five cents for every dollar that non-Hispanic white males earned. Hispanic females had the lowest median earnings of all race–gender groups in Table 14.2, earning 49 percent of what non-Hispanic white males earned.

In addition to median annual earnings by education level for race–gender groups, Table 14.2 also shows the number of persons with earnings

Table 14.2   Median Annual Earnings in 1999 by Educational Attainment for Persons Aged Twenty-five to Sixty-four by Race–Gender Groups: Year-Round, Full-Time Workers (in thousands)

	Total (all education levels)	Not high school graduate	High school graduate, incl. GED[a]	Some college, no degree	Bachelor's degree
All Races, male and female	$32,905	$19,862	$27,192	$31,853	$43,553
Number of persons with earnings	88,615	7,727	27,749	16,839	18,436
Percentage of total	100%	9%	31%	19%	21%
Non-Hispanic white males	$41,479	$26,900	$34,941	$40,024	$51,922
Number of persons with earnings	38,944	2,234	12,148	7,208	9,047
Percentage of total	100%	6%	31%	19%	23%
Non-Hispanic white females	$29,191	$17,902	$22,637	$27,164	$36,975
Number of persons with earnings	26,084	1,124	8,403	5,145	5,757
Percentage of total	100%	4%	32%	20%	22%
Non-Hispanic black males	$31,061	$22,061	$27,487	$31,910	$40,907
Number of persons with earnings	4,922	522	1,874	1,165	749
Percentage of total	100%	11%	38%	24%	15%
Non-Hispanic black females	$25,226	$15,545	$20,625	$25,304	$34,718
Number of persons with earnings	5,253	458	1,716	1,326	848
Percentage of total	100%	9%	33%	25%	16%
Hispanic males	$25,284	$19,010	$25,286	$31,487	$41,294
Number of persons with earnings	5,506	2,088	1,666	813	459
Percentage of total	100%	38%	30%	15%	8%
Hispanic females	$20,269	$13,766	$19,973	$24,220	$32,040
Number of persons with earnings	3,285	910	1,014	615	347
Percentage of total	100%	28%	31%	19%	11%
Asian/Pacific Islander males	$38,287	$20,405	$25,907	$31,282	$46,223
Number of persons with earnings	2,131	170	420	271	625
Percentage of total	100%	8%	20%	13%	29%
Asian/Pacific Islander females	$30,478	$19,334	$21,137	$26,912	$35,974
Number of persons with earnings	1,546	142	333	200	536
Percentage of total	100%	9%	22%	13%	35%

Source: U.S. Census Bureau (2000).
[a]GED: General Educational Development.

by education level for each race–gender group. Note that numbers of persons are in thousands. The percentages shown below the number of persons are row percentages, indicating what percentage of the total number of persons with earnings in that race–gender group belong to each educational category. For example, among non-Hispanic black males with earnings in 1999, the largest education category was high school graduate, including General Educational Development (GED), with 38 percent of non-Hispanic black males belonging to this education category. Hispanic males are concentrated in the category of those without a high school diploma, whereas Asian/Pacific Islander males and females are concentrated in the bachelor's degree category.

One way to understand the role of education

in earnings differentials by race and gender is to analyze earnings differentials by race–gender groups within educational attainment levels. To do so, one might inquire about the average earnings for those who have the same levels of education but belong to different race–gender groups. For example, how large are earnings differentials between black and white male high school graduates?

For each of the educational attainment levels included in Table 14.2, non-Hispanic white males have the highest median annual earnings. The rank order of race–gender groups from the next-highest to the lowest median annual earnings varies according to educational attainment category. For example, among persons who have not completed a high school diploma, the race–gender group with the highest median annual earnings after non-Hispanic white males ($26,900) is non-Hispanic black males ($22,061). Among persons who have completed high school, the race–gender group with the next-highest median annual earnings is non-Hispanic white females. The earnings differentials by race–gender group persist even for persons with the same levels of educational attainment. For example, black female high school graduates earn fifty-nine cents for every dollar that a non-Hispanic white male high school graduate earns.

For many race–gender groups, bachelor's degree holders are able to narrow the earnings gap with non-Hispanic whites to a greater extent than are members of the same race–gender group who have less education. For example, Asian/Pacific Islander male college graduates earn 89 percent of what non-Hispanic white male college graduates earn, but the Asian/Pacific Islander males with less education earn from 74 percent to 78 percent of what non-Hispanic males with the same education earn.[11] However, this pattern does not hold for black men or for Asian American/Pacific Islander women. Black male high school and college graduates earn 79 percent of what non-Hispanic white males with the same education earn; black males with less than high school diplomas earn 82 percent.

Earnings vary by educational outcome. Median earnings are higher for bachelor's degree

recipients than for those with lower levels of educational attainment. However, education does not fully explain differentials in earnings for race–gender groups. Differentials persist within levels of educational attainment.

CONCLUSION

This chapter documents how educational attainment critically matters for labor force participation, unemployment, occupation, and earnings. Across race–gender groups, education has a powerful impact on labor market outcomes: persons with college degrees have higher labor force participation rates, lower unemployment rates, and higher earnings than high school graduates or persons with less than a high school diploma. Finally, educational attainment matters for race and gender differences in the labor market. Observed differences in labor market outcomes across race–gender groups are clearly related to, and depend in part on, educational attainment.

NOTES

1. See Table 14.1 for statistics on labor force participation and unemployment rates.

2. This example refers to persons who have completed a high school diploma but no additional schooling.

3. The age group referred to in this section is twenty-five years and over. This age group is used because most persons have completed their formal schooling by age twenty-five.

4. The unemployment rates reported in this section are based on annual averages for the year 2001 published by the Bureau of Labor Statistics in 2002. The original data source is the Current Population Survey.

5. The median is one type of average that economists use to compare average earnings across demographic groups. Median annual earnings for a particular demographic group means that half of the persons in that group had earnings above the median and that the other half had earnings below the median.

6. These definitions come from the Census

Bureau's household-based survey, the Current Population Survey. More information on these and other definitions used in the Current Population Survey are available on the Internet at www.bls.census.gov/cps/ads/2002/sfiledif.htm.

7. Part-time workers would have lower earnings on average because they work fewer hours per week, and part-year or seasonal workers would have lower average earnings because they work fewer weeks per year.

8. The earnings estimates for high school graduates reported here include persons who have completed a General Educational Development (GED) equivalency certificate.

9. Here *college graduates* refers to persons who have completed a bachelor's degree or higher.

10. We calculate the relative earnings of Asian/Pacific Islander males (relative to non-Hispanic white males) by dividing the median annual earnings of Asian/Pacific Islander males ($38,287) by the median annual earnings of non-Hispanic white males ($41,479).

11. Asian/Pacific Islander males who have not completed a high school diploma earn 76 percent of what non-Hispanic white males with this level of education earn. Asian/Pacific Islander male high school graduates earn 74 percent of what non-Hispanic white male high school graduates earn. Earnings of Asian/Pacific Islander males with some college, no degree, are 78 percent of earnings of non-Hispanic white males with some college, no degree.

REFERENCES

U.S. Bureau of Labor Statistics. 1991. *Employment and Earnings.* January issue. Annual average tables. Washington, D.C.: Government Printing Office.

———. 2001a. *Employment and Earnings.* January issue. Available at www.bls.gov (accessed May 25, 2002).

———. 2001b. "Employment Status of the Civilian Noninstitutional Population by Sex, Age, Race, and Hispanic Origin: 2000 Annual Averages." Available at www.bls.gov/lau/table12full00.pdf (accessed June 5, 2002).

———. 2002a. Unpublished tabulations from the Current Population Survey.

———. 2002b. *Employment and Earnings.* January issue. Available at www.bls.gov (accessed December 20, 2002).

U.S. Census Bureau. 2000. "Educational Attainment in the United States, March 2000, Detailed Tables." Available at www.census.gov/population/www/socdemo/education/p20-536.html (accessed May 28, 2002).

———. 2001. *Statistical Abstract of the United States 2001.* Available at www.census.gov/prod/2002pubs/01statab/stat-ab01.html (accessed June 5, 2002).

———. 2002. *Current Population Survey (CPS): Definitions and Explanations.* Available at www.census.gov/population/www/cps/cpsdef.html (accessed January 15, 2003).

15

Persistent Racial Discrimination in the Labor Market
PATRICK L. MASON

Left to its own devices, competitive markets will not necessarily eliminate racial discrimination. During "the Nadir"—1877 to World War I—racial inequality in occupational status increased even as racial inequality in literacy declined. During 1974–2000, racial inequality in wages and access to employment expanded, even as racial inequality in the quantity and the quality of education declined. In both instances racial discrimination in the labor market more than offset the gains African Americans made in reducing the skills gap. Periods of declining racial discrimination in the labor market are characterized by strong social movements among African Americans, by declining or low national unemployment rate, and by vigorous action by the federal government aimed at attacking directly labor market discrimination against African Americans. Periods of progress were also initiated by substantial national crises that threaten the very existence of the nation.

The 1964 Civil Rights Act made it illegal for an employer to discriminate against an individual based on race, color, religion, sex, or national origin in terms of hiring, firing, compensation, conditions, and privileges. Among other objectives, this legislation sought to eliminate racial discrimination in the labor market. It failed. At least one-half of today's black–white inequality in compensation can be explained by racial discrimination in the labor market.

Racial discrimination in the labor market exists when there is differential treatment of workers because of nonessential differences in characteristics; that is, economically identical persons are treated differently within the market because of their race. Racial discrimination may affect all elements of the labor market process: establishment of employment pools, hiring practices, and requirements; wages and salaries; training opportunities; employment segregation within and between firms; evaluations; layoffs; working conditions and benefits; hours of work; and work schedule.

Economists make two distinctions that are important for our discussion in this chapter. One, racial inequality in the labor market is not the same thing as racial discrimination in the labor market. Accordingly, there is no disagreement that there are large and persistent racial differences in compensation, hours, and working conditions; but there is considerable disagreement among economists regarding how much—if any—of this inequality is due to racial discrimination within the labor market. Consider the fact that African American men earn about seventy cents for every dollar earned by white men. The issue in this instance is how much of the average difference in pay can be attributed to the average difference in skill, and therefore productivity, and how much of the difference in pay can be attributed to the racially differential treatment among equally skilled persons in the labor market. Second, economists are also careful to note the distinction between racial discrimination in the labor market and non-labor-market discrimination that contributes to racial inequality in labor market outcomes. No discrimination within the labor market means that individuals are paid in strict accordance with their level of skill, but non-labor-market discrimination may produce racial differences in skill. For example, a variety of activities may affect skill development before entering the labor market and skill enhancement after entering the labor market. Such activities include education and access to high-quality schools; access to information and capital via interpersonal relationships such as marriage; membership in private clubs; religious affiliation; and reduced parental resources—time, money, and education—because of past discrimination.

Accordingly, racial inequality in labor market outcomes may occur for four reasons:

1. racial discrimination within the labor market;
2. racial discrimination in non-labor-market activities that affect skill development and access to information and capital;
3. differences in the behaviors and values of individuals and families that affect skill accumulation; and
4. differences in the innate abilities of individuals.

Most economists agree that although the innate abilities of individuals may differ quite markedly, the average level of innate ability is equal for large aggregations, such as a racial group. Also, there is strong evidence that black–white income inequality cannot be linked to black–white differences in family values and behaviors. Accordingly, nearly all of the black–white racial inequality in earnings can be attributed to discrimination, either within the labor market or in non-labor-market activities that affect skill accumulation and other vital aspects of income attainment. The remainder of this chapter explores trends in racial inequality and racial discrimination in the labor market between 1964 and 2000.

RACIAL INEQUALITY: 1964–2000

Racial inequality in the labor market has been characterized by alternating periods of progress and retrenchment (see Table 15.1).[1] For example, during the years 1964–1973, African American men earned an average weekly wage of $447. By the period 1974–1980, this average had grown to $531, but the average weekly wage of African American men declined to $515 during the 1981–1990 period. Finally, during the years 1991–2000, the weekly wage of black men increased substantially, to $568.

The movement of African American men toward racial equality with white men has declined since 1974. In the years just after the end of Jim Crow—that is, 1964–1973—African American men earned sixty-five cents in weekly wages for every dollar received by white men. By the 1974–1980 period, African American men earned seventy-two cents for every dollar received by white men. This heady progress toward racial equality led liberal Harvard economist Richard Freeman to speak of a "collapse in labor market discrimination." Observing the same data, another highly respected scholar, sociologist William Julius Wilson, published a widely received manuscript entitled *The Declining Significance of Race* (1974). Nevertheless, by the mid-1990s, increasing racial inequality forced Freeman to openly query, "What went wrong?" During the 1980s and 1990s, African American men earned just sixty-nine cents for every dollar received by white men. So, rather than declining, male racial inequality in earnings actually increased during the years 1974–2000.

Access to employment also declined dramatically for African American men during the period 1964–2000. Average weeks worked fell by a month, dropping from thirty-seven weeks to thirty-three weeks. The employment:population ratio measures the fraction of working-age persons who are currently employed. For black men this ratio declined from 0.74 to 0.63. The unemployment:population ratio is the fraction of working-age persons who do not have jobs but are actively seeking employment. This ratio doubled during the late 1970s and 1980s, rising from 6 percent to 12

Table 15.1   Individual Labor Market Outcomes by Race and Gender, 1964–2000

	1964–1973	*1974–1980*	*1981–1990*	*1991–2000*
African American women				
Weekly wage	$277	$359	$396	$451
Weeks worked last year	24	24	27	31
Employment:population ratio	0.48	0.49	0.54	0.62
Unemployment:population ratio	0.05	0.08	0.09	0.06
Nonparticipation rate	0.47	0.43	0.37	0.32
African American men				
Weekly wage	$447	$531	$515	$568
Weeks worked last year	37	32	32	33
Employment:population ratio	0.74	0.63	0.61	0.63
Unemployment:population ratio	0.06	0.11	0.12	0.08
Nonparticipation rate	0.19	0.25	0.25	0.26
White women				
Weekly wage	$344	$371	$419	$503
Weeks worked last year	22	26	31	34
Employment:population ratio	0.45	0.54	0.62	0.69
Unemployment:population ratio	0.02	0.04	0.04	0.03
Nonparticipation rate	0.53	0.43	0.34	0.28
White men				
Weekly wage	$688	$735	$750	$828
Weeks worked last year	41	40	40	41
Employment:population ratio	0.82	0.79	0.79	0.80
Unemployment:population ratio	0.03	0.05	0.05	0.03
Nonparticipation rate	0.13	0.14	0.14	0.15

Source: Mason (2003).
Note: Weekly wages are adjusted for $2,000, using CPI-U-X1. The CPI-U-X1 is the Consumer Price Index, All Urban Consumers, Rental Equivalence housing adjustment. This schedule makes the CPI calculations for 1967–1982 compatible with the methodology used to calculate the CPI from 1983 to the present.

percent, before declining to 8 percent during the years 1991–2000. The fraction of working-age persons who do not have jobs but are not actively seeking employment is called the *nonparticipation rate*. This ratio increased from 19 percent to 26 percent, with nearly all of the increase initiated during the 1974–1980 period. The most severe increases in nonparticipation have been for the youngest and least educated black men; nevertheless, the nonparticipation rate has increased for college-educated African American men and for prime-aged males. For example, during the 1964–1973 period, the nonparticipation rate for African American men between twenty-five and fifty-four years of age was 3 percent. From 1974 to 1990, nonpar-

ticipation for this group rose to 5 percent, and from 1991 to 2000 the nonparticipation rate for African American men aged twenty-five and fifty-four years was 7 percent.

Black women improved their labor market earnings relative to black men, but they lost ground relative to white women. During the 1964–1973 period, African American women earned just sixty-two cents for every dollar earned by African American men. By the 1990s, this ratio was seventy-nine cents. The average weekly wage of African American women increased from $277 to $451 between 1965 and 2000. Mean weeks worked increased from twenty-four weeks to thirty-one weeks, with all of the growth occurring between the periods

1974–1980 and 1991–2000. The nonparticipation rate declined from 47 percent to 32 percent. The increase in labor force participation led to a large increase in the employment: population ratio and a modest increase in the unemployment:population ratio. The former rose from 48 percent to 62 percent, whereas the latter increased from 5 percent to 6 percent.

CURRENT RACIAL DISCRIMINATION IN THE LABOR MARKET

What are the long-term changes in the extent of racial discrimination in the labor market? More specifically, what fraction of the racial inequality in weekly wages in Table 15.1 can be attributed to racial discrimination within the labor market? Has discrimination increased or decreased over time? In this chapter, we examine racial discrimination among men and women separately, since men and women have different degrees of attachment to the labor market. Women often have greater housework and child care responsibilities than men do, so regardless of race one might reasonably expect a gender gap in weekly wages since men are able to direct more effort toward market work than women are. Next, for men and women both, we know that inequality in weekly wages occur because of differences in pay per region of the country. For example, wages are higher in California (West) and New York (Northeast) than they are in Mississippi (South). Over one-half of all African Americans live in the South versus about one-third of all whites; so, some racial inequality is related to racial differences in regional location and therefore does not represent racial discrimination within the labor market. Economists assume that pay is governed by productivity on the job and that individual productivity is directly related to individual skill. However, individual productivity and individual skill are difficult to measure; instead, economists assume that such factors as years of education and potential labor market experience are reasonable representatives of individual skill. We follow this practice.

Concluding, we measure racial wage discrimination in the labor market as the fraction of the racial weekly wage differential that remains, even when observing individuals of the same sex, living in the same region of the country, having the same years of education as well as identical years of work experience.

Table 15.2 presents the results of our analysis. The sample is limited to those who identified themselves as either African American or white. Hispanic status is treated as an ethnic identity; hence, Hispanics may belong to either racial group. African American women of the South show continuous improvement in the labor market during the years 1964–2000, whereas African American women outside the South show continuous deterioration from 1974 onward. African American men of the South show uneven and discontinuous change in the labor market during the 1964–2000 period, whereas African American men outside the South show continuous deterioration from 1964 onward. For example, outside of the South, African American men suffered a 10 percent wage penalty in the 1964–1973 period but a 17 percent wage penalty in the 1991–2000 period. During the same periods, the premium for non-Southern African American women moved from 14 percent to 9 percent. Regardless of gender, outside of the South, there is greater racial discrimination today than that observed during the late 1960s.

Within the South, in the years immediately following the end of Jim Crow (1964–1973), African American men were paid nearly 38 percent less than observationally identical white men, and African American women were paid 39 percent less than their respective counterparts. During the 1974–1980 period, the weekly wage penalty of the African American male of the South declined to 25 percent and that of the African American female of the South to just 7 percent. Clearly, the success of the civil rights and black power movements in eliminating Jim Crow had a dramatically positive effect on the relative wages of African Americans. However, since the years 1974–1980 the wage penalty of the African American male of the South has grown from 25 percent to 27 percent (1981–1990) before dropping to 22 percent (1991–2000).

Table 15.2. Extent of Discrimination by Race and Ethnicity, 1964–2000

Men	*1964–1973*	*1974–1980*	*1981–1990*	*1991–2000*
Non-South				
African American	−0.1010	−0.1052	−0.1537	−0.1720
Head is Hispanic	0.0085	−0.0211	−0.0098	−0.0245
South				
African American	−0.3773	−0.2548	−0.2715	−0.2153
Head is Hispanic	−0.0206	−0.1094	−0.1118	−0.1151
Women				
Non-South				
African American	0.1386	0.2213	0.1466	0.0866
Head is Hispanic	0.1953	0.1808	0.1480	0.0735
South				
African American	−0.3949	−0.0738	−0.0514	−0.0235
Head is Hispanic	0.0157	−0.0129	−0.0135	−0.0447

Source: U.S. Department of Labor, Current Population Survey, Annual Demographic Files, 1965–2001.

THE CONTINUING IMPACT OF THE NADIR

The current increase in racial discrimination within the labor market is not without historical precedent. Jim Crow was established throughout the South between the end of Reconstruction and the beginning of America's participation in World War I—that is, between 1877 and 1914. Civil rights historians refer to this era as "the Nadir," an era that witnessed a great increase in racial inequality and racial violence directed toward African Americans. During this time, between two and three blacks (usually men) were lynched per week. In 1895, Booker T. Washington gave his infamous Atlanta exposition speech. In 1896 the Supreme Court used the *Plessy v. Ferguson* case to establish "separate but equal" as the law of the land. Yet, the Nadir was also a period of impressive achievement among African Americans. Education, literacy, and entrepreneurship increased dramatically. The National Association for the Advancement of Colored People, the National Urban League, and scores of historically black colleges and universities were founded during this era. This period also saw the formation of each of the major black church organizations, such as the National Baptist Convention, African Methodist Episcopal, and Church of God in Christ.

Darity, Dietrich, and Guilkey (1997) have shown that in 1880 the labor market characteristics of African American men reduced their occupational status by nearly 30 percent relative to the average male (Table 15.3). However, racial discrimination in the market lowered African American occupational status by 31 percent. By 1910 the reduction in occupational status due to deficient labor market characteristics was just 19 percent, but the impact of labor market discrimination on occupational status increased from 31 to 44 percent. Darity, Dietrich, and Guilkey explain that

decreasing losses associated with deficient characteristics tracks well with the sharp rise in black male literacy, while increasing losses attributable to disadvantageous returns to characteristics track well with the hardening of Jim Crow practices in the U.S. South. This may suggest evidence of a simple pattern of endogenous discrimination: as blacks became harder to exclude from preferential employment and status positions on grounds of qualifications, outright exclusion intensified. (304)

Table 15.3   Impact of Racial Characteristics and Market Discrimination on the Occupational Status for African American Men, 1880–1990

	1880	1900	1910	1980	1990
Characteristics	− 0.297	− 0.224	− 0.185	− 0.148	− 0.110
Discrimination	− 0.312	− 0.385	− 0.439	− 0.165	− 0.139

Source: Darity, Dietrich, and Guilkey (1997).

In short, the researchers document that racial discrimination in the market increased during the Nadir even though African Americans were closing the gap in skill differences. This pattern of declining skill differences and increasing racial discrimination was reproduced during the years 1974–2000.

Darity, Dietrich, and Guilkey (1998) then assess whether group occupational status in 1880, 1900, and 1910 had an impact on individual occupational status in 1980 and 1990. At the turn of the century, African American men attained lower occupational status because of market discrimination and lower-skill-related characteristics compared to that of white men. The lower-skill-related characteristics among African American males were directly related to slavery and the rise and consolidation of Jim Crow in the South, where 90 percent of all African Americans resided as late as 1910. Darity, Dietrich, and Guilkey show that the effect of market discrimination and skill deficits continued to have a negative impact on the occupational status of African American males one hundred years later. Of course, some white men had skill characteristics similar to those of African Americans at the turn of the century; however, they also received race-based market premiums that they were able to pass on to their ethnic descendants some four generations later. Current generations of whites continue to benefit from past racism while current generations of African Americans are harmed by past racism.

ALTERNATIVE EXPLANATIONS AND ALTERNATIVE EVIDENCE

Does the weekly wage premium obtained by African American women represent market discrimination in favor of African American women? The conventional answer among economists is that actual labor market experience was higher among African American women than it was among white women until the mid-1990s. Hence, African American women enjoyed a small wage premium because they were more likely to participate in the labor market and because they worked longer hours per week. Married and college-educated African American women were much more likely to be market participants than their white counterparts were. The differential between African American and white females in actual experience and other aspects of labor force attachment declined with the massive entry into the labor force of married white women from the 1970s onward. As the racial differential in labor force attachment declined, the premium for African American women also declined.

Explanations of changes in male racial inequality have been more contentious. The orthodox explanation argues that male racial inequality has increased even as male racial discrimination in the labor market has been eliminated. Orthodox economists argue that the results of tables 15.1 and 15.2 do not reflect increasing racial and ethnic discrimination. Rather, the assertion is that racial and ethnic inequality increased because general inequality increased. General inequality increased because skill-biased technological progress created an increasing premium for skilled labor. According to Juhn, Murphy, and Pierce (1991), the average African American wage earner has less skill than the average white wage earner. Additionally, some time after the mid-1970s, economic growth became heavily biased toward highly skilled workers. The demand for such workers grew much faster than the supply did, while the demand for less-skilled workers grew at a slower rate and even declined. Hence, a rising premium for skill occurred as wages for the most skilled workers grew rapidly and as wages for the least skilled grew slowly. As inequality among whites increased, owing to a rising skill premium, interracial inequality between whites and African Americans and between non-Hispanics and Hispanics also increased because African Americans and Hispanics are disproportionately located in the lower half of the white and non-Hispanic skill distributions. The Juhn, Murphy, and Pierce argument preserves the orthodox faith that market competition will ensure that individual wage rates are determined strictly by individual productive ability.

An alternative explanation focuses on the role of power in determining labor market outcomes. Specifically, we may explain the changes presented in Tables 15.1 and 15.2 by arguing that the bargaining power of the average worker declined after the severe recession of 1974–1975, with the sharpest drops in bargaining power occurring for the least educated workers. The high levels of unemployment from the mid-1970s to the mid-1990s, combined with the foreign penetration of many domestic industries, greatly reduced the bargaining power of the least educated workers. Further, racial and ethnic discrimination increased as affirmative action among federal contractors was severely crippled after 1980, when antidiscrimination law enforcement became considerably lax. As the non-Hispanic white male unemployment rate increased in the wake of the 1974–1975 recession, racial job competition increased, and many African Americans were driven out of good jobs and stable employment.

There is not much evidence to support the skill-biased technological change explanation of racial inequality. I have presented evidence (Mason 2000) that the progress toward racial wage equality came to a halt by the mid-1970s; that is, there was declining racial wage discrimination within the labor market from the mid-1960s to the early or mid-1970s. However, the rising premium for skill did not begin until sometime between 1979 and 1983. Hence, one cannot say that increasing racial inequality is simply a reflection of an increasing premium for skill. Rodgers and Spriggs (1996) also find that skill-biased techno-

logical progress cannot explain much of the increasing racial wage inequality, though it can explain increasing inequality within racial groups. The difficulty with the skill-biased technical change explanation of increasing racial inequality is that the racial skills gap has declined dramatically since 1974; hence, one would expect that racial inequality would also have declined. But it has increased.

Audit studies and skin-shade studies also provide compelling evidence of racial discrimination in the labor market. Skin-shade studies take advantage of the fact that African Americans and Latinos have a variety of skin shades and phenotypes, ranging from dark complexions and African or Native American features to light complexions and European facial features. To the extent that there is racial discrimination in the labor market, we would expect that African Americans and Latinos with the darkest and most non-European phenotype would obtain lower income, employment, and occupational status than African Americans or Latinos with the lightest and most European phenotype.

Audit studies are labor market experiments where carefully matched pairs of individuals (black–white or Hispanic–non-Hispanic white) who are otherwise equal, except for their racial identity, are sent into the labor market to obtain employment at the same set of businesses. Typically, audit studies find rates of employment discrimination against African Americans and Latinos in excess of 25 percent (Riach and Rich 2002). For example, Bendick, Jackson, and Reinoso (1994) report that in a 1990 audit experiment carried out in Washington, D.C., testers found that black applicants were treated less favorably than equally qualified whites more than 71 percent of the time.[2] Raich and Rich (2002) summarize a series of audit studies that report similar results. In 1992, Hispanic testers in Washington, D.C., were treated less favorably than whites 25 percent of the time. Hispanic discrimination occurred in the process of individuals trying to obtain an interview, whereas discrimination against African Americans occurred as individuals attempted to obtain a job offer. In 1989, Hispanic testers in Chicago encountered interview discrimination 21 percent of the time. Hispanic testers in a 1990 San Diego audit faced job discrimination 11 percent of the time. Black testers in a 1990 Chicago study faced interview discrimination 8 percent of the time but were confronted with job discrimination 10 percent of the time in a 1990 Washington, D.C., study. Finally, a 1998 San Francisco audit study revealed that African Americans were confronted with job discrimination 38 percent of the time that they attempted to obtain employment.

Skin-shade studies have demonstrated sizable racial penalties within the labor market for those having a dark complexion. Keith and Herring (1991) examined the impact of skin-tone differences on individual and family income, years of education, and occupational status. Their data are taken from the 1979–1980 National Survey of Black Americans. They divided their sample into five skin-tone groups: very dark, dark brown, medium brown, light brown, very light. They found that an association between groups when comparing their relative physical similarity to "whiteness"—that is, comparing otherwise identical dark-brown African Americans with very dark African Americans, medium-brown African Americans with dark-brown African Americans, and so forth. Those who were "closer" to whiteness had higher levels of educational attainment, greater occupational status, larger personal income, and larger family income. The skin-tone effects on income, education, and occupation are in addition to other factors that also affect social status: parental education, sex, age, region, urban location, marital status, and personal education and occupation. Indeed, Keith and Herring found that skin tone had a larger impact on educational attainment than sex, region, or urban location did. Except for the individual's education, skin tone is the major determinant of occupational status. Similarly, skin tone has a larger impact on personal income and family income than parental education or urban location does.[3]

Among many others, Mark Hill (2000) confirms the results of Keith and Kerring's work. Specifically, he examined the occupational achievements of a sample of African American men who were young children in 1920. He divided his sample into "black" and "mulatto" according to the racial identity given by the head of household on the 1920 census. Mulattoes have very much lighter skin tones than blacks do. Hill found that mulattoes have more than two-and-a-half times greater odds of attaining a white-collar job than blacks do. Further, he found that differences in the social origins of blacks and mulattos are responsible for only 10 to 20 percent of the color gap in adult occupational attainment.

ARE IMMIGRANTS A SOURCE OF LABOR MARKET DISCRIMINATION AGAINST BLACKS?

Recent empirical studies have tried to examine the impact of immigration on the socioeconomic status of African Americans. There is little substantiation of the conventional wisdom that immigrants lower the earnings and income of African Americans. Borjas (1998) estimates that immigration has reduced the income of the typical African American worker by about one hundred dollars per year, even as immigration may have raised the overall level of American income.

There is a popular belief that "immigrants take undesirable jobs that native-born Americans are unwilling to take." Hamermesh (1998) shows this is a misconception. According to Hamermesh, immigrants and natives of similar characteristics—education, experience, gender, region of the country, and so forth—tend to hold equally desirable jobs. However, when compared to immigrants and native-born workers, African Americans are more likely to work in jobs with evening and night shifts, in jobs with a greater risk of injury, and in jobs where injuries are longer lasting when they do occur; and they are also less likely to report other amenities that increase the unpleasantness of work. In short, Hamermesh reports that African American workers take jobs that otherwise similar native-born whites, native-born Hispanics, and immigrants are unwilling to take. Reimers (1998) adds an important bit of evidence that shows how unskilled immigrants compete most directly with the highest-earning native-born high school dropouts. Specifically, Reimers finds that a 1 percent increase in the fraction of unskilled immigrants in the local labor force will lead to a 4 percent reduction in earnings for the highest-paid black high school dropouts.

CONCLUSION

Left to its own tendencies a capitalist economy with competitive markets will not necessarily eliminate racial discrimination. Indeed, we have seen that during the Nadir (1877–World War I) racial inequality in occupational status increased even as racial inequality in literacy declined. During the years 1974–2000, racial inequality in wages and access to employment expanded even as racial inequality in the quantity and the quality of education declined. In both instances racial discrimination in the labor market more than offset the gains African Americans made in reducing the skills gap. Reconstruction (1865–1877) and the civil rights and black power movements (1945–1973) were periods of declining racial discrimination in the labor market. Interestingly, both periods of progress were characterized by strong social movements among African Americans, declining or low national unemployment rates, and vigorous action by the federal government aimed at directly attacking labor market discrimination against African Americans. Both periods of progress were initiated by substantial national crises that threatened the very existence of the nation. Today, there is no national crisis threatening the nation's existence; the national unemployment rate is rising; the federal government and state governments have become increasingly uninterested in racial discrimination against African Americans; and social movements among African Americans have not demonstrated much political economic strength in recent years. Of course, the labor market is similar to the stock market; that is, past performance is not necessarily a predictor of future outcomes. Nevertheless, the current circumstances do strongly suggest that African Americans and others concerned with eliminating racial discrimination in the labor market should not accept the complacent conceit of conservatism that competitive markets will automatically end racial discrimination in the labor market.

NOTES

1. The period 1964–1965 marks the end of the Jim Crow era in the South, whereas the years 1974–1975, 1981–1982, 1991–1992, and 2001–2003 mark periods of deep recession.

2. The percentages for employment discrimination are taken from Raich and Rich (2002) rather than from Bendick, Jackson, and Reinoso (1994). Raich and Rich summarize several studies, and each has a slightly different way of computing the extent of discrimination. For consistency, each case in the text reports the discrimination fraction given by Raich and Rich.

3. For men, Keith and Herring (1991) find that skin tone affects only personal income status. For women, there are skin tone effects for education, occupation, personal income, and family income.

BIBLIOGRAPHY

Bendick, M., C. W. Jackson, and V. A. Reinoso. 1994. "Measuring Employment Discrimination through Controlled Experiments." *Review of Black Political Economy* 23, no. 1 (Summer): 25–48.

Borjas, George J. 1998. "Do Blacks Gain or Lose from Immigration?" In *Help or Hindrance? The Economic Implications of Immigration for Latin Americans,* ed. Daniel S. Hamermesh and Frank D. Bean, 51–74. New York: Russell Sage Foundation.

Darity, William, Jr., Jason Dietrich, and David K. Guilkey. 1997. "Racial and Ethnic Inequality in the United States: A Secular Perspective." *American Economic Association Papers and Proceedings* 87, no. 2 (May): 301–305.

———. 1998. "Persistent Advantage or Disadvantage? Decomposing the Effects of the Past on Present Patterns of Racial and Ethnic Inequality in the USA." Mimeo, Department of Economics, University of North Carolina, Chapel Hill.

Hamermesh, Daniel S. 1998. "Immigration and the Quality of Jobs." In *Help or Hindrance? The Economic Implications of Immigration for Latin Americans,* ed. Daniel S. Hamermesh and Frank D. Bean, 75–106. New York: Russell Sage Foundation.

Hamermesh, Daniel S., and Frank D. Bean, eds. 1998. *Help or Hindrance? The Economic Implications of Immigration for Latin Americans.* New York: Russell Sage Foundation.

Hill, M. E. 2000. "Color Differences in the Socio-economic Status of African American Men: Results of a Longitudinal Study." *Social Forces* 78, no. 4 (June): 1437–1460.

Juhn, C., K. Murphy, and B. Pierce. 1991. "Accounting for the Slowdown in Black-White Wage Convergence." In *Workers and Their Wages*, ed. M. Kosters, 107–143. Washington, D.C.: AEI Press.

Keith, V. M., and C. Herring. 1991. "Skin Tone and Stratification in the Black Community." *American Journal of Sociology* 97, no. 3 (November): 760–778.

Mason, P. 2000. "Persistent Discrimination: Racial Disparity in the US, 1967–1988." *American Economic Association Papers and Proceedings* 90, no. 2 (May): 312–316.

———. 2003. "Reproducing Racism: Reconstructing the Political Economy of Race from the Perspective of Stratification Economics." Unpublished manuscript.

Reimers, Cordelia W. 1998. "Unskilled Immigration and Changes in Wage Distributions of Black, Mexican American, and Non-Hispanic White Male Dropouts." In *Help or Hindrance? The Economic Implications of Immigration for Latin Americans,* ed. Daniel S. Hamermesh and Frank D. Bean, 107–148. New York: Russell Sage Foundation.

Riach, P. A., and J. Rich. 2002. "Field Experiments of Discrimination in the Market Place." Special issue, *Economic Journal* 112, no. 483 (November): F480–F518.

Rodgers, W. M., III, and William E. Spriggs. 1996. "What Does the AFQT Really Measure: Race, Wages and Schooling and the AFQT Score." *Review of Black Political Economy* 24, no. 4 (Spring): 13–46.

16

Racial Inequality and African Americans' Disadvantage in the Credit and Capital Markets

GARY A. DYMSKI and PATRICK L. MASON

This chapter explains how racial redlining and discrimination in credit and capital markets work to reproduce and even worsen racial inequality in the distribution of wealth and income. It then turns to historical experience. It first discusses the period before the 1960s; next, it focuses on blacks' access to credit during the post–Civil Rights Act period—in particular, on federal policies aimed at generating information on credit flows as well as creating equitable access to credit and capital. Finally, the chapter reviews the hard evidence of racial discrimination that has been found in recent studies and examines the public policy debate that this evidence has generated.

One of the primary economic legacies of slavery and racial oppression throughout U.S. history is an unequal racial distribution of wealth. This reflects not only patterns of inheritance but the operation of the credit and capital markets over time. Virtually all minority residents and business people have either experienced or heard of problems with access to credit and capital.

This chapter first explains how racial redlining and discrimination in credit and capital markets work to reproduce and even worsen racial inequality in the distribution of wealth and income. It then turns to historical experience. We briefly discuss the period before the 1960s; next, we turn our attention to blacks' access to credit during the post–Civil Rights Act period—that is, from the mid-1960s onward. In this period, pressure by the civil rights movement and by community-based activist organizations has led the federal government to establish nondiscrimination and community reinvestment principles for all banks. This, with the increased availability of standardized bank lending information (again, thanks to a federal mandate), has generated a public policy debate concerning whether banks engage in discriminatory practices. We briefly describe the status of this controversy, which involves several interrelated but separate questions: Is there discrimination against African Americans in the credit and capital markets? What about other minorities? What are the causes and effects of this discrimination? What have some of the responses to it been?

THE CREDIT MARKET, REDLINING, AND RACIAL DISCRIMINATION

Racial inequality in access to credit may occur because of racial differences in the economic characteristics of borrowers, racial discrimination, or redlining. If borrowers have economically different characteristics, they will be treated differently by the market. This type of differential treatment is not discrimination. Suppose there are two potential borrowers. They have identical income, identical debt, identical collateral; they live in the same neighborhood; they work in the same occupation; and they are the same age and gender. However, one borrower always pays bills on time while the second borrower has a much more spotty credit record. The second borrower frequently pays bills late and has some bills that are simply no longer being paid. Lenders make loans to make a profit. The borrower who does not pay on time or simply does not pay at all—that is, defaults on loan obligations—presents a less-profitable lending opportunity than the borrower who pays on time. Accordingly, the less-risky borrower has a higher chance of loan application approval and may even be given a loan at a lower interest rate than that to the risky borrower. So, if black and white loan applicants have different degrees of risk, they will not be treated equally in the market; but this unequal treatment does not reflect racial discrimination.

Redlining occurs when lenders charge higher interest rates or reject business loan applications to residents of one geographic area more so than to those of another geographic area, even when differences in the areas' economic characteristics are identical.[1] For example, white-owned businesses located in high-minority neighborhoods would have to pay higher interest rates on loans than white-owned businesses located in all-white neighborhoods. Similarly, when redlining occurs, black homeowners in a low-income inner-city neighborhood are more likely to be turned downed for a home-repair loan than economically identical black homeowners are in an affluent suburban neighborhood.

Racial discrimination in credit markets occurs when economically identical borrowers are treated differently by lenders. Suppose there are two sets of individuals, families, or businesses. They differ only according to race but not according to credit worthiness. Racial discrimination exists if these groups face different credit treatment by lenders—for example, one is charged a higher interest on loans, faces more stringent borrowing criteria, or has a lower probability of loan approval.

In general, racial discrimination in credit markets exists for three reasons:

Personal discrimination: unequal access to credit due to lenders' overt or covert big-otry—what economists like to call "racial preferences"—independent of applicants' credit worthiness, or ability and willingness to repay loans.[2] Personal discrimination can emphasize intentional behavior. Numerous court cases and congressional actions have declared this form of discrimination to be illegal, regardless of whether it is overt discrimination or disparate treatment. With overt discrimination a lender refuses to provide a loan to a person of color or charges a higher interest rate because of race. Disparate treatment occurs when a lender screens minority loan applications more harshly than white loan applications.

Rational discrimination: racially differential treatment because lenders use race or characteristics correlated with race to make predictions about borrowers' ability to repay debt and their probability of default.[3]

Structural discrimination: racially differential treatment in the credit market because of systematic disadvantages in the income, wealth, or other economic resources of minority applicants vis-à-vis white applicants.

Many analyses of discrimination in credit markets by economists focus almost entirely on the first type of discrimination. This means identifying racial perpetrators whose actions in markets result in unfair treatment of African Americans (or others).[4] But while they almost universally condemn unequal access to markets arising from personal discrimination, economists disagree sharply about whether the second two categories of discrimination are problematic and thus provide a context for corrective public policy.

Guttentag and Wachter (1981), for example, in one of the initial papers on redlining, acknowledge that because of the extensive segregation of American cities, together with the close correlation between race and differences in socioeconomic outcomes, banks may use neighborhood racial characteristics as a shorthand way of identifying neighborhoods in which economic risks are higher. If banks approve fewer loans in some neighborhoods on the basis of neighborhood race—that is, if banks implement statistical discrimination—this is simply a way of maximizing profits. Similarly, the asymmetric-information model of credit markets by Stiglitz and Weiss (1981) points out that banks might rationally redline minority neighborhoods if race is a signal of higher risk. These analysts do not morally condone statistical discrimination of this type; but their method of approaching issues on the basis of whether any given behavior can be understood as "rational" limits vary sharply the range of behaviors they can classify as requiring corrective action. Structural discrimination is completely off-limits in models like these, because it stems from resource differences that market participants have no responsibility to reduce.

This means that economists who base their thinking on agent-based models of behavior are unable to fully embrace the liberal paradigm to racial injustice described in chapter 3. Their modeling approach makes them reluctant to condemn statistical and structural discrimination, both of which follow from "rational" behavior.

The problem is that it is not so easy in practice to draw a line between the three types of discrimination in credit markets. At first glance, personal and structural discrimination seem quite different, but they are interlinked. Any personal discrimination that results in lower credit flows—and hence to lower rates of business creation, home ownership, and wealth accumulation for minorities in any one period—will increase structural discrimination in future periods.

Rational and structural discrimination are also interrelated. Suppose credit is allocated on the basis of current levels of wealth and prospective levels of earned income. Minorities are subject to structural discrimination if they have lower average wealth levels than whites do and are chosen less often for loans on this basis. If wealth levels are the same for minorities and whites, minorities are subject to rational discrimination if loans are based on prospective income and if minorities' average prospective incomes are lower than that of whites. Of course, the expected income of minorities might be lower because of labor market discrimination. Hence, it is true that discrimination in the credit market interacts perversely with discrimination in other markets.

It is also true that rational and structural discrimination may have a disparate impact on minorities. Disparate impact occurs when a lender's commercial practices disproportion-

ately harm a racial minority without being justified by a legitimate business need. The courts have declared illegal those lending actions that have a disparate impact.

THE 1964 CIVIL RIGHTS ACT AND BLACKS' ACCESS TO CREDIT AND CAPITAL

For a century after the Civil War, blacks were systematically denied equal access to wealth, jobs, education, insurance, and credit. They were largely excluded from the benefits of the federal legislation that made possible the huge postwar boom in home ownership among middle-class and working-class whites. Especially important in facilitating homeownership was the creation of mortgage underwriting by the Federal Housing Administration and by the Veterans Administration. These mortgages, which accounted for over half of all home mortgages in the 1940s and 1950s, explicitly discriminated against minority neighborhoods.[5]

From the mid-1960s onward, federal law mandated an end to racial discrimination; as of the mid-1970s, banks were given a mandate to meet the credit needs of all portions of their market area, including lower-income and minority neighborhoods. These developments created a different environment for the debate regarding access to credit and capital. These developments reflected the turn of the civil rights movement toward economic as well as social rights, propelled by the urgency of urban rebellions and insurrections, white flight, and urban neighborhood instability.

The Civil Rights Act of 1964 and its subsequent amendments established that race is a protected category under the U.S. Constitution's equal protection doctrine and due process rights. For example, the Fair Housing Act of 1968 provides that "it shall be unlawful for any person . . . engaging in residential real estate-related transactions to discriminate against any person . . . because of race." Similarly, the Equal Credit Opportunity Act of 1974 makes racial discrimination against loan applicants unlawful. In subsequent years, these new laws have opened the way for court decisions that have defined the different types of discrimination along the lines set out here.

In the early 1970s, a national coalition of community-based inner-city groups pressured Congress into passing two laws. The Home Mortgage Disclosure Act (HMDA) of 1975 requires lenders to report the number and dollar volume of residential loans by census tract. The Community Reinvestment Act of 1977 requires banks to meet credit needs in their entire market area; specifically, lenders "have a continuing and affirmative obligation to help meet the credit needs of the local communities in which they are chartered."[6] In effect, it banned redlining. When the thrift bailout bill passed in 1989, the HMDA was amended to require more detailed reporting.[7] As of 1990, banks must report every mortgage loan application, including the applicant's race and income and the disposition of the application. The Community Reinvestment Act and HMDA became tools that autonomous, decentralized groups have used frequently to support demands on banks and local governments for access to more credit and capital.

THE EMPIRICAL CONTROVERSY OVER REDLINING AND DISCRIMINATION IN THE CREDIT MARKET

This framework of antidiscrimination and antiredlining laws has given rise to a huge body of empirical research and an ongoing and unresolved debate among analysts and policymakers concerning evidence of unfair credit market outcomes.[8]

From 1979 to 1991, activists and academics carried out redlining studies using the census-tract-level HMDA data on loan numbers and loan amounts. These studies typically showed disparities between minority and white neighborhoods, even after controlling for differences in neighborhood median income. Activists took these results as evidence of unfair bank behavior; skeptical analysts asserted that these flows might reflect either a lack of demand for credit

in minority areas or the failure of HMDA data to cover nonbank lenders.

These were the gaps in HMDA reporting that were addressed by changes attached to the thrift bailout bill. Given that the HMDA data provided information on an application-by-application basis and further provided data on every applicant's income level, race, and gender, such information could be used to show that minority applicants had a lower probability of obtaining loans even after controlling for applicant income, loan amount, and other factors. The strongest systematic result, which holds in virtually every study, is that black applicants are at a statistical disadvantage in obtaining loan approval. Skeptics, however, continued to register objections to the inference that this statistical advantage implied discrimination. Instead, skeptics alleged that black applicants are less creditworthy than white loan applicants are and that HMDA data do not provide sufficient information on individual credit worthiness. Lenders have better information on loan applicants than that presented in HMDA data. Presumably, this information demonstrates that blacks pay higher interest rates or have a lower probability of loan approval because they are more likely to default than are whites who appear to be identical in HMDA data.

Using 1990 lending data, researchers from the Federal Reserve Bank of Boston sought to directly assess the validity of objections raised by skeptics who did not believe that there was evidence of racial discrimination in credit markets.[9] These researchers had access to every factor considered by banks in their decision-making processes; after controlling for all these factors, they found that blacks had a 60 percent higher chance of being denied credit. Surprisingly, even this apparently definitive result has been challenged by some researchers and analysts who cannot bring themselves to believe that racial discrimination is operative in credit markets.

The disagreement about the significance of empirical tests of discrimination is perhaps unresolvable. Some take the view that these studies are efforts to definitively identify perpetrators of racial bias. To the extent that they fall short of this standard—that is, in the absence of a smoking gun connecting racially differential outcomes to racial hostility—they reach no definitive conclusion. For most, this view is too narrow. Instead, the sheer cumulative weight of findings of disadvantage for blacks in loan markets constitutes prima facie evidence of discrimination, and both personal and structural discrimination provide grounds for policy interventions.

Aside from HMDA-based tests of discrimination, other tests have been tried, focusing primarily on personal discrimination. One approach (Turner and Skidmore 1999) is *paired testing*, comparing black and white applicants' loan or housing experiences in market interactions. Paired testing for racial discrimination involves setting up controlled real-world experiments. In these experiments, market participants who are virtually identical in their economic characteristics—for example, in their credit and employment histories, job experience, and so on—but who have different ethnicities attempt to obtain a loan, be hired for a job, or perform some other transaction. Differences in treatment then can be interpreted as due primarily to race. When tests of this sort are done on credit market transactions, they almost inevitably turn up strong evidence of racial bias.

Another approach (Becker 1993) is to evaluate black and white borrowers' default experiences—the idea is that if personal discrimination exists, then blacks should have lower default rates than whites do. These tests have not found differential default rates, suggesting that there was no personal discrimination when loans were made. This interpretation is however problematic—it assumes that all other conditions affecting loan repayment are the same for blacks and whites.

CONSEQUENCES OF RACIAL INEQUALITY IN CAPITAL AND CREDIT MARKETS

The balance of evidence from statistical tests of lending data and from paired-testing experiments has a clear, twofold message: personal discrimination exists against blacks, if not always against other minorities; and racial redlining is a continuing problem (Holloway and Wyly 2001). Further, structural discrimination operates systematically to the disadvantage of blacks in virtually every credit and capital market in the United States. Overall, racial inequality in credit and capital market outcomes widens the already huge differences in wealth between white and black households and between neighborhoods with many black residents and those with few or no blacks.

Personal and structural discrimination operate separately. If all personal bias against black applicants for capital and credit were to disappear tomorrow, the huge racial wealth gap would remain; this alone would ensure that credit and capital flows are lower in the black community, which leads to fewer opportunities for capital accumulation and wealth building. Since racial segregation remains a defining feature of American cities, credit and capital are therefore systematically less available for black applicants and minority communities, even today. Indeed, trends in banking—a strategic shift toward upper-income customers and communities, with the growth of informal financial firms and predatory lending in lower-income areas—have arguably worsened the hollowing-out problem of inner-city areas in recent years.

POLICY RESPONSES TO UNEQUAL OUTCOMES IN CAPITAL AND CREDIT MARKETS

The obvious solution to racial inequality in credit markets is for blacks to become as wealthy as whites. This would happen naturally if discriminators always paid, as Becker assumes; but they do not. Further, simply motivating blacks to start businesses or save more money will not suffice: given that many minorities live in inner-city communities and that these communities are caught up in market dynamics that tend to widen the extent of wealth inequality, encouragement alone will not be enough.

What to do, then?[10] Racial discrimination and redlining in credit markets are already illegal under the Civil Rights Act, the Equal Credit Opportunity Act, and the Community Reinvestment Act. Simply having this legislation on the books has not, however, stopped discrimination and redlining; but where communities have exercised vigilance and have actively monitored lender performance, lenders either have increased black applicants' access to their normal credit instruments or have participated in special lending programs for minority urban communities. Undoubtedly, these federal acts have provided the teeth that community people need to force changes in credit and capital flows. Across the United States, fair housing councils have worked hard to identify and punish cases of personal discrimination; these councils' work is a key element in guarding against unequal racial access to credit and capital.

Extending the Community Reinvestment Act to mortgage companies, finance companies, and other financial firms would help substantially in enhancing reinvestment flows into minority communities. Greenlining, as this phenomenon is now called, is beginning to include some venture capital firms oriented toward inner-city communities. Greenlining is a crucial element in building the financial resources available to residents of redlined neighborhoods.

In short, three rules apply toward the solution of racial inequality in the credit market: enforce the civil rights laws; protect and even expand the community reinvestment mandate that extends to a limited set of financial firms; and find ways to greenline funds into inner-city and lower-income areas.

NOTES

1. These definitions are discussed at length in Dymski (1995). Holloway and Wyly (2001) point out that spatial and individual effects can interact in subtle ways; for example, their study of Atlanta finds that middle- and upper-class black applicants have a lower probability of obtaining loans in white neighborhoods than they do in other neighborhoods.

2. Becker (1971) attributes racial inequality in market outcomes to racial preferences.

3. Arrow (1972) first suggested this idea in an essay on labor market discrimination.

4. See, for example, Cloud and Galster (1993) and Ladd (1998).

5. See Squires (1992).

6. Squires (1992) provides an overview of the U.S. community reinvestment movement.

7. High interest rates and macroeconomic instability in the 1980s led many savings and loan associations—at that time, the primary mortgage lenders—into severe financial difficulties. More than one-third became insolvent. The Financial Institutions' Reform, Recovery, and Enforcement Act of 1989 created institutions that permitted the reorganization of the savings and loan industry. This use of public monies and guarantees made it possible to increase bank reporting requirements as a component of this legislation.

8. Dymski (1996) and Turner and Skidmore (1999) provide two summarizes of the literature on discrimination in the credit market.

9. See Munnell and others (1992).

10. More policy suggestions for responding to racial discrimination and redlining in credit markets are contained in chapter 39, on inner-city economic development.

REFERENCES

Arrow, Kenneth. 1972. "Some Mathematical Models of Race Discrimination in the Labor Market." In *Racial Discrimination in Economic Life,* ed. Anthony H. Pascal. Lexington, Mass.: Lexington Books.

Becker, Gary. 1971. *The Economics of Discrimination.* 2nd ed. Chicago: University of Chicago Press.

———. 1993. "The Evidence against Banks Doesn't Prove Bias." *Business Week,* April 19, 18.

Dymski, Gary. 1995. "The Theory of Credit-Market Redlining and Discrimination: An Exploration." *Review of Black Political Economy* 23, no. 3 (Winter): 37–74.

———. 1996. "Why Does Race Matter in Housing and Credit Markets?" In *Race, Markets, and Social Outcomes,* ed. Patrick L. Mason and Rhonda Williams. Boston: Kluwer Academic Press.

Holloway, Steven R., and Elvin K. Wyly. 2001. "'The Color of Money' Expanded: Geographically Contingent Mortgage Lending in Atlanta." *Journal of Housing Research* 12, no. 1: 55–90.

Munnell, Alicia H., Lynn E. Browne, James McEneaney, and Geoffrey Tootell. 1992. *Mortgage Lending in Boston: Interpreting HMDA Data.* Working Paper 92-7. Boston: Federal Reserve Bank of Boston.

Squires, Gregory. 1992. "Community Reinvestment: An Emerging Social Movement." In *From Redlining to Reinvestment,* ed. Gregory Squires, 1–37. Philadelphia: Temple University Press.

Turner, Margery Austin, and Felicity Skidmore, eds. 1999. *Mortgage Lending Discrimination: A Review of Existing Evidence.* Washington, D.C.: Urban Institute.

17

Changes in the Labor Market Status of Black Women, 1960–2000

CECILIA A. CONRAD

This article focuses on the economic progress that black women made between 1960 and 1980 and on the reentrenchment from 1980 to 2000. The author examines the role of education, work experience, and the enforcement of equal opportunity laws as critical factors in explaining these economic trends for black women.

Black women have made enormous economic progress in the past four decades. However, most of the gains were realized between 1960 and 1980. The median earnings of black women who were year-round, full-time workers increased by 53 percent between 1960 and 1970, by 23 percent between 1970 and 1980, but by less than 10 percent between 1980 and 1990 and between 1990 and 2000. Table 17.1 reports median earnings over the past four decades.

So what explains the progress between 1960 and 1980 and the post-1980 slowdown? This chapter examines the role of education, work experience welfare reform, and the enforcement of equal employment opportunity laws in explaining changes in the labor market status of African American women.

TWO DECADES OF PROGRESS: 1960 TO 1980

In 1960, before the passage of the Civil Rights Act, black women occupied the bottom rung of the economic ladder. Black women were more likely to be in the labor force than white women were, but over a third worked as domestic servants. They earned less than did white women, black men, and white men. Many were not covered by minimum-wage laws; most were not part of the social security system. Very few had jobs in high-wage sectors such as manufacturing.

Against this backdrop, the economic achievements of the 1960s and the 1970s appear extraordinary. In 1960, black women earned sixty-three cents for every dollar earned by a white woman. By 1980, she earned ninety-two cents. Black women gained ground relative not only to white women but also to white men. In 1960, a black woman earned 38.7 cents for every dollar earned by a white man; in 1980, 53.5 cents. Three factors contributed to this relative earnings growth: the expansion of employment in clerical occupations; improvements in educational attainment; and the enforcement of equal employment opportunity laws.

Table 17.2 illustrates the dramatic changes in the occupational distribution of employed black women between 1960 and 1980. In 1960, 37.7 percent of employed black women worked as domestic servants, whereas only 3.2 percent of employed white women held these jobs. By 1980, 6.2 percent of black women were employed in this occupation.

Black women left domestic service primarily for higher-paying jobs as secretaries, clerks, typists, and stenographers. The proportion of black women employed as clerical workers more than

Table 17.1   Median Earnings of Year-Round, Full-Time Workers

	1960	1970	1980	1990	2000
Median earnings					
White male	27,619	35,635	38,188	37,082	38,869
White female	16,739	20,910	22,438	25,741	28,080
Black male	18,256	24,604	26,955	27,110	30,409
Black female	11,346	17,182	21,235	23,163	25,117
Female:male ratios					
White	0.61	0.59	0.59	0.69	0.72
Black	0.62	0.70	0.79	0.85	0.83
Black:white ratios					
Men	0.66	0.69	0.71	0.73	0.78
Women	0.68	0.82	0.95	0.90	0.89

Source: U.S. Census Bureau, Current Population Survey, March, Table P-36a and P-36b for 1960 median income and Table P-38a and P-38b for 1970, 1980, 1990, and 2000 median earnings. Available at www.census.gov/hhes/income/histinc/incperdet.html.

Note: The data for 1960 is median *income* for year-round, full-time workers; the data for the other years is median *earnings* for year-round, full-time workers. *Income* includes dollars received for employment and from all other sources (government transfers, dividends, etc.); *earnings* is money earned strictly from employment.

Table 17.2   Occupational Distribution of Black and White Women, 1960–2000

White women	1960	1980	2000
Professional/technical	15.8	20.1	22.1
Managers	4.3	6.4	14.8
Clerical	34.1	36.5	23.7
Sales	8.7	6.9	13.2
Crafts	1.4	3.3	2.1
Operatives/fabricators/laborers	18.4	9.7	6.4
Service	12.6	15.4	15.2
Private household	3.2	1.9	1.1
Agriculture	1.5	1.2	1.3
Total	*100.0*	*100.0*	*100.0*
Black women			
Professional/technical	7.7	16.1	18.3
Managers	1.1	2.5	10.7
Clerical	8.0	29.0	24.0
Sales	1.5	2.8	10.9
Crafts	0.8	3.1	2.1
Operatives/fabricators/laborers	16.0	14.1	9.1
Service	23.6	25.6	23.7
Private household	37.7	6.2	1.1
Agriculture	3.7	1.2	0.2
Total	*100.0*	*100.0*	*100.0*

Source: U.S. Bureau of Labor Statistics, *Employment and Earnings,* January 2002 (for 2000 data); January 1981 (for 1980 data); January 1961 (for 1960 data).

Note: Figures rounded to the nearest tenth.

tripled. The proportion of black women employed as professional and technical workers (teachers, librarians, and nurses) also increased.

Improvements in educational attainment explain part of the shift in occupations. In 1960, the average black woman had completed 8.9 years of schooling. Only 26.3 percent of black women had completed twelve or more years. By 1980, the average black woman had completed 11.9 years of schooling; and more than half, 12 years or more.

As black women completed more years of schooling, they narrowed the education gap between themselves and white female workers. In 1960, white female workers had on average two years more schooling; in 1980, less than one year.

Increases in the proportion of black women with college degrees contributed to their increased numbers in professional and technical occupations. In 1960, fewer than 8 percent of professional and technical workers were black women. In 1980, this percentage climbed to 16 percent.

However, education was clearly not the whole story. Before the civil rights legislation of the 1960s, a black woman could not get a job as a clerical worker, whatever her credentials. In a 1940 Women's Bureau survey, more than 50 percent of employers reported that they had a company policy against hiring black women as clerical workers (Goldin 1990). In 1960, less than 20 percent of black women with twelve years of schooling were clerical workers. The comparable statistic for white women was 54 percent.

Racial discrimination was a major obstacle to the employment of black women in these positions. Hence, the growth of black female employment in clerical positions and in professional and technical jobs must be partially credited to the enforcement of equal employment opportunity laws and to affirmative action (Fosu 1992). Title VII of the Civil Rights Act of 1964 prohibited discrimination on the basis of race and sex in any aspect of employment. In addition, in 1965 President Lyndon Johnson signed executive order 11246, which required that all federal contractors have affirmative action plans specifying goals and time tables for increasing the representation of women and minorities in their workforce. Although there is some debate about the magnitude of the impact of these laws, they clearly increased employment opportunities for black women (Betsey 1994; Heckman and Payner 1989; Leonard 1990).

Perhaps the impact of civil rights legislation was most strongly felt in the public sector. Much of the employment growth in clerical work and in professional and managerial occupations occurred in local, state, and federal governments and in nonprofit organizations such as hospitals. Lynn Burbridge reports that the percentage of black women in government and nonprofit employment grew 73 percent between 1960 and 1980 (1994). The percentage in the for-profit sector declined 36 percent. In contrast, for all workers, the percentage employed in the for-profit sector declined only 11 percent.

Indeed, some have argued that black women benefited more from affirmative action programs than black men did (Epstein 1973). The earnings of black men increased between 1960 and 1980, but the racial wage gap in earnings remained considerably larger among men than among women. By 1980, a larger percentage of black women were professional, managerial, and technical workers than were black men. However, black women continued to earn less than black men—seventy-nine cents for every dollar earned by a black man in 1980.

By 1980, almost 100 percent of the earnings differences between black and white women could be explained by differences in characteristics. Within occupations, there was little or no evidence of discrimination in pay (Blau and Beller 1992; Darity, Guilkey, and Winfrey 1996). Black women compensated for fewer years of schooling with more years of work experience. Black women tended to accumulate more work experience than white women did because the former had higher labor force participation rates. Labor force participation rates measure the proportion of persons who are either working or actively looking for work. In 1960, 50 percent of black women were in the labor force, compared with 37 percent of white women.

Despite parity in earnings, black women had not yet achieved economic equality with white women. In 1980, they were three times more likely to be unemployed and five times more likely to live in poverty. Only a small percentage had gained access to the highest-paying jobs.

Furthermore, within clerical work, they tended to occupy jobs requiring the least skill and offering the lowest pay (Anderson and Shapiro 1996; Power and Rosenberg 1993). Their concentration in entry-level jobs and in public employment left them vulnerable to the structural shifts in the economy that were on the horizon.

WIDENING GAP: 1980 TO 2000

Changes in the labor market status of black women since 1980 underscore this vulnerability to economic structural shifts. From 1980 to 2000, their earnings decreased relative to those of white women. The ratio of median earnings decreased from a peak of 96 percent in 1975 to 89 percent in 2000. Since 1992, the earnings of black women have also decreased relative to black men. In 1992, their median earnings were 88 percent of those of black men; in 2000, 83 percent.

One of the main factors contributing to the growth of the earnings gap between black and white women is the growth in the demand for college-educated workers. Technological change and global competition have increased the premium paid for skilled workers in the United States (Bound and Johnson 1995; Juhn and Murphy 1995).

Although the number of black women with college degrees is increasing, the racial gap in educational attainment persists. As of March 2000, only 19.7 percent of black women who were in the labor force and who were between the ages of twenty-five and thirty-four had college diplomas, compared with 39 percent of white women. In addition, young black women no longer have an edge in work experience. Labor force participation rates of white women increased dramatically over the 1970s and 1980s, particularly among the most educated. As a result, by 2000 the black–white difference in labor force participation had disappeared: 60 percent of white women were in the labor force, compared with 65 percent of black women. Among younger women, those aged sixteen to twenty-four years, labor force participation rates of white women exceeded those of black women.

As educated white women have entered the labor market, they have moved into high-paying jobs as officers and managers in the private sector. Black women in these occupations tend to be concentrated in lower-paying, public-sector employment (Burbridge 1994). Even white clerical workers appear to be more upwardly mobile than black clerical workers are (Power and Rosenberg 1993).

Once again, education is not the whole story. Audit studies of employer behavior suggest that discrimination remains a factor in employment and promotion even if workers receive the same pay once hired. In an audit study, pairs of testers are sent to respond to the same job announcement. The testers are carefully matched so that all employment relevant characteristics are the same. They differ only by race. Among men, audit studies have found evidence of discrimination in 20–25 percent of cases (Withers 1998). Given the decline in enforcement effort of equal employment opportunity laws (Leonard 1990) and the hostile environment for affirmative action, it would not be surprising to find increased labor market discrimination in the 1980s and the 1990s. In a study of the Los Angeles labor market, black women were more likely to report an experience of discrimination than were Latina, white, or Asian women (Suh 2000). Employment discrimination may partially explain why black welfare recipients appear to be having a particularly difficult time moving from welfare to work (DeParle 1998; Edin and Harris 1999). Surveys of employers reveal that many have negative opinions of the skills of black workers from low-income neighborhoods (Holzer 1996; Kirshenman and Neckerman 1991).

Macroeconomic fluctuations have also contributed to changes in the labor market status of African American women. During the economic expansion of the 1990s, employment rates for African American women increased while unemployment rates fell. However, even at the peak of the economic expansion (March 2001), the unemployment rate of African American women (6.4 percent) was double that of white women (3.2 percent).

More recently, welfare reform, which imposed stringent work requirements and time limits for recipients, has increased participation in the formal labor force by single mothers with children, roughly 31 percent of whom are

African American (Burtless as cited in Holzer and Stoll 2002).[1] The long-term effects of welfare reform are uncertain. On the one hand, the accumulation of work experience should increase earnings. On the other hand, because some recipients must forego formal schooling to meet the work requirements, investments in formal education may decrease and this could slow earnings growth in the future (Spriggs and Cox 2002).

Although progress toward racial equality stalled in the 1980s, working black women still enjoy higher economic status than before the Civil Rights Act of 1964. In 1960, the average working black women earned sixty-three cents for every dollar earned by a white woman; in 1980, she earned eighty-seven cents; and in 2000, eighty-nine cents. Black women moved out of low-status jobs as domestic servants into higher-status, clerical occupations. Their numbers in professional and technical occupations have also increased. Black women earn the same pay as white women when they are in the same jobs. Continued growth in employment and in wages of black women depends on increased investments in higher education and on improved access to jobs through vigilant enforcement of equal employment opportunity laws.

NOTE

1. Even before work requirements were imposed, many welfare recipients worked in the informal labor market, or "off the books," because welfare benefits were insufficient to cover basic subsistence (Edin and Lein 1997).

REFERENCES

Anderson, Deborah, and David Shapiro. 1996. "Racial Differences in Access to High-Paying Jobs and the Wage Gap between Black and White Women." *Industrial and Labor Relations Review* 49, no. 2: 273–286.

Betsey, Charles. 1994. "Litigation of Employment Discrimination under Title VII: The Case of African American Women," *American Economic Review* 84, no. 2 (May): 98–107.

Blau, Francine, and Andrea Beller. 1992. "Black-White Earnings over the 1970s and 1980s: Gender Differences in Trends." *Review of Economics and Statistics* 74, no. 2: 276–286.

Bound, John, and George Johnson. 1995. "What Are the Causes of Rising Wage Inequality in the United States?" *American Economic Review* 1, no. 1 (January): 9–17.

Burbridge, Lynn. 1994. "The Reliance of African-American Women on Government and Third Sector Employment." *American Economic Review* 84, no. 2 (May): 103–107.

Darity, William, David K. Guikey, and William Winfrey. 1996. "Explaining Differences in Economic Performance among Racial and Ethnic Groups in the USA: The Data Examined." *American Journal of Economics and Sociology* 55, no. 4 (October): 411–426.

DeParle, Jason. 1998. "Shrinking Welfare Rolls Leave Record High Share of Minorities." *New York Times,* July 27, A1.

Edin, Kathryn, and Kathleen Mullan Harris. 1999. "Getting off and Staying off: Racial Differences in the Work Route off Welfare." In *Latinas and African American Women and Work,* ed. Irene Browne. New York: Russell Sage Foundation.

Edin, Kathryn, and Laura Lein. 1997. *Making Ends Meet: How Single Mothers Survive Welfare and Low-Wage Work.* New York: Russell Sage Foundation.

Epstein, Cynthia. 1973. "Positive Effects of the Multiple Negative: Explaining the Success of Black Professional Women." *American Journal of Sociology* 78, no. 4 (January): 912–935.

Fosu, Augustin. 1992. "Occupational Mobility of Black Women, 1958–1981: The Impact of Post-1994 Antidiscrimination Measures." *Industrial and Labor Relations Review* 45, no. 2 (January): 281–294.

Goldin, Claudia. 1990. *Understanding the Gender Gap: An Economic History of American Women,* New York: Oxford University Press.

Heckman, James J., and Brook S. Payner. 1989. "Determining the Impact of Federal Antidiscrimination Policy on the Economic Status of Blacks: A Study of South Carolina." *American Economic Review* 79, no. 1 (March): 138–177.

Holzer, Harry. 1996. *What Employers Want: Job Prospects for Less-Educated Workers.* New York: Russell Sage Foundation.

Holzer, Harry, and Michael Stoll. 2002. "Employer

Demand for Welfare Recipients by Race." Urban Institute Discussion Paper 01-07, January.

Juhn, Chinhui, and Kevin M. Murphy. 1995. "Inequality in Labor Market Outcomes." *Federal Reserve Bank of New York Economic Policy Review* 1, no. 1 (January): 26–34.

Kirschenman, Joleen, and Kathryn M. Neckerman. 1991. " 'We'd Love to Hire Them, But . . .': The Meaning of Race for Employers." In *The Urban Underclass,* ed. Christopher Jencks and Paul E. Peterson. Washington, D.C.: Brookings Institution.

Leonard, Jonathan S. 1990. "The Impact of Affirmative Action Regulation and Equal Employment Law on Black Employment." *Journal of Economic Perspectives* 4, no. 4 (Fall 1990): 47–64.

Power, Marilyn, and Sam Rosenberg. 1993. "Black Female Clerical Workers: Movement toward Equality with White Women?" *Industrial Relations* 32, no. 2 (Spring): 223–237.

Spriggs, William, and Kenya Covington Cox. 2002. "Negative Effects of TANF on College Enrollment." National Urban League Special Report SRR-01-2002, New York.

Suh, Susan. 2000. "Women's Perceptions of Workplace Discrimination: Impacts of Racial Group, Gender and Class." In *Prismatic Metropolis: Inequality in Los Angeles,* ed. Lawrence D. Bob, Melvin L. Oliver, James H. Johnson Jr., and Abel Valenzuela Jr. New York: Russell Sage Foundation.

Withers, Claudia. 1998. "Coaching Employers and Job Seekers on Equal Employment Opportunity." Speech to the Annie E. Casey Foundation Jobs Initiative Race and Readiness Meeting, August 7.

18

Single-Mother Families in the Black Community: Economic Context and Policies

CECILIA A. CONRAD and MARY C. KING

A high proportion of black children live in families maintained by single mothers, and these families are more likely than other families to be poor. This chapter discusses the causes and consequences of the high rate of single motherhood in the black community and suggests public policies to improve the status of single mothers and their children.

The proportion of African American children living in families headed by single mothers is quite high by historical standards and by comparison with other groups. While many people think of family formation as primarily a social, cultural, or psychological issue, the causes and consequences of single motherhood may be profoundly economic. Many social scientists believe that men do not commit to marriage when they are unsure of their breadwinning potential. Women with more ability to earn an independent income may "drive a harder bargain"—or no bargain at all—with potential partners. And certainly the poverty rates of single mothers have severe social consequences for African American children and the future.

Marriage is a very personal choice and perhaps one that government policy should not attempt to affect. However, we certainly can implement policies that change the economic situation that leads to low marriage rates and high poverty levels of single-mother households. All other industrialized countries do a much better job than we do at fighting poverty. A decent antipoverty and employment program would allow more people to marry who would like to, would reduce economic stresses on marriages, and would sub-stantially decrease the economic penalties of single motherhood.

WHAT ARE THE FACTS?

Over half of African American children live in families headed by a single mother (Figure 18.1), and over 46 percent of these children are poor. Figure 18.1 depicts the percentage of children living in families maintained by women. As early as 1968, black children were roughly three times more likely to live in mother-only families than were white children.[1] The percentage of black children living in mother-only families increased dramatically into the 1980s then leveled off. Since 1995, the percentage of black children living in mother-only families has decreased slightly, yet the percentage of black children living in families maintained by women is nearly twice the percentage of Latino children and three times the percentage of white children.[2]

Regardless of race, families maintained by women have lower incomes and higher rates of poverty than do other families. Table 18.1 reports median income of family households by household type in 2000. For blacks, whites, and

Figure 18.1 Proportion of children under eighteen years of age living in mother-only families.

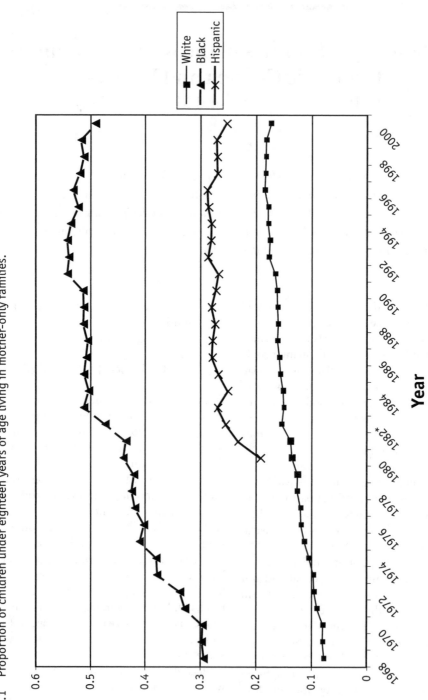

Year

Source: U.S. Census Bureau, at www.census.gov/population/socdemo/hh-fam/tabCH-2, www.census.gov/population/socdemo/hh-fam/tabCH-3, and www.census.gov/population/socdemo/hh-fam/tabCH-4.

Table 18.1 Median Income of Family Households with Children by Race, 2001

	Married couple	*Male householder*[a]	*Female householder*[a]
White, non-Hispanic	71,155	40,455	29,650
Black	55,618	32,213	20,494
Hispanic	40,839	32,349	22,579
Black:white ratio	0.78	0.80	0.69
Hispanic:white ratio	0.57	0.80	0.76

Source: U.S. Census Bureau, Detailed Household Income Package P60, available at http://ferret.bls.census.gov:80/cgi-bin/ ferret?&time = 11:35:02.
[a]No spouse present.

Latinos, families maintained by women have the lowest median incomes of all household types. Table 18.2 describes the poverty status of children by household type.

Again, across race and ethnicity, children in households maintained by women are at greater risk of poverty. The risk of poverty is especially high for black and Latino children. Over 45 percent of children in black and in Latino households maintained by women are poor. By comparison, 30 percent of children in white, non-Latino households maintained by women are poor. Nearly 20 percent of black children and over 25 percent of Latino children in households maintained by women live in extreme poverty (defined as less than 50 percent of the poverty line).[3]

Because these families have lower incomes, the high proportion of black families maintained by women contributes to the racial gap in family incomes. Furthermore, the racial gap is larger for this type of family.[4] For married-couple families, the ratio of median black-family income to median white-family income is 0.85. For mother-only families, the ratio is 0.78.

WHY DO SINGLE-MOTHER FAMILIES HAVE LOW INCOME?

The most obvious explanation for the low incomes of families maintained by women is the low number of earners in the family. Of families maintained by women, 15 percent include no workers (U.S. Census 2000, Table P48). Only 50 percent of children living in single-mother families have at least one parent employed full-time, year-round.[5] In contrast, 91 percent of children living in two-parent families have at least one parent employed full-time, year-round. Single mothers who work tend to earn low wages. When they work year-round and full-time, women still earn only seventy-six cents for each dollar earned by men.[6]

Women earn less than men who have the same amount of education and work experience, and

Table 18.2 Poverty Status of Children Living in Families, 2001

	Income under poverty threshold			Income under 50% of poverty threshold		
	MC	*MH*	*FH*	*MC*	*MH*	*FH*
Black	10.1	28.6	46.6	3.3	13.2	19.7
Latino	19.5	29.3	49.2	4.8	8.1	25.8
White[a]	4.7	14.6	29.0	1.5	4.5	8.3

Source: U.S. Census Bureau, available at http://ferret.bls.census.gov/macro/032002/pov/new02_004.htm.
Note: MC = married couple; MH = male householder; FH = female householder.
[a]Not Latino.

women tend to be crowded into "women's jobs," where pay has been set with the idea that women do not need to support families. More women than men work part-time—usually while their children are young—and part-time compensation is always substantially less per hour than it is for full-time work, even for the same work, and generally does not include benefits. And as obvious as the fact that single-parent households contain fewer earners, single-mother families include fewer parents so that single mothers are always the parent who must miss work when problems arise.

Table 18.3 reports median earnings for single mothers by marital status. Median earnings for single mothers who maintain families were $19,500 in 2001. In contrast, median earnings for all working women, regardless of family status, were $20,851; and median earnings for women who worked year-round, full-time were $29,215. Single mothers who have never married had especially low incomes, which is not surprising, as it is more common for poor women to bear children outside marriage than it is for more-affluent women.

Women who maintain families may have few resources to fall back on when work is unavailable. Less than half of single mothers receive any type of child support, and black single mothers were less likely to receive child support than white (Sorenson and Halpern 1999). According to a 1999 census survey, 44 percent of non-Latina white mothers received any child support payment; 25 percent of black custodial mothers received any child support; and 28 percent of Latina mothers received any payment.[7] These racial differences in the receipt of child support

can be explained in part by the low incomes of the absent fathers.

Child support payments, when paid, do reduce the risk of poverty for children in single-mother households, as does financial help from other family members. African American families, with less wealth and lower incomes than white families, cannot provide as much help to single-mother families, a fact that shows up in the differential experience of women trying to leave the welfare rolls (Edin and Harris 1999).

While some women who maintain families are eligible for transfer payments, these payments are typically inadequate to lift the family out of poverty. Social programs oriented toward the financial assistance of the elderly and the unemployed are geared toward keeping people above the poverty line; "welfare programs" for families without a male breadwinner are not.

The primary program to assist poor single-parent families is the Temporary Assistance to Needy Families (TANF) program. TANF replaced the long-running program Aid to Families with Dependent Children (AFDC) in Clinton's controversial "welfare reform." The gist of the reform was the shift of responsibility for the program from the federal to the state level, opening the way for individual states to significantly reduce assistance; the imposition of lifetime time limits on benefit receipt of a total of five years, regardless of age or circumstances; and to push mothers into full-time work immediately, without consideration of the age, training, health, or other needs of their children or themselves.

In the 1999–2000 period, the cash assistance received by the average family in TANF was $349 a month, or $4,187 a year.[8] In the same year, the

Table 18.3   Median Earnings of Single Mothers Who Maintain Families, 2001

	All groups, racial/ethnic	White non-Hispanic	Black non-Hispanic	Hispanic, any race
All single mothers	19,500	21,000	18,000	15,500
Married, spouse absent	19,240	20,000	23,000	15,000
Widowed, divorced, or separated	22,000	24,000	21,000	18,000
Never married	15,600	17,500	15,500	13,000

Source: Calculations using unpublished data from the U.S. Bureau of Census and the U.S. Bureau of Labor Statistics.

official poverty threshold for a mother and two children was $13,874. In other words, the mother would need to find $9,687 from other sources to climb out of poverty. Only one-quarter of TANF families had non-TANF income, and the average non-TANF income received was $6,980 a year.[9] In a study of low-income families, the Institute for Women's Policy Research found that, despite combining income from all sources, 80.2 percent of single-parent, TANF-recipient families live in poverty, and nearly half of those live in extreme poverty (Jones-DeWeever, Peterson, and Song 2003).

Another measure of the difficult economic situation of single-mother families is their low level of home ownership. Homes are the asset most commonly owned by American families, after vehicles. Homeowners can weather some economic storms by taking out home loans, using their equity for emergencies, such as unemployment and poor health; for college tuition; and for a new car. In 2002, 83 percent of married-couple families owned their own home, whereas only 49 percent of family households maintained by women owned their own home.[10]

WHY THE RISE IN SINGLE MOTHERHOOD?

The rise in single motherhood in the United States is the product of three interrelated demographic phenomena: decreasing marriage; increasing separation and divorce; and an increased proportion of children born outside of marriage. For white women, the growth in single motherhood is largely a product of the increase in divorce and separation rates; for black women, the growth in single motherhood is primarily the result of a decline in marriage rates and a growing proportion of children born outside of marriage (Ellwood and Crane 1990). Nearly 65 percent of black women who maintain families have never been married.

There are essentially four interrelated theories explaining why a high proportion of black families are maintained by women. One theory is that there are racial differences in social norms linked to the different historical experiences of blacks and other racial and ethnic groups. A second the-

ory is that there is a scarcity of black men who might make attractive marriage partners. A third is that the U.S. welfare system, specifically the AFDC, encourages poor mothers not to marry. A fourth is that increases in labor market opportunities for women relative to those for men have reduced the economic incentives for marriage and increased women's economic independence.

Some historians and other social scientists have identified the slave family as the precursor of the mother-only families of today. Slave families existed at the discretion of the slave owner. If a profit could be earned, a slave owner would separate husband from wife and children from parents. Sociologist E. Franklin Frazier, writing as early as 1939, asserted that slavery had impeded the development of monogamous nuclear families as a black social norm (Frazier 1939). Frazier's argument reappeared in the 1960s in the famous Moynihan report (Moynihan 1965). Moynihan's report *The Negro Family: The Case for National Action* sparked new research by historians who challenged the Frazier thesis. For example, Herbert Gutman's historical study *The Black Family in Slavery and Freedom, 1750–1925* argued that while slave families may not have followed the European norm, "upon emancipation most . . . ex-slave families had two parents, and most older couples lived together in long lasting unions" (1976, 9).

Although the prevalence of two-parent slave families remains a subject of controversy (Stevenson 1995), there is some consensus that slavery and the years of racial oppression since slavery have had an impact on black family structure. In the introduction of their edited volume *The Decline in Marriage among African Americans,* M. Belinda Tucker and Claudia Mitchell-Kernan conclude,

> We would argue, then, that the historical evidence demonstrates that situational factors have been disruptive of African American family life since the time that Africans first arrived here as slaves. This unique history may make black families even more vulnerable to new situational challenges, such as higher male mortality and economic decline, and may therefore help account for the very recent more dramatic changes in family

formation. That is, the absence of economic and ecological support for stable family life among African Americans, over a period of several hundred years, may have exacerbated the fragility of family forms. (1995, xx)

A similar line of argument asserts that African cultures place a lower premium on nuclear families and a higher emphasis on extended family kinship obligations than do European and white American culture. However, the idea that this cultural difference is behind differential marriage rates by race today would be more convincing if marriage rates had always been relatively low in the African American community rather than in marked decline over the last fifty years.

Sociologists William Julius Wilson and Kathryn Neckerman (1986) argue that the growth in single-mother families in the black community can be linked to a decline in the supply of marriageable black men. They argue that low employment rates among black men reduce their attractiveness as marriage partners.[11] High mortality rates coupled with high rates of incarceration also limit the supply of black men as marriage partners (Darity and Myers 1995). Several attempts have been made to test this hypothesis empirically, with mixed results. For example, Testa and Krogh (1995) find that employed black men have a significantly higher probability of marriage than black men without jobs. However, Wood (1995) finds that changes in the supply of marriageable men explained only 3–4 percent of the decline in marriage rates between 1970 and 1980. South and Lloyd (1992), in a study of women in seventy-five U.S. metropolitan areas, find that the nonmarital fertility rate is lower in cities with a high percentage of men without jobs.

Others have argued that U.S. welfare programs, primarily the AFDC program, sparked the growth in black families maintained by women (Murray 1984). The AFDC program was created in the 1930s as a program primarily to assist widows and their children. AFDC rules generally prevented two-parent families from collecting benefits, and children in two-parent families were also ineligible for health insurance through the Medicaid program. Hence, a poor family might be better off financially if an unemployed or low-wage father left the household. Before the 1960s, black families were systematically excluded from the program through discriminatory application of eligibility rules by local authorities.[12] However, after the 1960s, black participation in the AFDC program grew. In his book *Losing Ground*, Charles Murray observes that the growth in black participation in AFDC and the growth in the proportion of black families maintained by women occurred at roughly the same time. He concludes that AFDC actually worsened poverty in the black community by creating more mother-only families. The AFDC program, according to Murray and others, not only reduces incentives for marriage but increases incentives for childbearing outside of marriage.

Murray's thesis has been challenged on several grounds. First, after adjustment for inflation, AFDC benefits declined from 1970 through the 1980s, and a declining proportion of black families with children collected benefits; yet, the percentage of black children living in single-parent families continued to rise (Ellwood and Crane 1990). In statistical studies that examine variations in AFDC benefits across states as well as over time, AFDC benefits are found to have a negative impact on marriage, but the size of this effect is the subject of debate (Moffitt 1998). Similarly, AFDC benefits tend to have a positive impact on the probability of a birth outside of marriage, but the effects appear to be small (Foster and Hoffman 2001; Wolfe, Wilson, and Haveman 2001).

A fourth hypothesis for the decline in marriage and the increase in families maintained by women is an increase in the economic independence of women. For economists, marriage is an economic decision as well as a romantic one. One of the economic incentives for marriage is the increase in total household consumption that might be realized if one spouse specializes in home production (child care, meal preparation) and the other specializes in market work. Historically, because men commanded higher wages in the labor market, men specialized in market work and women focused on home production. This specialization is not without cost. In particular, a woman who specializes in home production is likely to see her earnings capacity diminished. As her opportunities outside of the marriage shrink, her bargaining power within the marriage is reduced. Furthermore, her economic vulnerability in the event of divorce is heightened. As women's wages and labor market opportunities increase relative to those of men, women may decide that the costs of specialization outweigh the benefits from marriage with a traditional division of labor.

Like the first three theories, this economic independence hypothesis has a few shortcomings. Among African Americans, a woman's employment has a positive effect on the likelihood of marriage, not a negative one (Burbridge 1995; Hartmann and Spalter-Roth 2003).

In qualitative studies, low-income single mothers focus as much on issues of power as on issues of income, but income and power within the relationship are obviously linked. Describing the results of interviews with a large number of low-income single mothers, Edin notes that the issues of "trust and control" figure importantly into the decision not to marry.

> Overall, the interview show that although mothers still aspire to marriage, they feel that it entails far more risks than rewards—at least marriage to the kind of men who fathered their children and live in their neighborhoods. Mothers say these risks may be diminished if they can find the "right" man—and they define "rightness" in both economic and noneconomic terms. In sum, they say they are willing and even eager to wed if the marriage represents a substantial economic upward mobility and their husband doesn't beat them, abuse their children, insist on making all the decisions, or "fool around" with other women. If they cannot find such a man, most would rather remain single. (2000)

Individually, these theories explain some of the factors contributing to the growth in mother-only families—but not all. For example, a scarcity of marriageable men or an increase in the economic independence of women might explain the decline in marriage but not the increase in nonmarital childbearing. Welfare is an attractive alternative to marriage only if potential marriage partners are jobless or work for low wages.

Single motherhood is on the rise worldwide. While the proportion of African American children living in mother-only households is unusually high, African Americans are by no means alone in this situation. Nancy Folbre (1994) has asserted that, globally, men are shifting the responsibility for children to women as the society makes a historic shift from an agricultural economy to an industrial one and as children become expensive rather than a source of family labor and old age security. While it is difficult to pin down one central explanation for the decline in the proportion of the population living in married-couple households, economic factors appear important. High unemployment rates and falling wages for men, particularly for young men, may undermine their financial ability to form their own households and to obtain the kind of "deal" from their partners that they may expect, based on what their fathers may have had in terms of the division of power and unpaid work in the family. Whether the African American community is also undergoing a more profound cultural shift regarding marriage and childrearing norms is a topic well beyond the ability of economists to assess.

CONSEQUENCES OF GROWING UP IN A POOR MOTHER-ONLY FAMILY

The consequences of growing up in a poor mother-only family are not completely understood. For starters, it is difficult to separate the effects of family structure from poverty. The correlation between growing up in a mother-only family and dropping out of high school could exist because a person growing up in a mother-only family is also likely to be poor. In addition, there may be unobservable differences between mother-only families and other families that contribute to differences in child outcomes. Differences in the psychological health of the parents or in exposure to racism, violence, and other external events could explain the different experiences of children in mother-only families but are often unaccounted for in studies of single-mother families.

Studies of the effect of family structure, controlling for family income, have found mixed results. The effects of single motherhood are stronger in adolescence than in early childhood and tend to be larger when the outcome is behavioral (skipping school) rather than cognitive (standardized test scores; McLanahan 1995). For example, children with a widowed parent do better than children with a divorced or never-married mother; but there is no evidence that children with a divorced mother do better than children with a never-married mother (McLanahan 1995).

Most research concludes that poverty has a negative impact on child outcomes.[13] Poverty reduces access to health care for a mother-to-be, leading to a higher incidence of low-birth-weight babies, which has long-term implications for educational achievement. Poverty also limits access to quality childcare (NICHD [National Institute of Child Health and Human Development] Early Child Care Research Network 1997) and might leave working parents with too little energy to interact with their children when they are home. As well, poverty limits housing choices, so poor families tend to live in neighborhoods with high crime rates, poor environmental quality, and in-adequately funded schools. And poverty often generates chaos in children's lives, resulting from frequent moves and makeshift child care arrangements. If kids are in and out of different classrooms and neighborhoods, it is hard for them to maintain the consistency in their school-work and in the relationships that helps kids thrive.

PUBLIC POLICY AND SINGLE MOTHERS

Single motherhood is increasing all over the globe. However, nowhere in the industrialized world is single motherhood so associated with poverty, and extreme poverty, as in the United States. The main reason is that the U.S. social safety net is much less effective than that in other countries in pulling single-mother families out of poverty; another important contributor is the relatively low level of wages earned by people in the bottom quarter of U.S. earners. As shown in Table 18.4, the result is an unconscionable rate of child poverty in the United States, created not by laziness but by low wages and a lack of support for children and parents.

Table 18.4   Comparative Poverty Rates, 1987–1998 (by percentage)

	Total population (%)	Children only (%)
United States	16.9	22.3
Australia	14.3	15.8
Italy	14.2	20.2
United Kingdom	13.4	19.8
Canada	12.8	16.3
Ireland	11.1	13.8
Austria	10.6	15.0
Spain	10.1	12.2
Switzerland	9.3	10.0
Denmark	9.2	8.7
Belgium	8.2	7.6
Netherlands	8.1	8.1
France	8.0	7.9
Germany	7.5	10.6
Norway	6.9	3.9
Sweden	6.6	2.6
Finland	5.1	4.2

Source: Mishel, Bernstein, and Boushey (2003, 416).

Whereas U.S. programs reduce the number of single-parent families with incomes below the poverty line by only 15 percent, Finnish social programs bring 82 percent of single-parent families who would otherwise be poor above the poverty line. The Belgians reduce the poverty rate of single-parent households by 72 percent, and the British bring it down by 59 percent (Smeeding 2004). For example, the countries with the lowest child poverty rates provide a child allowance to every family with children, regardless of income and family status. The United States and Italy, both at the top of Table 18.4, do not. The United States does offer a tax deduction for children through its income tax system. The deduction reduces a family's taxable income and, because of the progressivity of the tax system, is more valuable to rich families than it is to poor. For poor families, the earned income tax credit provides a refundable federal tax credit. A study by the Center on Budget and Policy Priorities (Greenstein and Shapiro 1998) found that the earned income tax credit lifts more children out of poverty than any other U.S. government program. Nevertheless, the United States is less successful in reducing child poverty than countries that combine universal family benefits with generous social insurance programs and policies to facilitate mothers' employment (Kamerman et al. 2003).

With the example of the rest of the world in front of us—not to mention Sweden, with a child poverty rate one-tenth of our own—we can clearly see how to reduce poverty rates of children and single-mother families. What is needed is income transfers that put families above the poverty line; subsidized, high-quality child care programs; public health insurance; active labor market policies to reduce unemployment; public housing programs; and higher wages in the bottom third of the earnings structure so that people concentrated in low wage work—whether due to low levels of education, skills, and experience; or discrimination based on race, sex, or age—can support their families.[14]

Each of these policies—as well as those to fight discrimination in education, housing, and employment—are worthy of chapters of discussion of their own. Luckily, a great deal of social science literature has been devoted to these pol-

icy prescriptions (e.g., Cantillon and Van den Bosch 2002; Kamerman et al. 2003; King 2001); and as the example of other nations show us, we need hardly reinvent the wheel.

What we do have to do is take responsibility for the condition of at least those other people who share our country and economy and implement policies that can radically alter the future by providing the nation's children with good food, comfortable shelter, safe neighborhoods, decent schools, and good health. Then we can leave the future in their hands.

NOTES

The authors would like to thank Rabia Ahmed for her excellent research assistance and Helen Beckon and Tony Tiu for their editorial assistance. The authors also thank Paula England and Tami Ohler for their comments on an earlier draft of the paper.

1. A *mother-only family* is defined here as a family household with a female householder, no spouse present. This definition could include some families that are not single-parent families. For example, if there are same-sex partners raising children together, the household would be grouped in this mother-only category. In addition, households could include other adults.

2. Other indicators of family structure paint a similar picture. According to the 2000 census, married-couple households constituted only 42 percent of black family households with children, compared with 78 percent of white family households and 86 percent of Asian family households.

3. For an explanation of the construction of the "poverty line," see the U.S. Census Bureau poverty website at www.census.gov/hhes/poverty/povdef.html. An excellent history of the poverty line is found at www.census.gov/hhes/poverty/povmeas/papers/orshansky.html. For a discussion on the need to change the way the official poverty line is constructed and on possible alternatives, see Citro and Michael (1995).

4. Curiously, the white–Latino gap is smaller for mother-only families than for married-couple families.

5. See the Federal Interagency Forum on Child and Family Statistics (ChildStats.gov) at http://childstats.gov/ac2002/tbl.asp?id=3&iid=16.

6. See U.S. Census Bureau, P-36, at www.census
.gov/hhes/income/histinc/incperdet.html.

7. See U.S. Census Bureau, at www.census
.gov/hhes/www/childsupport/chldsu99.pdf.

8. See Administration of Children and Families, Department of Health and Human Services, at
www.acf.dhhs.gov/programs/opre/characteristics/
fy2000/analysis.htm.

9. See Administration of Children and Families, Department of Health and Human Services, at
www.acf.dhhs.gov/programs/opre/characteristics/
fy2000/analysis.htm.

10. See U.S. Census Bureau at www.census
.gov/hhes/www/housing/hvs/annual02/ann02t15
.html.

11. Wilson and Neckerman implicitly assume
that the marriage market for black women consists
primarily of black men. This assumption is not unreasonable given the low incidence of interracial
marriage among African American women: 3 percent of black women were married to nonblack
men in 1994 (Sandefur et al. 2001).

12. Mink (1996), Piven and Cloward (1993),
and Robert Lieberman (2001) provide a lengthier
discussion of the treatment of black families under
U.S. social insurance systems.

13. The edited volume *The Consequences of
Growing Up Poor* (Brooks-Gunn and Duncan 1997)
provides extensive analysis of the links between
poverty and child outcomes. A different perspective
is offered by Susan Mayer in her book *What Money
Can't Buy*. She argues that extra money would not
make a big difference in the lives of poor children in
the United States (Mayer 1997).

14. There is remarkable international consensus
on this set of policies. In particular, UNICEF, the
United Nations agency responsible for children's
welfare, makes a similar recommendation (UNICEF
2000). An Organization for Economic Cooperation
and Development study by Sheila Kamerman and
others provides a survey (Kamerman et al. 2003).

REFERENCES

Brooks-Gunn, Jeanne, and Greg Duncan, eds. 1997.
Consequences of Growing Up Poor. New York:
Russell Sage Foundation.

Burbridge, Lynn. 1995. "Policy Implications of a
Decline in Marriage among African Ameri-
cans." In *The Decline in Marriage among African
Americans*, ed. M. Belinda Tucker and Claudia

Mitchell-Kernan. New York: Russell Sage Foundation.

Cantillon, Bea, and Karel Van den Bosch. 2002. "Social Policy Strategies to Combat Income Poverty
of Children and Families in Europe." Luxem-
bourg Income Study, Working Paper 336. Available at www.lisproject.org/publications/liswps/
336.pdf.

Citro, Constance F., and Robert T. Michael. 1995.
Measuring Poverty: A New Approach. Washington, D.C.: National Academy Press.

Darity, William, and Samuel Myers Jr. 1995. "Family
Structure and the Marginalization of Black Men:
Policy Implications." In *The Decline in Marriage
among African Americans*, ed. M. Belinda Tucker
and Claudia Mitchell-Kernan. New York: Russell
Sage Foundation.

Edin, Kathryn. 2000. "Few Good Men: Why Poor
Mothers Don't Marry or Remarry." *American
Prospect* 5, no. 11: 26–31.

Edin, Kathryn, and Kathleen Mullan Harris. 1999.
"Getting off and Staying off: Racial Differences
in the Work Route off Welfare." In *Latinas and
African American Women at Work: Race, Gender,
and Economic Inequality*, ed. Irene Browne. New
York: Russell Sage Foundation.

Ellwood, Daniel, and Jonathan Crane. 1990. "Family Change among Black Americans: What Do
We Know?" *Journal of Economic Perspectives* 5,
no. 4: 65–84.

Folbre, Nancy. 1994. *Who Pays for the Kids?* London:
Routledge.

Foster, E. Michael, and Saul D. Hoffman. 2001.
"The Young and the Not Quite So Young: Age
Variation in the Impact of AFDC Benefits on
Nonmarital Childbearing." In *Out of Wedlock:
Causes and Consequences of Nonmarital Fertil-
ity*, ed. Lawrence Wu and Barbara Wolfe. New
York: Russell Sage Foundation.

Frazier, E. Franklin. 1939. *The Negro Family in the
United States*. Chicago: University of Chicago
Press.

Greenstein, Robert, and Isaac Shaprio. 1998. "New
Research Findings on the Effects of the Earned
Income Tax Credit." Center for Budget and
Policy Priorities. Available at www.cbpp.org/
311eitc.htm.

Gutman, Herbert. 1976. *The Black Family in Slavery
and Freedom, 1750–1925*. New York: Pantheon.

Hartmann, Heidi, and Roberta Spalter-Roth.
2003. *Survival at the Bottom: The Income Pack-
ages of Low-Income Families with Children*.

Washington, D.C.: Institute for Women's Policy Research.

Jones-DeWeever, Avis, Janice Peterson, and Xue Song. 2003. *Before and after Welfare Reform: The Work and Well-Being of Low-Income, Single-Parent Families.* Washington, D.C.: Institute for Women's Policy Research.

Kamerman, Sheila, Michelle Neuman, Jane Waldfogel, and Jeanne Brooks-Gunn. 2003. "Social Policies, Family Types and Child Outcomes in Selected OECD Countries." Social, Employment, and Migration Working Paper 6, Organization for Economic Cooperation and Development.

King, Mary C., ed. 2001. *Squaring Up: Policy Strategies to Raise Women's Incomes in the United States.* Ann Arbor: University of Michigan.

Lieberman, Robert. 2001. *Shifting the Color Line: Race and the American Welfare State.* Cambridge, Mass.: Harvard University Press.

Mayer, Susan E. 1997. *What Money Can't Buy: Family Income and Children's Life Chances.* Cambridge, Mass.: Harvard University Press.

McLanahan, Sara. 1995. "The Consequences of Nonmarital Childbearing for Women, Children and Society." In *Report to Congress on Out-of-Wedlock Childbearing.* National Center for Health Statistics. Report PHS 95-1257. Washington, D.C.: U.S. Government Printing Office.

Mink, Gwendolyn. 1996. *The Wages of Motherhood: Inequality in the Welfare State, 1917–1942.* Ithaca, N.Y.: Cornell University Press.

Mishel, Lawrence, Jared Bernstein, and Heather Boushey. 2003. *The State of Working America, 2002–2003.* Ithaca, N.Y.: Industrial and Labor Relations Press.

Moffitt, Robert. 1998. "The Effect of Welfare on Marriage and Fertility: What Do We Know and What Do We Need to Know?" In *Welfare, the Family, and Reproductive Behavior,* ed. Robert Moffitt. Washington, D.C.: National Research Council, National Academy of Sciences Press.

Moynihan, Daniel Patrick. 1965. *The Negro Family: The Case for National Action.* Office of Policy Planning and Research, United States Department of Labor, March 1965. Available at www.dol.gov/asp/programs/history/webidmeynihan.htm.

Murray, Charles. 1984. *Losing Ground: American Social Policy 1950–1980.* New York: Basic Books.

NICHD [National Institute of Child Health and Human Development] Early Child Care Research Network. 1997. "Poverty and Patterns of Child Care." In *Consequences of Growing Up Poor,* ed. Jeanne Brooks-Gunn and Greg Duncan. New York: Russell Sage.

Piven, Frances Fox, and Robert Cloward. 1993. *Regulating the Poor: The Functions of Public Welfare.* New York: Vintage Books.

Sandefur, Gary, Molly Martin, Jennifer Eggerling-Boeck, Susan E. Mannon, and Ann M. Meier. 2001. "An Overview of Racial and Ethnic Demographic Trends." In *America Becoming: Racial Trends and Their Consequences,* ed. Neil J. Smelser, William J. Wilson, and Faith Mitchell. Washington, D.C.: National Research Council, National Academy of Sciences Press.

Smeeding, Timothy. 2004. "Government Programs and Social Outcomes: The United States in Comparative Perspective." Presented at the Smolensky Conference on Poverty, Income Distribution and Public Policy, University of California, Berkeley, December 12–13, 2003. Available at www.cpr.maxwell.syr.edu/faculty/smeeding/selectedpapers.htm.

Sorensen, Elaine, and Ariel Halpern. 1999. "Child Support Enforcement: How Well Is It Doing?" Assessing the New Federalism Discussion Paper 99-11. Urban Institute, December 1, 1999. Available at www.urban.org/url.cfm?ID=310324.

South, Scott, and Kim M. Lloyd. 1992. "Marriage Markets and Nonmarital Fertility in the United States." *Demography* 29, no. 2: 247–264.

Stevenson, Brenda E. 1995. "Black Family Structure in Colonial and Antebellum Virginia: Amending the Revisionist Perspective." In *The Decline in Marriage among African Americans,* ed. M. Belinda Tucker and Claudia Mitchell-Kernan. New York: Russell Sage Foundation.

Testa, Mark, and Marilyn Krogh. 1995. "The Effect of Employment on Marriage among Black Males in Inner-City Chicago." In *The Decline in Marriage among African Americans,* ed. M. Belinda Tucker and Claudia Mitchell-Kernan. New York: Russell Sage Foundation.

Tucker, M. Belinda, and Claudia Mitchell-Kernan. 1995. Introduction to *The Decline in Marriage among African Americans,* ed. M. Belinda Tucker and Claudia Mitchell-Kernan. New York: Russell Sage Foundation.

UNICEF. 2000. "A League Table of Child Poverty in Rich Nations." Report Card 7. Innocenti Center, Florence, Italy. Cited in Kamerman et al. 2003.

U.S. Census. 2000. "Summary File 3 (SF 3): Sample Data, Table P48." In *Family Type by Number of*

Workers in Family in 1999. Available at http://factfinder.census.gov.

Waite, Linda, and Maggie Gallagher. 2000. *The Case for Marriage: Why Married People Are Happier, Healthier, and Better Off Financially.* New York: Doubleday.

Wilson, William Julius, and Kathryn Neckerman. 1986. "Poverty and Family Structure: The Widening Gap between Evidence and Public Policy Issues." In *Fighting Poverty: What Works and What Doesn't,* ed. Sheldon Danziger and Daniel Weinberg. Cambridge, Mass.: Harvard University Press.

Wood, Robert G. 1995. "Marriage Rates and Marriageable Men: A Test of the Wilson Hypothesis." *Journal of Human Resources* 5, no. 30: 163–193.

Wolfe, Barbara, Kathryn Wilson, and Robert Haveman. 2001. "The Role of Economic Incentives in Teenage Nomarital Childbearing Choices." *Journal of Public Economics* 81:473–511.

19

The Racial Wealth Gap

THOMAS M. SHAPIRO and JESSICA L. KENTY-DRANE

In this chapter, addressing wealth inequality in the United States, Shapiro and Kenty-Drane describe the relationship between racial inequality and wealth accumulation. They highlight the importance of sociohistorical legacies in a family's ability to amass household wealth. The authors stress the significant impact of slavery and residential segregation on modern-day wealth inequality. Presenting recent national data on wealth, the authors document a black–white wealth gap ratio of 0.10 and an asset poverty rate of 25 percent for white households compared to 55 percent in black households. The black–white wealth gap can be explained by inequality in household income and differential distributions in inheritances by race. The authors conclude that the wealth gap is rooted in historical legacy: it is perpetuated by government policies and discrimination that result in residential and school segregation as well as a significant gap in potential inheritances between white and black households.

The past decade has proven to be an important period in understanding household economic stability. The financial security of a household has historically been measured by a family member's place in the labor market, including employment status and earnings. Since the work of Sherraden in *Assets and the Poor* (1991), the concept of wealth has become increasingly incorporated into modern measures of family economic well-being.[1] By itself, income is an insufficient measure of household socioeconomic status. Wealth accumulation has proven to be as important as income, if not more so, in discerning the life chances of household members.[2]

In recognizing the role of wealth, researchers have paved the way for a critical assessment of racial inequality in America. Wealth accumulation occurs via three pathways: inheritances, earnings, and savings. The work of Oliver and Shapiro in *Black Wealth/White Wealth* (1995)

documents how racial disparity accrues across these means of wealth accumulation. They demonstrate the structural barriers to wealth accumulation and the way these obstacles are connected to racial inequality, particularly for African Americans. Their work asserts that current disparities in wealth accumulation stem from historical racist policies, contemporary practices, and government policies.

OBSTACLES TO BLACK WEALTH ACCUMULATION

The impact of slavery on modern wealth distribution must not be underestimated. Slavery, the most extreme form of institutional racism, not only denied blacks freedom but also kept them from receiving appropriate compensation for their work and from improving the economic future of their families. Slaves were prohibited from entering into contracts and from purchasing property or land. These laws ensured that slaves were constrained from securing and accumulating assets. The outlawing of slavery did not rectify this matter. Institutional policies thwarted black wealth accumulation throughout U.S. history, as exemplified by residential segregation.

Blacks and whites continue living in separate neighborhoods long after official segregation, passage of major civil rights, fair housing and lending laws, and growth of a black middle class—a scenario some scholars call "American apartheid." In *Poverty and Place*, sociologist Paul Jargowsky details the importance of racial and economic segregation in determining inner-city poverty, noting a trend of increasing economic segregation alongside decreasing racial segregation. As of 2000, three-quarters of blacks live in highly segregated communities. Residential segregation persists at high levels: it remains a powerful force undermining the well-being of blacks, who are concentrated in communities with weak public services, such as hospitals, transportation, police, and fire protection; decreased housing appreciation; and inferior schools.

Federal housing, tax, and transportation policies helped to shape communities so that they would be highly segregated, racially as well as economically. Mortgage discrimination, redlining, and predatory lending practices reinforce residential segregation. Furthermore, racism remains a driving force behind community preference and white flight. Finally, neighborhoods remain highly segregated through deliberate acts of racial avoidance, violence and the threat of violence against minorities, local zoning decisions, and the isolation of public housing.[3]

In the twenty largest metropolitan areas, where 36 percent of all African Americans live, segregation pervades basic dimensions of community life. The residential color line means that blacks have greater difficulty overcoming problems associated with poor communities, especially crime, violence, housing abandonment, unstable families, poor health and high mortality, environmental degradation, and failing schools. No other group experiences segregation to the extent that blacks do. In many geographi-

cal areas, two decades of rising income inequality and budget cuts have produced a concentration of poverty that further compounds problems of segregation. Poor black neighborhoods are crowded, highly concentrated, and isolated far more severely than the neighborhoods of poor whites, Latinos, and Asians.[4]

The residential color line is the key feature distinguishing African Americans from all other groups in the United States. In *Black Identities*, Waters argues that African American segregation, especially in ghetto neighborhoods, is unlike the geographic separation that ethnic and immigrant groups face. The ramifications of such segregation are far more encompassing for African American children than they are for any other racial or ethnic group, leading to higher school dropout rates, lower college attendance, higher unemployment and lower earnings, and higher teenage pregnancy rates. Furthermore, effects of segregation are not limited to just poor blacks but are extended to middle-class blacks as well. Since middle-class black families tend to live in neighborhoods with poor people and share schools with lower-class blacks more than white middle-class families do, middle-class black students continue to face educational disadvantages.

The degree of residential segregation in America can be seen by looking at the typical metropolitan area in 1990, which was 13 percent black. To achieve a hypothetical semblance of integration, where 13 percent of one's neighbors were African American, almost two-thirds (64 percent) of black residents would have to move out of segregated communities and into white ones.[5] The evidence strongly suggests that segregation persists because of ongoing racial discrimination in real estate and mortgage markets, the persistence of white prejudice, and the discriminatory impact of public policies such as local zoning decisions and the isolation of public housing.

Residential segregation is the lynchpin of American race relations because so much else flows through community dynamics. One immediate consequence for wealth accumulation is that homes in white communities increase $28,600 more over a thirty-year-mortgage period than do comparable homes in black communities.[6] A community's racial composition appears to be the most salient feature determining home values. Homes lose at least 16 percent of their value when located in neighborhoods that are more than 10 percent black. Furthermore, properties decrease more steeply in neighborhoods with larger percentages of blacks. While white flight is a taken-for-granted social process, it is not just something that happens: it is propelled by family actions.

THE ASSETS AND INEQUALITY PROJECT

Our own research documents the present significance of race in wealth inequality. Using longitudinal data from the 1999 Panel Study of Income Dynamics (PSID),[7] we have demonstrated significant racial wealth disparities. We have also revealed the multiple mechanisms that propagate these inequities. For a full understanding of the data we present here, it is key that readers grasp the concepts we use to measure household wealth: net worth and net financial assets. Net worth is a measure of everything a household owns minus what they owe. Net financial assets is a measure of net worth minus home equity. Home equity is the value of the home net of mortgages. Net worth is a useful measure of wealth because it sums the households assets. We use net financial assets as well because the majority of most households wealth is built on their home equity. Using a measure that removes equity in a home allows us to see how much a family possesses besides their home.

The Black–White Wealth Gap

From our analysis of 1999 PSID data, we see in Figure 19.1 that the black-white wealth-gap ratio is 0.10, with typical white households having an overall median net worth of nearly $81,450 and blacks a median of just $8,000. The ratio for net financial assets is even lower, 0.09, with typical white families having median net financial assets of $33,500 and blacks possessing just $3,000. This disparity exists even when we compare whites and blacks in the top 20 percent category of income earners, as seen in Table 19.1. Top earners who are white have a net worth of $133,600 and net financial assets of $40,500, whereas top-earning blacks possess just $43,800 of net worth and a mere $7,500 in net financial assets.

Asset Poverty

Poverty thresholds for income have long been used to assess the economic well-being of households. The recognition of the impact of wealth has presented an opportunity to assess asset poverty as well. A concept of asset poverty helps us to understand the asset condition of American families. The fundamental idea is to determine the amount of assets needed so that a family can meet its basic needs over a specified period under the extreme condition that no other sources of income are available. We decided to tie this figure to the official income poverty standard. In 1999, the official U.S. government poverty line for a family of four stood at $1,392 a month. To live at the poverty line for three months, a family of four needed a

Table 19.1   Wealth by Income and Race

Income Class	White		Black	
	NW	NFA	NW	NFA
Highest fifth median	133,607	40,465	43,806	7,448
Second-highest fifth median	65,998	13,362	29,851	2,699
Middle fifth median	50,350	6,800	14,902	800
Second-lowest fifth median	39,908	3,599	6,879	249
Lowest fifth median	17,066	7,400	2,400	100

Note: NW = net worth; NFA = net financial assets.

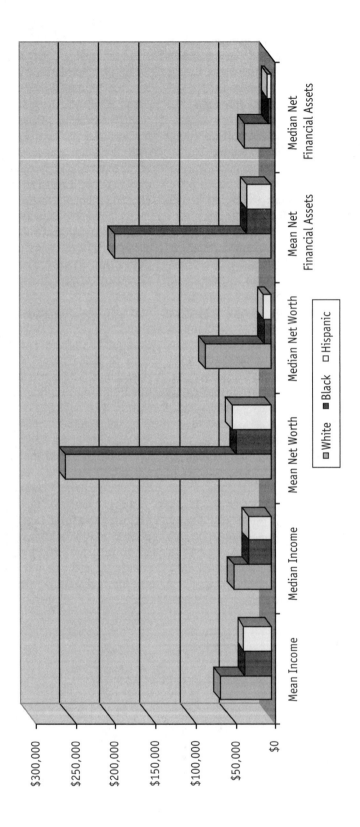

Figure 19.1 Family income and family wealth chart.

private safety net of at least $4,175. Families with less than $4,175 in net financial assets in 1999, then, were "asset poor." As the basis for our calculation, this is a conservative standard because it incorporates the official government poverty line, which many believe underestimates the actual scope of poverty. It also employs a three-month standard, even though one could argue just as reasonably for a six-month standard. Although we believe our built-in assumptions underestimate asset poverty among America's families, we want to stay focused on the basic idea of asset poverty. It is our hope that as these ideas are accepted, bold conceptions will follow.

Using data from the PSID, we found that relative to income poverty, asset poverty can be found in many households. In 1999, approximately 8 percent of white households were at the income poverty line, whereas nearly 25 percent were at the asset poverty line, as seen in Figure 19.2. For black families the numbers are even more dramatic. While 33 percent of black households are at the income poverty line, almost 55 percent suffer from asset poverty. When assets are examined, the fragility of American families is revealed, as is a huge disparity between asset-poor white and black families.

CONCLUSION: EXPLAINING THE BLACK–WHITE WEALTH GAP

Revealing the primary mechanisms related to wealth accumulation is vital if we hope to promote the growth of wealth among African American families. Our research has demonstrated several components important to asset accumulation. Several variables demonstrate a positive relationship with wealth: white households, age of head, having a college degree, middle-class occupational status, employment stability, retirement, home ownership, income, and receiving an inheritance. Several other variables demonstrate a negative relationship with wealth accumulation: living in the South, number of children, and being a widow. However, when combined, these variables explain a mere 17 percent of the variation in wealth accumulation.[8]

The most important contributor to wealth accumulation by far is household income. This finding provides us with an opportunity to explain some of the black–white wealth gap that exists. For each dollar of income a family earns, white families gain $3.25 in net worth. Contrast this amount with black families, who accumulate just under $2 of net worth for each dollar of income. Thus, not only are blacks earning less than whites are in terms of income (0.59 ratio), but they are accumulating less wealth for their earnings, dollar for dollar.

Another important explanation for the black–white wealth gap is the receipt of inheritances. The chance of receiving an inheritance is highly correlated with the economic wealth of one's parents. The greater the wealth of one's parents, the greater the inheritance a family is likely to receive. Inheritance provides us with a unique lens to examine the accumulation of wealth. Inheritances are sums of money that are distributed without regard to need or merit. They are gifts passed along from generation to generation. PSID data collected in 1988 documents a significant racial gap in parental wealth. White households estimated their parent's median wealth at $150,000, whereas black households valued theirs to be approximately $35,000. White families have a much greater chance of receiving a significant inheritance than do black families. Thus, white households will accumulate a greater proportion of wealth faster because of this inequity and the significance of inheritances for wealth accumulation.

African Americans cannot earn themselves out of the racial wealth gap. The huge racial wealth gap is a historical legacy that the past continually visits on current generations. But it is more than an obdurate past. The racial wealth gap also results from significant and continuing government policies and discrimination that result in residential and school segregation. Finally, the baby boomer generation—some of whose parents accumulated considerable wealth assisted by the Federal Housing Administration, home mortgage interest deduction, and other government policies—is passing to its adult children the largest wealth transfer in U.S. history. The racial wealth gap thus illustrates how hard-earned gains in

Figure 19.2 Asset poverty line; percentage below poverty line.

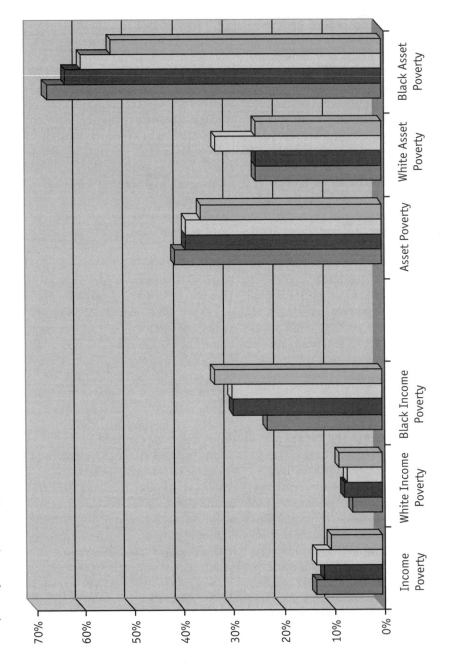

salaries, jobs, and education fail to improve racial inequality.

NOTES

1. The volume by Thomas Shapiro and Edward Wolff, *Assets for the Poor* (2001), provides a number of significant research papers that assume this challenge.

2. In addition to Michael Sherraden's work, Dalton Conley's book *Being Black, Living in the Red* (1999) and Lisa Keister's book *Wealth in America* (2000) have made important contributions to this discussion.

3. A good synopsis of these practices and policies can be found in Kenneth Jackson's *Crabgrass Frontier* (1985) and Guy Stuart's *Discriminating Risk: The U.S. Mortgage Lending Industry in the Twentieth Century* (2003).

4. Douglas Massey and Nancy Denton's *American Apartheid* (1993) provides ample evidence on the consequences of residential segregation and concentrated poverty.

5. See the analysis by Roderick Harrison and Daniel Weinberg, "Racial and Ethnic Segregation in 1990," working paper (Washington, D.C.: U.S. Bureau of the Census, 1992).

6. This figure comes from analysis of PSID data; the full analysis can be found in Shapiro, *The Hidden Cost of Being African American.*

7. See http://psidonline.isr.umich.edu.

8. The full regression models can be found in Shapiro, *The Hidden Cost of Being African American.*

BIBLIOGRAPHY

Jargowsky, Paul. *Poverty and Place.* New York: Russell Sage Foundation, 1997.

Oliver, Melvin, and Thomas M. Shapiro. *Black Wealth/White Wealth: A New Perspective on Racial Inequality.* New York: Routledge, 1995.

Patillo-McCoy, Mary. *Black Picket Fences.* Chicago: University of Chicago Press, 1999.

Shapiro, Thomas. *The Hidden Cost of Being African American: How Wealth Perpetuates Inequality.* New York: Oxford University Press, 2004.

Sherraden, Michael. *Assets and the Poor: A New American Welfare Policy.* Armonk, N.Y.: M. E. Sharpe, 1991.

Waters, Mary. *Black Identities.* Cambridge, Mass.: Harvard University Press; New York: Russell Sage Foundation, 1999.

PART V

*Globalization and Its Impact on
the Economic Well-Being of
African Americans and Latinos*

20

Globalization, the Transformation of Capital, and the Erosion of Black and Latino Living Standards
PETER DORMAN

Increased capital mobility has had large direct and indirect effects on the economic condition of black and Latino communities in the United States. Its direct effect has been to eliminate jobs on which these communities depend; indirectly, it has promoted a new "profit paradigm" for business, resulting in contingent and insecure employment, deunionization, and greater wage inequality—all of which have disproportionately harmed minority workers. Deregulated and outsourced production systems also provide fewer targets for political activism. These trends are exemplified by recent developments in the automobile, textile, and apparel industries.

A SUSPICIOUS COINCIDENCE

The era of neoliberal globalization has coincided with a striking deterioration in the prospects for minority workers in the United States—particularly blacks and Latinos. Since 1980, racial and ethnic economic inequality has increased, along with the ability of capital to take advantage of the most profitable investment opportunities worldwide. After a brief overview of the problem of racial justice in the context of globalization, I consider two ways that capital mobility has contributed to the hard times experienced by African American and other minority workers. First, many have lost their jobs in industries abandoned by domestic capital, such as textiles and apparel. Second, minority wages have declined because of changes in business strategy resulting from globalization. As we will see, a significant change in direction is required if these trends are to be reversed.

GLOBALIZATION AND RACIAL INEQUALITY

Economic struggles have always been an important part of the civil rights movement.[1] Living conditions for people of color have improved as a result of successful battles to remove discrimination in employment, wages, and training and promotion. Minority workers have fought to join unions and then fought again to be represented fairly by them. In so doing, workers of color have taken a political approach to economic institutions. The paradox of globalization, however, is that it removes political options even as it reverses the economic gains made by past generations.

Until recently, most firms concentrated on increasing productivity through increasing their overall size, bringing all the phases of production under one administrative structure, and managing in detail the work of their employees. It was a bureaucratic strategy: big, integrated organizations engaged in planning the entire work process. Most large corporations valued stability and predictability to make the long-term investments called for under this strategy. Firms were rooted in specific locations, and they preferred to see the same faces at work each morning. To discourage turnover, wages were set a little higher than necessary, and teamwork within the enterprise was encouraged by limiting the wage spread between higher and lower echelons. Unions, while seldom desired by business, were tolerated since they served as a potential force for order and stability. Although these traditional businesses had their considerable flaws, they did reduce to some extent the level of inequality as well as provide an institutional target for social justice movements.

All of this changed rather suddenly after the late 1970s. The new strategy was different: firms tried to reduce the layers of administration, and they treated each division as if it were a separate company, with its own financial accounting and control over production. In other words, the competitive logic of the market replaced the rule-making logic of administration. Operations were regarded as "assets"; a corporation might buy a product line one day and sell it the next. Every phase of the production process that could be performed more cheaply elsewhere was outsourced, meaning that parts of the company might be shut down and their operations farmed out to the lowest bidder. Even units that were not shut down were expected to prove they could do the work at less cost than outside suppliers. Workers, except for those thought to possess specialized and highly valuable skills, were regarded as expendable: there to be hired when needed and downsized when not. Wages were set at the lowest possible level, and unions were resisted at all costs. This was the new profit paradigm for the global marketplace.[2]

But competition is not an equal opportunity exploiter. Workers of color are subject to continuing discrimination and thus have a weaker bargaining position than nonminorities have and can be made to accept lower wages. For example, the differences in financial wealth between whites and people of color far exceed the differences in income, which removes a cushion that black and Latino workers could otherwise depend on during times of economic distress.[3] In the new world

of just-in-time, just-for-now employment, this translates into lower wages.[4]

THE DIRECT EMPLOYMENT EFFECTS OF INCREASED CAPITAL MOBILITY

In its simplest sense, capital mobility refers to the ease with which capital investment, in either its physical or financial form, can relocate from one region or country to another. This movement has occurred since the origins of capitalism, but it has accelerated in recent decades due to reduced costs of transportation and communication, as well as the elimination of political and cultural barriers. When it leaves, the outflow of capital takes the form of disinvestment; after it sets up shop abroad, the result is a flow of imports to replace the lost domestic production.

One measure of disinvestment is the use of international outsourcing, the strategy of shutting down portions of the production process in the home country (here the United States) that produce inputs into finished products and instead purchasing these inputs from abroad. Table 20.1 describes this trend.

This is rapid growth, particularly in transportation equipment, the sector that includes automobile production. As Feenstra and Hanson point out, this selective process of pruning the productive system probably concentrates its effects on workers with less education. These were once relatively good jobs. Now they have been eliminated because workers with similar qualifications in other countries are willing to do the same work for a fraction of the price.[5]

This highly targeted form of deindustrialization has had devastating impacts on African Americans and other communities of color, as described by William Julius Wilson. Cities such as New York, Detroit, Chicago, and Los Angeles depended on these industries for their economic base; the jobs fled, but the people remained, impoverished and without the means to address their spiraling social problems.[6]

Particular mention should be made of three industries profoundly affected by outsourcing: automobiles, textiles, and apparel. Table 20.2 traces

Table 20.1 Outsourcing, as Measured by the Share of Imported Inputs to Total Intermediate Inputs

	1974	1984	1993
All manufacturing	4.1	6.2	8.2
Chemical and allied products	3.0	4.5	6.3
Industrial machinery (nonelectrical)	4.1	7.2	11.0
Electrical equipment and machinery	4.5	6.7	11.6
Transportation equipment	6.4	10.7	15.7

Source: Feenstra and Hanson (2001, table 1).

overall and minority employment in these sectors during the period 1979–1999. Overall, the black and Latino shares of employment increased over these twenty years, but total employment grew slightly in automobiles and fell sharply in textiles and apparel.

As this table indicates, displacement from auto production in general was not a significant problem. Nevertheless, there were regional impacts, as production shifted from the original heartland, the region surrounding Detroit, and relocated to rural, largely white areas in other parts of the country. This restructuring had a profound effect on urban black communities in the upper Midwest; many are still struggling to return to their economic level of twenty-five years ago.[7]

Apparel and textiles were more directly affected by the decision to relocate portions of the production process abroad. Blacks constituted 14 percent of this combined sector in the United States in 1979, increasing to 16 percent by 1999, with women accounting for nearly half of these jobs. Black employment is particularly marked in textiles (almost 22 percent of the workforce in 1999), which has been the most important industrial employer in the rural South.[8] Fully two-thirds of all clothing production, by contrast, takes place in just two cities, New York and Los Angeles; in the latter, Latinos form 66 percent of the workforce, and Asian Americans another 14 percent.[9] By 1999 Latinos accounted for more than 30 percent of all workers in apparel. Between 1979 and 1999, however, total employment in the two sectors dropped precipitously from 2.1 million to 1.1 million.[10] As in other instances in which outsourcing has played a key role, the decline was

Table 20.2 Total, Black, and Latino Employment in Three Industries, 1979–2000 (in thousands of workers)

	1979	1989	1999
Automobiles	1,238	1,196	1,323
Black	187 (15.1%)	178 (14.9%)	206 (15.6%)
Latino	36 (2.9)	51 (4.3)	77 (5.8)
Textiles	823	127	524
Black	127 (15.4)	22 (17.3)	114 (21.8)
Latino	33 (4.0)	9 (6.9)	56 (10.6)
Apparel	1,279	1,172	583
Black	166 (13.0)	170 (14.5)	62 (10.7)
Latino	194 (15.2)	244 (20.8)	177 (30.4)

Source: U.S. Bureau of Labor Statistics (2003).
Note: The rows designated as *Automobiles, Textiles,* and *Apparel* give total employment per industry; percentages refer to the portion of each sector's labor force constituting black and Latino workers.

concentrated on production workers with the lowest qualifications, sparing some of the high-paid and highly trained occupations.[11] Thus, the impact on minority workers is probably greater than the overall numbers suggest.

CAPITAL MOBILITY AND THE NEW INEQUALITY

During the 1960s and 1970s, black workers made progress in closing the racial wage gap.[12] This was a period of civil rights activism, and as we have seen, pressure was brought to bear on employers to open up higher-paying jobs to black applicants and adopt equal-pay practices within existing job classifications. However, progress ended as the 1980s began, and the wage gap has slowly widened once more.

We can loosely distinguish between two factors that influence racial wage inequality. The first is the *sorting effect:* it measures the segmenting of workers of different races or ethnicities into the relatively better or worse jobs that our economy has to offer. Affirmative action in employment attempts to minimize this effect by bringing more minority workers into better jobs. Sorting is a product of the skills and qualifications that workers in each group bring to the labor market, as well as the ability or desire of employers to discriminate and choose members of one group over another. (It should be remembered, however, that the type of labor supplied by a group is strongly influenced by the demand—or lack of it—they encounter in the marketplace.[13]) The second factor can be called the *reward effect:* it captures the differences in pay and benefits between better and worse jobs. Thus, the racial wage gap, as a first approximation, can be viewed as the product of differential access to good jobs and the differential pay afforded by good versus bad jobs.

The weight of evidence suggests that, while hiring discrimination and unequal access to skills remain serious problems in American society, progress has continued on those fronts. Black workers in particular arrive in the labor market each year with a smaller education gap, and measures of overt hiring discrimination show gradual improvement.[14] Unfortunately, there has been an explosion of income and wage inequality over the past twenty years; thus, the Gini coefficient, a common measuring rod of inequality, rose 23.6 percent between 1979 and 1997.[15] This heightened inequality is fractal: it appears within specific occupations and industries as well as between them, such as among truck drivers and lawyers, as well as within and between every demographic group.[16] The combined result—slightly more equal sorting, vastly more unequal rewards—accounts for the dismal situation of black workers today. As Smith writes, "These last 20 years were actually a time during which the slowly evolving historical forces continued to close the wage gap between Black and White male workers. These forces were simply overwhelmed by the structural shift of rising wage dispersion."[17]

But the simple model of sorting and reward is too simple to capture the minority experience of the last two decades. Pay levels are not attached to jobs arbitrarily, irrespective of those who actually hold them. Pay reflects productivity, but it also reflects what employers can get away with. Recall the earlier discussion of the change in business strategies. Globalization has made it more profitable for companies to troll the market for the cheapest possible supplier, whether for labor or other inputs, than to make long-term investments in, and commitments to, a single supplier. This constant search for the lowest-cost alternative puts workers at a disadvantage, especially if they are already discriminated against.

Recent empirical evidence for the link between changes in business strategies and heightened wage inequality can be found in the work of McCall, whose study used a two-part method to examine inequality.[18] First, a statistical analysis was undertaken to determine what aspects of people's wages could be attributed to race, gender, or industry of employment. The residuals—the unexplained differences in wages—were then analyzed to see what factors account for these within-group differences. As in other studies, this one found that hard-to-explain within-group differences play a far greater role in wage inequality than between-group differences. For our purposes, what is particularly interesting are the factors associated with wider within-group spreads: contingent labor, unemployment rates, and employment in manufacturing (for men).

Direct measures are not available to the extent to which these workers' employers have adopted the new profit paradigm, but these findings are consistent with such a hypothesis.

In the remainder of this section, I touch on specific aspects of the transformation of capital and its impact on workers of color and then conclude with a closer look at the auto industry.

Contingent work. As we saw, contingent work—temp work, contract work, and other employment practices geared to short-term market conditions—is characteristic of the new paradigm. Every two years, the U.S. Bureau of Labor Statistics conducts a special survey to determine the extent and composition of contingent work in America. Since the series began in 1995, workers of color have been shown to be disproportionately contingent.[19] In the survey conducted in 2001, blacks were more likely than whites to be engaged in all forms of contingent work other than self-employment, and they accounted for a remarkable 24.5 percent of all temp agency personnel. A similar pattern holds for Hispanics, who make up 17.8 percent of all temporary help. Not surprisingly, most contingent work arrangements are associated with sharply lower pay and less provision of benefits such as health insurance and pensions.[20]

Deunionization. Firms making the transition to the competitive paradigm are extremely hostile to unions. Capital mobility itself contributes to their ability to resist unionization or defeat union demands where workers are organized. In a landmark study, Bronfenbrenner found that employers routinely used the threat of relocation abroad to subdue their workforces and that these actions were effective.[21] A more recent update confirms these findings, particularly for such mobile sectors of the economy as manufacturing, communications, and wholesaling.[22]

Union membership in the United States has been shown to benefit all workers, but it has had particularly positive effects on minority workers. Table 20.3 documents these effects using 2001 data. The wage premium in this table reflects the percentage increase in wages paid to unionized workers, controlling for experience, education, region, industry, occupation, and marital status.

Men in general tend to receive more benefits from unionization, presumably due to the nature of the jobs they are more likely to hold, but black and Latina women have higher wage premiums than their white counterparts do. It is also interesting to note that black men and women have unionization rates between 5 and 6 percentage points higher than do white men and women.

Displacement. A direct consequence of capital mobility in general, and the new profit paradigm in particular, is a higher rate of employment turnover. This has led to increased displacement of workers, defined as the involuntary separation (through layoffs or dismissal) of workers from their employers. Black workers have been displaced at significantly higher rates than whites. During the 1980s, for instance, 7.1 percent of all black workers were displaced, compared to 4.9 percent of all white workers. This declined somewhat during the soft recession of the early 1990s (which took a relatively larger toll on white-collar workers), but the black displacement rate was still higher at 5.1 percent, compared to the white rate of 4.4 percent. In addition, displacement has a different

Table 20.3   Union Wage Premium by Race/Ethnicity and Gender

	Percent union	*Wage premium*
White men	17.2	11.5
White women	13.1	9.5
Black men	22.8	13.6
Black women	18.8	11.3
Hispanic men	13.3	16.9
Hispanic women	12.3	12.8

Source: Mishel, Bernstein, and Boushey (2003, table 2.37).

meaning for black workers, since they face more obstacles to finding new jobs. During the initial recovery of 1982–1983, the white reemployment rate was fully 54 percent higher than the black rate, and the corresponding figure for 1992–1993 was 25 percent.[23]

The new profit paradigm in the auto industry. As mentioned, the auto industry has played a large role in the economic fortunes of black America. The industry was heavily unionized following the organizing drives of the 1930s, and the combination of union power and high productivity led to one of the highest wage levels in manufacturing. Nevertheless, the industry always had two tiers, the best-paid and most highly unionized work at the "big three"—Ford, Chrysler, and General Motors—and the less-lucrative work in the smaller plants that supplied components for later assembly. The biggest change that occurred during the past twenty years was the widening of this gap and the flow of jobs from the top tier to the bottom.

While overall employment in the auto industry held steady between 1978 and 1998, employment fell in the better-paying assembly and stamping plants from 320,000 to 258,000, while rising in the supplier plants from 352,000 to 437,000. Thus, as recently as the late 1970s, nearly half of the industry's jobs were in the top tier; by 1998 just over a third were. This reflects the outsourcing, low-cost supplier strategy associated with the new profit paradigm. At the same time, union representation of the supplier sector shrank, falling from a majority of all workers in this sector in 1981 to only 21.5 percent in 1998—less than half of whom were members of the United Auto Workers, the relatively powerful union representing the top tier.[24] This dramatic

restructuring of employment had equally dramatic effects on wages. Table 20.4 demonstrates the tight linkage between outsourcing, deunionization, and wages.

By outsourcing its work to a nonunion supplier, a "big three" producer can cut the unskilled portion of its labor costs nearly in half. Note also the impact that unionization plays in reducing wage inequality within the supplier sector, where the skilled–unskilled gap is only 16 percent, compared to 63 percent in the nonunion firms. Unionization would reduce the economic impact of any racial difference in access to the better, higher-skilled jobs for the small minority of such firms that still have unions. Incidentally, wages for auto parts production in Detroit's ironically named "empowerment zone" were only seven dollars an hour during this period, further evidence that the new profit paradigm is geared to take advantage of the vulnerability caused by discrimination.[25]

The other side of capital mobility in this industry is the influx of foreign-based capital, the so-called transplants that produce cars with Japanese or European nameplates here in the United States. These firms are almost entirely nonunion, and organizing drives fail against the argument that they are as ready to leave as they were to arrive.[26] Being nonunion, these firms typically pay less than union firms do, and they create wider divisions between higher- and lower-paid workers.[27]

The auto industry, long important for a large swath of black America, is a microcosm of the new, globalized workplace. Jobs are less likely to be unionized; less likely to be in large, stable businesses; and more likely to pay wages that are lower and less equal.

Table 20.4   Average Hourly Wage Rates in Michigan Automotive Production, 1998

Company	Skilled production	Unskilled production
Big three[a]	23.50	19.55
Union supplier	15.10	13.00
Nonunion supplier	16.41	10.06

Source: McAlinden, Smith, and Swiecki (1999).
[a]Ford, Chrysler, and General Motors.

CONCLUSION: A CASE OF MOTION SICKNESS

Flexibility and quickness help prey and predator alike. Firms that can move at a moment's notice to a distant location to take advantage of profit opportunities are the beneficiaries of an era of mobile capital. Workers who can move equally as quick between employers, owing to their valuable skills or social connections, also thrive. Left behind are those for whom a steady job once served as an oasis in a world of racial roadblocks. For economic change to benefit the majority of workers, especially those with least access to the labor market, there is an urgent need for the stability and procedural equity that only reinstitutionalization can provide. Capital needs to be rerooted in affected communities, and the organizational threads need to be rewoven—in particular, the unions and the training and promotion systems that bind enterprises and their workers. It is not in the market but in such a revitalized institutional framework that the struggle for justice can be carried to a successful conclusion.

NOTES

1. Examples include Martin Luther King's intervention on behalf of Memphis's striking sanitation workers, Operation PUSH's effort to pressure companies into ending employment discrimination, Cesar Chavez's campaign to upgrade wages and working conditions for Chicano and other farmworkers, and minority caucuses in the labor movement such as the League of Revolutionary Black Workers in the United Automobile Workers.

2. Harrison (1994), especially chapter 9, "The Dark Side of Flexible Production"; Kochan, Katz, and McKersie (1994), especially chapter 3, "The Emergence of the Nonunion Industrial Relations System."

3. Oliver and Shapiro (1995) document this inequality in wealth but examine its impact on what I later call the *sorting effect,* rather than the *reward effect,* in occupations and incomes.

4. Albelda, Drago, and Shulman (2001, 164–165); Bowles and Gintis (1992).

5. Feenstra and Hanson (2001).

6. Wilson (1996), especially chapter 2, "Societal Changes and Vulnerable Neighborhoods."

7. Farley, Danziger, and Holzer (2000), especially chapter 3, "The Evolution of Detroit's Labor Market Since 1940."

8. U.S. Bureau of Labor Statistics (2003).

9. Bonacich and Appelbaum (2000, 18, 169).

10. U.S. Bureau of Labor Statistics (2003).

11. Mittelhauser (1997).

12. Mishel, Bernstein, and Boushey (2003).

13. Mason (2000, 335).

14. Mishel, Bernstein, and Schmitt (2001, 163–165); Mishel, Bernstein, and Boushey (2003, 168–169).

15. The standard deviation of the distribution of wages (measured logarithmically), another useful measure, rose 25 percent for women and 18 percent for men between 1979 and 2001. Both data come from Mishel, Bernstein, and Boushey (2003, 50, 148).

16. McCall (2000); Mishel, Bernstein, and Boushey (2003, 163–167).

17. Smith (2000, 81).

18. McCall (2000).

19. Hipple (2001).

20. Mishel, Bernstein, and Schmitt (2003, 253–256).

21. Bronfenbrenner (1996).

22. Bronfenbrenner (2000).

23. Fairlie and Kletzer (1996).

24. Slaughter (1999).

25. Slaughter (1999).

26. Muller and Welch (2002).

27. Muller, Kerwin, and Welch (2002).

REFERENCES

Albelda, Randy, Robert W. Drago, and Steven Shulman. 2001. *Unlevel Playing Fields: Understanding Wage Inequality and Discrimination.* Cambridge, Mass.: Economic Affairs Bureau.

Bonachich, Edna, and Richard P. Appelbaum. 2000. *Behind the Label: Inequality in the Los Angeles Apparel Industry.* Berkeley: University of California Press.

Bowles, Samuel, and Herbert Gintis. 1992. "Power and Wealth in a Competitive Economy." *Philosophy and Public Affairs* 21, no. 4: 324–353.

Bronfenbrenner, Kate. 1996. "Final Report: The Effects of Plant Closing or Threat of Plant

Closing on the Right of Workers to Organize." Submitted to the Labor Secretariat of the North American Commission for Labor Cooperation, Washington, D.C.

———. 2000. "Uneasy Terrain: The Impact of Capital Mobility on Workers, Wages, and Union Organizing." Submission to the U.S. Trade Deficit Review Commission, Washington, D.C.

Fairlie, Robert, and Lori Kletzer. 1996. "Race and the Shifting Burden of Job Displacement: 1982–1993." *Monthly Labor Review* 19, no. 9: 13–23.

Farley, Reynolds, Sheldon Danziger, and Harry J. Holzer. 2000. *Detroit Divided*. New York: Russell Sage Foundation.

Feenstra, Robert C., and Gordon H. Hanson. 2001. "Global Production Sharing and Rising Inequality: A Survey of Trade and Wages." Working Paper 8372, National Bureau of Economic Research, Cambridge, Massachusetts.

Galbraith, James K. 1998. *Created Unequal: The Crisis in American Pay*. New York: Free Press.

Godley, Wynne. 2000. "Medium-Term Prospects and Policies for the United States and the World." Special report, Jerome Levy Economics Institute, Annandale-on-Hudson, New York.

Harrison, Bennett. 1994. *Lean and Mean: The Changing Landscape of Corporate Power in the Age of Flexibility*. New York: Basic Books.

Hipple, Steve. 2001. "Contingent Work in the Late 1990s." *Monthly Labor Review* 124, no. 3: 3–27.

Kochan, Thomas A., Harry C. Katz, and Robert B. McKersie. 1994. *The Transformation of American Industrial Relations*. Ithaca, N.Y.: Industrial and Labor Relations Press.

Mason, Patrick L. 2000. Understanding Recent Empirical Evidence on Race and Labor Market Outcomes in the USA. *Review of Social Economy* 58, no. 3: 319–338.

McAlinden, Sean P., Brett C. Smith, and Bernard F. Swiecki. 1999. "The Future of Modular Automotive Systems: Where Are the Economic Efficiencies in the Modular Assembly Concept?" University of Michigan Transportation Research Institute, Office for the Study of Automotive Transportation, Ann Arbor, Michigan.

McCall, Leslie. 2000. "Explaining Levels of Within-Group Wage Inequality in U.S. Labor Markets." *Demography* 37, no. 4: 415–430.

Mishel, Lawrence, Jared Bernstein, and Heather Boushey. 2003. *The State of Working America, 2002–2003*. Ithaca, N.Y.: Cornell University Press.

Mishel, Lawrence, Jared Bernstein, and John Schmitt. 2001. *The State of Working America, 2000–2001*. Ithaca, N.Y.: Cornell University Press.

Mittelhauser, Mark. 1997. "Employment Trends in Textiles and Apparel, 1973–2005." *Monthly Labor Review* 120, no. 8: 24–35.

Muller, Joann, Kathleen Kerwin, and David Welch. 2002. "Autos: A New Industry." *Business Week*, no. 3791 (July 15): 98–104.

Muller, Joann, and David Welch. 2002. "Can the UAW Stay in the Game?" *Business Week*, no. 3786 (June 10): 78–79.

Oliver, Melvin, and Thomas Shapiro. 1995. *Black Wealth/White Wealth: A New Perspective on Racial Inequality*. New York: Routledge.

Slaughter, Jane. 1999. "Modular Rage: Automakers Look to Revamp the Auto Industry—and Its Labor Relations." *Multinational Monitor* 20, no. 4: 24–27.

Smith, James P. 2000. "Race and Ethnicity in the Labor Market: Trends over the Short and Long Term." In *America Becoming: Racial Trends and Their Consequences*, ed. Neil J. Smelser, William Julius Wilson, and Faith Mitchell. Vol. 2. Washington, D.C.: National Academy Press.

U.S. Bureau of Labor Statistics. 2003. Unpublished Current Population Survey data.

Wilson, William Julius. 1996. *When Work Disappears: The World of the New Urban Poor*. New York: A. A. Knopf.

21

Globalization and African Americans: A Focus on Public Employment

MARY C. KING

The increased mobility of capital has strengthened the bargaining power of business with national governments and workforces around the globe. The result in the government arena has been lower taxes, fewer regulations, and a weakened public sector; and in the workplace, lower wages and less employment security. African Americans as a group are clearly hurt by cuts in public services, a shift of the tax burden from corporations to individuals, and lower wages overall. What is less clear is whether African Americans are being hurt by the cuts in the public-sector workforce. In the last ten years African Americans have become less concentrated in public employment: whereas in 1993 blacks were half as likely to work for the government as whites were, they are now only one-third as likely. At the same time, the racial wage gap has decreased—particularly in the private sector and particularly in the last five years—so that while the earnings gap between blacks and whites remains bigger in the private sector, the two sectors are now much more similar.

One of the most important aspects of the economic globalization of recent decades is the increasing pressure on national governments to reduce their demands on business, whether in the form of taxation or regulation (Rodrik 1998). Business—or capital, in another vocabulary— has disproportionately gained from globalization through increased mobility. Improvements in telecommunications and transportation allowed business to shift work—especially production and clerical work—to wherever it can be done most cheaply. Corporations are also shifting their nominal headquarters to low-tax nations, without losing their access to markets in the United States and in other affluent countries.

The consequence is that business has gained bargaining power with governments and with labor. With business more mobile than either, it is hard for governments to demand more in taxes or for labor to get more in wages. Business's increasing power relative to that of labor is a big part of the reason that real wages for production and nonsupervisory workers are no higher now than they were in the early 1970s; that the real purchasing power of the minimum wage is more than 20 percent lower than it was in 1979; and that unions are shrinking, hampered by an increasingly hostile legal environment (Mishel, Bernstein, and Schmitt 2001). Labor cannot demand higher wages directly from businesses, and they cannot compete with business lobbyists to get better legislation through Congress.

Although all economists see these changes in the relative bargaining power of business, government, and labor, Marxist economists describe them most explicitly. The reason is that Marxists view conflict between capital and labor over "shares of the pie" as the normal working of a market economy. The pie is divided at work and in the arena of government. At work, when business is strong and labor is weak—as is true now in the United States—profits and executive salaries are higher, and wages and benefits of most employees are lower. In the public forum, when business is strong and labor is weak, the burden of taxation is shifted from corporations and the wealthy to the poor, to the working people, and to the middle class; government services in the form of education and healthcare are cut; regulatory bodies monitoring safety, health, discrimination, and environmental degradation are disempowered and underfunded; and government expenditures are shifted to spending that benefits business, such as military contracts and agricultural subsidies of agribusiness.

Of course, all of this has clear implications for African Americans, whose current interests are much more in line with labor than with capital. Given the importance of race in our economic history, African Americans now disproportionately number among the poor, the working class, and the middle class rather than among the owners and managers of large corporations. Because of their class location, African Americans disproportionately rely on public services rather than private education, health care, or recreation—though it is also true that public programs were created and implemented in ways that served whites far better than they did blacks (Lieberman 1998; Oliver and Shapiro 1997; Quadagno 1994). Furthermore, because the public sector has been less discriminatory than the private sector has and because many African Americans have been oriented toward public service, African Americans are disproportionately employed by the public sector, including the military (Carrington, McCue, and Pierce 1996; Moskos and Butler 1996).

So, we would expect globalization to have disproportionately harmed African Americans since it has allowed business to put pressure on governments to reduce corporate taxes and taxes on the wealthy; to shrink the public sector; and to shift the focus of government spending from public services to activities that directly benefit business. One way to assess whether this line of logic is in fact true is to examine the history of African American employment in the public sector.

GOVERNMENT EMPLOYMENT AND AFRICAN AMERICANS

While it is certainly true now that there is less scope for discrimination against African Americans in the public sector than in the private sector, public employment has not always been open to blacks (Carrington, McCue, and Pierce 1996; Jones 1998). As late as the 1950s, African Americans—particularly women—were underrepresented in public employment, as is shown in table 21.1, which gives a quick overview of the history of black public employment. But by 1970, African Americans of both sexes were overrepresented in government work, until the early 1990s they were half again as likely as whites of the same sex to work for the government.

In 1980 Ronald Reagan was elected president and began to cut federal employment. The proportion of Americans who work for the government—whether federal, state, or local—has continued to fall ever since so that now fewer than one in five U.S. workers works in the public sector.

After the relative size of government labor forces began to fall, the proportion of African Americans in those labor forces began to decline, as is shown in table 21.2. The overrepresentation of African Americans in public employment has fallen through the 1990s, so that by 2001 African Americans were only one-third again as likely to work for the government as whites.

So, it is plainly true that African Americans hold a shrinking proportion of falling public-sector employment. On the face of it, these numbers by themselves need not be a bad thing for African Americans. Public employment for state and local governments is generally not as well paid as is work in the private sector—particularly for men—though the benefits may be better. "Female intensive" occupations are concentrated in the public and nonprofit sectors—including clerical, health, teaching, and social work. The higher the concentration of women in an occupation, the lower the pay, regardless of qualifications; so, a shift out of the public sector might be progress for African Americans (see England, Christopher, and Reid 1999).

Pay disparities between the public and the private sector are widest for people with college degrees, and professional African Americans

Table 21.1   Proportion of Employed African Americans and All Americans Working in Government, 1950–2001

	Black women	Black men	All women	All men
1950	10.1	10.0	14.4	11.1
1960	14.5	14.3	16.4	13.1
1970	24.3	19.1	20.0	15.7
1980	31.2	22.9	21.2	16.1
1990	26.1	20.8	18.4	14.7

	Black women and men	All women and men
1993	23.2	15.5
1994	22.3	14.9
1995	22.1	14.7
1996	21.2	14.4
1997	20.5	14.0
1998	19.8	14.0
1999	19.5	14.2
2000	19.1	14.1
2001	19.2	14.1

Sources: Figures for 1950–1990 come from public-use microdata samples of the census, as calculated by Lynn Burbridge (1994). Figures for 1993–2001 come from multiple issues of *Employment and Earnings*, January volumes (U.S. Bureau of Labor Statistics 1995, 1997, 1999, 2001).

Table 21.2   Proportion of Employed African Americans in Government Employment as a Proportion of all Americans Employed in Government, 1950–2001

	Black women	Black men
1950	.70	.90
1960	.88	1.09
1970	1.22	1.22
1980	1.47	1.42
1990	1.42	1.41

	Black women and men
1993	1.50
1994	1.50
1995	1.50
1996	1.47
1997	1.46
1998	1.41
1999	1.37
2000	1.35
2001	1.36

Sources: Figures for 1950–1990 come from public-use microdata samples of the census, as calculated by Lynn Burbridge (1994). Figures for 1993–2001 come from multiple issues of *Employment and Earnings*, January volumes (U.S. Bureau of Labor Statistics 1995, 1997, 1999, 2001).

have been almost "ghettoized" in public employment. As Lynn Burbridge (1994) has pointed out, in 1990 nearly 90 percent of black female professionals and nearly 70 percent of black male professionals worked either for the government or for nonprofits. Women and people of color in the United States and Britain have often found opportunities in new occupations in the public sector first, with the government performing some kind of "demonstration" for the lagging private sector (King 1993). Perhaps African Americans are less overrepresented in government work now because private-sector employers are hiring them in greater numbers than they have in the past. Many occupations and industries have become more integrated over the last thirty years so that black representation has increased broadly in niches where it was previously quite low (King 1998).

However, less-sanguine scenarios are possible. African American public employment may have been disproportionately hurt by government budget cuts. As budgets tighten, African Americans might be let go sooner or might not be hired at all. Public agencies are spinning off some of their lower-paid functions, such as janitorial, home health care, and cafeteria work, so that jobs that were once civil service positions—with the pay, benefits, promotion possibilities, and protections of the civil service—are now contracted out to private companies that compete for contracts by lowering wages and benefits. African Americans may be particularly found among people who once had a toehold in stable public employment but now work under far less-advantageous working conditions.

Despite some otherwise depressing developments in the labor market, including evidence of stagnant or growing wage gaps in the 1980s and early 1990s between black and white workers—particularly for young people—and low employment: population ratios for African Americans (Bound and Dresser 1999; Bound and Freeman 1992; Hertz, Tilly, and Massagli 2001), it appears that African American workers are gaining opportunities in the private sector. In the private and the public sector, blacks' earnings gained on whites' earnings during 1963–1977 but then held at the same ratio through the early 1990s. Much larger relative gains occurred in the private sector

because race differences in private-sector earnings were so massive, thereby making earnings gaps more similar in both sectors overall (Carrington, McCue, and Pierce 1996). This trend includes the college educated: whereas 83 percent of college-educated black women and 58 percent of college-educated black men worked for the government during 1968–1973, these figures were down to 51 and 40 percent, respectively, by 1988–1992 as compared with 35 and 21 percent of college-educated white women and men during this later period.

Another spurt of progress appears in the last five years or so, especially in the private sector, continuing to bring private-sector gaps closer to those of the public sector. The evidence for this progress is found in the Current Population Survey data shown in table 21.3. These data include all earners, part-time as well as full-time, and people of all education levels. Further, small sample sizes cause the figures to fluctuate more widely than would be true if we could sample the full population—particularly for African Americans, because their numbers are smaller; so, these figures should be read as suggestive rather than as definitive. Even with these caveats, it appears that the racial wage gap has decreased in recent years, particularly in the private sector, where it remains larger than that in the public sector.

On the strength of these figures, we may assume—until more evidence is in—that reductions in African American representation in public employment over the last ten years are a good thing, tied to increasing opportunities in the private sector rather than to discriminatory downsizing in the public sector.

Of course, it is a complex world, and many things often happen at once. It may well be that it is largely African American professionals finding more scope in the private sector in recent decades. Opposed to this largely positive development may be a shift in the other direction for less-educated African Americans, losing positions in a shrinking public sector that may be a relative haven for lower-wage workers, given the overall slide in wages in the lower half of the U.S. wage structure.

More detailed research is required to determine if people at all educational levels are benefiting from better opportunities for blacks in the private sector.

Table 21.3   Earnings of African Americans and White Women Relative to That of White Men, Public and Private Sectors, 1992–2001

	Private Sector			Public Sector		
	Black men	Black women	White women	Black men	Black women	White women
2001	.73	.58	.65	.78	.65	.70
2000	.70	.53	.60	.81	.70	.69
1999	.69	.49	.60	.78	.69	.69
1998	.71	.54	.58	.86	.65	.70
1997	.70	.53	.61	.82	.61	.67
1996	.64	.54	.60	.77	.62	.68
1995	.63	.53	.58	.73	.61	.67
1994	.65	.47	.61	.81	.65	.68
1993	.61	.47	.57	.67	.63	.67
1992	.59	.47	.57	.72	.57	.67

Source: Calculations based on Current Population Survey data (U.S. Bureau of Labor Statistics), as reported at www.unicon.com.

CONCLUSION

One aspect of globalization has put pressure on the public sector. Capital has gained bargaining power from its increased mobility and has used that power to increase profits and executive salaries at the expense of wages, taxes, and public services. It is clear that African Americans are hurt by the negative impact of globalization on American government services and wages overall. What is less clear is the meaning of the declining representation of African American workers in our shrinking public sector. We cannot really tell if the recent decline in black overrepresentation in government employment is a good or bad thing overall without further research into the changing nature of the jobs that African Americans are obtaining in all sectors. What evidence exists indicates that blacks are finding more opportunities in the private sector than they have in the past. However, it may be that less-educated African Americans are losing ground due to privatization and the reduction of public services.

REFERENCES

Bound, John, and Laura Dresser. 1999. "Losing Ground: The Erosion of the Relative Earnings of African American Women during the 1980s." In *Latinas and African American Women at Work: Race, Gender, and Economic Inequality,* ed. Irene Browne. New York: Russell Sage Foundation.

Bound, John, and Richard Freeman. 1992. "What Went Wrong? The Erosion of Relative Earnings and Employment among Young Black Men in the 1980s." *Quarterly Journal of Economics* 107, no. 1: 201–232.

Burbridge, Lynn. 1994. "Government, For-Profits, and Third-Sector Employment: Differences by Race and Sex, 1950–1990." Special report, Wellesley College Center for Research on Women, Wellesley, Massachusetts.

Carrington, William J., Kristin McCue, and Brooks Pierce. 1996. "Black/White Wage Convergence: The Role of Public Sector Wages and Employment." *Industrial and Labor Relations Review* 49, no. 3: 456–471.

England, Paula, Karen Christopher, and Lori L. Reid. 1999. "Gender, Race, Ethnicity and Wages." In *Latinas and African American Women at Work: Race, Gender, and Economic Inequality,* ed. Irene Browne. New York: Russell Sage Foundation.

Hertz, Tom, Chris Tilly, and Michael P. Massagli. 2001. "Linking the Multi-city Study's Household and Employer Surveys to Test for Race and Gender Effects in Hiring and Wage Setting." In *Urban Inequality: Evidence from Four Cities,* ed. Alice

O'Connor, Chris Tilly, and Lawrence D. Bobo. New York: Russell Sage Foundation.

Jones, Jacqueline. 1998. *American Work: Four Centuries of Black and White Labor.* New York: W. W. Norton.

King, Mary C. 1993. "Black Women's Breakthrough into Clerical Work: An Occupational Tipping Model." *Journal of Economic Issues* 27, no. 4: 1097–1125.

———. 1998. "Are African Americans Losing Their Footholds in Better Jobs?" *Journal of Economic Issues* 32, no. 3: 641–668.

Lieberman, Robert C. 1998. *Shifting the Color Line: Race and the American Welfare State.* Cambridge, Mass.: Harvard University Press.

Mishel, Lawrence, Jared Bernstein, and John Schmitt. 2001. *The State of Working America, 2000/01.* Ithaca, N.Y.: Industrial Labor and Relations Press.

Moskos, Charles C., and John Sibley Butler. 1996. *All That We Can Be: Black Leadership and Racial Integration the Army Way.* New York: Basic Books.

Oliver, Melvin L., and Thomas M. Shapiro. 1997. *Black Wealth/White Wealth: A New Perspective on Racial Inequality.* New York: Routledge.

Quadagno, Jill S. 1994. *The Color of Welfare: How Racism Undermined the War on Poverty.* New York: Oxford University Press.

Rodrik, Dani. 1998. "Has Globalization Gone Too Far? An Interview with Dani Rodrik." *Challenge: The Magazine of Economic Affairs* 41, no. 2: 81–94.

U.S. Bureau of Labor Statistics. 1995. *Employment and Earnings* 42, no. 1. Washington, D.C.: U.S. Government Printing Office.

———. 1997. *Employment and Earnings* 44, no. 1. Washington, D.C.: U.S. Government Printing Office.

———. 1999. *Employment and Earnings* 46 no. 1. Washington, D.C.: U.S. Government Printing Office.

———. 2001. *Employment and Earnings* 48, no. 1. Washington, D.C.: U.S. Government Printing Office.

22

Immigration and African Americans
STEVEN SHULMAN and ROBERT C. SMITH

This chapter reviews the impact of immigration on African Americans and discusses its political implications. Ethnographic and econometric studies show that immigration has reduced the wages and employment prospects of African Americans. Immigration has also increased the competition for public services such as education. However, African American political leaders have been reluctant to discuss immigration to build a "rainbow coalition." We argue that this stance is untenable. Instead, we propose several positive policies designed to reduce immigration and to improve the circumstances of immigrants.

The old employment by which we have heretofore gained our livelihood, are gradually and it may seem inevitably, passing into other hands. Every hour sees the black man elbowed out of employment by some newly arrived immigrant whose hunger and color are thought to give him a better title to the place.

—Frederick Douglass, circa 1880s

The massive influx of immigrants into the United States in the last several decades is an aspect of globalization that has had deleterious consequences for the economic, social, and political well-being of African American communities. This chapter reviews the research on the impact of immigration on urban black communities. It then discusses the implications of this research and several policies that might be proposed by African American leaders and others to deal with the flow of immigration and to meliorate its impact on black communities.

The size of the immigrant influx into the United States has been massive during the last two decades. More immigrants came to the country in the 1980s and 1990s than they have during any other period in history. Over eleven million persons from other countries were added to the population during the 1990s alone. In addition, almost seven million children were born to immigrant parents during this decade. Thus, the total number of immigrants added to the population during this decade was somewhere between eighteen million and twenty million people, representing nearly two-thirds of the U.S. population increase during the period.[1] By century's end the immigrant stock, which includes the children born to immigrants once they arrive in the United States, was fifty-six million.

THE IMPACT OF IMMIGRATION ON AFRICAN AMERICANS

Two types of studies examine immigration's impact on African Americans. Ethnographic studies focus on particular firms or industries to see if new immigrants have taken jobs traditionally held by African Americans. Quantitative studies use large data sets to discern the statistical relationship between immigration and African American wages and employment. Both types of studies are problematic in their own way. Ethnographic studies are usually able to show that immigrants have displaced African Americans in specific cases (Waldinger 1996; Waters 1999); but because immigration can also increase native employment (if it adds to economic growth) and because workers displaced by immigration can adapt by moving or acquiring new skills, ethnographic studies cannot conclude that the net effect of immigration on native workers is negative (Rosenfeld and Tienda 1999, 65).

Nonetheless, ethnographic studies have provided concrete evidence that immigrant employment often comes at the expense of African Americans, at least in the short run. Employers often view immigrants as docile, hard working, and cheap in comparison to African Americans (particularly males), who they view as threatening, demanding, and unreliable (Kirschenman and Neckerman 1991). Discrimination against African Americans and in favor of immigrants occurs even when the immigrants are of African descent (Waters 1998). Immigrant communities can establish strong social and informational networks that build an employment base for their own community while excluding outsiders. For example, Waldinger (1998, 255) notes that as immigrant densities in the low-skill sector grow, so do the obstacles to less-skilled African American workers. The "implantation of immigrant networks tends to detach vacancies from the open market, for reasons having to do with efficiency as well as the social-closure potential of immigrant networks. . . . Tension between African Americans and Latinos is rife . . . and that spells trouble for blacks, who find themselves not just a sociological but a quantitative, often very small, minority, needing to get along in a workplace where Spanish, not English, is often the lingua franca . . . and depending on others to learn skills and get jobs done" (255). Although the ethnographic studies cannot establish the aggregate effects of immigration on African Americans, they do provide telling evidence of ethnic competition and conflict in the low-wage sector that should be taken seriously by anyone concerned about African American employment opportunities.

That leaves the quantitative studies to establish the overall impact of immigration. Many of these studies have found only weak effects on the wages and employment of native workers. However, several reasons explain why the findings of negligible impact should not be taken at face value. First, it would not be surprising if immigration negatively affects low-wage workers but positively affects high-wage workers and employers. If this is the case, the aggregate effects can be slight even if the impact on low-wage workers is large. Second, these studies often use decennial census data, which means that they use a ten-year frame of reference. The impacts of immigration can be substantial over the short run but can wash out over the long run as workers adjust to immigration shocks. Third, much of the impact of immigration may take place in terms of labor supply and out-migration adjustments that offset the measured impact on wages and employment (Borjas, Freeman, and Katz 1997, 38; Johannsen, Weiler, and Shulman 2002). Fourth, these studies generally ignore variations in local labor market conditions that can affect the way in which immigration affects low-wage native workers (Bean, Fossett, and Park 2000). For these reasons the aggregate studies of the impact of immigration are not able to completely answer questions about the impact of immigration on low-wage native workers.

The quantitative studies focusing on low-wage workers have generally found negative impacts on their wages and employment. Hamermesh (1998) finds no evidence that immigrants are in a separate job market from natives or that they take jobs that natives reject, implying that immigrants and natives compete for many of the same jobs. Job competition then tends to drive wages down for the native workers who have similar skills as immigrants. Borjas, Freeman, and Katz (1997) conclude that immigration has had a marked adverse impact on the economic status of the least skilled U.S. workers, accounting for about half of the decline in their relative wages. Friedberg and Hunt (1995, 38) have reviewed studies showing that a 1 percentage point increase in the proportion of immigrants reduces the wages of high school dropouts by 1.2 percent. If they are correct, immigration in the Los Angeles metropolitan area over the 1990s (when the immigrant share of the population rose from 27.1 percent to 29.6 percent) lowered the wages of low-wage native workers by 3 percent. Although this would be a large negative effect, it is probably an understatement since natives respond to immigration by out-migrating and by dropping out of the labor force, responses that tend to mask the impact of immigration on natives' wages and employment. McCarthy and Vernez (1998, 69–70) calculate that in California 130,000 to 190,000 persons had dropped out of the labor force or were unemployed as a result of immigration. This represents 1.0 percent to 1.5 percent of the adult population of working age. They also show that immigration accounted for between 15 percent and 75 percent of the decline in real earnings of low-skill workers over the 1970s, with Hispanics and African Americans having been the most affected.

The evidence of a negative impact of immigration on earnings is even stronger when the focus is on African Americans. Espenshade (2000) uses data from New Jersey to show that each 1 percentage point increase in immigrants from Puerto Rico lowers the wages of African American males by 4 percentage points.[2] Kposowa (1998, chap. 6) shows that immigration has had a positive effect on native earnings, though he does not distinguish between its impact on low-wage workers and high-wage workers or on employers. However, he demonstrates that immigration has a significant negative effect on the earnings of minority workers. Briggs (1992, 211–215) argues that mass immigration has lowered the labor force participation of African American men despite other improvements in their economic opportunities. Rosenfeld and Tienda (1999, 97) show that immigration can benefit more highly educated African Americans (who face increased demand for their labor to provide services to immigrants) but that black workers who remain behind in the low-skill jobs confront fewer job opportunities and sharply increased rates of unemployment. Borjas (1998a, 1998b) argues that immigration hurts African Americans even if it produces net benefits for the economy as a whole. This is not to say that there is unanimous agreement that immigration harms African Americans (see Bean, Van Hook, and Fossett 1999; Butcher 1998; Fairlie and Meyer 1998). Nonetheless, the conclusion that immigration works to the detriment

of African Americans can be accepted with a reasonable degree of confidence.

This review has focused discussion on labor market outcomes. It is also of interest to examine the impact of immigration on public services. In an aggregate sense, the question is whether the cost of the public services used by immigrants is offset by the taxes they pay. If the net fiscal impact is negative, then immigrants are reducing the public resources available for native-born persons in general and for African Americans in particular.

This appears to be the case. Because immigrants are more likely than natives to have low incomes, they are more likely to be covered by means-tested programs. Of households with a foreign-born head, 21 percent collect noncash benefits such as food stamps and Medicaid, compared to 14.6 percent of households with native heads. Of households with a foreign-born head, 8 percent collect means-tested cash benefits such as welfare, compared to 5.6 percent of native households (U.S. Census Bureau 2001, 48). Immigrants are also more likely to depend on nonmeans-tested public services since their incomes are lower than that of natives, and for the same reason they are more likely to pay less in taxes. Consequently, the fiscal effect of immigration is negative.

McCurdy and colleagues (1998, 58–59) have surveyed a number of studies of the fiscal impact of immigration that come to this conclusion. In general, they find that immigration increases fiscal expenditures by about five times its increase to fiscal revenues. Garvey and Espenshade (1998, 78–79) use New Jersey–based data to show that the annual net fiscal impact of immigration varies from $1,101 to $3,142 per household. Clune (1998, 167) concludes that a California native's household provide net surpluses to all three levels of government while foreign-born households are a burden on the federal, state, and local governments. McCarthy and Vernez (1998, 76) conclude that immigrants in California contributed to, but were not the cause of, the state's fiscal deficit that developed when the economy entered a recession during the early 1990s. Borjas (1998) shows that under reasonable assumptions, immigration creates a net fiscal deficit on the order of $10 billion.

The impact of immigration on the educational attainment of minorities is of particular interest. If immigration absorbs educational resources that could otherwise be devoted to African Americans and other minority students, it would represent a serious cost to these students and to American society as a whole. Two recent studies find that educational crowding-out is real and substantial. Betts (1998) uses a variety of statistical tests on 1980 and 1990 census data to conclude that there is a negative link between immigration and the probability of high school graduation for blacks and Hispanics. The "effects are meaningful. The rise in immigrants share in the population observed in the 1980s is predicted to have decreased the probability that blacks graduate from high school by roughly 1 percent; for American-born Hispanics the predicted drop is closer to 3.5 to 4 percent. . . . Overall the results of this study are strongly suggestive of the hypothesis that immigrants crowd out investments in public education by American-born minorities" (276–277). Hoxby comes to similar conclusions with respect to higher education: "Disadvantaged natives and immigrants are sufficiently large groups relative to one another and relative to the resources devoted to improving their access to college that immigrants actually do crowd disadvantaged natives out of higher education. In particular, foreign-born blacks and Hispanics who are nonresident aliens are significantly better off than the native blacks and Hispanics, and we cannot reject the hypothesis that they crowd out native blacks and Hispanics one for one" (1998, 314). In other words, each immigrant who utilizes public resources to attend college prevents a native-born minority from doing the same. This is a striking and sobering finding. In the absence of dramatic expansions in educational resources, expansions that cannot realistically be expected, immigration is clearly harming the portion of the population that is most in need of educational assistance.[3]

The empirical evidence thus shows that large-scale, concentrated immigration is detrimental to African Americans in terms of their participation in the labor market and in the provision of public services. The effects vary with local conditions, but the overall conclusion of a negative impact seems warranted, particularly with respect to the impact of immigration on the educational resources available to native-born minorities.

POLITICAL AND POLICY IMPLICATIONS

If immigration has such deleterious effects on the economic and social well-being of African American communities, then why have African American leaders and others who are concerned about the plight of blacks and low-skilled workers generally been silent on this issue?[4] The most basic explanation is that since the 1970s, especially since Jesse Jackson's campaigns for the presidency, black leaders have been seeking to build a "rainbow coalition" of people of color, including immigrants (Smith 1996, 241–248). Thus, any effort to challenge or restrict the influx of immigrants runs the risk of undermining the potential viability of the coalition. Although immigration may harm low-wage workers and African Americans in the United States, it quite clearly benefits immigrants, their families, and their home countries. This scenario is probably the major reason that black leaders have been reluctant to speak out in favor of immigration restrictions. The conflict of interest between immigrants and blacks in the United States forces the coalition to define its constituency. Can a rainbow coalition respond to the interests of blacks and immigrants? If the benefits of immigration to immigrants outweigh the losses to blacks (as they probably do), does it follow that the coalition in the United States should favor immigration, or should it give some sort of priority to the well-being of blacks?

We believe that the answers to these questions must strike a balance between the interests of workers in other countries and the interests of blacks and low-wage workers in the United States. The coalition cannot simply ignore the interests of U.S. blacks without compromising its ability to form alliances with them. It is hopelessly abstract and unrealistic to expect that the most vulnerable people in the United States will favor policies that harm their own interests because these policies benefit poor people in other countries. A rainbow coalition that takes this tack will be perceived by blacks as out of touch, and in the long run this perception will undermine its potential viability. When the interests of blacks and low-income workers in the United States clash with workers in other countries, policies must attempt to reconcile the conflict, rather than to assume one side or sweep it under the rug, if they are to have any chance of building a movement of sufficient size and power to create progressive social change.

Several policies that recognize this conflict and attempt to balance the interests of African Americans and immigrants might be supported. For example, a policy to pay immigrants as much as native workers, protect them from exploitation, and provide them with labor rights is right in principle. If immigrant workers are paid and treated as U.S. citizens are, they will lose much of their comparative advantage. In other words, policies should be promoted that reduce economic advantages for immigrants in the United States to protect low-wage native workers. This is a realistic and just position, and it has the potential to strengthen the coalition between blacks and immigrants.

Another set of policies that could generate stronger domestic support among blacks, if their implications for immigration were explicitly emphasized, are the reform of international economic policy and the promotion of sustainable development and debt forgiveness. International Monetary Fund and World Bank reform; increased foreign aid; and international labor rights, land reform, microenterprise development, and the development of local markets are means of improving the standards of living of the world's poorest people. Most people who emigrate to the United States do so not because they want to be Americans but out of economic necessity. If they were more hopeful about their opportunities at home, they would be less likely to come to the United States. Increases in the amount of changes in the type of aid provided to poor countries (especially Mexico) are justifiable not only in terms of their beneficial impact on the people of those countries but also in terms of their beneficial impact on low-wage workers in the United States. The reluctance of black leaders, and progressives in general, to discuss immigration restrictions is palpable and odd. Open borders are supported by almost no one since

the effect would obviously flood the United States with immigrants and drastically lower the standards of living in this country. The question is not whether to impose immigration restrictions but to do so at what level. Conservative politicians such as Rudolph Giuliani, Newt Gingrich, and Dick Armey are outspoken in their support of more immigration and weaker restrictions. The most conservative economists, such as Milton Friedman, Thomas Sowell, and Julius Simon, also favor virtually open borders. They favor the free flow of people just as they favor the free flow of commodities and capital. If black leaders reject immigration restrictions, they will find themselves in uncomfortable political and intellectual company.

The appropriate level for immigration should take the interests of low-wage native workers into account, which means that current levels of immigration should be reduced. About two-thirds of immigration is legal and can be reduced simply by a policy decision to do so. The U.S. Commission on Immigration Reform (chaired by Barbara Jordan, a liberal African American Democrat from Texas) proposed reducing legal immigration to 550,000 per year, a reduction of one-third to one-half from recent levels. At a minimum, blacks and progressives could take up these proposals as a first step. Of course, given the high level of immigration in recent years, more stringent proposals are worth considering as well.

Although legal immigration is larger than illegal immigration as a whole, the opposite is the case among Mexican immigrants, of whom only 20 percent are estimated to be legal (Smith 2001, 84). Recent estimates show a dramatic increase in the number of illegal immigrants. According to Jeffrey Passel (2001) of the Urban Institute, over the 1990s approximately a half-million illegal immigrants settled in the United States each year, approximately double the annual flow of the previous decade. The large influx of low-skill illegal immigrants is especially important to control with respect to the well-being of low-wage African American workers. A reduction in illegal immigration can bring special benefits to these African American workers because they are especially likely to compete with illegal immigrants for jobs. Because illegal immigration is quite dangerous, a reduction in the incentives for it will reduce the hazards faced by illegal immigrants, up to and including the prospect of death from exposure. We emphasize incentives rather than punitive sanctions since the latter are inhumane, ineffective, and often increase the hazards faced by illegal immigrants.

The proposals to improve the economic circumstances in these immigrants' home countries would reduce the incentives to emigrate. In the United States, the same effect can be achieved by reducing the demand for illegal immigrant labor. The simplest way of achieving this goal is to penalize employers who employ illegal immigrants. The easiest way to hold employers accountable for the workers they hire is by making display of a national identification card (ID card) a normal part of the job application process. While the controversies surrounding this issue are too complicated to resolve here, it is worth noting that France, Greece, Belgium, Sweden, Spain, and some one hundred other nations have national ID cards. We already have an informal national ID card system in the form of drivers' licenses, and the technology now exists to produce these cards cheaply and without fear of forgery. The civil liberties concerns do not revolve around the cards themselves but in the way they can be used and the information that is collected to verify them. These are issues that can be addressed through legislative safeguards. A national ID card does not mean that the police can randomly stop people on the street and demand to see their papers, nor does it mean that persons who look Hispanic will necessarily be singled out. It can be voluntary in the sense that it facilitates, but is not necessarily required for, getting a job, boarding an aircraft, opening a bank account, and so forth. A national ID card system provides a means of reducing illegal immigration without increasing border controls or the risks of border crossings, which in their current form pose much greater risks to civil liberties and physical safety than does the national ID card alternative.

The point is that possibilities exist for reducing immigration, legal and illegal, should we choose to do it. The conversation about immigration reduction is worth having if we are serious about helping low-wage workers, African Americans as well as others. Unfortunately, the black leadership, which is so eloquent about virtually every other issue, is almost entirely silent about this one. In this respect it has found common ground with the free market fundamentalism it so vehemently opposes (Stiglitz 2002).

NOTES

1. Camarota (2001, fn1) argues that these figures understate the actual population impact of immigration, and Passel (2001) estimates that the foreign-born population consists of over thirty million, including eleven million to fourteen million during the 1990s.

2. Espenshade (2000) also demonstrates no significant effects of immigration as a whole on the wages of African American men, interpreting these results to mean that African Americans face job competition from Hispanic immigrants, with whom they are close substitutes, but not from non-Hispanic immigrants.

3. Fix and Zimmerman (2000) show that immigrants have not displaced low-income native-born minorities in Chapter 1 programs for the educationally disadvantaged because of sufficient expansions in program resources. However, they also show that immigration has caused per-pupil expenditures to fall in some cities. It could be argued that the resistance to increasing educational spending is the reason why immigrants educationally crowd out natives, but in practical terms this is not much consolation to students whose schools become less effective. Resources are limited, and even if they were increased to accommodate immigrants in the schools, the resources available for other needs would inevitably be reduced.

4. Although the political effects of immigration have not been addressed in this chapter, it is worth noting that immigration tends to dilute the political power of African Americans and creates conflicts between them and immigrant populations (see Alex-Assensoh and Hanks 2000; McClain and Karnig 1990; Miles 1992). Meyerson (2001) is enthusiastic about the emerging Latino–labor alliance in California but, tellingly, says almost nothing about the changing political status of blacks in the nation's most multicultural state. The reason is probably that, as a result of immigration, blacks are losing political power in the state, as both of the state's major newspapers have reported (see Barabak 2001; Ness 2001).

REFERENCES

Alex-Assanoh, Yvette, and Lawrence Hanks, ed. 2000. *Black and Multiracial Politics*. New York: New York University Press.

Barabak, Mark. 2001. "Blacks Losing Political Power in California." *Los Angeles Times*, May 20.

Bean, Frank D., Mark A. Fossett, and Kyung Tae Park. 2000. "Labor Market Dynamics and the Effects of Immigration on African Americans." In *Immigration and Race: New Challenges for American Democracy*, edited by Gerald D. Jaynes. New Haven, Conn.: Yale University Press.

Bean, Frank D., Jennifer Van Hook, and Mark A. Fossett. 1999. "Immigration, Spatial and Economic Change, and African American Employment." In *Immigration and Opportunity: Race, Ethnicity, and Employment in the United States*, edited by F. Bean and S. Bell-Rose. New York: Russell Sage Foundation.

Beck, Roy. 1998. "The High Cost of Cheap Foreign Labor." In *The Debate in the United States over Immigration*, edited by Peter Duignan and Lewis Gann. Stanford, Calif.: Hoover Institute Press.

Betts, Julian. 1998. "Educational Crowding Out: Do Immigrants Affect the Educational Attainment of American Minorities." In *Help or Hindrance: The Economic Implications of Immigration for African Americans*, edited by Daniel S. Hamermesh and Frank D. Bean. New York: Russell Sage Foundation.

Borjas, George J. 1998. "Do Blacks Gain or Lose from Immigration?" In *Help or Hindrance: The Economic Implications of Immigration for African Americans*, edited by Daniel S. Hamermesh and Frank D. Bean. New York: Russell Sage Foundation.

———. 1998b. "Immigration and Welfare." In *The Debate in the United States over Immigration*, edited by Peter Duignan and Lewis Gann. Stanford, Calif.: Hoover Institute Press.

Borjas, George J., Richard B. Freeman, and Lawrence F. Katz. 1997. "How Much Do Immigration and Trade Affect Labor Market Outcomes?" *Brookings Papers on Economic Activity* I.

Briggs, Vernon M. 1992. *Mass Immigration and the National Interest*. New York: M. E. Sharpe.

Butcher, Kristin F. 1998. "An Investigation of the Effect of Immigration on the Labor Market Outcomes of African Americans." In *Help or Hindrance: The Economic Implications of Immi-gration for African Americans*, edited by Daniel S. Hamermesh and Frank D. Bean. New York: Russell Sage Foundation.

Camarota, Steven A. 2001. "The Impact of Immigration on U.S. Population Growth: Testimony." Prepared for the House Judiciary Committee (August 2). Center for Immigration Studies. Internet release available at www.cis.org/articles/2001/sactestimony701.html.

Clune, Michael S. 1998. "The Fiscal Impacts of Immigrants: A California Case Study." In *The Immigration Debate: Studies on the Economic, Demographic, and Fiscal Effects of Immigration*, edited by James P. Smith and Barry Edmonston. Washington, D.C.: National Academy Press.

Espenshade, Thomas J. 2000. "Immigrants, Puerto Ricans, and the Earnings of Native Black Males." In *Immigration and Race: New Challenges for American Democracy*, edited by Gerald D. Jaynes. New Haven, Conn.: Yale University Press.

Fairlie, Robert W., and Bruce D. Meyer. 1998. "Does Immigration Hurt African American Self-Employment?" In *Help or Hindrance: The Economic Implications of Immigration for African Americans*, edited by Daniel S. Hamermesh and Frank D. Bean. New York: Russell Sage Foundation.

Fix, Michael, and Wendy Zimmerman. 2000. "Educating Immigrant Children in Changing Cities." In *Immigration and Race: New Challenges for American Democracy*, edited by Gerald D. Jaynes. New Haven, Conn.: Yale University Press.

Frey, William H. 1999. "New Black Migration Patterns in the United States: Are They Affected by Recent Immigration?" In *Immigration and Race: New Challenges for American Democracy*, edited by Gerald D. Jaynes. New Haven, Conn.: Yale University Press.

Friedberg, Rachel M., and Jennifer Hunt. 2000. "The Impact of Immigrants on Host Country Wages, Employment and Growth." *Journal of Economic Perspectives* 9 (Spring).

Garvey, Deborah L., and Thomas J. Espenshade. 1998. "Fiscal Impacts of Immigrant and Native Households: A New Jersey Case Study." In *The Immigration Debate: Studies on the Economic, Demographic, and Fiscal Effects of Immigration*, edited by James P. Smith and Barry Edmonston. Washington, D.C.: National Academy Press.

Hagan, John, and Alberto Palloni. 1998. "Immigration and Crime in the United States." In *The*

Immigration Debate: Studies on the Economic, Demographic, and Fiscal Effects of Immigration, edited by James P. Smith and Barry Edmonston. Washington, D.C.: National Academy Press.

Hamermesh, Daniel S. 1998. "Immigration and the Quality of Jobs." In *Help or Hindrance: The Economic Implications of Immigration for African Americans,* edited by Daniel S. Hamermesh and Frank D. Bean. New York: Russell Sage Foundation.

Hamermesh, Daniel S., Frank D. Bean, Richard B. Freeman, and Lawrence F. Katz. 1990. *Friends or Strangers: The Impact of Immigrants on the U.S. Economy.* New York: Basic Books.

———. 1995. "The Economic Benefits from Immigration." *Journal of Economic Perspectives* 9 (Spring).

———. 1997. "How Much Do Immigration and Trade Affect Labor Market Oucomes?" Brookings Papers on Economic Activity, No. 1.

———. 1998a. "Do Blacks Gain or Lose from Immigration?" In *Help or Hinderance: The Economic Implications of Immigration for African Americans,* edited by Daniel Hamermesh and Frank Bean. New York: Russell Sage Foundation.

———. 1998b. "Immigration and Welfare." In *The Debate in the United States over Immigration,* edited by Peter Duigan and Lewis Gann. Stanford, Calif.: Hoover University Press.

Hoxy, Caroline. 1998. "Do Immigrants Crowd Disadvantaged Natives Out of Higher Education?" In *Help or Hindrance: The Economic Implications of Immigration for African Americans,* edited by Daniel Hamermesh and Frank Bean. New York: Russell Sage Foundation.

Johannsen, Hannes, Stephan Weiler, and Steven Shulman. 2002. "Immigration and the Labor Force Participation of Low-Skill Native Workers." Manuscript under review at *Research in Labor Economics.*

Kirschenman, Joleen, and Kathryn M. Neckerman. 1991. "We'd Love to Hire Them But. . . . The Meaning of Race for Employers." In *The Urban Underclass,* edited by Christopher Jencks and Paul E. Peterson. Washington, D.C.: Brookings Institution.

Kposowa, Augustine J. 1998. *The Impact of Immigration on the United States Economy.* New York: University Press of America.

McCarthy, Kevin F., and George Vernez. 1998. "The Benefits and Costs of Immigration: The California Experience." In *The Debate in the United*

States over Immigration, edited by Peter Duignan and Lewis Gann. Stanford, Calif.: Hoover Institute Press.

McClain, Paula, and Albert Karnig. 1990. "Black and Hispanic Socioeconomic and Political Competition." *American Political Science Review* 84.

McCurdy, Thomas, Thomas Nechyba, and Jay Bhattacharya. 1998. "An Economic Framework for Assessing the Fiscal Impacts of Immigration." In *The Immigration Debate: Studies on the Economic, Demographic, and Fiscal Effects of Immigration,* edited by James P. Smith and Barry Edmonston. Washington, D.C.: National Academy Press.

Meyerson, Harold. 2001. "California's Progressive Mosaic." *American Prospect,* June 18.

Miles, Jack. 1992. "Black vs. Brown." *Atlantic Monthly* (October).

Ness, Carol. 2001. "Blacks Fear Losing Their Political Clout in State." *San Francisco Chronicle,* June 17.

Passell, Jeffrey. 2001. "The U. S. Population and Immigration." Testimony before the Subcommittee on Immigration and Claims Hearing, Committee on the Judiciary, U.S. House of Representatives, August 2.

Reimers, Cordelia W. 1998. "Unskilled Immigration and Changes in the Wage Distributions of Black, Mexican American, and Non-Hispanic White Male Dropouts." In *Help or Hindrance: The Economic Implications of Immigration for African Americans,* edited by Daniel S. Hamermesh and Frank D. Bean. New York: Russell Sage Foundation.

Rosenfeld, Michael J., and Marta Tienda. 1999. "Mexican Immigration, Occupational Niches, and Labor-Market Competition: Evidence from Los Angeles, Chicago, and Atlanta, 1970 to 1990." In *Immigration and Opportunity: Race, Ethnicity and Employment in the United States,* edited by Frank D. Bean and Stephanie Bell-Ross. New York: Russell Sage Foundation.

Smith, James P. 2001. "Race and Ethnicity in the Labor Market: Trends over the Short and Long Term." In *America Becoming: Racial Trends and Their Consequences.* Vol. II, edited by Neil J. Smelser, William Julius Wilson, and Faith Mitchell. Washington, D.C.: National Academy Press.

Smith, Robert C. 1996. *We Have No Leaders: African Americans in the Post Civil Rights Era.* Albany: State University of New York Press.

Stigilitz, Joseph E. 2002. *Globalization and Its Discontents.* New York: W. W. Norton.

U.S. Census Bureau. 2001. "Profile of the Foreign-Born Population in the United States: 2000." *Current Population Report P23-206.* Washington, D.C.: U.S. Government Printing Office, December.

Waldinger, Roger. 1996. *Still the Promised City? African Americans and New Immigrants in Post-Industrial New York.* Cambridge, Mass.: Harvard University Press.

———. 1998. "Network, Bureaucracy, and Exclusion: Recruitment and Selection in an Immigrant Metropolis." In *Immigration and Opportunity: Race, Ethnicity and Employment in the United States,* edited by Frank D. Bean and Stephanie Bell-Ross. New York: Russell Sage Foundation.

Waters, Mary C. 1998. "West Indians and African Americans at Work: Structural Differences and Cultural Stereotypes." In *Immigration and Opportunity: Race, Ethnicity and Employment,* edited by Frank D. Bean and Stephanie Bell-Ross. New York: Russell Sage Foundation.

23

African American Intragroup Inequality and Corporate Globalization

JESSICA GORDON NEMBHARD, STEVEN C. PITTS, and PATRICK L. MASON

Goods, services, capital, and people have always flowed across national borders. The current era can be characterized as "corporate globalization" because transnational corporations make the rules and benefit the most from their control of the internationalization. This chapter examines the linkages between corporate globalization during the latter part of the twentieth century and economic inequality within the African American community. Too often, discussion of the effects of globalization is detached from an analysis of the changing economic fates of black America. This separation reinforces racial insensitivities in policymaking and analysis, particularly among many progressive movements of the past. In addition, it circumscribes the nature of the struggle to transform black communities. Sections of this chapter define corporate globalization, present data on inequality among African Americans, outline possible causal relationships between corporate globalization and increased inequality in black America, and sketch programs designed to promote more equitable economic development.

Though international trade and investment have always been an integral part of the world economy, the extent to which all parties have benefited has depended on the circumstances in which they have taken place. The current process of globalization is no exception. . . . Fifty years ago [when the General Agreement on Tariffs and Trade was founded], few would have imagined that the exploitation of the world's abundant resources and a prodigious growth in world trade would have seen the gap between rich and poor widening.

—Nelson Mandela, 1998

Goods, services, capital, and people have always flowed across national borders. The cultural and commercial exchanges have often been beneficial—but not always, as in the case of the slave trade. The current manifestation of globalization over the past thirty years has specific characteristics whose combination distinguishes it from other eras of internationalization. This era combines rapid technological change, trade and investment liberalization (reduced barriers), financial instability (high volume of rapid, short-term financial transactions), a high volume of intrafirm trade, the increasing immobility of labor relative to capital, and a sectoral shift from manufacturing to service. Persuad and Lusane (2000) have found that the "new" globalized economy is characterized by the

> reconstitution of the labour market, away from the relative stability and predictability of the Fordist period to increasing "flexibility"; an increasing division in the labour market between core/protected and contingent/unprotected workers; and a realignment of state/society relations which has entailed a sustained attack on welfare provision and previous civil rights era legislations [in the USA]. (22)

Rapid technological change, particularly in communications and transportation, facilitates rapid physical and virtual movements of goods and services as well as capital. Advances in robotics and other manufacturing processes change the nature of work, the skills needed for particular jobs, the return to labor, and the locations where such work takes place.

With increases in technological innovations and decreases in national restrictions, capital—particularly money and finance—physically moves across sectoral and national boundaries much more easily and faster than labor does or can. The movement of human beings is physically more limited and difficult because it takes time and resources to move people from place to place. In addition, most countries have more stringent laws and regulations about how people enter than how money enters (if only for health reasons) and continue to restrict who and how many people are able to enter at one time. Labor is also less mobile, even across sectors, because people have to be retrained and retooled to change from one industry or profession to another, while most forms of capital can be used in most situations without much transformation. Despite these considerations, the United States has witnessed large-scale immigration since the middle 1970s. In addition, internal migration is rapid and varied.[1]

The rise of the service sector over manufacturing, and of knowledge production and technological change in the manufacturing that remains, exacerbates labor market inequality. Many middle-wage jobs, for example, have been eliminated, especially in the service sector. There are now mostly a few high-paying jobs for some types of knowledge production and highly technical skills, and most of the rest of the jobs pay little and may be more discriminatory. Wage inequality increased in manufacturing in the United States with the increased inequality in the service sectors (see Williams 2000).

This chapter examines the linkages between corporate globalization during the latter part of the twentieth century and economic inequality within the African American community. Too often, discussion of the effects of globalization is detached from an analysis of the changing economic fates of black America. This separation reinforces racial insensitivities in policymaking and analysis, particularly among many progressive movements of the past. In addition, it circumscribes the nature of the struggle to transform black communities. This chapter is part of a larger dialogue that seeks to unite the struggle for racial justice in the United States with the global struggle for economic justice. Succeeding sections of this chapter further define corporate globalization, present data on inequality among African Americans, outline possible causal relationships between corporate globalization and increased inequality in black America, and sketch programs designed to promote more equitable economic development.

CORPORATE GLOBALIZATION

We call the current era of globalization "corporate globalization" because transnational corporations make the rules, benefit the most, and control most of the internationalization. Anderson and Cavanagh (2000) summarize as follows:

> These giant firms and their counterparts in other countries are the principal drivers of the world economy. Their decisions shape the lives of most of the world's people and the directions of every national economy. They produce most of the world's goods and services, finance that production, and trade more and more of it across borders. In turn, they have steered the agendas of most governments at every level and have twisted the operations of the global institutions set up to govern the global economy in their interests. (65)

About one-third of world trade is intrafirm trade—that is, between one part of a transnational corporation and one of its affiliates, branches, or subsidiaries. Between 1982 and 1994, for example, exports shipped from U.S. parent companies to foreign affiliates increased from 31 percent to 42 percent of trade, and imports from foreign affiliates to U.S. parent companies increased from 36 percent to 50 percent of trade (Anderson and Cavanagh 2000, 29). One of the consequences is that competition between independent firms is much reduced while touted as a benefit of "free trade." However, the largest two hundred transnational firms controlled 26 percent of the world's gross domestic product in 1997 and employed only 0.74 percent of the world's workforce (66–67). Corporations exercise their power through lobbying, through corporate-sponsored think tanks, and through international corporate alliances and coalitions (Anderson and Cavanagh 2000).

At the same time, increased international competition over the past thirty years has led corporations to cut costs, particularly labor costs (sometimes wages but often benefits), break unions, locate across the globe-seeking profits without any local loyalty, and irresponsibly pollute and poison low-status and disenfranchised communities where they locate. Corporations have used increased competition and the technological ability to be footloose as an excuse and an opportunity to take the low road, pursuing profits no matter what the cost or who gets hurt (see Williams 2000 for more details). Transnational corporations operate through "global assembly lines" (Anderson and Cavanagh 2000), putting workers from different countries, living under different conditions, in competition with one another, driving wages down and increasing wage differentials around the world (also see Dorman 2003). In 1975, for example, the top fifteen exporters of goods were predominately rich nations who paid their workers comparable wages. The wage differential between the highest average hourly wage of $7.18 (Sweden) was less than two and one-half times the lowest average wage of $3.00 (Japan). By 1996 the composition of the top-fifteen exporters had changed, leaving the wage ratio 103

to 1: highest average hourly wage of $31.87, paid in Germany, compared with the lowest average hourly wage, in China, of $0.31 (Anderson and Cavanagh 2000, 30). In response, governments have promoted policies that support large companies and let corporations do what they want: deregulation, sweetheart deals to keep corporations in their jurisdictions, and a blind eye to union busting and environmental racism.

Unlike many previous periods, the current period is one in which growth "generates inequality" (Williams 2000; also see Wilson 1996, 153). All measures of income inequality in the United States, for example, show relatively smooth upward movement in inequality since the late 1960s (see *Left Business Observer* 1993; U.S. Census Bureau 2002e). The difference in per-capita income between industrial and developing countries tripled between 1960 and 1993. In 1999, the wealth of the 475 billionaires in the world was greater than the combined incomes of the poorest 50 percent of the world's population (Anderson and Cavanagh 2000, 53). Anderson and Cavanagh report that United Nations and World Bank studies find rising inequality in Australia, Belgium, Germany, Japan, Netherlands, Sweden, the United States, the United Kingdom, and in thirty-two developing and former communist countries (52).

The intercountry inequality reported here has been replicated within the United States. Income inequality has been increasing in the United States since the late 1960s. With respect to the black community, some African Americans were able to enjoy substantial income growth following the civil rights movement; however, by the mid-1970s, real economic progress for blacks as a group ended.[2] Black Americans suffer the same patterns of intragroup inequality as their counterparts, white or otherwise, in the United States. Persuad and Lusane point out that in this period, the state has withdrawn from "market regulation and oversight, and the provision of social welfare" to let monetarism and market ideology rule. This has meant that sustained growth in the United States has had differential class and racial impacts (2000, 22). We document this as follows.

INCOME INEQUALITY

Within the African American community, intragroup income inequality rose from the late 1960s to the mid-1990s. Two different measures of income inequality indicate this: the Gini coefficient and the ratio of aggregate income of the richest and poorest families. The Gini coefficient indicates how the current distribution of income deviates from complete equality. A ratio of zero represents a state of complete equality; a ratio of one represents a state of complete inequality. In 1966, the Gini coefficient for African American families was 0.375; in 1993, the figure had increased to 0.482 (U.S. Census Bureau 2002d). By way of comparison, the corresponding figures for white families were 0.34 and 0.42, respectively, meaning within-group black family inequality is higher than that of white families. Figure 23.1 shows an increasing trend of black–white income inequality through 1993, followed by a slight decreasing trend in inequality through 2000. The Gini coefficients for African Americans decrease slightly after 1993 to 0.45 in 2000—still above the lower levels in the late 1960s, 1970s, and early 1980s. (For white families, the Gini coefficient maintained a slow growth, reaching 0.42 in 2000, creating a decline in the gap between black–white inequality levels between 1997 and 1998, U.S. Census Bureau 2002d.) Also see Table 23.1, which provides the Gini coefficient for African American families by decade and shows persistent and increasing income inequality from 1970 to 2000.

A second measure of income inequality examines the distribution of aggregate income held by different percentages of a population. The nation's families (or households) can be ordered by income and divided into fifths (called *quintiles*)—that is, each 20 percent of the population. In a completely equitable society, each quintile would possess 20 percent of the national income. As inequality rises, the income shares deviate from 20 percent. A simple use of this data examines the ratio of the income share held by the richest quintile to the income share held by the poorest quintile. Within the African American community (using families as the basic unit), this ratio stood at 8.42 in 1966 (U.S. Census Bureau 2002b)—meaning that the rich-

est 20 percent of black families possessed $8.42 for every $1.00 possessed by the poorest 20 percent of black families. By 1993, this ratio was 17.00. After 1993, this ratio began to fall. In 2000 the ratio was 13.14, after spiking again in 1999. Figure 23.2 maps this upward trend for black and for white families. In comparison, the corresponding white figures were 6.80, 10.04, and 9.98, respectively (U.S. Census Bureau 2002a). The disparity among African Americans between the richest in the population and the poorest is higher than that for whites and has increased over the period more than it has among whites.

In addition, the black middle class has dwindled. There are two ways to demonstrate this phenomenon. The second section of Table 23.1 charts the distribution of aggregate income of black families for each quintile, every decade from 1970 to 2000. The lowest two-fifths of the population in income lost shares of income between 1970 and 1990. The middle fifth of the population lost their share of income each decade. The fourth quintile gained shares of aggregate income between 1970 and 1980 but lost after that. The top quintile and the top 5 percent of income earners increased their share of aggregate income every decade.

The dwindling black middle class can be demonstrated by examining the socioeconomic status of families from 1964 to 2000. Rising inequality during the 1964–2000 period has produced fewer African American families with middle incomes. At the same time the fraction of affluent families grew modestly. Moreover, the fraction of the poorest families increased dramatically. Table 23.2 shows that elite African American families—that is, those families whose income would place them in the top 10 percent of the national distribution of income—were 2 percent of all African American families for the years 1964–1973; by 1991–2000, they were 3 percent of all African Americans families. At the other extreme are African Americans families whose income is within the bottom 10 percent of the national income distribution. These very poor families were 24 percent of African Americans families in the 1964–1973 period, and this figure increased to 39 percent of African American families in the 1991–2000 period. Middle-

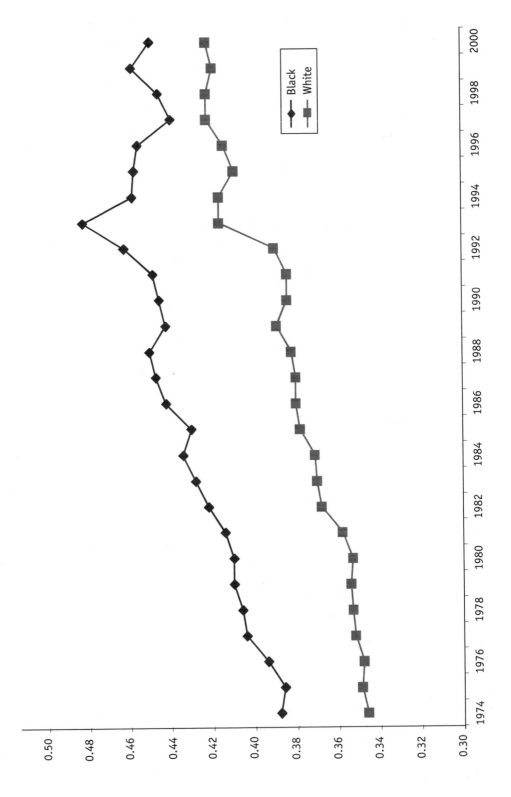

Figure 23.1   Black and white income inequality: Gini coefficients, 1974–2000.

Figure 23.2   The ratio of aggregate income of the richest and poorest family quintiles, 1974–2000.

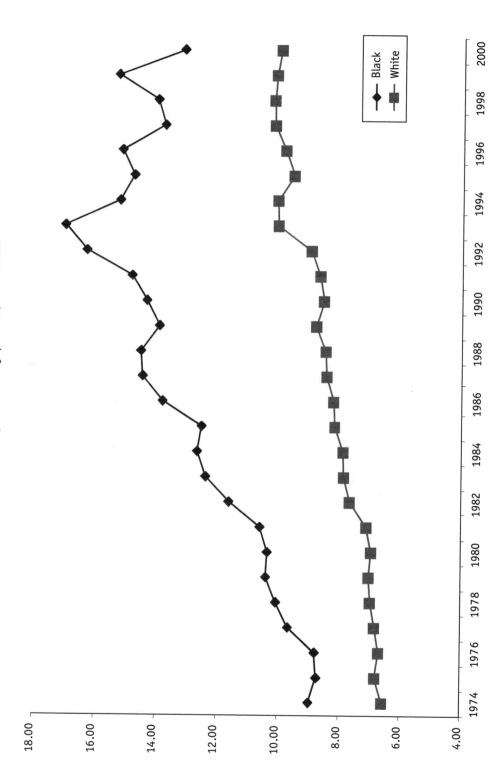

Table 23.1   Distribution of Aggregate Income Received by Each Fifth and Top 5 Percent of Black Families

	1970	1980	1990	2000
Gini coefficient	0.388	0.410	0.445	0.449
Distribution				
Lowest fifth	4.6	4.3	3.3	3.7
Second fifth	10.6	9.6	8.6	9.1
Middle fifth	16.8	16.1	15.6	15.2
Fourth fifth	24.9	25.5	25.3	23.4
Highest fifth	43.3	44.3	47.3	48.6
Top 5 percent	15.2	15.2	17.2	20.3

Source: U.S. Bureau of the Census.

income African American families (those between the twenty-sixth and seventy-fifth percentile of the national income distribution) declined noticeably from 40 percent to 35 percent. The entire decline occurred from the 1964–1973 period to the 1981–1990 period. From 1964 to 1973 lower-income (eleventh to twenty-fifth percentile) and very poor families constituted 51 percent of all African American families; by 1991–2000, they represented 53 percent of all African American families. Elite and upper-income (seventy-sixth to ninetieth percentile) families increased from 8 percent in the 1964–1973 period to 11 percent in the 1991–2000 period. This shows a decrease in the middle class while the upper and lower classes increased.

WEALTH

Disparity in wealth shows intragroup inequality as well. The poor lack income and have few assets to depend on. Even middle-class and well-to-do African Americans own few assets. Their status is based on income. A large wealth gap persists between African Americans and whites even when income levels, occupational status, and educational attainment are similar (Oliver and Shapiro 1997; also see Kunjufu 2002).

Table 23.2   Socioeconomic Status of Families, 1964–2000

African Americans	Elite	Upper income	Middle income	Lower income	Very poor
1964–1973	0.02	0.06	0.40	0.27	0.24
1974–1980	0.03	0.08	0.37	0.19	0.33
1981–1990	0.03	0.08	0.35	0.16	0.39
1991–2000	0.03	0.08	0.35	0.14	0.39
Whites					
1964–1973	0.11	0.15	0.50	0.14	0.11
1974–1980	0.12	0.16	0.43	0.11	0.19
1981–1990	0.11	0.15	0.41	0.10	0.24
1991–2000	0.10	0.14	0.40	0.09	0.27

Source: Mason (2003, Table 3-19).

Recent data from Wolff (2001) finds that the ratio of average wealth holdings between non-Hispanic white and non-Hispanic black households was 0.18 in 1998. In terms of financial wealth (which excludes home ownership), there is a 0.15 ratio between white and black average wealth, meaning that African Americans hold only fifteen cents of wealth to every dollar of wealth held by white households.

About 30 percent of black households own any stock, directly or indirectly; comparatively, over 50 percent of white households own stock (Wolff 2001). This means that two-thirds of blacks have no stock holdings. At higher incomes, more blacks do own stock, bringing the percentage closer to that of whites rates (Wolff 2001) and increasing intragroup differences in wealth holdings between rich and poor African Americans. Few blacks own interest-earning checking accounts: in 1991 only 14 percent of all black households did, compared to 41 percent of white households (Darity and Myers 2000, 102). Almost one-third of African Americans have either no wealth or negative wealth (Wolff 2001).

Home ownership and pension plans are two of the most important forms of wealth accumulation. Home ownership is the most common form of wealth for African Americans, but at its highest level, in 1998 (46.3 percent), less than half of the black population actually owned their own home. Among whites, two-thirds own their own home. Even many poor whites own homes and have assets. African Americans who reside in the Southern United States have traditionally had higher home ownership rates than African Americans outside of the South (Table 23.3). Regardless of region, home ownership declined among middle-income, lower-income, and very poor African American families during the 1976–2001 period. The largest declines were among the very poor. Home ownership declined by 3 percentage points among very poor Southern African American families and by 4 percentage points among non-Southern African American families. Lower-income families were able to maintain what they had, but middle-income families saw home ownership decline by 2 percentage points in the South and 3 percentage points outside the South.

Of Southern elite and upper-income African American families, 86 percent and 87 percent were homeowners during the years 1976–1981 and 83 percent and 89 percent during the 1992–2001 period, respectively. Of non-Southern upper-income African American families, 78

Table 23.3   African American Home Ownership by Economic Status and by Region

		All	*South*	*Non-South*
1976–1981	Very poor	0.38	0.42	0.32
1982–1991		0.34	0.40	0.27
1992–2001		0.34	0.39	0.28
1976–1981	Lower income	0.45	0.52	0.37
1982–1991		0.46	0.52	0.38
1992–2001		0.46	0.53	0.36
1976–1981	Middle income	0.65	0.70	0.61
1982–1991		0.64	0.68	0.58
1992–2001		0.64	0.68	0.58
1976–1981	Upper income	0.82	0.86	0.78
1982–1991		0.81	0.85	0.77
1992–2001		0.82	0.83	0.80
1976–1981	Elite	0.87	0.87	0.86
1982–1991		0.86	0.90	0.83
1992–2001		0.88	0.89	0.86

Source: Mason (2003, Table 3-25).

percent were homeowners during the years 1976–1981, but 80 percent were homeowners in the 1992–2001 period. Of non-Southern elite African American families, 86 percent of were homeowners during the 1976–1981 and 1992–2001 periods.

During 1979–2000, African Americans were increasingly likely to be employed at firms that offered a pension plan (Table 23.4). Except for a modest increase among very poor families during the 1981–2000 period, individuals from very poor and lower-income families had no increase in their inclusion in pension plans from 1979 to 2000.

Note in Table 23.4 that very poor Southern African American families showed a 4 percentage point gain during the 1990s whereas non-Southern families showed only a 1 percentage point increase. This regional differential also exists among middle-income families, as pension plan inclusion among middle-income Southern African American families increased from 29 percent to 35 percent. At the same time, non-Southern African American families' pension plan inclusion moved from 32 percent to 34 percent with no increase occurring after the 1980s.

Regardless of region, upper-income and elite African American families were increasingly likely to be included in pension plans, but Southern families were much more likely. Southern upper-income family pension plan inclusion increased from 46 percent to 53 percent, whereas Southern elite family pension inclusion increased from 41 percent to 52 percent.

POVERTY

Poverty data also help to describe within-group inequality. In 1974, 26.9 percent of black families had incomes below the official poverty line.[3] This percentage drifted slightly upward until 1993, when the poverty rate peaked at 31.3 percent (U.S. Census Bureau 2002g) and then dropped to 19.1 percent in 2000. Black family poverty rose to higher than one-third of the population, as globalization increased through the early 1990s. Rates for Latinos are similar to those for blacks, and white rates are about a quarter of black rates.

There is a considerable diversity of experiences with poverty in black communities, which

Table 23.4   Existence of and Inclusion in Employer Pension Plan by Socioeconomic Status, 1979–2000

		Job Has Pension Plan			Individual Included in Plan		
		All	South	Non-South	All	South	Non-South
1979–1980	Very poor	0.41	0.35	0.48	0.16	0.13	0.19
1981–1990		0.43	0.38	0.49	0.15	0.13	0.18
1991–2000		0.49	0.47	0.52	0.18	0.17	0.19
1979–1980	Lower income	0.36	0.34	0.40	0.14	0.14	0.13
1981–1990		0.37	0.35	0.39	0.13	0.14	0.13
1991–2000		0.43	0.43	0.44	0.14	0.14	0.13
1979–1980	Middle income	0.51	0.47	0.56	0.31	0.29	0.32
1981–1990		0.56	0.54	0.58	0.33	0.33	0.34
1991–2000		0.60	0.59	0.60	0.34	0.35	0.34
1979–1980	Upper income	0.66	0.63	0.68	0.47	0.46	0.48
1981–1990		0.69	0.68	0.69	0.50	0.51	0.50
1991–2000		0.71	0.71	0.72	0.52	0.53	0.52
1979–1980	Elite	0.66	0.59	0.71	0.47	0.41	0.50
1981–1990		0.69	0.70	0.68	0.52	0.54	0.50
1991–2000		0.73	0.73	0.74	0.55	0.52	0.56

Source: Mason (2003, Table 3-22).

supports the analysis of inequality among African Americans. The aggregate rate for family poverty does not tell the whole story. Among African American children under eighteen years old who reside in families, the poverty rate was 39.6 percent in 1974 (U.S. Census Bureau 2002f). By 1993, the figure for African American children rose to 45.9 percent—almost half of all black children—and back down to one-third of black children (30.4 percent) in 2000.

Another way to disaggregate the experience of poverty in black communities is to examine family structure. Among single-parent families headed by women, the poverty rates were 52.2 percent in 1974, about 49.9 percent in 1993, and 34.6 percent by 2000—much higher than the rates among black married couples. The dichotomy between the high rates of poverty for some groups in the black community alongside groups with high incomes indicates intragroup inequality.[4]

New statistics from the U.S. Census Bureau show that nearly every measure of poverty rose between 2000 and 2001, after having fallen during the expansion years. Poverty rates for all black families stood at 20.7 percent in 2001, up from the 2000 level of 19.1 percent (U.S. Census Bureau 2002i).[5] The increase in poverty that occurred in 2001—reflecting the beginning of the recession—may last for several years beyond the end of the recession and so will continue to plague black communities. Poverty increases during recessionary periods, and the rise persists for several years after the official beginning of an economic expansion (a pattern that held after the recessions of 1974–1975, 1980–1982, and 1990–1991).

INTERNATIONAL TRADE AND AFRICAN AMERICAN INEQUALITY

The squeezing of the middle class can be partially attributed to the negative impact of trade on jobs. At the height of the industrial period, "good" manufacturing jobs were responsible for allowing the least educated and least skilled workers to obtain a middle-class standard of living, a situation from which African Americans began to benefit. Nembhard (2000) notes the "biasness" of postin-

dustrial economic "tides" from 1973 to 1993. Rather than "high tides lifting all boats," or good times benefiting all, postindustrial economic high tides did not lift all boats; they were biased against local businesses, low-skilled workers, workers without a college degree, and people of color (especially black men). African Americans, particularly black men, were disproportionately in industries that had suffered from increased trade or competition from abroad. They also disproportionately lost jobs from reductions in defense expenditures and declines in durable manufacturing (even though whites were more concentrated in that sector). In addition, black workers suffered severely from the shift in economic activity away from inner cities to the suburbs, away from the manufacturing belt (New York to Chicago) to the South and the West, and away from the United States to Mexico and other countries. This is one beginning of the correlation between corporate globalization and African Americans' increasing income inequality. Blacks lost what was once considered "good" jobs, often replaced by inferior jobs or no job at all.

In a study of the potential effects of the North American Free Trade Agreement (NAFTA) on African Americans, Henry and Nembhard (1993) point out that in the 1980s and early 1990s firms were employing other ethnic groups at much higher rates than they were African Americans. In particular, the industries that traditionally gain the most from increased international trade were employing a lower percentage of people of color than those adversely affected by trade (Aho and Orr 1981). Even in the case of some U.S. companies returning from Mexico, they located their operations in towns or suburbs with small African American populations, as suburbanization of manufacturing had already become the norm. In the case of job losses, evidence at the time found that workers of color were overrepresented in trade-induced job losses. In Chicago, for example, between 1987 and 1991, workers of color accounted for 50 percent of the total jobs lost because of plant closing and layoffs by transnational corporations in the region (Ranney and Cecil 1993). Ranney and Cecil found that transnational corporations in the Chicago area actually reduced jobs at a time when trade was accelerating. Industries that lose the most from trade agreements such as NAFTA are those associated with low-level services, textiles, and apparel—all low-wage and low-skill jobs in which African Americans are concentrated.

In 1985, about 20 percent (2,085,000) of the 10,501,000 employed African American workers were employed in manufacturing—10 percent in durable goods manufacturing and 10 percent in nondurable goods manufacturing. By 2000, there were 15,106,000 employed black workers, but just 12 percent (1,775,000) of these workers were employed in manufacturing—6 percent in durable goods manufacturing and 6 percent in nondurable goods manufacturing. These manufacturing jobs were the employment that allowed individuals and families to move from lower- to middle-income status.

The ten trade-affected industries listed in Table 23.5 show large declines in African American employment between 1985 and 2002.[6] Borjas and Ramey (1995) show that these industries lost a total of 672,000 jobs during the 1976–1985 period. Change in trade explains 68 percent of the total decline in employment between 1976 and 1985. These industries lost another 126,000 jobs during years 1985–1990, a period when their trade status actually improved. The improved trade status had a positive impact on employment, cutting employment losses by 54 percent. Overall, trade accounted for over 48 percent of decline in employment in these industries during the 1976–1990 period.

Trade-related job losses affected inequality among African Americans in several ways. First, jobs located in trade-affected industries, such as the automobile and steel industries of the Midwest, were high-wage jobs. Indeed, the automobile and steel industries were among the industries in the country with the highest wages and benefits. African American and other job losers employed in these industries were disproportionately males without a college degree. Between 1979 and 1982 the United Automobile Workers union lost 450,000 members. Traditionally, these were the kinds of jobs that provided the path to a middle-class standard of living for European immigrants and Southern African American migrants. Some low-education workers were fortunate enough to find new employment in the growing service sector; however, service-sector jobs often paid only a fraction of the weekly wages earned by workers in trade-affected industries. Simultaneously, the increasing competitiveness of international trade and the growth in service-sector employment increased the demand for college-educated and other highly skilled workers, leading to a dramatic increase in their compensation from 1982 to the present.

Second, African American male job losers during the 1976–1994 period—the period of most intense job loss from trade—were quite likely to be prime-aged men (between the ages of twenty-five and fifty-five). These are men with children, spouses, and mortgages. Their job losses contributed to marital instability and reduced family functioning, as well as personal bankruptcies and mortgage foreclosures. In addition, the average level of income and wealth of African American families with low incomes and low levels of education declined during the 1980s. At the same

Table 23.5   Black Employment in Select Trade-Affected Manufacturing Industries

	1985	2002
Glass	21,000	13,000
Primary iron and steel	17,000	16,000
Engines and turbines	5,000	7,000
Farm equipment	9,000	4,000
Construction equipment	17,000	8,000
Household appliances	19,000	15,000
Motor vehicles and parts	149,000	165,000
Ships and boats	50,000	36,000

Source: U.S. Bureau of Labor Statistics.

time, the wealth level of high-income and high-education African American families increased.

The increased mobility of capital and the surge of competitive cost-cutting among increasingly mobile transnational corporations have resulted in a profound shift in corporate strategy that disproportionately affects African Americans. With the advent of hypermobile capital and increased competitive pressure beginning in the 1970s, corporate practice began to shift. It became less profitable to centralize, coordinate, and make long-term commitments to particular workers or operations (a necessary aspect of administrative coordination). Instead, firms, particularly global corporations, increased their outsourcing, letting producers around the world bid for portions of the work process and compete with one another over how cheaply to do it. Advances in communications technology permitted corporations to manage a global network of low-cost suppliers while still seeing to it that the pieces fit together and that production schedules were maintained. Even for the production units remaining within the corporate enclave, the threat of shifting work elsewhere was used to decrease wages and increase work intensity. In sum, exploiting the availability of extremely low-wage or highly compliant workers around the globe became so profitable that corporations were willing to give up the advantages of a tightly managed but stable workforce.[7]

The results have been disadvantageous for black and Latino workers in two ways. First, they have been hit directly by the downsizing and wage-cutting effects of the new profit paradigm. Particularly in such regionally important industries as automobiles, textiles, and apparel, employment that sustained working-class communities has been lost, and the jobs that remain are less likely to afford the incomes needed to sustain families and improve prospects for the next generation. The widening split in the labor force, between the professionally trained workers who benefit from corporate globalization and the far more numerous lower-level workers who are the victims of it, has typically found workers of color on the losing side. But just as insidious is the second effect: the replacement of administrative control by market competition

has made it more difficult to apply the established remedies of the civil rights movement. While business owners and managers continue to make discriminatory decisions that can be challenged in court or on the picket line to an ever-greater extent, the economic hardships experienced by black and other communities of color are the result of the market practice of buying at the lowest price—a practice much harder to challenge.

FUTURE PROSPECTS, POSSIBLE SOLUTIONS

I have tried to relate many of the economic woes in the African American community to fundamental shifts in the demand for labor in the global economy. Whereas the more educated and highly trained African Americans, like their counterparts among other racial groups, have very likely benefited from the shifts in labor demand, those with lesser skills have suffered.[8]

—William Julius Wilson (1999, 63)

Inequality has been a trend for all groups in the United States but appears to be more pronounced in black communities. Increased inequality within the African American population appears to coincide with increasing corporate globalization. Several of the authors cited see connections—especially Anderson and Cavanagh (2000), Makhijani (1992), Persuad and Lusane (2000), Williams (2000), and Wilson (1996, 1999). We find that income inequality among African Americans has increased, wealth inequality is high, the quality of many of the jobs available to African Americans has decreased, the African American middle class has declined, and black children and female-headed families are disproportionately poor. However, some black business owners and some well-educated and well-connected blacks are doing quite well.

Solutions that lessen the adverse effects of corporate globalization in general are applicable, as are specific remedies directed at African American communities who are disproportionately affected. These solutions can be categorized into those that affect the demand and supply sides of the labor market and those that affect the institutional context within which these market forces operate. Approaches to ameliorating the affects of globalization too often limit the scope of the policies to some combination of supply-side (worker characteristics and productivity) and demand-side (microeconomic and macroeconomic demand for labor). Liberals and conservatives often battle over the relative weight of the two market forces in the policy portfolio. However, without examining the institutional environment and the power relationships that this environment reflects, any singular focus on market forces will not qualitatively alter the impacts of globalization.

With respect to a set of general policy prescriptions, those with an institutional thrust include attempts to reduce corporate power through accountability measures, shareholder initiatives, and managed trade policies that balance the rights of capital with the rights of labor. Other important policies include the development of global labor standards and the enhancement of the right to organize unions. In addition, policies are needed to support anti-sweatshop businesses and a broader movement for economic justice—including an anti-sweatshop movement. Finally, policies are needed that promote economic development that is generated by and supports communities and not the corporate elite. This would include fiscal and monetary policies with a clear goal of full employment at living wages. Given this institutional backdrop, policies to affect labor market supply and demand, such as trade adjustment programs and business and investment creation, can be enacted.[9]

History, however, has shown that race-neutral policies will be insufficient in a race-conscious world. Consequently, policies that recognize the specificity of the racial inequality and discrimination in the twenty-first-century world are needed. These include the vigorous enforcement of antidiscrimination laws through the strengthening of designated government agencies and the empowerment of individuals and groups to seek remedies. Affirmative action programs should continue to take into account continuing and historical discrimination and unequal outcomes. In the context of "minority" set-aside programs, these programs would be more effective if they were expanded to promote the hiring of African American workers, rather than rely on black contractors to "do the right thing." Finally, community-based asset building and wealth creation require explicit resource redistribution measures and strategies for expanded democratic ownership.[10]

NOTES

Many thanks to the editors—Cecilia Conrad, James B. Stewart, and especially John Whitehead—for reading several drafts, providing important feedback and ideas, and connecting us with innovative research in this area. We would also like to thank Tom Hale of the U.S. Bureau of Labor Statistics and David Burns for their valuable research assistance.

1. Immigration is clearly a feature of globalization. This chapter, however, focuses on corporate globalization and its effects on African Americans—in particular, effects stemming from flows of goods, services, and capital across national borders, as well as corporate practices related to those flows.

2. See for example Darity and Mason (1998) and Darity and Myers (2000) for more details.

3. While the topic is beyond the scope of this chapter, it is important to note that most social scientists recognize that the thresholds used by the U.S. Census Bureau to measure poverty increasingly understate the level of economic hardship in the United States. See Persuad and Lusane (2000).

4. A note about the changing level of poverty: Encouragingly, the poverty rates dropped between 1993 and 2000—the most recent period of economic expansion. It is important to realize that any decline in poverty that is associated with expansion is very much dependent on the nature of the expansion and the institutional forces providing the context for economic growth. The 1960s, 1980s, and 1990s were all decades with long periods of economic growth. While poverty rates declined sharply in the 1960s and 1990s, however, the rates were virtually stagnant during the 1980s. In addition, Persuad and Lusane explain that while poverty rates declined during the Clinton years, in the 1990s, "the benefits of a lower poverty rate, while welcome,

have not corrected the attacks on the poor that existed during the 1980s," and millions of African Americans continue to be poor (2000, 28). Poverty rates began to increase again in 2001.

5. Even if one disaggregates these figures by family structure, poverty still rises. For African American married couples, the poverty rate was 7.8 percent; for single-parent female-headed households, the poverty rate was 35.2 percent. Among black youth in families, 30.0 percent were poor in 2001 (U.S. Census Bureau 2002h).

6. The Bureau of Labor Statistics altered its industrial classification system in 1987. Hence, some of the table's employment changes between 1985 and 2000 may be the result of classification changes rather than actual employment change in a particular industry. Nevertheless, the employment changes do capture the overall trend of employment in these and other trade-affected industries.

7. Thanks to Peter Dorman, Evergreen State College, for some of the concepts and the wording in this and the following paragraph. See Dorman in this volume (chapter 20).

8. Wilson adds, "It is important to note that in the United States the sharp decline in the relative demand for low-skilled labor has had a more adverse effect on blacks than on whites because a substantially larger proportion of African Americans is unskilled" (1999, 63).

9. See Anderson and Cavanagh (2000) for more details. Also see Henry and Nembhard (1993).

10. Also see Nembhard (1999, forthcoming) and Kunjufu (2002).

REFERENCES

Aho, C. Michel, and James A. Orr. 1981. "Trade-Sensitive Employment: Who Are the Affected Workers?" *Monthly Labor Review* (February): 29–36.

Anand, Nikhil, and Henry Holmes. 2000. "Failed Promises: Why Economic Growth and the Global Economy Cannot Achieve Social Justice and Ecological Sustainability, and What Can." Manuscript prepared for the Earth Island Institute, San Francisco.

Anderson, Sarah, and John Cavanagh. 2000. *Field Guide to the Global Economy*. With Thea Lee and the Institute for Policy Studies. New York: New Press.

Borjas, George, and Valerie A. Ramey. 1995. "Foreign Competition, Market Power, and Wage Inequality." *Quarterly Journal of Economics* 110, no. 4 (November): 1075–1110.

Collins, Chuck, and Felice Yeskel. 2000. *Economic Apartheid in America: A Primer on Economic Inequality and Insecurity*. With United for a Fair Economy. New York: New Press.

Darity, William A., Jr., and Patrick Mason. 1998. "Evidence on Discrimination in Employment: Codes of Color, Codes of Gender." *Journal of Economic Perspectives* 12, no. 2 (Spring): 63–90.

Darity, William A., Jr., and Samuel L. Myers Jr. 2000. "Languishing in Inequality: Racial Disparities in Wealth and Earnings in the New Millennium." In *New Directions: African Americans in a Diversifying Nation*, ed. James S. Jackson, 86–118. Ann Arbor: University of Michigan, Program for Research on Black Americans; and Washington, D.C.: National Policy Association.

Dorman, Peter. 2003. "Globalization, the Transformation of Capital, and the Erosion of Black and Latino Living Standards." Chapter 20 of this volume.

Henry, Lester, and Jessica Gordon Nembhard. 1993. "What's in It for U.S.: The Economic Impact of NAFTA on African Americans." Working Paper. Medger Evers College, City University of New York, November.

Kunjufu, Jawanza. 2002. *Black Economics: Solutions for Economic and Community Empowerment*. 2nd ed. Chicago: African American Images.

Left Business Observer. 1993. "Gini Says: Measuring Income Inequality." *Left Business Observer*, October 18, available at www.panix.com/~dhenwood/Gini_supplement.html.

Makhijani, Arjun. 1992. *From Global Capitalism to Economic Justice: An Inquiry into the Elimination of Systemic Poverty, Violence, and Environmental Destruction in the World Economy*. New York: Apex Press.

Marshall, Ray. 2000. *Back to Shared Prosperity: The Growing Inequality of Wealth and Income in America*. Armonk, N.Y.: M. E. Sharpe.

Mason, Patrick L. 2003. "Reproducing Racism: Reconstructing the Political Economy of Race from the Perspective of Stratification Economics." Unpublished manuscript, Florida State University, Tallahassee.

Nembhard, Jessica Gordon. 1999. "Community Economic Development: Alternative Visions for the 21st Century." In *Readings in Black Political Economy*, ed. John Whitehead and Cobie Kwasi

Harris, 295–304. Dubuque, Iowa: Kendall/ Hunt Publishing.

———. 2000. "Postindustrial Economic Experiences of African American Men, 1973–1993." In *Advances in Education in Diverse Communities: Research, Policy, and Praxis,* ed. C. Yeakey, 1:241–261. Stamford, Conn.: Jai Press.

———. Forthcoming. "Toward Democratic Economic Participation." In *Facing the New Millennium: A Transformative Research and Action Agenda in Black Education,* a monograph edited by Joyce King. Commission on Research in Black Education, American Educational Research Association, Washington, D.C.

Oliver, Melvin, and Thomas Shapiro. 1997. *Black Wealth/White Wealth: A New Perspective on Racial Inequality.* New York: Routledge.

Persuad, Randolph B., and Clarence Lusane. 2000. "The New Economy, Globalization and the Impact on African Americans." *Race & Class* 42, no. 1 (July–September): 21–34.

Ranney, David C., and William Cecil. 1993. "Transnational Investment and Job Loss for Chicago: Impacts on Women, African-Americans and Latinos." Center for Urban Economic Development, University of Illinois at Chicago, January.

Staveteig, S., and A. Wigton. 2000. "Racial and Ethnic Disparities: Key Findings from the National Survey of American's Families." New Federalism: National Survey of America's Families Series, no. B-5. Urban Institute, Washington, D.C.

Stewart, James B., ed. 1997. *African Americans and Postindustrial Labor Markets.* New Brunswick, N.J.: Transaction Publishers.

U.S. Census Bureau. 2002a. "Table F-2A. Share of Aggregate Income Received by Each Fifth and Top 5 Percent of White Families: 1947 to 2000." Available at www.census.gov/hhes/income/histinc/f02a.html.

———. 2002b. "Table F-2B. Share of Aggregate Income Received by Each Fifth and Top 5 Percent of Black 3/ Families: 1966 to 2000." Available at www.census.gov/hhes/income/histinc/f02b.html.

———. 2002c. "Table F-2C. Share of Aggregate Income Received by Each Fifth and Top 5 Percent of Families of Hispanic Origin: 1972 to 2000." Available at www.census.gov/hhes/income/histinc/f02c.html.

———. 2002d. "Table F-4. Gini coefficients for Families, by Race and Hispanic Origin of Householder: 1947 to 2000." Available at www.census.gov/hhes/income/histinc/f04.html.

———. 2002e. "Table IE-6. Measures of Household Income Inequality: 1967 to 2000." Available at www.census.gov/hhes/income/histinc/ie6.html.

———. 2002f. "Table 3. Poverty Status of People, by Age, Race, and Hispanic Origin: 1959 to 2000." Available at www.census.gov/hhes/poverty/histpov/hstpov3.html.

———. 2002g. "Table 4. Poverty Status Status of Families, by Type of Family, Presence of Related Children, Race, and Hispanic Origin: 1959 to 2000." Available at www.census.gov/hhes/poverty/histpov/hstpov4.html.

———. 2002h. "Table 16a. Poverty Status of Families by Type of Family, Age of Householder, and Number of Children: 2001." Available at http://ferret.bls.census.gov/macro/032002/pov/new16a_000.htm.

———. 2002i. "Table 1. Age, Sex, Household Relationship, Race and Hispanic Origin—Poverty Status of People by Selected Characteristics in 2001." Available at http://ferret.bls.census.gov/macro/032002/pov/new01_003.htm.

Williams, Rhonda. 2000. "If You're Black, Get Back; If You're Brown, Stick Around; If You're White, Hang Tight: Race, Gender and Work in the Global Economy." Working Paper for the Preamble Center (Washington, D.C.), University of Maryland, College Park, May.

Wilson, William Julius. 1996. *When Work Disappears: The World of the New Urban Poor.* New York: A. A. Knopf.

———. 1999. *The Bridge over the Racial Divide: Rising Inequality and Coalition Politics.* Berkeley: University of California Press.

Wolff, Edward N. 2001. "Recent Trends in Wealth Ownership, 1983–1998." In *Assets and the Disadvantaged: The Benefits of Spreading Asset Ownership,* ed. T. Shapiro and E. Wolff, 34–73. New York: Russell Sage Foundation.

24

Globalization, Racism, and the Expansion of the American Penal System

ANDREW L. BARLOW

This chapter argues that the exponentially growing incarceration rates of black men and women in the United States is a central component of the political economy of globalization today. Globalization is causing rapidly growing inequality that is disrupting the stability of the post–World War II middle-class social order and is leaving large numbers of people of color outside the global economy. Unable to redistribute resources downward, political elites have turned to repressive means to maintain order in dangerously polarized cities and to appease panicky middle-class whites. The sweeping social consequences of the criminalization of black and brown America are assessed, as are the possibilities that globalization may also create conditions favorable to efforts to challenge the prevailing politics of repression and fear.

One of the most significant trends in American society since the 1980s has been the construction of a massive penal system. The growth of this penal system is so rapid, its scope is so vast, and its effects on American society are so profound that we are compelled to reconsider the role of prisons in American society. The purpose of this chapter is to delve into the causes and consequences of the expanding role of the criminal justice system in American society today.

The numbers are themselves staggering. In 2002, some 2.1 million people were incarcerated; over 4.0 million were on parole or probation.[1] The rate of incarceration for the United States is 702 for every 100,000 people, the highest in the world. The rate of incarceration for black men, however, was 3,109 for every 100,000 in 1990.[2] Some 72 percent of all people incarcerated in the United States are people of color, with African Americans by far the most numerous, constituting 46 percent of all people in state prisons.[3]

Black men have over eight times the chance to be incarcerated at some point in their lives than do white men. An estimated 12 percent of all African American men aged twenty to thirty-four are currently in jail or prison, as compared to 1.6 percent of white men in the same age group. Including men awaiting trial, on bail, on parole, or on probation, some 32 percent of all black men aged twenty to twenty-nine are currently under some type of correctional control.[4] Latino, Native American, and Asian American men are also disproportionately incarcerated. Latino men have four times the chance of serving time in prison than white men.[5]

The likelihood of imprisonment is so great that one study of black men reports that 56 percent of all African American men aged eighteen to thirty-five in Baltimore were under some form of criminal justice system supervision on any given day in 1992.[6] The expansion of prisons and the lack of educational opportunities have made it likelier that a young black man today is under the control of the criminal justice system (prison, jail, bail, parole, probation) than he is in college. A 2003 Bureau of Justice Statistics report calculates that 28 percent of all black men in the United States will be incarcerated at some point in their lives.[7]

The facts are not in dispute; the question is what they mean.[8] Why did incarceration rates mushroom since the 1980s? The prevalent view in the United States is that the so-called war on crime was needed to respond to an alarming rise in crime rates. Quite the opposite, however, crime rates have been generally falling since the late 1970s.[9] Further, the people who are incarcerated are only a small subset of those who might be called "criminals." Most people who commit crimes are never apprehended or charged for their transgressions.[10] As well, many people who are incarcerated are being punished for acts whose criminal status is at best debatable, such as drug possession and parole violations, the two acts likeliest to lead to incarceration.[11] Those who are charged, tried, convicted, and incarcerated are thus a subset selected from a vast pool of potential criminals, a pool that at one time or another might include the majority of the U.S. population.

The rising rate of incarceration cannot be explained by simplistic ideas that it is a response to a rising rate of criminal behavior in society. Why, then, has government increasingly criminalized social behavior for the last twenty-five years? And why are people of color much more likely than whites to be selected out of the sea of eligible candidates for criminal arrest, prosecution, and incarceration?

One answer to these questions is that the driving force behind prison expansion comes from a *prison–industrial complex,* a political and economic interest group formed by private companies who build and run prisons, corporations that exploit prison labor, prison employees' associations, and politicians who receive donations from these entities. While the existence of such an interest group cannot be denied, neither can it explain the profound reorganization of American society that is manifest in the expanding penal system. The rising incarceration rate represents nothing less than a fundamental change in the state's role in society. Mass incarceration is the

product of a political tidal wave of mandatory minimum-sentencing laws, tough new sentences for an array of crimes, and a tripling of the number of prison beds and police in the United States. All of these were changes that took place in less than a single generation and were enabled by a shift in funding from social programs such as schools and public health to prisons and police. Such a systemic change cannot be laid at the feet of a special interest group. The prison–industrial complex is more a result than a cause of prison expansion, one that seeks to maximize prison spending within a sociopolitical context in which the criminal justice system plays a central role.

Here I propose a different type of explanation for the expansion of the criminal justice system. The systemic changes that make the criminal justice system increasingly prominent are rooted in new dynamics of globalization that have in recent years reshaped the political economy and culture of the United States and the rest of the world. U.S. politicians, more so than political elites in other nations, have responded to globalization by avidly embracing criminalization and incarceration because of the deeply structured racism in American society.

GLOBALIZATION AND THE CRIMINALIZATION OF BLACK AND BROWN AMERICA

It is well established that globalization is reshaping the American political economy in new and vastly important ways. The most pronounced features of the current stage of globalization in all of the most developed countries are growing inequality, the reduced capacity of the state to regulate the economy or redistribute resources downward, and the rising rates of immigration into the United States and Europe. Globalization's impact on the United States is destabilizing the preexisting (post–World War II) middle-class social order. Growing inequality is making the rich richer and the poor poorer than at any other time in American history.[12] The American dream, long the stabilizing ideology for most Americans, is becoming unattainable for growing cross-sections of American society.[13]

But these trends are not affecting all people in the United States equally. The burdens of globalization are racialized, with whites using whatever privileges they can muster to buffer themselves from the pressures toward downward mobility.[14] For many, but not all, African Americans and other people of color, globalization has had negative consequences. The growing mobility of capital has initially enabled big businesses and well-paid, mostly white workers to abandon the central cities, via the phenomenon termed *white flight*. A lethal combination of high housing prices and restrictive zoning laws excluded millions of African Americans and a growing number of Latino and Asian immigrants from the suburbs where the high-paying jobs were located.[15] The growing importance of higher educational credentials for access to these jobs further excluded many people of color, who were remanded to inferior schools with declining tax dollars.[16] By the 1980s, ghetto and barrio residents were largely cut off from access to the high-paying jobs of the global economy.[17] As government cut funding for social services and public education, inner-city ghetto and barrio residents found themselves in an increasingly desperate situation, with little hope for good-paying jobs and decent housing, education, and health care.

It is this context—the racialized marginalization or outright separation of poor African American, Latino, Asian American, and Native American communities from the emergent global economy—that allows us to determine why the prison population has tripled during the last twenty-five years. As a racially exclusive social order emerges, the use of repressive force to keep communities of color in "order" becomes increasingly necessary. Troy Duster suggests that the growing use of repressive force against communities of color is necessitated by the exclusion of people of color from access to jobs, education, social services, and decent housing.[18] One way to understand this phenomenon is to look at where the police concentrate their activities: in wealthy white communities and in poor inner-city neighborhoods comprised of people of color. There are two ways for people to be convinced that it is in their interests to conform to a social order: one way is to give them a chance to improve their standard of living; the other is to use

repressive force to keep them in line. As globalization widens the gap between the rich and the poor and as government programs to ameliorate poverty are terminated—that is, as the avenues out of poverty are closed off—the only way to maintain order in ghettos and barrios is through the use of more and more repressive force.

William Chambliss offers a second type of explanation for the expansion of the criminal justice system, one consistent with this analysis of globalization.[19] Chambliss argues that wars on crime are used by political elites to deflect peoples' understanding of the source of the threats to their well-being away from the economy and the state. The incarceration of millions of people of color can thus be understood by looking at the difficulties experienced by much of the white middle class. Globalization exerts a downward pressure on most whites' standards of living, forcing many middle-class whites to work longer hours, to have difficulty paying their mortgages or credit cards, and in general to feel that the quality of their lives is declining. These problems are compounded by the inability of government to ameliorate these problems through regulation of corporate behavior and redistributive programs. Political elites, whose positions depend on the votes of the white middle class, have found it virtually irresistible to pander to the anxieties of white voters by putting a black or brown face to their fears. By whipping up a frenzy of fear of the black criminal (made notorious by George Bush Senior's Willie Horton ads in the 1988 Presidential campaign),[20] the illegal immigrant (California's proposition 187 in 1994), or the dreaded Muslim terrorist (post-2001 Homeland Security America), politicians appear to be "doing something" about the insecurities of the "good" (white) people. In this way, as with Duster's analysis, the growing number of incarcerated people of color can be read not as the result of a crime wave, but as an indicator of the growing crisis engulfing the middle class in the global era.

THE SOCIAL CONSEQUENCES OF INCARCERATION

The deployment of an army of police in ghettos and barrios and along the U.S. borders, the militarization of the borders in the name of a war on drugs in the 1980s and 1990s and a war on terrorism in the twenty-first century, and the tripling of inmates—all in the last twenty-five years—have had dramatic effects on American society. The direct public expenditures on the massive new prison–industrial complex are enormous: all levels of government now spend over $150 billion on criminal justice expenditures, representing a 369 percent increase in state spending since 1982.[21] These soaring expenditures have forced state and local governments to cut other programs, including public education and public health. These cutbacks are racialized, as white suburbs buffer their schools and social services by passing local bond issues to replace state funds, which inner cities are unable to do, given their weak tax bases. But even as the growing expenditure on police and prisons has stripped inner cities of much-needed funds, it has sparked a fierce competition for prison siting in hundreds of depressed, predominantly white rural communities, who hope prisons will revitalize their local economies. Recent research suggests that these hopes are in vain, as the rate of unemployment and the rate of inequality are as high in rural counties with prisons as such rates are in those without them.[22]

The impact of the increasing use of repressive state power is highly corrosive of fundamental democratic rights, a process that is also highly racialized. Police can now search people with almost complete disregard for the Fourth Amendment. An array of people can be held without bail awaiting trial or deportation hearings.[23] The laws of many states disenfranchise convicted felons for the rest of their lives: one estimate suggests that some 15 percent of black men have been permanently stripped of the right to vote by this provision.[24]

Finally, the broadest impact of the new penal system is to greatly exacerbate a culture and a politics of fear within the United States. Certainly, the expansion of the police presence in communities of color, as well as the traumas of incarceration on inmates and their families, has greatly intensified fear within communities of color. Police sweeps, such as those associated with the war on drugs in south central Los Angeles or the shootings and beatings of black men by the New York police department, have a calculated intimidating impact on entire communities.[25] However, fear of the black criminal, the illegal immigrant, or the Arab terrorist is purposely utilized by politicians seeking to appeal to white suburban voters. In sum, the increasing use of crime and punishment as a way to address social problems in the global era is having a dramatic effect on Americans as a whole, undermining social programs such as public education and public health; eroding fundamental democratic rights; and making people everywhere afraid, ineffectual, and ready to strike out at anyone seen as a potential threat.

Fortunately, globalization is producing new conditions that make these reactionary responses to social problems less palatable. As globalization reshapes societies everywhere, the kinds of racist and xenophobic reactions to globalization described here are increasingly perceived as illegitimate to people in other parts of the world. As human rights regimes become more important to address global problems, we can expect evermore forceful condemnations of violations of human rights in the United States—namely, the death penalty, "three strikes" laws, and the military tribunal system created by President Bush in 2001. Globalization is also transforming the population of the United States, rapidly increasing the numbers of people of color. In the most globalized regions, such as California and New York, whites are already a minority of the population. As these trends continue, it might become possible for those excluded from the current global arrangements to mobilize the political power necessary to make demands on transnational corporations and governments for different, more humane policies toward communities of color. If globalization is the context for the rise of the American penal system, it might also be the context for challenging it in the decades to come.

NOTES

1. U.S. Department of Justice, Bureau of Justice Statistics, *Annual Report* (Washington, D.C.: Government Printing Office, 2002).

2. "Nation's Inmate Population Exceeds 2 Million for First Time," Sentencing Project, Washington, D.C., April 6, 2003.

3. Theodore G. Chiricos and Charles Crawford, "Race and Imprisonment: A Contextual Assessment of the Evidence," in *Ethnicity, Race and Crime*, ed. Darnell F. Hawkins (Albany: State University of New York Press, 1995), 281–309.

4. Fox Butterfield, "Prison Rates among Blacks Reach a Peak," *New York Times*, April 7, 2003, 1.

5. Steven R. Donziger, ed., *The Real War on Crime* (New York: Harper, 1996), 102.

6. Jerome G. Miller, *Hobbling a Generation: Young African American Males in the Criminal Justice System of America's Cities: Baltimore, Maryland* (Alexandria, Va.: National Center on Institutions and Alternatives, 1992).

7. Butterfield, "Prison Rates among Blacks," 1.

8. Indeed, whites tend to overestimate the amount of crime in black communities.

9. Steven R. Donziger, ed., *The Real War on Crime* (New York: Harper Perennial, 1996).

10. Jeffery Reiman, *The Rich Get Richer and the Poor Get Prison*, 6th ed. (Boston: Allyn and Bacon, 2001).

11. Craig Reinarman and Harry G. Levine, eds., *Crack in America: Demon Drugs and Social Justice* (Berkeley: University of California Press, 1997).

12. Harold R. Kerbo, *Social Stratification and Inequality*, 3rd ed. (New York: McGraw-Hill, 1996).

13. Katherine S. Newman, *Falling from Grace* (Berkeley: University of California Press, 1988).

14. Andrew L. Barlow, *Between Fear and Hope: Globalization and Race in the United States* (Lanham, Md.: Rowman & Littlefield, 2003).

15. David L. Kirp, John P. Dwyer, and Larry A. Rosenthal, *Our Town: Race, Housing, and the Soul of Suburbia* (Rutgers, N.J.: Rutgers University Press, 1997).

16. Margaret Weir, "The American Middle Class and the Politics of Education," in *Social Contracts Under Stress*, ed. Oliver Zunz, Leonard Schoppa,

and Nobuhiro Hiwatari (New York: Russell Sage Foundation, 2002), 178–203.

17. William Julius Wilson, *The Truly Disadvantaged* (Chicago: University of Chicago Press, 1987).

18. Troy Duster, "Pattern, Purpose, and Race in the Drug War" in Reinarman and Levine, *Crack in America*, 260–287.

19. William Chambliss, "Crime Control and Ethnic Minorities: Legitimizing Racial Oppression by Creating Moral Panics," in *Ethnicity, Race, and Crime*, ed. Darnell F. Hawkins (Albany: State University of New York Press, 1995), 235–258.

20. Willie Horton was a convict in Massachusetts who was participating in a program that furloughed prisoners for weekends. While on furlough, he reportedly raped a white woman and murdered her husband. The Bush campaign created an advertisement depicting Bush's Democratic opponent, Massachusetts governor Michael Dukakis, as soft on crime. The ad was reportedly shown four times an hour in the South at the end of the campaign.

21. These numbers underestimate the cost, as they do not include new prison construction, contracts to private corporations, or interest payments on bond issues related to prison construction. U.S. Department of Justice, Bureau of Justice Statistics, *Judicial Expenditures and Employment Extracts 1982–1999*, tables 1–3 (Washington, D.C.: Government Printing Office, 2003).

22. Ryan S. King, Marc Mauer, and Tracy Huling, "Big Prisons, Small Towns: Prison Economics in Rural America," Sentencing Project, Washington, D.C., 2003.

23. *Demore v. Kim* 539 U.S. 2003 (April 29, 2003).

24. Jeff Manza and Chris Uggen, *Locked Out: Felon Disenfranchisement and American Democracy* (forthcoming, 2004).

25. Mike Davis, *City of Quartz* (New York: Verso, 1990).

PART VI

*Black Capitalism: Entrepreneurs
and Consumers*

Pictured above (left to right) are Tony Davis, director of facilities, Snap Appliances, Inc; Alicia Davis, owner, Forever After Wedding Consulting and Photography; and Eric Kelly, founder, CEO, and president of Snap Appliances, Inc. Snap Appliances has one of the most diverse management teams in the high-tech industry. Tony Davis, one member of this team, chooses locations for Snap Appliance facilities, including its headquarters in San Jose, California. Snap Appliances is an example of the new breed of black-owned businesses; this global enterprise is the leading provider of network-attached storage. Using venture capital, Mr. Kelly purchased Snap Appliances for $15 million in September 2002. He more than doubled the size of the company before selling it for $100 million in summer 2004. Alicia Davis's business is another example of the new type of black-owned businesses. Her company is local and consumer-oriented, but her clientele is diverse. *Photo courtesy of Dillard L. Davis, Photography.*

25

History of Black Capitalism
MANNING MARABLE

This chapter traces black capitalism back to the pre–Civil War period and contends that black businesses grew most rapidly during periods of rigid racial segregation when white corporations had no interest in black consumers. Also discussed are the current challenges to black businesses from white corporations' targeting of black consumers.

The origins of black capitalism are found in the development of a small, but affluent, propertied black elite, which emerged before the Civil War. In Northern cities, some blacks owned surprisingly large amounts of real estate. Properties owned by blacks in Philadelphia were valued at $400,000 in 1847 and $800,000 in 1856. In 1840, blacks in Cincinnati had accumulated real property, excluding church and personal property, valued at $209,000. Real estate owned by blacks in New York City and Brooklyn in 1853 was valued at $755,000 and $790,200, respectively. Black entrepreneurs were involved in a variety of antebellum commercial activities. In the 1840s, one black clothing and tailoring firm in Detroit, owned by James Garrett and Abner H. Frances, boasted annual gross profits of $60,000. Black entrepreneurs in Cincinnati were particularly successful. Samuel T. Wilcox, a black boat steward on the Ohio River, initiated a wholesale grocery store in the downtown business district in 1850. He quickly became "the largest dealer of provisions in the city," establishing commercial links with New Orleans and New York. By the mid-1850s, Wilcox's annual gross profits were estimated at $140,000.

Under the slavery regime, black entrepreneurial activities were difficult in the South but not impossible. In 1860, there were 348 free blacks in Baltimore whose total property was worth $449,000. In New Orleans in 1836, 855 free blacks owned 620 slaves as well as real estate worth $2,462,470. The majority of blacks engaged in activities that provided goods and services to white patrons—tailoring establishments, saloons, eating houses, barbering, and stables. The total value of all establishments owned by free blacks and all personal wealth in the United States in 1860 was at least $50 million dollars—half of which was based in the slave South.[1]

Of course, black business was not without certain risks in a racist society. Northern and Southern whites found it difficult to tolerate the economic success of any individual black person, fearing that even isolated instances of black financial ability would threaten the racist order. White insurance companies usually refused to do business with blacks, and white bankers drew the color line against blacks desiring credit. Black businessmen usually could not sue white creditors in Northern courts and were often legally restricted from engaging in certain commercial activities.

Despite these obstacles, the relatively successful record of some early black business efforts prompted many blacks to conclude after the Civil War that private enterprise was the only means to achieve black economic advancement. Booker T. Washington reflected on these isolated instances and proceeded to postulate a general theory of group upward mobility via capitalism. Writing in 1906, the black educator insisted that black artisans "had a monopoly of the common and skilled labor throughout the South" in 1865. "By reason of contact [between] whites and blacks during slavery, the Negro found business and commercial careers open to him at the beginning of his freedom."[2]

In slavery, when the master wanted a pair of shoes made, he went to the Negro shoemaker for those shoes; when he named a suit of clothes, he went to the Negro tailor for those clothes; and when he wanted a house built, he consulted the Negro carpenter and mason about the plans and cost—thus the two races learned to do business with each other. It was an easy step from this to a higher plane of business; hence immediately after the war the Negro found that he could become a dry goods merchant, a grocery merchant, start a bank, go into real estate dealing, and secure the trade not only of his own people, but also of the white man, who was glad to do business with him thought nothing of it.

Washington concluded, "for these reasons . . . the Negro in the South has not only found a practically free field in the commercial world, but in the world of skilled labor."

But emancipation and Reconstruction did not usher in a new period of black economic expansion. Washington's interpretation of black economic history is sharply contradicted by the evidence of the destruction of most black artisans after the war. Several factors limiting black economic opportunity were present. First, the majority of black millers, blacksmiths, carpenters, and other potential entrepreneurs were illiterate. A second factor is suggested in DuBois's *The Negro Artisan*. Slavery permitted blacks to develop skills as master craftsmen but seldom permitted black artisans to acquire training as entrepreneurs— placing advertisements in local newspapers, hiring and firing employees, purchasing supplies, and maintaining profit-and-loss records.[3] A third and decisive factor was white racism. In late 1865 many Southern states passed "black code" regulations declaring that any black man who did not have an employer was subject to arrest as a vagrant. Working independently for themselves, some black artisans were fined, jailed, and even sentenced to work as convict laborers.

The older black business elite—barbers, butlers, caterers, tailors, blacksmiths, carpenters, furniture makers, and other skilled artisans—had been dependent on white patrons for much, if not all, of its business. With the expansion of racial segregation after 1890, many of these artisans disappeared. The new generation of black entrepreneurs was a by-product of racial segregation, developing goods and services for black consumers, embracing Washington's rhetoric of self-help and racial upliftment. A conservative black nationalist ideology was promoted aggressively by black bankers, insurance agents, and small merchants precisely because they "depended upon the Negro community for their support," observed historian August Meier.

The number of black capitalist success stories multiplied with the proliferation of Jim Crow restrictions. The total number of black businesses in the United States doubled in a little more than a decade, reaching forty thousand in 1914. Two of the most influential black entrepreneurs of the period were John Merrick of North Carolina and Isaiah T. Montgomery of Mississippi. A former slave and brick mason, Merrick established the North Carolina Mutual Insurance Company. By 1915, the company was insuring black customers in twelve states and the District of Columbia. Montgomery, the former slave of Jefferson Davis's brother, established an all-black town, Mound Bayou. In less than ten years the city possessed several banks and real estate firms, a trades and technical education school modeled after the Tuskegee Institute, a newspaper, a power and light company, and a sawmill.[4]

Much of this sudden growth of black business could not have occurred without the critical assistance of the black press. Between 1865 and 1900 over twelve hundred black-owned newspapers were established, about 70 percent of them in the South. Without adequate advertising support, most of these papers disappeared within ten years. But in the age of black business growth after 1900, a series of black entrepreneurs succeeded in creating a number of politically influential newspapers.

The golden age of black business occurred in the decade 1919–1929, which not coincidentally was also the period of the most extensive racial segregation.[5] By 1929 the number of black-owned firms exceeded seventy thousand. Virtually every black neighborhood or town in the United States could claim a number of independent black entrepreneurs providing goods and services to an exclusively black consumer market: barbers and beauty parlors, laundries, restaurants, grocery stores, newspapers, shoeshine and shoe repair shops, automotive service and repair, funeral parlors, insurance companies, and small banks.

It was not until the Great Depression and its aftermath that black leaders and intellectuals grew pessimistic about the long-term possibility of a "black capitalist solution" to the Negro's plight. Few, if any, black intellectuals and political leaders recognized the extreme economic instability of black firms. A National Business League survey of 1,534 black enterprises in thirty-three large cities in 1928 found that 666, 43.4 percent, recorded annual gross profits below $5,000 and that only 137, or 8.9 percent, had annual gross receipts above $25,000.[6]

For the black banking industry, the Depression was disastrous. The Douglass National Bank of Chicago, which in 1929 had a capital investment of $293,212.70 and deposits totaling $1,507,336.70, failed in May 1932, despite a $200,000 loan from the Reconstruction Finance Corporation. The Chicago African Methodist Episcopal Church lost $18,000 with Douglass's collapse; a black fraternal order lost $20,500. Of the 135 black banks founded between 1888 and 1934, not more than twelve were operating in 1938.[7] Thousands of other black businesses also went bankrupt during the Great Depression.

As the black sharecropper in the South became a blue-collar or service worker in the East Coast and Midwest, the bulk of black business activity moved with the massive migration North. Gradually, black entrepreneurs who traveled North discovered that small Jewish, Irish, Italian, and Slavic business owners did not often sell their establishments after their old ethnic neighborhoods had been racially transformed. Most of these firms were engaged in retail trade, had stable lines of credit with small banks established by their own ethnic groups, and had absolutely no intention of surrendering the growing ghetto consumer market to upstart black petty capitalists. Adding insult to injury, many of these Northern stores had an informal Jim Crow hiring policy well into the 1950s.[8]

The black response to white ethnic economic hegemony within the ghetto's retail market took distinct political form in the "don't buy where you can't work" movement. Local black leaders picketed white establishments, first in Chicago in late 1931, demanding jobs for blacks. The movement swept rapidly to Pittsburgh, Atlanta, Boston, Baltimore, and Richmond. Blacks initiated the Citizens' League for Fair Play of New York and initiated selective boycotts of major white establishments in Harlem. The aspiring black petty capitalists profited from this racial discontent. The closing of a single Jewish grocery store in a small black neighborhood potentially meant thousands of dollars in added gross receipts to struggling black entrepreneurs.

In the 1950s and 1960s, the political prospects for black capitalism began to improve. White corporate leaders and politicians, anxious to improve their standing within the burgeoning black urban communities of the North and the West, began serious efforts to cultivate a stable, class-conscious black elite. The general pattern that emerged was corporate and philanthropic support for local development corporations and "conomic resource centers" that provided fiscal and technical assistance to black businesses. In Los Angeles, for example, the Economic Resource Corporation was created with white corporate assistance. It guaranteed loans made by black entrepreneurs at local banks, extended generous grants, and purchased property and machinery for blacks. Despite these and other paternalistic efforts, the general pattern of U.S. black business in the 1980s reveals a systematic underdevelopment that extends across geographical and regional boundaries.

Census research on black-owned businesses also indicates a profound pattern of concentrated wealth and power in the hands of a relatively small number of black capitalists. Only 164,177 workers (mostly blacks) found employment in the 39,968 black firms that hired personnel in 1977. Within this figure, however, 32,581 businesses (81.5 percent of firms hiring workers) employed between one and four persons during the year. These firms hired an average workforce of 1.45 employees, paid average annual gross payrolls of $9,695, and recorded average gross receipts totaling $68,831. Moving up the employment scale, a different picture emerges. Only 230 black firms in the United States in 1977 hired between fifty and ninety-nine employees. This group retained an average workforce of 67.6 employees, had average annual gross payrolls of $540,035, and average yearly gross receipts of $2,357,909. At the pinnacle of black capitalism were the 113 black U.S. firms that employed one hundred or more workers in 1977. This tiny elite is marginally part of the dominant U.S. capitalist class. With an average workforce of 247.5 employees, these firms met average annual payrolls of $1,960,221. Average annual gross receipts for the elite in 1977 were $8,952,469. Throughout the United States, there were 1,060 black-owned corporations and partnerships that hired twenty or more employees. Representing a small fraction of blacks engaged in private enterprise, these 1,060 affluent black firms had gross receipts totaling $2,467,958,000—38.6 percent of all gross receipts acquired by black firms with employees and 28.5 percent of the gross receipts received by all black-owned businesses.

Black capitalism in the 1970s and 1980s may be subdivided into three distinct constituencies: the "proletarian periphery," the intermediate black petty entrepreneurs, and the black corporate core. Over four-fifths of all black-owned U.S. firms, 82.7 percent of the total number, belong to the proletarian periphery. These 191,235 enterprises have several common characteristics:

1. almost all are sole proprietorships, unincorporated firms owned by a single black individual;
2. most are started by black blue-collar or marginally white-collar employees;
3. the firms are undercapitalized from the outset, and owners are forced to subsidize business activities by drawing on personal savings, by taking out loans from friends and relatives, and by allocating a portion of their salaries at their other place of employment;
4. all of these firms have no paid employees;
5. the majority are concentrated in two traditional sectors of the segregated black economy, human services and retail trade;
6. at least 75 percent become bankrupt within three years; and
7. average annual gross receipts vary between $3,000 and $15,000.

Economically and politically, these blacks are essentially workers who are attempting to become small-business persons, struggling against massive odds to leave the ranks of the proletariat.

Those fortunate enough to survive, by legal or even illegal means, become part of the black petty bourgeoisie, the intermediate level of black entrepreneurship. These black businesses constitute about 38,900 firms, or 16.8 percent of all black enterprises. The common traits they share are the following:

1. all retain paid personnel, with an annual workforce between one and nineteen employees;
2. average gross receipts are between $30,000 and $300,000;
3. almost all employers work full-time in their enterprises;
4. almost all firms receive loans from banks and from savings and loan establishments to continue business expansion; and
5. a substantial minority of these firms are involved in real estate, finance, manufacturing, and other traditionally all-white sectors of private enterprise.

In *Black Capitalism*, Timothy Bates outlines the financial characteristics of 285 black "high-caliber" firms in Chicago, Boston, and New York that received loans through the Small Business Administration in the early 1970s. Mean value for the group's total sales was $74,101; mean total assets, $30,029; the mean number of years of the black owner's management experience, 8.45 years; mean total liabilities, $19,528; mean amount of Small Business Administration loan, $27,740.[9]

Black businesses with a workforce of twenty or more employees form the corporate core of black capitalism, as listed by *Black Enterprise* magazine's top one-hundred firms. First on the list is Motown Industries of Hollywood, producers of soul records, films, and tapes, with 1979 gross receipts of $64.8 million. Holding the second spot through the fifth spot are Johnson Publishers ($61 million), Fedco Foods supermarkets ($45 million), H. J. Russell Construction of Atlanta ($41 million), and Johnson Cosmetics of Chicago ($35.4 million). This select group also includes Independence Bank of Chicago ($98.3 million in 1979 assets); Seaway National Bank of Chicago ($80.9 million in assets); Industrial Bank of Washington, D.C. ($59.9 million in assets); Freedom National Bank of New York City ($57.9 million in assets); United National Bank of Washington, D.C. ($56.2 million in assets); North Carolina Mutual Life Insurance Company ($5.1 billion insurance policies in force); and Golden State Mutual Life of Los Angeles ($2.7 billion insurance policies in force). Although these figures seem impressive, all of these major black corporations combined could be purchased, for instance, by Mobil Oil Corporation with its liquid assets. It could be argued that white corporations allow these black companies to exist for symbolic value alone.

A major obstacle to a present-day black capitalist strategy is the newly found interest of white corporations in controlling and capturing the black consumer market. The white corporate strategy of gaining control of the black consumer market occurred first with Pepsi-Cola Company. In the early 1950s the majority of black soft-drink customers purchased Pepsi, approximately three times more frequently than they selected Coca-Cola, Pepsi's chief competitor. Overall profits for Pepsi sagged from the black market throughout the 1950s. Between 1960 and 1964, after spending several million dollars solely in black-oriented advertising, Pepsi-Cola's annual profits rose from $157.6 million to $250 million.[10] The Pepsi-Cola campaign not only reaped almost $100 million but illustrated to the entire white corporate and advertising world the enormous profits at stake in the black consumer market.

The modern paradox confronting the prospective black capitalist is the process of desegregation. No black nation in history has acquired the economic growth potential of the total black consumer market in the United States. Total black income had grown from $98.6 billion in 1978 to $125.8 billion in 1980. Almost half of the aggregate black income, roughly $56 billion in 1980, was earned by less than one-fifth of all black families.[11] Theoretically, black enterprise activities should have entered an unprecedented period of capital growth in the 1970s and 1980s. But in real terms, the opposite occurred. Between 1900 and 1930, the number of black firms increased 700 percent; between 1930 and 1969, the number of black firms grew by 233 percent; between 1969 and 1977, growth was 70.5 percent. The number of black businesses with paid employees in 1969—38,304—amounted to 23.4 percent of all black firms in operation; by 1977, black firms with employees totaled 39,968, only 17.3 percent of all black businesses. Gross black business receipts climbed from $4.5 billion in 1969 to $8.6 billion in 1977, but inflation and other factors actually reveal an overall stasis in real net profits. Historically, rapid black business growth occurred only during the period of rigid racial segregation, when relatively few white corporations made any attempts to attract black consumers. The civil rights movement and desegregation permitted the white private sector to develop a variety of advertising strategies to extract billions in profits from black consumers, all in the name of "equality." The net result was the increased marginalization of the black entrepreneur, the manipulation of black culture and social habits by white corporations, and a new kind of economic underdevelopment for all blacks at all income levels.

NOTES

1. Abram L. Harris, *The Negro as Capitalist: A Study of Banking and Business among American Negroes* (New York: Haskell, 1936; reprinted 1970), 8–9.

2. Booker T. Washington and W. E. B. DuBois, *The Negro in the South* (1907; repr., New York: Citadel Press, 1970), 26–28.

3. W. E. B. DuBois, *The Negro Artisan: A Social Study* (Atlanta, Ga.: Atlanta University Press, 1902), 22.

4. August Meier, *Negro Thought in America, 1880–1915* (Ann Arbor: University of Michigan Press, 1963), 144–145; Timothy Bates, *Black Capitalism: A Quantitative Analysis* (New York: Draeger, 1973), 9; Earl Ofari, *The Myth of Black Capitalism* (New York: Monthly Review Press, 1970), 30.

5. Bates, *Black Capitalism*, 9.

6. Harris, *The Negro as Capitalist*, 55.

7. Harris, *The Negro as Capitalist*, 60–61, 145, 153.

8. David Caplovitz, *The Poor Pay More: Consumer Practices of Low-Income Families* (New York: Free Press, 1963), 4–5.

9. Caplovitz, *The Poor Pay More*, 169; Bates, *Black Capitalism*, 24–25. The real status of the black entrepreneur is not unlike that of a factory foreperson. As Lenin observed, a foreperson is not a boss; he or she is a worker who controls only a minute aspect of the process of production. His or her status, at least in the estimation of those who own the plant, is not as an equal partner or investor. The intermediate entrepreneur, only one out of every six black businesspersons, is not a worker but is also not part of the capitalist class. The periphery is sustained by "bourgeois illusions," whereas intermediate entrepreneurs do have a real material interest in private enterprise.

10. C. Orphen, "Reactions to Black and White Models," *Journal of Advertising Research* (October, 1973): 75–79.

11. Lerow W. Jeffries, *Facts about Blacks, 1980–1981* (Los Angeles: Jeffries and Associates, 1980), 18–20.

26

Black-Owned Businesses:
Trends and Prospects
CECILIA A. CONRAD

This chapter examines historical trends in the number, size, and distribution of black-owned businesses. In the 1990s, black-owned businesses experienced rapid growth in sales and in employment. They have diversified their activities beyond their traditional niche of personal services and have expanded their markets beyond black consumers. Because black-owned businesses tend to be more likely to hire black workers than white-owned firms with similar profiles are, the continued growth of this sector is likely to have positive benefits for the African American community as a whole.

The typical black-owned business today has a quite different profile than its forebears. At the beginning of the 1960s, most black-owned businesses were small mom-and-pop operations with few, if any, nonfamily employees. These businesses concentrated primarily in retail sales and personal services, including beauty parlors and barbershops. Today, a black-owned business is just as likely to deliver services to businesses as to individual consumers. According to the most recent government statistics, 11.3 percent of black-owned firms in 1997 had paid employees; 889 firms employed more than one hundred workers (U.S. Census Bureau 2001). Black-owned firms with paid employees accounted for 79.2 percent of all black-owned business receipts (U.S. Census Bureau 2001). This diversification and growth has revived interest in black capitalism as one component of an overall strategy for African American economic advancement.

HISTORICAL TRENDS IN
BLACK BUSINESS OWNERSHIP

Before the 1960s, racial segregation assured black barbers, beauticians, and restaurateurs a protected market for their services, but there was little opportunity for growth. The black business community consisted primarily of small-scale operations that served an exclusively localized black clientele. A 1944 survey of black businesses in twelve cities found that beauty parlors and barber shops accounted for 27.3 percent of black businesses; eating and drinking places, 19.2 percent; food stores, 7.6 percent; cleaning and pressing establishments, shoe shine and repair, and funeral parlors, 15.5 percent (Bates 1973).

The concentration of blacks in activities such as shoe shine and repair and funeral parlors is an outgrowth of racial hierarchy in the post-Reconstruction United States. To preserve their racial identity, whites could not provide certain services to blacks. They could not launder their clothes, serve them meals, fix their hair, or embalm their bodies. Black-owned businesses emerged to provide these services, and they rarely faced competition from white-owned firms.

Bates (1973) attributes the black presence in retailing to post–World War I "Buy Black" campaigns. In addition, white entrepreneurs may have been slow to recognize profit opportunities in black communities, or black entrepreneurs may have had lower costs because they had better information about which community members were good credit risks and which were not.[1] Black ownership of retail establishments may have been the result of limited employment opportunities outside of the black community. An individual will choose self-employment when the expected income from being self-employed, adjusted for risk, is greater than the income he or she might expect to earn as a wage or salary worker. Because of discrimination in labor markets, the expected income from operating a food store may have been attractive for a black entrepreneur as compared to the next best alternative (the opportunity cost) but may have been unattractive to most whites.[2]

The industrial composition of black businesses changed only slightly between 1944 and the 1960s. Using U.S. Decennial Census of the Population, Andrew Brimmer (1997) describes the distribution of black self-employed businessmen in 1950 and 1960. In 1950, 24.3 percent of black self-employed businessmen owned food and dairy retail stores, and 25.1 percent owned eating and drinking establishments. In 1960, 18.8 percent operated food and dairy retail stores, and 24.5 percent operated eating and drinking establishments. Although the percentages in food and dairy declined between 1950 and 1960, there was a slight growth in the share of total sales in this sector. Of black self-employed businessmen, 10 percent in 1950 and 9.4 percent in 1960 were in personal services, including beauty and barbershops. (Brimmer's data do not separate beauty and barber shops from the provision of other personal services.)

The concentration of blacks in a limited range of businesses is most graphically illustrated by comparing their distribution with that of all self-employed. In 1960, 24.45 percent of black self-employment businesses operated eating and drinking establishments; only 11.18 percent of self-employed businessmen of any race operated eating and drinking establishments. In 1960, 18.84 percent of black self-employed businessmen operated food and dairy stores; the comparable percentage for all businesses was 15.54 percent (Brimmer 1997). Black self-employed businessmen were overrepresented in eating and drinking establishments, in food retail stores, and in personal services. They were underrepresented in manufacturing and in the retailing of durable goods (including motor vehicles.)

Traditional black-owned businesses were unable to expand beyond their niche markets for several reasons. One, white consumers would generally not patronize black-owned businesses. Two, government regulations limited some black businesses to black neighborhoods. Licensing requirements tended to exclude black plumbers, barbers, and physicians from the general market, whereas a black plumber or barber could serve black customers without a license (Bernstein 2001). Finally, lack of access to capital and lack of managerial skill were obstacles to black business growth (Bates 1973).

A few black-owned businesses founded before the 1960s grew to serve a national market, but they were concentrated in three industries: insurance, publishing, and health and beauty products. Atlanta Life Insurance Company began in the 1880s as a mutual aid society, the Afro-American Benevolent Society. Alonzo Franklin Herndon oversaw the transformation of this society into the Atlanta Mutual Association in 1905, which became Atlanta Life in 1922 (Weare 1991). In 2002, Atlanta Life's assets totaled $98.68 billion. The largest black-owned insurance company, North Carolina Mutual, was founded in 1899. Its assets totaled $209.91 billion in 2002 (*Black Enterprise* 2000). Of the top-ten black-owned insurance companies, as listed in *Black Enterprise Magazine*'s list of top black-owned insurance companies, nine were founded before 1950. In publishing, a company founded in the 1940s has appeared on *Black Enterprise Magazine*'s top-one-hundred list since its inception—Johnson Publishing. Madame C. J. Walker (Sarah J. Breedlove) founded a national beauty product business in the early 1900s that survived into the Great Depression.

With desegregation, the traditional black business sector (food stores, eating and drinking establishments, and personal service establishments) shrank in relative size and importance. In 1972, 32 percent of black-owned firms operated in this traditional sector (Boston 2001). By 1982 this percentage declined to below 20 percent and by 1992 to less than 18 percent (Boston 2001).[3] These firms experienced a slower growth rate than the average for all black-owned firms (Brimmer 1995). Overall, between 1969 and 1982, black business' share of the U.S. market shrank from 0.362 percent to 0.301 percent (Brimmer 1995).

Although government loan guarantees and loan programs gave minority-owned firms greater access to capital, the traditional black-owned retail establishments and personal service providers lost their monopoly over the black consumer market. Many middle-class black families moved out of black neighborhoods and increased their patronage of retailers outside the traditional neighborhood. As social prohibitions against intermingling of the races weakened, white-owned businesses increased competition for the black consumer dollar. In this more competitive environment, traditional black-owned businesses suffered from several disadvantages. One, white-owned retailers were larger and better able to exploit economies of scale and offer low prices. There has been a long-term trend in the U.S. retail sector toward increased domination by large national chains. Large chain retailers can take advantage of economies of scale—per unit cost of production and distribution that decrease as output expands. For example, a large retail chain may pay a lower wholesale price for cornflakes because it buys in larger quantities compared with that of a single store. In addition, a large retail chain is likely to realize cost savings in transportation of the cornflake boxes to its stores. With lower costs of operation, the chain retailer can set a lower price for its cornflakes than can an independent store operator. Hence, a small retailer, regardless of race, is disadvantaged.

Even if a black-owned company could price competitively, it might not be able to attract customers from outside of the black community. A white consumer with tastes of discrimination would buy from a black-owned firm only if the firm's price was lower than its white-owned competitors. Traditional black-owned businesses faced other disadvantages as well, including limited managerial experience and lack of access to the social networks where many deals were made—for example, country clubs, golf courses, and service organizations (Boston 2001).

Ironically, affirmative action initiatives in white-owned businesses may have contributed to the decline in black business' share of total receipts. As discussed, some black business owners may have initially chosen self-employment because of a lack of opportunity in the white corporate sector. As the rewards to salaried employment grew (and the profit margins in food stores and restaurants shrank) some blacks, who might have opted for self-employment in an earlier era, chose salaried positions instead (Brimmer 1971).

While the desegregation effort hurt traditional black businesses, it also created opportunities. Government procurement programs and minority contracting programs expanded demand for the products and services of black business outside of their traditional niche. For example, Section 8 (a) of the Small Business Act was used to award contracts to small minority-owned businesses. The Public Works Employment Acts of 1977 and the 1978 Omnibus Small Business Act created set-asides for minority contractors in public works projects. The result was an increase in the share of federal procurement expenditures received by black, Latino, and Asian American firms (Boston 2001).

In addition to the federal programs, many state and local governments initiated minority-contracting programs. One of the pioneers was Atlanta, Georgia. In 1975, mayor Maynard Jackson issued an administrative order mandating the use of minority contractors on the construction of the then-proposed Hartsfield International Airport. These local set-aside programs were especially effective in urban areas with black mayors (Bates 1993). There were also private initiatives to support black business development.[4] For example, the Ford Motor Company established its Minority Dealer Training Program in 1967 to develop candidates for Ford and Lincoln-Mercury dealerships (Ford Motor Company 2002).

The civil rights movement had an indirect impact on minority business development through the creation of a new pool of skilled labor. With desegregation of public universities and colleges and with the implementation of affirmative action plans at elite universities, the number of blacks with college educations and with master's degrees in business expanded. Affirmative action programs in corporate America increased the pool of African Americans with managerial experience. Thomas Boston stresses the importance of this growth in human capital in the creation of a new group of entrepreneurs (2001).

Against this backdrop, the character of black business ownership slowly began to change. Table 26.1 describes the distribution of black-owned firms by industry in 1977 and 1997, using data from the Survey of Minority-Owned Business Enterprises (SMOBE).[5] In his work, Andrew Brimmer (1995) divides black-owned businesses into two broad categories, those serving the black consumer market and those serving the general, open market. Table 26.1 uses a similar framework. Firms serving the black consumer market are divided into three subcategories: those serving black consumers with a national market, those serving a local black clientele, and those firms engaged in ethnic marketing. The ethnic marketing category includes firms who sell goods identified with African Americans to black and to white consumers. For example, Motown Records, which topped the *Black Enterprise* list of top black-owned companies from 1973 to 1983, sold black music to black and to white audiences. The ethnic marketing category might also include firms that sell access to the black community, such as market research and advertising agencies. For firms serving the general open market, table 26.1 reports data for five subcategories: business services (including engineering and technical consulting), human services (health, educational, and social services), construction, transportation, and communications.

As the data in table 26.1 show, firms selling to the black consumer market in 1997 account for a smaller percentage of the total receipts of black-owned enterprises than they do in 1977. They also represent a smaller proportion of the firms. The primary reason for the decline in share is a decrease in the relative importance of firms serving a local black consumer market. This change in share of receipts would be even more dramatic if automotive dealers and gas stations were excluded. Automotive dealers and gasoline service stations accounted for 2 percent of total receipts in 1977 and almost 10 percent of that in 1997 (U.S. Census Bureau 1977, 2001). If we exclude these receipts from the total for local black consumer markets, its share declines from 0.334 in 1977 to 0.154 in 1997.[6] Within the general open market, the sector experiencing the greatest growth in share of receipts is business services. Although there is still a large number of black-owned beauty parlors and barbershops (103,865 in 1997), there are even more engaged in the de-

Table 26.1   Distribution of Black-Owned Firms in 1977 and 1997

	Receipts		Number of Firms	
	1997	1977	1997	1977
Black consumer market, national	0.019	0.004	0.004	0.004
Black consumer market, local	0.250	0.356	0.230	0.356
Auto dealers/gasoline service stations	0.096	0.022	0.005	0.022
Ethnic goods/access to ethnic markets	0.028	0.025	0.039	0.025
Black products or consumers	0.297	0.385	0.278	0.407
Transportation	0.069	0.085	0.082	0.101
Human services	0.117	0.074	0.154	0.074
Business services	0.152	0.067	0.173	0.067
Communications	0.009	0.000	0.004	0.000
Construction	0.108	0.091	0.068	0.091
All other	0.248	0.296	0.246	0.297
General open market	0.703	0.615	0.727	0.630
Total receipts ($billion)	$79.76	$25.68		
Total number of firms			823,499	231,203

Source: Author's calculations using U.S. Census 1977, 1994, 1996, and 2001.
Note: Total receipts in 2002 dollars.

livery of business services and technical consulting (144,142 in 1997; U.S. Census Bureau 2001).

Black Enterprise magazine's list of the one hundred largest black-owned firms (the *BE*100) offers another snapshot of black business diversification. Table 26.2 compares the distribution of *BE*100 firms by industry in 1977 and in 2002. Again, firms selling to the black consumer market account for a declining share of total receipts. However, among larger firms, those selling to a national black consumer market experienced the biggest decline in total share. This is explained in part by the disappearance of several large beauty product manufacturers. In 1977, the *BE*100 included health and beauty product manufacturers Johnson Products and Pro-Line Corporation. These firms disappeared from the list in 1997 not because they experienced a decline in sales but because they were taken over by larger, white-owned conglomerates.[7] Although the share of receipts accounted for by ethnic product firms has not changed significantly, there has been a change in the source of those revenues. In 1977, music production companies dominated this category. The 1977 list included Motown Industries, which topped the list with sales of fifty million, and Philadelphia International. In contrast, only one music company appears on the 2002

list. As well, black-owned advertising agencies generated a large percentage of the revenues in this category in 2002.

Other changes between 1977 and 2002 include the decline in receipts from construction and a growth in receipts from communications. The decline in construction receipts for black-owned firms may reflect the diminished role of affirmative action in government contracting programs.[8]

Diversification has been accompanied by growth. The receipts of black-owned businesses grew by 103 percent between 1977 and 1997, an average annual rate of 5.1 percent (U.S. Census Bureau 2001). By comparison, U.S. gross domestic product grew at an average annual rate of 2.8 percent over this period. Nevertheless, the black-owned business sector remains small, accounting for less than one-half of 1 percent of total business receipts in 1997 (U.S. Census Bureau 2001).

OBSTACLES TO GROWTH

Economists have identified several obstacles to continued growth and viability of black-owned business enterprises. One is the small scale of most businesses. A larger firm, measured either by sales or employment, has a greater chance of

Table 26.2 Industry Share of Receipts Derived from *Black Enterprise*'s List of the One Hundred Largest Black-Owned Firms

	2001	1977
Black consumer goods, national market	0.034	0.168
Black consumer goods, local market	0.045	0.096
Ethnic marketing	0.083	0.097
Black consumer market	0.162	0.361
Auto dealers	0.384	0.290
Transportation	—	—
Human services	—	—
Business services	0.143	—
Communications	0.049	—
Construction	—	0.086
All other	0.262	0.263
General open market	0.454	0.349
Total sales ($billion)	16.88	2.31

Source: Black Enterprise (1977, 2002a, 2002b).
Note: Dashes indicate zero value. Total sales in 2002 dollars.

survival (Bates 1973; Christopher 2002). Black-owned firms are small relative to all U.S. firms. In 1997, the average receipts per firm were $86,000 for black-owned businesses and $891,000 for all businesses. In other words, the average black-owned firm was less than one-tenth the size of the average U.S. business. The size differential was greatest in manufacturing, where the average black-owned firm is less than a hundredth the size of the average U.S. manufacturer.

A second obstacle to black business growth and development is the lack of financial capital. Christopher (2002) shows that a significant factor contributing to business survival is the amount of start-up capital, of which African American entrepreneurs generally have less when compared to the average start-up for all small businesses. Because access to capital is limited for black-owned businesses, Christopher predicts that black-owned firms would be most successful in industries that have low capital requirements. This is certainly consistent with the observed distribution of black-owned companies as compared with that of all U.S. firms. Black-owned businesses are overrepresented in services—personal services, business services, and human services—with low capital requirements, and they are underrepresented in industries with high capital requirements, such as manufacturing.

The lack of financial capital reflects racial inequality in earnings and in wealth as well as the discriminatory practices of lenders. Blanchflower, Levine, and Zimmerman (1998) report that after controlling for differences in credit worthiness and other relevant factors, black-owned firms are about twice as likely to be denied credit as white-owned firms. Bates (1993) also finds evidence of discrimination against black-owned businesses in commercial lending.

The retrenchment of government set-aside programs may also prove an obstacle to black business expansion. Boston (2001) attributes some of the diversification and growth during the past two decades to mandated government minority contracting and set-aside programs. Minority-owned firms earn a higher percentage of their revenues from local, state, and federal governments than do nonminority-owned firms (Boston 2001). Unless there is an offsetting increase in sales to private entities, black-owned firms in construction, transportation, and some business services are likely to see a drop in revenues as a result of the elimination of these programs.

In the past, a major obstacle to black business development was the lack of human capital among black business owners. Although college completion rates for African Americans continue to lag behind those of whites, the number of African Americans with college degrees has increased dramatically over the past forty years. Furthermore, more black college graduates appear to be choosing to become entrepreneurs. Historically, black college graduates tended not to choose business ownership as a career path (Bates 1973). According to 1992 data, 24.6 percent of black business owners are college graduates compared with 12 percent of the black population as a whole (U.S. Census Bureau 1994, 2002). The educational attainment of black business owners compares favorably with that of white business owners, 34.9 percent of whom have bachelor's degrees or higher. Of black business owners, 14 percent hold degrees in business compared with 17 percent of white business owners (U.S. Census Bureau 2002).

BLACK CAPITALISM

During the late 1960s and early 1970s, "black capitalism" was espoused as a magic potion to cure the economic ills of the black community.[9] One of its most prominent advocates was president Richard Nixon, who created the Office of Minority Business Enterprise in the Department of Commerce and backed a number of other initiatives to support black business development—including federal contracting programs. The strategy was "to transfer ownership of ghetto business from white to black control" and "to create jobs and profit centers inside the ghetto" (Cross 1974, 211). Advocates of black capitalism listed among its benefits the creation of a black middle class, an increase in political power, improvements in the physical and social infrastructure of black communities, reduced dependence of African Americans on whites, and an increase in employment opportunities. Critics of Nixon's strategy argued that an increase in the incomes and wealth of individual black entrepreneurs would do little to increase the prosperity of most blacks.

> The creation of a middle class of Black capitalists would make the distribution of income inside the Black community less equal, not more equal. It would be the source of greater chaos and disorder inside the Black community, because the layer at the bottom of the Black community, far from seeing these Black capitalists as models and symbols to be admired and imitated, would be hostile to and strike out at them. (Boggs 1971, 154)

Andrew Brimmer, an economist and the first black member of the Board of Governors of the Federal Reserve System, questions the employment capacity of traditional black-owned businesses and expressed concerns about encouraging blacks " to seek careers as self-employed, small businessmen" rather than as managers in large corporations (1971, 164; 1997).

The recent growth and diversification of black-owned businesses has revived interest in black capitalism, but with a twist. The focus has shifted from the creation of a black middle class and a self-sufficient ghetto economy to the expansion of employment opportunities, especially for black youth. Black-owned businesses have a higher propensity to hire African Americans than do other businesses (Bates 1997; Simms and Allen 1996). Historically, the propensity of black-owned firms to hire black workers was linked to their location in black communities. However, even as black-owned businesses have moved to suburban locations, they continue to be more likely to hire black workers, other things being equal (Boston 2001; Raphael, Stoll, and Holzer 1998).

Economist Thomas Boston has proposed a strategy he calls *twenty by ten*. As described by Boston, *twenty by ten* "calls for the government and private sector to pursue policies that are designed to create a sufficient number of black-owned firms such that their combined employment capacity will equal 20 percent of the black labor force by the year 2010" (Boston 1998, 86). Total employment in black-owned firms in 1997 (718,341 workers) equaled nearly 5 percent of the black civilian labor force. Between 1977 and 1997, black-owned businesses added 554,614 employees, an average of 27,731 employees per year for an annual average growth rate of 6.3 percent (U.S. Census Bureau 2001). To achieve Boston's goal, black businesses would have to add 107,751 jobs each year between 1997 and 2010. The implied rate of growth may be unrealistic. Nevertheless, even at more modest rates, job growth in black-owned businesses could help reduce black joblessness and serve as a point of entry into the formal labor market for many young black workers.

CONCLUSION

Black-owned businesses have experienced rapid growth over the past decade in sales and in employment. They have diversified their activities beyond their traditional niche of personal services and have expanded their markets beyond black consumers. Despite these changes, black-owned businesses tend be more likely to hire black workers than are white-owned firms with similar profiles. Hence, even though this sector is small relative to the U.S. economy, its continued growth is likely to have positive benefits for the African American community as a whole. Obstacles to black business growth include limited access to financial capital and a retrenchment in government assistance programs.

NOTES

1. According to Bates (1973), white insurance companies would not sell insurance to blacks because of their belief, based on an 1886 study, that blacks were poor insurance risks. Black insurance companies later prospered in this market.

2. This line of reasoning would also explain the ownership of retail stores in black communities by immigrant groups and other ethnic groups who at one time or another have been the subject of labor market discrimination.

3. The Survey of Minority-Owned Business Enterprises is conducted every five years by the U.S. Bureau of the Census. It is the primary data source

on the distribution and size of minority owned businesses in the United States. A business is defined as black-owned if over 50 percent of the ownership was held by blacks. Because of changes in survey methodology, the 1992 figure is not strictly comparable to the data for 1972 and 1982. The 1987 and 1992 SMOBEs excluded 1,120 subchapter C corporations that were included in the 1982 survey. Because subchapter C corporations tend to be larger, the exclusion of these firms reduced reported black business receipts and employment. Excluding subchapter C corporations, 21.5 percent of black-owned businesses in 1982 were food stores, eating or drinking establishments, personal service establishments or auto repair garages.

4. Appendix II of Theodore Cross's book *Black Capitalism: Strategy for Business in the Ghetto* (1974) offers a listing of private initiatives.

5. As noted, the 1982, 1987, and 1992 SMOBEs included only sole proprietorships, partnerships, and subchapter S corporations. The 1997 SMOBE returned to the earlier practice of including subchapter C corporations. Because the 1977 and 1997 SMOBEs included these larger companies, this chapter analyzes trends by comparing those two years.

6. The classification of these businesses as serving a local black consumer market is somewhat questionable. While gasoline service stations are likely to be located within a black community and hence have a primarily black clientele, automobile dealers probably service a broader audience.

7. Johnson Products was sold to IVAX in 1994 (IVAX later sold Johnson Products to Carson Products). Pro-Line was sold to Alberto Culver in 2000. Another *BE*100 company, Soft Sheen (eighteen on the 1998 list), was sold to Paris-based L'Oreal in 1998. McDonald (1998) discusses the entry of major white-owned companies into the ethnic hair-care market.

8. For a discussion of court decisions affecting government set-aside programs, the interested reader should look at Boston (2001).

9. For a summary of the debate over black capitalism and its historical antecedents, the interested reader is referred to Bailey (1971).

REFERENCES

Bailey, Ronald. 1971. "Black Business Enterprise: Reflections on Its History and Future Development." Introduction to *Black Business Enter-prise: Historical and Contemporary Perspectives,* ed. Ronald Bailey. New York: Basic Books.

Bates, Timothy. 1973. *Black Capitalism: A Quantitative Analysis.* New York: Praeger Publishers.

———. 1993. *Banking on Black Enterprise: The Potential of Emerging Firms for Revitalizing Urban Economies.* Washington, D.C.: Joint Center for Political and Economic Studies.

———. 1997. "Utilization of Minority Employees in Small Business: A Comparison of Nonminority and Black-Owned Urban Enterprises." In *African Americans and Postindustrial Labor Markets,* ed. James B. Stewart. New Brunswick, N.J.: Transaction Publishers.

Bernstein, David E. 2001. *Only One Place of Redress: African Americans, Labor Regulations, and the Courts from Reconstruction to the New Deal.* Durham, N.C.: Duke University Press.

Black Enterprise. 1977. "The Top 100." June, 63.

———. 2000. "B. E. Insurance Companies." June, 229.

———. 2002a. "B. E. Auto Dealer100." June, 167–174.

———. 2002b. "B. E. Industrial/Service 100." June, 138–146.

Blanchflower, David, Phillip B. Levine, and David J. Zimmerman. 1998. "Discrimination in the Small Business Credit Market." National Bureau of Economic Research, Working Paper 6840.

Boggs, James. 1971. "The Myth and Irrationality of Black Capitalism." In *Black Business Enterprise: Historical and Contemporary Perspectives,* ed. Ronald W. Bailey. New York: Basic Books.

Boston, Thomas D. 1998. "An Employment and Business Strategy for the Next Century: A Comment." *Review of Black Political Economy* 25, no. 4: 85–90.

———. 2001. "Trends in Minority-Owned Businesses." *America Becoming: Racial Trends and Their Consequences,* vol. 2, ed. Neil J. Smelser, William Julius Wilson, and Faith Mitchell. Washington, D.C.: National Academy Press.

Brimmer, Andrew. 1971. "Small Business and Economic Development in the Negro Community." In *Black Business Enterprise: Historical and Contemporary Perspectives,* ed. Ronald W. Bailey. New York: Basic Books.

———. 1995. "Economic Growth and Diversification of Black-Owned Businesses." Paper presented at the National Economic Association, Washington, D.C. January 6.

———. 1997. "Preamble: Blacks in the American

Economy: Summary of Selected Research." In *A Different Vision: African American Economic Thought,* ed. Thomas D. Boston. New York: Routledge.

Christopher, Jan. 2002. "Minority Business Formation and Survival: Evidence on Business Performance and Viability." In *Leading Issues in Black Political Economy,* ed. Thomas D. Boston. New Brunswick, N.J.: Transaction Publishers.

Cross, Theodore. 1974. *Black Capitalism: Strategy for Business in the Ghetto.* New York: Atheneum.

Ford Motor Company. 2002 "Minority Dealer Operations Training Programs." Available at www.dd.ford.com/training.asp.

McDonald, Kimberly Seals. 1998. "Hair Care Firms Get Ownership Makeover." *Black Enterprise,* September, 19.

Raphael, Steven, Michael A. Stoll, and Harry J. Holzer. 1998. "Are Suburban Firms More Likely to Discriminate against African Americans?" University of California, San Diego, Department of Economics, Working Paper 98/05.

Simms, Margaret, and Winston J. Allen. 1996. "Is the Inner City Competitive?" In *The Inner City: Urban Poverty and Economic Development in the Next Century,* ed. Thomas D. Boston and Catherine L. Ross. New Brunswick, N.J.: Transaction Publishers.

U.S. Census Bureau. 1977. *Minority Owned Businesses: Black.* Washington, D.C.: U.S. Superintendent of Documents.

———. 1994. *Blacks in America—1992.* Statistical brief SB/94-12. Available at www.census.gov/apsd/www/statbrief/sb94_12.pdf.

———. 1996. *1992 Economic Census: Survey of Minority Owned Business Enterprises; Black.* MB92-1. Washington, D.C.: U.S. Superintendent of Documents.

———. 2001. *Black: 1997 Economic Census; Survey of Minority Owned Business Enterprises.* Company Statistics Series EC97CS-3. Washington, D.C.: U.S. Superintendent of Documents.

———. 2002. "Characteristics of Business Owners: Summary Characteristics of Business Owners and Their Businesses 1992." Available at www.census.gov/csd/cbo/1992/www/cbo9201.html.

Weare, Walter B. 1991. "Atlanta Life Insurance Company: Guardian of Black Economic Dignity." *Journal of Southern History* 57 (November): 756–757.

27

Black-Owned Banks: Past and Present
GARY A. DYMSKI and ROBERT E. WEEMS JR.

The creation of black-owned banks stands as one of the most important historical responses of the black community to their virtually complete exclusion from bank credit and capital markets from the post–Civil War period through the 1960s. This chapter describes the historical emergence of black-owned banks in the nineteenth century and summarizes their responses to a variety of challenges in the twentieth century. It further argues that black-owned banks can play a key role in minority community wealth creation in the twenty-first century.

The creation of black-owned banks stands as one of the most important historical responses of the black community to their virtually complete exclusion from bank credit and capital markets from the post–Civil War period through the 1960s. This chapter describes this history and then turns to the challenges facing black-owned banks in this contemporary period. We conclude with some suggestions for policies that can support the fiscal solvency of black-owned banks while supporting their effectiveness in community wealth creation.

THE HISTORICAL EMERGENCE OF BLACK-OWNED BANKS

For a significant part of the African American experience, access to financial services appeared irrelevant, given that the majority of blacks were enslaved. To be succinct, most African American slaves did not have money to deposit into a bank.

Notwithstanding this historical reality, not all African Americans before 1865 were slaves. Moreover, some antebellum free blacks were involved in the banking industry. As Juliet E. K.

Walker asserts in her classic 1998 work *The History of Black Business in America: Capitalism, Race, Entrepreneurship,* not only did Northern free blacks buy stock in "mainstream" banks, but wealthy Southern free blacks, especially barbers, established their own private banks to lend money to blacks as well as whites.[1] Even more significant, the National Negro Convention movement, which commenced in 1830, advocated the establishment of a national black bank. In an apparent response to Northern blacks' patronage of white-owned banks, the organization's Banks and Banking Institutions Committee noted in an 1847 report that "a Banking Institution originating among the colored people of the U.S. [is needed] because they at present contribute to their own degradation by investing capital in the hands of their 'enemies.'"[2]

Significantly, the notion of a national bank for blacks achieved fruition immediately following the Civil War. Ironically, the Freedman's Savings and Trust Company, established in 1865, was white controlled (hereafter Freedman's Bank). This financial institution was ostensibly founded with the support of the U.S. government to instruct newly freed blacks in the nuances of financial planning; ultimately, however, it hindered rather than assisted African American economic development.[3]

Between 1865 and 1870, Freedman's Bank established branches throughout the country. Unfortunately, by the early 1870s, Freedman's Bank white directors lost sight of their earlier missionary intent and became caught up in the speculative fever of the period. Using the savings of African Americans, the bank's officers engaged in a number of questionable financial maneuvers, such as granting large unsecured loans to railroads and other white corporations.[4]

With the onset of the panic of 1873, Freedman's Bank lost huge sums of money because of bad loans. Yet, the bank's directors intentionally kept this information from the general public and the institution's black depositors. Their subterfuge included appointing the venerable Frederick Douglass as president of the institution. In fact, the directors encouraged Douglass, who was not informed of the bank's crisis situation, to make a well-publicized personal deposit to help maintain depositor confidence.[5]

This tragic charade ended in June 1874, when an audit forced Freedman's Bank to close its doors. The $31,000 in available cash deposits must have shocked Douglass and the institution's sixty-one thousand other depositors because their passbooks verified that African Americans had deposited nearly $3.3 million into Freedman's Bank.[6]

About one-half of the creditors and depositors of Freedman's Bank eventually received partial compensation of approximately $18.51 each, per under normal bankruptcy procedures. The remainder, who had failed to follow the procedures necessary to get their partial reimbursement, received nothing. Well into the twentieth century, Freedman's Bank depositors sent appeals to Washington, D.C., seeking the balance of their funds.[7]

It would be difficult to overestimate the negative effect that the demise of Freedman's Bank had, not just on its unfortunate depositors, but on the psyche of the entire African American community. Nevertheless, shortly following the Freedman's Bank debacle, blacks began establishing their own, independent banking institutions. The motivation for these efforts was to combat the era's overt and explicit racial discrimination in financial services: white-owned banks systematically denied blacks and other minorities any access to credit and capital markets. While bank branch networks thickly covered urban areas, minority areas had virtually no bank branches and no access to credit. In many U.S. cities and rural areas, this exclusion led to the creation of a large number of black-owned banks and other financial institutions, such as insurance companies.

Abram Harris's seminal 1936 work *The Negro as Capitalist: A Study of Banking and Business among American Negroes* remains a key source on the post-Reconstruction history of black-owned banks in America. According to Harris, "the first banks that were actually organized and administered by Negroes were the Savings Bank of the Grand Fountain United Order of True Reformers at Richmond, Virginia March 1888 and the Capital Savings Bank at Washington, D.C., October 1888."[8] Indeed, "no fewer than twenty-eight banks were organized by Negroes from 1899–1905. Nearly all of these early institutions were created to serve as depositories for Negro fraternal insurance orders."[9] It is also worth noting that the majority of these pioneer black banks were established in the South.[10]

With the onset of the World War I "great migration" and the growing proliferation of African Americans in Northern cities, the epicenter of the African American banking industry moved north of the Mason-Dixon line. For instance, in 1929, there were twenty-one black-owned banks in the United States, with combined assets of $11 million. Yet, Chicago's Binga State Bank and Douglass National Bank had combined assets of nearly $4 million (36 percent of the national total).[11]

The Great Depression of the 1930s had an especially negative effect on black-owned banks. Only six African American banks survived this dramatic economic downturn.[12] Among the casualties were Chicago's once-proud Binga State Bank and Douglass National Bank.

BLACK BANKS FROM THE CIVIL RIGHTS ERA TO THE AGE OF FINANCIAL GLOBALIZATION

Black banks were not alone in experiencing high failure rates in periods of severe economic downturn in the pre–World War II period—the entire U.S. banking system suffered severe boom–bust swings. Changes in Federal Reserve powers, deposit insurance, and other protections addressed the systematic weaknesses in the banking system and helped to stabilize the banking population. Banking was heavily regulated, with many restrictions on movement of banks into new geographic or product markets. As a result of these changes, many minority communities were again left with few or no banking services.

Against this background, the civil rights movement, mobilizing black pride and community organization, led to the founding of a new wave of black banks. At least seventeen black banks, including the Freedom National Bank of New York, were founded in the 1962–1969 period.[13] The founding of Independence Bank and of Seaway National Bank in Chicago, in December 1964 and January 1965, respectively, helped the city to again achieve preeminence in the black banking industry.[14] An even bigger surge in the number of black banks occurred in the 1970s: at least thirty-four were founded between 1970 and 1978.[15] As Juliet E. K. Walker asserts, "Both the Civil Rights Movement and federal affirmative action policies were significant in contributing to the growth of black banks."[16] For instance, part of President Nixon's widely publicized "black capitalism" initiative was a program that encouraged federal agencies and private corporations to deposit funds into black-owned banks. This encouraged the rapid growth of deposits in minority-owned banks.[17] Indeed, assets and deposits in this period grew faster at black banks than they did in the banking system as a whole.[18]

At the same time, new challenges emerged for black banks. Some of these challenges were specific to the urban communities in which these institutions were located. By the 1960s, the population of U.S. cities began to shift from central cities into rapidly growing suburban areas. More-

over, a large portion of this population shift involved white flight. The urban job base soon followed—many stable working-class jobs disappeared from areas with high minority populations to be reestablished in the suburbs, in right-to-work states, or abroad. Meanwhile, the 1964 Civil Rights Act marked a major benchmark in efforts to break down the walls of strict residential segregation and overt economic and social discrimination on the basis of race. Consequently, some of the more affluent African Americans began moving into suburban areas in search of better schools, jobs, and public services. Another significant development during the mid-1970s was the passage of federal legislation requiring banks to reinvest in lower-income—hence, heavily minority—areas.

Because of these shifts, black-owned banks were serving a local customer base with lower incomes and less-stable jobs than they did in previous years. Because many of these banks' better customers were relocating outside of their immediate service areas, it became more costly for bank and customer alike to engage in banking services—thereby causing a serious problem, since smaller banks (a category including all black-owned banks) must already overcome inconvenience costs in their efforts to compete with larger, white-owned banks. The bank reinvestment legislation of the 1970s, in turn, shifted the attention of many community activists from using black banks as engines of community development to inducing large banks to provide needed financial services in inner-city and minority communities.

Another set of recent challenges affecting black-owned banks were related to pressures on the entire U.S. banking system. Beginning in the 1970s, the 1930s structure of banking regulations began to break down because of a disorganized macroeconomy and the competition from non-bank financial firms. By the 1980s, a full-scale process of bank deregulation was underway, nationally and globally. Bank mergers dramatically increased in the United States, spurred on by occasional lending crises and by large banks' search for increased market share.[19]

In the 1980s, the rate of black bank formation slowed considerably relative to that of the 1970s.[20] Through the early 1990s, the number of black-owned banks declined, as some institutions closed and others were purchased by other banks; however, the number of black-owned banks then stabilized.[21]

The industry-wide pressures on banks pose a real challenge for black-owned banks; the fact that they operate primarily in lower-income urban areas, in which other banks have reduced their exposure, adds another dimension to this challenge. This leads to two questions: first, are these banks viable as business entities? second, can they play a significant role in stimulating economic growth in the heavily minority communities they serve?

Economic studies have found that, overall, black-owned banks are somewhat less profitable than other banks. Black-owned banks fall into two groups in terms of profitability: the larger and better capitalized black banks, which outperform their peers among nonminority banks; and the smaller and undercapitalized black banks, which do less well.[22] In sum, black-owned banks can survive if they attain adequate scale. One manager of an African American bank pointed out that the bank merger wave has opened some market niches because of branch closures by the megabanks that increasingly dominate the U.S. banking market.[23]

What about black-owned banks' impact on African American community development? Andrew Brimmer, a former member of the Federal Reserve Board, has pointed out that these institutions face the dilemma of "lending risks versus community service."[24] These banks can redress the discrimination that minority borrowers have often experienced at other institutions and can use the personal touch to develop strong ties with community residents and businesses; but these institutions must be cautious, since their customers include many undercapitalized households and firms that are operating in minority communities with many structural challenges. Further, these banks face competition by nonminority banks for a portion of their customer base. Black banks have reacted in various ways to these challenges. Some have used the Small Business Administration loan guarantee programs to make loans to local businesses while minimizing credit risk. Some black banks have entered into partnerships of various kinds with other lenders. Others use conservative lending criteria, in some cases more conservative than that of other banks.[25]

CONCLUSION: LESSONS OF OTHER ETHNIC BANKS' EXPERIENCE FOR BLACK BANKS?

Historically, part of the rationale for the establishment of black-owned banks was that these institutions provided financial services that were unavailable to black consumers in mainstream banks. Yet, by the late twentieth-century, white-owned financial institutions no longer openly discriminated against potential black depositors and borrowers. So as has happened with their counterparts in the insurance industry, black-owned banks found themselves openly competing with white-owned banks for black consumer support. Similarly, as in the insurance industry, economy-of-scale disadvantages have put many black banks at a competitive disadvantage in their quest for depositors. Considering that white consumers have never seriously considered patronizing African American financial institutions, this raises questions about black-owned banks' chances for survival in the landscape of twenty-first-century American business.[26]

The experiences of other minority-owned banks in the United States may contain some lessons for black-owned banks. On a population-adjusted basis, the black-owned banking sector is actually relatively small relative to other minority banking sectors. Using the Federal Reserve's list of minority-owned banks, as of December 31, 2001, there were four black-owned bank offices for every one million blacks. By contrast, per population of one million, there were seven offices of Hispanic-owned banks, eight offices of Native American banks, and fifteen offices of Asian American banks.[27]

The Hispanic-owned banking sector is quite centralized—77 percent of all its offices are operated by just three institutions. The largest of these, Banco Popular, is based in Puerto Rico. The Latino/Chicano population in the United States, like the African American population, includes a large proportion of "unbanked" households who operate entirely outside of the banking system. Banco Popular has grown aggressively in recent years in part by implementing a strategy of recruiting lower-income, unbanked workers and households. This strategy involved first providing convenient check-cashing services, often on work sites, and then converting these informal banking customers into depositors and eventually borrowers.[28]

The Asian American banking sector also deserves study. This sector, like the Asian American population itself, is concentrated in a small number of urban areas. This population's banking sector is concentrated in Los Angeles and Orange counties in Southern California. A sizable Asian American banking sector has emerged in Los Angeles, fueled especially by the steady inflow of people and capital from East and Southeast Asia over the past three decades. Currently, about one-quarter of all bank branches in Los Angeles County are Asian American, and most of these are Chinese American. The first Chinese American banks had the same community-based roots as did black-owned banks, but the recent growth of this sector is due primarily to cross-border population and money shifts.[29] Recent entrants have generally had high education and wealth levels and have deposited their financial resources, at least initially, into Asian American banks. This sizable banking sector has focused on providing banking services and loans in areas with heavy Asian American populations, just as black-owned banks focus on areas of concentrated African American population.[30] The difference, however, is scale of operation. For example, whereas heavily black areas of Los Angeles County usually have less than half the bank branches per person that other areas do, the heavily Asian American areas of the county have nearly double the number of per-capita bank branches, with Asian American institutions accounting for all of this difference. This concentrated and capable ethnic banking sector has been able to engage in or leverage substantial commercial and residential development.

In sum, the banking industry's reduction of services for lower-income customers and inner-city areas confronts black-owned banks with a dilemma—either shift with the overall banking market to protect their solvency or buck these trends and fill the social need for banking in neighborhoods other banks are reluctant to serve. The experience of other ethnic banks suggests that recruiting new customers, attracting significant inflows of money, and focusing and concentrating their financial strength will enhance their impact on community economic development and improve their long-run prospects.

NOTES

Gary A. Dymski is a professor of economics at the University of California, Riverside. Robert E. Weems Jr. is professor of history at the University of Missouri, Columbia.

1. Juliet E. K. Walker, *The History of Black Business in America: Capitalism: Race, Entrepreneurship* (New York: Twayne Publishers, 1998), 87–88.

2. Walker, *The History of Black Business*, 88.

3. Eric Foner, *Reconstruction: America's Unfinished Revolution, 1863–1877* (New York: Harper & Row, 1988), 531.

4. Foner, *Reconstruction*, 531.

5. Foner, *Reconstruction*, 532; Carl R. Osthaus, *Freedmen, Philanthropy, and Fraud: A History of the Freedman's Savings Bank* (Urbana: University of Illinois Press, 1976), 138.

6. Foner, *Reconstruction*, 532.

7. Foner, *Reconstruction*, 532; Osthaus, *Freedmen, Philanthropy, and Fraud*, 221.

8. Abram L. Harris, *The Negro as Capitalist: A Study of Banking and Business among American Negroes* (1936; repr., Chicago: Urban Research Press, 1992), 57.

9. Harris, *The Negro as Capitalist*, 57.

10. Harris, *The Negro as Capitalist*, 236–237.

11. Harris, *The Negro as Capitalist*, 195.

12. Walker, *The History of Black Business*, 313. It is worth noting that in the prologue to the 1992 reprinting of *The Negro as Captialist*, Dempsey Travis asserts that only eight black banks survived the Great Depression (xix). Although there is a discrepancy between Walker's and Travis's numbers, one fact remains indisputable: the Great Depression had a very negative effect on black-owned banks in America.

13. By contrast, just four black banks were founded in the 1947–1961 period. See Lila Ammons,

"The Evolution of Black-Owned Banks in the United States between the 1880s and the 1990s," *Journal of Black Studies* 26, no. 4 (March 1996): 474–478.

14. Harris, *The Negro as Capitalist*, xviii–xix, xxviii. Chicago's situation was special in part because Illinois was a unit-branching state—that is, commercial banks could have just one office and no branch offices.

15. Ammons, "The Evolution of Black-Owned Banks," 479.

16. Walker, *The History of Black Business*, 314.

17. Dean J. Kotlowski, "Black Power—Nixon Style: The Nixon Administration and Minority Business Enterprise," *Business History Review* 72 (Autumn 1998): 437. Kotlowski documents an increase in the number of minority-owned banks from twenty-eight to fifty between 1970 and 1974, a substantially lower number than that from Ammons. He also reports that deposits at minority-owned banks increased from $400 million in 1970 to $1 billion in 1973—attributable in part to this federal program.

18. Andrew Brimmer, "Recent Developments in Black Banking (1970–71)," *Review of Black Political Economy* 58 (1972).

19. See Gary A. Dymski, *The Bank Merger Wave: Economic Causes and Social Consequences of Financial Consolidation* (Armonk, N.Y.: M. E. Sharpe, 1999), chaps. 2–5.

20. Ammons, "The Evolution of Black-Owned Banks," 483.

21. Sam Q. Ziorklui, "The Performance of Black-Owned Commercial Banks: A Comparative Analysis," *Review of Black Political Economy* 23, no. 2 (Fall 1994): 7.

22. Ziorklui, "The Performance of Black-Owned Commercial Banks," 21–22.

23. See Matthew Scott and Wendy C. Pelle, "Must Black Banks Merge or Be Purged?" *Black Enterprise* 26, no. 11 (June 1996): 162.

24. Andrew F. Brimmer, "The Dilemma of Black Banking: Lending Risks vs. Community Service," *Review of Black Political Economy* 20, no. 3 (Winter 1992): 5–29.

25. One recent paper has asserted that black banks' conservative lending practices may constitute a form of black-on-black discrimination. See Harold A. Black, M. C. Collings, and K. B. Cyree, "Do Black-Owned Banks Discriminate against Black Borrowers?" *Journal of Financial Services Research* 11, no. 1–2 (February 1997): 189–204.

26. Desegregation in the realm of business has been a one-way phenomenon in recent decades. For instance, in the early 1960s, African American insurance companies actively sought to diversify their workforce to reach white consumers. Some black companies actually paid the training costs of white agents. However, when white consumers discovered that these agents worked for a black-owned company, they refused to do business with them. See Robert E. Weems Jr., *Black Business in the Black Metropolis: The Chicago Metropolitan Mutual Assurance Company, 1925–1985* (Bloomington: Indiana University Press, 1996), 103–104.

27. These figures are based on the list of minority-owned banks participating in the same federal program mentioned in note 17. As of December 2001, there were ninety-eight banks on this list, with assets of $37 billion; this represents substantial growth, much of it accounted for by Asian American banks.

28. See Carolyn Aldana, Gary Dymski, and Barbara Wiens-Tuers, "Molding the Market or Following It? African American and Latino Banks in Los Angeles County," unpublished manuscript, University of California, Riverside, October 2000.

29. The growth of this banking sector is analyzed in Wei Li, Yu Zhou, Gary Dymski, and Maria Chee, "Banking on Social Capital in the Era of Globalization: Chinese Ethnobanks in Los Angeles," *Environment and Planning A* 33 (2001): 1923–1948; and in Wei Li, Gary Dymski, Yu Zhou, Carolyn Aldana, and Maria Chee, "Chinese American Banking and Community in Los Angeles County: The Financial Sector and Chinatown/Ethnoburb Development," *Annals of the American Association of Geographers* 92, no. 4 (2002): 777–796.

30. See Gary Dymski and Lisa Mohanty, "Credit and Banking Structure: Asian and African-American Experience in Los Angeles," *American Economic Review* 89, no. 2 (May 1999): 362–366.

28

"Bling-Bling" and Other Recent Trends in African American Consumerism
ROBERT E. WEEMS JR.

"Bling-bling," or conspicuous consumption, represents one of the most striking characteristics of contemporary African American consumerism. Moreover, while African Americans' collective buying power continues to rise, the amount of money that blacks spend with black-owned businesses continues to decline. This chapter suggests that African Americans' focus on bling-bling—through excessive spending on such items as fancy cars, jewelry, and gold teeth—contributes little to the actual wealth of the African American community. Thus, a major challenge facing contemporary African American consumers is to develop spending strategies that advance black economic well-being.

One of the most striking characteristics of contemporary African American consumerism is an increased focus on "conspicuous consumption." Significantly, this phenomenon appears to be fueled by the "bling-bling" genre of hip-hop. While so-called gangsta rap correctly generated a public outcry, bling-bling—which glorifies the acquisition of "ice" (jewelry), big cars, and fancy clothes—may be even more insidious in its effect on black youth.

Before we examine the bling-bling phenomenon in greater detail, a survey of the broader demographics of recent African American consumerism would be useful and illuminating. As illustrated in table 28.1, between the years 1996 and 2001, the collective buying power of black America increased by 64 percent (from $367 to $601 billion).[1] On the surface, this represents good news and is a concrete indication of African Americans' growing economic clout. Yet, in studying African American consumerism, it is perhaps more important to examine how blacks spend their money.

Table 28.2 provides a striking cross-section of African American spending patterns in recent years. Between 1996 and 2001, African Americans spent $27.1 billion on alcoholic beverages and tobacco products and smoking supplies. Yet, during the same period, blacks spent only $9.5 billion on books, computers, and computer-related equipment.[2] There was a similar striking disparity between African American expenditures on clothing and education. Between 1996 and 2001, African Americans spent $135.2 billion on apparel products and services. Conversely, blacks spent only $19.6 billion on education during the same period.[3] While black consumers have the right to spend their hard-earned money as they see fit, this data raises legitimate concerns about African Americans' spending priorities.

Where are African Americans spending their more than a half-trillion dollars of collective buying power? Although the African American consumer dollar is now fully "desegregated" in the U.S. economy, many black-owned businesses

Table 28.1   The Buying Power of Black America, 1996–2001 (in billions)

1996	$367.0
1997	391.0
1998	441.0
1999	491.0
2000	543.0
2001	601.0

Source: Target Market News, consumer expenditure data from "The Buying Power of Black America," at www.target marketnews.com/numbers/index.htm.

must still rely exclusively on the black consumer market for clients and customers as a result of ongoing white racism. Thus, as African American consumers spend more money with non-black-owned businesses, black businesses in America steadily decline. The insurance industry provides perhaps the most stark case study of this development.

Between 1996 and 2001, African Americans spent $38 billion on insurance.[4] Yet, during the same period, the premium income of the top-ten black insurance companies was a relatively paltry $899.1 million.[5] Thus, it is not surprising that the contemporary African American insurance industry is fighting a desperate and apparently losing battle to survive.[6]

To return to the bling-bling phenomenon, since African Americans do not own, in significant numbers, large jewelry stores, luxury car, yacht dealerships, or designer fashion businesses—notwithstanding FUBU, Phat Farm, and P. Diddy's Sean Jean label—many of today's

hip-hop artists, despite their bravado, are little more than "foot soldiers" for the interests of corporate America. This is paradoxical in that hip-hop, early on, celebrated and promoted African American independence from the embellishments of Madison Avenue. For instance, as Run DMC's 1984 song "Rock Box" declared, "Calvin Klein's no friend of mine, don't want nobody's name on my behind."[7]

Perhaps the most troubling aspect of hip-hop's evolution toward conspicuous consumption is that the promoters of bling-bling and their fans are being overtly exploited by corporate America. Since the 1930s, corporate marketers have known that African Americans, because they are the only group to have been enslaved in this country, suffer from an especially acute case of status anxiety. Thus, large U.S. companies know that blacks, in an attempt to distance themselves from their slave past, have sought to buy respect and dignity.[8] If any group should be ashamed of slavery, it should be the

Table 28.2   Selected Characteristics of the Buying Power of Black America, 1996–2001 (in billions)

	1996	*1997*	*1998*	*1999*	*2000*	*2001*
Alcoholic beverages	$1.8	$1.9	$1.7	$1.9	$2.2	$2.9
Tobacco products and smoking supplies	2.1	2.2	2.1	2.4	2.7	3.2
Books	0.3	0.3	0.3	0.3	0.4	0.3
Computers and related equipment	0.8	0.6	1.3	1.2	1.6	2.1
Apparel products and services	21.3	25.2	20.5	21.2	24.7	22.3
Education	0.3	3.9	3.3	4.4	3.3	4.4

Source: Target Market News, consumer expenditure data from "The Buying Power of Black America," at www.targetmarket news.com/numbers/index.htm.

descendants of former slaveholders, not the descendants of former slaves. Nevertheless, as noted in my 1998 book *Desegregating the Dollar: African American Consumerism in the Twentieth Century,* "increasingly sophisticated market research and advertising campaigns have helped American corporations to continually profit from blacks' lingering social and psychological hang-ups."[9]

Notwithstanding such socially conscious hip-hop artists as Public Enemy, KRS 1, and Dead Presidents, hip-hop began to sell out to corporate interests shortly after Run DMC's famous Calvin Klein rhyme, despite a façade of defiant bravado. As one of the contributors to *The Vibe History of Hip Hop* (1999) noted,

> Ironically, the hip-hop nation, once so proudly self-sufficient, became obsessed with the finer things in life: designer clothing, imported champagne, Cuban cigars, luxury automobiles, and fine jewelry—all the things that prove how successful you are by American Dream standards. Now everybody in hip hop is donning gold or platinum pendants, watches, and rings encrusted with diamonds—"Name-brand niggers," as the late Notorious BIG put it on his hit single "Hypnotize."[10]

George E. Curry, the former editor in chief of the now sadly defunct *Emerge* magazine, provides another thoughtful analysis of this phenomenon. In an editor's note entitled "Walking Billboards," he wrote,

> After conducting successful campaigns to remove certain billboards from our neighborhoods, perhaps, it's time to launch a campaign against another kind of billboard in our community—our youth (and some adults) who are walking advertisements for Nike, Polo, Tommy Hilfiger, Nautica, and too many other labels to list in this space.... There is an obsession with having someone else's name plastered on our baseball caps, shirts, bags, and the back of our jeans. In addition to spurring some of our youth to commit violent crimes against African Americans in order to sport these expensive brand-name items, we're lining the pockets

of designers who show contempt for us, but not for our \$400 billion per year spending power.[11]

To buttress his assertions, Curry cited a Tommy Hilfiger quote that appeared in the April 21, 1997, issue of *Forbes* magazine, where Hilfiger told *Forbes* "many of these people [blacks] would rather have a Rolex than a home."[12]

While Curry and others were justifiably outraged at Hilfiger's flippancy regarding black consumers, young blacks—fueled by hip-hop's increased focus on flashing brand names—did indeed exhibit distorted notions of "status." For example, how much can one respect a person who wears pants literally falling off his buttocks to reveal the brand of underwear he's wearing (a practice introduced by hip-hop artists and later imitated by their fans)? Sadly, again in a historical sense, this type of outrageous behavior and dress had tragic similarities to the minstrel and "coon" shows of the past.

While not all hip-hop artists are ambassadors of bling-bling, there are enough proponents of African American conspicuous consumption to cause real concern about the future of black America. As the *Target Market News* revealed in a recent demographic profile of African Americans, "nearly one-third of the nation's black population was under 18 years of age in 1999, versus 24 percent of the white population."[13] Since hip-hop's primary audience is young people under the age of twenty-five, hip-hop artists, because of their wide media exposure, are shaping the worldview of a future generation. For example, when today's ten-year-old African American child is fed a steady stream of messages glorifying individualistic conspicuous consumption, how will this manifest itself when he or she becomes an adult? While it is impossible to answer this question with precision, let's ponder another possible scenario, presented by Curry in his essay "Walking Billboards":

> Instead of showcasing clothing designed by people who disrespect our race, why not start a campaign that will replace the likes of Hilfiger, Ralph Lauren, and Donna Karan with respected African-American figures. We could have trend setters like rappers

sport W. E. B. DuBois suits (preferably three-piece ones, if we're going to be true to his spirit) at their concerts, Ida B. Wells-Barnett baseball caps, William Monroe Trotter sneakers, Frederick Douglass eyeglasses and Harriet Tubman jogging suits. Not only would we be showing respect for those who fought for rights we now take for granted, we might develop enormous pride along the way.[14]

To elaborate upon Curry's sense of possibility, if hip-hop artists (using their widespread visibility and influence) began encouraging their fans to build wealth by acquiring land, stocks, and bonds—instead of encouraging them to acquire such trinkets as "ice" (jewelry), big cars, fancy clothes, and gold-plated teeth—how would this affect the present and future African American community? Moreover, if hip-hop artists told their fans of the importance of supporting black-owned businesses, how would this affect black America? As it stands, the conditioning of young African Americans to be concerned only with securing as many flashy trinkets as possible has dire consequences for the African American community. First, bling-bling's focus on individual accumulation diminishes and trivializes any notions of collective social, political, and economic activity. Finally, since African American–owned companies do not produce the items that the promoters of bling-bling glorify (big cars, yachts, jewelry), bling-bling is directly contributing to the destruction of what's left of black America's business infrastructure.

While this chapter places a special focus on bling-bling, this subgenre within the realm of hip-hop represents just one nuance of contemporary black consumers' declining support of black business. Historically, black businesses had gained the patronage of black consumers partially because of the discriminatory hiring practices of white businesses. Yet, beginning in the 1960s, enhanced black employment opportunities with white companies contributed to a dramatic increase in collective African American spending power. Consequently, black consumers, apparently unwilling to bite the proverbial hand that feeds them, began spending more of their earnings with white-owned businesses.

An important essay on African American consumption, which appeared in the National Urban League's *State of Black America 1994*, clearly conveys the marginality of black-owned businesses in the minds of contemporary African American consumers. Marcus Alexis and Geraldine R. Henderson, citing a 1993 study of African American consumer attitudes, disclosed that only 26 percent of black consumers considered African American ownership of a business as an important factor in deciding where to shop.[15]

For their part, today's black-owned companies can only look on in helpless dismay as black consumers increasingly dismiss the importance of African American–owned enterprises. Unfortunately, for black-owned enterprises, the evidence clearly indicates that they have contributed relatively little to the dramatic rise in African American workers' disposable income since the 1960s. For instance, the most recent U.S. government survey of African American business, conducted in 1997, revealed that 90 percent of black-owned firms were individual proprietorships. In fact, out of the 823,499 black-owned businesses enumerated in 1997, only 889 had one hundred or more employees.[16] This reality, coupled with African American occupational gains in white-owned companies, seemingly helps to explain why the percentage of African American disposable income spent with black-owned business has dipped to approximately 7 percent in recent years.

Also, even before the advent of bling-bling, scholarly research revealed that African American consumerism and wealth accumulation are not intrinsically linked. Billy J. Tidwell's important 1988 essay "Black Wealth, Facts and Fiction" suggests that increased African American consumerism since the 1960s did not necessarily reflect substantive economic progress. Tidwell, then director of research for the National Urban League, offered a bleak assessment of contemporary black America in the league's *State of Black America 1988*. He noted,

Based on current census data, the total net worth of all U.S. households is approximately $6,830 billion. Blacks account for $192 billion, or a minuscule 2.8 percent of the total. By contrast, the aggregate net worth of white households is $6,498 billion or 95 percent of the national total. . . . Thus, the net worth estimate for black households is more than eight percent below their proportion of the population, while the net worth of white households exceeds their proportion of the population by a considerable margin. Converted into dollar terms, black households are "undervalued" by some $559 billion, relative to their proportion of the U.S. population.[17]

Moreover, Tidwell lamented that "on a per-household basis, whites enjoy about 12 times the net worth of blacks. The average net worth of black households is $3,400, compared to $39,000 for white households. Viewed from any perspective, the position of black America is very marginal."[18]

However, U.S. Census Bureau statistics related to asset ownership of households in 1993 do reveal a slight improvement. Compared to that of 1988, when the average net worth of black households ($3,400) stood at 8 percent of the average net worth of white households ($39,000), African Americans' average household net worth in 1993 ($4,418) represented 9 percent of the average net worth of white households ($45,740).[19] If this represents a trend that in every five years, African Americans will close the wealth gap with European Americans by a single percentage point, the parity should be reached, *ceteris paribus*, by the year 2448!

The economic stature of present-day black America suggests a reference to Charles Dickens's classic work *A Tale of Two Cities*, in which he declares, "It was the best of times, it was the worst of times." Clearly, as the data suggest, black consumers possess an ever-growing access to the goods and services offered by the American economy. Yet, ironically, black-owned businesses are attracting an ever-shrinking percentage of African American consumer dollars.

As I noted in *Desegregating the Dollar*, African Americans must unflinchingly address the following question: "Is the slow, but steady, destruction of urban black America (and its businesses) too steep a price to pay for unre-stricted African American consumerism?"[20] For the sake of generations to come, I hope we come up with the right answer.

NOTES

1. "The Buying Power of Black America," *Target Market News* (1996–2001), available at www.targetmarketnews.com/numbers/index.htm.
2. "The Buying Power of Black America."
3. "The Buying Power of Black America."
4. "The Buying Power of Black America."
5. "Black Insurance Companies," *Black Enterprise* 27 (June 1997): 196; "Black Insurance Companies," *Black Enterprise* 28 (June 1998): 187; "Black Insurance Companies," *Black Enterprise* 29 (June 1999): 216; "Black Insurance Companies," *Black Enterprise* 30 (June 2000): 206; 31 (June 2001): 206; "Financial Services Summaries Overview," *Black Enterprise* 32 (June 2002): 220.
6. For historical perspective on the decline of black insurance companies, see Robert E. Weems Jr., "A Crumbling Legacy: The Decline of African American Insurance Companies in Contemporary America," *Review of Black Political Economy* 23 (Fall 1994): 25–37.
7. Emil Wilbekin, "Great Aspirations: Hip Hop and Fashion Dress for Excess and Success," in *Vibe History of Hip Hop*, ed. Alan Light (New York: Three Rivers Press, 1999), 277. I want to offer special thanks to Vernon C. Mitchell Jr., my unofficial research assistant, for alerting me to this source.
8. Robert E. Weems Jr., *Desegregating the Dollar: African American Consumerism in the Twentieth Century* (New York: New York University Press, 1998), 27.
9. Weems, *Desegregating the Dollar*, 27.
10. Wilbekin, "Great Aspirations," 288.
11. George E. Curry, "Walking Billboards," *Emerge* 9 (December 1997–January 1998): 8.
12. Curry, "Walking Billboards," 8. Hilfiger's quote in the April 21, 1997, *Forbes*, is at 144.
13. "The African American Market: A Demographic Profile," *Target Market News*, at www.targetmarketnews.com/demographics/htm.
14. Curry, "Walking Billboards," 8.
15. Marcus Alexis and Geraldine R. Henderson, "The Economic Base of African American Communities: A Study of Consumption Patterns,"

in *The State of Black America 1994,* ed. Billy J. Tidwell (New York: National Urban League, 1994), 67.

16. U.S. Department of Commerce, *1997 Economic Census: Survey of Minority-Owned Business Enterprises—Black* (Washington, D.C.: U.S. Department of Commerce, 2001), 9, 17, 77.

17. Billy J. Tidwell, "Black Wealth: Facts and Fiction," in *The State of Black America 1988,* ed. Janet Dewart (New York: National Urban League, 1988), 195.

18. Tidwell, "Black Wealth," 195.

19. U.S. Census Bureau, "Asset Ownership of Households: 1993," available at www.census.gov:80/hhes/www/wealth/with93f.html.

20. Weems, *Desegregating the Dollar,* 131.

29

A Critical Examination of the Political Economy of the Hip-Hop Industry
DIPANNITA BASU

Rap and other forms of urban music are the fastest-growing music genres in major markets. This chapter describes the complex economic relationships that form the hip-hop industry, the role of independents, and the competitive advantage of the major record labels. I argue that despite the hypervisibility of a few African American rap artists and entrepreneurs, African Americans lack control and ownership of their music.

Every hip-hop CD sold, every dollar made from urban gear, every buck generated from TV shows, radio programs, films and even video games with a bit of "flava" contribute to this 5 billion burgeoning sector.

—*Black Enterprise* (2002a, 72)

Despite a sustained interest by academics of hip-hop in the politics of race, identity, and representation, relatively little attention has been paid to the entrepreneurial and economic dynamics of hip-hop (Kelley 2002). However, in the spring and summer of 2002, *Black Enterprise* magazine paid tribute to the phenomenal success of the hip-hop industry and its black rap moguls. The magazine profiled a cadre of successful and streetwise hip-hop entrepreneurs who negotiated favorable deals with record companies and who demonstrated an understanding of the importance of cultural industries as a system of interconnected multimedia services—namely, radio, television, publications, Internet, and advertising[1] (*Black Enterprise* 2002a, 2002b). Table 29.1 summarizes the activities of some of these rap moguls. On the surface it would appear that the success of these hip-hop entrepreneurs is changing the rules of the game. They are

in positions of control and autonomy of their multimillion-dollar-generating businesses. However, I argue that major corporate conglomerates control the music industry; that independents are not really independent; and that the increasing fragmentation of production economies results in exploitive and racist labor practices. Black rap moguls exist, but the industry is white controlled and yields little of hip-hop's economic power to its black creators and entrepreneurs. Before examining this contention more closely, we turn to the definitions and features of *hip-hop culture, hip-hop industry,* and *indies* (independent record companies). In doing so, we see how these terms are unclear and subject to a variety of interpretations. But first, I provide a brief overview of hip-hop as a culture and a commodity, with particular emphasis on rap music, its most commodifiable component.

THE HISTORY OF HIP-HOP AS CULTURE AND COMMODITY

In her seminal study on hip-hop culture, Tricia Rose (1994) details how black and Latino youth in the South Bronx combined technology, oral

Table 29.1   Hip-Hop Moguls

Name: Russell Simmons, 45, chairman and CEO, Rush Communications
Ventures: Def Jam Records (1983–2000), Russell Simmons Television, Def Pictures, Phat Fashions, Oneworld Magazine

Name: Sean "Puffy" Combs, 33, chairman and CEO, Bad Boy Entertainment
Ventures: Bad Boy Entertainment (founded 1994), Combs Music Publishing (joint venture with EMI Music Publishing), Janice Combs Management, Sean John clothing, Justin's Restaurants (New York and Atlanta), Daddy's House Studios

Name: Jermaine Dupri, 29, CEO So So Def Recordings
Ventures: So So Def Recordings (founded 1993)

Name: Damon Dash, 31, and Shawn (Jay-Z) Carter, partners, Roc-a-Fella Enterprises
Ventures: Roc-a-Fella Records (founded 1995), Rocawear apparel, Roc-a-Fella Films

Name: Bryan and Ronald Williams
Ventures: Cash Money Records (founded 1991)

Name: Percy "Master-P" Miller, 32, CEO, New No Limit Enterprises
Ventures: New No Limit Records (founded 1990), No Limit Gear, No Limit Film, Real Estate

Name: Andre "Dr Dre" Young, 37, CEO, Aftermath Records
Ventures: Aftermath Records (founded)

Name: Marion "Suge" Knight, CEO, Tha Row Records
Ventures: Tha Row Records (founded as Death Row Records in 1992)

traditions, vernacular language, dance, and attitude to create hip-hop culture and community. Amidst the fiscal and social crisis of New York City in the late 1970s, hip-hop provided an escape from gangs, drugs, racism, and poverty.[2] *The Zulu Nation*, a 1970s hip-hop collective of DJs, graffiti artists, and breakers established by Afrika Bambataa (Kevin Donovan), had the political purpose of urban survival through cultural empowerment and peaceful social change.

One of the distinctive features of hip-hop is its continual reconfiguration of its expressions, genres, and practices (Cross 1994; Forman 2002). Hip-hop's early urban practices are conventionally understood as comprising five elements: *emceeing* (rapping), *b-boying* (break dancing), *deejaying* (spinning and scratching records on a turntable), *beat boxing,* and *graffiti art* (appropriating public spaces). Over the years the cultural forms and expressions of hip-hop have evolved. Today, it is arguably the case that it is constituted by nine elements: emceeing, deejaying, graffiti art, breaking, beat boxing, street fashion, street

language (Ebonics), street knowledge, and street enterprise. Although graffiti and break dancing were influenced and performed by the Spanish-speaking communities of Puerto Rico and Dominica, rap music, the most commodifiable component, continues to be dominated by African Americans. Aided by technology, hip-hop culture has been celebrated as a style "no one can deal with." It is authentic and commercial (Rose 1994), revolutionary and renegade, radical yet conservative (Gilroy 1994), confirming white stereotypes of black criminality, yet symptomatic of the sexism and racism of white patriarchal society (hooks 1994). Despite its distinct and localized cultural origins, hip-hop needs no passport to travel around the world or to transgress the boundaries between music, advertising, film, dance, television, and the new digital–multimedia culture. From Barney's rapping in a Fruity Pebbles breakfast cereal commercial to rap music in McDonald's, Coca-Cola, and Sprite commercials, it is the sound of our present-day technocultures.

Rap music is the most castigated and commodified element of hip-hop. Drawing on a canon of black musical history from funk, jazz, disco, rock, Afro-beat, dance hall, and beyond, the MC (*master of ceremonies*, later known as the *rapper*), once secondary to the DJ became ascendant. Either by memorizing poetry (*writtens*) or by improvising lyrics on the spot (*freestyle*), the MC flowed, bragged, and generally raised havoc on the "mic." Throughout rap music's twenty-five-year-plus tenure, it has consistently been seen as an "internal threat." For much of middle black and white America, its moral bankruptcy, unbridled materialism, misogyny, sexism, homophobia, and swaggering sexuality is a moral affront. Ignored, vilified, and exploited by the black middle classes; relegated to a passing fad by the mainstream record industry; incurring the wrath of religious groups, censors, the FBI, two presidents, and senate hearings, its profits have nonetheless "phattened."[3]

In 1998, rap outsold country music, which had previously been America's top-selling genre. In 1998, rap music sold eighty-one million CDs and country music, seventy-two million. Sales increased 31 percent from 1997 to 1998. In contrast there was a 2 percent gain for country and 6 percent for rock. It is estimated that between 60 percent to 70 percent of rap music is sold to suburban white youth. In the United States and the United Kingdom (ranked first and third worldwide in consumers of music) rock and heavy metal accounted for one in four record sales in 2000, but the share of rap and hip-hop rose to 13 percent in the United States and doubled to 4 percent in the United Kingdom.[4] In 2001, the national sales of hip-hop music constituted 11.7 percent of the U.S. market (762.8 million albums sold). It ranked third behind rhythm and blues and alternative music.[5] In 2002, rap and other forms of urban music (black music, essentially) are the fastest-rising music genres in major markets. Rap music has also made a major impact in a number of other countries.[6]

KEEPING IT REAL: MEASURES AND MISMEASURES

Mapping a dynamic cultural process and practice such as hip-hop into a static musical genre

has limitations. First, consumption and production are not separate activities. Hip-hop relies on the recycling of previously existing sounds. Until the early 1980s, the hip-hop community made "clandestine tapes made by would-be bootleggers at parties and clubs, or tapes made by groups themselves and given out to friends, to cab drivers or to kids with giant tape boxes just to get their music out" (Toop 1991, 78). Today, the DJ culture (*turntablism*) in hip-hop not only stimulates direct consumption (record collecting) but also creates complementary economic activity through the demand of specialist services, such as secondhand record shops, mail-order businesses, and record fairs.

It is difficult to acquire statistical data on the number of employees in the music industry, never mind the nebulous entity known as the hip-hop industry. For one, the industry comprises a number of entities that are enmeshed with one another. As they are separate identities, no integrated industry records are kept. The contemporary music industry incorporates four major activities: creative rights and intellectual property, publishing, talent development, and consumer electronics. Creative and intellectual property rights activities consist of legal regulation of ownership and licensing of a host of musical works. It is the copyright system that enables artists to be compensated for their work. They license their work for use by the public for a fee. The copyright system is set up by publishers and composers to collect data on every time a piece of music is played on air or radio so they can get paid. Publishing companies bring works to the public and are dependent on the creativity of the artist. This involves agents, promoters, publishers, and record companies. Talent companies provide effective management of artists (musicians and composers) and the development of a star system.[7] Consumer electronics companies market various kinds of equipment for producing and creating rap music and other products (Shukur 2001; Vogel 2004).

The music industry operates with very little federal regulations or public pressure. Although the largest organized group, the Record Industry Association of America, represents about 85 percent of the country's record companies, it has no control or influence over the practices and activities of its members. While each company is required to report employment statistics to the U.S. Equal Employment Opportunity Commission, the agency combines statistics from the broad recording industry so that figures from individual companies cannot be recorded. It is then even harder to monitor the small business and individuals that are connected under contract or on a project-by-project basis as art directors, sound engineers, make-up artists, and so forth. With the cultural infusion of hip-hop culture to the stratosphere of popular and youth culture globally and the undetected economic activity that it incorporates, it would be difficult to measure the extent to which the estimated $5 billion market generates employment, entrepreneurship, and profits within the black community.

If we define the hip-hop industry as those persons and businesses that seek to profit from the marketing and sales of rap music and hip-hop culture, it would include record companies, music publishers, recording studios, talent brokers, performance venues, artists, engineers, producers, personal attorneys, promoters, managers, publishers, marketing, hair and set stylists, DJs, attorneys, accountants, musical publications, websites, party planners, limousine services, personal assistants—many of whom go undocumented, as they are ancillary workers who have contractual relationships with larger businesses but may not be recorded by the U.S. census. Within the rap industry, transformations in the various cultural industries have produced spaces for creative and entrepreneurial skills that are not always measurable. They can be part of an independent production company's street marketing team to being hired as a freelance stylist on a video or magazine shoot (Basu 1997, 1998). The census regards the existence of an employment relationship as most readily, but not exclusively, shown by a person's appearance on the employer's payroll. This includes part-time and temporary workers. Independent contractors are not counted as employees and thus escape documentation.

Although some rap moguls are middle class and have gone to college, many within the hip-hop industry possess few social and economic resources, such as accumulated wealth, education beyond high school, and so forth. They have to fund their businesses in the informal economy because of their lack of access and success in the formal institutions of banking. They appear to have even greater difficulty than do other small black-business start-ups because of the perceptions of the music industry in general (high risk) and of rap music in particular (violent, deadly, corrupt). Many of the respondents have actively sought advice about bookkeeping, marketing, product developments, contract negotiation, office management, and so forth to conduct their affairs efficiently and to gain leverage with formal banking and insurance companies.[8] In this regard many have mentioned the importance of having a white front person (or a "middle-class sister") who can bring "credibility" to business dealings with insurance companies, record attorneys, performance venues, and so forth.

While the term *hip-hop industry* is applied liberally, it is seldom defined. Established companies such as Nike, Timberland, Helly Hansen, Ralph Lauren, Puma, McDonald's, Coca-Cola, and Sprite are not part of the hip-hop industry. But the immense sales boosts given to their products by rap artist endorsements or by the infusion of a hip-hop aesthetic or a sartorial style in its selling strategies means that even the largest multinational companies are influenced by hip-hop culture. (According to Pina Sciarra, the marketing director of the Sprite brand, the rap campaign has quadrupled the number of people saying it is their favorite soda.) If we consider the number of rap songs that exalt consumer brands and lifestyles in their songs, from "My Adidas" to "Pass the Courvoisier," the boundaries of hip-hop's economic potency are immeasurable.[9]

When rappers endorse products through love of the product or because of the money they are getting in exchange for their endorsement, they are, according to rapper Xhibit, "acting as billboards for corporate America," even though corporate America may be making many bills from them in their record contracts. Verbal endorsements in lyrics (*shout-outs*), such as Jay-Z's mention of Motorola in "I Just Wanna Love U," or blatant product placements in videos—Bentleys, Cadillacs, and Crystal are a staple of rappers in their videos and in their real lives—save millions in advertising for companies. According to Urban IQ, an urban research firm, there are forty-five million consumers of urban culture, about two-thirds of Americans between the ages of eighteen and thirty-five. Hip-hop stylistic and aesthetic distillations are central to that marketing (Spiegler 1996).

The standard method of measuring record sales is SoundScan, which is an information system that tracks sales of music and music video products throughout the United States. Sales data from point-of-sale cash registers are collected weekly from over sixteen thousand retail, mass merchant, and nontraditional outlets such as online stores and other venues. Tricia Rose (1994) argues that SoundScan underestimates hip-hop consumers in poor black neighborhoods. The majority of the record stores that possess the system are outlets of major retailers located in malls and the suburbs. Many small independent, "ma and pa" shops in poorer neighborhoods do not have SoundScan devices but sell a lot of rap music. Rap music consumers also obtain their music through such means as bootlegging, copying cassette tapes, and buying CDs and cassettes at local swap meets, all of which escape formal measurement. These buyers constitute a cadre of consumers who easily escape statistical analysis. *Ghetto SoundScan*, or more commonly *ghetto platinum*, is the term that many in the rap music industry use to refer to the actual sales rather than to the sales recorded by SoundScan. Straw argues that "statistics only measure the consumption habits of those who continue to acquire music through old fashioned means" (2001, 54). Their use in determining trends can be regarded with some suspicion because those trading music through online downloading, burning CDs, visiting secondhand specialist stores are not "registered within the industry's official measures of success" (Straw 2001, 54). Furthermore, a substantial part of the recording industries profits come from back catalogues of stars, such as Prince, Michael Jackson, the Rolling Stones, and so forth. Hence, popularity as measured through pop charts is a measurement of popularity that is artificially contrived. In short, music's popularity does not dance to the rhythm of the week, but its measurement does.

THE STRUCTURE OF OPPORTUNITIES AND CONSTRAINTS IN THE HIP-HOP INDUSTRY

An entrepreneurial spirit and energy has always accompanied hip-hop culture, which has been marked by independent labels, a hip-hop press, and mass media dissemination. In the late 1970s and early 1980s the local demand for rap music created the market conditions in which black entrepreneurs could cater to the black cultural tastes of rap fans. Blacks were best positioned to serve the specific cultural needs, tastes, and preferences of their coethnic consumers. These entrepreneurs operated at the local, underground level, where local swap meets, "ma and pa" shops, local clubs, and local DJ battles were all social spaces used to sell or promote mixed tapes, DJs, records, and artists. In addition, there was little interest and therefore competition from the established music industry. In 1980 *Billboard* was still asking the question "Rap records: Are they fad or permanent?"

The corporate blindness to rap's potential was due to its complicated status in the industry. It was perceived to have its primary appeal to a young black audience. Keith Negus (1999) points out that the genre of rap was considered a "wild cat" by the major record companies, who were uncertain about its aesthetics, its "potential market growth," and for some its politics of black representation. This is exactly the area where independents are well placed to serve and where majors, when the time is right, are ripe to exploit. Because the majors were asleep at the wheel in rap's formative years, it spent most of its young life promoted and recorded by independent labels run by hustling entrepreneurs. During the 1980s, it was primarily young white entrepreneurs at the helm of the independents that made rap music. Corey Robbins, who started Profile Records in 1981; DJ Tommy Silverman, who founded Tommy Boy Records; Arthur Baker, who founded Streetwise; and Aaron Fuchs, who founded Tuff City took up the space between white corporate disinterest and black middle-class disdain.[10]

When these entrepreneurs became successful, the initial music industry rejection of rap music was supplanted by attempts to produce and control the rap market.[11] Table 29.2 provides examples of the growth in involvement of major music companies such as Columbia/Sony and Vivendi Universal in the rap music business.

This pattern of initial industry rejection, followed by industry absorption and consolidation, has been the repeated theme for black musical genres.[12] This annexation is part of a process in which major companies have over the years changed to make themselves more responsive to innovative and higher-risk work. The record industry has shifted from a "closed" system to an "open" system. The open system incorporates strategies such as hiring independent producers on a short-time basis and incorporating independent companies (indies) into their organizational structure through a number of strategies. Independents are by definition those record companies distributed through independent networks rather than by the majors. A label can be partially owned by a major but still be considered independent. An independently owned label is not considered so if it uses a major distributor; yet, nowadays some independent distributors are partially owned by majors (Roberts 2002). Independents facilitate the co-option of new and underground musical movements by amalgamation, joint ventures, or complete buyouts with majors. By absorbing successful independent labels through consolidation, the difference between them is opaque.

Major labels and independents utilize five basic strategies. First, majors can create a spin-off label, sending it through independent and major distributors. This label is called "independent" even though it remains under the control of the major. Second, equity deals are established when a major buys a successful indie label but sends the records through an exclusively independent distribution network, such as Warner Brothers, which owns 50 percent of Tommy Boy (which has De La Soul and Coolio on their roster). Third, a major will buy into an indie and send its records via major distribution. Fourth, majors buy some or all of independent distributors so

that they can access smaller local markets and retailers—for example, Sony purchased RED distributions. Fifth, a major may also launch its own indie distribution.

As joint ventures, equity deals, production company contracts, and pressing and distribution deals between independents and major distributors, record labels, and publishers increase, so does the process of outsourcing. There is little doubt that successful rap music entrepreneurs have indeed been able to wrestle favorable deals from the "big five" record companies and distributors—Sony, BMG, Universal, WEA, and Cema—which include joint ventures that give latitude in decision making and a split of the profits. Suge Knight and Master P have been adamant about 100 percent ownership of their master recordings and continued autonomy over the daily operations and release schedules.

THE COMPETITIVE ADVANTAGE OF DISTRIBUTION

Black record company—White distribution.

—Public Enemy, "White Heaven/Black Hell"

The competitive advantage of the major record labels is in their control of distribution. They have the capital and networks to get a record from the pressing plant to the retail stores. It is very hard for labels to manufacture, distribute, market, sell, and collect on a record beyond one hundred thousand units, so the prospect of a major organization handling this is attractive. It also means exposure to a wider market, better distribution and promotion, and hit records. The distributor's job is to make the buyers at retail outlets aware of a label's product. If a specific title sells, it is the job of the distributor, in cooperation with the label, to provide the retailers with a continuous flow of the product. Each of the majors maintains a system of wholesale dealerships, distribution warehouses, and record jobbers. Their control of distribution means that they can get the product out regionally, nationally, and internationally.

Table 29.2   Major Company Involvement with "Independent" Rap and Hip-Hop Labels

Def Jam	*Current status:* Island Def Jam Music Group, a division of Universal Music Group (Vivendi Universal SA). *Ownership history:* Founded by Russell Simmons and Rick Rubin in 1983. 50/50 production deal with Columbia Records/Sony in 1985. Simmons sold his interest to Universal in 1999–2000. *Artist roster:* DMX, LL Cool J, Ludacris
Roc-a-Fella	*Current status:* 50/50 venture with Island Def Jam Music Group, a division of Universal Music Group (Vivendi Universal SA); 50/50 ownership of master recordings. *Ownership History:* Founded 1995–1996 by Shawn (Jay-Z) Carter, Kareem "Biggs" Burke and Damon Dash. *Artist roster:* Jay-Z, Cam'ron
Bad Boy	*Current status:* Three year distribution deal with Universal Music Group signed in 2003. Combs retains ownership of masters. *Ownership History:* Founded by Sean Combs, 1994. Joint venture with BMG's Arista Records terminated in June 2002. *Artist roster:* P Diddy
Cash Money	*Current status:* Three-year pressing and distribution deal with Universal Records; signed Cash Money; retains ownership of masters. *Ownership History:* Founded by Ronald and Bryan Williams in 1991. *Artist roster:* Baby #1 Stunna, Turk, Juvenile
Tommy Boy	*Current status:* Independent, but Warner owns master recordings *Ownership History:* Founded by Tom Silverman. Subsidiary of Warner Records through 2002.
No Limit	*Current status:* Ten-year distribution agreement with Universal Music Group signed in 2002. No Limit owns master recordings *Ownership History:* Founded by Percy "Master P" Miller in 1996. *Artist roster:* Master P, Lil Romeo, Currancy, Silkk
So So Def	*Current status:* Joint Venture with Sony's Columbia Records. Columbia owns master recordings. *Ownership History:* Founded by Jermaine Dupri. *Artist roster:* Jermaine Dupri
Aftermath	*Current status:* 80% owned by Vivendi Universal SA's Interscope Records. *Ownership History:* Founded by Dr. Dre. *Artist roster:* Dr. Dre, Eminem

Sources: Black Enterprise (2002a, 2002b), Muhammad (1999), Rhea (2002).

The relationship between the label and the distributor is important. The distributors can advertise record releases extensively through advertisements in magazines and video play; they can coordinate the marketing and the merchandizing; and they can have the mechanisms in place for distributing popular songs. Distributors can use their sales tools—promos, one-sheet flyers, airplay, press, and live performance reports—to try to persuade the buyers that they should stock the product they carry. Their direct links to radio, music video, and other industries of cultural dissemination provide "advertising" for its product.

In essence, hip-hop labels such as Def Jam, Roc-a-Fella, and Bad Boy are not really "independent." They cannot distribute without being part of a major label's network, which means that they are beholden to large corporations whose interest is spurred by the attraction of hip-hop cool to major advertisers who want to attract a mostly white demographic (Kelley 1999). These deals mean that the major provides financing, manufacturing, and distribution in exchange for a share of the profits. In 1998 the William's Brothers (Cash Money) signed a three-year, $30 million pressing and distribution deal with Universal Records. The deal provided financing up front and, most important, guaranteed complete ownership of the masters. The Cash Money splits with Universal are, respectively, 80 percent–20 percent, yet the major earns profit with little risk and relatively small investment. Wendy Day, the attorney who worked on the deal makes the following calculations (Day 2002).[13] If Cash Money's split of the record sales is $69,606,235—before marketing expenses, promotions (radio, retail, video production, street marketing), publicity, and overhead— Universal's portion of the split would be $17,401,559 plus whatever they charge Cash Money to utilize their internal departments. Wendy Day points out that this is not bad for a $2 million recoupable investment in July 1998, split into four quarterly payments by the major. She also points out the importance of Cash Money's catalogue deal with the same label putting out their current projects. Such an arrangement results in little if any incentive for Universal to advertise the back product. Conse-

quently, the deal has done a poor job of exploiting the catalogue, which consists of platinum hits and hip-hop classics. This highlights the importance of negotiations around the publishing and past catalogues in joint ventures.

The millions involved in these joint ventures, as reported in publications such as *Black Enterprise* magazine (2000a, 2002b; Muhammad 1999), are in general exaggerating the figures by virtue of not pointing out that those large amounts are not necessarily monies that the artist or independent label is guaranteed to receive. As several music attorneys have pointed out, when you hear an artist has just renegotiated a multimillion-dollar deal, they do not just get that money up front. It is the amount that the record company *might* have to pay over a period of years—that is, if it were to choose to exercise all the relevant options for every possible recording delivered under contract and if every recording were as commercially successful as anticipated in the contract.

A few entrepreneurs and artists have energized and established groundbreaking joint ventures generating millions of dollars in profits. Yet, there is a multitude of artists stuck in unfair contracts that find themselves in debt to their label for expenses they have little say in or knowledge of. In the music industry, failure is the norm, with 90 percent of all ventures generating losses. To control for the uncertainty, the star system develops, which provides the majority of the labels' profits. Taking the burden of the risk are artists who have developed their skills at their own costs and who, before they see any money from their record sales, have to pay a plethora of people.

An up-and-coming record producer told me that whenever he was offered anything to eat while recording in the studio of the record company to which he was signed, he would ask if he was paying for it. "You don't know how many times I just bought my own food, even though pizza had been ordered in by the dozens." His actions can be understood if we examine the notion of advancements and recoupments, an integral part of the contractual obligation in record deals. The tab for the delivered pizzas might come out of his pocket. When artists get record contracts with advancements, they are exactly that—*advancements*. Specifically, an advance is a prepayment against future royalties, a process referred to as *recoupment*. Essentially, any monies paid to the artist as advances by the record company will be deducted from royalties earned by the artist before the artist actually receives any royalty payments. According to BlackBritishMusic.com, the principal difference between a loan and an advance is that there is no obligation on the artist to repay any unrecouped advances on termination of the agreements, whether the artist is dropped or otherwise. Signing fees, living expenses, tour support, and recording costs are all deemed to be advances as the record company funds them. Marketing costs are not treated as advances, except in rare instances. Typically, those who are paid first are the manager (15 percent–20 percent), the lawyer (by the hour or 5 percent–10 percent of the deal), the accountant (by the hour or 5 percent of all income), and the IRS (28 percent–50 percent, depending on the tax bracket). Afterward, the artists have their own payroll responsibilities, such as running a fan club, maintaining offices and studios, and supporting family members.

Once again, Wendy Day from the Rap Coalition provides some sobering facts on the reality of the music industry on most rap artists and labels. Very few rap records make enough to recoup their costs—that is, to make enough money from their sales to see a profit. Since 1995, there have been around five hundred rap records released each year except 1999, when the numbers doubled (1995, 469 releases; 1996, 482 releases; 1997, 497 releases; 1998, 477 releases; 1999, 997 releases). Yet only such a small percentage of those releases sell at the gold or platinum level (respectively, a half-million copies or a million copies). In 1998, only 5 percent, or 26 releases, went platinum and gold (respectively, 12 and 14). In 1999, there were 997 records released, and only 51 sold more than a quarter-million units. Of those 51 releases, 11 went platinum and 20 went gold. About 90 percent of recording artists never sell enough records to earn royalties beyond that initial advance. Some are unable even to afford health insurance just months after signing a so-called big deal.

For the average music lover, the indies are perceived as a system of creative production and product unbridled by capitalistic concerns and as truly outside the mainstream of major companies. In reality, indies are complicit in the capitalist machinations of major companies and have found themselves in the ironic position of being the "antiestablishment" component of the establishment while facilitating renegade labor practices. Outsourcing, the practice of subcontracting work to outside companies, enables the façade of indies as antiestablishment and masks their role as nonunion contractors. It allows the recording industry to divest itself of the physical means of producing records without foregoing at least partial ownership and the right to distribute independent labels. This situation has led to a decline in pay standards for all musicians, since indies are not signatory to agreements between the union and the major labels (Roberts 2002).

With the development of raw talent, street marketing, talent spotting, and production left to independent operators, they have in effect become the research and development departments for major companies. Between 1994 and 1996, Cash Money Records sold roughly one hundred thousand cassettes and CDs per year. With no video support or major promotional campaigns they consistently sold records, entering the *Billboard* charts in 1997. Juvenile's *400 Degreez* alone sold three million copies in 1998. The riskier aspects of the business—such as sleeve design, public relations, and radio plugging—are bought in on a project-by-project basis, according to the whims of the market (Frith 2002).

CONCLUSION

The difficulties in defining hip-hop culture, rap music, and the hip-hop industry go beyond academic debate. The categorization of music (genre)and its audience (marketing) affects the resources allocated to it (Forman 2002; Harvard Report 2002; Negus 1999). As a musical genre, hip-hop's fusion with a host of other genres—from rhythm and blues to bhangra, from reggae to rock—complicates its categorization and hence marketing. The infusion of the hip-hop's cadences and tones into the marketing of otherwise bland products (drinks, burgers) and luxurious goods (Moet designer clothes) further complicates matters.

In the words of Russell Simmons, of Def Jam Records, "Black culture is too significant in American culture for Blacks to be glorified employees" (quoted in Kelley 1999, 1). On the surface, Russell's own success and the success of other hip-hop entrepreneurs are living testaments to this statement (*Black Enterprise* 2000a, 2000b). On closer analysis, we have seen that the cycle of castigation, commodification, crossover, and counter-crossover—that is, the white appropriation of music, from Eminem to Justin Timberlake—continue to mark the experience of black music.

Hip-hop labels such as Def Jam, Roc-a-Fella, and Bad Boy, are not really "independent." They act as intermediaries within the production of music. They cannot distribute without being part of a major label's network. Yet, as intermediaries, the owners are far richer than the average hip-hop neophytes (Kelley 2002). In essence, they are no more than titular CEOs who are "media moguls by name, millionaires by bank balance, but paid staff nevertheless" (Cashmore 1997, 176). The power of the corporate music industry has been catalogued by a number of scholars, arguing that the music industry is run by conglomerates whose increasing ownership "colonizes leisure" (Frith 1988; Kelley 2002; Walker 1998). This becomes more ominous in the case of rap music because of the historical dynamics of race in the processes of capital accumulation and cultural credibility in the music industry.

There is no doubt that highly profiled rap moguls have benefited from the increased exposure. It provides endorsements, large publishing deals, and a plethora of other opportunities that lead to increased record sales, thereby extending the reach of the entire rap genre. However, as Al Sharpton points out, "The record industry at the top needs to become more inclusive. There are no Black presidents, distributors, or Black-owned advertising firms used despite millions in promotion money spent." Examining the hip-hop industry in terms of only the visible successes tends to simplify and obscure the diversity of the black entrepreneurism that goes undetected. It is, after all, much easier to be a sound engineer, a dress designer, or owner of a record store than it is to sell platinum hits.

Fortunately, there is a growing consciousness of the systematic exploitation in which rappers and producers submit to contracts that turn nearly all creative rights and profits over to the record company, just so that the artists' records are widely available. The entertainment lawyer Londell McMillan noted how "it has become part of hip-hop culture now to be a business mogul. Rappers are talking about everything from recoupment status to publishing percentages and ownership of their music" (Muhammad 1999, 79). For artists and producers, there is a growing awareness of the importance of the entrepreneurial dynamic to the impulses of hip-hop culture and industry. A slew of successful artists have established their own record companies.[14] There have been numerous conventions, workshops, and websites on the music industry, sponsored by the hip-hop industry, nonprofit organizations, and colleges and universities.[15] Chuck D, the "rebel without a pause," is a champion and unofficial spokesman for freely trading music on the Internet and thus bypassing major distributors. Ice T has released his music online. The Beastie Boys have not only released several songs in MP3 format, but their record label, Grand Royal, produces an entire "shoutcast" station online (www.rapstation.com). As mayoral hopeful Robb Pitts of Atlanta poignantly notes: hip-hop's contribution is "not only from a cultural point of view, but from an economic development point of view. It is labor intensive, and builds on the talents of individuals. It doesn't pollute the air or the water, and it can continue to grow." In which direction, and in whose favor, remains to be seen.[16]

NOTES

1. The headlines for the four issues include "Russell Simmons' Phat Profits," "The Hip-Hop Economy Explodes," "Hip-Hop Economy Part 2: Rap Stars in Hollywood," and "Music Moguls Take Control." Two of the four issues of *Black Enterprise*

magazine had rap entrepreneurs Russell Simmons, Damon Dash, and Jay-Z on the cover.

2. On the relationship between hip-hop and rap and for various accounts of their historical genesis and significance, see George (1998), Lipsitz (1994), Rose (1994), and Toop (1991).

3. Most recently, Texas Republican John Cornyn overcame African American Democrat Ron Kirk's November Senate bid by linking him to police-hating rappers. When Jam Master Jay, the well-respected, peacemaking DJ of rap group Run DMC, was murdered in October, police and federal investigators intensified their surveillance of rappers. Based on what it claims is a "culture of violence" in the hip-hop world, the police's gang intelligence unit had already begun watching nightclubs frequented by celebrity musicians as well as compiling a dossier on rappers and others in the music industry with criminal histories before the murder.

4. See the International Federation of the Phonographic Industry at www.ifpi.org.

5. This is according to SoundScan, a method measuring record sales (discussed in detail on p. 262).

6. French music awards have been given to French hip-hop artists for best new band (IAM in 1995, Alliance Ethnik in 1996), best artist (MC Solaar in 1995), and best newcomer (Ménélik in 1996). Alliance Ethnik achieved national and international success within a year (one hundred thousand units sold abroad). In part this was due to the boost given to French rap by the Ministry of Culture, which mandates that 40 percent of music played should be in French. Due to linguistic and social factors, French language and realities substitute for English language and American realities, making hip-hop more amenable to a French aesthetic and narrative and, hence, a French public (Rutten 1996).

7. "Stars" are those defined as musicians whose past sales successes are taken to guarantee their future sales.

8. These observations are based on my current research into the hip-hop industry.

9. Run DMC's "My Adidas" song (distributed by Def Jam) netted a $1.5 million deal with the shoe company. Other artists on the same label made similar deals: Whoduni, with Sportif; and LL Cool J, with Troop. In the new millennium, Russell Simmons's marketing firm Rush continues the spirit of the marketing mechanism, given that it was hired by a French spirits company to refurbish the staid image of one of its products. As a consequence, Busta Rhymes has a top-twenty hit and continual airplay with a tribute to the drink Courvoisier.

10. The distancing of the black middle classes from hip-hop cultures stymied rap's economic and cultural potential within the black community. *Rolling Stone, Spin,* and *People* highlighted hip-hop before black-owned companies such as *Ebony* and *Jet* did. While black-owned radio stations took pride in proclaiming that they played no rap, top-forty stations proclaimed their station was where "hip-hop lives." MTV (*Yo! MTV Raps*) played rap videos before BET did.

11. One illustration is provided by the case of disagreements over marketing between So So Def and Columbia Records, as reported in 2002 (Rhea 2002) Another is the dispute between Island Def Jam Music Group (Vivendi Universal SA) and the independent label TVT, which sued Island Def Jam for copyright infringement, breach of contract, and fraud. A New York federal court jury ruled against Island Def Jam in March 2003.

12. The notorious Harvard Report commissioned by Colombia Records Group in 1971 heralded the appropriation of black music and talented black artists and music executives as a deliberate marketing strategy to compete in the market for soul music. In realizing that the company was missing a lucrative opportunity in the black market, the report determined that the soul market constituted at least $60 million in annual sales and a market potential well beyond the black community. The study found the soul music market to be dominated by three small record firms—Atlantic, Motown, and Stax—when soul music was considered "peripheral" by executives at the larger, established record firms. As a consequence, major records augmented their roster of African American artists through making distribution deals—for example, Stax's distribution deal with Atlantic Records in 1965—or through buying contracts of artists whose records were already hits—for example, RCA's acquisition of Sam Cooke from Keen Records in 1960.

13. Wendy Day founded the Rap Coalition, which is a nonprofit organization that is dedicated to "addressing the way urban artists are unfairly exploited in the music industry to support, educate, protect, and unify hip-hop artists and producers—in other words, to keep artists from getting jerked" (see www.rapcoalition.org).

14. They include Kurrupt's Antra Record, Missy

Elliot's Gold Mine, Lil Kim's Queen Bee Records, Mos Def and Talib Kweli's Good Tree Records, and Queen Latifah's Flava Unit.

15. Sponsors include Loud Records, the Source, Motown Records, Island Def Jam, the nonprofit organization Rap Coalition, University of California–Berkeley, Howard University, and New York University.

16. There are a number of policies that support popular music production and circulation as part of local economic development policies. While there are very few in the United States, the examples of government support in Britain are quite remarkable and are based on stimulating the economy. In Liverpool, for example, the Labor Party–dominated city council strongly advocated cultural policies as a central tenant for local economic development as the economy went from a manufacturing base to the service sector (Cohen 1991; Frith 1993).

REFERENCES

Basu, Dipannita. 1997. "The Economics of Rap Music: An Examination of the Opportunities and Resources of African Americans in the Business of Rap Music." Paper presented at the American Sociological Association annual meeting, Toronto, Ontario.

———. 1998. "What Is Real about Keeping It Real?" *Postcolonial Studies* 1, no. 3: 371–387.

Black Enterprise. 2002a. "Hip-Hop Economy." *Black Enterprise,* May, 70–75.

———. 2002b. "Music Moguls Take Control." *Black Enterprise,* August, 86–91.

Cashmore, Ellis. 1997. *The Black Cultural Industry.* New York: Routledge.

Cohen, Sarah. 1991. "Popular Music and Urban Regeneration: The Music Industries of Merseyside." *Cultural Studies* 5, no. 2: 332–346.

Cross, Brian. 1994. *It's Not about a Salary: Rap, Race, and Resistance in Los Angeles.* London: Verso.

Day, Wendy. 2002. "Interview: Wendy Day, Advocate for Rappers." In *Rhythm and Business,* ed. Norman Kelley. New York: Akshic Books.

Dingle, Derek. 2002. "The Producers." *Black Enterprise,* August, 76–98.

Frith, Simon. 1988. *Music for Pleasure: Essays in the Sociology of Pop.* Cambridge, Mass.: Polity Press.

———. 1993. "Popular Music and the Local State." In *Rock and Popular Music Politics, Policies, and Institutions,* ed. Tony Bennett, Simon Frith, Lawrence Grossberg, John Shepherd, and Graeme Turner. New York: Routledge.

———. 2002. "The Popular Music Industry." In *Pop and Rock,* ed. Will Straw, Simon Frith, and John Street. Cambridge: Cambridge University Press.

Forman, Murray. 2002. *The Hood Comes First: Race, Space, and Place in Rap and Hip-Hop.* Middletown, Conn.: Wesleyan University Press.

George, Nelson. 1998. *The Death of Rhythm and Blues.* New York: Pantheon Books.

Gilroy, Paul. 1994. *"There Ain't No Black in the Union Jack": The Cultural Politics of Race and Nation.* Chicago: University of Chicago Press.

Harvard Report. 2002. "A Study of the Soul Music Environment Prepared for Columbia Records Group [May 11, 1972]." In *Rhythm and Business,* ed. Norman Kelley. New York: Akshic Books.

hooks, bell. 1994. *Outlaw Culture: Resisting Representations.* New York: Routledge.

Kelley, Norman. 1999. "Rhythm Nation: The Political Economy of Black Music." *Black Renaissance* 2, no. 2.

———. 2002. "Notes on the Political Economy of Black Music." In *Rhythm and Business,* ed. Norman Kelley. New York: Akshic Books.

Lipsitz, George. 1994. *Dangerous Crossroads: Popular Music, Postmodernism, and the Poetics of Place.* London: Verso.

Muhammad, Tariq. 1999. "Hip-Hop Moguls: Beyond the Hype." *Black Enterprise,* December, 78–90.

Negus, Keith. 1999. *Music Genres and Corporate Cultures.* London: Routledge.

Rhea, Shawn E. 2002. "Music Masters." *Black Enterprise,* August, 86–92.

Roberts, Michael. 2002. "Papa's Got a Brand New Pig Bag: Big Music's Post-Fordist Regime and the Role of Independent Music Labels." In *Rhythm and Business,* ed. Norman Kelley. New York: Akshic Books.

Rose, Tricia. 1994. *Black Noise: Rap Music and Black Culture in Contemporary America.* Middletown, Conn.: Wesleyan University Press.

Rutten, Paul, ed. 1996. "Music, Culture and Society in Europe." Part II of *Music in Europe,* 129–134. Brussels: European Music Office.

Shukur, Roy. 2001. *Understanding Popular Music.* London: Routledge.

Speigler, Mark. 1996. "Marketing Street Culture: Bringing Hip-Hop Style to the Mainstream." *American Demographic,* November, 28–34.

Straw, Will. 2001. "Consumption." In *The Cambridge Companion to Pop and Rock,* ed. Simon Frith, Will Straw, and John Street. Cambridge: Cambridge University Press.

Toop, Davis. 1991. *Rap Attack 2.* London: Serpent's Tail.

Walker, Juliet. 1998. *The History of Black Business in America.* New York: Macmillan.

Vogel, Harold. 2004. *Entertainment Industry Economics.* Cambridge: Cambridge University Press.

30

Black Capitalism: Self-Help or Self-Delusion?
EARL OFARI HUTCHINSON

*In recent years, black organizations have shifted emphasis from politics to eco-
nomics, citing the recent economic success of other ethnic groups in the United
States. This chapter explains why analogies to recent immigrant groups may
not be applicable to the situation of African Americans. Proponents of black
capitalism have touted the rise of the black consumer dollar, but the author
points out that black consumer dollars may not necessarily translate into significant investments in black communities. Further, black capitalism may exacerbate class divisions among African Americans. The author asserts that
only the federal government can provide the necessary resources to revitalize
African American communities and concludes that political and economic
strategies are necessary to advance black socioeconomic well-being.*

Nearly a century ago, Booker T. Washington argued that political rights and social legislation
should take a back seat to building black wealth
and economic self-sufficiency. Washington's
backers—primarily black businesspeople, farmers, ministers, and Republican politicians—
agreed with his view that "brains, property and
character for the Negro will solve the question of
civil rights." Washington founded the National
Negro Business League in 1900 with the express
goal of organizing support for a business-
oriented approach to black advancement.

Militant black leaders led by W. E. B. DuBois
of the National Association for the Advancement of Colored People (NAACP) roundly
condemned Washington's philosophy. His critics—upwardly mobile college-educated Northern professionals—believed that his approach
amounted to little more than a shameful accommodation to segregation and exploitation.
DuBois put it bluntly: "Washington's program
practically accepts the alleged inferiority of the
Negro races!"[1]

As the NAACP grew in strength and as the civil

rights movement gathered steam during the
1960s, Washington's program was discredited as
outdated and reactionary. During the 1960s,
Washington's name became an epithet that young
black militants flung at anyone they considered
an "Uncle Tom."[2]

But times have changed, and the pendulum
has swung back. At the NAACP's national conference in 1988, executive director Benjamin Hooks
gave the first hint that the political winds had
shifted. Hooks noted, "We know that black America must do much of the work itself for it is our
future we must save." As of 2002, the NAACP had
launched its Financial Empowerment Initiative in
eleven cities.[3] Other organizations, such as Operation Push and the National Urban League, have
also focused on business development. Both organizations have formed partnerships with major
corporations to develop minority businesses as
suppliers.[4] Dozens of local and national black organizations have followed this lead to make black
business development and economic self-help the
centerpiece of the black agenda.[5]

Three reasons form the basis for this shift.

First, during the Reagan era, massive cuts in job programs and social services, coupled with the assault on affirmative action and civil rights, left black leaders frustrated and dismayed with government. The conviction grew among black leaders that government had become an enemy rather than an ally of the black poor. A second reason is the spectacular growth of the black middle class since 1980. According to 2001 U.S. Census Bureau figures, 39.4 percent of black high school graduates went on to enroll in college; 47 percent of blacks owned homes; and 28 percent of black families were earning more than $50,000 per year.[6]

The middle-class advance has also brought a sharp rise in black purchasing power. According to the Consumer Expenditure Survey, black consumers spent $384 billion dollars on goods and services—dollars that can be "recycled" into thriving businesses and community programs to provide jobs and social services for the black poor.[7] Black economic strength, black leaders say, will ultimately translate into greater political power for blacks in general.[8] Third, black leaders point to the phenomenal economic success of Korean, Chinese, Vietnamese, and Cuban immigrants. These groups have prospered in business, finance, real estate, manufacturing, and retail trade. They have built powerful business and trade associations that provide capital, credit, and technical training for their members. Equally important, their political influence—particularly in Miami, New York, Los Angeles, and San Francisco—has grown with their economic clout.[9]

At first glance, these are powerful reasons for which economic self-help appears to be a vibrant and attractive goal. But let's probe deeper. Asian and Hispanic immigrants did not start at the bottom. A study of Korean small business in Atlanta in 1984 found that 79 percent were able to secure loans or credit from banks.[10] Many of the merchants had operated successful businesses in Korea, were highly trained in management and retailing, and had strong family and business ties. These immigrants also got an added boost from the Korean government when it permitted them to take up to $100,000 from the country to start new businesses. The immigrants as well made skillful use of the *kye* system, which operates as a kind of rotating credit association in which Korean entrepreneurs receive loans, subsidies, business training, and investment information.[11]

The pattern was repeated with the first wave of Vietnamese immigrants who came to America immediately after the fall to the communists of the United States–backed South Vietnamese government in 1974. Many held college degrees and had either owned businesses or were employed in the professions or skilled trades in South Vietnam. In addition, the federal government poured millions into a comprehensive and costly resettlement program for these refugees from "communist terror."[12]

Far from being a model of "bootstrap" uplift, the Cuban refugees who fled Castro in the early 1960s benefited from the largesse of the American government. They received substantial sums for resettlement, welfare and income subsidies, as well as business loans and grants. Like the Vietnamese, many of the Cubans were college educated and had been technicians, managers, and business owners or landowners in Cuba.[13]

How important to their business success was the political and economic help the immigrants received? One only has to compare the figures for economic growth among African Americans, Latinos, and Asians. In 1997, black firms averaged $86,478 in sales. The average of Asian American companies was $336,195, and the average of Cuban American companies was $211,476.

Even if blacks have not enjoyed the instant entrée into business and government that immigrants have experienced, black self-help advocates argue that they can still fashion into a formidable power base the billions of consumer dollars spent by blacks. The problem, however, is that black consumer dollars are just that—consumer dollars, not investment dollars.

And despite the increased numbers of blacks in managerial, technical, and professional positions in corporations, more than 70 percent of the nearly twelve million black workers in America are still concentrated in clerical, service, and trade jobs. A sizable portion of blacks are employed as unskilled laborers. In 2001, the median household income for blacks was $29,420, which was much less than the $46,305 for whites and considerably less than the $33,565 median income of Hispanic households.[14]

With respect to median net wealth, the gap

between blacks and whites is even more glaring. In 1999, median net wealth for white households was nearly $81,450, whereas for blacks the median was just $8,000.[15] Moreover, African Americans own less than 1 percent of the nation's stock holdings."[16]

The consolidation of conservative economic policy and the acceleration of the global economy since the 1980s have pushed increasing numbers of blacks into the ranks of the unemployed. African Americans as a group are clearly being hurt by the continual strangling of social spending and the lack of commitment by the Bush administration to fund educational services that prepare the black urban poor for entry-level jobs in the new economy. The failure of the federal government to fund effective job training in America's inner cities has contributed to the black underclass becoming even more marginalized and unemployable. Unable to effectively compete for jobs in the new global economy, many poor inner-city blacks have turned to minimum-wage jobs and crime as their only means of survival.

The growing impoverishment and disparity in wealth means that most blacks have very little discretionary income or savings. They spend their paychecks almost exclusively on basic household goods and services. The major corporations exercise nearly monopolistic domination over this consumer market, controlling production, supply, and transport of all basic food and household items.

This is no accident. Historically, the economic infrastructure of African American communities has never been designed for capital inflow or retention. The iron-clad control of domestic markets by major corporations is akin to a kind of domestic colonialism. Black consumers buy goods from white producers, for whom black workers serve as a low-wage pool of labor. This reality, with the fact that most black consumers do not see any benefits from shopping at black-owned businesses, helps to explain why black consumers only spend 5 percent of their disposable income with black-owned businesses.[17]

A look at recent black business patterns reveals that traditional black businesses continue to have a significant presence in the ghetto economy. The small mom-and-pop stores, catering businesses, beauty and barber shops, video and record shops, service enterprises, and small grocery stores still represent a large number of the older, start-up businesses in African American communities. As sole proprietorships in general, capable of providing employment only to the owner and family members, they are plagued by the problems of small business: higher prices, limited stocks, and a narrow consumer base. More than 80 percent fail within two years.

The expansion in the 1990s by black entrepreneurs into automotive sales, business services, communications, transportation, and other emerging fields did not provide large-scale employment for blacks. Indeed, these capital and skill-intensive industries tend to create few jobs. For instance, the top-one hundred black industrial and service companies of 2003, per *Black Enterprise* magazine, provided employment for only 74,966 blacks—less than 1 percent of the general black workforce.[18]

Although some black firms have prospered, most prospective black entrepreneurs still find the door shut when they seek either credit and capital from lending agencies or managerial and technical training from corporations. The result is that black capitalism is still largely a myth. The $16.6 billion combined sales of the *Black Enterprise* 100 in 2002 pales beside the $4.1 trillion in sales racked up by *Fortune* 100 companies during the same year.[19] In fact, the combined sales of the *Black Enterprise* 100 is less than the sales of the one-hundredth ranked company of the *Fortune* 500. Moreover, the average receipts per firm of $86,000 for black-owned businesses were less than one-tenth of the $891,000 average per firm for U.S. businesses.[20]

Overall, the gross receipts for black-owned businesses hover at about 0.5 percent of total business receipts.[21] The relative strength of black business vis-à-vis the American economy did not change much even during the early 1990s, a period of high black-business growth.

The immediate prospects for change are hardly much better. The collapse of the high-tech-inspired speculative bubble, years of overinvestment, corporate financial scandals, and a weak international economy have contributed to growing business pessimism and a sluggish U.S. economy. And it can get worse. The increasingly unequal distribution of income, high consumer household debt, and declining employment may lead to a severe decline in consumer spending. This outcome would launch another round of belt-tightening by the major corporations, rendering them even less able or willing to assist minority businesses.

Given the problems of national economic decline and the continuing impoverishment of African Americans, black leaders will have to do some deep soul-searching and ask themselves, What are the limits of race loyalty? They expect black consumers to support black businesses because they are black, too; yet, they do not say what black businesses are willing to give in return. Indeed, they have presented no visible blueprint that shows how the black dollars in their hands will be used to provide tangible economic and social benefits.[22]

Black leaders constantly point to the example of the Jews. They say that Jews support Jews, and that is why they have advanced. But the Jewish experience is completely different from that of African Americans. Jewish consumers know that many Jewish merchants have a deeply ingrained sense of responsibility and duty to their communities. This economic bonding is the product of centuries of religious and social persecution suffered in the ghettos of Russia and Eastern Europe. Jewish consumers expect that a portion of the dollars they spend in transactions with Jewish merchants will be recycled into an array of social, cultural, and educational programs and services that benefit Jewish communities. If anything, this is the lesson that African Americans must learn in the context of ethnic success.[23]

But in the bigger context of changing American capitalism and the global economy, if black businesses are to have any prospect of becoming competitive, they must adopt the following three strategies:

1. *Pool capital into a development fund.* The fund can then provide African Americans with loans, credits, resources, training, and a contact network for new business development.
2. *Become more efficient and continue to diversify.* Black firms must concentrate more capital in research and development to upgrade products and services. Mergers, joint ventures, stock trading, and expansion into international markets are critical mechanisms for growth.
3. *Expand their consumer base.* Black firms must provide efficient service and sell quality goods at competitive prices to generate patronage by all segments of the consumer market—not just by blacks.

The growth of efficient black business and socially responsible black entrepreneurs is desirable, of course, but black leaders must be realistic. Black business and self-help programs cannot magically cure the ills of African Americans. The danger also exists that black business, given its inherent capitalist nature, will create greater wealth for a small black elite. The resultant deepening of class divisions among African Americans would simply perpetuate the exploitation of African American workers and the poor.

Despite the massive assault on government programs and services since the Reagan years, the hard truth is that only the federal government can provide the mass resources needed to revitalize African American communities. Since the New Deal, the World War II military buildup, and the postwar recovery, government spending—not private industry—has fueled economic growth and job development in America. The federal entitlement program, civil rights legislation, equal opportunity statutes, and affirmative action goals enacted during the Lyndon Johnson administration broke down the barriers for blacks to universities and corporations.[24]

It was hardly coincidental that black business experienced its single biggest period of growth from 1977 to 1980. Sales for the *Black Enterprise* 100 nearly doubled, from $886 million to $1.53 billion. This increase was due largely to the initiatives advanced during president Jimmy Carter's administration in an effort to strengthen federal programs that provided grants, loans, and technical training to minority businesses.

The centerpiece of the federal action toward minority business during the Carter term was the "8a set-aside" program. This plan mandated that national, state, and local agencies allocate a fixed percentage of their contracts exclusively to minority firms. By the time Carter left the White House in 1980, the government had nearly tripled the amount of business it did with black firms—from $1 billion to $2.7 billion.[25]

Under Reagan, the federal government rapidly backpedaled from its commitment to minority business. Cuts in Small Business Administration funds and programs, with adverse Supreme Court rulings on minority contracting and affirmative action, knocked many black firms out of the economic box. The economic plans offered by the George H. W. Bush administration, as well as by the Democrats in the wake of the Los Angeles uprising in 1992, indicate a continuation of the policy of federal withdrawal from direct aid to urban areas.

Both Congress and the White House have touted "enterprise zones" as the answer to the urban economic crisis. In his 1992 State of the Union address, Bush told Congress that these zones "will empower the poor." Both Bush and Congress proposed the use of federal and state tax incentives to induce businesses to locate in designated "enterprise zones."

There was nothing new here. The enterprise zone concept was first approved by Congress in 1980. The idea was to create special business zones in or near economically depressed, low-income neighborhoods. The businesses themselves would then provide skills training and jobs for local residents. Supposedly, they would also stimulate the growth of minority business.

Do enterprise zones work? Evidence of their success is at best spotty. A 1991 study by the National Center for Enterprise Zone Research found that the 155 zones in twenty-eight states created minimal employment for local residents and few business opportunities for minority firms. From 1987 to 1990, the Watts enterprise zone in Los Angeles generated a meager 159 jobs and almost no new black business growth. A study released in 2002 by two noted professors of urban and regional planning, Alan H. Peters and Peter Fisher, evaluates seventy-five zones in thirteen states. The authors' overall assessment of enterprise zones is negative: enterprise zones do little to improve the job prospects of local residents and have very limited impact on minority business development.[26] Eleanor Holmes Norton, District of Columbia congressional representative, bluntly dismissed enterprise zones as a conservative scheme to evade expenditure of money on the poor and on the development of "a comprehensive urban policy."[27]

The failed conservative economic policies of the past two decades are precisely the reason African Americans have no choice but to put government back on their agenda. They must mount a massive black pro-democracy-style campaign to pressure the White House and Congress to commit resources, and they must initiate new programs toward the economic rebuilding of African American communities. Black leaders and organizations must spearhead that effort by organizing community task forces, political action groups, and mass protest drives.

The funds are certainly there. The George W. Bush administration had no difficulty digging up the estimated $350 billion to wage the Iraq War and fund the subsequent occupation and reconstruction. So African Americans need not be ashamed to demand more federal dollars and programs to meet their needs. After all, they pay billions yearly to the government in taxes and fees. When they insist that the government create jobs, supply skills training and business development programs, and provide income support as well as quality health care, they are not asking for charity. On the contrary, they are asking only for a fair share return on their own money. Likewise, these demands will not encourage dependency, as claimed by many Republican and Democratic conservatives and some blacks. Despite the rhetoric of many business leaders, corporations are not antigovernment. Savvy corporate heads regard government as a necessary arbiter to protect their economic interests.

Certainly representatives from the airlines, banking, and steel industries did not consider themselves wards of Uncle Sam when they asked for government bailout funds. Defense contractors do not regard the billions they receive in weapons manufacturing contracts as encroachments on their economic sovereignty and decision-making ability. And agribusiness does not complain that price supports and crop subsidies are stunting its growth.

This "corporate welfare" costs taxpayers billions annually. If corporations can look to the federal government for help keeping their bootstraps up, then why should African Americans (who have much less) not do the same?[28]

Black leaders must continue to demand that the multibillion-dollar "peace dividend" from the Cold War's end be used to tackle the massive problems of the black underclass. These funds could provide low-interest home loans, stimulate small business expansion, fund a national health insurance plan, rebuild the crumbling infrastructure of the inner cities, and support art and cultural projects. Such measures alone would create thousands of private- and public-sector jobs for African Americans.

Self-help and "black capitalism" must not be regarded as the sole plans for economic rescue of African Americans. The problems of crime, drugs, poverty, and institutional racism that confront African American communities demand economic and political solutions. African Americans cannot afford to forget that.

NOTES

1. See W. E. B. DuBois, *The Souls of Black Folks* (New York: Fawcett), 48. See also Emma I. Thornbrough, ed., *Booker T. Washington* (Englewood Cliffs, N.J.: Prentice-Hall, 1969), 59; Louis R. Harlan, *Booker T. Washington: The Wizard of Tuskeegee, 1901–1915* (New York: Oxford University Press, 1983), 359–378; and Arnold Rampersad, *The Art and Imagination of W. E. B. DuBois* (New York: Schocken, 1990) 81–84.

2. For a fuller discussion of why Booker T. Washington became a pariah in the eyes of 1960s black power advocates, see Robert L. Allen, *Black Awakening in Capitalist America* (Garden City, N.Y.: Doubleday, 1969), 79–85; Harold Cruse, *Rebellion or Revolution* (New York: William Morrow, 1968), 156–166; and Nathan Hare, "How White Power Whitewashes Black Power," in *The Black Power Revolt*, ed. Floyd B. Barbour (Boston: Porter Sargeant, 1968), 182–188.

3. The program is described at www.naacp.org.

4. The Detroit Bureau of Operation Push has a program with the automobile industry described at www.rainbowpush.org/detroit/index.html. The National Urban League has partnership with Enterprise Rent-a-Car, described at www.nul.org/programs/econ_self_sufficiency/enterprise.htm.

5. *Los Angeles Times*, July 13, 1988; July 10, 1990; July 8, 1991. *Milwaukee Journal Sentinel*, September 18, 2000. *Washington Post*, September 16, 2002. *St. Petersburg Times*, February 2, 2003.

6. U.S. Department of Commerce, Bureau of Census, at www.census.gov/population/socdemo/school/ppl-148/tab13.xls (education); www.census.gov/hhes/www/housing/hvs/annual02/ann 02t20.html (home ownership); www.census.gov/population/socdemo/race/black/ppl-164/tab15.xls (income).

7. See the U.S. Bureau of Labor Statistics, at www.bls.gov/cex/home.htm#tables.

8. See Dorothy J. Gaiter, "Short-Term Despair, Long-Term Promise," *Wall Street Journal*, April 4, 1992, 1; and Guy Halverson, "Minorities Have Purchasing Clout," *Christian Science Monitor*, November 24, 1991, 8. See also *Black Enterprise* magazine, which regularly features how-to articles detailing methods by which black entrepreneurs can better tap the black consumer market.

9. For background on and analysis of the success that recent Asian immigrants have enjoyed in business and politics, see Ronald Takaki, *Strangers from a Different Shore* (New York: Penguin, 1989).

10. P. G. Min, *Ethnic Business Enterprise: Korean Small Business in Atlanta* (New York: Center for Migration Studies, 1988).

11. Pyong Gap Min, "Filipino and Korean Immigrants in Small Business: A Comparative Analysis," *Amerasia* 13, no. 1 (1986–1987): 54–60; Takaki, *Strangers from a Different Shore*, 436–445.

12. Barry N. Stein, "Occupational Adjustment Refugees: The Vietnamese in the United States," *International Migration Review* 13, no. 1 (Spring 1979): 29–40; Takaki, *Strangers from a Different Shore*, 458–459.

13. Frank D. Bean and Marta Tienda, *The Hispanic Population of the United States* (New York: Russell Sage Foundation, 1987), 30–40; Alejandro Portes and Robert Bach, "Immigrant Earnings: Cuban and Mexican Immigrants in the United States," *International Migration Review* 14 (1980): 315–341; David Treadwell, "Hard Road for Black Businesses," *Los Angeles Times*, September 20, 1991, 20.

14. U.S. Department of Commerce, Bureau of Census, at www.census.gov/population/socdemo/race/black/ppl-164/tab15.xls.

15. These figures are derived from 1999 longitudinal data in the Panel Study of Income Dynamics. For a full analysis of this data, see Thomas Shapiro, *The Cost of Being African American: How Wealth Perpetuates Inequality* (New York: Oxford University Press, 2003).

16. *Los Angeles Times,* July 25, 1992, A19; "The Black Middle Class," *Business Week,* March 14, 1988, 64; U.S. Census Bureau, "The Black Population of the States, March 1990 and 1989" (Washington, D.C.: Government Printing Office, 1991), 15–16.

17. See Thomas Boston, "Black Patronage of Black-Owned Businesses and Black Employment," in this volume (chapter 42).

18. Calculated from data in *Black Enterprise,* June 2003, and from the U.S. Bureau of Labor Statistics, at www.bls.gov. As of 1997, all black-owned firms combined employed just over 5 percent of the black workforce.

19. Dawn M. Baskerville, "One Step Forward, Two Steps Back," *Black Enterprise,* November 1991, 49; Frank McCoy, "Weathering a Weak Economy," *Black Enterprise,* January 1991, 46.

20. "The Fortune 500," *Fortune Magazine,* April 14, 2003, F-1; *Black Enterprise,* June 2003.

21. U.S. Census Bureau, *Black: 1997 Economic Census; Survey of Minority Owned Business Enterprises,* Company Statistics Series EC97CS-3 (Washington, D.C.: U.S. Superintendent of Documents, 2001).

22. Karen Tumulty, "Global Competition: Can the U.S. Still Play by Its Rules?" *Los Angeles Times,* June 8, 1992, A1, A8; Joel Kurtzman, *The Decline and Crash of the American Economy* (New York: W. W. Norton, 1988), 99–119; Donald Bartlett and James B. Steele, *America: What Went Wrong?* (Kansas City, Mo.: Andrews and McNeel, 1992), 89–104.

23. Geral Krefetz, *Jews and Money: Myths and Reality* (New Haven, Conn.: Ticknor & Fields, 1982), 207–231; Nathan Glazer, "The American Jew and the Attainment of Middle-Class Rank: Some Trends and Explanations," in *The Jews: Social Patterns of an American Group,* ed. Marshall Sklare (Glencoe, Ill.: Free Press, 1968), 138–146; and Fred L. Strodtbeck, "Family Interaction, Values and Achievement," in Sklare, *The Jews,* 147–168.

24. William Appleman Williams, *The Great Evasion* (Chicago: Quadrangle Books, 1964), 84–85; Forest Chrisman and Alan Pifer, *Government for the People* (New York: W. W. Norton, 1987), 59–115.

25. Derek T. Dingle, "What Happened to Black Capitalism?" *Black Enterprise,* August 1990, 162, 164.

26. Alan H. Peters and Peter Fisher, *State Enterprise Zones: Have They Worked?* (Kalamazoo, Mich.: W. E. Upjohn Institute, 2002).

27. Eleanor Holmes Norton, "Whatever Happened to Enterprise Zones?" *Black Enterprise* (April 1992): 20; John Schwada, "L.A.'s Zone Program Is Unproven," *Los Angeles Times,* June 14, 1992, A39.

28. Donald L. Bartlett and James B. Steele detail the high cost of domestic and foreign bailouts, defense industry waste, and their impact on the economy in *America: What Went Wrong?* (Kansas City, Mo.: Andrews and McMeel, 1992), 40–65, 105–124, 143–161, 189–211.

PART VII

Education, Employment, Training, and Social Welfare: Alternative Public Policy Approaches in the Struggle to Achieve Racial Equality

31

Black Power: The Struggle for Parental Choice in Education
HOWARD FULLER

There is a growing national public policy debate about the potential effects of tax-supported education voucher programs. This chapter contributes to this debate by linking it to the educational crisis facing black Americans. The author focuses on the experience of the Milwaukee Parental Choice Program to show how tax-supported vouchers lead to improved educational outcomes for low-income black children. The author suggests that the school choice debate is in part about whether parents of low-income black children should have the power to make educational choices that a majority of middle- and upper-income parents routinely exercise on behalf of their own children.

A deep canyon divides America when it comes to parental choice in education. On one side, with a narrow range of options, are low-income parents, mostly of color. On the other side, with a much broader array of choices, are middle- and upper-income parents, mostly white. A variety of options are available to parents, including tax-supported vouchers, tax credits and deductions, charter schools, public–private partnerships, home-schooling, and innovative options in the existing system. This chapter focuses on the most controversial of these options: tax-supported education vouchers. According to Indiana University professor Martha M. McCarthy, no education "topic is generating more volatile debate . . . than voucher systems to fund schooling" (2000).

For many, the voucher debate is highly nuanced, often featuring arcane discussion of scholarly methodology. But that is not what this debate is really about. This is a debate about power. This debate is largely about whether parents of low-income black children should obtain a power that many critics of the choice movement exercise every day on behalf of their own children. In de-

scribing the struggle of African Americans for expanded educational opportunity, this chapter defines the core issue of the parental choice debate; highlights the educational crisis facing black Americans; describes how tax-supported vouchers have led to improved educational outcomes for thousands of low-income children, most of whom are black; and uses Milwaukee's experience as an illustration of the struggle of black Americans for the power to make the best choices for their children's education.

THE CORE ISSUE IS THE POWER TO MAKE CHOICES

The current debate about vouchers is not about choice per se but who has it. Many American parents take school choice for granted (Henig and Sugarman 1999). As Richard Elmore and Bruce Fuller (1996) explain:

> Choice is everywhere in American education. It is manifest in the residential choices

made by families [and] in the housing prices found in neighborhoods [and] when families, sometimes at great financial sacrifice, decide to send their children to private schools. . . . In all instances, these choices . . . are strongly shaped by the wealth, ethnicity, and social status of parents and their neighborhoods.

The central question confronting elected and appointed officials and, indeed, all citizens of America is, Should low-income American parents (most of whom are black) be empowered to make educational choices that a majority of Americans cherish and take for granted?[1] While any answer but yes is unacceptable, powerful forces want decision makers to say no. These forces—led by teachers unions and school boards—now have key roles in deciding where large numbers of low-income children (predominately black) attend school. They do not want to surrender that power. They have committed substantial energy and resources to keep it. The status quo is very important to them.

For black people, the stakes are huge. If those opposed to providing low-income parents with more educational power prevail, historical obstacles to black advancement will be even more entrenched. As African Americans, we cannot lose this struggle!

THE CRISIS IN EDUCATION FOR BLACK AMERICANS

Critical problems in urban America will worsen unless young black men and women gain a quality education. Low high school graduation rates and poor academic achievement relative to white students demonstrate that black students are not receiving a quality education.

Graduation rates of black children are one of the indicators that highlight the tragic and unacceptable circumstances facing the black community—and indeed America. Researcher Jay Greene's groundbreaking study of graduation rates documents the problem. He reports, "For white students the graduation rate is 78%, but for black students it is 56%. . . . Seven states and 16 of the largest 50 districts were unable to

graduate *more than half* of their black students" (Greene 2001b).

This staggering graduation rate is reinforced by other national data showing that blacks as a group perform well below national norms. Data from the 1999 National Assessment of Educational Progress details the continuing achievement gap between white students and black students. In reading, math, and science, whites are much more likely than are blacks to score at proficient or advanced levels. Just consider that in math, where the percentile gap between blacks and whites is closest, 18 percent of whites scored proficient whereas only 4 percent of blacks did. This fourteen-point gap compares to a twenty-three-point gap in reading and a twenty-point gap in science (College Board 1999). The National Assessment of Educational Progress (2001) reports, "These large gaps between sub-groups' performance have remained relatively unchanged since 1990."

Low levels of academic achievement lead to a lack of preparation to participate in the labor market. There are countless research studies showing that the level and quality of an individual's education is positively linked to economic attainment. Greene (2001b) outlines the importance of high school graduation to an individual's economic future:

Students who fail to graduate from high school face a very bleak future. Because the basic skills conveyed in high school and higher education are essential for success in today's economy, students who do not receive these skills are likely to suffer with significantly reduced earnings and employment prospects. . . . For people reporting any earnings the median income for those who left school without a high school diploma or GED is $15,334 compared to $29,294 for people with at least a high school degree or GED.

VOUCHERS LEAD TO IMPROVED EDUCATIONAL ATTAINMENT

One lever of power for addressing the educational problems of black students is the use of vouchers, which research has shown improves the academic achievement of voucher recipients. Some studies specifically demonstrate that the use of vouchers improves the educational achievement of black children (Howell 2001). Recent reports also demonstrate the potential for voucher programs to improve the local public school district, thereby improving the achievement of all students in an urban area (Greene 2001a; Hoxby 2001). A recent Brookings Institution report (Loveless 2001) characterizes the overall findings of scholarly research on vouchers: "Although controversial, research generally shows positive effects for students using vouchers to attend private schools."

In Milwaukee, researchers Jay Greene, Paul Peterson, and Jiangtao Du (1999) found statistically significant math and reading score gains for the city's voucher students. Describing this research, Greene said that the research team "compared the test scores of applicants . . . accepted to the choice program by lottery to those who were rejected by lottery. We found significant test score gains . . . after three or four years of participation in the choice program. The . . . gains were quite large, 11 normal curve equivalent (NCE) points in math and 6 NCE points in reading" after four years. Economist Cecilia Rouse (1998) of Princeton University found "quite large" statistically significant math gains for Milwaukee choice students as well.

The research trends are summarized by Greene (2000) in a paper presented at a Harvard University conference on school choice:

Researchers who have served as evaluators of the publicly funded choice programs in Milwaukee and Cleveland as well as the privately-funded programs in Washington, D.C., Dayton, New York, and San Antonio agree that these programs have been generally positive developments and have supported their continuation if not expansion. If one only examined the competing interest group and research community spin on the various evaluations instead of reading the evaluations themselves, one might easily miss the level of positive consensus that exists. This positive consensus is all the more remarkable given the politically contentious nature of the issue and the rewards scholars have for highlighting disagreements with one another. [Yet] there is largely agreement among the researchers who have collected and analyzed the flood of new

data on school choice that these programs are generally positive in their effects and ought to be continued if not expanded.

THE MILWAUKEE EXPERIENCE

In January 1976, a federal judge ruled that Milwaukee's black children were unlawfully confined in segregated schools. The Milwaukee public schools (MPS) responded with a forced busing plan that explicitly gave the best choices to middle- and upper-income parents (mostly white) and uprooted a disproportionate number of low-income children (mostly black) and assigned them to distant schools (Fuller 1985). Through this plan, some African Americans received more power to choose. However, they were far outnumbered by those who were forced to choose, because of their race, from distant schools to which they were bused. All the while, a larger proportion of white students either stayed in neighborhood schools or transferred to magnet schools (schools with specialized curricula and superior facilities), many of which had selective admission practices.

As for placing the disproportionate burden of desegregation on African Americans, the plan's rationale was specific and haunting. According to MPS, "the psychological guarantee of not having to attend a school that is predominantly minority will tend to stabilize the [white] population in the city" (Fuller 1985). Describing the plan, University of Wisconsin–Milwaukee professor William Kritek (1977) describes the "optimum percentage of minority students in a desegregated school." He writes that 15 percent "is a minimum if the minority group is . . . to exert pressure without constituting a power threat to the majority." He quotes another educator: "As long as the proportion of black pupils is small . . . and expected to remain so, there is no reason for white pupils to experience stigma, relative deprivation, social threat, marginality, or a change in norms, standards, or . . . expectations of their significant others."

It was not until 1999 that a former MPS official, and one of this plan's architects, acknowledged that the unequal burden was not accidental. The occasion was a forum at the Helen Bader Foundation, part of a series of events aimed at discussing race relations in Milwaukee.

The former MPS administrator said that "white benefit" was a central consideration in the plan's development (Williams 1999). This admission some thirty years after the fact only confirmed what many people in the black community had always known. Beginning in the 1960s, Mikel Holt has traced growing discontent among African Americans with the unacceptable educational achievement of African American students. Discontent grew in the late 1970s once it was clear that the court-ordered integration plan placed a disproportionate, involuntary burden on African American students (Holt 2000).

MILWAUKEE'S TAX-SUPPORTED VOUCHER PROGRAM

Sponsored by black state representative Annette "Polly" Williams, black state senator Gary George, and by governor Tommy Thompson, the Milwaukee Parental Choice Program (MPCP) was enacted in 1990 to create more options for poor parents, better achievement for their children, and improved performance in MPS.

The MPCP was the nation's first program to provide low-income families with publicly funded vouchers that enabled them to send their children to private schools. While opponents in 1990 sought a court order to halt the program, the Wisconsin Supreme Court in 1992 upheld its constitutionality. MPCP enrollment was initially restricted to 1 percent of the approximately one-hundred-thousand-student enrollment of the MPS. In 1993, the Wisconsin legislature raised the enrollment limit to 1.5 percent.

In 1995, the governor and the legislature—responding to a bipartisan coalition of parents, employers, and civic leaders—raised the MPCP participation limit to 15 percent and allowed religious schools as well as secular schools to participate. Teachers unions and other voucher opponents sued. A Wisconsin court injunction blocked the expansion, placing thousands of children in limbo until a private fund-raising drive created a private scholarship program that allowed many of the students to remain in the schools they had chosen. In 1998, the Wisconsin Supreme Court upheld the constitutionality of the expansion. Opponents appealed to the U.S.

Supreme Court, but the Court allowed the decision to stand.

The injunction and the three-year court battle typify the environment of hostility and uncertainty for parental school choice in Milwaukee that opponents have generated. Beginning with the unsuccessful suit in 1990, they have pursued multiple legislative, regulatory, and legal strategies to keep low-income parents from having the power to make educational choices for their children.

Despite the opposition and resulting uncertainty about the MPCP's future, parent interest has grown steadily. MPCP participation has increased from 341 students at seven schools in 1990–1991 to 10,882 students at 106 schools in 2001–2002. Of participating students, 81 percent are of color: 62 percent, African American; 19 percent, Hispanic, Asian, and other (Legislative Audit Bureau 2000). The state's official evaluator confirmed that the program has been serving the student population for which the program was intended:

> The demographic profile [of MPCP students] was quite consistent over each of the [first] five years. . . . Students who ultimately enrolled . . . were from very low-income families, considerably below the average [MPS] family and about $500 below the low-income (free-lunch-eligible) MPS family. . . . Blacks and Hispanics were the primary applicants . . . both being overrepresented compared with [MPS]. . . . Choice students were considerably less likely to come from a household in which parents were married. . . . Prior test scores of Choice students [showed they] were achieving considerably less than MPS students and somewhat less than low-income MPS students. (Witte 1995)[2]

He also affirmed that the program was an outlet for parents dissatisfied with the schooling their children were formerly receiving:

> There was evidence that Choice parents were very dissatisfied with their former (MPS) schools; there may have been good reason for it, as indicated by test scores taken in MPS prior to students enrolling in Choice. . . . [The] judgment of Choice parents of their

child's prior public school was especially harsh in contrast with the MPS control groups. . . . Satisfaction of Choice parents with private schools was just as dramatic as dissatisfaction was with prior public schools. . . . The results were a dramatic reversal— high levels of dissatisfaction with prior public schools, but considerable satisfaction with private schools. . . . There was also, in each year, overwhelming support among participants that the Choice program should continue. . . . Finally, parental involvement, which was clearly very high for Choice parents before they enrolled in the program, increased while their children were in private schools. (Witte 1995)

There is no honest dispute that the MPCP has successfully encouraged and empowered urban parents to make major decisions about their children's education.

THE CONTINUING STRUGGLE

The MPCP gave low-income parents an inkling of the broader power long valued by more affluent parents. First in Milwaukee, and later in Cleveland and Florida, the result has been more educational options for a small but growing number of low-income parents, most of whom are black. Black support for vouchers has grown in tandem with their concern about the failure of public schools. For example, according to the Joint Center for Political and Economic Studies, "among African Americans, support for school vouchers in the 1999 survey shows a 25 percent increase . . . from last year. . . . A substantial majority of the black respondents (60 percent) supported school vouchers, while only a third . . . rejected them" (2000).

While the nation's black community does not need to be of one mind, the future of our children requires an open discussion focusing on the core issue: the urgent need to expand the educational power of low-income black parents. The history described in this chapter shows how our community and its children suffer when we lack the power to make educational choices and when the range of those choices is controlled by anyone other than parents.

When some public school educators and their supporters argue that choice will hurt black children, it is important to see where their own children go to school. For example, consider this information from the October 4, 1996, edition of the *Washington Times*: "The percentage of public school teachers . . . who enroll their children in private school is staggering . . . Boston (44.6 percent); Cleveland (39.7 percent); San Francisco (36.7 percent); Chicago (36.3 percent); Philadelphia (35.9 percent); and Pittsburgh (35.4 percent)." Fuller and White (1995) show that while a third of teachers in Milwaukee choose private schools for their children, the lower income in many African American families explains why only 6 percent of African American parents chose private schools.

Educators' choices are not unique. Millions of American parents—beginning with those at the very top of our government through those representing all political persuasions—benefit from the power of educational alternatives. While 14 percent of school-age children are in private school, that rate for the children of representatives and senators is 40 percent and 49 percent, respectively (Shokraii 2000). These parents have exercised their rightful power to select the school they believe is best for their children. However, the question that remains is, Why is this power that is so highly valued and widely used by many of our government's top leaders so controversial when applied to low-income parents, most of whom are African American?

CONCLUSION: POWERFUL GUIDANCE

Sara Lightfoot (1980) writes that "a critically important ingredient of educational success . . . lies in the power relationship between communities and schools, rather than in the nature of the student population." In comments that would apply well to the history of educational options in Milwaukee, she continues: "Mixing black and white bodies . . . in the same school and preserving the same relationships and perceptions between the schools and the families they serve is unlikely to substantially change . . . the quality of the educational process." In words that speak directly to the need for expanded educational alternatives, she says, "The nature and distribution of power among schools, families and communities is a crucial piece of the complex puzzle leading toward educational success of all children."

Kenneth B. Clark is one of this century's most distinguished African American leaders. Three decades ago, long before school choice was the controversial topic it has become today, he wrote forcefully of the need for expanded educational alternatives. Clark said such alternatives would only arise if "competitive public school systems" replaced the public "education monopoly" (1968). He added that "truly effective competition [i.e., more educational alternatives for parents] strengthens rather than weakens that which deserves to survive. . . . Public education need not be identified with the present system . . . of public schools. [It] can be more broadly and pragmatically defined in terms of . . . an educational system which is in the public interest."

The words of Clark and Lightfoot provide powerful guidance. Black Americans must continue to organize and act decisively to attain the power to make educational choices that are best for our children. They must be inspired by—and never forget—the clear and powerful words of Milwaukee parent Val Johnson: "I think I know what's best for my children. Yes, I do."

NOTES

1. For decades there has been a myriad of tax-supported and privately endowed programs for students attending public and private colleges. In addition, middle- and upper-income parents have always had the resources to exercise K–12 choice. What has changed is the more recent development of K–12 choice as a meaningful option for low-income parents. Recent court cases have suggested that educational assistance programs are constitutional if they treat religious and nonreligious options neutrally and if funds are directed by the private choices of individual parents.

2. John Witte is a University of Wisconsin political scientist who evaluated Milwaukee's program from 1991 to 1995. In a new book, he endorses targeted voucher programs such as the MPCP (Witte 2000). Witte urges observers of this debate "to read [his] original reports."

REFERENCES

Clark, K. 1968. "Alternative Public School Systems." *Harvard Educational Review* 38 (Winter): 110–111.

College Board. 1999. "Reaching the Top." A report of the National Task Force on Minority High Achievement. New York.

Elmore, R., and B. Fuller. 1996. *Who Chooses? Who Loses? Culture, Institutions, and the Unequal Effects of School Choice.* New York: Teachers College Press.

Fuller, H. 1985. "The Impact of the Milwaukee Public Schools System's Desegregation Plan on Black Students and the Black Community (1976–1982)." Doctoral diss., Marquette University, Milwaukee, Wisc.

Fuller, H., and S. White. 1995. "Expanded School Choice in Milwaukee." Wisconsin Policy Research Institute report.

Greene, J. 2000. "A Survey of Results from Voucher Experiments: Where We Are and What We Know." Prepared for the Conference on Charter Schools, Vouchers, and Public Education. Sponsored by the Harvard Program on Education Policy and Governance and the Manhattan Institute for Policy Research, Cambridge, Mass.

———. 2001a. "An Evaluation of the Florida A-Plus Accountability and School Choice Program." Prepared for Florida State University, the Manhattan Institute for Policy Research, and Harvard University Program on Education Policy and Governance.

———. 2001b. "Graduation Rates in the United States." Prepared for the Manhattan Institute for Policy Research, New York.

Greene, J., P. Peterson, and J. Du. 1999. "Effectiveness of School Choice: The Milwaukee Experiment." *Education and Urban Society* (February).

Henig, J., and S. Sugarman. 1999. "The Nature and Extent of School Choice." In *School Choice and Social Controversy, Politics, Policy and Law,* ed. S. Sugarman and F. Kemerer. Washington, D.C.: Brookings Institution Press.

Holt, M. 2000. "Not Yet 'Free at Last.'" Institute for Contemporary Studies, Oakland, Calif.

Howell, W. 2001. "Vouchers in New York, Dayton, and D.C." *Education Matters* (Summer): 46–54.

Hoxby, C. 2001. "School Choice and School Productivity (or, Could School Choice Be a Tide
That Lifts All Boats?)." *Education Next* (Winter).

Joint Center for Political and Economic Studies.
2000. *1999 National Opinion Poll—Education.*
Washington, D.C.: Joint Center for Political and
Economic Studies.

Kritek, W. 1977. "Voluntary Desegregation in Wisconsin." *Integrated Education* (November–
December).

Legislative Audit Bureau, State of Wisconsin. 2000.
"An Evaluation—Milwaukee Parental Choice
Program." Report 00-2.

Lightfoot, S. 1980. "Families as Educators: The For-
gotten People of *Brown*." In *Shades of Brown:
New Perspectives on School Desegregation,* ed. D.
Bell. New York: Teachers College Press.

Loveless, T. 2001. "How Well Are American Students Learning?" Brown Center report on American education. Washington, D.C.: Brookings
Institution Press.

McCarthy, M. 2000. "What Is the Verdict on School
Vouchers?" *Phi Delta Kappa* (January): 371–378.

National Assessment of Educational Progress.
2001. "The Nation's Report Card: Mathematics
Highlights 2000." National Center for Education Statistics, Washington, D.C.

Rouse, C. 1998. "Private School Vouchers and Student Achievement: An Evaluation of the Milwaukee Parental Choice Program." *Quarterly
Journal of Economics* (May).

Shokraii, N. 2000. "How Members of Congress
Practice School Choice." The Heritage Foundation, Washington, D.C.

Williams, J. 1999. "'White Benefit' Was Driving
Force of Busing 20 Years Later, Architects of
MPS Plan Admit They Didn't Want to Disrupt
City's White Residents." *Milwaukee Journal Sen-
tinel,* October 19.

Witte, J. 1995. "Fifth Year Report: Milwaukee Parental
Choice Program." Department of Political Sci-
ence and Robert M. La Follette Institute of Public
Affairs, University of Wisconsin–Madison.

———. 2000. *The Market Approach to Education:
An Analysis of America's First Voucher Program.*
Princeton, N.J.: Princeton University Press.

32

School Choice: A Desperate Gamble
LOUIS SCHUBERT

The school voucher, or "school choice," debate in the African American com-munity represents a conflict between the immediate needs of children in failing schools and the viability of universal public education in the United States. While pilot programs show that motivated students and parents can benefit from voucher programs, the system must also give consideration to those students who are left behind. Vouchers do not provide the full cost of private tuition and related expenses but merely expand the availability of private and religious education to a wider population. Children deemed in-eligible to attend private schools for any reasons—financial, behavioral, or otherwise—would be forced into increasingly underfunded public schools as money is diverted away from public education.

American public education is failing to meet the needs of many of the nation's African American children. Whether considering standardized test scores, graduation rates, or other measures of student achievement, one discovers a clear prob-lem. While the system of American public edu-cation is failing to provide quality education to all American children, the problem is particu-larly serious for poor African American children who must develop the skills needed to compete in an increasingly globalized, high-technology economy. One proposal to improve African American children's educational opportunities centers on the use of school vouchers, a proposal that purports to provide so-called school choice.

School choice is a term derived from the eco-nomic concept of consumer choice in the market-place. In sum, school choice endorses the idea that public school funds should be given directly to parents so that they can choose the best schools for their children. This approach allows parents to direct public money to private and religious schools. Voucher advocates argue that doing so will create healthy competition for these public funds and will ultimately pressure public schools to improve or be shut down.

A diversity of views on school vouchers exists among African Americans, some strongly favor-ing vouchers and others vigorously opposing them. In some ways, this range of opinion re-flects the general trends on the issue, but the poor quality of inner-city public schools has led a disproportionate number of African Ameri-cans to put greater hope in the voucher system. The purpose of this chapter is to investigate the reasons for this support and the consequences of voucher plans for African American children.

THE DEBATE

The debate over school vouchers raises a range of issues. In the largest sense, the debate over vouch-ers is also a debate over the role of government in American society. One side, generally regarded as conservative, believes that government involve-ment limits individual freedom and disrupts the efficient allocation of scarce resources. Therefore, government intervention should be limited whenever and wherever possible. Vouchers are thus depicted by advocates as a way to get government out of the education "business" unless it can provide an educational "product" that can favorably compete with private-sector schools. The opposing side, generally those who are liberal, sees government as an institution whose responsibility is to regulate the market economy. According to liberals, an unregulated free market economy would reinforce conditions for monopoly domination of markets, economic inequality, and other socially undesirable economic outcomes. The goal of public education—to ensure that all children receive access to quality schooling through universal education—is a bedrock component of the liberal belief that government intervention is essential to create a society based on the principle of equal opportunity for all. Liberals believe that more tax-supported privatization of educational markets would allow children of privileged families to have far greater opportunities for an education, a fact that would exacerbate race and class inequities in a high-technology society.

The different conceptions of the role of government in society reflect the political identities of the participants in the school choice debate. The ideologically conservative Republican Party favors school vouchers and champions school choice, although president George W. Bush was willing, for tactical reasons, to drop vouchers from the 2001 No Child Left Behind education reform law. The more-liberal Democratic Party usually opposes proposals to use public money for private schools. The political nature of the school choice debate is apparent in the funding sources of both sides. The antivoucher movement is led by the nation's teachers' unions—most notably, the National Education Association and the American Federation of Teachers—whose members (mostly public school teachers) clearly have a stake in government funding and the improvement of public schools. Both unions channel millions of dollars to Democratic candidates and antivoucher campaigns in different states. The traditional African American political leadership, such as the National Association for the Advancement of Colored People and the large majority of black elected officials, are allied with the teachers' unions on this matter.

The provoucher movement is largely financed by a handful of extremely wealthy benefactors and foundations, such as the Walton Family Foundation; the Milton and Rose Friedman Foundation; and, most prominently, the Lynde and Harry Bradley Foundation, which is the major contributor to the most active African American school-choice lobbying group, the Black Alliance for Educational Options. The Bradley Foundation is perhaps the largest and most influential conservative source of funding in the United States, having also contributed to the anti–affirmative action National Association of Scholars and the American Enterprise Institute, whose affiliates include Charles Murray, author of the racially controversial *The Bell Curve*. Rather than have school vouchers linked with rich whites, such as Silicon Valley tycoon Tim Draper (sponsor of the defeated provoucher proposition 38 in California in 2000), the new tactic of the conservatives seems to be to associate school choice with poorer urban blacks.

There is, however, another aspect of the school choice debate among African Americans that has little to do with conservative and liberal positions. Overwhelmingly Democratic, African Americans who voted in 2000 supported Democratic presidential candidate Al Gore. Yet there exists significant support for school vouchers in the African American community. A 1998 study by the Joint Center for Political and Economic Studies showed that 48 percent of African Americans support vouchers, with even higher numbers for those between the ages of twenty-six and thirty-five (64.6 percent).

Why have so many African Americans taken on a position on school vouchers championed by the conservative Right? The answer clearly has to do with the real-life experiences of having children in substandard public schools, rather than political ideology in general. Ideology is secondary to every parent's hope for the best education for their children. If the present state of public education is not working for the children in school today, it is only rational for their parents to look for alternatives. At this level, the debate centers on what will work. Parents and students want schools that educate. African Americans have every reason to ask whether public schools can be sufficiently reformed or if privatizing education would serve some students better. The question for many African American parents is, Will vouchers work to give my child better opportunities right now?

DO VOUCHERS PROVIDE OPPORTUNITIES FOR AFRICAN AMERICAN SCHOOLCHILDREN?

Studies of the effects of vouchers on test scores show some improvement for selected African American students who used vouchers to switch to private schools. One recent study demonstrates that black students who used vouchers to enroll in private schools in Dayton, Ohio; Washington, D.C.; and New York City saw a 6.3-point improvement in their national percentile ranking after two years when compared to black students who did not use vouchers (Howell et al. 2000). Although voucher programs can help some students, they certainly are not the only way to improve student performance. A study of African American students who were in a class-size reduction program in Tennessee public schools saw an increase in national percentile ranking of 4.9 points after two years. These studies raise several questions: Should improvements such as lower class size be sought within the public education system or outside it? Can vouchers offer immediate relief through making funds available to all parents?

In the largest scale-voucher experiment in the United States, the Milwaukee (Wisconsin) public schools funded a small voucher program for over a decade involving several thousand black and Latino students in an urban school district of close to one hundred thousand students. This limited program (similar to another in Cleveland) tended to attract parents who were actively looking to support their children's education. Critics have noted that one unintended effect of the voucher program has been to weaken efforts to improve all the public schools in Milwaukee by diverting involved activist parents to a limited public–private "choice" program. Rather than becoming models for improving other urban districts, the schools that accept vouchers bolster their students' (termed "customers" by voucher advocates) chances by seeking supplementary private funding and by implicitly rejecting broader systemic educational change. The Milwaukee program and its advocates may claim success in raising student achievement, but the program includes only a small, select percentage of this urban district's students. Indeed, one key initial supporter of the Milwaukee experiment, state representative Polly Williams, has become a major critic since it became clear that conservatives were using black children as "cover" for their privatization plans (Peterson and Miner 2000, 819).

Another problem with vouchers relates to the inequities of private education. Most voucher programs propose that $3,000–$4,000 in funds be made available to parents to be used in their choosing any school. Such an amount may be enough to pay for some cheaper, generally religious, private schools, but the best private schools cost well over $10,000 a year. This is not meant to suggest that a quality education is impossible to find in less-expensive schools, such as those that keep down costs by using unpaid members of religious orders as teachers. But in general, schools—whether private or public—are of uneven quality in large part because of variations in the amount of dollars per student a school has available. In a comprehensive voucher system, a three-tier private school system can be expected (Visnick 1993), ranging from minimally equipped storefront schools that could be paid for with voucher money alone, to more costly schools that would take the voucher funds and then require several thousand dollars more, to expensive schools that would remain out of the reach of most parents with or without vouchers. In this system, vouchers would only re-create the inequalities of the public schools for poor children, while subsidizing rich and middle-class families already sending their children to private schools. This economic reality is reflected by the fact that within the African American community, vouchers are most popular with the wealthiest families, those earning over $90,000 a year (65 percent of whom are in favor of the voucher system) and are least popular with those earning under $15,000 a year (only 28 percent in favor; Joint Center for Political and Economic Studies 1996).

Another problem with the voucher system is that its advocates ignore many of the costs of education absorbed by public schools. Los Angeles Board of Education president Genethia Hudley-Haysas points out that the voucher funds used toward private school tuition do not factor in transportation costs, school lunches and breakfasts for most poor children, and before- and after-school programs, all of which are presently provided for free by public schools (Williams 2000, A9). This only serves to underscore the fact that vouchers give their main benefit to those that need it the least while still excluding the poorest. Certainly, the top African American students without the money to pay for private schools can and do get scholarships. Still, those not in the "talented tenth" will either need additional money or be limited to underfunded public schools or underfunded private schools, a lack of choice that is the exact opposite of the "free" choice that proponents of school vouchers use as their main argument.

Yet another problem with vouchers is that they encourage private schools to be highly selective in their admissions policy. School choice is a two-way street: just as parents are supposed to be able to choose the school to which they want to send their children (assuming the voucher covers enough of the cost), so the schools will be able to choose which children they admit. Many private schools require entrance exams. Others accept students of all aptitude levels but specifically exclude children with histories of disciplinary problems, a factor that particularly affects African American boys, who are disproportionately classified as having "behavioral disorder" by schools that cannot afford to give them more attention (Kunjufu 1992, 11). For the parents of such children, there may be no choice whatsoever regarding which school will accept their sons: only public schools are based on the principle of education for all children. Public schools cannot legally deny admission on the basis of race, religion, ethnicity, scholastic ability, "family values," ability to pay, or physical or mental disability.

An additional potential problem with vouchers resides in the differential ability of parents to make school choices. School choice is based on the economic model of rational decision making. To make decisions about which school to select, the first thing a child's family needs is quality information, something that low-income families

sometimes lack (Wells 1993, 30–31). One limitation is in the ability to obtain information, which requires considerable time and ability. Low-income parents are at a disadvantage in this regard as they are often working long hours. Furthermore, low-income parents may not be as readily able to gain access to the Internet or to other information sources. Some parents may also be limited in their ability to analyze information, again partly due to time but also related to the parents' own level of education.

In conclusion, the best way to understand the support for school choice that does exist in the African American community is to understand the desperation parents feel knowing that their sons or daughters are going to public schools that are not meeting their children's educational needs. Mothers and fathers do not have as a first interest to save universal public education; parents want a better education for their child *now*. Vouchers have been shown to help those students whose parents work hard to get them into voucher programs and help them make the most of that opportunity. While a full voucher or school choice program will only offer African American children a slightly improved chance of a better education, this chance becomes a risk that a parent may be willing to take based on the level of desperation they feel. If their son or daughter is accepted by a high-quality private school; if the family can afford the tuition in excess of what the voucher pays; and if the family can afford all the other hidden costs of private education in terms of money, time, and commitment, then the school choice program may work for that child in that family.

ALTERNATIVES TO VOUCHERS: FIXING THE PUBLIC SCHOOLS

Individualized decision making carries a great cost for the large majority of African American children who are likely to be left out of these arrangements. The American ideal of equal-quality education for all children has been optimistically embraced for the past forty-eight years by the movement to end school segregation after *Brown v. Board of Education*. A fundamental precept of that movement is that solutions to educational inequities must help all students and ensure that American society will, as the Children's Defense Fund says, "leave no child behind." However, voucher supporters reply that "this is the 'if the Titanic doesn't have enough lifeboats for everybody, nobody should use one' argument" (Cordell 1998). This is the crux of the question: American schools may sometimes appear to be a sinking boat, but is it so desperate a situation that the nation needs to apply the lifeboat ethics of sacrificing some so that others can succeed? Or is the real issue to continue to search for ways to provide quality public education to all American children?

It is clear that many public schools can and do work well. The question is how to help all public schools replicate the success of the best public schools. Within most large urban school districts (those with enrollment over fifty thousand), the quality of the public education offered depends on two factors: first, the socioeconomic and educational levels of the parents in the local elementary school neighborhood; and second, the academic magnet programs offered to the secondary students citywide (grades sixth through twelfth). For example, in Oakland, California, public school standardized test scores in the fifteen elementary schools in the affluent Oakland Hills are at the seventy-fifth percentile or above, whereas the lower socioeconomic and educational-level "flatland" schools are usually under the twenty-fifth percentile. Yet, all of these schools are part of the same, public Oakland Unified School District! The primary problem is economic segregation, not "public school monopoly."

Given the dismal record of African Americans' access to quality education, there can be no doubt that American public schools must engage in an ongoing learning process to improve. Many proposals being examined to improve public education do not include a resort to moving public funds outside public schools:

Smaller classes. Smaller class size (fifteen to twenty students per class rather than thirty-five to forty-five) has been widely embraced as a positive approach that gives teachers greater time to spend on each student.

Magnet schools. Magnet schools, charter schools, and special academies have been shown to be motivators of student success.

Cooperative programs. A viable strategy for helping improve rates of graduation and college matriculation for African American students is the development of cooperative college preparatory programs. These programs involve universities working with high school administrators and teachers to improve teaching competence, and curriculum design and implementation.

Faculty compensation. Of basic importance is increasing teacher pay to make the teaching profession more attractive to recruit better teachers. Teacher competence is always a central concern.

Parental involvement. Also needed are creative approaches for promoting parents as partners in education. The greatest factor in student success is support from home, and parents cannot expect public schools to assume total responsibility for their children's education. In some cases this might mean aggressive adult education for parents.

These and other possibilities for improving universal public education are being explored and adopted in the nation's schools as individual districts search for improvement. Schools should be willing to learn from one another. Abandoning over two centuries of American public education in favor of privatization would at best help only a select few, who would still then live in a society where the majority of students would remain in increasingly underfunded public classrooms.

NOTE

The author wishes to thank George Moss, Timothy Killikelly, Deborah Goldsmith, and Laura Walsh for their comments and suggestions on earlier drafts of this chapter. Special thanks goes to John Whitehead for his invitation to contribute to this volume and his patience and understanding as an editor.

REFERENCES

Britt, Barato. 2000. "Parents, Community Leaders Take School Choice Advocacy to Statehouse: BAEO Joins Local Movement for Increased Options." *Indianapolis Recorder,* December 1.

Cordell, Dorman E. 1998. "Answering Objections to School Vouchers in D.C." Brief Analysis 266,

National Center for Policy Analysis, Washington, D.C., available at www.ncpa.org/ba/ba266.html.

Fuller, Howard. 2000. "The Continuing Struggle of African Americans for the Power to Make Real Educational Choices." Presented at the Second Annual Symposium on Educational Options for African Americans, March 2–5, available at http://edreform.com/school_choice/Fuller_choice.htm.

Joint Center for Political and Economic Studies. 1996. Study on school vouchers, at www.joint center.org/databank/NOP/NOP_1996/VOUCHERS7.htm.

———. 1998. Study on school vouchers, available at www.jointcenter.org/selpaper/pdffiles/educ98/04tbl_ed.pdg.

Howell, William G., Patrick J. Wolf, Paul E. Peterson, and David E. Campbell. 2000. "Test-Score Effects of School Vouchers in Dayton, Ohio, New York City, and Washington, D.C.: Evidence from Randomized Field Trials." Prepared for the annual meeting of the American Political Science Association, September, Washington, D.C., available at www.ksg.harvard.edu/pepg/dnw00r.pdf.

Kaminer, Wendy. 1997. "The Hidden Agenda of School Vouchers." November 13, available at www.speakout.com/Content/ICArticle/4920.

Kunjufu, Jawanza. 1992. *Countering the Conspiracy to Destroy Black Boys.* Vol. 2. Chicago: African American Images.

Peterson, Bob, and Barbara Miner. 2000. "Vouchers, the Right, and the Race Card." In *Civil Rights since 1787,* ed. Jonathan Birnbaum and Clarence Taylor. New York: New York University Press.

Visnik, Ben. 1993. "The Voucher Initiative/Proposition 174 and Privitization . . . Why in 1993 . . . ? Why in California . . . ?" Statement as president of Oakland Education Association and State Council Delegate to the California Teachers Association, September 13.

Wells, Amy Stuart. 1993. "The Sociology of School Choice." In *School Choice: Examining the Evidence,* ed. Edith Rasell and Richard Rothstein. Washington, D.C.: Economic Policy Institute.

Whitaker, Charles. 1991. "Do Black Males Need Special Schools?" *Ebony*, March.

Williams, Samuel, Jr. 2000. "Minorities Have Much to Learn about Prop. 38." *Los Angeles Sentinel*, November 1.

33

The Black Youth Employment
Problem Revisited
MICHAEL A. STOLL

This chapter examines the massive and persistent racial gap in employment among youth in the 1990s. It examines whether the 1990s economic boom led to a reduction in this racial gap in employment, and it offers the major explanations for the gap as well as potential policy responses to help solve this problem. The findings include that the economic boom over the 1990s did little, on most accounts, to significantly reduce the racial gap in employment, especially among young men. This chapter concludes by suggesting that policies that directly target the unique labor market problems of black youth must be pursued to close the racial gap in employment.

Since the 1960s, a massive racial gap has existed in employment among young people. Over this period, scholars of labor market trends have shown that black youths' employment rates have been persistently and significantly lower than those of their white counterparts. The consequences of these employment problems for black youth are not trivial. The lack of regular employment prevents their attaining consistent income and limits their accumulation of work experience and job contacts that are necessary for securing future labor market opportunities. Indeed, many researchers have shown that youth who are unable to gain steady employment and develop on-the-job skills through work experience are more likely to experience relatively lower wages and higher unemployment as they age in the labor market.[1]

In the 1970s and 1980s, academics and policymakers alike gave a great deal of attention to this black youth employment crisis. During this period, academics wrote a number of widely cited books and articles addressing the nature, scope, causes, and potential remedies of this problem. Furthermore, policymakers began to implement a number of programs—including Job Corps and the Youth Employment and Demonstration Project Act of 1977—designed to address the youth employment problem generally and the black youth employment crises indirectly. Unfortunately, these efforts were met with mixed-to-limited success, and the attention given by policymakers to addressing this problem was relatively short-lived. The consequence has thus been an enduring racial inequality in the youth labor market.

In this chapter, we revisit the black youth employment problem, paying special attention to its scope over the 1990s. In particular, we seek to understand whether the economic boom over the latter half of 1990s, which pushed overall unemployment rates in the United States to their lowest levels since the 1960s, extended employment benefits to African American youth and helped close the racial youth employment gap. We also explore and evaluate current explanations of black youth's poor employment outcomes. Finally, we consider relevant policies to reduce this problem.

THE EVIDENCE

The employment rates of young people have always been lower than those of adults. The reasons for this are multiple. First, young people are much more likely to be enrolled in school and are more likely to be searching for their occupational niche; therefore, they are more likely to move in and out of jobs. In addition, employers prefer to hire adults, meaning that young people are often competed out of many jobs. Although there is some worry over youth employment in general, the focus of concern in this chapter is that, within the youth population itself, there is a large racial gap in employment. What is the magnitude of this gap?

In figures 33.1 and 33.2, we present evidence on the employment:population ratios (or employment rates) of young men and women between the ages of sixteen and twenty-four.[2] Employment:population ratios measure the fraction of the relevant youth population that is employed; thus, this measure includes those young people that are in and out of the *labor force,* defined as the employed and unemployed—with the latter being those actively searching for work but not working. We present this measure rather than the unemployment rate, which is calculated as the fraction of the labor force that is unemployed, since for youth there is little difference between being unemployed and out of the labor force.[3]

Figures 33.1 and 33.2 show these employment rates for young men in and out of school, respectively. Two clear patterns are apparent in these figures. First, for in- and out-of-school young men alike, there is a large and persistent racial gap in employment throughout the 1980s and 1990s, though overall employment rates are higher for out-of-school young men than they are for those in school. These gaps range from 20 percentage points to nearly 25 percentage points. The employment rates are lower for in-school youth in part because of the obvious reason that most of their time is devoted to school activities.[4]

Second, the employment rate of young black men is much more sensitive to business-cycle fluctuations than that of young white men, as has been shown elsewhere and is consistent with the "last hired, first fired" syndrome.[5] That is, young

black men are last to be hired during an upswing in the economy but are first to be let go during a downswing, a trend that occurred in the early 1990s. For both in- and out-of-school youth, young black men's employment was hit harder by the early-1990s recession and, in the case of in-school youth, responded more dramatically to the late-1990s economic boom. But their employment took much more time to reach its cyclical peak than that of young white men. Still, at the end of the boom economy in 2000, the racial gap in employment remained and, in the case of out-of-school youth, was as large as that seen over the past fifteen years.[6]

Figures 33.3 and 33.4 show the employment rates for young women in and out of school, respectively. A careful glance at these figures reveals that the patterns for young women are slightly different than those for young men. Like young men, a persistent and large racial gap in employment exists for young women through the 1980s and 1990s, ranging from 10 percentage points to 20 percentage points. Moreover, young black women's employment is also much more sensitive to business fluctuations than that of young white women. But unlike what happened for young men, the economic boom over the late 1990s closed much of the racial employment gap for young out-of-school women. Whether welfare reform policies of 1996 help explain these trends is an open question, as is whether the racial gap in employment has continued, and will continue, to close for these women through and after the recession of 2001.

In short, by the end of 2000, a massive and persistent racial employment gap among youth remained, despite the recent ending of the longest peacetime growth in our economy since the 1960s. Furthermore, this gap remained larger for young men than it did for young women. Still, it is fairly clear from these data that African American youth continue to experience disproportionate employment difficulties. It is unlikely that another economic expansion as long, deep, and significant as the one we just experienced over the 1990s will occur in the near future. It is safe to say, then, that without direct policy intervention, this racial gap in employment is likely to remain an intractable and permanent feature of American economic and social life. But before we analyze

Figure 33.1   Employment:population ratios, males aged sixteen to twenty-four, in school.

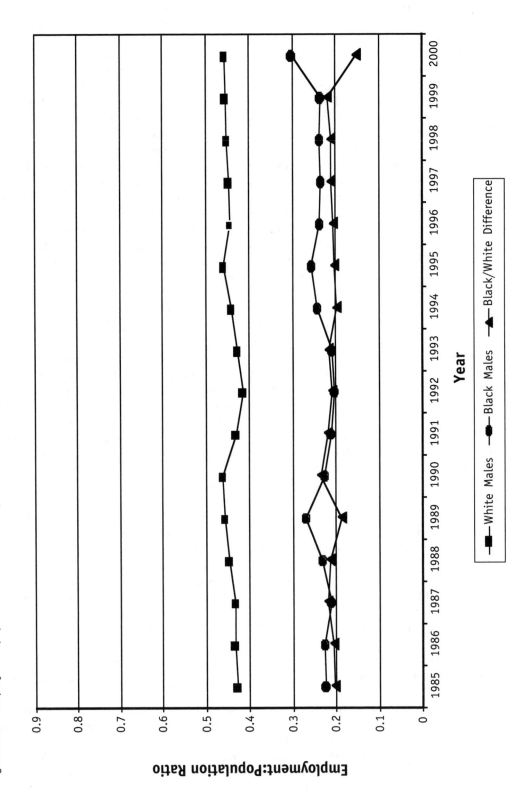

Figure 33.2   Employment:population ratios, males aged sixteen to twenty-four, out of school.

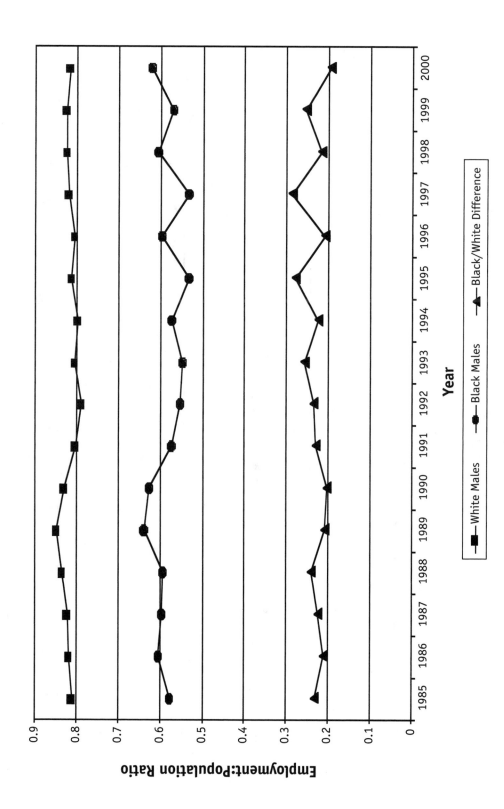

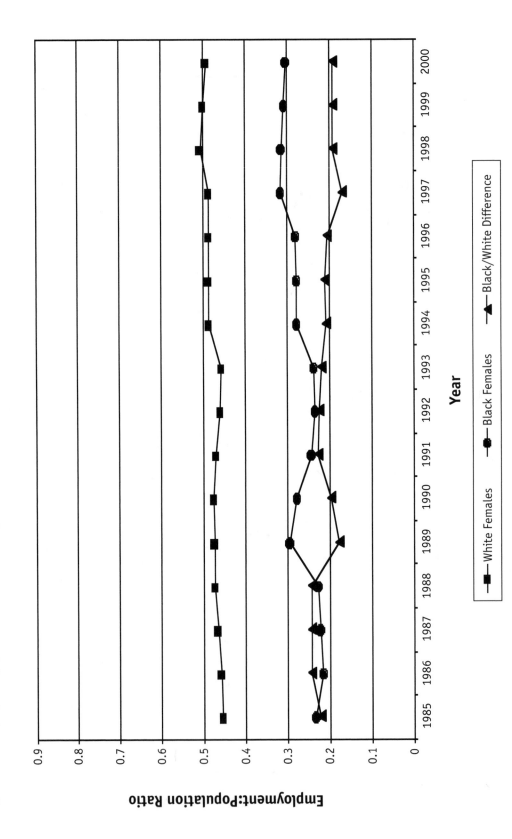

Figure 33.3   Employment:population ratios, females aged sixteen to twenty-four, in school.

Figure 33.4   Employment:population ratios, females aged sixteen to twenty-four, out of school.

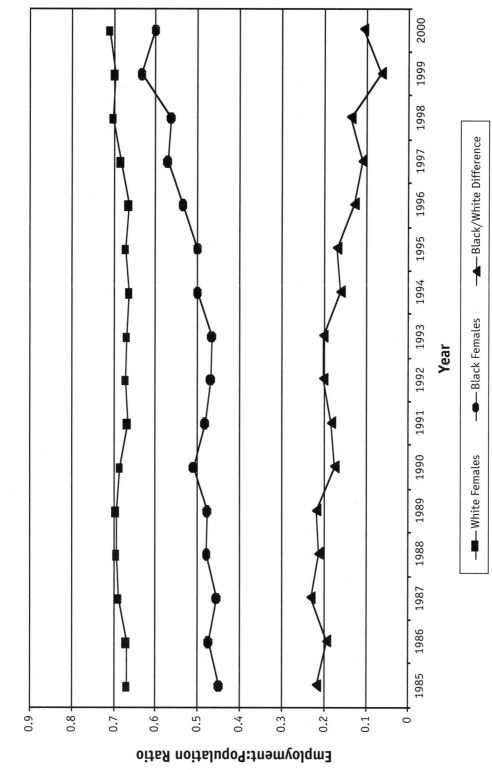

White Females — Black Females — Black/White Difference

relevant policies to address this black youth employment problem, it is first important to provide an overview of the major explanations for it.

THE EXPLANATIONS

A number of explanations of black youths' employment problems have been offered and studied. These can be most conveniently organized into supply- and demand-side explanations. Supply-side explanations refer to the characteristics, behaviors, and choices of the youth themselves, whereas demand-side explanations include the characteristics, behaviors, and choices of employers who hire youth into jobs.

The most prominent supply-side explanations of black youth employment problems include skills mismatch, reservation wage, cultural or urban underclass behavior, crime, and (in the case of women) government dependency. The skills mismatch hypothesis holds that the skill requirements of jobs are rising faster than black youths' acquisition of skills through education, training, and work experience. Thus, a persistent skills gap between job skill requirements and black youths' human capital prevents many of them from qualifying for most jobs. However, the reservation wage argument posits that many black youth have a higher reservation wage (or the lowest wage for which an individual is willing to work) than that of other similar youth and thus price themselves out of many jobs. This hypothesis suggests that black youths' employment problems stem from the fact that black youth are unwilling to take the same low-pay jobs that other youth are willing to accept.

The final supply-side explanations are somewhat related. The cultural or urban underclass hypothesis argues that black youth are more likely than other youth to exhibit qualities that are unattractive to employers. These include low motivation and aspirations as well as "ghetto" styles of dress, presentation, and language.[7] These kinds of behaviors are argued to be products of living in neighborhoods that are characterized by extreme poverty and racial concentration, ones typically isolated from "mainstream" society. Black youth are more likely than other youth to live and grow up in such neighborhoods; thus, these behaviors are reinforced through contact with neighborhood peers.

These same neighborhood effects are argued to extend to criminality and welfare dependence among black youth. Some suggest that these same neighborhoods have high concentrations of criminal activity, such as petty drug dealing, that serve as employment alternatives to the formal labor market, especially for young black men. Finally, others argue that these neighborhoods have high concentrations of welfare use, so much so that such use is seen as the norm and thus influences young women's decisions to choose welfare over work—that is, until welfare reform in 1996.[8]

On the demand-side, prominent explanations of black youth's employment problems include racial discrimination, spatial mismatch, aggregate demand, and job competition hypotheses. The racial discrimination argument holds that employers discriminate against young blacks in hiring either through statistical discrimination or racial animus. Statistical discrimination refers to employers' use of real or perceived information about groups when making hiring or recruiting decisions among individuals. If, for example, employers view young blacks as less-desirable workers for any number of reasons—including employer perceptions that they are untrustworthy, unmotivated, and so on—they may be reluctant to hire any black youth applicants. This is particularly true if employers cannot access full information about this youth, despite the fact that he or she might be the most qualified. Or, they may use recruitment methods that bias the applicant pool toward nonblacks.

The spatial mismatch hypothesis refers to the idea that blacks are physically distant from the locus of employment opportunities because of the continuing suburbanization of jobs and the persistent racial segregation of blacks in the central city as a result of housing market discrimination. The consequence is that young blacks have difficulty attaining employment in suburbs, where the majority of low-skill jobs are locating. These location-specific jobs impose significant disadvantages on black youth. For one, inner-city blacks have limited information about these jobs. In addition, blacks cannot travel to these jobs easily, especially if they have to do so by public transit, which a disproportionate share of black youth use to travel.[9] Of course, employers could be locating to suburbs to distance themselves from blacks, whom they may deem as less-favorable workers.

The final demand-side explanations are closely linked. The aggregate demand hypothesis posits that black youth employability is much more sensitive to the strength of the overall economy than that of other groups, as we saw in the data presented in the figures. The reason is that black youth, in the eyes of the employer, may be a least preferred group of workers. If this is true, then black youth are likely to be hired only when there is tightening in labor markets, which occurs when the economy is in a boom cycle and when there are fewer workers available for employment. Similarly, the job competition hypothesis holds that there are other demographic groups, in particular women and immigrants, who compete with black youth for employment and whom employers prefer. In this scenario, black youth are pushed further down the hiring queue as a consequence of these labor substitutes and employer preferences.[10]

A careful review and evaluation of the mountainous research on the black youth employment crisis published over the last decade or so reveals that, on balance, demand-side factors appear to be relatively more important explanations than supply-side explanations are. Audit studies, or studies using equally qualified and trained pairs of black youth and white youth posing as applicants for the same jobs, show convincing evidence that black youth are treated less favorably and hired less frequently than their equally qualified white counterparts are.[11] But they cannot show whether the source of this discrimination is from employer racial animus or statistical discrimination. Other studies using employer interviews show that employers statistically discriminate against black youth in part on the basis of residential location and that they consciously use employee recruitment methods that yield few blacks.[12] Moreover, a convincing body of work has recently been produced showing that spatial mismatch is a significant factor of black youths' employment problems.[13] However, there is less-convincing evidence on the influence of aggregate demand on black youths' employment, especially for young black men, and even less evidence on job competition.[14]

Still, some supply-side considerations do matter. Job skill requirements continue to rise quite rapidly in the modern economy, and despite the fact that young blacks have substantially increased their high school completion rates over the 1970s and 1980s (to the point where they are now in near parity with those of whites), their college enrollment rates still lag well behind, especially for young men.[15] Furthermore, the rapid rise in the incarceration rates of young black men over the 1990s suggests that a large fraction of civilian young black men in the labor force in the present and near future will be ex-offenders, whom employers seem leery of hiring for a variety of reasons, a few of which having nothing to do with race.[16] But the jury is still out on whether neighborhood effects influence black youths' employment, and convincing evidence demonstrates that black youths' reservation wages are no different than those of similar white youth.[17]

THE POLICY RESPONSE

In an ideal world, policies that are designed and implemented to solve a particular problem should address the major causes of the problem; otherwise, they are unlikely to be effective. Given this and our evaluation of the evidence, policies that are likely to be most effective in addressing the black youth employment crisis include those that address the demand-side of the labor market. What might these policies be?

First, the evidence on discrimination against black youth suggests that antidiscrimination efforts in labor markets must be enforced vigorously to improve black youths' employment opportunities. Currently, the Office of Federal Contract Compliance and Equal Employment Opportunity Commission are charged with monitoring discrimination in the workplace, but they usually and by law target their efforts toward bigger firms.[18] It is likely that black youth come into contact more with small firms; thus, these antidiscrimination efforts must begin to target smaller employers.

Second, policies should be tailored to close the spatial divide between black youth and jobs. To accomplish this, policies that enhance blacks' residential and transit mobility should be pursued. These could include antidiscrimination efforts in housing markets, development of low-income housing in the suburbs, and moving assistance—all of which would allow blacks to have geographic flexibility in housing choices. Programs to enhance transit possibilities would be effective in raising black youths' employment as well. These could include policies that lead to effective public transit, provide public transit subsidies, expand van pools, and improve car access. At the same time, bringing jobs to where black youth live would have the same effect.[19] In particular, a subsidized job creation program targeting black youth would be especially effective. In fact, the Youth Demonstration Act of 1977 included publicly subsidized employment for youth, and its programs were successful in eliminating employment differences between the young whites and blacks who participated.[20]

Aggregate demand policies, such as those that pursue full employment, are likely to raise black youths' employment but are not likely to close the racial employment gap. Consider, for example, demand-side expansionary policies that increase government spending or those that increase the monetary supply to reduce interest rates. These policies, *ceteris paribus,* are likely to create new jobs in the macroeconomy but are not likely to have the required impact on black youth employment to significantly close the black–white youth employment gap. This is true since such demand-side policies may not stimulate investment or increase demand in economically distressed communities, where many black youth live. However, they may not disproportionately help black youths' employment since, for example, such efforts may not stimulate investment or increase demand in economically distressed communities, where many black youth live.

Finally, on the supply-side, policies that continue to foster black youths' skills are likely to enhance their employment opportunities as well. Thus, policies that improve the quality of schools that black youth attend, lower their high school dropout rates, and raise their college enrollment rates are likely to have positive effects. So too would increasing their participation in effective employment and training programs, particularly those that are school-to-work based. However, the latter programs must guard against the practice of *tracking,* in which potential college-bound black youth are tracked into training programs for noncollege jobs.

All of this suggests that to raise the employment of black youth and to eliminate the racial employment gap among young people, polices must be developed that target black youth. This strategy would allow policymakers to design programs that directly address the complex factors that uniquely affect black youths' employment. But in this era of challenges to affirmative action and to race-specific policies in general, some would argue that such a targeting strategy might not receive the political support it needs to work. These concerns, however, are likely to be tempered since these targeting efforts are aimed at enhancing participation in an activity about which Americans seem to care a great deal—namely, work.

CONCLUSION

Even by the year 2000, the racial gap in employment among young people still remained and in some instances remained as large as that observed in the 1970s and 1980s. More disturbing is the fact that in the 1990s, the longest and most significant period of economic growth that occurred in over thirty years did little, on most accounts, to significantly reduce this gap, especially among young men. The consequence is that black youth continue to suffer disproportionate employment difficulties. This suggests that without direct policy intervention that targets the unique set of factors that contribute to black youths' employment problems, racial inequality in youth labor markets is likely to endure. Policies most likely to address this problem correctly include those that target the demand-side of the labor market, especially those that address racial discrimination and spatial mismatch. Supply-side policies that foster black youths' skill acquisition will be effective as well.

NOTES

1. Paul Osterman, *Getting Started: The Youth Labor Market* (Cambridge, Mass.: MIT Press, 1980).

2. The data for all figures shown in this chapter come from the U.S. Bureau of Labor Statistics, *Employment and Earnings*, vols. 33–48 (Washington, D.C.: U.S. Department of Labor).

3. Kim Clark and Lawrence Summers, "The Dynamics of Youth Unemployment," in *The Youth Labor Market Problem: Its Nature, Causes, and Consequences*, ed. Richard Freeman and David Wise (Chicago: University of Chicago Press, 1982).

4. Some would argue that the racial gap in employment for in-school youth is a less-important concern since schooling is and should be the major activity for these youth. In this view, the lower employment rates for in-school black youth as compared to that of in-school white youth would be seen as an even less concern if in fact they reflect increasing investments in schooling by black youth. There is, however, no analysis of which we are aware that addresses these claims.

5. Harry J. Holzer and Paul Offner, "Trends in Employment Outcomes of Young Black Men, 1979–2000," paper prepared for the Extended Opportunities Project, 2001. Richard Freeman and William M. Rodgers III, "Area Economic Conditions and the Labor Market Outcomes of Young Men in the 1990's Expansion," in *Prosperity for All? The Economic Boom and African Americans*, ed. Robert Cherry and William M. Rodgers III (New York: Russell Sage Foundation, 2000), 50–87.

6. It is important to remember that over the 1990s the incarceration rates of young black men rose dramatically. Those who are incarcerated are also likely to be those who experience employment difficulties; but they do not appear in the data presented here. If they did, the trends in employment of young black men would appear much worse than that shown here (see Bruce Western and Becky Pettit, "Incarceration and Racial Inequality in Men's Employment," *Industrial and Labor Relations Review* 54, no. 1 (2000): 3–16.

7. Linda Datcher-Loury and Glenn Loury, "The Effects of Attitudes and Aspirations on the Labor Supply of Young Men," in *The Black Youth Employment Crisis*, ed. Richard Freeman and Harry J. Holzer (Chicago: University of Chicago Press, 1986), 377–402.

8. For more on these arguments, see William J. Wilson, *The Truly Disadvantaged: The Inner City,* the Underclass, and Public Policy (Chicago: University of Chicago Press, 1987).

9. Harry J. Holzer, Keith R. Ihlanfeldt, and David L. Sjoquist, "Work, Search, and Travel among White and Black Youth," *Journal of Urban Economics* 35 (1994): 320–345.

10. Elijah Anderson, "Some Observations on Black Youth Unemployment," in *Youth Employment and Public Policy*, ed. Bernard Anderson and Isabel Sawhill (Englewood Cliffs, N.J.: Prentice-Hall, 1980), 37–46. Robert Cherry, "Black Youth Employment Problems," in *The Imperiled Economy*, ed. Robert Cherry et al. (New York: Union for Radical Political Economics, 1988), 2:121–132.

11. Marc Bendick Jr., Charles W. Jackson, and Victor A. Reinoso, "Measuring Employment Discrimination through Controlled Experiments," *Review of Black Political Economy* 23 (1994): 25–48. Jerome Culp and Bruce Dunson, "Brothers of a Different Color: A Preliminary Look at Employment Treatment of White and Black Youth," in *The Black Youth Employment Crisis*, ed. Richard Freeman and Harry J. Holzer (Chicago: University of Chicago Press, 1986), 233–260. Michael Fix and Raymond J. Struyk, *Clear and Convincing Evidence: Measurement of Discrimination in America* (Washington, D.C.: Urban Institute Press, 1993).

12. Joleen Kirshenman and Kathryn M. Neckerman, "'We'd Love to Hire Them, But ...': The Meaning of Race for Employers," in *The Urban Underclass*, ed. Christopher Jencks and Paul E. Peterson (Washington, D.C.: Brookings Institution, 1991), 203–232. Kathryn M. Neckerman and Joleen Kirshenman, "Hiring Strategies, Racial Bias, and Inner-City Workers," *Social Problems* 38, no. 4 (1991): 801–815.

13. Michael A. Stoll, Harry J. Holzer, and Keith R. Ihlanfeldt, "Within Cities and Suburbs: Racial Residential Concentration and the Distribution of Employment Opportunities across Sub-metropolitan Areas," *Journal of Policy Analysis and Management* 19, no. 2 (2000): 207–231. Michael A. Stoll, "Spatial Mismatch, Discrimination, and Male Youth Employment in the Washington, DC, Area: Implications for Residential Mobility Policies," *Journal of Policy Analysis and Management* 18, no. 1 (1999): 77–98. Keith R. Ihlanfeldt and David L. Sjoquist, "Job Accessibility and Racial Differences in Youth Employment Rates," *American Economic Review* 80, no. 1 (1990): 267–276. Harry J. Holzer, Keith R. Ihlanfeldt, and David L. Sjoquist, "Work, Search, and Travel among White and Black Youth," *Journal of*

Urban Economics 35 (1994): 320–345. Katherine M. O'Regan and John M. Quigley, "Labor Market Access and Labor Market Outcomes for Urban Youth," *Regional Science and Urban Economics* 21 (1991): 277–293.

14. Harry J. Holzer and Paul Offner, "Trends in Employment Outcomes of Young Black Men, 1979–2000," paper prepared for the Extended Opportunities Project, 2001. Krisin Butcher, "An Investigation of the Effect of Immigration on the Labor-Market Outcomes of African Americans: Help or Hindrance?" in *The Economic Implications of Immigration for African Americans*, ed. Daniel S. Hamermesh and Frank D. Bean (New York: Russell Sage Foundation, 1998), 149–182.

15. John D. Kasarda, "Urban Change and Minority Opportunities," in *The New Urban Reality*, ed. Paul E. Peterson (Washington, D.C.: Brookings Institution, 1985), 33–67. John D. Kasarda, "Jobs, Migration, and Emerging Urban Mismatches," in *Urban Change and Poverty*, ed. Michael G. H. McGeary and Lawrence E. Lynn (Washington, D.C.: National Academy Press, 1988). Reynolds Farley, "Demographic, Economic, and Social Trends in a Multicultural America," in *New Directions: African Americans in a Diversifying Nation*, ed. James S. Jackson (Washington, D.C.: National Policy Association, 2000), 11–44.

16. Harry J. Holzer, Steven Raphael, and Michael A. Stoll, "Will Employers Hire Ex-offenders? Employer Preferences, Background Checks, and Their Determinants," in *The Impact of Incarceration on Families and Communities*, ed. Mary Patillo, David Weiman, and Bruce Western (New York: Russell Sage Foundation, 2002).

17. Harry J. Holzer, "Reservation Wages and Their Labor Market Effects for Black and White Male Youth," *Journal of Human Resources* 21, no. 2 (1986): 157–177.

18. Harry J. Holzer, "Employer Hiring Decisions and Antidiscrimination Policy," in *Generating Jobs: How to Increase Demand for Less-Skilled Workers*, ed. Richard B. Freeman and Peter Gottschalk (New York: Russell Sage Foundation, 1998).

19. Helen Ladd, "Spatially Targeted Economic Development Strategies: Do They Work?" *Cityscape: A Journal of Policy Development and Research* 1, no. 1 (1994): 193–218.

20. Michael A. Stoll, *Race, Space, and Youth Labor Markets* (New York: Garland Publishing, 1999).

34

Employment and Training Solutions for the Economically Disadvantaged

BERNARD E. ANDERSON

For several decades, U.S. public policymakers have struggled over ways to improve the employability and standard of living of the urban poor. This chapter examines key social science research on the effectiveness of past programs aimed at increasing the employment and training of economically disadvantaged urban groups. The findings of this research support continued investment in employment and training programs as well as experimentation with people-based programs designed to address the needs of specific target groups. Also encouraged is the need to combat urban poverty through linking job-training programs with job creation and economic growth initiatives.

For more than thirty years, national policymakers have grappled with the problem of urban poverty but thus far have not found a fully satisfactory solution. The quest for ways to improve the income of the least fortunate among urban dwellers is a vexing task that will continue to challenge the capacity of social and behavioral scientists. In searching for remedies to improve the economic status of the urban poor, it is necessary to begin with a clear understanding of the cause of the barriers to the urban poor's participation in the economy. The search is not made easier by use of the term *urban underclass,* and I refuse to use it. *Underclass* implies that some people are poor because of their attitudes, values, and behavior. It further implies that poverty is imbedded in the folkways and mores of a cultural lifestyle.

Rather than accept such a view of the problem, it is important that one recognize how urban poverty is grounded in the limited economic opportunities available to the economically disadvantaged urban population. The attitudes, values, and behavior that might seem endemic to the ur-

ban poor reflect the inevitable adaptation to blocked opportunities that characterize the lives of many who live in low-income urban areas.

As Daniel Patrick Moynihan said some years ago while serving as the White House domestic policy adviser for president Richard M. Nixon, "the reason people are poor is that they don't have money." Urban poverty has little to do with values, attitudes, and behavior. The urban poor would like to be income maximizers as described in economic theory, but many factors conspire to block their opportunity to achieve that goal.

THE STRATEGY: LABOR MARKET SOLUTIONS

An important and indispensable requirement for improving the economic status of the urban poor is to increase the quality and quantity of their participation in the labor market. Increased labor market participation will generate increased income and contribute to an improvement in the standard of living of the economically disadvantaged.

Over the past quarter-century, many efforts have been made to improve the labor market experience of the economically disadvantaged in urban areas. Most efforts were initiated and funded by the federal government, but other institutions played an important role as well. For instance, credit must be given to private foundations such as the Ford, Rockefeller, and MacArthur foundations, each of which has funded important demonstration projects aimed at finding solutions to the problems of urban poverty. The Carnegie Corporation and the Edna McConnell Clark, Mott, and William Penn foundations also played an important role in providing seed money to test the effectiveness of promising interventions designed to address the problem. Virtually no stone has been left unturned in the search for innovative and creative ways to improve the economic status of the urban poor. But as is evident in most urban areas throughout the nation, progress has been slow, and success has been limited in finding effective ways to improve the income of the economically disadvantaged.

KEY STRATEGIES

In pursuing the employment and training option, the strategy has been to target resources toward services for specific groups. The major programs fall into four groups:

1. *Employability development for youth,* which includes the summer youth employment programs and out-of-school youth programs. In-school programs should be classified under education initiatives rather than employment and training.
2. *Adult training programs aimed at young adults,* many of whom have limited work experience.
3. *Welfare-to-work programs,* efforts that include workfare and initiatives aimed at job training and transition to work.
4. *Direct job creation.*

At various times these categorical program strategies played a major role as weapons in the arsenal of the federal government that aimed at increasing the employment and at raising the income of the economically disadvantaged. But although other employment and training programs, especially the dislocated worker initiatives, served as important devices for improving the labor market conditions facing workers, they were not designed to address the problem of urban poverty.

IMPACT OF EMPLOYMENT AND TRAINING

The central policy question that should be raised concerning employment and training programs and the urban poor is, What impact have these efforts had in helping to expand economic opportunity for the economically disadvantaged? Does the experience with such programs justify continued investment in them? Indeed, should the investment in employment and training be increased, perhaps at the expense of support for other strategies, to improve the income of the urban poor? The answers to these questions can be gleaned from the results of the voluminous social science research on the impact of employment and training programs. Several research summaries on this issue were prepared over the past two decades.

The first was prepared by a labor market research group at the Wharton School, University of Pennsylvania, in the late 1970s.[1] The review assessed the research on the impact of government "manpower" programs from their initiation during the War on Poverty in the mid-1960s to 1974, the year in which federal policy shifted from categorical program funding to the Comprehensive Employment and Training Act. This act reduced the role of the U.S. Department of Labor in designing program strategies and greatly increased the role of state and local government in determining how federal funds would be used.

More recent summaries of the research literature on employment and training programs include the National Research Council study of youth employment programs[2] and the U.S. Department of Labor study of employment and training economic impacts.[3] Finally, much of what we know about the impact of this strategy in recent years is based on the national Job Training Partnership Act study conducted by Abt Associates and the Manpower Demonstration Research Corporation under contract to the Department of Labor.[4]

The research summaries cover more than one hundred studies of categorical programs, demonstration projects, and pilot programs funded by private foundations and by federal, state, and local governments. Collectively, the social science evidence contained in these studies tell us what is working and what is not in producing an economic impact on the income status of the economically disadvantaged population in urban areas. In contrast to the oft-repeated claim that nothing works, the social science evidence tells us a great deal about the opportunities and the limitations of the employment and training solution to the problem of urban poverty.

LESSONS FROM THE RESEARCH

Four key lessons can be drawn from the social science research.

Lesson 1. Small but important victories are possible from the employment and training strategy. The net impacts for men and women are modestly positive, and employment and training programs pay for themselves in terms of increased earnings for the two adult groups. But the results for out-of-school youth are disappointing. There is little evidence that such youth, most of whom are economically disadvantaged, are better off from participating in the Job Training Partnership Act program than they would be in the absence of such participation. Similar modest or even negative income results were found among youth who participated in the Manpower Demonstration Research Corporation's Supported Work and JobStart demonstration studies. None of the training programs designed and implemented thus far show statistically significant, positive results in improving the earnings of disadvantaged youth.

Studies of state work–welfare programs for women on Aid to Families with Dependent Children in the early 1980s found statistically significant, positive impacts that ranged up to $1,000 per year in the first two years of the program.

These findings are similar to those observed in the Supported Work demonstration project, but the Supported Work costs per participant were much higher.

Lesson 2. The replication of successful intervention models is quite difficult; as a result, replication is rarely achieved. For example, one of the most successful programs identified in the national search for effective models is the Center for Employment and Training (CET) in San Jose, California. CET serves a predominantly Hispanic population, many of whom have limited English-speaking proficiency; but CET has shown the capacity to provide skills training in a variety of occupational fields while improving participants' basic communication and computation skills. The program's job placement rate remains consistently high, and former participants have a high rate of job retention.

Still, it has been difficult to replicate the successful CET experience in other communities on the West Coast, much less other regions of the country. Is the reason that the vibrant Silicon Valley labor market is unique? Are there other locational factors that limit the replicability of a successful model? Experience has shown that many successful community-based job-training programs are sui generis; it is not easy to identify the key factors that contribute to their success. For that reason, the knowledge learned in one place seems limited in its application elsewhere.

Lesson 3. Public job creation is indispensable to success, especially for out-of-school youth. Even successful job-training programs rarely live up to all the expectations placed on them. Training programs alone cannot lift disadvantaged participants entirely out of poverty. For some groups, direct job creation might be necessary. Support for this conclusion can be found in the experience of minority group youth during the summer of 1978. At that time, the federal government supported a range of youth employment programs, including some funded under the Public Service Employment program, which was expanded to more than five hundred thousand jobs in 1977. Through a variety of grants made to state and local governments and to nonprofit community-based organizations, nearly 80 percent of all minority group youth who were employed during the summer of 1978 held publicly subsidized jobs.

The policy that was designed to saturate selected low-income communities with public jobs for disadvantaged youth paid off, as reflected by the significant increase in the employment:population ratio for minority youth. But the program was only temporary: when funding was cut at the end of the summer, the minority youth employment rate reverted to its previous low level.

Lesson 4. The market will not solve the problem. A conclusion that logically follows lesson 3 is that public policy intervention is indispensable to success in addressing the economic problems of the urban poor. No automatic market adjustment to reduced operating costs, low-cost labor from inner-city communities, or other neoclassical economic nostrums will stir the backwaters of depressed urban areas, where large numbers of the economically disadvantaged jobless reside.

Publicly funded economic incentives are vital to the process of community economic development through which locally based, private-sector jobs might be created. The employment requirements of welfare reform, combined with the persistent long-term joblessness of economically disadvantaged youth, have produced a formidable job creation challenge in the cities. In Philadelphia alone, city officials expect a shortfall of thirty-five thousand jobs below what is required to meet the welfare-reform job-placement goal during the next two years. A variety of public initiatives, including empowerment zones and enterprise communities, are necessary to stimulate job creation aimed at increasing the income of the urban poor. Market forces alone will not do the job.

CONCLUSION

The persistence of urban poverty and the presence of economically disadvantaged families in our cities is a continuing challenge to national aspirations for equal opportunity and economic justice. What is unacceptable is a continuing bifurcation of society between those who enjoy an increasing share of economic prosperity and others who are stuck on the lowest rung of the economic ladder. The search must continue for ways to improve the productivity and earning power of those who need assistance in getting a foothold on the escalator to a middle-income standard of living.

Employment and training programs remain one of the options necessary to achieve such a goal. While past programs have not been a panacea, they have contributed to a modest improvement in income among many who participated in them. In the choice of weapons required to combat urban poverty, employment and training programs should be part of the arsenal. The experience of the past, while limited, justifies continued investment in the employment and training option and the continued experimentation with programs to address the needs of specific target groups. Only by testing new and increasingly comprehensive training models will we find the right mix to accelerate the decline of urban poverty. To achieve success in reducing urban poverty, we must maintain steady, balanced economic growth and persist in the experimentation of job-training models.

NOTES

This chapter originally appeared as Bernard E. Anderson's "Employment and Training Solutions for the Economically Disadvantaged," in *Leading Issues in Black Political Economy*, ed. Thomas D. Boston (New Brunswick, N.J.: Transaction Publishers, 2002), 75–80.

1. Charles R. Perry, Bernard E. Anderson, Herbert R. Northrop, and Richard L. Rowan, *The Impact of Government Manpower Programs: In General and for Minorities and Women* (Philadelphia: University of Pennsylvania Press, 1975).

2. Charles Betsey, Robinson Hollister, and Mary Papageorgius, *An Evaluation of Youth Employment Programs* (Washington, D.C.: National Research Council, 1985).

3. L'awrence Katz and Alan Krueger, *Youth Employment Programs: What Works and What's Not?* (Washington, D.C.: U.S. Department of Labor, 1994).

4. James J. Kemple, Fred Doolittle, and John W. Wallace, *The National JTPA Study* (New York: Manpower Demonstration Research Corporation, 1993).

35

Racism in U.S. Welfare Policy:
A Human Rights Issue
LINDA BURNHAM

Welfare policy in the United States has always been fraught with racism. Many scholars believe that our family and welfare policies are among the worst in the industrialized world because Americans are unwilling to support programs that they perceive—and are encouraged to perceive—as benefiting people of color. The so-called welfare reform of the late 1990s is no exception, as politicians manipulated racist images to bolster support for tearing down the meager family assistance programs we had, with consequences particularly dire for women, children, and communities of color. Activists working for better welfare programs in this country are increasingly demonstrating the extent to which current policies result in violations of the United Nations' Universal Declaration of Human Rights, though the effectiveness of this strategy is not yet clear.

The complex interplay of race and class in the United States ensures that certain areas of domestic policy are suffused and tainted with racial bias; that they bear the imprint of a racist past; that they are particularly prone to political manipulation to preserve racial privilege; and that they serve as touchstones for galvanizing key elements of a racist consensus. U.S. social welfare policy is one such area.

The 1996 passage of the Personal Responsibility and Work Opportunity Reconciliation Act (PRWORA), commonly known as welfare reform, underscored how deeply embedded racial bias and xenophobia are in U.S. domestic policy. Welfare reform does not affect all women or all racial groups equally; women of marginalized racial groups are disproportionately represented among those now receiving welfare. These women, with their families and communities, bear a disproportionate share of the burden of welfare reform's negative effects simply by virtue of their overrep-resentation on the rolls. Furthermore, among women receiving welfare, women of color bear the brunt of the racially discriminatory implementation of regulations and sanctions.

To more fully understand the particular vulnerability of women of color and communities of color to the negative effects of welfare reform requires an exploration of the dynamics of racism within welfare policy.

PREPARING THE GROUND

The strength of U.S. racism resides in the ability of the government to sustain and justify, in different historical periods, the economic, social, political, and cultural aspects of white privilege while proclaiming itself as the world's most advanced democracy. Central to racial subordination are the economic and political mechanisms that re-create racial economic disparities. Today's clear racial differentials in income, wealth, educational attainment, and health status are grounded in the government-sanctioned subordination of people of color. Contemporary welfare policy reaffirms and strengthens the dynamic polarization of racial privilege and disadvantage. The official stance of those who advocated welfare reform is that the legislation was neither motivated by racial considerations nor discriminatory in substance. This self-serving claim is not supported by the facts.

The decline in support for welfare assistance coincides with a darkening of the welfare rolls. As the historically higher proportion of white recipients fell and the proportion of African Americans and Latinas rose, the program became increasingly vulnerable to being cut back; to being used as a political cudgel by antitax, anti–big government conservatives; and to being wielded on behalf of white backlash and racial polarization (Williams 1997). Generations of right-wing ideologues evoked the image of the lazy, sexually irresponsible African American welfare cheats until that image was strong enough to shift public policy. The political conversation evolved from "unmarried Negro women who make a business of producing children . . . for the purpose of securing easy welfare money" (Allen 1961) to the "welfare queen" of the Reagan era, whose race was unspecified but universally understood.

Highly charged debates among social analysts and politicians during the 1980s about the so-called underclass prepared the way for welfare reform. The term *underclass* masquerades as race neutral, but from the beginning, concerns about the "underclass" were concerns about "ghetto poverty" and "inner-city poverty"—that is, black poverty. The widespread use of the word *underclass* continued a longstanding U.S. tradition of using class to talk about race, using race to talk about class, and thoroughly confusing the two. It also paved the way for the welfare reform debate in important ways. First, poverty was linked to racial identity, which in turn was connected by scholars with deviance and distance from the social values and sexual norms that supposedly are common in mainstream America. *Underclass* served as a summarizing term for black deviance, encompassing, at the least, criminality, promiscuity, irresponsibility, sloth, and dependence. This

directly relates to the way in which "underclass" theory anticipated the conceptual framework for welfare reform: poverty is regarded as a result of individual choices, behaviors, and failings—"personal responsibility"—not as a structural social dynamic resulting from an economic history and from economic institutions for which race has been very important.

The public conversation just before the passage of PRWORA was anchored in and dependent on the long, ignoble history of the radicalization of poverty and poverty policy. It was a conversation whose deep, historical roots created the basis for subtle forms of ideological dissembling, making possible the simultaneous evocation and denial of racist content and rendering a profoundly regressive policy palatable to a distressingly broad swath of the political spectrum. But, whether frankly evoked or not, the PRWORA is steeped in racist intent; is racially biased in its implementation; and, not surprisingly, has racially differentiated impacts.

IMPACT

It should come as no surprise that women of color and their communities disproportionately bear the burden of PRWORA's negative consequences. Data on welfare reform's impact are seldom disaggregated by race, so it is currently not possible to demonstrate statistically that PRWORA is deepening racial inequality on a national scale. However, a number of trends point toward such a conclusion.

Welfare reform is exacerbating vulnerabilities that were already racially marked. Even before the passage of PRWORA, women of color and their families were disproportionately represented among the homeless, among those who experience food insecurity and hunger, and among those receiving low wages and working in substandard conditions. Welfare reform has heightened women's exposure to each of these situations.

Homelessness. Widespread family homelessness rose steeply in the 1980s, as the value of the welfare grant and the minimum wage dropped, as low-wage work expanded, and as housing costs ballooned—all of which put shelter beyond the reach of many welfare recipients. Negligible in the 1970s, family homelessness climbed to 27 percent of the total homeless population in 1985 and on to an estimated 37 percent in 1999 (United States Conference of Mayors 1999). The majority of homeless families are composed of a single mother and her children.

Some communities of color experience homelessness at exceptionally high rates. African American women, for example, are massively overrepresented in the urban homeless population, constituting over 80 percent of homeless women with children in some cities; as well, Puerto Rican women are homeless in highly disproportionate numbers (Burt and Cohen 1989; Bassuk et al. 1996).

Immigrant female recipients are likely to experience severe overcrowding in their housing situations and are likely as well to devote a huge portion of their income to housing. Many share housing with relatives or unrelated adults; many live in garages or other makeshift, substandard dwellings; and many worry constantly about paying the rent.

There is increasing evidence that welfare reform has further jeopardized poor women's access to housing. The author of one recent study noted, "Young children are without homes in the largest numbers since the Great Depression. Welfare reform has made things much worse. Shelters are overflowing and gridlocked" (Griffin 1999, 4A). A social service worker in a Salvation Army shelter in New Orleans observed, "When I started here three years ago, we had plenty of family space. Since welfare reform, I don't have a bed" (Cobb 1999, 1).

A few studies are beginning to confirm the anecdotal evidence of what happens when families hit the two-year time limit or are removed from the rolls for noncompliance with work requirements. A survey conducted by social service agencies in six states found that 8 percent of the single parents who had stopped getting welfare in the previous six months had to turn to homeless shelters to house their families (Sherman et al. 1998). Of former recipients in Illinois who were not working, 7 percent became homeless. Prospects were not much better for former recipients who *were* working, of whom 5 percent became homeless (Work, Welfare, and Families 2000). Home-

lessness widens the chasm between those who prosper and those who fall ever further behind. There are far more people of color on one side of that chasm than there are on the other. Welfare policy has narrowed poor women's access to safe and affordable housing, and in doing so has intensified the already disproportionate vulnerability of women of color.

Food insecurity and hunger. Food insecurity and hunger are also racially weighted conditions. One study by a national food bank network revealed that African Americans were represented among those using soup kitchens and food pantries at three times the rate of their representation in the population overall, whereas Native Americans were also substantially overrepresented (VanAmburg Group 1994, cited in Poppendieck 1999). Insofar as welfare reform exaggerates the vulnerability to hunger of poor women and their families, it may also be expected to deepen this racial divide. And the evidence is accumulating that PRWORA has indeed made women's struggles to obtain food for themselves and their families more difficult. Many former recipients cannot pay for sufficient food; they and their families skip meals; they go hungry; and they use food pantries or other emergency food assistance.

The figures are astoundingly high. In New Jersey, half of former recipients surveyed reported an inability to sufficiently feed themselves or their children (Work, Poverty, and Welfare Evaluation Project 1999). In an Illinois study, the population reporting the most difficulty with food insecurity was former recipients who were participating in the labor force, of whom 63 percent said that there was a time when they could not buy the food they needed (Work, Welfare, and Families 2000). The costs of transportation and child care associated with participating in the labor force, combined with reduction or elimination of the food stamp allotment, meant that many women's access to adequate food becomes more precarious as they move from welfare to work.

Welfare reform has also contributed to the underutilization of the food stamp program. Many families that leave the welfare system do not know that as long as their income remains below a certain level, they can continue receiving food stamps. Not having been correctly informed by their caseworkers, former recipients mistakenly believe that the termination of their Temporary Assistance for Needy Families benefits means an end to food stamps as well. According to one study, among families that left welfare, only 42 percent of those who were eligible for food stamps were receiving them. Immigrant families have been hit particularly hard. A study of San Francisco immigrant households whose food stamps had been cut found that 33 percent of the children were experiencing moderate to severe hunger (Venner, Sullivan, and Seavey 2000, 21).

From welfare to low-wage work. As others have convincingly argued, welfare policy is also labor policy (Piven and Cloward 1971). Indeed, within months of the passage of PRWORA, evidence was already emerging that workfare and Work First programs were depressing wages and displacing low-wage workers. In the boom economy of the mid- to late 1990s, employers recognized that "everyone has been raising wages to get people . . . and this [influx of welfare recipients] will make it possible to hold pay steady" (Uchitelle 1997, A10).

The work requirements and time limits that coerce women into the paid labor force, where race and sex discrimination are ongoing, cannot be expected to be neutral with respect to race and sex. Thus, while the surge of former welfare recipients into the low-wage sector of the economy will worsen wages and working conditions for the poorest strata of the working class as a whole, some communities will be hit harder than others. Communities of color, with traditionally higher unemployment and underemployment rates, higher proportions of very low-wage workers, and lower median incomes will be further disadvantaged by PRWORA policies, which force women into a labor market in which they have virtually no bargaining power.

There are substantial racial differences among working women. Full-time, year-round Latina workers earned a median annual income of $19,817 in 1998, considerably less than the $23,864 earned by African American women or the $27,304 white women earned (U.S. Department of Labor Women's Bureau 2000). All women are far more likely than white men are to earn poverty level wages. But, again, racial differentials are substantial. More than half of Latina workers—51.8 percent—earn poverty level

wages, compared to 40.7 percent of black women and 29.7 percent of white women. African American women with less than a high school education faced 1996 unemployment rates nearly twice as high as those of white women—20.9 percent versus 10.8 percent—while 15.9 percent of Hispanic women at this educational level were unemployed. Underemployment rates were even higher (Bernstein 1997). Analyzing the labor market conditions facing women receiving welfare benefits, one researcher concluded, "Such high rates of un- and under-employment, which persist in a labor market that has experienced overall unemployment rates below 6% for over two years, suggest that it may be difficult for welfare recipients to meet the work requirements of the new welfare law" (Bernstein 1997, 4).

Former welfare recipients generally end up in low-paid, entry-level jobs in the gender ghettos of service, sales, and clerical work. A study of the first two years of welfare reform in New Jersey found that the average hourly wage of those former welfare recipients who were working was only $7.31. More than one-third were holding jobs that paid less than $6.00 per hour (Rangarajan and Wood 1999). A 1997 national survey found that adults who left the welfare system and were employed had a median hourly wage of $6.61 (Loprest 1999). This would bring a family just above the official poverty level but far short of a "living wage." Most former recipients who enter the labor force work at jobs that do not provide them with benefits. According to one national survey, less than one-quarter of these workers were covered by health benefits (Loprest 1999).

Far too many families end up in worse economic circumstances than they endured while receiving welfare benefits. For example, a study that tracked families who left Wisconsin's welfare system found that during the first year off welfare, only half of the families had higher income than they had while receiving welfare benefits, even if they had been working while receiving welfare (U.S. General Accounting Office 1999).

Many women have been pushed off welfare but have not found employment. Several studies show that from 20 percent to 40 percent of former recipients find no work (Loprest 1999; Rangarajan and Wood 1999; U.S. General Accounting Office 1999). As more and more women reach their two-year and five-year limits in an economy that is far less robust than it was when welfare reform was passed, they will face an even less-welcoming labor market.

The passage from welfare to work is beset with difficulties. Women are forced into jobs earning poverty-level wages that leave them worse off than they were while receiving welfare benefits. With no benefits, transportation problems, and high child care costs, they struggle with the complex logistics of caring for their families while clinging to the bottom rungs of the economic ladder. Other women are sanctioned off the rolls, or they reach their time limits but find no place in the paid labor force.

Welfare reform is being implemented in ways that follow well-worn patterns of racial and immigrant discrimination. Furthermore, the negative impacts of welfare reform are unequally shared. Left unchallenged, we cannot but expect that this policy will bolster white privilege and deeply inscribe racial subordination.

HUMAN RIGHTS

Targeting U.S. welfare policy as a violation of human rights is one way in which welfare reform is being challenged. Scholars and activists alike are increasingly considering welfare policy within the framework of international human rights. Many have concluded that the PRWORA is a violation of UN human rights conventions. For example, aspects that are identified as violations of the Universal Declaration of Human Rights (UDHR) include the imposition of the "family cap," which denies an increase in the welfare grant to cover children born to women who are already receiving welfare; and the denial of assistance to teen mothers who are not living with their parents. These provisions run contrary to the states' obligation to support families regardless of their structure or their "legitimacy" of children. "Under the UDHR . . . the family, in general, and motherhood and childhood, in particular, are entitled to special care and assistance from the state regardless of the marital status of the parents" (Crooms 2000, 9).

Time limits and sanctions, which may deepen family poverty, are condemned as undermining the rights of children to equal treatment without distinction to birth or other status (UDHR, article 2; Unitarian Universalist Service Committee 2001). Furthermore, those excluded from assistance—including those convicted of drug felonies, children born after the "family cap," and immigrants without documents—"are guaranteed no economic and social rights at all" (Mittal, Rosset, and Borchardt 1999, 131). The coercion of women off welfare and into joblessness or jobs paying poverty-level wages is also a clear violation of the right to "free choice of employment, to just and favourable conditions or work and to protection against unemployment" (UDHR, article 23[1]). The PRWORA runs directly contrary to the UDHR; the International Convention on Economic, Social, and Cultural Rights; and the Convention on the Elimination of All Forms of Discrimination against Women. Welfare reform is also incompatible with the objectives of the 1995 Beijing Platform for Action, a document that provides substance to the claim that "women's rights are human rights" and directs UN member states to take action to relieve "the persistent and increasing burden of poverty on women" (para. 44).

The International Convention on the Elimination of All Forms of Racial Discrimination (CERD)—ratified by the United States in 1994 and premised on the rights articulated in the UDHR—specifically condemns racial discrimination and enjoins states to eliminate "any distinction, exclusion, restriction or preference based on race, colour, descent or national or ethnic origin" (article 1[1]). The convention condemns incitement to racial discrimination and, in article 5(e), identifies the range of economic, social, and cultural rights to be guaranteed on a nondiscriminatory basis, including the rights to free choice of employment, just and favorable remuneration, housing, public health, medical care, social security, and social services.

Far from condemning and working to eradicate incitements to racial discrimination, U.S. government officials have built on a long tradition of such incitements to turn public opinion against social assistance for poor women and their families. By targeting women of color in intent, implementation, and impact, welfare reform substantially violates CERD, actively undermining racial equality in the enjoyment and exercise of human rights.

It is not difficult to demonstrate that U.S. welfare policies deny women of color access to their full range of human rights. More difficult is to develop strategies, using the human rights framework, that effectively mobilize the political power necessary to create change. But local, statewide, and national welfare rights organizations and networks are increasingly engaging in human rights education, in documenting violations, and in exploring ways to hold the government accountable for abandoning its treaty obligations. For example, the Kensington Welfare Rights Union launched a 1997 national campaign to document violations of the UDHR. After accumulating testimony from poor people's organizations nationwide, the union published the *Poor People's Human Rights Report* (1999), which addresses violations of the human rights to employment, an adequate standard of living, and education as articulated in the UDHR.

The international human rights framework has great moral force and has been skillfully used by activists worldwide to bring violators to justice. What has yet to be demonstrated is its ability to force changes in U.S. domestic policy, particularly those policies that undermine economic rights. Many challenges remain, and the grassroots human rights movement is relatively young. Mechanisms of accountability are highly complex and time-consuming, requiring technical and financial resources well beyond the reach of most grassroots organizations. Hard issues must be confronted: the balance and relationship between strategies aimed at winning tangible victories and those that expose the U.S. government's moral and political hypocrisies; between local organizing and international advocacy; between reforming domestic legislation and enforcing accountability to international human rights norms.

The challenge for U.S. human rights activists is not only to arrive at a balance—where education, organizing, documentation, advocacy, and litigation at all levels can reinforce rather than eclipse one another—but also to convince others of the value of this integrated advocacy approach (Women's Institute for Leadership Development 2000, 20). Welfare rights organizations have be-

gun to tackle these challenges. In doing so, they open a new chapter in the struggle for racial, gender, and economic justice.

RECOMMENDATIONS

Organizations that advocate and mobilize for welfare rights, economic and racial justice, and women's rights have formulated a range of demands and recommendations for government action. Among the most important recommendations are as follows:

- End the two-year and five-year time limits.
- Restore entitlement to assistance based on need.
- Count education as a work activity.
- Increase funding for child care subsidies.
- Raise the minimum wage.
- Support job development for living-wage jobs with benefits.
- Increase funding for housing assistance.
- Increase the food stamp allotment.
- Ensure that all welfare recipients are informed of their rights and the full range of services to which they are entitled.

These measures would significantly improve economic circumstances for all women receiving welfare benefits. However, given the racially discriminatory intent, implementation, and impact of welfare reform, it is crucial that the government "take effective measures to review governmental, national and local policies, and to amend, rescind or nullify any laws and regulations which have the effect of creating or perpetuating racial discrimination wherever it exists" (CERD, article 2[1][c]). Among these measures must be the following:

- Disaggregate data on the impact and outcomes of welfare reform by race and ethnicity at the county, state, and federal levels.
- Monitor the provision of welfare services and the implementation of sanctions for racially discriminatory practices, and institute measures to eliminate such practices.
- Abolish the family cap.
- Eliminate the "illegitimacy bonus."

- Restore benefits to teen mothers, whether living with their parents or not.
- Restore benefits to immigrants, and provide equal access to all information and services, regardless of immigrant status.
- Provide translation services at welfare offices, and translate all forms and notices.
- Fund educational programs, including adult basic education and English as a Second Language, that address the particular needs of immigrant women.

These recommendations are made within the context of the existing legislation. However, it must be noted that nothing short of a complete overhaul of the U.S. social welfare system—a true reformation that makes human needs central—can eradicate the racially discriminatory, gender biased, anti-immigrant, and anti-poor foundations of a policy that so powerfully shapes the lives of so many U.S. women of color.

NOTE

This chapter draws on "Working Hard, Staying Poor" (Burnham and Gustafson), a report produced for Beijing+5, the special session of the UN General Assembly convened to assess member states' progress in implementing the 1995 Beijing Platform for Action.

REFERENCES

Allen, Marilyn R. 1961. *Beacon Light-Herald,* March–April. Cited in Lucy Williams, *Decades of Distortion: The Right's 30-Year Assault on Welfare.* Somerville, Mass.: Political Research Associates, 1997.

Bassuk, Ellen, et al. 1996. "The Characteristics and Needs of Sheltered Homeless and Low-Income Housed Mothers." *Journal of the American Medical Association* 276, no. 8: 640–646.

Bernstein, Jared. 1997. "The Challenge of Moving from Welfare to Work: Depressed Labor Market Awaits Those Leaving the Rolls." *EPI Issue Brief* no. 116 (March).

Burt, Martha R., and Barbara E. Cohen. 1990. "A Sociodemographic Profile of the Service-Using Homeless: Findings from a National Survey." In *Homelessness in the United States.* Vol. 2: *Data and Issues,* ed. Jamshid A. Momeni. New York: Greenwood.

Cobb, Kim. 1999. "Homeless Kids Problem Worst in Louisiana; Welfare Reform, Housing Crunch Are among Reasons." *Houston Chronicle,* August 15.

Crooms, Lisa. 2000. "The Temporary Assistance for Needy Families Program and the Human Rights of Poor Single Women of Color and their Children." Unpublished paper.

Equal Rights Advocates. 1999. *From War on Poverty to War on Welfare: The Impact of Welfare Reform on the Lives of Immigrant Women.* San Francisco: Equal Rights Advocates.

Griffin, Laura. 1999. "Welfare Cuts Leaving More Families Homeless, Study Finds." *Dallas Morning News,* July 1.

Kensington Welfare Rights Union. 1999. *Poor People's Human Rights Report on the United States.* Philadelphia: Kensington Welfare Rights Union.

Loprest, Pamela. 1999. *How Families That Left Welfare Are Doing: A National Picture.* Washington, D.C.: Urban Institute.

Mittal, Anuradha, Peter Rosset, and Marilyn Borchardt. 1999. "Welfare Reform Violates Human Rights." In *America Needs Human Rights,* ed. Anuradha Mittal and Peter Rosset. Oakland, Calif.: Food First Books.

Moore, Thomas, and Vicky Selkowe. 1999. *The Impact of Welfare Reform on Wisconsin's Hmong Aid Recipients.* Milwaukee: Institute for Wisconsin's Future.

Piven, Frances Fox, and Richard A. Cloward. 1971. *Regulating the Poor: The Functions of Public Welfare.* New York: Vintage.

Poppendieck, Janet. 1999. "Hunger in the Land of Plenty." In *America Needs Human Rights,* ed. Anuradha Mittal and Peter Rosset. Oakland, Calif.: Food First Books.

Rangarajan, Anu, and Robert G. Wood. 1999. *How WFNJ Clients Are Faring under Welfare Reform: An Early Look.* Princeton, N.J.: Mathematica Policy Research.

Sherman, Arloc, Cheryl Amey, Barbara Duffield, Nancy Ebb, and Deborah Weinstein. 1998. *Welfare to What: Early Findings on Family Hardship and Well-Being.* Washington, D.C.: Children's Defense Fund and National Coalition for the Homeless.

Uchitelle, Louis. 1997. "Welfare Recipients Taking Jobs Often Held by the Working Poor." *New York Times,* April 1.

Unitarian Universalist Service Committee. 2001. "Welfare and Human Rights Monitoring Project." Available at www.uusc.org/WelfareReport3-01/Whrmp.txt.

United Nations. 1948. *Universal Declaration of Human Rights.* Available at www.unhchr.ch/udhr/lang/eng.htm.

———. 1965. *International Convention on the Elimination of All Forms of Racial Discrimination.* Available at www.unhchr.ch/html/menu3/b/d_icerd.htm.

———. 1995. *Beijing Platform on Women.* New York: United Nations.

U.S. Conference of Mayors. 1999. *A Status Report on Hunger and Homelessness in America's Cities.* Washington, D.C.: U.S. Conference of Mayors.

U.S. Department of Labor Women's Bureau. 2000. "Women of Hispanic Origin in the Labor Force." *Facts on Working Women,* no. 00-04 (April).

U.S. General Accounting Office. 1999. *Welfare Reform: Information on Former Recipients' Status.* Washington, D.C.: U.S. General Accounting Office.

VanAmburg Group. 1994. *Second Harvest National Research Study.* Erie, Penn.: VanAmburg Group. Cited in Janet Poppendieck, "Hunger in the Land of Plenty." In *America Needs Human Rights,* ed. Anuradha Mittal and Peter Rosset (Oakland, Calif.: Food First Books, 1999).

Venner, Sandra H., Ashley F. Sullivan, and Dorie Seavey. 2000. *Paradox of Our Times: Hunger in a Strong Economy.* Medford, Mass.: Center on Hunger and Poverty, Tufts University.

Williams, Lucy. 1997. *Decades of Distortion: The Right's 30-Year Assault on Welfare.* Somerville, Mass.: Political Research Associates.

Women's Institute for Leadership Development for Human Rights. 2000. *Making the Connections: Human Rights in the United States.* San Francisco: Women's Institute for Leadership Development for Human Rights.

Work, Poverty, and Welfare Evaluation Project. 1999. *Assessing Work First: What Happens after Welfare?* Edison, N.J.: Study Group on Work, Poverty, and Welfare.

Work, Welfare, and Families. 2000. *Living with Welfare Reform: A Survey of Low-Income Families in Illinois.* Chicago: Chicago Urban League and University of Illinois–Chicago Center for Urban Economic Development.

PART VIII

Understanding Black Reparations

36

Past Due: The African American Quest for Reparations

ROBERT ALLEN

A growing social movement within the African diaspora has heeded the call for reparations. Much of the analysis generated by this movement focuses on reparations as a form of compensation for centuries of unpaid slave labor and for the negative lingering effects of slavery and ongoing discrimination in the United States. This chapter examines the history of the U.S. reparations movement and focuses on reparations as a matter of social justice for African Americans. Also discussed are reparations to address the effects of state-sanctioned discrimination.

In recent years the quest for reparations for Africa and Africa's children in the diaspora has emerged as an important issue. A growing number of activists, scholars, and political leaders, such as British member of parliament Bernie Grant and U.S. congressman John Conyers, have heeded the call for reparations. Organizations have been formed to press the issue, and a foundation for engagement with governments, particularly in Britain and perhaps the United States, is being laid. The issue of reparations is truly global and has many dimensions—moral, cultural, social, psychological, political, and economic. In this chapter, I focus chiefly on reparations as a matter of social justice for African Americans, but I am cognizant of the fact that the struggle for reparations is a global issue requiring an internationally unified mobilization.

HISTORY OF THE QUEST FOR REPARATIONS

As early as 1854 a black emigrationist convention called for a "national indemnity" as a "redress of our grievances for the unparalleled wrongs, undisguised impositions, and unmitigated oppression which we have suffered at the hands of this American people."[1] After the Civil War the antislavery activist Sojourner Truth organized a petition campaign seeking free public land for the former slaves.[2] In support of her campaign, Sojourner Truth said, "America owes to my people some of the dividends. She can afford to pay and she must pay. I shall make them understand that there is a debt to the Negro people which they can never repay. At least, then, they must make amends."[3] Her valiant campaign was unsuccessful.

In the 1890s another black woman, Callie House, filed lawsuits and petitioned Congress for reparations payments to African Americans. Her efforts were endorsed by Frederick Douglass, but again there was no success.[4]

Religious leaders have also called for reparations. Bishop Henry McNeal Turner once declared, "We have worked, enriched the country and helped give it a standing among the powers of the earth." Turner estimates that the United States owes black people $40 billion for unpaid labor.[5] More recently, the Reverend Amos Brown, pastor of the Third Baptist Church in San Francisco, called for reparations in the form of tax credits and automatic tuition for African American youths who qualify for higher education.[6]

The Nation of Islam also made a reparations demand. In its program for establishing a separate state, the nation asserted that "our former slave masters are obligated to provide such land and that the areas must be fertile and minerally rich. We believe that our former slave masters are obligated to maintain and supply our needs in this separate territory for the next 20 to 25 years—until we are able to produce and supply our own needs."[7]

The quest for reparations was voiced in the Ten-Point Program of the Black Panther Party. Point 3 states,

> We believe that this racist government has robbed us and now we are demanding the overdue debt of forty acres and two mules. Forty acres and two mules was promised 100 years ago as restitution for slave labor and mass murder of Black people. We will accept payment in currency which will be distributed to our many communities. The Germans are now aiding the Jews in Israel for the genocide of the Jewish people. The Germans murdered six million Jews. The American racist has taken part in the slaughter of over fifty million Black people; therefore, we feel that this is a modest demand that we make.[8]

In the late 1960s, two of the most dramatic demands for reparations were put forward by former Student Nonviolent Coordinating Committee leader James Forman and by the nationalist Republic of New Africa. In 1969 Forman strode into Riverside Church in New York City and presented a "Black Manifesto" calling for $500 million in reparations from white Christian Churches and Jewish synagogues. The manifesto stemmed from a Black Economic Development Conference held in Detroit under the auspices of Christian churches. Commenting on the thinking behind the reparations demand, Forman wrote in *The Making of Black Revolutionaries*, "Reparations did not represent any kind of long-range goal to our minds, but an intermediate step on the path to liberation. We saw it as a politically correct step, for the concept of reparation reflected the need to adjust past wrongs—to compensate for the enslavement of black people by Christians and their subsequent exploitation by Christians and Jews in the United States. Our demands—to be called the Black Manifesto—would not merely involve money but would be a call for revolutionary action, a Manifesto that spoke of the human misery of black people under capitalism and imperialism, and pointed the way to ending these conditions."[9] The Manifesto proposed that reparations be used for helping black farmers, establishing black print and electronic media, funding training, research and community organizing centers, assistance in organizing welfare recipients and black workers, funding research on black economic development and links with Africa, and funding a black university.

The Republic of New Africa (RNA) was founded in 1968 with the purpose of establishing an independent black republic in five Southern states with large black populations: South Carolina, Georgia, Alabama, Mississippi, and Louisiana. In 1972 the RNA developed what it called an Antidepression Program, which called for $300 billion in reparations from the U.S. government, part of which would be used to finance the establishment of new communities in the proposed black republic.[10] The program featured three "legislative requests" to be presented to the U.S. Congress. One proposal called for the ceding of land to the RNA in areas where black people voted for independence. A second proposal called for reparations of $300 billion. The third proposal called for negotiations between the U.S. government and the RNA with regard to the details of reparations.

The RNA reparations proposal noted that reparations are commonly paid by one nation to another to compensate for damage caused by unjust acts of war. For example, the document pointed to payments made to various nations by the Federal Republic of Germany for damage caused by the Nazi regime during World War II. The document argued that slavery constituted a form of unjust warfare against the African nation in America, and the damage caused by this warfare provided the basis for a demand for reparations.[11]

In comparing the Black Manifesto and the RNA Antidepression Program, several things stand out. The Black Manifesto was directed not at the government but at church institutions, and its monetary demands were much more modest. Reparations payments were to be used to fund a Southern land bank; independent media, training, and organizing efforts; and educational initiatives. The RNA demand was directed to the government and sought reparations to fund new self-sustaining communities as part of an independent black nation. These communities were to develop their own industries, health and educational systems, media, and public infrastructure. The Black Manifesto and the RNA program stressed the need for independence from white control. However, Forman and the RNA deployed the concept of domestic colonialism. For the RNA, reparations were a means of establishing a separate black nation. For Forman reparations were a step in the process of liberating an oppressed black community and transforming America into a socialist regime.

In 1974, economist Robert S. Browne, at the time the director of the Black Economic Research Center, wrote of reparations as requiring "a massive capital transfer of a sizable chunk of America's wealth to the black community."[12] According to Browne, racial disparities between the black and the white community in economic status and political power could be traced to disparities in ownership of capital assets. Echoing the position that was most widely adopted by black advocates of reparations, Browne said a moral justification for reparations derived from "the debt owed to Blacks for the centuries of unpaid slave labor which built so much of the early American economy, and from the discriminatory wage and employment patterns to which Blacks were subjected after emancipation." When Browne further suggested that such "gross inequities" in wealth distribution would exacerbate racial tensions if not redressed, he invoked white America's "national self-interest" and desire for racial peace.

NEW ACTIVISM EMERGES

In the last decade, reparations have again become an activist issue with the establishment of the National Coalition of Blacks for Reparations in America[13] and with the international Africa Reparations Movement.[14] Founded in 1989, the coalition is an umbrella group that sponsors a Reparations Awareness Day each February 25 and holds an annual convention. The organization has done much to create public awareness in the United States about the issue of reparations.[15] Similarly, the Africa Reparations Movement, founded in 1993 as an outgrowth of a conference on reparations held in Nigeria, has worked in the international arena to promote the idea of reparations, including cancellation of the external debt of African nations and the return of stolen art objects to their home countries. British member of parliament Bernie Grant is chairperson of the Africa Reparations Movement, and he has taken an active role in pushing the British government to begin to take the issue of reparations seriously.[16]

In the arena of public policy in the United States, there have been growing efforts to get reparations on the agenda. In 1987 the Republic of New Africa again drafted a reparations bill and circulated it to members of Congress.[17] In 1989, seventeen years after the Gary Black Political Convention, congressman John Conyers introduced a bill in Congress, calling for creation of a presidential commission to study the question of reparations for African Americans. The Conyers bill (originally HR 40, now HR 891) followed the passage of the Civil Liberties Act of 1988, which granted reparations to Japanese Americans who were unjustly interned during World War II. With the success of the reparations effort by Japanese Americans, black activists succeeded in getting several cities—including Detroit, Cleveland, and the District of Columbia—to pass resolutions endorsing the tenets of reparations.[18] The Conyers bill, which has been put forward every year since 1989, presents findings that "the institution of slavery was constitutionally and statutorily sanctioned by the Government of the United States from 1798 through 1865" and that slavery "constituted an immoral and inhumane deprivation of Africans' life, liberty, African citizenship rights, and cultural heritage, and denied them the fruits of their own labor." So far, every year the Conyers bill has been bottled up in committee and prevented from coming before Congress. Nevertheless, the bill has become a significant rallying point for those individuals and organizations seeking to get a serious hearing for reparations.

The Conyers bill calls for appropriating $8 million to establish a commission to study reparations proposals for African Americans. Specifically the commission would:

1. examine the institution of slavery that existed from 1619 through 1865 within the United States and the colonies that became the United States, including the extent to which the federal and state governments constitutionally and statutorily supported the institution of slavery;
2. examine de jure and de facto discrimination against freed slaves and their descendants from the end of the Civil War to the present, including economic, political, and social discrimination;
3. examine the lingering negative effects of the institution of slavery and the discrimination (as described in the second point) on living African Americans and on society in the United States;
4. recommend appropriate ways to educate the American public of the commission's findings;
5. recommend appropriate remedies in consideration of the commission's findings; and
6. submit to Congress the results of such examination, with recommendations.[19]

If deemed appropriate, the remedies to be considered include the possibility of a formal apology from the government and a payment of compensation to the descendants of African slaves. The commission would recommend what form any compensation should take and who would be eligible. The commission would have seven members: three appointed by the president, three by the Speaker, and one by the president pro tempore.

POLITICAL ECONOMY AND REPARATIONS

With the destruction of affirmative action programs, the quest for reparations gains added urgency. However, let me stress that my discussion of reparations is not meant to dismiss issues of access to employment and the necessity of challenging racial discrimination in education and other areas of social life. Social movements and public policies that address racial discrimination in employment, education, and elsewhere are clearly important in bringing about any progressive change; yet, such remedies do not address the systematic long-term decapitalization of the African American community. Struggles for civil rights are important but not sufficient. Transfers of capital resources into the African American community must occur. To be most effective, such transfers must be class-based, aimed at benefiting first and foremost the black working class—those who have been most ravaged by the depredations of capitalism and who have benefited least from the social reforms of the civil rights era.

From the standpoint of political economy I think that the process of underdevelopment of the African American community and the role of the state in this process of underdevelopment are critical in understanding the unfolding of the quest for reparations.

Manning Marable has argued convincingly that capitalism is the fundamental cause of the underdevelopment of black America. At the same time, the wealth produced by slave labor enormously enhanced the economic and political development of North America. In his seminal book *How Capitalism Underdeveloped Black America*, Marable writes, "Capitalist development has occurred not in spite of the exclusion of Blacks, but because of the brutal exploitation of Blacks as workers and consumers. Blacks have never been equal partners in the American Social Contract, because the system exists not to develop, *but to underdevelop Black people.*[20]

He goes on to write,

The ordeal of slavery was responsible for accelerating the economic and political power of Europe and North America over the rest of the mostly nonwhite world. Since the demise of slavery, and the emergence of modern capitalism, the process of Black underdevelopment has expanded and deepened. To understand this dynamic of degradation, first, is to recognize that development itself is comparative in essence, a relationship of inequality between the capitalist ruling class and those who are exploited. Underdevelopment is not the absence of development; it is the inevitable product of an oppressed population's integration into the world market economy and political system. Once "freed," Black Americans were not compensated for their 246 years of free labor to this country's slave oligarchy. The only means of survival and economic development they possessed was their ability to work, their labor power, which they sold in various forms to the agricultural capitalist. Sharecropping and convict leasing were followed by industrial labor at low wages.... Throughout the totality of economic relations, Black workers were exploited—in land tenure, in the ownership of factories, shops, and other enterprises; in the means of transportation, in energy, and so forth. *The constant expropriation of surplus value created by Black labor is the heart and soul of underdevelopment.*[21]

Underdevelopment manifests in the restriction of black labor to certain functions: chattel slavery, sharecropping, low-paid industrial work, a reserve army of labor (the "underclass"). It manifests in the restricted and distorted development of black landownership, home ownership, and black business enterprises. It manifests in chronic impoverishment, the fostering of retrograde political leadership, the destruction of black education, the spread of racist violence, and the wholesale incarceration of black youth.

The role of the state, as Marable and others have noted, was critical to the process of underdevelopment. Specifically, the underdevelopment of black America occurred not because of the "normal" operation of capitalist economic and property relations; rather, the state apparatus was directly and intimately involved in the expropriation of surplus value from black workers and in the blocking of capital accumulation by African Americans.

From the earliest colonial period, the passage of laws establishing racial slavery ensured that black labor could be exploited without compensation and in perpetuity. (By the 1640s, de facto African slavery became institutionalized in law.) Virginia colony, with a plantation economy based on tobacco, led the way. First, laws were passed effectively excluding Africans as non-Christians from a limit of the number of years they could be held in bondage.[22] A Virginia law in 1661 regarding punishment of runaway servants recognized that some black workers were already enslaved for life; it referred to "any Negroes who are incapable of making satisfaction by addition of time."[23] Second, the status of slavery was made hereditary. In 1662 the Virginia Assembly decreed that the children of a slave mother shall themselves be slaves, regardless of the status of the father.[24] This law flew in the face of English patriarchal tradition, but it guaranteed that African bondage could be passed down through the generations without interruption.

At the same time, European indentured servants were granted privileges based on whiteness. They were protected from enslavement by statutes limiting the period of servitude (typically four to six years). Moreover, capital accumulation by whites was privileged. In 1705 the Virginia colonial assembly passed a law granting white servants fifty acres of land, thirty schillings, a musket, and food on completion of their term of service.[25] No such land stake would be granted to black workers.

Free black people found their freedom circumscribed by the state. Licensing was used to exclude them from certain occupations. They could not own land in many areas, and they were largely excluded from the franchise. In California and elsewhere, they could not testify in court against whites, further undermining their ability to protect themselves.[26] In 1668 Virginia—seemingly always in the forefront of new ways to oppress black people—made free African American women liable to taxes on the ground that black women should not be admitted to the "exemptions and impunities of the English."[27]

Theodore Allen, in the second volume of his important work *The Invention of the White Race*, notes one consequence of such state intervention. He reports that in Virginia, landholding by blacks declined from 11 percent in 1666 to one-quarter of 1 percent in 1860. Allen concludes that this precipitous decline was the result not of normal capitalist economic development but of a system of racial oppression enforced by the state.[28]

IMPACT ON WEALTH ACCUMULATION

Melvin Oliver and Thomas Shapiro in *Black Wealth/White Wealth* note that the much-celebrated progress of the new black middle class that has emerged since World War II is highly deceptive. The authors observe that although it is true that middle-class blacks are approaching middle-class whites in terms of annual income, the black middle class lags far behind when it comes to wealth and capital assets. White families typically have a net worth eight to ten times as large as the net worth accumulated by black families.[29] This discrepancy remains even when occupation and income are comparable. Oliver and Shapiro contend that this disparity does not result from the normal operation of a capitalist economy but results from what they call the "racialization of the state," by which they mean systematic, state-sanctioned mining of the wealth created by black labor and by the blocking of asset accumulation by African Americans. For example, in the period from 1933 to 1978, over thirty-five million American families benefited from home owner equity accumulation as a result of suburban home ownership polices of the federal government. Blacks were largely excluded from this process due to such practices as restrictive covenants and "redlining" (refusing to make loans in certain areas). The Federal Housing Authority endorsed restrictive covenants on the grounds that "if a neighborhood is to retain stability, it is necessary that properties shall continue to be occupied by the same social and racial classes."[30]

"The FHA's actions have had a lasting impact on the wealth portfolios of black Americans," Oliver and Shapiro write. "Locked out of the greatest mass-based opportunity for wealth accumulation in American history, African Americans who desired and were able to afford home ownership found themselves consigned to central city communities where their investments were affected by the 'self-fulfilling prophecies' of the FHA appraisers: cut off from sources of new investment their homes and communities deteriorated and lost value in comparison to those homes and communities that FHA appraisers deemed desirable."[31]

The difficulty of gaining access to credit has enabled banks and finance companies to strip-mine black communities of housing equity through unscrupulous backdoor loans and by charging higher interest rates and points for conventional mortgages. As many as half of borrowers who must opt for high-interest loans end up losing their homes through foreclosure.[32]

Home ownership is the primary means for accumulating capital among middle-class Americans. Housing equity can underwrite the cost of college education for children and provide for a comfortable retirement for parents. It is a major form of inheritance passed on to the next generation. Oliver and Shapiro calculate what they refer to as the cost of being black in the housing market in terms of higher interest rates, lost home equity, and mortgages denied to qualified borrowers. That cost came to $82 billion in 1992.

CONCLUSION: THE COST OF BEING BLACK

The cost of being black amounts to a tax unfairly imposed solely because of race. It is analogous to the tax that Virginia imposed on free black women in 1668. The state must bear responsibility for abolishing such an unjust tax and for making restitution for the period that it was imposed. Not only does the race tax harm the present generation, its effects are cumulative—it deprives the present generation and denies an inheritance to the next. Imposed by the state, the burdensome and unfair race tax can only be remedied by the federal government. More than a matter of individuals or regions, the state must be held accountable to remove the burden and make appropriate restitution for value lost.

As many advocates of reparations have argued, if we are seeking a more economically just society, a society in which equality (or parity) is more than rhetoric, then the issue of reparations must be addressed. Reparations provides a framework for the redistribution of wealth within the existing political economy, thereby moving toward economic equality between whites and blacks. Transfers of wealth in the form of capital assets and resources—black community ownership of national and local economic enterprises, housing and home ownership, educational scholarships—

are critical to the success of any effort aimed at reversing the present underdevelopment of the black community. In my view, such transfers must first and foremost benefit the black working class and the poor.

I argue that the quest for reparations also raises questions about the nature and legitimacy of the capitalist political economy—most fundamental, capitalist alienation of labor from ownership of the wealth that labor produces and the role of the state in this process. At its most radical, the demand for reparations stands as a critique of capitalist property relations. It also underscores the need for general redistribution of wealth and resources. Seen in this light, the struggle for racial reparations can be convergent with the struggle for a socialist society in which black people would have full and equal access to the total wealth and resources of society. Only in the presence of such full and equal access to the total wealth and resources of society could we conclude that racial discrimination has been eliminated.

Finally, it must be said again that the issue of reparations is a global issue, for the enslavement of Africans and the colonization of Africa constitute a global issue. The situation of African Americans cannot be divided from the situation of Africans in Africa and the diaspora. If civil rights alone are insufficient to ensure full equality for black Americans, then national independence alone is insufficient to ensure national liberation for the former colonies. As Frantz Fanon commented in *The Wretched of the Earth,*

We are not blinded by the moral reparation of national independence; nor are we fed by it. The wealth of the imperial countries is our wealth too. . . . Europe is literally the creation of the Third World. The wealth which smothers her is that which was stolen from the under-developed peoples. The ports of Holland, the docks of Bordeaux and Liverpool were specialized in the Negro slave-trade, and owe their renown to millions of deported slaves. So when we hear the head of a European state declare with his hand on his heart that he must come to the help of the poor under-developed peoples, we do not tremble with gratitude. Quite the contrary; we say to ourselves: "It is a just reparation which will be

paid to us." . . . This help should be the ratification of a double realization: the realization by the colonized peoples that it is their due, and the realization by the capitalist powers that in fact they must pay. For if, through lack of intelligence . . . the capitalist countries refuse to pay, then the relentless dialectic of their own system will smother them.[33]

The African American quest for reparations is part of a much larger, global reparations movement by black people in Africa, the Caribbean, South America, and Britain. This global movement has been gaining strength in recent years. Africa and black people in the diaspora represent a powerful force, a sleeping giant, that has been drugged by the poisons of colonialism, slavery, and racism. But the giant is awakening fitfully but certainly from the nightmare, and justice must be served. In the words of Fanon, a just reparation must be paid for the lives that were lost and for the wealth and labor that were stolen.

NOTES

1. Mary Frances Berry and John W. Blassingame, *Long Memory: The Black Experience in America* (New York: Oxford University Press, 1982), 405.

2. Berry and Blassingamc, *Long Memory,* 406; Nell Irvin Painter, *Sojourner Truth: A Life, a Symbol* (New York: W. W. Norton, 1996), 244.

3. Quoted in Jeanette Davis-Adeshote, *Black Survival in While America* (Orange, N.J.: Bryant and Dillon Publishers, 1995), 87.

4. Berry and Blassingame, *Long Memory,* 406.

5. Berry and Blassingame, *Long Memory,* 405

6. *San Francisco Chronicle,* February 10, 1998.

7. John H. Bracey Jr., August Meir, and Elliot Rudwick, *Black Nationalism in America* (New York: Bobbs-Merrill, 1970), 404.

8. Huey P. Newton, *To Die for the Purple: Selected Writings and Speeches* (New York: Writers and Readers Publishing, 1995), 3.

9. James Forman, *The Making of Black Revolutionaries* (Seattle: University of Washington Press, 1997), 545.

10. Imari Abubakari Obadelc I, *Foundations of the Black Nation* (Detroit, Mich.: House of Songhay, 1975), 68.

11. Obadelc, *Foundations of the Black Nation*, 80–89.

12. Quoted in William Darity Jr., "Forty Acres and a Mule: Placing a Price Tag on Oppression," in *The Wealth of Races: The Present Value of Benefits from Past Injustices,* ed. Richard F. America (New York: Greenwood Press, 1990), 5.

13. Address: National Coalition of Blacks for Reparations in America, P.O. Box 62622, Washington, D.C. 20020-2622. Website: www.ncobra.com.

14. Address: Africa Reparations Movement, 3 Devonshire Chambers, 557 High Road, Tottenham, London, N17 6SB, United Kingdom. Website: http://the.are.co.uk/arm/home.html.

15. Lori Robinson, "Righting a Wrong," *Emerge* 8, no. 4 (February 1997): 44, 46.

16. Interview in *West Africa* magazine, October 27–November 9, 1997.

17. William L. Van Deburg, ed., *Modern Black Nationalism* (New York: New York University Press, 1997), 333.

18. Van Deburg, *Modern Black Nationalism,* 333.

19. U.S. House of Representatives, HR 891.

20. Manning Marable, *How Capitalism Underdeveloped Black America* (Boston: South End Press, 1983), 2 (emphasis in original).

21. Marable, *How Capitalism Underdeveloped Black America,* 7 (emphasis in original).

22. Theodore W. Allen, *The Invention of the White Race: The Original of Racial Oppression in Anglo-America* (New York: Verso, 1997), 2:179. The loophole allowing possible freedom for Christian Africans was closed in 1662 (197).

23. Allen, *The Invention of the White Race,* 187.

24. Allen, *The Invention of the White Race,* 197.

25. Ronald Takaki, *A Different Mirror: A History of Multicultural America* (Boston: Little, Brown, 1993), 66.

26. Berry and Blassingame, *Long Memory,* 35.

27. Allen, *Invention of the While Race,* 187.

28. Allen, *Invention of the While Race,* 184–185.

29. Oliver and Shapiro, *Black Wealth/White Wealth,* 116–117.

30. Oliver and Shapiro, *Black Wealth/White Wealth,* 16–18.

31. Oliver and Shapiro, *Black Wealth/White Wealth,* 16–18.

32. Oliver and Shapiro, *Black Wealth/White Wealth,* 20–21.

33. Frantz Fanon, *The Wretched of the Earth* (New York: Grove Press, 1963), 80–81.

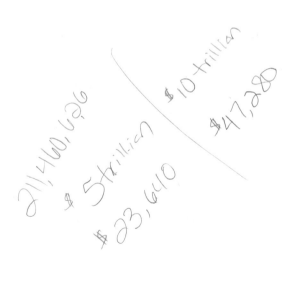

37

The Theory of Restitution
RICHARD AMERICA

This chapter defines the theory of restitution and applies it to the case of African Americans in the United States. The author concludes that past and present economic injustices have occurred that have benefited whites and suggests several remedies as part of paying restitution to African Americans for these unjust enrichments.

Whenever nations, races, or other large social groups have chronic grievances, a fundamental issue is invariably the sense that one party has perpetrated unremedied historical economic injustices. The theory of restitution is based on the intuition that it is possible

- to reconstruct historic economic relations;
- to specify "fair" standards—prices, wages, terms of trade, interest rates, return on investment—that were violated, usually by force;
- to audit the historical pattern of transactions between the groups and compare the actual with the "fair" standard;
- to then estimate the deviation from "fairness";
- to designate the result as unjust enrichment and estimate its present value and distribution; and
- to then draw policy implications usually in the form of lump sum or other redistributive income and wealth transfers, in-kind subsidies, or investments in real and human capital.

For over 370 years, income and wealth have been coercively diverted from Africans and African Americans to the benefit of Europeans and European Americans. This was primarily done through slavery and then discrimination in education, housing, and labor and capital markets. It is possible now to reconstruct that history in some detail, and it is possible to not only develop theory and method to measure the magnitude of the income and wealth transfers but also to estimate their present value and distribution.

These unjust enrichments were not dissipated. They were transferred intergenerationally and are currently enjoyed by whites in the top 30 percent of the income and wealth distribution. Since the processes that produced the benefits are now widely regarded as wrong, illegal, and illegitimate—violating current standards of fairness—the benefits that have been produced are unjust. They should therefore be returned to those who were harmed or to their collective descendants.

The actual debt, which amounts by some estimates from $5 trillion to $10 trillion, can be paid through adjustments in tax and budget policies over the next forty years. The debt should be paid primarily through investments in human capital, housing, and business formation.

THE PROBLEM

Many of the other contributors in this volume have exhaustively reviewed the economics of poverty, and they have chronicled the disparities by race in economic life. The inequalities are well known, and the basic reasons for the continuing chronic economic distress among a significant minority of African Americans have been thoroughly analyzed. But the descriptions and analyses have not produced behavior changes or innovative policies sufficient to eliminate the phenomenon of gross disparities in income and wealth by race. It is possible that the real problem is still not properly specified.

The race problem can be accurately defined as such. It is, for all practical purposes, the coerced and manipulated diversion of income and wealth from blacks to whites. Racism is a social mechanism that justifies and helps make possible a range of decisions that occur in education, housing, finance, employment, and training. They also make possible and reinforce the wrongful accumulation of wealth by the beneficiaries of racism as a class. So racism, whatever else it might be, is an instrument for creating and maintaining economic dominance and unjust economic relationships. It has persisted because, among other reasons, it is beneficial to many people.

Solving the primary American social problem—the race problem—is therefore a matter of making racism less economically attractive. Part of the solution is to retrieve some or all of the wrongful benefits that racism has produced for the white majority and to intervene in markets and educational processes so that they do not generate further benefits.

But the focus should be keenly on the benefits side—the benefits accruing to white Americans from continuing racial discrimination against blacks. For too long, we have focused simply on the costs of racism. Such a way of looking at the problem is one reason relatively little progress has been made against intransigent, chronic economic underperformance and persistent poverty.

DISCUSSION

For generations the idea has persisted that whites owe blacks money. It has never been a mainstream idea; it has never had strong adherents in high places; and it has never had strong theoretical or practical support among economists and policy analysts. Nonetheless, the idea has enough intuitive power that it never completely went away.

The idea that forty acres and a mule had somehow been promised after emancipation—rather than simply proposed—has endured. That notion has kept alive the feeling that there really is something to the idea that even such a vast amorphous injustice as racial exclusion, exploitation, and discrimination in many forms and in many markets can lead to a kind of debt. This obligation has also been felt but not articulated by many whites, and it seems to underlie many acts of altruism, compassion, and charity. Some whites have gone further and said that they acknowledge some kind of moral debt, but few have gone all the way to this idea: that the past produced tangible benefits to the white majority; that these benefits were accumulated, compounded, and bequeathed; and that today there is a measurable unjust enrichment that should be surrendered and transferred back in an orderly, democratically agreed-on way. But that is the most obvious policy implication of the concept of restitution.

Note that the word used here is *restitution* rather than *reparations*. Reparations has inflammatory connotations and is associated commonly with the aftermath and consequence of military victory and defeat. Losers in war pay reparations under duress—that is not what we have in mind. Instead, the concept is that justice and morality are operating broadly and that these are not compatible with holding in perpetuity benefits derived from past immoral and wrongful systemic transactions and processes. So, at the beginning of the twentieth-first century, Americans have the opportunity to look at their collective history. They can acknowledge that much wealth has been built by methods that cannot stand scrutiny by today's standards. Although they may have been acceptable at the time, moral people cannot accept the fruits of wrongful actions that were committed on their behalf—as posterity—by their collective, if not direct, biological ancestors.

Boris Bittker's 1972 book *The Case for Black Reparations* examines these questions thoroughly and successfully. In it, Bittker deals with all the common objections—that raising these issues now, so late in the game, is ex post facto and that we do not mete out justice that way, under our system. Bittker says that, on the contrary, there is ample precedent for finding retroactive guilt and for correcting it, if practicable.

Incidentally, guilt, in the emotional sense, is not the point. That is another common objection: "Why try to play on guilt?" No. The point is that a careful examination leads to a finding of guilt but that it does not matter whether culprits feel emotional guilt or not. They are guilty in any event. So restitution, when all is said and done, depends on a majority of Americans concluding that the distribution of income and wealth, by race, cannot be justified. Restitution is based on wrongful acts. It implies an obligation to make restitution, and the key is to find ways that are politically feasible and practical in the actual circumstances.

BACKGROUND AND HISTORY

Slavery produced benefits for over two hundred years. Agricultural slavery was primary. But many Americans think of slavery only in terms of agricultural commodity production. In fact, slavery generated great benefits in other ways as well. Slaves were used in manufacturing services and in activities that today would be regarded as the responsibility of municipal or state government, such as running transportation, utility, and emergency services. Also vitally important, slaves cleared land and built infrastructure—roads, dams, levees, canals, railroads, and bridges.

It can be argued that without this labor the nation would not have expanded west as it did. Indeed, it is possible and perhaps probable that the United States would never have become a continental nation. It likely would not have been able to complete the Louisiana Purchase nor gain the territories that became the Southwest and the West Coast states, so vital to twentieth-century growth. The United States could well have ended territorially at the Mississippi River and never emerged as a world power. The point is not to speculate on counterfactual history, but the crucial role of slave labor in creating the basis for expansion and total continental development is worth underlining.

Slave-produced goods and services benefited most whites indirectly and passively. This happened through the process of human capital for-

mation. Slaves made it possible for many whites to go into more rewarding occupations, gain increased skills, and generate greater lifetime earnings for themselves and their descendants. In these indirect and passive ways, slavery produced enormous benefits beyond those that flowed directly from production.

DISCRIMINATION

After slavery, exclusion and discrimination allowed millions of Americans and immigrants to enter occupations with greater prospects. In these ways, racism generated income and wealth that flows to present-day recipients. That is an important reality. It should not be minimized.

Theodore Hershberg, at the University of Pennsylvania, has studied immigration. He found that successful, accomplished black tradespeople and skilled operators were displaced by immigrants. So it is not simply a matter of black entrance being blocked. Black earnings were established and then forcibly discontinued by private practice and by conscious, active, wrongful interventionist public policy.

Discrimination continued through the mid-twentieth century, and in the past one hundred years it has produced far greater benefits than those accumulated during the preceding 270 years—namely, because of the far greater population and size of the economy. So the most significant sources of unjust enrichments have fairly recent origins, notwithstanding the dramatic effects of compound interest on the earlier, longer stream of coercively, interracially diverted income.

PROCESSES

Exploitation, exclusion, and discrimination were mechanisms that produced unjust enrichment. *Exploitation,* however, is a loaded term. It carries great emotional baggage with the general public, even when used in a technical sense. Here it simply refers to super benefits over and above "normal" returns on investment or above a unit of labor's marginal productivity. *Exclusion* refers to what is usually known as occupational discrimination, in which whites occupy jobs that in a freely competitive market would have otherwise been occupied by blacks of equal ability and training. *Discrimination* refers to three other phenomena, in addition to occupational discrimination. First, employment discrimination is commonly seen in the "last hired, first fired" practice; that is, blacks and whites of equal endowments experience different lengths of employment in similar economic cycles. Second, wage discrimination refers to equally endowed whites and blacks receiving different wages for the same occupational and skill contribution. Third are other forms of discrimination, as outlined by Lester Thurow in *Generating Inequality* (1975), including capital, housing, medical health, and other subtle modern practices.

RESULT

All of these differential practices produce a diversion of benefits by race. All of them made whites better off relative to blacks in the aggregate than they otherwise would have been in a society and in markets using free and openly competitive selection processes. The total consequence of these direct and indirect, active and passive methods of diverting income and wealth interracially have resulted in a massive unjust enrichment that is measurable and that is enjoyed by whites, even to the present. The important objective is to refine the theory, locate and organize the data, and create an econometric technique that can shed light on the processes' quantitative impact.

MEASUREMENT

There have been estimates; they have been preliminary and illustrative, not final and conclusive. For example, in my edited volume *The Wealth of Races* (1990), Marketti, Neal, Swinton, and Chachere and Udinsky each apply contrasting methods covering differing periods. There is room for much more work of this kind. The National Association for the Advancement of Colored People, the National Urban League, the Joint Center for Political and Economic Studies, and other civil rights groups should systematically engage in this task. Furthermore, govern-

ment organizations such as the Bureau of Labor Statistics, the Federal Reserve Board, the Congressional Budget Office, the Office of Management and Budget, General Accounting Office, the House Ways and Means Committee, the House and Senate Budget Committees, and the Joint Economic Committee should do this research as well. Finally, the National Bureau of Economic Research, the Brookings Institution, the American Enterprise Institute, the Progressive Policy Institute, the Upjohn Institute, the Urban Institute, the Center for Budget and Policy Priorities, the Economic Policy Institute, the Committee on Economic Development, and other think tanks and research centers should also make it a priority to track this issue. They should produce measurements of the unjust enrichment over the entire period, 1619 to the present, and they should track the annual consequences of discrimination—costs and benefits.

Indeed, someone should create and produce an annual discrimination index. This would give readings on the economic consequences of discrimination much the same as readings on prices, corporate securities, employment, interest rates, output, and other important aggregate and sectoral activities. This quantification of harmful behavior would help reduce it; that is, the announcement of monthly, quarterly, and annual results would tend to shed light on discrimination as never before. The victims have always known, intuitively, that they have been hurt, but they have never had any idea by how much.

The beneficiaries do not seem to realize that they are beneficiaries. The information will be salutary for all concerned, although it might produce grumbling among technicians, who will quibble over technique and method. But that will be healthy. It will sharpen the analyses, and it will focus policy discussion on constructive alternatives.

POLICY IMPLICATIONS

The discussion thus far leads us to the *So what?* question. What difference will this information make? What practical value will restitution theory have?

Reasonable minds may differ. One school of

thought says, "There is this debt, and civil rights groups and their friends should militantly demand that it be paid." How do they want it paid? Some say, via lump sum cash—so much per individual. Others say, through government programs—invest in a domestic Marshall Plan of some kind.

A second school of thought says, "Demanding payment will be counterproductive." In reply, I argue that the United States is suffering prolonged economic stagnation for complex reasons—one of which is this historic imbalance caused by past injustices. If we look carefully, we see that economic underperformance is caused in part by the alienation of millions of people who believe they are victims of injustice, and so they withhold their best efforts in response. The argument goes on that getting the entire country back on the healthy track requires that all lagging sectors receive overdue attention. They should be targets of investment, especially in human capital. This argument says, "Demands will not work, but logic will." If there is restitution to be paid, most voters will come to accept, acknowledge, and respond if they see paying it as in their best interests collectively.

So it is a fundamentally moral issue—but it is also a practical matter. Restitution probably only stands a chance of gaining wide practical acceptance if it is presented in the context of the overall management of the economy and its long-term health. Thus, it may in fact gain broad support if it is understood as a matter of general social importance. What follows are ways it can be paid.

Affirmative Action

Restitution should be approached as a matter of broad income and wealth redistribution from the haves to the have-nots and especially, though not only, from white haves to black have-nots. Affirmative action is essentially about income and wealth redistribution, but it has not been discussed as such. It has not been debated explicitly as a means of changing income and wealth distributions. It has been muddled. Discussion is based on the mistaken concept that restitution is intended to help "make up for past discrimination." That is the wrong formulation, and that is a major reason the concept is so confused in the public mind.

The correct rationale is that we can correct a current injustice, not a past one. The current injustice is that the top 30 percent of the income distribution is overwhelmingly white and enjoys this $5 trillion to $10 trillion unjust enrichment at the expense of blacks. The remedy includes affirmative action that will shift occupation, wage, and employment distributions from whites in favor of blacks.

To put it bluntly, this will not produce an immediate, enthusiastic embrace, but it will put the matter properly on the table. Afterward, the discussion can be rational and can be focused on the real problem and its solutions. No more evasion, euphemism, half-truths, and half-measures. Affirmative action should be pursued because it is a good way to pay restitution. But it should also have a sunset. It should end in a limited time—say, two generations. That way, it is recognized not as an open-ended process. It will be expected to even the playing field and then no longer be needed.

Set-Asides

Business programs that provide entry to previously exclusionary markets are frequently attacked as unfair to white businesses. Those who make that argument generally, though not always, know better. They are dissembling. But the feelings among many disappointed white business owners are real and have political force. The programs should be explicitly seen and presented as paying restitution. That will produce angry reactions at the outset as well. But when passions subside, there will be a clean reason to redistribute opportunities interracially, which is what set-asides should do. They, too, should have a sunset provision. Two generations should be long enough to produce a large group of competitive African American businesses, able to compete in most sectors at small, medium, and large scale.

Other Preferences

Other kinds of preference programs should be clearly labeled as justified ways to pay restitution. Housing mortgages, employment and training, scholarships, and so on all are justified as make-whole remedies. They are, or should be, intended to put African Americans collectively in their

Table 37.1   Current Income Distribution in the United States, by Quintile

Quintile	Total income received
Lowest 20%	5%
Second	9
Middle	14
Fourth	28
Top	44

rightful place, which means that they will be helped to raise their income and wealth to levels they would have achieved but for the wrongful interference of discriminatory practices that favored and benefited whites. This concept of rightful place should be asserted confidently. Let it be clear.

INCOME AND WEALTH REDISTRIBUTION

The quintiles now receive earned income roughly in the proportions shown in table 37.1. In a fair world they would probably receive shares as shown in table 37.2. This would still provide ample incentives to the haves to produce and take risks, but the effects of past injustice and gross exclusion, exploitation, and domination would be greatly reduced. This kind of distribution is one objective of a program of restitution. The poor would still be poor, but the disparities would not be nearly so overwhelming, formidable, and wrongful. Restitution thus helps to create incentives for full participation by the 20 percent to 40 percent of the population who are now underutilized, underrepresented, and underappreciated and who—most important—unjustly enrich those at the top.

CONCLUSION: THE THEORY OF RESTITUTION

This entire discussion can be incorporated into a concept statement: systemic economic arrangements are often imposed by dominant social groups on less-powerful groups. Invariably, these patterns of transactions produce costs for the latter and benefits for the former. Economic injustices, sustained over time, produce cumulative benefits. These can be measured. When they are, the results can then be introduced into public policy discussion for the purpose of acknowledging the transgressions; admitting the consequences; and accepting the fact that remedies are proper, feasible, and just.

So restitution theory offers a basis for correcting the lopsided results of distortions in markets characterized by coercion, exclusion, and discrimination. It raises the prospect of reducing the offending behavior by simply illuminating the economic relationships and their ramifications. A major reason that the injustices were perpetrated in the first place and then perpetuated was that a veil of ignorance rested over the phenomena. Restitution theory lifts that veil, which in itself will make it harder for eco-

Table 37.2   Income Distribution in the United States If It Were More Fairly Shared, by Quintile

Quintile	Total income received
Lowest 20%	10%
Second	9
Middle	20
Fourth	25
Top	30

nomic injustices to become systemic in the future because this time their magnitude will be well understood. In most cases, political and social forces will then mobilize to stop the practices and to retrieve the unjust enrichments that have been produced.

NOTE

This chapter previously appeared as Richard D. America's "The Theory of Restitution," in *A Different Vision: Race and Public Policy*, II, ed. T. D. Boston, 154–162. London: Routledge, 1997.

— These ideas seem to operate under the assumption that there are only 2 races in the US. How do these reparations factor in other races?

— How do you determine who qualifies for reparations?
  — all blacks?
    — all slave decendents?
    — do recent immigrants qualify?

38

The Economics of Reparations
WILLIAM A. DARITY JR. and DANIA FRANK

There is a nationwide movement and debate over the claim by African Americans for compensation for the enslavement of their ancestors. This chapter presents a brief introduction to the economics of reparations to African Americans for slavery and decades of Jim Crow practices. We first explore the black–white wealth differential as a basis for the reparations movement. We then propose two criterions to determine eligibility for reparations. Finally, we discuss the size of a reparations payment and how the way in which it is financed and distributed effects the incomes of blacks as well as nonblacks.

REPARATIONS AND SLAVERY

The U.S. government's posture at the 2001 World Conference against Racism—where the transatlantic slave trade was declared a crime against humanity—evaded a warranted claim by African Americans for compensation for the enslavement of their ancestors. This evasive posture is anomalous in light of U.S. government support for, and administration of, reparations for other groups subjected to recent or historical grievous wrongs.

Indeed, the U.S. government has undertaken numerous reparations payments to American Indian tribes for atrocities and treaty violations. Two examples include the 1971 grant of $1 billion and forty-four million acres to Alaskan natives and the 1986 grant of $32 million to the Ottawa tribe of Michigan (Benton-Lewis 1978, chart). In addition, in 1990 the U.S. government issued a formal apology to Japanese Americans subjected to internment during World War II and made a $20,000 payment to each of sixty thousand identified victims (Benton-Lewis 1978, 1, chart).

In a non–United States precedent, the 1952 German *Wiedergatmachung* established group-based indemnification for Jewish people worldwide in the aftermath of Nazi persecution. Compensation included payment of more than $800 million to "the State of Israel, on behalf of the half million victims of the Nazis who had found refuge in its borders, and the Conference on Jewish Material Claims against Germany, on behalf of the victims of Nazi persecution who had immigrated to countries other than Israel" (Westley 2003, 120). Thus, German reparations payments went to institutional entities (Israel and the claims conference); to survivors of the Holocaust who could reasonably establish specific harms or losses, such as property lost through confiscation; and relatives of those killed in the concentration camps. Similar principles governed the much later payment of $25 million by the Austrian government in 1990 to Jewish claimants.

Almost 250 years of domestic enslavement of African people and their descendants have not elicited a similar response from the U.S. government. The paradox has not been lost on Robert Westley (2003, 122):

Blacks have never received any group compensation for the crime of slavery imposed upon them by the people and government of the United States. As in the case of the Japanese, Jews received not only material compensation for their losses, but their victimization was also publicly memorialized in Germany, Israel, and the United States (even though there was no legitimate claim of oppression or genocide that Jewish survivors of the Holocaust might assert against the United States). The only "memorial" dedicated to the suffering of Black slaves and the survivors of slavery in the United States is contained in a series of legislative enactments passed after the Civil War. The history of Black Reconstruction shows how these enactments were successively perverted by the courts, and by Congress itself.

JIM CROW OVERLOOKED?

Another compelling pillar of the case for reparations for African Americans is the practice of nearly a century of state-sanctioned apartheid in the United States. The harms of Jim Crow practices are extensive; moreover, unlike U.S. slaves, direct victims of Jim Crow practices are still living.

Particularly in the U.S. South, the post-Reconstruction period gave way to a climate of terror that allowed whites to take black lives and black-owned property with impunity. An Associated Press report documented 406 cases of black landowners who had twenty-four thousand acres of farms and timberland stolen from them in the first three decades of the twentieth century (Lewan and Barclay 2001, A1, A3).

Raymond Winbush (2003, 48–49) has referred to "'whitecapping' as denoting the habit of night riders who confiscated land from vulnerable blacks during the era of Jim Crow." James Grossman reports that 239 cases were recorded in Mississippi alone between 1890 and 1910. Furthermore, perpetrators of black property theft "often colluded with local, state and even the federal government to defraud African Americans of property. . . . Wholesale burning of courthouses, Black churches, and homes were common ways of destroying evidence of Black land ownership illegally obtained by white terrorists" (1997, 48).

The process of white destruction of black wealth reached its apex in the literal annihilation of prosperous black communities in Wilmington, North Carolina, in 1898; in Tulsa, Oklahoma, in 1921; and in Rosewood, Florida, in 1923. Moreover, lynching may have often conjoined the murder of blacks with property theft. Winbush speculates that the lynching trail was a trail of stolen black land, contending that lynching victims frequently were black landowners (Barclay 2001, A3).

Today, while the black–white per-capita income ratio is in the 50 percent range, the black–white wealth disparity is far wider. The highest estimates of the racial wealth ratio run in the 15 percent to 25 percent range (Chiteji 1999; Chiteji and Stafford 1999). Since the major source of wealth for most persons today is inheritance (Blau and Graham 1990), the forced deaccumulation of black wealth during the Jim Crow era has to have played a key role in producing contemporary racial wealth differentials.

American apartheid subjected three successive generations of African Americans to separate schools with inferior facilities and resources. Patterns of systematic residential segregation in the North and the South restricted black access to neighborhood amenities, quality housing, and hospital services. Differential sentencing and punishment of blacks, extending from slavery times to the present, has imposed immense costs on individual blacks and on communities of black persons (Betsey 2001).

Employment discrimination has further constrained the opportunity of blacks to transform their skills and credentials into incomes comparable with that of whites with similar levels of attainment. Moreover, in a recent study using data from the Integrated Public-Use Microdata Series (a national census database), Darity, Dietrich, and Guilkey (2001) showed that labor market discrimination and imposed schooling deficits faced by blacks in the interval 1880–1910 significantly weighed down the occupational attainment of their descendants in 1980 and 1990, a century later. Furthermore, current labor market discrimination continues to penalize black earners (Darity, Dietrich, and Guilkey 2001), affording a further justification for reparations.

ECONOMICS AND REPARATIONS

Given the suitability of reparations to compensate blacks for having been subjected to slavery, Jim Crow practices, and ongoing discrimination, economics can provide useful insights in determining eligibility for reparations, types of reparations programs, the long-term effects of reparations, methods of financing reparations, and the magnitude of reparations.

The moral hazard principle alerts us to potential problems in establishing criteria for eligibility for receipt of African American reparations.[1] Reparations create a premium for being black in America that previously did not exist. Thus, individuals who had not previously been self-identified as black will have an incentive to suddenly declare their African ancestry. To mitigate this problem, we propose two criteria for eligibility: first, an individual would have to provide reasonable documentation that they had at least one ancestor who was enslaved in the United States; and, second, an individual would have to demonstrate that at least ten years before the onset of the reparations program, they self-identified as black, African American, colored, or Negro on a legal document.

Economics also leads us to contemplate a reparations program taking a number of forms, none mutually exclusive. One approach would be lump-sum payments to eligible individual African Americans. A second approach would be the establishment of a trust fund to which eligible blacks could apply for grants for various asset-building projects, including home ownership, additional education, or start-up funds for self-employment. A third option would be the provision of vouchers that could be used for asset-building purposes, including the purchase of financial assets. Thus, reparations could function as an avenue to undertake a racial redistribution of wealth akin to the mechanism used in Malaysia to build corporate ownership among the native Malays. In that case, shares of stock were purchased by the state and placed in a trust for subsequent allocation to the native Malays. A fourth approach would be reparations in kind—for example, guaranteed schooling beyond the high school level or medical insurance. Still, a fifth approach would be use of reparations to build entirely new institutions to promote collective well-being in the black community. Finally, any combination of these five approaches is yet another possibility.

The venerable transfer problem (Johnson 1955; Keynes 1929) in international trade theory provides a warning that reparations payments to blacks need not have the long-term effect of closing the racial income or wealth gap.[2] In an extended theoretical inquiry (Darity and Frank 2002), we examined how different methods of reparations payments to African Americans would affect the black and nonblack populations in the United States. We found that reparations payments that either mandate or provide incentives for blacks to spend on goods and services produced by nonblacks would raise the relative incomes of nonblacks. Without significant productive capacity in place before reparations, a lump-sum payment could actually result in an absolute decline in black income. Thus, the structure of a reparations program is critical if it is to close the black–white economic gap in the United States.

How are reparations to be financed? Public finance theory suggests that nonblacks could finance the transfer by paying additional taxes, borrowing (dissaving), or by lowering their spending. Or the United States government could borrow by issuing bonds to finance the reparations program. In general, African Americans should not bear the tax burden of financing their own reparations payments. Blacks paid local, state, and federal taxes for more than eighty years while being disenfranchised in the U.S. South, a paradigmatic case of "taxation without representation." If, however, taxes are levied universally to finance reparations, guarantees must be put in place that the reparations payment net of the tax is substantial for black taxpayers. Furthermore, reparations income should be tax-free.

Finally, economic analysis can be mobilized to establish the magnitude of the reparations payment. Contributors to Richard America's *Wealth of Races* (1990) used a variety of procedures to calculate the debt owed to blacks for slavery. Ransom and Sutch computed the difference between the market value of slaves' net of food, shelter, and other consumption over the last fifty years of slavery, which led them to an estimate of $3.4 billion by 1860. Larry Neal used a similar measure of unpaid wages to slaves between 1620 and 1840 compounded at 3 percent of 1983 dollars to reach a figure of $1.4 trillion. James Marketti's estimate of Africans' income foregone via slavery came to a present value estimate by 1983 of $3 trillion to $5 trillion. Vedder, Gallaway, and Klingaman sought to estimate the accumulated gains in wealth to white Southerners from ownership of enslaved blacks to arrive at a bill of $3.2 million as of 1859. In current dollars these procedures generally lend themselves to present-value estimates in the range of $5 trillion to $10 trillion for the debt for slavery. These numbers do not take into account the costs of Jim Crow or the costs of present discrimination. Estimates by David Swinton (1990) and by Chachere and Chachere (1990) of the costs of labor market discrimination during the forty-year period 1929–1969 alone run between $500 billion and $1.6 trillion in 1983 dollars. Suffice it to say, the damages to the collective well-being of black people have been enormous and, correspondingly, so is the appropriate bill.

NOTES

This chapter previously appeared as William Darity and Dania Frank's "The Economics of Reparations," *Papers and Proceedings of the American Economics Review* (May 2003).

1. *Moral hazard* refers to incentives associated with a policy that induce people to alter their behavior dishonestly to take advantage of the benefits provided by the policy—for example, setting a fire to get the insurance benefit.

2. In international trade, the transfer problem poses the following question: Does a unilateral transfer from one country to another impose a secondary burden or a blessing on the paying country through an adjustment in the terms of trade? If the paying country experiences an increase in their terms of trade or in their balance of payments account due to the transfer, then the receiving country necessarily receives a decrease in their terms of trade or a decrease in their balance of payments account. It is possible that a transfer payment could result in a real income loss to the receiving country. In the case of reparations, a payment to blacks could result in a real income loss.

REFERENCES

America, Richard F. 1990. *The Wealth of Races: The Present Value of Benefits from Past Injustices.* Westport, Conn.: Greenwood Press.

Barclay, Dolores. 2001. "Torn from the Land: The Lynching Trail." *Sunday Herald-Sun* (Durham, N.C.), December 2, A1, A3.

Benton-Lewis, Dorothy. 1978. *Black Reparations NOW!* Rockville, Md.: Black Reparations Press.

Betsey, Charles. 2001. "Income and Wealth Transfer Effects of Discrimination in Sentencing." Paper presented at a National Economic Association meeting, New Orleans, Louisiana, January.

Blau, Francine, and John Graham. 1990. "Black-White Differences in Wealth and Asset Composition." *Quarterly Journal of Economics* 105 (May): 321–339.

Chachere, Gerald, and Bernadette Chachere. 1990. "An Illustrative Estimate: The Present Value of the Benefits from Racial Discrimination, 1929–1969." In America, *The Wealth of Races.*

Chiteji, Ngina. 1999. "Wealth Holding and Financial Marketplace Participation in Black America." *African-American Research Perspectives* 5, no. 1 (Fall): 16–24.

Chiteji, Ngina S., and Frank P. Stafford. 1999. "Portfolio Choices of Parents and Their Children as Young Adults: Asset Accumulation by African-American Families." *American Economic Review* 89, no. 2: 377–380.

Darity, William, Jr., Jason Dietrich, and David Guilkey. 2001. "Persistent Advantage or Disadvantage: Evidence in Support of the Intergenerational Drag Hypothesis." *American Journal of Economics and Sociology* 60, no. 2 (April).

Darity, William, Jr., and Dania Frank. 2002. "Reparations for African Americans as a Transfer Problem." Unpublished manuscript, Duke University, August.

Grossman, James. 1997. *A Chance to Make Good: African Americans, 1900–1929.* New York: Oxford University Press.

Johnson, Harry G. 1955. "The Transfer Problem: A Note on the Criteria for Changes in the Terms of Trade." *Economica* 22, no. 86 (May): 113–121.

Keynes, J. M. 1929. "The German Transfer Problem." *Economic Journal* 39, no. 153 (March): 1–7.

Lewan, Todd, and Dolores Barclay. 2001. "Inquiry: Black Landowners Cheated." *Sunday Herald-Sun* (Durham, N.C.), December 9, A3.

Marketti, James. 1990. "Estimated Present Value of Income Diverted during Slavery." In *America, The Wealth of Races*.

Neal, Larry. 1990. "A Calculation and Comparison of the Current Benefits of Slavery and an Analysis of Who Benefits." In *America, The Wealth of Races*.

Ransom, Roger, and Richard Sutch. 1990. "Who Pays for Slavery?" In *America, The Wealth of Races*.

Swinton, David. 1990. "Racial Inequality and Reparations." In *America, The Wealth of Races*.

Vedder, Richard, Lowell Gallaway, and David Klingaman. 1990. "Black Exploitation and White Benefits: The Civil War Income Revolution." In *America, The Wealth of Races*.

Westley, Robert. 2003. "Many Billions Gone: Is It Time to Reconsider the Case for Reparations?" In *Should America Pay? Slavery and the Raging Debate over Reparations*, ed. Raymond Winbush. New York: Harper Collins.

Winbush, Raymond. 2003. "The Earth Moved: Stealing Black Land in the United States." In *Should America Pay? Slavery and the Raging Debate over Reparations*, ed. Raymond Winbush. New York: Harper Collins.

PART IX

*African American Economic Development
and Urban Revitalization Strategies*

39

Inner-City Economic Development and Revitalization: A Community-Building Approach

JOHN WHITEHEAD, DAVID LANDES, and JESSICA GORDON NEMBHARD

Conservative free-market revitalization models have always been based on the assumption that the private business sector holds the key to inner-city economic development. This chapter, while recognizing the importance of involving the private sector in urban revitalization campaigns, focuses on a community-building approach to inner-city economic development. The authors suggest that several principles are needed to achieve successful urban revitalization: the adoption of collaborative and holistic strategies; active involvement and participation by local residents; social justice; employment creation and training for local residents; and special attention to increasing capital and wealth formation in America's inner cities.

Reversing the economic decline and misery facing many inner-city communities is one of the nation's most pressing challenges. The apparent failures of past efforts to meet this challenge have contributed to extraordinary high rates of urban poverty and an enormous waste in human resources. This chapter outlines a community-building approach to inner-city economic development that is fundamentally different from past efforts and that reflects the new realities of America's inner cities and the global economy.

This chapter begins with a summary and critique of Michael Porter's proposal for inner-city revitalization, which focuses on attracting non-minority-owned mainstream firms to the inner city. We then offer an alternative vision of inner-city economic development that is informed by economic and social principles that receive little attention or outright rejection in conservative/free-market revitalization models such as Porter's. This vision entails the implementation of various

strategies—including minority-owned business development, inner-city job creation and workforce development, and cooperative enterprise development—and focuses on the necessity to attract capital into, and create wealth in, inner-city communities of color.[1]

THE PRIVATE BUSINESS–CENTERED DEVELOPMENT MODEL: A SUMMARY OF MICHAEL PORTER'S PROPOSAL FOR INNER-CITY REVITALIZATION

Michael E. Porter advances a model in which the private sector holds the key to the revitalization of America's inner cities. In his May 1995 *Harvard Business Review* article, Porter argues that government economic development policies have failed for four major reasons:

1. they place too much emphasis on delivering relief programs, such as food stamps and income assistance;
2. they have been fragmented, piecemeal, and void of an overall strategy;
3. they represent a mix of social *and* economic programs; and
4. they have focused on redistributing income and wealth.[2]

Porter claims that these policies "have encouraged and supported small businesses designed to serve the local community but ill-equipped to attract the community's own spending power, much less *export* outside of it."[3] In short, Porter believes that government economic development policies and their emphasis on social programs "undermine the creation of economically viable companies."[4]

Porter claims that the only way to promote viable inner-city companies and sustainable inner-city economic development is through "private, for profit initiatives and investments based on economic self-interest and genuine competitive advantage—not through artificial inducements, charity, or government mandates."[5] To be viable, inner-city companies must be able to compete within the general macroeconomy, not just within the local economy, and must be export oriented.[6] In the model, businesses must not only be able to identify and exploit the competitive advantages of inner cities but also be able to overcome the disadvantages. On this note, Porter identifies four major competitive advantages:

1. *Strategic location.* Inner cities enjoy ready access to interstate freeways, harbors, airports, and entertainment facilities.
2. *Local market demand.* Thanks to a large population concentration, even low-income neighborhoods have large incomes per acre.
3. *Integration with regional clusters.* Most inner cities are near clusters of companies that are in the same industry and region—for example, the automobile industry.
4. *Human resources.* Inner cities offer large pools of workers.[7]

Porter also points out the other side of the economic balance sheet where inner cities have some real disadvantages: high building and security cost; underdeveloped, fragmented, and costly land; lack of debt and equity capital; a scarcity of managerial and labor skills; poor infrastructure, often inadequate for transport of goods; and antibusiness attitudes on the part of various workers, community-based organizations (CBOs), and social activists.

Large "mainstream" private-sector firms have the resources and capital to exploit the competitive advantages of inner cities.[8] To attract them, government should deliver financial and business-related services through private-sector institutions and not through government agencies or CBOs. Moreover, government "people-based" policies, which focus on individuals and firms, should be replaced with "place-based" policies, which target areas of greatest economic need.[9] Government must also stop implementing policies that combine social and economic goals, such as subsidized housing construction. In particular, Porter calls for the elimination of long-term direct subsidies and preference programs. Last, local governments must reduce and simplify regulations, offer tax exemptions, improve infrastructure, and bundle land into larger parcels.

Porter argues that inner-city firms must begin to develop relations with large mainstream firms. Large firms have the resources, first, to develop joint job-training programs with inner-city firms; and, second, to hire locally, though Porter admits that most of the local hiring will center on low- to moderate-wage jobs with limited opportunities for advancement.[10] Large firms are also in a position to develop joint business ventures, as well as a variety of customer–supplier relationships, with inner-city firms.

New and traditional inner-city firms are encouraged to take advantage of nearby regional clusters. The advantage of regional clusters is the potential they offer inner-city businesses to compete in the delivery of "downstream" products and services.[11] Additionally, the formation of regional clusters and joint business ventures will increase the capacity of participating inner-city firms to compete and export outside of the local economy. Furthermore, according to Porter, new income flows from regional clusters will be created within, not simply redistributed to, the inner city.

Finally, in Porter's view, CBOs should stay out

of business development because of their abysmal track record in this area. Instead, CBOs should focus on teaching the workforce and the community to respect and value business. They should also work with private-sector institutions in preparing, screening, and referring workers to local business employers and in providing work-readiness training. CBOs are also encouraged to facilitate commercial site improvement and development.

Porter is especially critical of some community-development corporations and banks, which he says try—and fail—to take the place of mainstream private lending institutions. In his view, only private mainstream financial institutions have the expertise and resources to be major business lenders. Consequently, Porter believes that "government must help create the conditions necessary for private, mainstream financial institutions to be profitable in minority and inner-city business lending."[12] As Porter sees it, government must begin to address the high cost of delivering a relatively small, minority or inner-city business loan.[13]

CRITIQUE OF PORTER

Though well argued, Porter's proposal is not without its limitations and blind spots. What follows are four points of contention regarding Porter's model of inner-city revitalization.[14]

Government policies should promote wealth creation rather than wealth redistribution. Porter's model calls for a market-driven process of inner-city revitalization in which the government helps to facilitate wealth creation but is prevented from promoting wealth redistribution.[15] Porter's negative view of government-induced redistribution fails to take into account that market forces have redistributed wealth from the inner city to the suburbs and, as a result, have retarded wealth and capital formation in America's inner cities.[16] The process by which market forces reproduce huge suburb–inner city differentials in incomes, real estate values, equity capital, and transportation infrastructure amounts to what Gary Dymski calls "market-driven wealth redistribution, with a vengeance."[17] One

study in Brooklyn, New York, for example, found that for every dollar deposited in personal accounts in commercial banks in Bedford Styuvesant and in Crown Heights, only one cent was returned in home lending.[18]

A second study by Brent Fairbairn and colleagues at the University of Saskatchewan Center for the Study of Co-operatives diagrams ways in which dollars and wealth from chain and outside firms leave communities: most of the salaries are paid to nonresidents; supplies are purchased outside communities; and the corporation does its banking outside of the community in which it is located, leaving a net outflow of income and wealth.[19] The above studies suggest that the market-driven practices of most private firms owned by nonresidents contribute to the recirculation of dollars outside of the community—that is, the transfer of income and wealth from inner-city to suburban areas. Unfortunately, Porter's model completely fails to account for this direction of redistribution and hence, fails to see the need for government-sponsored redistribution as a counterbalancing force.

Market forces should replace long-term direct subsidies. Porter's approach to government subsidies is deceptive. Porter strongly criticizes government programs such as affirmative action and Urban Enterprise Zones, yet he would replace them with various "short-term" subsidies to large corporations and private lending institutions.[20] This form of corporate welfare serves to redistribute income in favor of owners of corporations and to ultimately facilitate the outflow of wealth from the inner city.[21] Typically, as noted previously, large subsidized corporations operating in the inner city recruit their workforce from candidates outside the inner city, purchase their supplies from vendors outside the inner city, and circulate their profits outside of the inner city.

Moreover, Porter proposes a "single government entity charged with assembling parcels of land and with subsidizing demolition, environmental cleanup, and other costs."[22] This proposal recalls the ill-fated urban renewal programs of a generation ago that provided subsidies to large corporate interests while devastating and displacing the low-income residents they were supposedly designed to serve.[23] If they have not worked well in the past, why should they work now? It is interesting that Porter selectively favors only certain kinds of government involvement and support—that is, the kind that subsidizes and sustains large corporations.

The private sector should lead employment development activities in the inner city. Porter's private-sector job-creation strategy, which focuses on attracting white-owned mainstream firms to the inner city, is weakened by the findings of recent research. The most compelling findings against Porter's job-creation proposal are provided by Timothy Bates.[24] Using data from the U.S. Bureau of the Census, Bates's pioneering study concludes that white-owned firms that are physically located within the inner city hire very few people of color.[25] The study also supports a different generalization: black-owned businesses tend to hire a large percentage of local nonwhite residents even when their firms are not located within the inner city.[26] Clearly, then, a job-development strategy that centers on businesses owned by people of color rather than on attracting white-owned firms to the inner city would likely go further toward creating new jobs for inner-city residents of color. However, a comprehensive strategy aimed at developing "minority" firms is not the centerpiece of Porter's model.[27]

A related problem that even Porter acknowledges is that his job-development proposal centers on low-wage jobs with limited opportunities for advancement.[28] On this issue, Michael Henry observes that "Porter fails to distinguish between creating jobs and creating jobs that permit the poor to work their way out of poverty."[29] In effect, Porter's proposal reinforces the existing suburb–inner city disparities in income and fails to provide many inner-city workers access to the education, job training, and decent jobs that would improve their career paths and earning capacities. The thrust of any community economic development campaign should be to generate momentum toward self-sustained economic and social development of the inner city that provides a range of jobs paying a "living wage" (with the benefits that it entails).[30]

Community development banks should stay out of economic development efforts and inner-city lending. Porter argues that government pro-grams and community development banks should stay out of inner-city lending since they hinder private, for-profit financial institutions from providing the capital necessary for inner-city development. A look at the history of private capital in the inner city reveals just the opposite. Contrary to Porter's argument, it is precisely due to private lending institutions' having such a poor history serving inner-city businesses and residents that community development banks have gained such an important role in providing a vital source of capital. The restructuring of the financial sector since 1980 has further exacerbated the lack of sufficient sources of household and small-business credit.[31] Community development banks such as Chicago's South Side Bank and Oakland's Community Bank of the Bay were designed to fill the vacuum created by the redlining practices of the corporate banking in the current system—that is, the refusal of lenders to make loans in specific inner-city neighborhoods—and the recent financial restructuring that has in effect cut off the inner city from reliable sources of credit.[32] These community development banks grow out of existing community networks and serve to empower local communities by creating jobs and by lending to local minority business.[33] Credit unions (financial institutions owned by their depositors) also have a proven track record of providing affordable financial services and loans to their members and constitute a viable alternative to commercial banks.[34]

COMMUNITY ECONOMIC DEVELOPMENT: CONCEPT AND PRINCIPLES

The Concept of Community Economic Development

Community economic development is a multifaceted, comprehensive process. That it is a process aimed at qualitative positive change involving economic, political, social, and cultural goals and that it is based on local control are important elements in understanding the concept. One basic definition of community economic development is the process of economic change resulting in sustained qualitative improvements in the production, distribution, and consumption of goods and services for people who live in the same geographic area.[35] Other definitions focus on maintaining sustainability and on increasing residents' capacities, financial equality, and independence.[36] Still others focus more on community empowerment and local control of resources, such as the following: "Community economic development seeks to change the way a local economy relates to external markets and political forces by mobilizing local resources and reinforcing local control to better capture broader opportunities, rather than passively relying on the benevolence of government or private enterprise."[37]

When applied to inner-city African American communities, economic development entails a holistic process to create economic and social institutions that enable African American inner-city residents to repair and heal from the damage generated by centuries of enslavement and legalized segregation and oppression. Community economic development also involves the formation of new institutions that fundamentally rupture patterns of external market and "nonminority" domination over the economic life of inner-city residents of color. In this context, community economic development involves a process leading to

- the ability of inner-city communities of color to significantly reduce their dependence on outside mainstream firms for jobs, household credit, and capital resources;
- new inner-city retail establishments' being responsive to the community's need for goods and services at fair market prices;
- greater local control of institutions and resources vital to the community's socioeconomic well-being; and
- the development of new institutions that attract and transfer wealth into, rather than out of, the inner city.

A critical aspect of the community economic development process is advancing linkages among community manufacturing and retail establishments, including cooperative and privately owned firms. Such relationships will facilitate economies-of-scale outcomes and continuing development and growth within the inner city. Finally, the community development process, guided by the community-building approach, provides community residents with the tools, knowledge, and resources to increase their capacity to democratically plan and determine the socioeconomic arrangements, goals, and practices within their communities. Hence, community economic development addresses the social goals of local residents and not just economic growth.

Principles of Community Economic Development

In private, business-centered development models, the principles of democratic participation, empowerment, and equity receive very little attention, if any at all.[38] We believe, however, that these principles and the goals to which they give rise deserve serious attention and should be integrated into new urban economic development initiatives. Having said that, we now give a brief outline of seven core principles of community economic development, with the first three falling under the category of democratization and the subsequent four under social justice.

Democratization and Empowerment

Democratic participation. Local residents and community-based organizations (CBOs) must be active participants and partners in all phases of community economic development (CED). The failure to involve local residents and CBOs "leaves essential resources untapped, ignores local priorities, and misses opportunities to strengthen the communities' own problem-solving capabilities."[39] Economic enterprises that are cooperatively and democratically owned and governed increase productivity, generate income and wealth, provide leadership opportunities and job mobility, and teach skills that enhance civic engagement.[40]

Empowerment. Local economic development initiatives must be designed to give local residents avenues to increase their capacity to democratically plan and control the way in which their communities are run, particularly in the following areas: the types of industry and businesses that should be encouraged and recruited; employment conditions and benefits; land use; allocation of local resources; forms of ownership of community enterprises; and the distribution of their profits.[41] Local residents also need access to finance, asset ownership, and wealth accumulation.

Mobilization and education. CBOs involved in CED must be involved in the mobilization and education of local residents if the process of democratization and empowerment is to be implemented.

Social Justice

Meeting basic needs. CED initiatives should focus on meeting the basic needs of all members of the community. Among these needs are health, education, child care, transportation, shelter, food, clothing, and recreation. Meeting the needs of all members of the community can be accomplished through some combination of goods and services being provided for free or through a redistributive, income-generating system in which incomes for all members of the community are sufficient to purchase basic necessities.[42] In addition, economic enterprises such as cooperative businesses can be formed to meet the needs of residents by pooling resources to make available high-quality goods and services at affordable prices.

Equity. CED initiatives should be implemented with a focus on achieving equitable development.[43] This form of development gives priority to reducing gross inequities within local and regional boundaries; to widening the choices and opportunities available to residents of disadvantaged neighborhoods; and to ensuring that these residents receive an equitable share of the benefits from local and regional growth. A realistic community-building approach to these goals would mean that local and regional development projects should not be judged by whether they achieve equitable distributional results but rather by whether they develop meaningful opportunities for achieving equity based-goals.[44]

Environmental health and justice. CED initiatives should not contribute to local pollution, intro-duce toxic materials into neighborhoods, or create other forms of environmental degradation that negatively affect the health, safety, and lives of urban residents. CED activities must be sustainable. CED initiatives should also be part of efforts to stop environmental racism, the practice of using African American and Latino neighborhoods as dumping grounds for toxic waste. Promoting environmental justice and the end of socially unacceptable environmental degradation can begin to be accomplished through providing education to local residents about environmental health risks and the need for community action.

Social needs over profits. Local development initiatives should support the creation of a new type of economic development that does not place profits over social needs. Local economic development initiatives that focus on private profit instead of social needs exacerbate socially inefficient outcomes and gross inequalities. Many goods that are needed to achieve equitable development—such as goods that generate positive externalities (education, child care, and health care) and public merit goods (parks, libraries, and streets)—would be underproduced by profit-maximizing firms in the private market. In addition, the needs of low-income communities would be underserved, as private firms would find it more profitable to cater to high-income communities.

URBAN REVITALIZATION STRATEGIES

If African Americans and other minorities are to compete effectively in today's global economy, new urban revitalization strategies must be developed to reverse economic decay in the inner city. While comprehensive efforts to reduce inner-city social problems—such as gang violence, drug abuse, and inferior schooling—are essential and must continue, new economic development strategies are needed to improve minority business and job development. Moreover, increasing financial capital flows and the availability of household credit in the inner city must be a major priority of new economic development campaigns. In effectively addressing these challenges, it is crucial, we believe, that the following strategies be implemented.

Private-Sector Job Creation

There is a critical need to develop employment anchor inner-city businesses that are linked to the high-growth sectors of the U.S. economy.[45] Unlike Porter's job-creation strategy of attempting to lure nonminority-owned businesses to inner-city locations, employment anchor businesses must be developed from the growing pool of skilled and talented entrepreneurs, managers, and professionals of color. Talented nonwhites must be provided with incentives to develop large-scale businesses that employ a significant number of inner-city residents and pay a "living wage." In the absence of such employment anchor businesses, traditional businesses owned by people of color—namely, retail and personal services—will continue to generate below-normal profits and have high failure rates.[46] However, if a continual supply of jobs paying decent wages were generated by large-scale enterprises, these small-scale businesses would likely experience higher rates of profit and growth, as their customers would have more income to spend. More important, the growth of these traditional businesses will also create new jobs for inner-city residents.

Job and Wealth Creation through Cooperative Enterprises

The important fact about the cooperative society is the purpose to increase the economic well-being of the whole *community. The basic purpose is increased income for all. Increasing the income of the people means not only enabling them to live more decent and fuller lives but also to provide the savings without which there can be no capital for anything.*

—Chancellor Williams[47]

Cooperative economic development is a viable strategy for community economic development, business development, and job creation. Cooperative firms are successful and competitive methods of enterprise organization.[48] Cooperatives are businesses collectively owned by groups of people to meet certain needs. Members pool their resources to leverage other resources and to govern and distribute surpluses democratically. They operate according to the principles of open membership; democratic control ("one person, one vote" rather than "one share, one vote"); member economic participation; autonomy and independence; continual education, training, and information; concern for community; and cooperation among cooperatives.[49]

Haynes and Nembhard contend that cooperative economic development is an important strategy for inner-city revitalization, in part, because it satisfies many of the principles delineated here.[50] Nembhard, for example, examines the history of African American cooperatives and provides examples of successful African American credit unions as well as cooperatives based on farming, food, home health care, crafts, and cleaning services.[51] African Americans have come together to create alternative economies throughout history by pooling resources, taking control of productive assets, and sharing business ownership in the face of poverty and racial discrimination. These cooperatives have saved and sustained jobs—good jobs; they have created jobs; and they have helped members enhance their product or service. At the same time, they have generated income and wealth, and they have educated and trained their members in specific skills as well as in business ownership and management. These cooperatives give benefits back to their communities in the form of consumer education, economic stability, affordable prices, and quality goods and services that might not otherwise be offered. Cooperative enterprises address many urban and economic development challenges because their mission is to serve members' needs using business ownership that creates and sustains jobs as well as wealth.

Fairbairn and colleagues explain the cooperative advantage: "For decades, cooperatives in market economies have arisen where there are market deficiencies—imperfect competition, excessive concentrations of power and unmet needs. They have arisen, too, where the costs of adjustment to economic change have threatened to destroy communities, where local people needed power to control the pace and direction of change in order to preserve what they valued."[52] Nevertheless, cooperative strategies tend to be overlooked and undervalued in the design of policies to create jobs and wealth in inner-city communities of color. Recommended first steps to build broad-based community and local government interest, support, and trust in this area include the following:

- Use an asset model, rather than a deficit model, that focuses on utilizing community residents' existing skills, capacities, and resources (even if nontraditional); and on building wealth and tangible assets through pooling of resources, cooperative ownership, and democratic economic participation.
- Begin building trust through low-risk, high-return tangible collaborative neighborhood victories. A playground project is one example: a neighborhood designs and builds a playground and in the process identifies skills, pools resources, and develops a camradery that can be carried over to long-term projects, even to business development.[53]
- Develop workshops about alternative community-based economic development and cooperative enterprises; explain the principles of economic cooperation; and share best practices so that residents and policymakers can learn about this model, its implementation, and its strengths and weaknesses.
- Support programs for youth that include their opening credit union accounts, being representatives on a board of directors, starting their own cooperative businesses and encouraging them to work with adults on entrepreneurial community development projects and advocacy based on the need for specific goods and services within a sustainable development model for the inner city.
- Develop public policies to support cooperative economic development, such as tax incentives, cooperative economic curricula in public schools, government set-asides for cooperative and community-owned businesses, credits for the recirculation of capital within communities, and networking among cooperative businesses in the region. Provide support for using cooperatives and community-owned businesses to address underserved areas: environmental and recycling issues; the effects of environmental racism; and affordable housing, senior housing, day care, and other quality services that have been overlooked or deemed not profitable in the inner city.

Cooperative economic strategies can expand employment, training, and educational opportunities. Participation in cooperative enterprises builds social capital and develops skills transferable to other activities and economic pursuits. Therefore, cooperative economic strategies should be a significant component of urban revitalization campaigns.

Job Training in the Inner City

A critical part of the solution to the human capital deficit in the inner city is providing effective job training. Unfortunately, many job-training programs that focus on inner-city residents are ineffective. Too often, training programs are fragmented, noncollaborative, and removed from the needs of industry and local labor markets. Moreover, many programs provide training for dead-end jobs in the low-growth sectors of the economy.[54]

In recent years, government planners, private-sector organizations, and community service providers have formulated a range of public policy recommendations and job-development strategies to narrow the human capital gap between suburban and inner-city communities of color. Among the most important recommendations and strategies are the following:

- Develop and implement effective certification procedures that require government-sponsored programs to link their training to specific job opportunities and local labor market demand as determined by industry-wide benchmarks.[55]
- Design customized job-training programs that link residents of economically dis-

tressed inner-city communities with real job prospects in emerging business ventures. Provide free customized job training for new high-growth and emerging minority companies bringing large investments to inner-city locations.[56]

- Develop opportunities for inner-city residents to receive on-the-job training with classroom instruction. Reimburse participating companies for all costs, including the cost of replacement workers, while program participants are involved in classroom activities.[57] In return, participating companies should provide a structured, long-term curriculum leading to a degree or credential in a field with a range of jobs paying a "living wage" and with opportunities for career advancement.

- Reward local programs that facilitate genuine collaboration between CBOs, government planners, the private sector, local schools, and research universities in the design and implementation of training programs.[58]

The inner-city human capital problem can and must be solved. Effectively addressing this problem will require a broad, holistic, and innovative approach to education and job training in which the needs of inner-city residents and employment anchor businesses are paramount. Finally, the complete range of the nation's assets—including the resources of government, the private sector, CBOs, and (especially) local schools—must be mobilized if we are to substantially improve human capital formation in America's inner cities.

Financing Inner-City Economic Development

A monumental problem facing inner-city neighborhoods is lack of access to credit and financial capital for business enterprises, home ownership, and household credit needs. The legacy of redlining continues. Increasing access to business capital and household credit must be at the center of any strategy to revitalize inner-city communities.

Government Programs
Since the start of the Nixon administration's Minority Enterprise Small Business Investment

Company (MESBIC) program in 1969, several federal programs have attempted to intervene in credit and capital markets to increase the availability of capital to inner-city neighborhoods and to encourage business development.[59] These programs include the Community Reinvestment Act of 1977, which required that inner-city-based lenders participate in mortgage and business lending in previously redlined, underserved communities. More recently, the Clinton administration's 1994 Community Development Financial Institutions initiative provided subsidized government funding to a diverse range of lending institutions, including community development banks, loan funds targeted at minority borrowers, and community-based credit unions. Among those that these institutions serve are housing developers building affordable housing, small businesses, community groups providing community services, and child care providers.

Lessons from the MESBIC program
An important study by Timothy Bates analyzes the 1987–1993 track record of MESBIC investment in inner-city-located and minority-owned small businesses.[60] Companies participating in the MESBIC program are federally chartered venture-capital and private-equity investment firms that provide debt and equity capital to minority businesses. Bates observes that there is a greater need for the more risky equity capital investments than there is for debt capital (loans). His data show that although the majority of MESBICs that provided equity capital were unsuccessful, "others thrived by making equity investments in large-scale minority business enterprises operating in emerging fields."[61] These investments, though a small proportion of total MESBIC lending, have encouraged the expansion of these large-scale minority business enterprises.

Financing Emerging Minority Businesses
Recent research and the pioneering studies of Timothy Bates suggest that the greatest roadblock to minority business development is equity capital, not debt, and that existing government-sponsored equity capital sources tend to overlook emerging minority businesses that are likely to

Debt capital: Money borrowed by a firm by procuring loans or selling bonds. The borrower agrees to repay the loan or bond plus interest. The owners of the firm maintain control over the firm. Bondholders and other lenders do not gain a share of ownership. Disadvantage of debt capital is that it must be repaid with interest at scheduled times.

Equity capital: Money raised by a new or existing company in exchange for an ownership interest in the company. It is more flexible than debt capital is because it does not require scheduled repayment with interest. Equity capital can come from many sources, including venture capital firms, public stock offerings, and institutional or individual investors. In the case of corporations, private equity is often raised from issuing shares of stock ownership.

Venture capital: Venture capital is a form of equity investment from professional investors whose interest is to provide start-up capital for new businesses perceived to have excellent growth potential. Venture capital is typically expensive with the venture investor seeking higher returns than normal equity investors seek, as well as significant proportions of ownership in the company. Managerial and technical expertise is often provided by venture capital firms. This form of private equity became important during the 1990s in emerging fields such as "high technology" and Internet development firms.

succeed. Therefore, we propose the creation of new government incentives and policies that lead to the expansion of private-equity investment firms that serve the equity capital needs of large-scale emerging minority businesses operating in the finance, insurance, and real estate business services; and in communications, wholesale, and transportation sectors. Government policies that successfully assist the more capable, emerging minority businesses with high-growth potential produce a related benefit—job creation—for inner-city minority communities.

As well, we recommend significant tax reductions on capital gains and dividends from equity capital investment in minority businesses that employ a minimum percentage of inner-city residents. This proposal would, we believe, result in new flows of equity capital to emerging minority businesses. The economic cost of our proposal, which should be relatively modest, would be greatly outweighed by increased tax revenues from the creation of new jobs for inner-city residents.

Increasing Funding to Small Businesses and Inner-City Residents

What strategies and institutions are necessary to increase lending to diverse inner-city constituencies such as small businesses, potential homeowners, and household borrowers? Clearly, this requires new and expanded methods of attracting—and requiring—funds from the private sector, in addition to increased government subsidies and funding. We propose several financial *push mechanisms* necessary to increase available capital in the inner city:[62]

- strengthening the Community Reinvestment Act of 1977 and extending it beyond banks and savings and loan institutions to all financial institutions (unfortunately, this act was weakened in 1999 by the Gramm-Leach-Bliley Act);
- creating additional government incentives and requirements to increase private-sector funding of community development banks, credit unions, and other sources of lending;
- increasing funding sources for mortgage loans to provide inner-city residents with opportunities to purchase a range of housing, including homes and condominiums and that these options be broadened to give inner-city residents a greater range of alternatives to begin building home equity wealth in the way that the Federal Housing Administration programs subsidized and promoted suburban home ownership (98 percent white) after World War II; and

• subsidizing microenterprise funds—which provide funding to small, often individual businesses, targeting the very poor—coupled with grants for day care and health benefits.

Financing inner-city community development requires a diverse and creative mix of new government requirements and incentives. Only then can we begin to redress the historical draining of capital from the inner city and address the enormous needs for new sources of capital. As Gary Dymski notes, this initiative must be coupled with additional government spending for infrastructure improvements, education, and training.[63]

CONCLUSION

It is likely that the private, business-centered development model proposed by Porter and other conservative free-market advocates will not have a significant impact on the economic revitalization of inner-city communities. Inner-city economic revitalization requires considerably more than provision of a favorable environment for attracting private, profit-seeking mainstream firms. In fact, the more than thirty years of research on inner-city revitalization suggest that revitalization initiatives must be comprehensive and holistic, extending beyond economic issues. The motor of a local revitalization initiative may be economic development, but crucial to its success may be programs in such areas as family support, improved public education, drug rehabilitation, mental health, environmental cleanup, community policing, and cooperative enterprise development.

Local revitalization initiatives must also promote positive core social values that raise the consciousness of the people and their commitment to community involvement. Inner-city revitalization initiatives must not only create material benefits but also increase the "social energy" of the community, forge a sense of real togetherness, and "establish a sense of accountability and ownership within the community."[64] Moreover, our vision, as summarized in this chapter, calls for social justice, consciously equitable development and cooperative development strategies, and a social safety net for those in

deepest need during the period of transition. Our approach assigns primary importance to attracting debt and equity capital to support businesses owned by people of color and household needs in communities of color. Our approach emphasizes the development of businesses owned by communities of color, which are linked to the high-growth sectors of the economy and principles of democratic ownership and governance. Last, we believe that without a broad-based community-building approach—which involves mobilizing the entire range of the nation's assets, including the resources of government—America will not make significant progress toward solving the "inner-city problem."

NOTES

We are indebted to our colleagues at City College of San Francisco who read all or parts of this chapter, particularly Marc Kitchel, Deborah Goldsmith, and George Moss. We are also especially grateful to Peter Bohmer for his valuable advice and encouragement throughout the development of this work.

1. The term *minority* has less and less meaning, particularly in the United States, as demographic shifts show increasing numbers and percentages of people of color, particularly Latinos, in the population. Although sometimes more cumbersome, in this chapter we generally use terms such as *people of color, communities of color,* and *nonwhite populations* instead of the word *minority*.

2. Michael F. Porter, "The Competitive Advantage of the Inner City," *Harvard Business Review* (May–June 1995): 55–71.

3. Porter, "The Competitive Advantage," 55.

4. Porter, "The Competitive Advantage," 55.

5. Porter, "The Competitive Advantage," 56.

6. Porter, "The Competitive Advantage," 56.

7. Porter adds to this feature his expectation that cadres of minority MBA holders (currently twenty-eight hundred African Americans and fourteen Hispanics per year) will return to the inner cities to provide much-needed managerial skills.

8. Porter uses the terms *inner city* and *mainstream* without defining them. The term *inner city* often refers to low-income urban areas where there are a heavy concentration of African Americans and Latinos. However, the term *mainstream firms* is

quite ambiguous and appears to apply to large, heavily capitalized firms.

9. There has been an ongoing debate, a "people versus place" debate, in economic development research and practice regarding the strategies of targeting places (e.g., inner cities) or targeting people (e.g., the poor, especially minorities). See, for example, R. Bolton, "Place Prosperity vs. People Prosperity Revisited: An Old Issue with a New Angle," *Urban Studies* 29, no. 2 (1992): 185–203; M. Edel, "People versus Place in Urban Impact Analysis," in *The Urban Impacts of Federal Policies*, ed. N. Glickman (Baltimore: Johns Hopkins University Press, 1980) 175–191; L. Snow, "Economic Development Breaks the Mold: Community-Building, Place-Targeting, and Empowerment Zones," *Economic Development Quarterly* 9, no. 2 (1995): 185–198.

10. Porter, "The Competitive Advantage," 61.

11. Porter, "The Competitive Advantage," 61. The term *downstream product* or *service* is most commonly employed by marketing professionals in the technology sector to denote an upcoming product that is a derivative of an existing product. While this term is used in other sectors, such as biotechnology, to denote a medical correlation between product lines, its use in the technology sector does not indicate a specific phase of the product development cycle.

12. Porter, "The Competitive Advantage," 60.

13. For example, Porter suggests that a bank that closes a minority loan could be awarded a transaction fee to offset the high cost associated with making such a loan.

14. For a critique of the conservative (neoclassical) theoretical base of Porter's model and for alternative solutions, see Curtis Haynes Jr. and Jessica Gordon Nembhard, "Cooperative Economics: A Community Revitalization Strategy," in *Leading Issues in Black Political Economy*, (New Brunswick, N.J.: Transaction Publishers, 2002): 457–464. For additional discussion of the Porter model and its weaknesses, see the contributions in *The Inner City*, ed. Thomas Boston and Catherine Ross, (New Brunswick, N.J.: Transaction Publishers, 1997).

15. Porter, "The Competitive Advantage," 62.

16. Gary Dymski, "Business Strategy and Access to Capital in Inner-City Revitalization," in *The Inner City*, ed. T. Boston and C. Ross (New Brunswick, N.J.: Transaction Publishers, 1997), 54–55. Market forces leading to, and influenced by, deindustrialization and financial restructuring have devastated the inner-city economy. For example, industrial job losses have been particularly heavy in the inner city, and many financial intermediaries have discontinued their operations and services there as a result of financial restructuring.

17. Dymski, "Business Strategy and Access to Capital," 55.

18. From a feasibility study conducted for the Central Brooklyn Federal Credit Union, quoted in the *New York Times*, April 25, 1993; see Jessica Gordon Nembhard, "Entering the New City as Men and Women, Not Mules," working paper, University of Maryland, College Park, 2003.

19. Brett Fairbairn, June Bold, Murray Fulton, Lou Hammond Ketilson, and Daniel Ish, *Co-operatives and Community Development: Economics in Social Perspective* (Saskatoon, Saskatchewan: University of Saskatchewan Centre for the Study of Co-operatives, 1995), 23, 27.

20. Michael E. Porter, "New Strategies for Inner-City Economic Development," *Economic Development Quarterly* 11, no. 1 (February 1997): 20.

21. Jessica Gordon Nembhard, "Community Economic Development: Alternative Visions for the 21st Century," *Readings in Black Political Economy* (DuBuque, Iowa: Kendall/Hunt Publishing, 1999), 297–299.

22. Porter, "The Competitive Advantage," 68.

23. See Susan S. Fainstein and Mia Gray, "Economic Development Strategies for the Inner City: The Need for Government Intervention," in *The Inner City*, ed. T. Boston and C. Ross (New Brunswick, N.J.: Transaction Publishers, 1997), 30, for a critique of the history of government subsidies to the business sector and their impact on communities of color.

24. Timothy Bates, "Utilization of Minority Employees in Small Businesses: A Comparison of Nonminority and Black-Owned Urban Enterprises," *Review of Black Political Economy* (Summer 1994): 113–121.

25. Bates, "Utilization of Minority Employees," 113.

26. Bates, "Utilization of Minority Employees," 114.

27. Dymski, "Business Strategy and Access to Capital," 53.

28. Porter, "The Competitive Advantage," 61.

29. C. Michael Henry, "The Porter Model of Competitive Advantage for Inner-City Development: An Appraisal," in *The Inner City*, ed. T. Boston and C. Ross (New Brunswick, N.J.: Transaction Publishers, 1997), 144.

30. An additional roadblock to employment development in the inner city is strong overseas competition for many of the industries that Porter suggests are promising, such as electronic assembly and data processing. This competition deepens the crisis of structural unemployment that resulted from the departure of blue-collar industries, such as autos and steel, for cheaper labor abroad. This deindustrialization devastated the labor market for good-paying blue-collar jobs that had been the underpinning of the inner-city working class for decades. Edward J. Blakely and Leslie Small, "Michael Porter: New Gilder of the Ghettos," in *The Inner City*, ed. T. Boston and C. Ross (New Brunswick, N.J.: Transaction Publishers, 1997), 168, 170.

31. Dymski, "Business Strategy and Access to Capital," 58–60.

32. In addition to overt race discrimination, people of color are more likely to face perceptions of lack of credit worthiness in home-loan and home-equity applications as a result of racially "neutral" acts that are economically "rational." See Dymski, "Business Strategy and Access to Capital," 55. A recent study by the Association of Community Organizations for Reform Now demonstrates continuing, and in some cases growing, economic and racial disparities in home purchase and mortgage lending. The report found that although the disparity between white and minority denial rates decreased nationally from 1998 to 1999, these gains were not realized in Chicago or in many of the nation's biggest metropolitan areas with large minority populations, including Oakland, Miami, Atlanta, Detroit, Baltimore, Memphis, Milwaukee, St. Louis, and Washington, D.C. "While financial modernization allowed banks to expand into a number of new businesses, they still fail to provide lower income and minority families with one of the most basic and needed services-loans to realize their dream of home ownership" ("Minority Mortgage Rejection Decline Nationally, but Racial Gap Widens in Chicago," *Chicago Citizen* 35, no. 27 [October 12, 2000]: 5).

33. These institutions are private grassroots organizations with long-term commitments to the communities they serve. Richard Taub of the University of Chicago reports that "the process of community revitalization takes a long time. In the South Shore community [of Chicago], my measurements show that it's taken eight years for things to really have changed. Government programs can't wait that long" (at www.pbs.org/capital/cdfi/not.html, for *Faith, Hope, and Capital* video).

34. See the Credit Union National Association website, at www.cuna.coop; and the National Federation of Community Development Credit Unions website, www.natfed.org.

35. This definition is derived from Pat Barringer, "Community Economic Development: Principles, Practices, and Strategies," course material for Neighborhood Reinvestment Corporation training workshop (Boston: OKM Associates, 1998).

36. See Nembhard, "Community Economic Development," 297–298.

37. P. Pietgoff, "Child Care Enterprise, Community Development and Work," *Georgetown Law Journal* 81, no. 5 (June 1997): 1916.

38. These principles receive little if any credibility from private business advocates because, according to Porter, they place "inappropriate" demands on businesses that are simply trying to pursue their profit-maximizing objectives.

39. Committee for Economic Development, Research and Policy Committee, *Rebuilding Inner-City Communities: A New Approach to the Nation's Urban Crisis* (New York: Author, 1995), 4. See Jessica Gordon Nembhard, "Democratic Economic Participation and Humane Development," *Trotter Review* (2000): 26–31, for further discussion of democratic participation when applied to urban revitalization.

40. See Jessica Gordon Nembhard and Anthony A. Blassingame, "Economic Dimensions of Civic Engagement and Political Efficacy," working paper for the Democracy Collaborative–Knight Foundation Civic Engagement Project, University of Maryland, December 2002, at www.democracycollaborative.org; and Nembhard, "Democratic Economic Participation."

41. Jessica Gordon Nembhard posits that empowering inner-city residents by giving them democratic control "over decisions about economic activity and policy . . . enhances [local] productivity and profitability." See Nembhard, "Democratic Economic Participation."

42. In either case, the market mechanism often does not provide a means for these goods and services to be affordable to all. Local and national movements that push for universal health care, free education from preschool through college, free or affordable child care, affordable and high-quality public transportation, and affordable housing are steps in that direction. Movements for economic

justice that win demands for a livable income also go part of the way toward creating the necessary purchasing power.

43. The term *equity* has several meanings since it is defined by the customary standards and norms of different communities. Thus, equity may not mean absolute income equality. The income and wealth inequality within the United States is by most standards quite unjust. One way of measuring income inequality is to look at the proportion of income that the 20 percent of the population with the highest income receives compared to the 20 percent with the lowest income. The difference in the United States is about ten to one: the highest 20 percent of all households receive almost 50 percent of all income; the poorest 20 percent receive less than 5 percent of the national income. These gaps are growing. An equitable community economic development policy reduces these huge gaps within and between communities. This requires the redistribution of income and wealth on a substantial scale.

44. June Manning Thomas, "Rebuilding Inner Cities: Basic Principles," in *The Inner City*, ed. T. Boston and C. Ross (New Brunswick, N.J.: Transaction Publishers, 1997), 72.

45. *Employment anchor* refers to an industry or a specific class of businesses ("emerging minority businesses") that serve as the primary employer of workers in a geographical location or of those belonging to a specific social group. Before deindustrialization, the manufacturing industry was the employment anchor for blue-collar workers in most inner cities.

46. Traditional minority businesses are frequently compared to minority businesses in the "emerging fields." The so-called emerging lines of minority business enterprise are business services; finance, insurance, and real estate; transportation and communication; and wholesale trade. According to Timothy Bates, "emerging black firms . . . are larger, fail less often, and generate more jobs" than traditional firms. See Timothy Bates, "Traditional and Emerging Lines of Black Enterprise," in *Race and Ethnic Conflict* (Boulder, Colo.: Westview Press, 1994), 251.

47. Chancellor Williams, "The Economic Basis of African Life," *The Rebirth of African Civilization* (1961; repr., Chicago: Third World Press, 1993), 178.

48. Haynes and Nembhard, "Cooperative Economics," 47.

49. See the National Cooperative Business Association website for more information, www.ncba .coop.

50. See Haynes and Nembhard, "Cooperative Economics"; Nembhard, "Community Economic Development"; and Nembhard, "Entering the New City as Men and Women, Not Mules."

51. Nembhard, "Entering the New City as Men and Women, Not Mules."

52. Fairbairn et al., *Co-operatives and Community Development*, 1.

53. See Nembhard, "Community Economic Development."

54. Porter, "The Competitive Advantage," 66.

55. The limited success of the now-defunct Job Training Partnership Act was partially due to its failure to link training to local labor market demand. Moreover, the failure of many employment training programs to train to industry standards has contributed to many workers not acquiring general skills that are transferable across a significant range of jobs.

56. Customized training programs connected to specific job opportunities have generally been successful in improving job placement rates for inner-city workers. Customized training programs have also been an effective tool in attracting new companies with employment creation potential to inner-city locations. See Rosabeth Moss Kanter, *World Class: Thriving Locally in the Global Economy* (New York: Simon and Schuster, 1995).

57. See James Fitzgerald and William Patton, "Race, Job Training, and Economic Development: Barriers to Racial Equality in Program Planning," *Review of Black Political Economy* 23 (1994): 93; Bennett Harrison and Amy K. Glasmeire, "Why Business Alone Won't Redevelop the Inner City: A Friendly Critique of Michael Porter's Approach to Urban Revitalization," *Economic Development Quarterly* 11, no. 1 (February 1997): 33.

58. Allowing the private sector to take the lead in developing training services has not significantly improved the quality of training and placement in urban minority communities. In contrast, genuine collaboration between community-based organizations, government planners, the private sector, training venders, public schools, community colleges, and (sometimes) research universities has produced measurable superior placement and training outcomes. See Bennett Harrison, Marcus Weiss, and Jon Grant, *Building Bridges:*

Community Development Corporations and the World of Employment Training (New York: Ford Foundation, 1995).

59. The MESBIC name was changed several years ago to Specialized Small Business Investment Company (SSBIC); it refers to the same program.

60. Timothy Bates, "Financing the Development of Urban Minority Communities: Lessons of History," *Economic Development Quarterly* (August 2000).

61. Bates, "Financing the Development," 231.

62. The term *push mechanism* and some of these proposals are made by Dymski, "Business Strategy and Access to Capital," 61–62.

63. Dymski, "Business Strategy and Access to Capital," 63.

64. Nair Reichert, "Revitalizing the Inner-City: A Holistic Approach," in *The Inner City*, ed. T. Boston and C. Ross (New Brunswick, N.J.: Transaction Publishers, 1997), 72. The term *social energy* is described by Nembhard as "a non-material resource stimulated by the strategic use of cooperative action and consensus seeking" ("Community Economic Development," 227). This conception is based on work by Curtis Haynes Jr. ("A Democratic Cooperative Enterprise System: A Response to Urban Economic Decay," *Ceteris Paribus* 4, no. 2 [October 1994]: esp. 21 and n. 3, for an in-depth discussion of this term). Haynes likens the term *social energy* to DuBois's formulation of transforming the "cooperative spirit" into an economic resource (*Economic Cooperation among Negro Americans* [Atlanta, Ga.: Atlanta University Press, 1907]).

BIBLIOGRAPHY

Barringer, Pat. "Community Economic Development: Principles, Practices, and Strategies." Course material for Neighborhood Reinvestment Corporation training workshop. Boston: OKM Associates, 1998.

Bates, Timothy. "Financing the Development of Urban Minority Communities: Lessons of History." *Economic Development Quarterly* (August 2000).

———. "Traditional and Emerging Lines of Black Enterprise." In *Race and Ethnic Conflict*. Boulder, Colo.: Westview Press, 1994.

———. "Utilization of Minority Employees in Small Businesses: A Comparison of Non-minority and Black-Owned Urban Enterprises." *Review of Black Political Economy* (Summer 1994).

Blakely, Edward J., and Leslie Small. "Michael Porter: New Gilder of the Ghettos," in *The Inner City*, ed. Boston and Ross. New Brunswick, N.J.: Transaction Publishers, 1997.

Boston, Thomas D., and Catherine L. Ross, eds. *The Inner City: Urban Poverty and Economic Development in the Next Century*. New Brunswick, N.J.: Transactions Publishers, 1997.

Bruyn, Severyn T., and James Meehan, eds. *Beyond the Market and the State: New Directions in Community Development*. Philadelphia: Temple University Press, 1987.

Committee for Economic Development. Research and Policy Committee. *Rebuilding Inner-City Communities: A New Approach to the Nation's Urban Crisis*. New York: Committee for Economic Development, 1995.

Conley, Dalton. *Being Black, Living in the Red: Race, Wealth, and Social Policy in America*. Berkeley: University of California Press, 1999.

DuBois, W. E. B. *Economic Cooperation among Negro Americans*. Atlanta, Ga.: Atlanta University Press, 1907.

Dymski, Gary A. "Business Strategy and Access to Capital in the Inner City," in *The Inner City*, ed. Boston and Ross. New Brunswick, N.J.: Transaction Publishers, 1997.

Fainstein, Susan S., and Mia Gray. "Economic Development Strategies for the Inner City: The Need for Government Intervention," in *The Inner City*, ed. Boston and Ross. New Brunswick, N.J.: Transaction Publishers, 1997.

Fairbairn, Brett, June Bold, Murray Fulton, Lou Hammond Ketilson, and Daniel Ish. *Cooperatives and Community Development: Economics in Social Perspective*. Saskatoon, Saskatchewan: University of Saskatchewan Centre for the Study of Co-operatives, 1995.

Fitzgerald, James, and William Patton. "Race, Job Training, and Economic Development: Barriers to Racial Equality in Program Planning." *Review of Black Political Economy* 23 (1994).

Harrison, Bennett, and Amy K. Glasmeire. "Why Business Alone Won't Redevelop the Inner City: A Friendly Critique of Michael Porter's Approach to Urban Revitalization." *Economic Development Quarterly* 11, no. 1 (February 1997): 33.

Harrison, Bennett, Marcus Weiss, and Jon Grant.

Building Bridges: Community Development Corporations and the World of Employment Training. New York: Ford Foundation, 1995.

Haynes, Curtis, Jr. "A Democratic Cooperative Enterprise System: A Response to Urban Economic Decay." *Ceteris Paribus* 4, no. 2 (October 1994).

———. "An Essay in the Art of Economic Cooperation: Cooperative Enterprise and Economic Development in Black America." Ph.D. diss., University of Massachusetts, Amherst, 1993.

Haynes, Curtis, Jr., and Jessica Gordon Nembhard. "Cooperative Economics: A Community Revitalization Strategy," in *Leading Issues in Black Political Economy.* New Brunswick, N.J.: Transaction Publishers, 2002.

Henry, C. Michael. "The Porter Model of Competitive Advantage for Inner-City Development: An Appraisal," in *The Inner City,* ed. Boston and Ross. New Brunswick, N.J.: Transaction Publishers, 1997.

Kanter, Rosabeth Moss. *World Class: Thriving Locally in the Global Economy.* New York: Simon and Schuster, 1995.

Karsinitz, Philip, and Jan Rosenberb. "Why Enterprise Zones Will Not Work: Lesson from a Brooklyn Neighborhood." *City Journal* (Autumn 1993).

Nembhard, Jessica Gordon. "Community Economic Development: Alternative Visions for the 21st Century." *Readings in Black Political Economy* (DuBuque, Iowa: Kendall/Hunt Publishing Company, 1999), 295–304.

———. "Democratic Economic Participation and Humane Development." *Trotter Review* (2000): 26–31.

———. "Cooperatives and Wealth Accumulation: Preliminary Analysis." *American Economic Review* 92, no. 2 (May 2002; American Economic Association papers and proceedings): 325–329.

———. "Entering the New City as Men and Women, Not Mules." Working paper, University of Maryland, College Park, 2003.

Nembhard, Jessica Gordon, and Anthony A. Blassingame. "Economic Dimensions of Civic Engagement and Political Efficacy." Working paper for the Democracy Collaborative–Knight Foundation Civic Engagement Project, University of Maryland, College Park, December 2002, at www.democracycollaborative.org.

Porter, Michael E. "The Competitive Advantage of the Inner City." *Harvard Business Review* (May–June 1995).

Reichert, Nair. "Revitalizing the Inner City: A Holistic Approach," in *The Inner City,* ed. Boston and Ross. New Brunswick, N.J.: Transaction Publishers, 1997.

Sawicki, David S., and Mitch Moody. "Deja-vu All Over Again: Porter's Model of Inner-City Redevelopment," in *The Inner City,* ed. Boston and Ross. New Brunswick, N.J.: Transaction Publishers, 1997.

Whatley, Warren C., and Tia Wells. "Community Economic Development: Potentials and Challenges." In *Readings in Black Political Economy,* ed. John Whitehead and Kobi Kwasi Harris. Dubuque, Iowa: Kendall/Hunt Publishing, 1999.

Williams, Chancellor. "The Economic Basis of African Life." *The Rebirth of African Civilization* (1961; repr., Chicago: Third World Press, 1993), 151–181.

Williamson, Thad, David Imbrosio, and Gar Alperovitz. *Making a Place for Community: Local Democracy in a Global Era.* New York: Routledge, 2002.

WEBSITES

Acorn: www.livingwagecampaign.org

Credit Union National Association: www.cuna.coop

Democracy Collaborative: www.democracycollaborative.org

Faith, Hope and Capital video: www.pbs.org/capital/cdfi/not.html

National Cooperative Business Association: www.ncba.coop

National Federation of Community Development Credit Unions: www.natfed.org

40

Combating Gentrification through Equitable Development

KALIMA ROSE

While the expanding economy of the last decade accelerated the pace of displacement in revitalizing communities, the current recession has not reversed gentrification trends. Low-income and people-of-color communities remain particularly vulnerable to the larger trends of disinvestments, reinvestment, and displacement. This chapter discusses strategies to stabilize community revitalization by dealing with regional development patterns, housing affordability challenges, the lack of jurisdictional commitment to production of affordable housing, and the fiscal pursuit of sales tax and property tax.

The Fifth Avenue Committee has worked for fifteen years to revitalize the lower Park Slope neighborhood of Brooklyn by building affordable housing, rehabbing dilapidated buildings, and training residents to own cooperative businesses in the neighborhood. The success of these efforts has forced the committee into unanticipated arenas, including a Displacement-Free Zone campaign, its fierce effort to defend tenants within the thirty-six-block neighborhood from evictions; and a local and state policy campaign with other New York City organizations to give landlords incentives to keep their tenants in place and to require developers to include affordable housing in market rate developments. "Our work has made the neighborhood nicer, which was the point," reflects the Fifth Avenue Committee's director of organizing Benjamin Dulchin, "but it's meant that evictions are on the rise."[1]

Even though the expanding economy of the last decade accelerated the pace of displacement in revitalizing communities, the current recession has not reversed that trend. Thus, low-income and people-of-color communities such as lower Park Slope, working hard for equitable development, remain vulnerable to the larger trends and economic realities that come with revitalization. What exactly are these trends, and how can communities respond to make the improvements benefit existing residents?

DEVELOPMENT TRENDS

Regional development patterns play a significant role in gentrification and displacement in particular neighborhoods. As regions grow and sprawl into a network of economically interdependent jurisdictions, the abandoned or disinvested communities become attractive to residents and developers. Workers who tire of commuting long distances and who want to be closer to effective mass transit systems seek to move back toward the core. In an effort to stem hemorrhaging municipal budgets, public officials promote regional developments that will draw people back to the core for shopping and entertainment. Because the initial abandonment and disinvestment were spurred by segregationist practices such as "white flight," mortgage preferences, and redlining by banks and insurance companies, the new influx of people and capital has a distinct racial impact when displacement begins to occur.[2] For instance, gentrification in San Francisco's Mission District displaced residents and businesses from the Latino cultural nexus of the Bay Area; the expansions of Los Angeles' Staples Center entertainment complex and the University of Southern California threaten a historic African American community and a newer Latino community as land values escalate; Chinatowns of New York, Oakland, and Portland have felt the loss when seniors and low-income members of historic Asian communities can no longer afford the rents or taxes on their housing.

Housing affordability problems in the United States have become pervasive. A shrinking investment in affordable housing by the federal government limits the affordable supply and concentrates low-income housing in disinvested communities. The federal investment in the Department of Housing and Urban Development and low-income housing programs has declined as much as 60 percent over the last quarter century. These cutbacks have placed upward pressure on the affordability of existing private units. In 1999, over fourteen million households (owner and renter) spent more than half their incomes on housing. Contributing to these pressures is the ongoing loss of affordable rentals. More than three hundred thousand units affordable to households with low incomes were lost and not replaced between 1997 and 1999 alone.[3]

Not all jurisdictions are committed to producing affordable housing, and enforcement mechanisms are the exception rather than the rule. When jurisdictions undergoing growth do not tie development to affordability commitments, they place increasing pressure on units in affordable neighborhoods. Restrictions on land development and exclusionary zoning practices make it difficult for the market to produce housing that low-income people can afford. As household growth adds to demand, the mismatch between the supply of low-cost rentals and the number of households who need them will likely grow.[4]

Jurisdictions chase sales tax and property tax to increase local revenues. Jurisdictions make development decisions based on revenue instead of community need. Urban core jurisdictions increasingly opt for large-scale developments such as "big box" retail stores, hotels, and stadiums that draw visitors from across the region. These developments often directly displace community-serving and culturally oriented businesses, opening wounds for communities that were negatively affected by earlier urban renewal. The urban renewal programs of the 1960s and 1970s—also known as "urban removal"—caused widespread condemnation of African American commercial districts. To residents of New York's Harlem, Cincinnati's Over the Rhine, and Portland's Interstate neighborhood, revitalization efforts all portend the loss of community-serving enterprises. With this tangible history, however, the biggest champions for community continuity—the residents—are mobilizing to direct positive neighborhood and regional changes to ensure that their visions of equitable development come to life, rather than gentrification and displacement.

INDICATORS OF GENTRIFICATION

Specific community attributes that create the greatest vulnerabilities to displacement include a high proportion of renters; ease of access to job centers, such as freeways, public transit, reverse commutes, new subway stations, and ferry routes; location in a region with increasing levels of metropolitan congestion; and comparatively low housing values, particularly for housing stock with architectural merit.[5]

While the story of gentrification within each community is unique, the process tends to unfold in a series of recognizable stages. The first stage involves either a significant public or nonprofit redevelopment investment or a private newcomer's buying and rehabbing vacant units. In the next stage, the neighborhood's low housing costs and other amenities become known, and housing costs rise. Displacement begins as landlords take advantage of rising market values and evict longtime residents to rent or sell to the more affluent. Increasingly, newcomers are more likely to be homeowners, and the rising property values cause down payment requirements to increase. With new residents come commercial amenities that serve higher income levels.

As rehabilitation becomes more apparent, prices escalate and displacement occurs in force. New residents have lower tolerance for existing social service facilities that serve homeless populations or other low-income needs as well as industrial and other uses they view as undesirable. Original residents are displaced with their industries, commercial enterprises, faith institutions, and cultural traditions. In San Francisco's Mission District, rents escalated so rapidly in the past few years that nonprofit health clinics, Latino cultural arts organizations, and the ubiquitous auto-repair shops have been forced to close. In their place, dot-coms and other offices neither serve nor employ the historic residents of the community.

STRATEGIES TO RESPOND TO GENTRIFICATION

Gentrification and displacement are felt most severely in historic communities of color. While community advocates have worked tirelessly to attract new investment to their capital-starved communities, they concede that just recently they have begun to wield the tools or power to substantively intervene and redirect development projects that may bring harm to the community. The Fifth Avenue Committee's Displacement-Free Zone campaign, although effective as a community education and mobilization strategy, is enormously time-consuming and localized in impact. But organizers from San Francisco's Mission Antidisplacement Coalition, from Los Angeles' Figueroa Corridor Coalition for Economic Justice, from Portland's Interstate Alliance to End Displacement, and from the District of Columbia's Colombia Heights and Shaw neighborhoods are adopting similar campaigns to heighten community awareness of the problem. They are also mobilizing tremendous policy gains that include new housing trust funds, inclusionary housing or zoning campaigns, real estate transfer taxes that dedicate sources of new affordable housing revenue, and campaigns for historic tax credits—all

of which provide for the revitalization of commercial districts with the explicit charge of meeting current residents' needs for jobs, services, contracts, and so forth.[6]

First, Assess

A strategic assessment of the situation is a crucial first step because it not only helps a community figure out what is taking place but will provide a baseline of information that communities can then compare to their community goals.[7]

The very best time to start dealing with displacement is at the beginning of community revitalization efforts. Most communities, however, begin to focus on displacement when the elders, the disabled, and those with the most limited incomes start facing eviction or when the indigenous businesses and service organizations can no longer afford rent in the neighborhood. An assessment usually involves community-mapping efforts that identify renter-to-home owner rates; vacancy and abandonment rates; affordability indexes, or rent and mortgage as percentage of household income; and spatial analyses of race and poverty.

Action on Four Fronts to Preserve and Expand the Supply of Affordable Housing

After an assessment, communities will have a better sense of their priorities and will be ready to take action. Four major categories of action form the basis for an antidisplacement strategy that can help to stabilize a gentrifying neighborhood. Whether communities are working to rehab and fill vacant buildings in depopulated urban cores or to improve community infrastructure in fully populated low-income neighborhoods, an explicit housing affordability plan should always be in place first. A comprehensive housing affordability plan has several integral objectives, such as those that follow.

Stabilize existing renters. This can include assessing displacement rates, creating emergency funds for rental assistance, removing discriminatory barriers that renters face, and creating rent stabilization policies such as eviction controls and rent increase schedules.

On the proactive side, developing limited-equity housing cooperatives and other forms of resident-controlled housing allows a neighborhood to stabilize by turning some of the high proportion of renters into home owners. The democratic organization of co-ops also creates a structure that enables co-op members to play significant roles in neighborhood development. Harlem has the largest proportion of cooperative housing of any community of color in the United States. With over three hundred buildings under cooperative ownership in Harlem, residents can stay in their community as land values rise, and use their savings on housing to accrue other assets. The Harlem Community Congregations is working to acquire vacant land held by the city and to develop the equivalent of real estate investment trusts with residents of the neighborhood as shareholders.

With resident-controlled housing, building and preserving affordable housing can involve all three sectors: nonprofit-owned, public-sector developed, and private housing with long-term affordability restrictions. In particular, legal mechanisms to ensure long-term affordability can preserve public investment in housing and take properties off the commercial market. San Francisco has one of the highest rates of non-profit-owned housing in the country. In the Tenderloin neighborhood, over a dozen nonprofit organizations focus on specific racial minority communities or special-needs populations and keep culturally relevant, service-appropriate housing available for the long-term.

Control land for community development. Land use, tax, and zoning policies all shape equitable developments; a housing affordability plan cannot succeed without taking them into account. Communities need to evaluate zoning and public-land giveaways and steer them in the direction of their aspirations. To do so will include promoting inclusionary zoning ordinances, mixed-use and transit-oriented development, and density provisions—all of which can encourage affordability and mixed-income areas. One of the Fifth Avenue Committee's policy campaigns is for a citywide New York inclusionary zoning policy that would require developers to include the low-income housing within the market rate development, rather than simply contribute to a fund dedicated to affordable housing. The latter

can have the effect of concentrating low-income housing rather than spreading it across jurisdictions wherever development is occurring. The Balanced Development Coalition in Chicago, which has a similar goal, is negotiating with developers building by building until they have the power and public will to win through legislation.

When communities take the initiative to map out the commercial, industrial, service, and arts amenities they want to hold onto and negotiate with public and private actors, they find creative ways to do this. "We approached [Staples Center developers and city officials] with neighborhood residents and a large coalition of community organizations, churches, and unions," recounted Jafari Eayne, organizer for the Figueroa Corridor Coalition. "It took a two to three year campaign, but after a lot of media pressure, a lot of organizing, and a lot of good coalition work, we managed to get a community benefits package that includes things like local hiring, affordable housing, money for parks, and the first ever low-income parking district."[8]

ACORN California and PolicyLink are two groups working to advance a regional tax-sharing campaign in the Sacramento region that pools future tax increments and redistributes them via a formula of population and incentives for affordable housing and open space.

Build income and assets creation. Although stabilizing housing affordability and ensuring appropriate amenities are crucial components of neighborhood planning, income and asset creation are critical to ensuring the residents' well-being as the neighborhood economy improves. One precondition for success is to provide needed residential services—child care, transportation, a retail sector, and access to health care. Tying public investment to local-hire and living-wage provisions or otherwise connecting land use decisions to local asset creation can significantly mitigate negative displacement pressures by bringing some of the benefits of the new investment to existing residents.

The Interstate Alliance to End Displacement in Portland has a three-pronged policy campaign to advance their equitable development aspirations. A short-term local campaign is focused on the city budget to win rental assistance to residents facing rent escalations as high as 200 percent. A statewide campaign for real estate transfer taxes is underway to provide revenue for affordable housing production on a scale commensurate with demand for the entire Portland metro region. The asset-building campaign may prove the most innovative in its delivery of direct community benefits. Led by coalition member Hacienda Community Development Corporation, it proposes a mixed-use development at one of the new light-rail transit stations in the city's redevelopment plan. This prospective development would provide ownership opportunities for the current residents of Interstate; a credit union for the burgeoning Latino community; home ownership opportunities in 20 percent of the 107 affordable housing units; a worker-owned cooperative for parking at the transit stop; and resident ownership of other commercial and cultural aspects of the plan. The plan brings together innovative policy, community organizing, and physical development to realize the fullest benefits of equitable development.[9]

Develop financing strategies. Proactive financing strategies can provide neighborhood-specific ways to fund the other three categories of action. They are generally most effective in communities that anticipate gentrification pressures before redevelopment, since communities already suffering displacement face escalated real estate prices and limited available capital. Options for funding are numerous and can be directed at nonprofits, private developers, and even landlords. They include investments from labor union pension funds and regional business associations; exactions and fees on commercial developments; tax increment financing and eminent domain; bank investments under the Community Reinvestment Act; community credit unions and tax abatements; credits and deferments. In Washington, D.C., activists just succeeded in capitalizing a new housing trust fund being supported by an annual $15 million from a real estate transfer tax that is indexed for speculation.

Core Tools in Action

Within each of these four categories lie dozens of tools. What follows is a list of some of the most important tools, as well as ideas about how they

can connect to one another and to other strategies to redirect the development trends that yield gentrification and displacement and undermine equitable development goals:

Community land trusts take real estate off the speculative market and ensure long-term affordability for renters, low-income homeowners, community arts and nonprofit institutions, and community-centered businesses. The Sawmill community of Albuquerque, for example, is building its vision of mixed income, Latino-rooted, mixed-use development on a brownfield turned community land trust. Community-based organizations in Oakland, California, are crafting a citywide trust with neighborhood equity and representation. They have won a $5 million commitment from the city to initially capitalize the trust.[10]

Limited-equity housing cooperatives are another affordability mechanism, providing a method for renters to acquire their buildings and share in permanently affordable and democratically controlled home-ownership opportunities. A group of renters in a class action lawsuit over the uninhabitable conditions of their Colombia Heights apartments in Washington, D.C., reached a settlement to acquire ownership of their building for the cost of one dollar. With a limited-equity cooperative, they will formalize resident ownership and make long-needed improvements to the building. If Columbia Heights can achieve the scale of cooperatives found in Harlem (which has more than three hundred) and combine that with rent stabilization and zoning protections, the neighborhood will have strong antidisplacement protection.[11]

Housing trust funds, created by legislation that dedicates ongoing revenue streams to affordable housing, are one of the most promising financing strategies for combating gentrification, particularly if they are used to provide housing that includes long-term affordability restrictions. San Francisco, for example, channels fees from commercial development into a housing trust fund, with federal HOME and Community Development Block Grant money as well as state and city revenues allocated to housing. These funds target households that earn 30 percent to 50 percent of the area median income.

Inclusionary zoning and below–market rate ordinances provide an ongoing framework for ensuring mixed-income communities. East Palo Alto, a historically African American and growing Latino community on the edge of Silicon Valley, recently enacted a below–market rate ordinance that requires one of every four units to be made available to people making no more than 30 percent of area median income. With significant new development underway, this provision will provide home ownership opportunities for many residents who would otherwise be forced to leave their community. These ordinances combine particularly well with the three core tools listed here.[12]

Organizing

Achieving any of these objectives takes political will, however, which means organizing. Brooklyn's Fifth Avenue Committee called together two hundred actors in community development, neighborhood associations, and urban planning to develop a proposal for a broad policy response to displacement in their community. The Fifth Avenue Committee has garnered leadership commitments to propose joint action on inclusionary zoning, tax abatements for rental support, and mortgage conditions that hold new owners of apartment buildings accountable under agreements that prohibit eviction for specified periods.

There is no reason why people who have worked so hard to build lives and improve their neighborhoods should not be able to stay there. The types of dynamic policy responses to the forces of investment and development described here bode well for holding communities together, especially as they revitalize and thrive.[13]

NOTES

Kalima Rose is senior associate at PolicyLink in Oakland, California. See PolicyLink's Beyond Gentrification Toolkit, a web-based resource for equitable development, at www.policylink.org.

1. Interview at Equitable Development Policy Conference, March 16, 2002, Kansas City, Mo.

2. Maureen Kennedy and Paul Leonard, *Dealing with Neighborhood Change: A Primer on Gentrification and Policy Choices* (Washington, D.C.: Brookings Institution Center on Urban and Metropolitan Policy; Oakland, Calif.: PolicyLink, April 2001), 29.

3. National Low-Income Housing Coalition, "Out of Reach 2002: Rental Housing for America's Poor Families: Farther Out of Reach Than Ever," Washington, D.C., September 2002.

4. Nonprofit Housing Association of Northern California, "The Bay Area Housing Crisis Report Card," June 2002, San Francisco, available at www.nonprofithousing.org.

5. Kennedy and Leonard, *Dealing with Neighborhood Change*, 9.

6. PolicyLink has been working with many coalitions across the country to draw new capital resources to these communities while allowing enough community control of development to enable current residents and appropriate commercial, industrial, and community service amenities to remain. PolicyLink's web-based "Equitable Development Toolkit: Beyond Gentrification" (www.policylink.org) provides a roadmap to the most effective policies and practices that are emerging from innovative campaigns across the country.

7. Kennedy and Leonard, *Dealing with Neighborhood Change*, 31.

8. Interview at Equitable Development Policy Conference, March 16, 2002, Kansas City, Mo.

9. From field visits conducted March 2002–March 2003.

10. See www.policylink.org/equitabledevelopment, Community Land Trust tool.

11. See www.policylink.org/equitabledevelopment, Housing Trust Fund tool.

12. See www.policylink.org/equitabledevelopment, Inclusionary Zoning tool.

13. For more information, see the Beyond Gentrification Toolkit (note 6).

41

The Black Church and Community Economic Development

SHONDRAH NASH and CEDRIC HERRING

The black church has long been one of the major institutions in the struggle to achieve African American socioeconomic development and progress. This chapter examines the historical and current involvement of the black church in black economic development and the revitalization of American inner cities. It discusses the role of the black church in African American social capital formation, the black church's use of cooperative and holistic strategies, and examples of successful black church–sponsored community economic development ventures and campaigns. The chapter concludes by suggesting that the black church may be poised as never before to carry out successful strategies to revitalize inner-city communities.

At various times in history, the black church has been in the forefront in generating community economic development and empowerment. The church has also been one of the few institutions where African Americans could construct their own interpretations and understandings of the world and develop social structures independent of the greater society. In addition to giving birth to several black colleges and universities, black churches have been the birthplace of notable entrepreneurial ventures. In addition, black churches have been instrumental in establishing alternatives to discriminatory financial institutions. All across the United States, churches from different denominations are forming partnerships to fight institutionalized discrimination and to combat social problems such as drug abuse, crime, and illiteracy.

This chapter presents an overview of the historical and contemporary role of the black church in community economic development. It then shows how the black church has been engaged in community outreach and community development. As well, this chapter shows that although the role of the black church has evolved, it continues to be a center of social and political involvement in America's black communities. Increasingly, the black church has been a primary source of economic and community development as well as empowerment in cities and towns across the United States.

Community economic development is generally designed to empower community residents. This often means identifying ways of generating job opportunities, reducing poverty, ridding neighborhoods of social problems, and strengthening neighborhoods. Some efforts focus on increasing levels of education; others center on growing businesses and building wealth; still others concentrate on employment issues. These efforts share the view that community residents themselves are central to formulating and carrying out strategies to revitalize their communities.

THE BLACK CHURCH AS THE HISTORICAL IMPETUS FOR ECONOMIC DEVELOPMENT IN THE AFRICAN AMERICAN COMMUNITY

Before community action toward economic development could be forged, African Americans had to develop a basis from which they could envision and consequently galvanize their efforts. Perhaps unknowingly, religion was one of the first institutions that inspired early blacks to establish economic development initiatives. Indeed, the efforts of early African American church folk resemble a model of economic community development whose utility has remained important. Church folk combined their meager economic resources, purchased property, constructed or bought buildings, and collectively acquired their "church homes." The beginnings of collective strides in black social welfare and development, however, did not come without difficulties.

The Black Church's Inspiring Social Justice and Economic Initiatives in Slavery and Post–Civil War America

Many African slaves in America had to secretly craft a religious doctrine to subvert their owners' gospel of docility or objection to the slaves' religious enfranchisement. Often risking severe punishment or death, slaves gathered in secluded places or in the secrecy of their quarters to devise a Christianity and an "invisible institution" that was empathic to their voicelessness and oppression. Despite these constraints, emancipation was most frequently highlighted in the discourse and practices of slave religion. Biblical narratives and adages told by slave preachers or ministers hired by slave masters were interpreted in light of the slaves' daily experiences, distress, and desire for freedom. Moreover, religion was perceived as a withdrawn, yet proactive means of social resistance. Black slaves, for example, prayed for the success of Union forces during the American Civil War, despite urging from slaveowners and slave mistresses to the contrary (Raboteau 1967).

On the dismantling of slavery, emancipatory preachings were parlayed into collaborative efforts between White House officials and black religious leaders vying for economic initiatives for the newly freed slave. In 1865, president Abraham Lincoln's abolitionist secretary of war, Edwin Stanton, consulted an audience of black religious leaders who advocated land allowances for African Americans in light of the pending Emancipation Proclamation. Special Field Order 15 was drafted four days after the meeting. The federal injunction set aside forty acres of coastal, tillable ground for freed slaves that stretched from South Carolina to northern Florida (Billingsley 1999). Although tabled after Lincoln's assassination, the order suggests the black religious sector's influence and the importance it placed on property ownership in securing economic stability and community development.

Mutual Aid and Beneficial Societies, Fraternal Orders and the Black Economic Ethos

In areas settled by blacks, quasi-religious mutual aid and beneficial societies and fraternal organizations were established in response to racial discrimination, white philanthropic neglect, and black economic disenfranchisement (Lincoln and Mamiya 1990; Loescher 1948). Many have disbanded over time. Nevertheless, these orders demonstrate the importance of economic cooperation in answering black community needs. Perhaps the earliest, Philadelphia's Free African Society, was organized in 1787 by two Methodist leaders, Absalom Jones and Richard Allen. Described as a sort of "ethical and beneficial brotherhood," the Free African Society offered support for infirmed African American men, their widows, and fatherless children (Frazier 1963). Beneficial societies ("sickness and burial" associations) held close ties to black churches and populated cities throughout the United States. Black-owned funeral parlors and mortuaries grew from such enterprises and today constitute a noted economic base in the African American community. In the post–Civil War North, orders such as the Reverend Moses Dickson's Temple and Tabernacle of the Knights and Daughters of Tabor advised its members to avoid intemperance and to acquire real estate. In the South, the True Reformers—a Virginia fraternal order led in part by church men—produced an array of enterprises, including a real estate firm, a weekly newspaper, a bank, and a hotel (Frazier 1963). However, black self-help initiatives were also promoted in more discursive ways. In the pulpit, black ministers extolled the value of saving portions of earnings, while print publications such as the American Methodist Episcopal's *Christian Recorder* urged blacks to replicate the economic advancements of European Jews. Collectively, the efforts of black Protestant leaders and the Christian media helped to form and internalize a Protestant economic ethos of sorts, which rationalized the benefits of industry, discipline, sobriety, long-term sublimation over immediate gratification, and racial solidarity (Lincoln and Mamiya 1990).

The early twentieth century marked migrations from the South, the black church's emphasis on education issues, and the effects of the Great Depression and federal social welfare programs. All these factors, in part, took a toll on the black church's economic initiatives. Nevertheless, remaining intact were small- and large-scale religious-based initiatives aimed at fostering the social welfare of African Americans. Depression-era black churches, for example, held classes for newly arrived rural immigrants on the fundamentals of job seeking and household management. Many pre–Civil Rights era ministers negotiated for blacks' access to jobs. Particularly reflective of Protestant values, innovative educator Booker T. Washington espoused a philosophy of moral gradualism, whereby blacks could demonstrate their marketability to prospective white employers. To this end, Washington extolled the benefits of economic accumulation and black support of black businesses (Lincoln and Mamiya 1990). In Detroit during the early 1930s, Wali Fard Mohammad and, later, Elijah Mohammed promoted the Nation of Islam as an alternative to black mainstream religion, especially among black males. Although its social and religious philosophies remain controversial, the Nation of Islam has been successful in embedding a behavioral discipline that regards self-help enterprising over mainstream capitalist ventures (Lincoln 1974).

From Societies to Strip Malls: Gains in Black Economic and Community Development during the Late-Twentieth and Early-Twenty-First Century

During the late twentieth century, the black church continued to push for the creation of black businesses and wealth accumulation in African American communities. In the 1960s, Philadelphia pastor Leon Sullivan's Opportunities Industrial Centers established the "10–36" plan. Congregants gave ten dollars for thirty-six months to a community investment cooperative. Consequently, a shopping complex, garment plant, and shopping center were erected. In response to claims of racial discrimination in lending, the Southern Christian Leadership Conference in 1988 campaigned for black churches to withdraw their monies out of white banks and deposit them in black-owned financial institutions (Lincoln and Mamiya 1990). Currently in Atlanta, the Wheat Street Plaza and its two strip malls house ten small businesses. The enterprise is the product of the Wheat Street Charitable Foundation, a nonprofit organization that is the developmental arm of the Wheat Street Baptist Church. The foundation does not own any of the businesses; however, all of the merchants are members of the church, four of whom have been in the mall since its construction over twenty-five years ago. Most of the businesses are owned by African Americans (DePriest and Jones 1997).

WHY THE BLACK CHURCH?

In contemporary America, faith-based organizations often find themselves distinctively positioned to provide leadership in many communities. In distressed urban neighborhoods and in depressed rural towns, local religious groups often represent the best hope for community development and empowerment. But not all faith-based organizations are involved in community development. In fact, "relatively few faith-based organizations participate in community development activities" (Vidal 2001, i). Among African American congregations, it is fairly common practice to spin off separate nonprofit organizations in which the local pastor may play a key role. Congregations with a predominantly African American membership are more likely than Anglo-dominated congregations to be involved in community development activities (McDougall 1993; McRoberts 2001).

In their book *The Black Church in the African American Experience,* Lincoln and Mamiya (1990) report on the results of surveys encompassing nearly nineteen hundred ministers and over twenty-one hundred churches. Some 71 percent of black clergy reported that their churches engaged in community outreach programs, including day care, job search, substance abuse prevention, food and clothing distribution, and many others. Black urban churches, they find, are generally more engaged in outreach than rural ones are. Size is also an important variable because large congregations are likely to have financial resources, paid staff, and members willing to serve as unpaid volunteers. Theological orientation also makes a difference, as liberal congregations are more than twice as likely than are conservative congregations to engage in social services and to carry out community-oriented activities. Congregations located in areas where more than 30 percent of the residents live below the poverty line also are more likely to be involved in work in their communities. Finally, the presence of charismatic leadership in a congregation committed to community work is a significant factor in a congregation's participation.

Beyond these characteristics are several reasons why the black church is often involved in community economic development. First, the black church remains the most stable institution in the black community. It also has the ability, through members' tithes and offerings, to raise money. Lincoln and Mamiya (1990) show that churches and religion receive the highest percentage of charitable donations and volunteer time. Moreover, church-born enterprises and the cumulative property value of churches run into the billions of dollars. These resources can be leveraged and can provide seed funding for development projects that will generate additional assets that can be used to provide needed services such as low-cost child care, food pantries, and antidrug programs (DePriest and Jones 1997).

In addition, because the church generates collective goods that are owned by members of a cooperative enterprise rather than by an individual, it is more able to tap into voluntary efforts that allow it to accumulate assets more rapidly than would be the case with paid labor. Such voluntary efforts depend on goodwill and the idea that the church is being responsiveness to local needs. Nevertheless, because many black churches are embedded in national and international networks, they are able to form coalitions with others involved in similar efforts, to become major actors in urban revitalization planning and development, and to take advantage of economies of scale that result from collective endeavors (Stewart n.d.).

EMPLOYMENT

The intractable nature of inner-city joblessness has presented one of the greatest challenges to those concerned with community economic development. In many inner-city neighborhoods, communities struggle to retain their employment bases, and large numbers of residents have difficulty securing work. Increasingly, the long-term unemployed have become concentrated in neighborhoods that are physically and socially isolated from emerging employment centers. When combined with the decline of inner-city economies, this isolation creates great hardships for residents. Workers with few employment opportunities near their homes are forced to find employment in distant job centers.

With this current age of government downsizing and skepticism about the ability of elected officials to solve complex and unwieldy societal ills, there has been a renewed interest in involving the black church in tackling illiteracy, insufficient day care, inadequate job training, and other barriers to job readiness. As mentioned, the black church has historically offered a welcoming place of empowerment and encouragement.

Despite concerns that the black church is embarking on areas where its competence and effectiveness are in question, it increasingly offers job skills and placement services. For example, those providing job training and transportation include New York congregations such as the Bronx Christian Fellowship, Abyssinian Baptist Church in Harlem, Allen A. M. E. Church in Queens, Grace Baptist Church in West Chester, and Greater Centennial A. M. E. Zion Church in Mount Vernon, as well as New Jersey churches such as First Baptist of Lincoln Gardens and Elmwood United Presbyterian of East Orange (Webber 2001). These are not just menial, dead-end jobs. They often involve computer literacy, training in the use of various software programs, accessing the Internet, sending and receiving e-mail, HTML design, graphics applications, and webpage design; television production and editing; culinary arts; and events planning. In addition, job-training efforts focus on increasing professionalism and personal productivity through sessions that introduce skills that strengthen commitment to organizational goals and missions. In other words, these efforts are usually geared toward meeting the labor force and the technological needs of local businesses in the twenty-first century. These efforts have gone a long way toward reducing the joblessness and underemployment that expose workers to economic insecurity and that ultimately weaken local communities.

COMMUNITY DEVELOPMENT CORPORATIONS AND WEALTH CREATION

Wealth creation is another common goal of community development. Usually, African American churches establish community development corporations (CDCs) to operate their community projects (Orr 2000; Owens 2000). CDCs are organizations engaged in planning, entrepreneurial, and management activities involving community economic development. They typically concern themselves with community organizing as well as physical and economic growth that often takes the form of encouraging home ownership. For blacks, home ownership is the most important type of wealth. Homes account for 65 percent of blacks' total wealth, compared to 40 percent for others in the nation.

African American churches "have traditionally worked . . . to preserve ownership of projects that are 'in, of, and for' the African-American community" (Day 2001, 193). Depending on the

needs of their communities, CDCs may be involved in a range of activities, including housing renovation and construction, economic development, and social services. As a result, entrepreneurial churches are able to tackle whole neighborhoods and "a plethora of issues within them—education, business development, housing, commercial development, job training, crime and safety, and so on" (194).

Although several churches have been successful in implementing the CDC model to bring about community economic development and wealth accumulation, they are not always a good idea. Because a majority of their boards must be composed of representatives from the beneficiary community, they tend not to work when the majority of the congregation members are scattered miles from the church or have little personal knowledge of the service area. They may also not be desirable when the church is desperate for funds so that much of the funding will go to administration, staff, utilities, and so forth.

Church-based CDCs are not without their problems. They do not always produce identifiable goods. Their outcomes, which are often how CDCs justify their existence to potential funders, are at times hard to measure. Sometimes, excessively narrow missions have left the organizations vulnerable to shifts in funding priorities and to overreliance on single sources of funding. At other times, CDCs have experienced tension between obtaining funding and maintaining grassroots ties (Ferguson and Dickens 1999). In addition, researchers have found excessive turnover among CDC directors and other employees because of higher pay elsewhere and poorly balanced or passive boards that include few community residents. Other problems include poor communications between directors and boards, funders, and policymakers. Still another issue is a lack of strong and continual community support.

A disturbing paradox about some CDCs is that, although virtually everyone agrees that jobs form the greatest need in the communities in which CDCs are implemented, the majority of CDCs give out the best jobs and contracts to outsiders, who come in and work while many residents of the communities are left jobless (Rohe, Bratt, and Biswas 1999). Some critics charge that even the name is misleading since many CDCs are not controlled by residents and in fact have been organized and run by people who are not part of the community (Rohe, Bratt, and Biswas 1999). Nevertheless, CDCs have proven to be a viable mechanism for dealing with community issues for more than thirty years, and their popularity has grown over the past several years. Thus, in neighborhoods where the loss of private businesses has been widespread and where investments have been extremely low, CDCs have become key vehicles for providing better housing and for promoting development.

CHURCH-SPONSORED COOPERATIVE ENTERPRISES

Examples of successful cooperative ventures by black churches are plentiful. They include such community development efforts as providing housing for low- and moderate-income residents, establishing credit unions for congregation members and community residents, providing child care to area communities, offering job training and employment services to the unemployed, establishing drug abuse rehabilitation and services, and supplying care for the elderly. The examples are too numerous to detail, but the following cases are illustrative.

Bethel New Life, a faith-based CDC in Chicago, opened its doors in 1979 to increase the availability of affordable housing. Ten years later, Bethel established Project Triumph to provide more comprehensive services, including a home-visiting program for pregnant mothers and parents with children up to three years of age. The program helps mothers and grandparents obtain information about, and services for, housing, education, employment, child care, and health care. Among its other services, Project Triumph provides periodic developmental screening for children, as well as home visits by a child development specialist. In addition, the program holds regular meetings for parents and grandparents, during which a meal is served so that staff can observe interactions with children; after the meal, parents meet in support groups while a child development specialist works with the children.

Atlanta is home to "the nation's oldest congregation-based, African American credit union, established in 1956 by Wheat Street Baptist Church. The operation now has 1,000 members and assets of more than $1 million" (Slutz 2000). The church used the credit union to launch other areas of community economic development, and it now holds housing developments, an office building, a shopping center, and real estate assets that are worth more than $30 million.

In New York, Allen A. M. E. Church created the Allen Housing Development Fund Corporation, with assets in excess of $2 million. It also owns a newly built cathedral, eighteen commercial rental properties, a printing operation, twelve investment clubs, and a Pathmark Grocery. In addition, the church owns a school in a $3.8 million complex (Webber 2001).

In Los Angeles, the First African Methodist Episcopal Church owns a $4 million facility for housing the physically handicapped, a $35 million housing unit for low-income residents, two units to provide housing for those infected with HIV/AIDS, and a $5 million transportation program for seniors and the handicapped. In addition, it offers education for grades K–8, a health care (AIDS/tobacco) ministry, free tutoring, legal aid, computer training, and job training and placement. It also offers a prison ministry, an oil-recycling and environmental program, a business incubator for multimedia production, a twenty-four-hour child care and youth program, and a monthly feeding program that provides groceries for six hundred families. Finally, it offers a $5 million microloan program and another $500,000 that is invested in economic development.

Finally, the Rainbow/PUSH Coalition, under the leadership of the Reverend Jesse Jackson, launched a Wall Street project to encourage church-based investing. Arguing that financial empowerment and independence are extensions of the black church's historical role, Jackson challenged one thousand churches to develop finance ministries and to establish investment clubs and financial education programs for their members (Jackson and Jackson 1999). This initiative was aimed at helping churches and their members strengthen their communities by reducing their debt, building their equity, and gaining increased ownership in their communities. This relatively new initiative offers the promise of increased economic power, and it is an "illustration of how churches can play a leadership role in the economic emancipation of [black] people" (9). In short, through its economic activities and efforts, the black church is a significant economic institution in its own right.

THE BLACK CHURCH AND SOCIAL CAPITAL

Social capital describes relationships among people. It consists of cohesive community networks that indicate trust and cooperation based on a common culture and goals, group loyalty, a sense of identity and belonging, and coordinated action. It generally refers to concern for one's family, friends, and neighbors and to a willingness to live by the norms of one's community. It focuses attention on what groups do rather than on what people own. It is reflected in how people interact in their daily lives and in their families, neighborhoods, and work groups—and not just as buyers, sellers, and citizens.

Churches build and sustain more social capital—and social capital of more varied forms—than any other type of institution in America does. Churches provide a vibrant institutional base for civic good works and a training ground for civic entrepreneurs. Churches run a variety of programs for members, from self-help groups to job-training courses to singles' clubs. Churches also spend more than an estimated $15 billion each year on social services such as food and housing for the poor and elderly (Putnam 2000, 10). Regular religious services attenders meet many more people weekly than nonworshipers do, making religious institutions a prime forum for informal social capital building. At the same time, religious faith provides a moral foundation for civic regeneration. Faith gives meaning to community service and goodwill, forging a spiritual connection between individual impulses and great public issues—that is, religion helps people to inter-

nalize an orientation to the public good. Because faith has such power to transform lives, faith-based programs can enjoy success where secular programs have failed.

Faith-based organizations are especially important to the generation of social capital within the African American community (Lincoln and Mamiya 1990; Putnam 2000). Blacks are more likely than whites to attend church and are less likely to be members of other types of voluntary associations. Hence, the black church is a main forum for the development of civic skills—how to deal with intergroup conflict, manage budgets, write committee reports, organize meetings, and mobilize communities. Church involvement is correlated with political activism and voting (Brown and Brown 2003). Further, the black church has been an important source of informal support for the elderly and for other community members (Chatters et al. 2002). Southern black churches provide many more mental health and social services to congregations than do Southern white churches (Blank et al. 2002). These church-provided services are often the primary source of support for those who have limited access to publicly provided assistance or are reluctant to seek help from government agencies. Also, the black church has been enlisted to reduce youth violence (Berrien and Winship 2002). Black churches are increasingly becoming directly involved in providing alternatives to public education through the establishment of charter schools. Many of these church-based schools have proved to be more successful than traditional public schools have in fostering educational achievement.

African Americans cannot depend on Eurocentric institutions to bring about the kind of resources required to prepare African American people to compete and succeed in the twenty-first century. It is the obligation of black people to foster the growth of such resources in their families, their communities, and their civic associations. The black church in particular has been useful in this respect. As mentioned, the black church has been involved in community economic development and empowerment for years. Although the emphasis is somewhat different today, its role has been similar over the years.

SHOULD THE BLACK CHURCH CONNECT WITH PRESIDENT BUSH'S "FAITH-BASED" INITIATIVES?

In 2001, one of president George W. Bush's first official acts was to create the White House Office of Faith-Based and Community Initiatives. Under this initiative, churches and other community-based organizations were invited to take an active role in combating the nation's social problems, such as housing, health care, at-risk youth, substance abuse, employment, and elder care. Given the black church's longstanding tradition of involvement in such issues, many saw President Bush's faith-based initiative as an opportunity to receive additional funding to continue doing what they were already doing or to expand and improve their efforts.

Others view the faith-based initiative more critically. They see it as a way to bolster the conservative agenda to redefine and privatize the entire public sector—from education to welfare to housing. They see Bush's faith-based initiative as a classic case of diversion. By focusing on the need for religiously based social services to receive government funding, Bush obscures the reality that public services are woefully underfunded, a status that his administration has little intention of changing. They are also wary of terms such as "charitable choice," which have been used to describe legislation allowing religious groups to receive taxpayer funding for programs such as job training or drug treatment that have religious teachings as a main component. Indeed, it is unclear how to resolve conflicts over the extent to which religious groups will be allowed to overtly proselytize using public taxpayer dollars as long as payments to religious groups are disguised as vouchers to individuals.

For the African American community, Bush's faith-based initiative poses particular problems. Critics suggest that Bush's faith-based initiative is a clear attempt to silence African American churches and to divert them from their traditional role as a voice for social justice. They argue that Bush is trying to buy the allegiance, or at least cooperation, of the black church to reduce the black church's opposition to the Republican Party. While many realize the political downsides, the lure of money is powerful. Given the black church's tradition of community empowerment and independence, it would be more than ironic if these religious institutions were to give in to temptation and become dependent on government funds.

Opponents of the faith-based initiative also see it as a means for Bush to increase his share of votes from African Americans, further the conservative goal of privatizing public services, woo black ministers and churches, and divert attention from the fact that the administration's focus on a military buildup and tax cuts for the wealthy leaves little money for social programs. Although black churches will receive funds under the faith-based initiative, the major winners probably will be the religious Right and fundamentalist churches with connections to Republican power brokers. Such groups do not have a history of community economic development in the black community.

CONCLUSION

The black church has long been a social and economic force in the African American community. During slavery, in the post–Civil War era, at the turn of the twentieth century, and through the Great Depression, it led the way in attempts to improving the social welfare and quality of life for African Americans. In addition to giving birth to several black colleges and universities, black churches have been the birthplace of notable entrepreneurial ventures. In addition, it has been central to the creation and survival of other institutions in the black community. In the contemporary era, its role has been expanded to combat social problems such as unemployment, drug abuse, crime, and illiteracy. Increasingly, it has been engaged in community outreach and community development. Such engagement has led to even more innovations and activism. If anything, these functions are likely to expand, as institutions such as the family, the school, the courts, and government seem to have fallen off as protectors of well-being and security. Indeed, with president George W. Bush's faith-based initiative, it is likely that more services to the needy will be privatized and that religious and community organizations will be called on to do even more. There may be fewer resources to combat social problems in troubled communities, and most of the funds for the faith-based initiative may go to conservative causes. Nevertheless, with the infusion of new resources, if black churches can maintain their independence, they may be poised as never before to work with community residents to formulate and carry out strategies to revitalize their communities.

REFERENCES

Berrien, Jenny, and Christopher Winship. 2002. "An Umbrella of Legitimacy: Boston's Police Department—Ten-Point Coalition Collaboration." In *Securing Our Children's Future: New Approaches to Juvenile Justice and Youth Violence,* ed. Gary S. Katz. Washington, D.C.: Brookings Institution.

Billingsley, Andrew. 1999. *Mighty Like a River: The Black Church and Social Reform.* New York: Oxford University Press.

Blank, Michael B., Marcus Mahmood, Jeanne C. Fox, and Thomas Guterbock. 2002. "Alternative Mental Health Services: The Role of the Black Church in the South." *American Journal of Public Health* 92, no. 10 (October): 1668–1672.

Brown, R. Khari, and Ronald E. Brown. 2003. "Faith and Works: Church-Based Social Capital Resources and African American Political Activism." *Social Forces* 82, no. 2 (December): 617–641.

Chatters, Linda M., Robert Joseph Taylor, Karen D. Lincoln, and Tracy Schroeper. 2002. "Patterns of Informal Support from Family and Church Members among African Americans." *Journal of Black Studies* 33, no. 1 (September): 66–85.

Day, Katie. 2001. "Putting It Together in the African American Churches: Faith, Economic Development, and Civil Rights." In *Religion and Social Policy,* ed. Paula D. Nesbitt, 181–195. Walnut Creek, Calif.: AltaMira Press.

DePriest, Tomika, and Joyce Jones. 1997. "Economic Deliverance thru the Church." *Black Enterprise* (February): 195+.

Ferguson, Ronald F., and William T. Dickens, eds. 1999. *Urban Problems and Community Development.* Washington, D.C.: Brookings Institution.

Frazier, E. Franklin. 1963. *The Negro Church in America.* Liverpool, England: University of Liverpool.

Jackson, Jesse L., Sr., and Jesse L. Jackson Jr. 1999. *It's About the Money: The Fourth Movement of the Freedom Symphony; How to Build Wealth, Get Access to Capital, and Achieve Your Financial Dreams.* With Mary Gotschall. New York: Random House.

Lincoln, C. Eric. 1974. *The Black Church since Frazier.* New York: Schocken Books.

Lincoln, C. Eric, and Lawrence H. Mamiya. 1990. *The Black Church and the African American Experience.* Durham, N.C.: Duke University Press.

Loescher, Frank S. 1948. *The Protestant Church and the Negro.* Westport, Conn.: Negro Universities Press.

McDougall, Harold A. 1993. *Black Baltimore: A New Theory of Community.* Philadelphia: Temple University Press.

McRoberts, Omar M. 2001. "Black Churches, Community and Development." *Shelterforce Online* (January/February): 1–8, available at www.nhi.org/online/issues/115/McRoberts.html.

Orr, Marion. 2000. "Baltimoreans United in Leadership Development: Exploring the Role of Governing Nonprofits." In *Nonprofits in Urban America,* ed. Richard C. Hula and Cynthia Jackson-Elmoore, 151–167. Westport, Conn.: Quorum Books.

Owens, Michael Leo. 2000. "Political Action and Black Church-Associated Community Development Corporations." Paper prepared for the Meeting of the Urban Affairs Association, Los Angeles, May 3–6.

Putnam, Robert D. 2000. *Bowling Alone: The Collapse and Revival of American Community.* New York: Simon and Shuster.

Raboteau, Albert J. 1967. *Slave Religion.* New York: Oxford University Press.

Rohe, William M., Rachel G. Bratt, and Protip Biswas. 1999. "Factors Influencing the Performance of Community Development Corporations." *Journal of Urban Affairs* 21, no. 3: 325–329.

Slutz, Ted. 2000. "Congregations and Community Banking." *Responsive Communities* 2, no. 3. At www.polis.iupui.edu/ruc/newsletters/responsive/vol2no3.htm#.

Stewart, James. n.d. "The Black Church as a Religio-Economic Institution." Unpublished manuscript.

Vidal, Avis C. 2001. "Faith-Based Organizations in Community Development." Report prepared for U.S. Department of Housing and Community

Development, Office of Policy Development and Research, August, available at www.huduser.org.

Washington, Joseph R. 1964. *Black Religion: The Negro and Christianity in the United States.* Boston: Beacon Press.

Webb, Susan. 2001. "To Help the People: Worker Transit in Black Belt South Carolina." Coastal Carolina University.

Webber, Brenda. 2001. "The Church and the Money." *Network Journal* 9: 20.

42

Black Patronage of Black-Owned Businesses and Black Employment

THOMAS D. BOSTON

In 2002, black-owned businesses provided jobs for 6.8 percent of the black workforce. This figure is projected to increase to 10 percent by 2010. Our results reveal that quality of employment provided to blacks in black-owned firms is superior to that provided by white-owned firms. Nevertheless, we estimate that blacks spend only five cents out of every dollar with black-owned businesses. This amount is distressingly low, especially in light of the fact that every $1 million in revenue to black-owned firms generates about ten jobs, eight of which go to black workers. We argue that blacks must increase their patronage of black-owned businesses as a fundamental way of increasing black employment, income, and community development.

In 2002 black buying power in the United States reached $645.9 billion, or 8.5 percent of total U.S. buying power. More important, while the buying power of all whites increased by 67.2 percent between 1990 and 2002, the buying power of blacks increased by 104 percent.[1] In 1997 (the year of the latest available business census) the 823,499 black-owned businesses in the country employed 718,341 workers. Since employment in these businesses grew at an annual rate of 9.8 percent between 1982 and 1997, in 2003, we estimate that these businesses employ 1,258,765 workers. More important, given that about eight out of every ten workers employed in these businesses are black, we estimate that black-owned businesses employ approximately one million black workers, or about 6.8 percent of the U.S. black workforce.[2]

The percentage of the black workforce employed in black-owned firms is not a trivial number. In fact, this percentage has increased significantly over the previous two decades. In 1982, black-owned firms employed only 165,765 workers and about 1.4 percent of the U.S. black workforce. But if the trend in employment growth of the last two decades continues until 2010, black-owned firms are projected to employ 2,421,927 workers, by which time the black labor force will number 20,041,000 (per U.S. Department of Labor projections).[3] If by that time the workforce in black-owned firms is still 80 percent black, these firms will as a result employ 1,937,541 black workers, or 9.7 percent of the 2010 projected black workforce. Another way to look at this is that, by 2010, the percentage of black workers employed in black-owned businesses will be equivalent to the average percentage of blacks that are currently unemployed. Now the importance of the number becomes clearer.

BLACK PATRONAGE AND BLACK EMPLOYMENT

Given the growing contribution of black-owned businesses to black employment, a reasonable question is, How much do black consumers support black-owned businesses? This question is commonly asked as follows: How many times does the black dollar turn over in the black community? There is perhaps not one black economist in the country who has not been asked this question at some point, yet the structure of the question defies an answer; therefore, I will restructure the question and provide a simple, yet commonsense, answer to it.

An alternative way of phrasing the question is this: How much total black purchasing power is spent with black-owned businesses? The greater our expenditures with black-owned businesses, the greater their business revenue. This added revenue translates into greater black employment, income, and community development.

As such, we answer the question as follows. First, in 2002, the total disposable income (buying power) of blacks in the United States was $645.9 billion.[4] Also in 2002, the total revenue of black-owned businesses was $123.3 billion.[5] Further, we conducted a national survey in 2002 focusing on the CEOs of 350 randomly selected black businesses. Having a margin of error of plus or minus 4 percent, the survey indicated that 26 percent of the total revenue of black-owned businesses is derived from black customers and clients.[6] This means that $32.1 billion of the $123.3 billion in total black business revenue comes from black consumers. This $32.1 billion represents 5 percent of the total buying power of blacks in 2002. Therefore, we can conclude that five cents out of every one dollar that blacks spend is with black-owned businesses. Now imagine if this amount were doubled to ten cents on the dollar. This would increase total black business revenue by 26 percent. Further, since black firms create ten jobs for every million dollars in revenue, this would translate into about 320,000 more jobs for black workers.

At present, black businesses represent 4.0 percent of all businesses in the country but receive only 0.9 percent of all business revenue. These are not encouraging numbers, and they are not helped by the low patronage of black consumers. Therefore, the central argument of this chapter is that blacks must increase their patronage of black-owned businesses. Remembering that every $1 million in revenue creates ten jobs and

that eight out of every ten jobs go to blacks, there appears to be a compelling necessity to do so.

The remainder of this chapter examines some recent trends in black-owned businesses, focusing specifically on employment related trends.

BLACK EMPLOYMENT BUSINESS TRENDS

Over the last quarter-century the industry distribution of black-owned businesses has undergone a significant change. The predominance of small-scale personal service and retail establishments ("mom and pop" stores) has diminished. For example, in 1972, at least 35 percent of all black-owned businesses operated in just four industries: food stores (6.3 percent), eating and drinking places (7.6 percent), personal service establishments (18.5 percent), and auto repair and garages (2.9 percent). Between 1982 and 1997, the share of all black businesses in these four industries declined from 35.3 percent to 20.2 percent (a 42.7 percent decrease). Likewise, the share of revenue of black businesses in these four industries decreased from 25.9 percent to 18.9 percent (a 27.1 percent decrease). Between 1992 and 1997 the number of black-owned businesses increased by 26 percent compared to a 7 percent increase for all U.S. businesses.[7]

For black-owned businesses the trend toward more diversified industries and the movement away from "mom and pop" establishments represented a new development, which began with the decline of racial segregation in the 1960s. However, it accelerated during the 1970s and 1980s as blacks gained managerial and executive experience in the corporate sector and pursued business degrees in greater numbers. In general, during this period blacks accumulated a greater endowment of experiences, skills, and human capital attributes that are associated with successful self-employment activities.

By the late 1980s and early 1990s, the typical black business owner was younger, better educated, had more managerial and supervisory experience, and relied to a greater extent on public-sector markets than he or she had in previous decades. Increasingly, the growing industries for black enterprises were construction contracting, transportation, architectural and engineering services, management and consulting services, services to buildings, data processing, computer sales and services, public relations, and health and other social services. Most of these were all newly emerging industries for blacks. Many businesses prospered as a result of the availability of public sector contracting opportunities.

Table 42.1 examines the changing industry distribution of black-owned businesses by evaluating the share of employment per industry. The table also presents total employment in black-owned firms per industry in 1982 and 1997, and it illustrates the percentage change in employment during this period as well as the share of employment by industry.

In 1982, the largest share of employment in black-owned businesses was in services, 38.8 percent; and retail, 26.0 percent. The third-largest share was in manufacturing, 9.2 percent; followed by construction, 8.7 percent. By 1997,

the share of employment in services had increased to 54.1 percent, and retail had decreased to 17.5 percent. Similarly, construction had increased to 9.9 percent, and manufacturing had dropped to 3.7 percent. Transportation, communication, and utilities increased to 6.6 percent from 4.1 percent in 1982. Employment in this latter industry experienced the largest percentage increase, 594 percent during the period. Services (504 percent) and construction (390 percent) followed.

To analyze these trends in more detail, we disaggregated the three industries that experienced the largest percentage increases in employment: construction; transportation, communications, and utilities; and services (see Table 42.2). The greater detail reveals that among the service industries, social services (1,941.8 percent), health services (913.7 percent), motion pictures (600.0 percent) and business services (583.4 percent) have experienced the largest percentage increases. Because of the large share of employment in business services

Table 42.1   Employment Changes by Industry in Black-Owned Firms

	1982	1997	% change 1982–1992	% share 1982	% share 1997
Agricultural services	2,032	5,457	169	1.2	0.8
Mining	323	186	− 42	0.2	0.0
Construction	14,470	70,928	390	8.7	9.9
Manufacturing	15,186	26,624	75	9.2	3.7
Transp., commun., utilities	6,813	47,289	594	4.1	6.6
Wholesale	4,391	13,746	213	2.6	1.9
Retail	43,140	125,480	191	26.0	17.5
Finance, insurance, real estate	13,454	18,379	37	8.1	2.6
Services	64,355	388,398	504	38.8	54.1
Not classified	1,601	21,854	—	1.0	3.0
Total	165,765	718,341	333	100.0	100.0
Black civilian employment	9,189,000	13,969,000	52		
Total civilian employment	99,526,000	129,588,000	30		
Black business employment as a % of total black employment	1.8	5.1			
Black business employment as a % of total U.S. employment	0.2	0.6			

Source: U.S. Department of Commerce, Bureau of the Census, *Survey of Minority-Owned Business Enterprises: Black, 1997* [SMOBE: Black, 1997] (Washington, D.C.: Government Printing Office, 2001). See also SMOBE: Black, 1982.

and health services, these two industries are obviously the most important. Among transportation, communication, and utilities, air transportation (2,791.8 percent) and local and interurban transportation (2,032.4 percent) increased most significantly. However, their share of overall employment is rather small, at 0.25 percent and 3.8 percent, respectively. Finally, within the construction industry, special trades contracting (406.1 percent) experienced the largest percentage increase and accounts for a significant share of total employment, 6.9 percent.

WHAT KINDS OF JOBS ARE BEING CREATED IN BLACK-OWNED FIRMS?

Studies have consistently found that about three-fourths or more of the employees in black-owned businesses are black. The obvious question this raises is, What kinds of jobs are these businesses creating? To give a partial answer to this question, we compiled primary data from equal employment opportunity reports (EEO-1 reports) submitted by businesses located in met-

Table 42.2   Employment Changes in Black-Owned Firms by Detailed Industry

	1982	1997	% increase 1982–1997	% share 1982	% share 1992
Industry					
General building construction	3,292	15,045	357.0	1.99	2.09
Heavy construction	1,357	6,346	367.6	0.82	0.88
Special trades contracting	9,773	49,463	406.1	5.90	6.89
Subdividers and developers	48	75	56.3	0.03	0.01
Transp., Commun., Utilities					
Local and interurban	950	20,258	2,032.4	0.57	2.82
Trucking and warehousing	3,463	14,872	329.5	2.09	2.07
Water transportation	214	832	288.8	0.13	0.12
Air transportation	61	1,764	2,791.8	0.04	0.25
Pipelines	—	—	—	—	—
Transportation services	464	2,566	453.0	0.28	0.36
Communications	1,077	5,557	416.0	0.65	0.77
Electric, gas, sanitary services	584	1,440	146.6	0.35	0.20
Services					
Hotel and lodging	2,287	—	—	1.38	—
Personal services	9,170	23,882	160.4	5.53	3.32
Business services	22,971	156,974	583.4	13.86	21.85
Auto repairs	2,817	8,922	216.7	1.70	1.24
Misc. repairs	879	2,784	216.7	0.53	0.39
Motion pictures	192	1,344	600.0	0.12	0.19
Amusement and recreation	1,182	3,307	179.8	0.71	0.46
Health services	9,909	100,450	913.7	5.98	13.98
Legal services	1,651	7,954	381.8	1.00	1.11
Education services	655	4,262	550.7	0.40	0.59
Social services	2,078	42,428	1,941.8	1.25	5.91
Museum, botanical	—	—	—	—	—
Engineering and management	10,564	34,463	226.2	6.37	4.80

Source: U.S. Department of Commerce, Bureau of the Census, *Survey of Minority-Owned Business Enterprises: Black, 1997* [SMOBE: Black, 1997] (Washington, D.C.: Government Printing Office, 2001). See also SMOBE: Black, 1982.
Note: Dashes indicate zero value.

ropolitan Atlanta that pursued work with the city of Atlanta. Specifically, data was collected on 1,381 firms (all located in the Atlanta metropolitan area) that sought contracts with the city of Atlanta between 1996 and 1998. Each firm was required to file an EEO-1 report detailing the ethnicity and gender of its employees. Of these firms, 802 (58.1 percent) were owned by African Americans; 437 (31.6 percent) were owned by whites; 49 (3.5 percent) were owned by Asian Americans, 38 (2.8 percent) were owned by Hispanic Americans; 2 were owned by Native Americans; and the remainder, 3.8 percent, were owned by minorities whose specific group identity could not be determined. The industries having the largest number of black-owned companies was business services (159), general building contracting (140), and engineering and management services (79).

In total, these firms employed 23,298 workers, but the employment pattern between black-owned and white-owned firms differed significantly. For example, 76.0 percent of the employees in black-owned firms were black (8,107 employees) and 16.0 percent were white (1,702 employees); the remainder was from other minority groups. By contrast, 29.4 percent of the workforce in firms owned by whites was black and 62.6 percent were white.

An examination of the employment pattern within black firms indicates that blacks were much more likely to be employed by black firms in professional service industries as opposed to white firms in professional service industries. For example, 1,095 black workers employed by black firms worked in engineering and management service industries. This represented 13.5 percent of all black workers. By contrast, only 1.6 percent of black workers employed in white-owned firms worked in engineering and management service industries. In general, our examination reveals that the quality of employment of black workers

in black-owned firms is superior to that of black workers in white-owned firms.

In light of the fact that black-owned firms provide an increasingly significant share of employment opportunities for blacks and that the quality of employment is greater than what is provided by white-owned firms, five cents out of every dollar is too little support from the black community. Blacks must increase their patronage of black-owned businesses as one fundamental way of increasing black employment, income, and community development.

NOTES

1. Jeffrey Humphreys, "The Multicultural Economy 2002: Minority Buying Power in the New Century," *Georgia Business and Economic Conditions* 62, no. 2 (2002).

2. Past studies and surveys indicate that about 80 percent of the workforce in black-owned firms is black. See Thomas D. Boston, *Affirmative Action and Black Entrepreneurship* (New York: Routledge, 1999), 56; and Timothy Bates, *Banking on Black Business: The Potential of Emerging Firms for Revitalizing Urban Economies* (Washington, D.C.: Joint Center for Political and Economic Studies, 1993), 77.

3. Labor force projections are cited at www.bls.gov/news.release/ecopro.t05.htm.

4. Humphreys, "The Multicultural Economy 2002."

5. This estimate is derived by extrapolating annual average black business revenue growth rate between 1982 and 1997. The annual rate was 11.6 percent.

6. For more information on this new national quarterly survey, see www.inggazelleindex.com.

7. Thomas D. Boston, "Minority Business Trends," in *America Becoming: Racial Trends and Their Consequences,* ed. N. Smelser, W. J. Wilson, and F. Mitchell (Washington, D.C.: National Academy of Science Press, 2001).

43

African American Athletes and Urban Revitalization: African American Athletes as a Funding Source for Inner-City Investments
JOHN WHITEHEAD and JAMES STEWART

High-earning African American athletes constitute one of the potential pools of sizable black capital available for inner-city investments. This chapter provides several models for a broad-based inner-city investment movement led by African American athletes. It identifies specific industries with significant potential for investment ventures initiated by black athletes and examples of successful inner-city investment activities by this group. Also presented are specific barriers to the formation of substantial inner-city investments by black athletes and economic development initiatives that include members of this group.

This chapter examines the potential role of professional African American athletes as a funding source for inner-city economic development initiatives. The extraordinary earnings of African American athletes constitute a valuable, but largely untapped, community economic development resource. Rationales for greater involvement of athletes in supporting economic development efforts are presented and discussed. Barriers to the creation of community economic networks that include African American athletes are described, and strategies to overcome these obstacles are offered. Successful pilot ventures undertaken by Earvin "Magic" Johnson are suggested as models for a broad-based inner-city investment movement spearheaded by African American athletes. Industries with significant potential for investment ventures initiated by black athletes include business services, transportation, real estate, and banking and insurance.

EARNINGS OF AFRICAN AMERICAN ATHLETES IN MAJOR U.S. SPORTS

It is no secret that professional African American athletes are handsomely paid—and the best of them extravagantly paid—for their performance in arenas, stadiums and ballparks. This is evident from the figures in table 43.1, which show the 2000–2001 average annual salaries for African American athletes in the three major sports (football, basketball, and baseball). (The measure of earnings used to calculate these figures does not include earnings from commercial endorsements and nontaxable items.) African Americans in the National Basketball Association (NBA) had the highest average annual salary at $3,585,818; those in the National Football League (NFL) had the lowest at $990,225; and those in Major League Baseball (MLB) fell

Table 43.1 Earnings (before taxes) of African American Athletes in Major U.S. Sports

	NFL	*NBA*	*MLB*
Number of African American athletes	1,087		114
Average annual salary: Black	$0.99	$3M	$2.92M
Average annual salary: All players	$1.20	$3M	$2.26M

Source: Prepared by John Whitehead and Associates. Data from USAToday.com, InsideHoops.com, and sportsline.com.
Note: NFL = National Football League, NBA = National Basketball Association, MLB = Major League Baseball. Figures are based on 2000 NFL salaries, 2000–2001 NBA salaries, and 2001 MLB salaries.

between, at $2,920,751. The total annual earnings of black NBA players were 1.14 billion (3,585,818 multiplied by 318), the highest of the three groups. Black NFL players earned 1.1 billion, whereas black MLB players had the lowest total of 0.3 billion ($332,965,614). The lower total earnings of black MLB players reflect the comparatively small number (114) who played during the 2001 season. The combined annual salaries of African American athletes in the three major sports totaled nearly $2.6 billion.

The data summarized in Table 43.1 indicate that African American professional athletes earn an enormous amount of income, potentially available for capital formation in America's inner cities. It is important to recognize, however, that these earnings are not distributed equally among athletes.

Despite significant inequality in earnings

among black athletes across the three major sports, inequality in earnings has been much more pronounced within each major sport since the advent of free agency. Table 43.2 shows the distribution of earnings among African American athletes within each major sport. The data are presented by *quintiles*—that is, the total number of African American athletes within each major sport is first ranked by earnings and then split into five groups of equal size. In the NFL, the top quintile earned 56.7 percent of total earnings, while the bottom quintile earned just 4.4 percent. Thus, black players in the top quintile earned nearly 13.0 times as much as the bottom quintile. The remaining middle three quintiles, or 60 percent of the total, received 38.9 percent of all earnings. In the NBA, players in the top quintile earned 53.8 percent of total earnings and 19.7 times more than the bottom quintile,

Table 43.2 Distribution of Earnings among African American Athletes in Major U.S. Sports

Earnings rank by quintile	*NFL* Share of earnings	*NFL* Average annual salary	*NBA* Share of earnings	*NBA* Average annual salary	*MLB* Share of earnings	*MLB* Average annual salary
Lowest fifth	4.4%	$ 219,030	2.7%	$ 487,778	1.5%	$ 220,148
Second fifth	7.3	363,206	7.2	1,303,651	2.7	396,196
Middle fifth	10.5	519,534	13.3	2,365,625	11.3	1,637,263
Fourth fifth	21.1	1,040,045	23.1	4,100,313	29.2	4,078,485
Highest fifth	56.7	2,800,739	53.8	9,577,656	56.3	8,154,245

Source: Prepared by John Whitehead and Associates. Data from USATODAY.com, InsideHoops.com, and sportsline.com.
Note: Because figures are rounded, the sum of the five fifths in each column may not add to 100. Figures are based on 2000 NFL salaries, 2000–2001 NBA salaries, and 2001 MLB salaries. Figures do not include earnings from commercial endorsements.

which earned only 2.7 percent of the total. However, the earnings gap was widest in the MLB: players in the top quintile earned 37.7 times more than those in the bottom quintile.

The inequality in earnings reflected in Table 43.2 suggests a great potential for significant large-scale inner-city investments by wealthy African American athletes. The reason is that large-scale business ventures usually require outside financing from those with wealth or from mainstream financial institutions. It is generally easier to amass investment capital from one or a few wealthy individuals, who can be persuaded to move on a particular investment, than it is from many less-wealthy individuals. This is especially true if the particular investment is perceived as involving initial short-run losses, which is often the case with inner-city investments. Therefore, high-earning African American athletes who have accumulated substantial wealth offer one of the few potential pools of sizable black capital available for inner-city investments.

WHY AFRICAN AMERICAN ATHLETES SHOULD SUPPORT INNER-CITY ECONOMIC DEVELOPMENT

The Communitarian Argument

A compelling argument calling for African American athletes to support community economic development initiatives is presented by Pennsylvania State University economist James B. Stewart.[1] In Stewart's view, high-earning African American athletes have a responsibility to support community economic development initiatives as repayment for the community's investments toward the athletes' income-generating human capital endowments. Stewart summarizes his reasoning as follows:

In the course of the growth and development of prospective big-time athletes, communities (individuals, families, churches, schools, etc.) typically make special investments over and above those made for individuals with fewer physical endowments.

These investments take a variety of forms including early nurturance of athletic skills through specialized instruction, provision or maintenance of public facilities to provide special access to hone skills, special support to ensure adequate academic performance to allow access to major collegiate sports programs, specialized monitoring of behavior to discourage involvement in activities that pose risk to future earnings capacity, public support and psychological reinforcement for athletic accomplishments that induce additional investments and signal potential value to the sports industry. As a consequence, communities have a legitimate claim for repayment of these investments including a reasonable return.[2]

Many conservative/free-market economists, of course, reject some or all of Stewart's arguments. Some emphasize the individualistic character of athletic performance and the process by which skills or human capital is developed. This argument suggests that individual effort, manifested in part as intense individual training, is the primary contributor to the development of extraordinary athletic skills. As a result, the income generated reflects a return to the individual's investments rather than a derivative of community investments.

A second line of criticism maintains that the existing earnings inequalities between athletes and nonathletes and among athletes are socially efficient in channeling people into the occupations for which they are best suited. These critics contend that efforts to reduce inequality lead to resource misallocation. This argument is based on the following reasoning. Suppose that there were some type of artificial limit on athletes' earnings. This limitation would discourage some potential athletes from pursuing professional athletics as an occupation. This disincentive might lead to a reduction in the quality of the "product" generated by the remaining athletes, leading to lower revenues and lower overall and average earnings. These losses would be significantly greater than the additional income generated by the discouraged athletes who entered other professions. "Displaced athletes" would not bring comparable extraordinary skills to their new jobs, and hence their earning capacity would not be unusual. As a consequence, society as a whole would be worse off because the allocation of persons across occupations would produce less value than would be the case without the artificial limitations on athletes' earnings.

A third criticism of the communitarian argument focuses on the absence of any contractual relationship between athletes and their communities of origin. This criticism suggests that the community has no collective property rights to any portion of the athletes' stream of earnings. Athletes can choose to contribute to community development initiatives, but they have no formal obligation to do so.

A fourth challenge asserts that athletes already contribute to community economic development, broadly defined, because the progressive tax system appropriates significant portions of their earnings. To the extent that some of these tax receipts are channeled into publicly funded antipoverty and development programs, any moral responsibility of athletes to their communities of origin has been met.

A response to these criticisms should first reemphasize the importance of social capital in producing high-caliber athletes. Consider, for example, why certain countries regularly produce athletes who excel in specific sports. It is evident that specialization in producing athletes in certain sports has occurred on a global scale. For instance, Cuba and the Dominican Republic have specialized in the production of baseball players; Cuba and Mexico have excelled in cultivating talented boxers; Jamaica is responsible for a disproportionate number of sprinters; and specific regions of Kenya continue to be a source of world-class long-distance runners. It would be difficult to maintain that this pattern results purely from individual choice and effort. There are clearly institutional arrangements, traditions, and social support networks that reinforce the athletic specialization process in these countries. The reproduction of similar social capital networks exists in many U.S. inner-city communities and have contributed to the income-generating human capital endowments of many African American athletes.

Legitimate issues can be raised about the social efficiency of the existing choices of African American youth. As the data in tables 43.1 and 43.2 indicate, few individuals actually enter professional athletics; yet, there is clearly an overinvestment in the cultivation of athletic skills among African American youth, relative to the likely returns to these investments. Consequently, existing patterns of human capital accumulation are themselves socially inefficient. The operative question, then, is whether it is possible to structure support systems that address this source of social inefficiency while not limiting the income-generating opportunities for prospective athletes with the potential to succeed as professional athletes.

While there are currently no formal contractual relationships between prospective athletes and their communities, the question is whether such an arrangement could be developed in a way that benefited all parties. One such model, suggested by University of Nebraska economist Richard Edwards, proposes a "group contract," or a multiperson commitment, that a group of black athletes would sign. This contract entails an agreement "that when a specified number had signed . . . all signatories would be obligated to contribute a prescribed percentage of their earnings to community economic development initiatives."

There is no question that athletes are currently socialized to think of their financial relationship to inner-city communities as a form of charity. There are a few examples of black athletes establishing foundations, presumably to support worthwhile community development and antipoverty projects. However, many of these foundations are shells designed as tax shelters with few assets and virtually no grant-making activity. Thus, it is not clear that the charitable contribution model can generate the sustained investment required to foster large-scale community development.

Finally, the progressive tax/reallocation argument is unconvincing. Substantial portions of athletes' earnings are sheltered from taxation. In addition, there is no mechanism to target tax receipts to inner-city development projects.

The Economic Self-Interest Argument

In addition to the communitarian rationales presented here, African American athletes should support community development initiatives by investing in undercapitalized inner-city locations based solely on genuine opportunities for profit.[3] In most inner cities, a variety of competitive advantages and opportunities to build highly profitable businesses remain unrecognized and untapped. Harvard business professor Michael E. Porter brings attention to several fundamental, but often overlooked, inner-city competitive advantages.[4] They include the following:

> *Strategic location:* Inner cities are near major business centers, harbors, airports, entertainment facilities, and transportation infrastructure.
> *Unmet local demand:* Given high population density, inner-city neighborhoods have large incomes per acre; yet, local inner-city markets are relatively untapped and poorly served.
> *Human resources:* Inner cities offer large pools of workers who have the potential to be industrious, loyal employees.[5]

Many African American athletes are in a strategic position to exploit the competitive advantages and market potential of the inner city. First, high-income athletes have easy access to a range of financial institutions that can provide the capital needed most to create and sustain economically viable inner-city companies. Second, socially conscious athletes with business savvy and roots in the inner city often possess local knowledge and unbiased market information, useful for penetrating the local market. For example, many have valuable insights regarding the ethnically diverse cultural patterns within the urban milieu and the products suited to meet the unique yet diverse needs of African American consumers. Third, high-profile athletes are in a position to use their high visibility and stature within the community to advertise and promote their products and services in the local market and elsewhere.[6] Fourth, African American athletes can leverage their celebrity status, social capital, and financial resources to assemble top-flight management teams with the capacity to identify, integrate, and exploit highly profitable business opportunities on a local, national, and global scale. In short, many African American athletes are in a good position to exploit the economic potential of the inner city, to create or invest in economically viable inner-city companies, and to reap significant economic benefits as a result.[7]

WHY HAVE WEALTHY AFRICAN AMERICAN ATHLETES NOT SIGNIFICANTLY INVESTED THEIR FINANCIAL RESOURCES IN AMERICA'S INNER CITIES?

Many skeptics have asked, "If the inner city has genuine economic potential and competitive advantages, why hasn't it attracted more capital from wealthy minorities, including star athletes?" There are several reasons.

One major roadblock stems from popular misconceptions and negative stereotypes about the inner city and its economic potential, or what economists call *information imperfections.* Influenced by the U.S. media and a variety of racial assumptions, many Americans see inner cities as drug-infested war zones devoid of viable economic activity, inhabited only by low-income residents who have very little ambition, discipline, or marketable skills. Unfortunately, these misperceptions have influenced many African American athletes and retarded their investments in inner-city locations with obvious market potential. Most high-earning black athletes channel their investment funds into nonminority wealth managers who view inner-city investments as risky and use asset-allocation models that focus on investments in stocks, bonds, and mutual funds, which provide capital only for mainstream companies operating outside of the inner city.[8]

Conspicuous consumption, usually interpreted as lavish spending to display wealth and status, is also a major factor averting African American athletes' investments in the inner city. Most African American athletes spend an exceedingly high proportion of their newly acquired wealth and high earnings on expensive jewelry, $80,000-plus cars, cultural entertainment, and other luxury items. This practice is legitimated by a market-oriented value system that stresses the acquisitive spirit and personal fulfillment through material acquisition, now spreading around the world as one aspect of globalization.[9] More important, high levels of conspicuous consumption by most black athletes have resulted in their spending a large portion of their discretionary funds that would otherwise be available for savings and potentially productive inner-city investments.[10]

Another major factor inhibiting investments in the inner city by African American athletes is their lack of social consciousness and commitment to activism.[11] This can be partially explained by the absence of black political institutions, paradigms, and resources that effectively challenge all African American social classes and groups—including black professional athletes—to identify with, and actively support, African American socioeconomic development and progress.[12] Moreover, as noted by University of California sociology professor Harry Edwards, the African American press lacks the relative autonomy and resources to serve as ideological and institutional agents for increasing social consciousness and activism among athletes and other wealthy African Americans.[13]

Therefore, irrespective of how critical the need may be for the inner city to attract financial capital from wealthy minorities, there are very few black institutions in place to articulate this message to African American athletes. Not surprisingly, then, there is very little serious discussion or support among African American athletes for any strategy that would increase their investments in the inner city.

The challenge of increasing the participation of African American athletes in urban revitalization campaigns is further complicated by the negative and individualistic attitudes held by many athletes toward the inner city. Typically, African American athletes either unwittingly or consciously embrace the view that breaking their identification and involvement with the inner-city community is a necessary step in moving up the socioeconomic ladder.[14] This and other "abandon the inner city" strategies have been embedded in the individual psyche of African American athletes and are legitimized and reinforced by prevailing American attitudes toward the inner city and by the capitalist ideology of rugged individualism. Consequently, these strategies and their supposed benefits have been accepted by most African American athletes and other upwardly mobile blacks as conventional wisdom and common sense.[15] Furthermore, the present attitudes, behaviors, and advancement strategies of African American athletes suggest that currently most members of this group will invest in the inner city only on the basis of economic self-interest or individual idiosyncratic motivations and not out of any historical–moral duty or obligation.

STRATEGIES FOR AFRICAN AMERICAN ATHLETES TO SUPPORT INNER-CITY ECONOMIC DEVELOPMENT

Start Viable Businesses That Create New Jobs for Inner-City Residents

African American athletes can best support inner-city economic development by starting economically viable businesses with significant employment creation potential. Currently, the viable large-scale minority businesses are operating outside of the traditional lines of minority business enterprise (retail and personal services); they are concentrated in the so-called emerging lines of minority business enterprise: business services; finance, insurance, and real estate; transportation and communication; and wholesale trade.[16] According to Timothy Bates, "emerging black firms, started by better-educated owners who invest more money in them than do traditional owners, are larger, fail less often, and generate more jobs" than traditional black firms.[17] Moreover, firms in emerging fields are oriented toward marketing products and services to a racially diverse clientele.[18] Thus, recent trends in black business support an important generalization: wealthy African American athletes can best support urban revitalization by starting businesses in the emerging fields that target a racially diverse clientele and facilitate job, income, and wealth creation for urban minority residents.

There are specific niches in business services and other emerging fields where African American athletes would face few obstacles in building profitable, job-generating inner-city companies. For example, African American athletes with substantial wealth and quality college educational backgrounds would have a reasonable chance of success in starting large-scale companies in the skill-intensive business services, such as advertising, contract employment recruitment, marketing, printing, and upscale recreation and sports event planning for business clients. In addition, most African American athletes can effectively start and sustain businesses in semiskilled areas such as security, maintenance, and janitorial services. Within the broad category of transportation and communication, specific industries in which African American athletes can start economically viable companies include trucking and basic telecommunications.[19] However, if African American athletes are to compete effectively in the skill-intensive emerging fields, they will have to possess hands-on work experience in these industries or form partnerships with those skilled in the applicable fields.[20] Nonetheless, linking the substantial financial capital of African American athletes to specific high-growth emerging fields where they are likely to succeed can potentially produce a large derivative benefit—namely, the creation of new jobs for inner-city residents.[21]

Untapped opportunities remain in some traditional fields as well, such as construction, which is evolving into a significant employment anchor and growth area.[22] As in the emerging fields, growth in the construction industry has been most pronounced among large firms that serve a racially diverse clientele.[23] There is, however, one crucial difference between construction firms and firms in the emerging industries; to wit, very few owners of construction firms have college degrees.[24] Therefore, African American athletes with or without a college education can start large-scale firms in several construction subindustries, including general contracting, heavy construction, and demolition with a reasonable expectation of success.[25] At the same time, entrepreneurs planning to pursue urban construction projects must be mindful of changes in the urban landscape associated with the globalization process. Contemporary urban development policies are attempting to reallocate inner-city space to support the needs of the information economy. Employees in this sector, sometimes referred to as "knowledge workers," have expressed preferences to live near their places of employment. One result has been increasing displacement of inner-city residents through redevelopment projects. Advocates of African American inner-city community development must be cognizant of these trends and associated tendencies to exclude African American developers from redevelopment projects.[26]

Invest in Private Investment Firms Providing Equity Capital to African American Businesses

A major obstacle to sustained inner-city economic development is the undercapitalization of African American firms. The relatively low infusion of equity capital into emerging African American firms limits their employment creation potential and ability to serve as inner-city employment anchors.[27] The average private-equity-backed firm creates nearly twice as many jobs as its non-equity-backed peers.[28] Moreover, the burgeoning growth of emerging African American firms cannot be sustained without a major infusion of equity capital into these firms.[29]

A crucial part of the solution to the problems discussed here is channeling capital from wealthy minorities into targeted investment funds that are accessible to private equity investment firms focused on minority markets. Unfortunately, private-equity funds that focus on ethnic and gender-specific businesses and markets receive relatively little capital from banks, corporations, insurance companies, private pension funds, and other institutional sources.[30] Consequently, minority-focused private-equity investment firms manage less than 4 percent of the available capital within the U.S. private-equity market and currently lack the ability to fully serve the equity capital needs of emerging minority firms as a whole.[31] Thus, targeted investment funds and alternative sources of equity capital must be made available to private-equity firms focused on the ethnically diverse marketplace. One way this can be accomplished is through pooling the capital of wealthy African American athletes into targeted "fund-of-funds."

Targeted Fund-of-Funds
Recently, private-equity fund-of-funds have experienced a surge in popularity because of their

low minimum-investment requirements and the reemergence of individual investors as a source of private-equity capital.[32] These funds raise money primarily from wealthy individual investors and less frequently from institutional investors. Typically, these funds are structured as limited partnerships and are managed by an experienced fund manager, who is responsible for selecting, managing, and exiting deals.[33] More important, fund-of funds do not invest directly in private companies but instead invest in other specialized private-equity funds that are managed by private-equity fund managers who have specialized industry knowledge and proven track records. As a general rule, fund-of-funds managers who only possess basic equity investing or specific industry experience rely more on private-equity fund managers than they do on individual investors for technical assistance or information. This allows fund-of-funds managers to bring together a diverse group of investors, who may have little or no specialized knowledge of a particular industry or of the private-equity market.[34]

One example of a fund-of-funds involving investors with little experience and industry knowledge is Champion Ventures. This fund is run by managing partners Harris Barton, Ronnie Lott, and Joe Montana—all formerly of the San Francisco 49ers. Champion operates by pooling investment capital from wealthy sports figures and institutional investors and by investing directly in leading venture capital funds focused on the high-technology sector. To ensure success, Barton, Lott, and Montana have created an advisory board of leading members of the venture capital community. These board members provide Champion's managing members with guidance and connections to other important figures in the venture capital community.[35]

The fund structure created by Champion Ventures serves as a viable model through which wealthy African American athletes can pool their capital and invest in minority-focused private-equity funds. By investing in a number of private-equity funds, primarily focused on minority markets, this fund structure would provide investors with the diversification they require to mitigate risk. This minority-focused fund-of-funds could be run by either a professional fund

manager with experience in minority markets or, as with Champion, by athletes who rely on a well-connected advisory board with years of experience. In either case the fund would possess the required experience and management to ensure success.

Although the Champion model has potential applicability for organizing economic development initiatives involving black athletes, it also highlights several of the problems raised previously regarding biases against inner-city investments. While the Champion venture may have symbolic importance as an example of interracial cooperation, it does not itself address the problem of inner-city economic development. The high-technology sector, the focus of this venture, is notorious for limited representation of African Americans. Passive investments in this and other sectors will not alter employment patterns. While new types of organizational models are certainly necessary to mobilize capital, it is even more important to identify and analyze existing examples of successful ventures undertaken by black athletes that focus specifically on inner-city communities and provide direct benefits to inter-city minority residents.

EXAMPLES OF SUCCESSFUL INNER-CITY INVESTMENT ACTIVITIES BY BLACK ATHLETES

755 Restaurant Corporation/755 Doughnut Corporation

Ventures that either increase access to goods and services or provide employment meet the objective of providing direct benefits to community residents. Former major league baseball player Hank Aaron has been successful in using franchise agreements to penetrate the market for fast food in predominantly black communities. Aaron organized the 755 Restaurant Corporation in 1995, named for the number of home runs he hit as an active player. The company, based in Atlanta, operates thirteen Church's Chicken franchises and three Popeye's Chicken and Biscuits franchises in Atlanta and Charlotte, North Carolina.[36] Aaron's latest venture is the formation of the 755 Doughnut Corporation.

According to the June 9, 2002, issue of the *New York Times*, Aaron has established this corporation to operate a Krispy Kreme franchise slated to open June 25, 2002, in the predominantly black west end of Atlanta.[37]

Magic Johnson Enterprises

The initiatives undertaken by the Johnson Development Corporation, founded by former basketball star Earvin "Magic" Johnson, provide an even broader range of benefits to community residents. These initiatives are the premier existing examples of how athletes and former athletes can serve as major catalysts for inner-city economic development. The corporation was formed in 1993 to develop a shopping plaza in west Las Vegas. Subsequently, it has focused much of its energies on creating entertainment complexes, restaurants, and retail centers in underserved urban and suburban communities across the country. These projects are generally undertaken via fifty–fifty partnerships with mainstream corporations.[38] One example is the 1994 partnership with what is now Loews Cineplex Entertainment, which operates multiplex theatres in inner-cities in several metropolitan areas. Similar partnerships were established with Starbucks Coffee and Carlson Restaurants (TGIFriday's) in 1998.[39] As of 2001, Johnson announced the acquisition of the Fatburger chain as part of the corporation's expansion plans. In contrast to the earlier ventures, Johnson announced an intention to open new Fatburger restaurants in suburban as well as urban areas.[40]

The Johnson Development Corporation is also involved in urban development projects via the Canyon–Johnson Urban fund. This is a special-purpose closed-end real estate fund managed by Canyon–Johnson Realty Advisors, a partnership between Canyon Realty Advisors and Johnson Development Corporation. The fund's investment strategy is to identify, enhance, and capture value through the acquisition, development, redevelopment, and repositioning of urban real estate and the origination of mortgages secured by urban real estate.[41]

Johnson has also become involved in the development of financial intermediaries that are targeting lending and other activities in inner-city communities. He and other investors, including diva Janet Jackson, holds controlling interests in the Los Angeles–based Founders Bank of Commerce. In 2001 Founder's Bank merged with the Boston Bank of Commerce to create the first bicoastal African American bank. The Johnson–Jackson group is one of the bidders to acquire the troubled Family Savings Bank in south Los Angeles.[42]

Black Athletes and Black-Owned Financial Institutions

The banking initiative spearheaded by Magic Johnson and Janet Jackson addresses one of the most difficult challenges to sustaining a development initiative—namely, cultivating strong financial institutions serving African American communities. The formidable challenges hampering the viability of black-owned banks are discussed in detail in the chapter in this volume by Gary Dymski and Robert Weems (chapter 27).

There may be similar opportunities for African American athletes to shore up the African American insurance industry, which has traditionally been one of the major institutions promoting African American socioeconomic development and progress. Despite their historic importance, African American insurance companies in recent decades have been engaged in an increasingly difficult struggle to survive. Since the early 1960s, the black insurance industry has suffered steep decreases in the number of firms, total assets, premium income, and personnel.[43] Except for coverage in the annual special edition of *Black Enterprise*, the decline of the contemporary black insurance industry has gone unnoticed by most blacks.[44] African American athletes and entertainers can help save this industry by becoming active participants in its current marketing campaign to attract new customers.

Any campaign to save and resuscitate the black banking and insurance industries, spearheaded by African American athletes and entertainers (by contributing their time and by purchasing financial products), must consist of more than merely bombarding African American consumers with messages of *Buy black*. It must include efforts urging existing black banks and insurance companies to streamline their operations to better serve an increased clientele. In the case of insurance companies, according to Robert E. Weems Jr., this could be accomplished by having most of the current black-owned insurance companies merge into a "mega" black insurance company. Among other benefits, such a maneuver would take advantage of economies of scale, having them work for, rather than against, the black-owned insurance industry.[45] Another major benefit from the creation of a mega black insurance company would be a greater capacity to penetrate new markets. For example, a consolidated large-scale African American insurance company could enter the growing health insurance market more aggressively than could small-scale black-owned insurance companies.[46]

CONCLUSION

It is evident that there are significant unrealized opportunities for African American athletes to play a major role in undergirding economic development initiatives in inner-city communities. Successful models of involvement have been identified to provide guidance in establishing community investment initiatives. However, the fact remains that one of the principal hurdles that makes such examples anomalies is the ongoing tension between the individualistic aspirations and motivations of athletes and the needs of communities fostered by dominant societal values.

As a consequence, increasing the involvement of African American athletes in supporting community economic development will require short- and long-term strategies. In the short term there is a need for information about current economic development initiatives in which African American athletes are involved. To the extent that a complete database can be generated, opportunities to take advantage of economies of scale may be identified that would allow large collaborative ventures. Such ventures could be pursued using various organizational models including the fund-of-funds model discussed here.

A comprehensive database would also allow systematic dissemination of information to potentially interested athletes regarding how to establish organizations, identify ventures, and implement projects. This could be accomplished

through the creation of an ongoing seminar series developed through a collaboration involving organizations such as the National Urban League as well as current and former athletes, such as Magic Johnson, who are currently involved in economic development initiatives.

In the longer term there is a need for new community institutions that provide alternative venues for socialization and values formation, with the goal of fostering communitarian values among prospective athletes. Such institutions should be structured to establish long-term relationships with prospective athletes to mobilize their engagement in community development ventures. One possible strategy could entail the creation of special nonprofit community institutions that would develop the idea of "group contracts" discussed previously. These institutions would offer special supplemental academic tutoring and other personal support, as well as personalized athletic training. These services would be provided to prospective student athletes through a formal contractual relationship. The contract would require that the prospective athlete pledge to return a fixed percentage of future professional earnings to the organization. Such an arrangement would, of course, not be attractive to all prospective athletes. Athletes with more individualistic orientations could continue to follow existing models of personal development.

This approach does not attempt to alter existing patterns of earnings inequality. Instead, it provides a mechanism for any interested prospective athlete to develop and sustain involvement in community development efforts. It would improve social efficiency by providing counseling to prospective athletes whose skills are not likely to qualify them for the professional ranks, and it would assist them in developing alternative occupational aspirations. In some respects this approach can be thought of as an extension of the "Jack and Jill" club model used by African American elites to guide the socialization of their offspring.

The celebrated athlete, actor, singer, scholar, and activist Paul Robeson provides the best exemplar of the potential outcomes derived from the socially efficient socialization processes envisioned for contemporary African American athletes. The excellence Robeson exhibited in a range of activities remains a standard worth pursuing. And Robeson himself provided guidance regarding the type of athlete capable of contributing significantly to inner-city community development efforts—namely, "a new kind of human being—one shaped in conditions where deep concern for others is basic, where there is a sense of real togetherness, joined with deep concern for the highest development of individual excellence and initiative."[47]

NOTES

We wish to acknowledge the valuable assistance of George Moss, Deborah Goldsmith, Marc Kitchel, Jeff Gagnon, and Laura Walsh who read and reread all parts of this chapter. We are also especially indebted to Robert Weems, Michael Best, and Richard Edwards for their valuable advice and commentary.

1. James B. Stewart, "A Communitarian Model of the Optimal Economic Relationship between Black Athletes and Entertainers and Black Communities," unpublished paper, Penn State University, University Park, Pennsylvania, September 2001.

2. Stewart, "A Communitarian Model," 1.

3. Inner cities are a window into the future American economy. As we move into the twenty-first century, more and more U.S. cities will have populations that are multiethnic, multilingual, and multifaith. Inner-city companies that serve an ethnically diverse base will have a powerful competitive advantage in the future.

4. Michael E. Porter, "The Competitive Advantage of the Inner City," *Harvard Business Review* (May–June 1995): 55–71.

5. Integration with regional clusters is a fourth competitive advantage discussed by Porter. Porter's research shows that most inner cities are near clusters of companies that are in the same region and industry, such as health care. The main advantage of regional clusters is the potential they offer inner-city businesses to compete in the delivery of "downstream products."

6. Earvin "Magic" Johnson is the best example of a sports figure undertaking profitable ventures in the inner city. In South Central Los Angeles, Magic Johnson Theaters consistently rank in the top five theaters among the 21,800 surveyed nationwide, and plans are underway to open similar complexes in Atlanta, Houston, and Harlem (see *New York Times*, January 8, 1996).

7. A large percentage of an athlete's income is based on his or her marginal revenue product, which in turn depends on the athlete's potential to generate additional sales revenue. The ability of an African American athlete to generate additional sales revenue will depend in part on the income of his or her African American fan base. Hence, it is in the economic self-interest of African American athletes to support community economic initiatives that generate additional income and wealth in the African American community.

8. A significant number of "low earning" black athletes, especially football players, have a relatively high precautionary demand for money (to cover unexpected expenses and emergencies) and will usually only allocate a small percentage of their discretionary funds to the equity portion of their portfolio. Their low-risk tolerance behavior can be explained by the fact that the average black male professional athlete is released from professional sports within four years of signing his first contract and will need to hold onto whatever cash and other liquid assets he may secure to meet his uncertain future financial needs. Harry Edwards, "Playoffs and Payoffs: The African American Athlete as an Institutional Resource," in *The State of Black America 1994* (New York: National Urban League, 1994), 105.

9. Conspicuous consumption may be spreading even faster among African Americans because, as Derrick Z. Jackson recently reported (*Austin American-Statesman*, August 29, 2001), the typical African American household is watching television 10.5 hours per day, or a full 3.0 hours per day more than that in all other households.

10. Athletes' discretionary funds, which could be available for inner-city investments, are further reduced by the athletes' enormous financial commitments to immediate family members and other relatives. Harry Edwards ("Playoffs and Payoffs," 105) makes this point clear: "Often operating under woefully ill-informed assumptions and expectations relative to the amount of money that an athlete has at his disposal, family members and other relatives will typically besiege upon him with requests for what is often desperately needed financial assistance. The parents and siblings of most black athletes expect that professional sports success will raise the entire family above their accustomed circumstances and station in life. . . . Seldom do family members consider the tax bill and agent's fees confronting the average black athlete, or the athlete's own lifestyle aspirations, or his plans for the use of his money."

11. Several African American scholars have noted that certain parties with vested interests in maintaining the subordination of black athletes in sports would likely view any significant involvement of black athletes in community development efforts as a potential black power threat to the reproduction of the existing plantation system of organized sports. For a provocative analysis of this view, see Edwards, "Playoffs and Payoffs," 85–111.

12. African American athletes would definitely not participate in community economic development initiatives if other wealthy African Americans were seen as giving little support to African American economic and institutional development. Clearly, then, the formation of a new African American political struggle dedicated to social and economic justice would help to facilitate the collective participation of African American athletes in urban revitalization campaigns. As well, mass education is needed to raise the social consciousness and activism among all African American social groups—including black doctors, engineers, lawyers, teachers, entertainers, and other affluent blacks.

13. Edwards, "Playoffs and Payoffs," 103.

14. Edwards, "Playoffs and Payoffs," 103.

15. Edwards, "Playoffs and Payoffs," 103.

16. Timothy Bates calls these four broad industrial areas "emerging lines of minority business enterprise" because the number of black-owned firms operating within them have, until recently, been quite limited. See Timothy Bates, "Minority-Owned Businesses: Public Policy Approaches," unpublished paper, July 2001; Timothy Bates, "Traditional and Emerging Lines of Black Enterprise," in *Race and Ethnic Conflict* (Boulder, Colo.: Westview Press, 1994).

17. Bates, "Traditional and Emerging Lines," 243.

18. Bates, "Traditional and Emerging Lines," 243.

19. Deregulation has had a significant impact on the long-haul trucking market, where unionization is common. However, black-owned trucking firms are concentrated in local and regional markets and have not been affected much by deregulation.

20. College-educated African American athletes could assemble top-flight management teams to identify and exploit viable businesses opportunities in the so-called FIRE sector of the economy (finance, insurance, and real estate). Most high-earning African American athletes have sufficient discretionary funds to meet the start-up capital requirements for the three industrial areas in the FIRE sector. Generally speaking, capital requirements are modest in insurance and real estate and highest in finance. Although the growth potential in the FIRE sector is less than that in the business services, minority-owned firms have substantially increased in this sector. The growth of minority firms in this sector can be partially explained by the following reasons. One, firms in the FIRE sector provide services that are used by all households, regardless of income. Two, African American churches—the core institutions in all black neighborhoods—heavily utilize FIRE services. Three, the financial mediation activities of minority-owned firms provide them enormous leverage of firms in the real sector of the economy.

21. The growth of black-owned firms in the business services and in the transportation and communication area has coincided with significant employment creation. The total employee members operating in the business services industries grew from 12,432 employees in 1982 to 32,636 in 1987; 72,130 in 1992; and 156,974 in 1997. The total employment of black-owned firms in the transportation and communication area—dominated by trucking—grew 594 percent over the 1982 to 1997 period, from 6,813 to 47,289 employees nationwide.

22. Timothy Bates, "Traditional and Emerging Lines," 251.

23. Bates, "Traditional and Emerging Lines," 251.

24. Bates "Minority-Owned Businesses," 6.

25. The distribution of minority-owned firms in construction subindustries has substantially changed since the 1960s. For example, the number of minority-owned firms in heavy construction and general contracting has risen sharply, whereas minority firms in special trade areas such as carpentry and painting have decreased substantially.

26. For perspectives on the effect of globalization on the allocation of space in urban areas see C. Abbott, "Through Flight to Tokyo: Sunbelt Cities and the New World Economy, 1960–1990," in *Urban Policy in Twentieth Century America,* ed. A. Hirsch and R. Mohl (New Brunswick, N.J.: Rutgers University Press, 1993), 183–212; R. Knight, "City Development and Urbanization: Building the Knowledge-Based City," in *Cities in a Global Society,* ed. R. Knight and G. Gappan, Urban Affairs Annual Review (Newbury Park, Calif.: Sage Publications, 1989), 35: 223–242; and N. Pressman, "Forces for Spatial Change," in *Technological Change and Urban Form,* ed. J. Brotchie et al. (New York: Nichols Publishing, 1985), 349–361.

27. *Employment anchor* refers to an industry or specific class of business (e.g., "emerging minority businesses") that serve as the primary employer of workers in a geographical location of workers belonging to a specific social group. Before deindustrialization, the manufacturing industry was the employment anchor for blue-collar workers in most inner cities.

28. Glen Yago and Aaron Pankratz, "The Minority Business Challenge—Democratizing Capital for Emerging Domestic Markets," Milken Institute, U.S. Department of Commerce, Minority Business Development Agency, September 25, 2000, vs. Private-equity venture-backed companies experience close to a 41 percent growth in jobs compared to a 2.5 percent job decline for *Fortune* 500 companies (Yago and Pankratz, "The Minority Business Challenge," v).

29. Yago and Pankratz, "The Minority Business Challenge," iii.

30. "Private Equity Analyst," December 1998; *Forbes*, August 25, 1998.

31. Of the $95 billion in estimated assets under management by all private equity funds in 1999, just $2 billion were managed by investment companies with a focus on minority markets. Yago and Pankratz, "Minority Business Challenge," 16.

32. Yago and Pankratz, "Minority Business Challenge," 19. Professionally managed fund-of-funds will generally not accept from an individual investor an investment of less than $200,000. Many have higher minimums; few have lower. The money raised from individual investors is pooled and then invested in larger amounts (usually a minimum of $5 million to $10 million) in various private-equity funds.

33. Limited partnerships most commonly comprise a general partner, who manages a fund; and limited partners, who invest money but have limited liability and are not involved with the day-to-day management of the fund. In most private-equity funds, the general partner receives a management fee and a percentage of the profits for selecting, managing, and exiting deals. *Exiting* refers to the method by which an investor or fund manager withdraws from investments. In most private-equity arrangements, this typically includes either the initial public offering of stock or the acquisition of the portfolio by another company (usually one larger and wealthier). To target new companies in emerging markets, the manager of the fund would ideally have specific knowledge, comfort, and experience in this area, including the ability to work constructively and efficiently with various minority entrepreneurs.

34. A second way for African American athletes to invest in emerging minority businesses and markets is through *angel funds*. These funds raise money from wealthy individuals and are usually invested directly into start-up or seed-stage private companies. They are typically structured as limited partnerships and managed by an experienced professional, who is responsible for selecting, managing, and exiting deals. In addition, angel funds leverage the experience of their investors to aid in deal flow, offering new companies access to experienced professionals who can provide them with ongoing management and marketing assistance. For example, an angel fund focused on investments in emerging minority companies could benefit from investment by wealthy African American athletes, by leveraging their high visibility, corporate and media resources, and community connections to generate quality deals. In general, angel funds carry a high level of risk for investors, as they typically represent the first infusion of capital into a new company and are rarely backed by other capital providers.

35. Champion Ventures has successfully raised $250 million from such well-known sports figures as Andre Agassi, Troy Aikman, Barry Bonds, Wayne Gretzky, and Jerry Rice.

36. "Take Me Out to the Krispy Kreme," *New York Times*, sec. 3, June 9, 2002, 2.

37. "Take Me Out to the Krispy Kreme," 2.

38. The following website contains general information about the Magic Johnson Development Corporation: www.magicjohnson.com.

39. For additional information go to www.johnsondevelopmentcorp.com/theaters/index.html and "Magic Johnson Adds Fatburger Business Ventures," SportingNews.com, October 2, 2001, at http://tsn.sportingnews.com/nba/articles/20011002/384077.html.

40. "Magic Johnson Adds Fatburger Business Ventures."

41. This venture is described at www.magicjohnson.com.

42. Karen Robinson-Jacobs, "Four Submit Offers for Family Savings," latimes.com, February 25, 2002, at www.ltimes.com/templates/misc/printsory.jsp?slug=la percent2D00014360feb25.

43. See Robert E. Weems Jr., "A Crumbling Legacy: The Decline of African American Insurance

Companies in Contemporary America," *Review of Black Political Economy* 23 (Fall 1994): 25–37.

44. Special editions are issued every June. In 1989, *Black Enterprise* informed its readers (in bold black letters) that African American insurance companies had two options: FORTIFY OR DIE. "Fortify or Die," *Black Enterprise* 19 (June 1989): 285.

45. Weems, "A Crumbling Legacy," 33–35.

46. In addition, a mega black insurance company would have sufficient financial capital to penetrate burgeoning markets in Africa and the Caribbean. In fact, a mega black insurance company would be able to join existing efforts to promote economic "Pan-Africanism."

47. Philip S. Foner, *Paul Robeson Speaks: Writings, Speeches, Interviews, 1918–1974* (New York: Brunner-Mazel, 1977), 464.

Index

About the Editors

Cecilia A. Conrad is the Stedman-Sumner Professor of Economics at Pomona College. She has authored, coauthored, edited, or coedited several monographs, including *Building Skills for Black Workers: Preparing for Future Labor Markets, Critical Path Analysis of California's S&T Education System: California's Demand for a Science and Technology Workforce, The Workforce in the New Millennium: The Growing Demand for Skills,* and *Soft Skills and the Minority Workforce: A Guide of Informed Discussion.* She is the current editor of the *Review of Black Political Economy* and is an associate editor of *Feminist Economics.* She is a recipient of the 2002 California Professor of the Year Award, an honor presented by the Carnegie Foundation for the Advancement of Teaching.

John Whitehead is professor of economics and African American studies at City College of San Francisco. He has written extensively on racial economic inequality and community economic development and is the coeditor, with Cobie Kwasi Harris, of *Readings in Black Political Economy.* He is the founder and chairperson of the Committee on the Impact of Globalization on U.S. Minorities.

Patrick Mason is associate professor of economics and director of the African American Studies Program at the Florida State University. He is coeditor of *International Encyclopedia of the Social Sciences; African Americans, Labor and Society: Organizing for a New Agenda* (2001); and *Race, Markets and Social Outcomes* (1997). Dr. Mason has also published over forty economics and black studies refereed journal articles, book chapters, and professional studies. He is currently chair of the Committee of the Status of Minorities in the Economics Profession and is the past president of the National Economics Association.

James Stewart is professor of labor studies and industrial relations, African and African American studies, and management and organization at Penn State University. He has authored, coauthored, edited, or coedited numerous books, including *Black Families: Interdisciplinary Perspectives, The Housing Status of Black Americans, African Americans and Post Industrial Labor Markets,* and *Managing Diversity in the Military.* He has served as editor of the *Review of Black Political Economy* and president of the National Economics Association. Dr. Stewart recently completed two terms as president of the National Council for Black Studies (1998–2002).